LEADERSHIP

Theory, Application, & Skill Development

LEADERSHIP

Theory, Application, & Skill Development

5e

ROBERT N. LUSSIER, PH.D.
Springfield College

CHRISTOPHER F. ACHUA, D.B.A.
University of Virginia's College at Wise

SOUTH-WESTERN
CENGAGE Learning·

Australia • Brazil • Japan • Korea • Mexico • Singapore • Spain • United Kingdom • United States

SOUTH-WESTERN
CENGAGE Learning·

Leadership: Theory, Application, & Skill Development, **Fifth Edition**
Robert N. Lussier, Christopher F. Achua

Vice President of Editorial, Business: Jack W. Calhoun

Publisher: Erin Joyner

Acquisitions Editor: Scott Person

Senior Developmental Editor: Julia Chase

Marketing Manager: Jonathan Monahan

Marketing Coordinator: Julia Tucker

Media Editor: Rob Ellington

Manufacturing Planner: Ron Montgomery

Senior Art Director: Stacy Jenkins Shirley

Rights Acquisition Director: Audrey Pettengill

Interior Design, Production Management, and Composition: PreMediaGlobal

Cover Designer: Red Hangar Design LLC

Cover Image: © John Kershner, Shutterstock

For product information and technology assistance, contact us at
Cengage Learning Customer & Sales Support, 1-800-354-9706

For permission to use material from this text or product,
submit all requests online at **www.cengage.com/permissions**
Further permissions questions can be emailed to
permissionrequest@cengage.com

Library of Congress Control Number: 2011941648

ISBN-13: 978-1-111-82707-6

ISBN-10: 1-111-82707-9

South-Western

5191 Natorp Boulevard
Mason, OH 45040
USA

Cengage Learning products are represented in Canada by Nelson Education, Ltd.

For your course and learning solutions, visit **www.cengage.com**

Purchase any of our products at your local college store or at our preferred online store **www.cengagebrain.com**

Printed in the United States of America
1 2 3 4 5 6 7 15 14 13 12 11

To my wife Marie and our six children:
Jesse, Justin, Danielle, Nicole, Brian, and Renee
— *Robert N. Lussier*

To my family, especially my wife (Pauline),
the children (Justin, Brooke, Jordan, Cullen, Gregory and Zora)
and my mother (Theresia Sirri).
— *Christopher F. Achua*

Brief Contents

Contents

PART ONE   **INDIVIDUALS AS LEADERS   1**

CHAPTER 4

Contingency Leadership Theories 111

CHAPTER 7

Leader–Member Exchange and Followership   239

PART THREE   ORGANIZATIONAL LEADERSHIP   321

CHAPTER 10
Leadership of Culture, Ethics, and Diversity 356

CHAPTER 11
Strategic Leadership and Change Management 393

CHAPTER 12

Crisis Leadership and the Learning Organization   428

Preface

Target Market

This book is intended for leadership courses offered at the undergraduate and graduate levels in schools of business, public administration, health care, education, psychology, and sociology. No prior coursework in business or management is required. The textbook can also be used in management development courses that emphasize the leadership function, and can supplement management or organizational behavior courses that emphasize leadership, especially with an applications/skill development focus.

Goals and Overview of Competitive Advantages

In his book *Power Tools,* John Nirenberg asks: "Why are so many well-intended students learning so much and yet able to apply so little in their personal and professional lives?" Is it surprising that students cannot apply what they read and cannot develop skills, when most textbooks continue to focus on theoretical concepts? Textbooks need to take the next step, and develop students' ability to apply what they read and to build skills using the concepts. I (Lussier) started writing management textbooks in 1988—prior to the call by the Association to Advance Collegiate Schools of Business (AACSB) for skill development and outcomes assessment—to help professors teach their students how to apply concepts and develop management skills. Pfeffer and Sutton concluded that the most important insight from their research is that knowledge that is actually implemented is much more likely to be acquired from learning by doing, than from learning by reading, listening, or thinking. We designed this book to give students the opportunity to learn by doing.

The overarching goal of this book is reflected in its subtitle: theory, application, skill development. We developed the total package to teach leadership theory and concepts, to improve ability to apply the theory through critical thinking, and to develop leadership skills. Following are our related goals in writing this book:

- To be the only traditional leadership textbook to incorporate the three-pronged approach. We make a clear distinction between coverage of theory concepts, their application, and the development of skills based on the concepts. The Test Bank includes questions under each of the three approaches.
- To make this the most "how-to" leadership book on the market. We offer behavior models with step-by-step guidelines for handling various leadership functions (such as how to set objectives, give praise and instructions, coach followers, resolve conflicts, and negotiate).
- To offer the best coverage of traditional leadership theories, by presenting the theories and research findings without getting bogged down in too much detail.
- To create a variety of high-quality application material, using the concepts to develop critical-thinking skills.
- To create a variety of high-quality skill-development exercises, which build leadership skills that can be used in students' personal and professional life.

- To offer behavior-modeling leadership skills training.
- To make available a video package, including 7 Behavior Model Videos and 12 Video Cases.
- To suggest self-assessment materials that are well integrated and illustrate the important concepts discussed in the text. Students begin by determining their personality profile in Chapter 2, and then assess how their personality affects their leadership potential in the remaining chapters.
- To provide a flexible teaching package, so that professors can design the course to best meet the leadership needs of their students. The total package includes more material than can be covered in one course. Supplemental material is included, thus only one book is needed—making it a low-cost alternative for the student.

Flexibility Example

The textbook, with 12 chapters, allows time for other materials to be used in the leadership course. The textbook includes all the traditional topics in enough detail, however, to use only the textbook for the course. It offers so much application and skill-development material that it cannot all be covered in class during one semester. Instructors have the flexibility to select only the content and features that best meet their needs.

Specific Competitive Advantage— Pedagogical Features

Three-Pronged Approach

We created course materials that truly develop students into leaders. As the title of this book implies, we provide a balanced, three-pronged approach to the curriculum:

- A clear understanding of the traditional theories and concepts of leadership, as well as of the most recently developed leadership philosophies
- Application of leadership concepts through critical thinking
- Development of leadership skills

The three-pronged approach is clear in the textbook and is carried throughout the Instructor's Manual and Test Bank.

Theory

Leadership Theories, Research and References, and Writing Style: This book has been written to provide the best coverage of the traditional leadership theories, presenting the theories and research findings clearly without being bogged down in too much detail. The book is heavily referenced with classic and current citations. Unlike the textbooks of some competitors, this book does not use in-text citations, to avoid distracting the reader and adding unnecessary length to the text chapters. Readers can refer to the notes for complete citations of all sources. Thus, the book includes all the traditional leadership topics, yet we believe it is written in a livelier, more conversational manner than those of our competitors.

The following features are provided to support the first step in the three-pronged approach—theory.

Learning Outcomes: Each chapter begins with Learning Outcomes. At the end of the chapter, the Learning Outcomes are integrated into the chapter summary.

Key Terms: A list of key terms appears at the beginning and end of each chapter. Clear definitions are given in the text for approximately 15 of the most important concepts from the chapter (with the key term in bold and the definition in italic).

Chapter Summary: The summary lists the Learning Outcomes from the beginning of the chapter and gives the answers. For each chapter, the last Learning Outcome requires students to define the key terms of the chapter by writing the correct key term in the blank provided for each definition.

Review Questions: These questions require recall of information generally not covered in the Learning Outcomes.

Product Support Web Site: The product support Web site, www.cengage.com/management/lussier, has information for both professors and students. Students can take interactive quizzes, written by Kenneth Zula of Keystone College, and quiz themselves on key terms.

Test Bank (Assessment of Understanding of Theory/Concepts) and Instructor's Manual: The Test Bank includes traditional assessment of student knowledge. It also includes the Learning Outcomes and Review Questions for each chapter. The Instructor's Manual includes the answers to all Review Questions.

Application

The second prong of our textbook is to have students apply the leadership theories and concepts so that they can develop critical-thinking skills. Students develop their application skills through the following features.

Opening Case Application: At the beginning of each chapter, information about an actual manager and organization is presented. The case is followed by four to eight questions to get students involved. Throughout the chapter, the answers to the questions are given to illustrate how the manager/organization actually uses the text concepts to create opportunities and solve problems through decision making. A distinctive head (Opening Case APPLICATION) appears when the opening case is applied in the text.

OPENING CASE *APPLICATION*

1. What Big Five and leadership personality traits does Ellen Kullman possess?

To a large extent, Ellen Kullman is a successful leader because of her strong personality in the Big Five.

She has a strong need for *surgency* that helped her climb the corporate ladder at DuPont, which is dominated by men. It took energy and determination to become the first woman CEO of DuPont. Further evidence of her being powerful follows: *Forbes* listed Kullman number 18 on its list of the World's 100 Most Powerful Women. *Fortune* ranked Kullman seventh on its list of 50 Most Powerful Women, and fifth on its Businessperson of the Year list.

Work Applications: Open-ended questions, called Work Applications, require students to explain how the text concepts apply to their own work experience; there are over 100 of these scattered throughout the text. Student experience can be present, past, summer, full-time, or part-time employment. The questions help the students to bridge the gap between theory and the real world. The Work Applications are also included in the Test Bank, to assess students' ability to apply the concepts.

Concept Applications: Every chapter contains a series of two to six Concept Application boxes that require students to determine the leadership concept being illustrated in a specific, short example. All the recommended answers appear in the Instructor's Manual with a brief explanation. In addition, the Test Bank has similar questions, clearly labeled, to assess students' ability to apply the concepts.

CONCEPT APPLICATION 1
Big Five Personality Dimensions

Identify each of these seven traits/behaviors by its personality dimension. Write the appropriate letter in the blank before each item.

a. surgency   d. conscientiousness
b. agreeableness   e. openness to experience
c. affiliation

_____ 1. A leader is being very quiet when meeting some unexpected visitors in the work unit.

_____ 2. A leader is giving in to a follower to avoid a conflict.

_____ 3. A manager is influencing the follower to do the job the way the leader wants it done.

_____ 4. A sales representative submitted the monthly expense report on time as usual.

_____ 5. A leader is saying a warm, friendly good morning to followers as they arrive at work.

_____ 6. A leader is seeking ideas from followers on how to speed up the flow of work.

_____ 7. As a follower is yelling a complaint, a leader calmly explains what went wrong.

Critical Thinking Questions: There are more than 80 critical-thinking questions (an average of 7 per chapter) that can be used for class discussion and/or written assignments to develop communication and critical thinking skills.

Cases: Following the Review Questions and Critical Thinking Questions, students are presented with another actual manager and organization. The students learn how the manager/organization applies the leadership concepts from that chapter. Each Case is followed by questions for the student to answer. Chapters 2 through 11 also include cumulative case questions. Cumulative questions relate case material from prior chapters. Thus, students continually review and integrate concepts from previous chapters. Answers to the Case questions are included in the Instructor's Manual.

Video Cases: All chapters include one Video Case. Seeing actual leaders tackling real management problems and opportunities enhances student application of the concepts. The 12 Video Cases have supporting print material for both instructors and students, including a brief description and critical-thinking questions. Answers to the Video Case questions are included in the Instructor's Manual.

VIDEO ▶❚ CASE
Motivation at Washburn Guitars

Founded in the late 1800s in Chicago, Washburn Guitars boasts a rich tradition of fine instrument making. Today the company sells more than 50,000 guitars annually, totaling about $40 million in revenue. Washburn Guitars produces a variety of acoustic and electric guitars. Washburn craftsmen also enjoy making custom guitars. In recent years, custom shop production has grown dramatically from 20 to 300 guitars per month. Having a motivated workforce is essential because guitar making is labor intensive and requires attention to detail.

Quality materials combined with quality craftsmanship are necessary to produce quality guitars. Washburn Guitars' workforce is motivated because they love music and care about the instruments.

1. What motivates most employees at Washburn Guitars?
2. What kinds of guitars do employees most like to produce?
3. What is the connection between quality guitars and workforce motivation?

Test Bank (Assessment of Application Ability) and Instructor's Manual: The Test Bank includes Work Applications and Concept Application questions. The Instructor's Manual contains detailed answers for all of the application features.

Skill Development

The difference between learning about leadership and learning to be a leader is the acquisition of skills, our third prong. This text focuses on skill development so students can use the leadership theories and concepts they learn to improve their personal and professional life.

Self-Assessments: Scattered throughout the text are 37 Self-Assessments. Students complete these exercises to gain personal knowledge. All information for completing and scoring the assessments is contained within the text. Students determine their personality profile in Chapter 2, and then assess how their personality affects their leadership in the remaining chapters. Self-knowledge leads students to an understanding of how they can and will operate as leaders in the real world. Although Self-Assessments do not develop a specific skill, they serve as a foundation for skill development.

SELF-ASSESSMENT 3   Personality and Charismatic and Transformational Leadership

Charismatic leaders have charisma based on personality and other personal traits that cut across all of the Big Five personality types. Review the ten qualities of charismatic leaders in Exhibit 9.3 on page 336. Which traits do you have?

_____

_____

If you have a high surgency Big Five personality style and a high need for power, you need to focus on using socialized, rather than personalized, charismatic leadership.

Transformational leaders tend to be charismatic as well. In Self-Assessment 1 on page 332 you determined if you were more transformational or transactional. How does your personality affect your transformational and transactional leadership styles?

_____

_____

You Make the Ethical Call. The boxes present issues of ethics for class discussion, with many presenting actual situations faced by real companies. Each dilemma contains two to four questions for class discussion.

YOU
Make the ETHICAL Call

1.1   *Is Leadership Really Important?*

Scott Adams is the creator of the cartoon character Dilbert. Adams makes fun of managers, in part because he distrusts top-level managers, saying that leadership is really a crock. Leadership is about manipulating people to get them to do something they don't want to do, and there may not be anything in it for them. CEOs basically run the same scam as fortune-tellers, who make up a bunch of guesses and when by chance one is correct, they hope you forget the other errors. First, CEOs blame their predecessors for anything that is bad, then they shuffle everything around, start a new strategic program, and wait. When things go well, despite the CEO, the CEO takes the credit and moves on to the next job. Adams says we may be hung up on leadership as part of our DNA. It seems we have always sought to put somebody above everybody else.[25]

1. Do you agree with Scott Adams that leadership is a crock?

2. Do we really need to have someone in the leadership role?

Case Role-Play Exercise: Following each Case are instructions to prepare students to conduct an in-class role-play, based on a situation presented in the Case. Through role-playing, students develop their skills at handling leadership situations. For example, students are asked to conduct a motivational speech and to develop a vision and a mission statement for an organization.

Step-by-Step Behavior Models: In addition to traditional theories of leadership, the text includes behavior models: how-to steps for handling day-to-day leadership functions, such as how to set objectives, give praise, coach, resolve conflicts, delegate, and negotiate.

Behavior Model Videos: There are seven Behavior Model Videos that reinforce the development of skills. The videos demonstrate leaders successfully handling common leadership functions, using the step-by-step behavior models discussed earlier in the Theory section. Students learn from watching the videos and/or using them in conjunction with the Skill-Development Exercises. Material in the text integrates the videos into the chapters. Ideas for using all videos are detailed in the Instructor's Manual.

Behavior Model Video **6.1**

Situational Communications

Objectives

To better understand the four situational communication styles and which style to use in a given situation

Video *(12 minutes)* Overview

You will first listen to a lecture to understand how to use the situational communications model. Then, you will view two managers, Steve and Darius, meeting to discuss faulty parts. You are asked to identify the communication style

Darius uses in four different scenes. Write the letters of the style on the scene line after each scene. This may be completed as part of Developing Your Leadership Skills Exercise 2.

Scene 1. _____ Autocratic (S1A)

Scene 2. _____ Consultative (S2C)

Scene 3. _____ Participative (S3P)

Scene 4. _____ Empowerment (S4E)

Developing Your Leadership Skills: There are between one and four Exercises at the end of each chapter. We use the term *developing your leadership skills* only in referring to an exercise that will develop a skill that can be used in the students' personal or professional life at work. Full support of 30 activities can be found in the Instructor's Manual, including detailed information, timing, answers, and so on. There are three primary types of exercises:

Individual Focus. Students make individual decisions about exercise questions before or during class. Students can share their answers in class discussions, or the instructor may elect to go over recommended answers.

Group/Team Focus. Students discuss the material presented and may select group answers and report to the class.

Role-Play Focus. Students are presented with a model and given the opportunity to use the model to apply their knowledge of leadership theories through role-playing exercises.

Behavior Model Skills Training: Six of the Developing Your Leadership Skills Exercises may be used as part of behavior modeling by using the step-by-step models in the text and the Behavior Model Videos. Meta-analysis research has concluded that behavior modeling skills training is effective at developing leadership skills. For example, students read the conflict resolution model in the text, watch the video in class, and then complete an Exercise (role-play) to resolve a conflict, using the model and feedback from others.

Behavior Model Skills Training 2

Session 2

In this behavior model skills training session, you will perform three activities:

1. Read "Improving Performance with the Coaching Model" (to review how to use the model).

2. Watch Behavior Model Video 6.2, "Coaching."

3. Complete Developing Your Leadership Skills Exercise 3 (to develop your coaching skills).

For further practice, use the coaching model in your personal and professional life.

Test Bank (Assessment of Skill Development) and Instructor's Manual. The Test Bank includes skill-development questions. The Instructor's Manual contains detailed answers for all of the skills featured in the text, including timing, information, answers, logistics, and so on. It also explains how to test on the specific Skill-Development Exercises, and provides information that can be shared with students to help them prepare for exams.

Ancillary Support

Instructor's Resource CD (ISBN: 9781133494836)

Place all the key resources you need at your fingertips with this convenient, powerful instructor's resource. This CD-ROM includes the Instructor's Manual, Test Bank, ExamView, and Microsoft® PowerPoint® slides. It's the ultimate tool for customizing lectures and efficiently creating memorable presentations.

The accompanying Instructor's Manual, prepared by Robert Lussier and Christopher Achua, contains the following for each chapter of the book: a detailed outline for lecture enhancement, Review Question answers, Concept Application answers, Case and Video

Case question answers, instructions on use of videos, and Developing Your Leadership Skills Exercise ideas (including setup and timing). The Instructor's Manual also contains an introduction that discusses possible approaches to the course, and provides an overview of possible uses for various features and how to test and grade them. It explains the use of permanent groups to develop team leadership skills, and provides guidance in the development of a course outline/syllabus.

Quickly and accurately assess your students' understanding of management concepts with this edition's ExamView Test Bank prepared by Louis Jourdan, Clayton State University. You'll find more than 2,000 questions. Each question is clearly identified by level of difficulty, by type of question; and by corresponding AACSB guidelines, making it simple to create a balanced student exam. This Test Bank is available on both the instructor's Web site and the Instructor's Resource CD-ROM. ExamView allows you to create customized tests or study guides for your course in minutes. Add or edit questions, instructions, and answers, and select questions (randomly or numerically) for the assessment that best fits your students and course.

The PowerPoint Lecture Presentation, prepared by Charlie Cook, University of Alabama, enables you to easily customize your multimedia classroom presentation. You'll find slides with figures and tables from the text as well as outside materials that supplement chapter concepts. Material is organized by chapter and can be modified or expanded.

CourseMate (ISBN: 9781133317500)

Visit www.cengagebrain.com to find the dedicated Lussier/Achua, Leadership 5e Web site. Here instructors will find all of the materials available on the Instructors CD, along with a complete e-book and Engagement Tracker tool. The tracker tool provides instructors with the ability to identify at-risk students while it's still early enough to help, and also allows you to see what resources your students find most valuable. It goes beyond the book to deliver what you need!

The student interactive Web site helps students make the most of study time. This new CourseMate provides an interactive e-Book that allows students to take notes; highlight, bookmark, and search a complete e-book; and reference in-context glossary definitions. Numerous interactive learning tools, such as quizzes, flashcards, videos, and more, help students master today's leadership concepts.

DVD (ISBN: 9781133494843)

The DVD includes 2 types of videos: Behavior Model Videos and Chapter Videos. The Behavioral Model Videos are integrated into the text. They reinforce student skill development as they demonstrate managers successfully performing common leadership functions. Students learn from watching the videos and/or using them in conjunction with the Skill Builders exercises in the text. The Chapter Videos center around topics key to leadership understanding within a profile of a real business organization solving real-world problems. The Video Cases add variety to the classroom presentation and stimulate students to learn about organizations, teams, and leadership.

WebTutor on WebCT or Blackboard

Instructors can jumpstart their courses with rich content that's specific to LEADERSHIP 5e in this Course Management System. Full instructor and student support includes interactive course materials, including lecture outlines, discussion items, quizzes, and flashcards. All content has been updated to accompany this edition.

Summary of Key Innovations

Our goal is to make both students and instructors successful by providing learning features that not only teach about leadership but also help students become leaders. Here are the special ways in which this is done:

- Three-pronged approach (theory, application, skill development) in the textbook, and corresponding assessment of the three areas in the Test Bank
- Unique skill-development materials that build leadership skills for use in students' personal and professional life
- Unique application material to develop critical-thinking skills in applying the leadership concepts and theories
- Unsurpassed video package, with 12 Video Cases and 7 Behavior Model Videos
- Flexibility—use any or all of the features that work for you!

Changes to the Fifth Edition

The fifth edition has been thoroughly revised:

- While keeping the classic theory references, this edition has been thoroughly updated by including the latest research and business press facts to support the leadership theory and concepts. Over 80 percent of the references are new to this edition.
- Chapter 5, Contingency Leadership Theories, from the 4e is now Chapter 4. The change puts the three major theories of traits, behavior, and contingency in sequence.
- Chapter 4, Influencing: Power, Politics, Networking, and Negotiation is now Chapter 5.
- The skill development exercises indicate which updated 2011 AACSB Competency is developed through the exercise.
- Over half of the chapter opening and end-of-chapter cases are new, and the remaining cases have been updated.
- All of the Applying the Concept boxes have been changed to include new situations and re-sequence others so that all answers have changed.
- The names of some of the features have been changed. Applying the Concept is now Concept Applications. Ethical Dilemmas are now You Make the Ethical Call. Communication Skills is now Critical Thinking Questions. Skill Building Exercises are now Developing Your Leadership Skills.
- All chapters have new and updated Test Bank questions.

Chapter 1

The Chapter title has been changed to include the skills leaders need. There is a new major section "Leadership Skill" to identify and describe the three important skills that leaders need to be successful. In this section, there is a new Learning Outcome, three new Key Terms, a new Exhibit, one Work Application, five new Concept Application questions, and a new Self-Assessment for better understanding one's leadership skills. The subsection "AACSB Assurance of Learning Standards" has been rewritten to include a new list of standards published in 2011.

Chapter 2

There has been a major reorganization of the first two sections. The Big Five and traits of effective leaders are now combined with a new major heading "The Big Five Including Traits of Effective Leaders." The discussion of the Big Five has been moved to this new section with the nine traits listed under their Big Five classification. The nine traits have been expanded to 12, adding determination, sociability, narcissism, and dependability. The definitions of the Big Five have been changed to include the individual traits of effective leaders. The discussion of several individual traits has been rewritten. Several of the questions in Self-Assessment 1 Personality Profile have been changed to coincide with the reorganization list of traits. There is a new subsection for the topic Leadership and Neuroscience.

Chapter 3

The introduction to the chapter has been rewritten with all new references. The subheading "Differences between Leadership Models—and Their Contributions," has been changed to Differences, Contributions, and Applications of Leadership Models," with a new discussion on the applications of the models. The discussion on "Using Goal Setting to Motivate Employees" has been expanded to include the need for planning with an example. In the "Types of Reinforcement" subsection, the sequence of punishment and extinction has been reversed. A new discussion has been added for each of the four types of reinforcement to explain which type to use when. In the "Motivating with Reinforcement" subsection, there is a new heading "Changing Behavior" with a discussion on how to change behavior using reinforcement theory.

Chapter 4

It has been changed to Chapter 5 in the 5e. The subsection "Research" within each of the leadership theories has been expanded to "Research, Criticism, and Applications" to more clearly include and expand on these two new topic areas in all five sections. In the "Global Contingency Leadership" section, Theory Z has been replaced with GLOBE, so the critical thinking question about Theory Z has been taken out.

Chapter 5

It has been changed to Chapter 4 in the 5e. With the updating of content with references, there are many changes in paragraphs throughout the entire chapter. A new subsection "Social Networking at Work" has been added to the networking section to discuss this trend and challenges for business. Almost all of the Ethics and Influencing section has been rewritten.

Chapter 6

The Communication section opening and subsection "Communication and Leadership" have been rewritten and updated with new references. It now includes a brief discussion of the changing use of technology in communication. The subsection "Coaching and Leadership" has been dropped and its content merged with the introduction to the section "Coaching," which has been rewritten. In step 1 of the Conflict Resolution BCF statement, new material stating what not to say, to prevent the person from getting defensive, has been added to the opening comment.

Chapter 7

Vertical Dyadic Linkage (VDL) Theory and Leader-Member Exchange (LMX) theory underwent some rewriting and restructuring to simplify and improve content flow. Some of these changes include:

- Retitling of Exhibit 7.1 from "Dyadic Approach: Stages of Development" to "Evolution of Dyadic Theory" and deleting the last stage (Systems and Network) from the exhibit.

- Changing the sequencing of the subsections in LMX Theory to a new sequence as follows: Factors that Influence LMX Relationships, Developing High Quality LMX Relationships, The Benefits of High Quality Relationships (new) and Strengths and Limitations of LMX Theory (new).
- Effective Leader-Follower Feedback, that was presented as a sub-section under LMX Theory in the 4e, has been moved to the section on Delegation. Also, the title has been changed to "Effective Leader Evaluation and Feedback." This change is to put the focus on the leader's actions during the evaluation process.
- As part of the Followership presentation, we have added two new subsections – "Defining Followership" and "The Effective Follower."

Chapter 8

In Chapter 8, we added new sections, reorganized some sections and deleted some sections in an effort to streamline the flow of the discussion for easier comprehension. Here are the main changes:

- Added a new subsection titled "What is an Effective Team?"
- Complete overhaul of the section on the "Characteristics of Effective Teams." Instead of 7 characteristics, we now have ten. Team Leadership and Creativity Driven that were listed as characteristics of effective teams are now separated and presented as standalone subsections.
- The section on Decision Making in Teams has been scaled back to focus on the Normative Leadership Model (discussed in Chapter 4) and Team-Centered Decision Making.
- Added a new subsection titled "Advantages and Disadvantages of Team-Centered Decision Making."
- Exhibit 8.5 – Differences between Self-Managed Team and Conventional Teams – has been updated with new a dimension added and an old dimension redefined.
- Finally, a number of subheading titles were changed and parts of the content rewritten for clarification. For example, "Guidelines for Improving Self-Managed Team Effectiveness" has been changed to "Improving the Success Rate of Self-Managed Teams" and "The Changing Role of Leadership in Self-Managed Teams" has been changed to "The Role of Leadership in Self-Managed Teams." Also, we scaled back the discussion in this subsection.

Chapter 9

Charismatic and Transformational Leadership, theories do share quite a bit in common. To reflect this reality, we reorganized the chapter to focus on the uniqueness of Charismatic Leadership, Transformational Leadership and a separate section that focuses on the similarities of both theories. This new section is titled "Charismatic and Transformational Leadership – An Integrated Perspective." Under this new section, we added the following three sub-sections: Qualities of Effective Charismatic and Transformational Leaders, Charismatic and Transformational Leader Behaviors and Differentiating Between Charismatic and Transformational Leadership. This change has resulted in the deletion of redundant content (such as the subsection on "Differentiating between Charismatic and Non-Charismatic Leaders"). Another significant change worth mentioning is the fact that "Personal Meaning" and "Charisma" were changed from primary headings to subheadings. Personal meaning is now scaled back and presented simply as one of the factors distinguishing charismatic from transformational leadership.

Chapter 10

The Leader's role in influencing culture has been updated and expanded and focused on actions (symbolic and substantive) that impact culture creation and adoption. Added a new subsection titled "Authentic Leadership" to highlight the increasing relevance and interest in the topic. Finally, some subheading titles were changed and parts of the content rewritten for clarification. They include the following:

- "Changing Demographics and Diversity" is now "Diversity Leadership."
- "Current State of Workforce Diversity" is now "Changing Demographics and Workforce Diversity."
- "The Impact of Globalization on Diversity" is now "The Effects of Globalization on Diversity."
- "Reasons for Embracing Diversity" is now "Benefits of Embracing Diversity."
- "Diversity Awareness Training and Leadership Education" is now "Training and Education." It is now presented simply as one of the factors supporting a culture of diversity.
- Deleted the subsection titled "Obstacles to Achieving Diversity." It was repetitive given that the subsection on "Creating a Pro-Diversity Culture" centered on the same discussion and objectives.

Chapter 11

Chapter 11 opens with a new section titled "Globalization and Environmental Sustainability." Strategic Leadership is discussed as a subheading under this section rather than a primary heading as was the case in the 4e. The reason for this change is to underscore the significance of globalization and environmental sustainability as trends affecting business performance and competitiveness; and also to highlight the role of strategic leadership in managing these trends. "The Strategic Management Process" was changed to "The Strategic Management Framework." The basic steps of the strategic management process are organized under the strategic management framework. The strategy formulation subsection has been reorganized and updated to highlight the key components of this step. On the topic of Leading Change, we combined "People-Centered" and "Task-Centered" Recommendations for Minimizing Resistance (from 4e) into one subsection and renamed it "Recommendations for Minimizing Resistance." With this change, we also combined Exhibit 11.4 and 11.5 (from the 4e) into one exhibit titled "Ten Recommendations for Minimizing Resistance."

Chapter 12

In Chapter 12, we added to the discussion on crisis leadership the debate on the debt ceiling and the potential crisis of default that it created. A new subsection titled "Crises Training for Leaders" has been added. To highlight the key steps in the crises management process, a new exhibit (12.1) titled "The Three-Stage Crisis Management Model" has been added. We concluded the section on crisis leadership with a focus on crises on the African Continent. We called this subsection a "A Spotlight on the African Crisis." The concept of the Learning Organization has been updated and expanded with a new subsection titled "What Is Knowledge Management?"

Acknowledgments

I'm deeply honored that Judi Neal, Executive Director, Association for Spirit at Work (**http://www.spiritatwork.org**), wrote the Appendix, "Leadership and Spirituality in the Workplace." I also want to thank my mentor and coauthor of many publications, Joel Corman, for his advice and encouragement during and after my graduate education at Suffolk University.

I hope everyone who uses this text enjoys teaching from these materials as I do.

Robert N. Lussier, *Springfield College*

As it has been with past editions of this book, working with Bob Lussier is always a learning and growth experience that I value very much. He is a good friend and a mentor. To my students, friends, and colleagues who have encouraged and supported me morally, I say thanks. And, finally, I give recognition and thanks to the leadership of my institution, the University of Virginia's College at Wise, for their support of scholarship of this kind.

Christopher F. Achua, *University of Virginia's College at Wise*

Finally, we both would like to acknowledge the superb assistance we received from our editorial team. The guidance, support, and professionalism of Scott Person (acquisitions editor), Jonathan Monahan (marketing manager), Jennifer Ziegler and Joseph Malcolm (content project managers), Tippy McIntosh (senior art director), Kristen Meere (media editor), and Ruth Belanger (editorial assistant) were invaluable to the completion of this project. We would also like to thank the individuals who assisted in the preparation of support material (John Bowen, BJ Parker, Charlie Cook, and Louis Jourdan.) Special thanks to Julia Chase (developmental editor) for all her help in updating and upgrading this new fifth edition. We sincerely acknowledge the reviewers and survey respondents of this and past editions who provided feedback that greatly improved the quality of this book in many areas.

Reviewers

Chris Adalikwu, *Concordia College—Selma, Alabama*

Josje Andmore, *Camosun College School of Business*

Kathy Bohley, *University of Indianapolis*

John Bonosoro, *Webster University*

Brenda D. Bradford, *Missouri Baptist University*

Brian W. Bridgeforth, *Herzing College*

Carl R. Broadhurst, *Campbell University*

Jon Burch, *Trevecca Nazarene University*

Debi Cartwright, *Truman State University*

Don Cassiday, *North Park University*

Ken Chapman, *Webster University*

Felipe Chia, *Harrisburg Area Community College*

Valerie Collins, *Sheridan College*

George W. Crawford, *Clayton College & State University*

Janice Cunningham, *Indiana Tech*

Sue Cunningham, *Rowan Cabarrus Community College*

Joseph Daly, *Appalachian State University*

Frederick T. Dehner, *Rivier College*

Melinda Drake, *Limestone College*

Rex Dumdum, *Marywood University*

Ray Eldridge, *Freed-Hardeman University*

Debi Carter-Ford, *Wilmington College*

Dave Foster, *Montana State University*

Gerald A. Garrity, *Anna Maria College*

Thomas Garsombke, *Northland College*

Ronald Gayhart, *Lakeshore Tech College*

Michele Geiger, *College of Mount St. Joseph*

James Gelatt, *University of Maryland University College*

Don R. Gibson, *Houston Baptist University*

Eunice M. Glover, *Clayton College & State University*

Garry Grau, *Northeast State Community College*

Wade Graves, *Grayson County College*

Ray Grubbs, *Millsaps College*

Frank Hamilton, *Eckerd College*

Deborah Hanson, *University of Great Falls*

Nathan Hanson, *Palm Beach Atlantic*

Mary Ann Hazen, *University of Detroit Mercy*

Linda Hefferin, *Elgin Community College*

Marilyn M. Helms, *Dalton State College*

Mary Hogue, *Kent State University, Stark Campus*

Carol Himelhoch, *Siena Heights University*

Donny Hurwitz, *Austin Community College*

Stewart Husted, *Virginia Military Institute*

Dr. Katherine Hyatt, *Reinhardt University*

Gale A. Jaeger, *Marywood University*

Lori Happel-Jarratt, *The College of St. Scholastica*

David Jones, *North Carolina State University*

Thomas O. Jones, Jr., *Greensboro College*

Louis Jourdan, *Clayton State University*

Paul N. Keaton, *University of Wisconsin–La Crosse*

Gary Kleemann, *Arizona State University East*

Susan Kowalewski, *D'Youville College*

Bill Leban, *DeVry University*

Chet Legenza, *DeVry University*

Sondra Lucht, *Mountain State University*

Cheryl Macon, *Butler Community College*

James Maddox, *Friends University*

Kathleen B. Magee, *Anna Maria College*

Charles Mambula, *Suffolk University*

Gary May, *Clayton College & State University*

David McCalman, *University of Central Arkansas*

Lee E. Meadows, *Walsh College*

Ken Miller, *Mountain State University*

Michael Monahan, *Frostburg State University*

Steve Morreale, *Worcester State College*

Lorrie Mowry, *McCook Community College*

Jamie Myrtle, *MidAmerica Nazarene University*

Rhonda S. Palladi, *Georgia State University*

Patricia Parker, *Maryville University*

Jeff Pepper, *Chippewa Valley Tech College*

Nicholas Peppes, *St. Louis Community College*

Melinda Phillabaum, *Indiana University*

Laura Poppo, *Virginia Tech*

William Price, *North County Community College*

Dr. Kanu Priya, *Arkansas State University*

Gordon Rands, *Western Illinois University*

Kira K. Reed, *Syracuse University*

Marlys Rizzi, *Simpson College*

Mary Sacavage, *Alvernia College Schuylkill Center*

Khaled Sartawi, *Fort Valley State University*

Christopher Sieverdes, *Clemson University*

H. D. Sinopoli, *Waynesburg College*

Thomas G. Smith, *Fort Valley State University*

Emeric Solymossy, *Western Illinois University—Quad Cities*

Martha C. Spears, *Winthrop University*

Shane Spiller, *Morehead State University*

Karen Stephens, *Camosun College*

Bill Tracey, *Central Connecticut State University*

Dr. Robert Trumpy, *Central Washington University*

Robin Turner, *Rowan-Cabarrus Community College*

John Waltman, *Eastern Michigan University*

Fred A. Ware, Jr., *Valdosta State University*

Kerr F. Watson, *Mount Olive College*

Kristopher Weatherly, *Campbellsville University*

Amy Wojciechowski, *West Shore Community College*

Mike Woodson, *Northeast Iowa Community College*

Jan Wyatt, *Hesser College*

Benjamin R. Wygal, *Southern Adventist University*

Kimberly S. Young, *St. Bonaventure University*

Kenneth J. Zula, *Keystone College*

Joseph E. Zuro, *Troy State University*

About the Authors

ROBERT N. LUSSIER is a professor of management at Springfield College and has taught management for more than 25 years. He has developed innovative and widely copied methods for applying concepts and developing skills that can be used in one's personal and professional life. He was the director of Israel Programs and taught there. Other international experiences include Namibia and South Africa.

Dr. Lussier is a prolific writer, with over 350 publications to his credit. His articles have been published in the *Academy of Entrepreneurship Journal, Business Horizons, Entrepreneurship Theory and Practice, Journal of Business Strategies, Journal of Management Education, Journal of Small Business Management, Journal of Small Business Strategy, SAM® Advanced Management Journal,* and others. His other textbooks include *Management Fundamentals: Concepts, Applications, Skill Development* 4e (South-Western/Cengage); *Human Relations in Organizations: Applications and Skill Building* 7e (Irwin/McGraw-Hill); *Business, Society and Government Essentials: An Applied Ethics Approach* (Waveland); *Sport Management Principles and Applications: A Skills Approach* 2e (Human Kinetics); and others.

When not writing, Dr. Lussier consults to a wide array of commercial and nonprofit organizations. In fact, some of the material in the book was developed for such clients as Baystate Medical Center, Coca-Cola, Friendly's Ice Cream, the Institute of Financial Education, Mead, Monsanto, Smith & Wesson, the Social Security Administration, the Visiting Nurses Associations of America, and the YMCA.

Dr. Lussier holds a bachelor of science in business administration from Salem State College, two master's degrees in business and education from Suffolk University, and a doctorate in management from the University of New Haven.

CHRISTOPHER F. ACHUA is a Professor in the Department of Business and Economics at the University of Virginia's College at Wise. His teaching has centered on three disciplines: strategic management, marketing, and organizational leadership. Dr. Achua's interest in engaging students in real-life learning opportunities led him to create and direct programs such as the Center for Entrepreneurship, Leadership, and Service and the Small Business Institute at his university. These programs focused on developing students' leadership and entrepreneurial skills by applying theory to real-world situations.

Dr. Achua has presented scholarly papers at regional and national conferences. His papers have been published in many refereed proceedings, the *Small Business Institute Journal,* and the *Journal of Small Business Strategy.* When not involved in academic pursuits, he lends his expertise to community development programs and initiatives. He has served on several boards of organizations in the local community, and was chair of the Mountain Empire Regional Business Incubator Board of Directors.

Dr. Achua received his undergraduate degree in business administration and accounting from the University of Sioux Falls, South Dakota; his MBA from the University of South Dakota; and his doctorate from the United States International University (now Alliant International University) in San Diego, California.

LEADERSHIP

Theory, Application, & Skill Development

PART ONE

INDIVIDUALS AS LEADERS

1

Who Is a Leader and What Skills Do Leaders Need?

Learning Outcomes

After studying this chapter, you should be able to:

1. Briefly describe the five key elements of leadership. p. 5

2. Identify and define the managerial leadership skills. p. 9

3. List the ten managerial roles based on their three categories. p. 13

4. Explain the interrelationships among the levels of leadership analysis. p. 18

5. Describe the major similarity and difference between the trait and behavioral leadership theories. p. 19

6. Discuss the interrelationships between trait and behavioral leadership theories and contingency theories. p. 20

7. Define the following **key terms** (in order of appearance in the chapter):

leadership	leadership theory
influencing	leadership theory classifications
technical skills	leadership paradigm
interpersonal skills	leadership trait theories
decision-making skills	behavioral leadership theories
managerial role categories	contingency leadership theories
interpersonal leadership roles	integrative leadership theories
informational leadership roles	management to the leadership theory paradigm
decisional leadership roles	
levels of analysis of leadership theory	evidence-based management (EBM)

OPENING CASE *APPLICATION*

We begin each chapter by introducing an exceptional leader and company, followed by some questions for you to answer, and we answer the questions throughout the chapter. At age 29 Andrew Mason became the founder and CEO of Groupon (the name is a combo of group and coupon), a Chicago-based Web site.

Launched in November 2008 during the recession, Groupon features a daily deal on the best stuff to do, see, eat, and buy in more than 500 markets and 44 countries in local markets across North America and regional offices in Europe, Latin America, Asia, and throughout the world, and soon beyond.[1] It has been called the fastest-growing Web company ever (yes, faster than Google, Facebook, Amazon.com, etc.), and it has also become profitable much faster. More than a third of its sales already come from overseas.[2]

Mason grew up in Mt. Lebanon, Pennsylvania, a suburb of Pittsburgh. He started his entrepreneurial career at age 15 when he started a Saturday morning delivery service in his neighborhood called Bagel Express, and changed to the more profitable selling of Costco candy bars. He went to Chicago to attend Northwestern University where he earned a degree in music in 2003. After graduating, he was still in a band and the self-taught computer programmer landed a coding gig at Inner-Workings. In 2007 he founded The Point and in 2008 Groupon.[3]

Although he has been described as "hyperkinetc" and "a tough negotiator," he isn't your typical CEO yet. That is part of his charm. He's not used to talking about himself, and said "it feels strange." "I just like to build things and do things."[4] Headquarters in Chicago is a large open room with row upon row of shiny white desks without cubical walls, and Mason's desk, no different from any other, is in the middle of the hubbub.[5]

OPENING CASE QUESTIONS:

1. Why is Groupon so successful?

2. Does Groupon use our definition of leadership ("the influencing process of leaders and followers to achieve organizational objectives through change")?

3. What managerial leadership skills does CEO Andrew Mason use at Groupon? Can leadership skills be developed, and can you develop your leadership skills through this course?

4. What managerial leadership roles does CEO Andrew Mason perform at Groupon?

Can you answer any of these questions? You'll find answers to these questions about Groupon and its leadership throughout the chapter.

To learn more about Groupon, visit the company's Web site at **http://www.Groupon.com/about**.

The focus of this chapter is on helping you understand what leadership is and what this book is all about. As you can see in the chapter outline, we begin by discussing why leadership is important and defining leadership. Then we explain the three managerial leadership skills and the ten roles that managerial leaders perform. Next we explain the three levels of leadership analysis, which provides the framework for the book. After explaining the four major leadership paradigms that have developed over the years, we end this chapter by stating the objectives of the book and presenting its organization.

Leadership Is Everyone's Business

Let's begin with a discussion of the importance of leadership.

Here are just a few reasons why leadership is so important:

- Leadership remains one of the oldest domains of management research.[6] And research clearly links managerial leadership to positive consequences for both the individual and organizations, including financial performance. Also, substantial evidence demonstrates that sound managerial leadership practice is critical to creating effective organizations.[7]

- Leadership is one of the most debated and discussed topics and receives extensive coverage in the popular business press as well.[8] In the *Academy of Management Journal*, the number of organizational behavior articles researching leadership is second only to groups/teams.[9]

- Effective global leaders are a vital asset for organizations today as they can offer a competitive advantage.[10] CEO Mike Duke of Walmart® stated that his biggest challenge is to continue to develop the leadership talent to grow the company around the world.[11]

- Effective leadership can make a positive difference in the lives of people, the functioning of groups, and the success of organizations. Effective leadership has been shown to enhance employees' satisfaction with their jobs, motivation at work, and task performance. Some scholars have even suggested that effective leadership is essential for societies to progress in positive directions, and without it, the social fabric of our communities and organizations would fall apart.[12] On the other side, a bad boss can cause employees a lot of stress and heath-related problems.[13]

- The great debate over how much a chief executive officer (CEO) matters rages on.[14] CEOs like Steve Job of Apple have the power to make or break a company.[15] We will discuss how Jobs came back and saved Apple in the end-of-chapter case. During and coming out of a recession is a brutal time for anyone in leadership.[16] Studies show that the right person in the CEO position may be more important in bad times.[17] Nokia hired Stephen Elop and Yahoo hired Carol Bartz to be the CEOs to turn these companies around.[18] Only time will tell if they can succeed.

As the examples illustrate, leadership matters, and there is a great need for better leaders.[19] If we want to be successful, we must develop our leadership skills.[20] To this end, the focus of this book is to help you develop your leadership skills, so that you can become a successful leader in your personal and professional life.

OPENING CASE *APPLICATION*

1. Why is Groupon so successful?

Founder and CEO Andrew Mason is the key to Groupon's success. Groupon's company philosophy is pretty simple: We treat our customers the way we like to be treated.[21] Mason is the one who came up with the idea to fundamentally change the way that people buy from local businesses in the same way that e-commerce has changed the way that people buy products. Mason says it's like Amazon for small businesses. Groupon gives small business the opportunity to advertise their products and services without paying any up-front costs, along with the opportunity to get repeat business from new customers; at the same time, Groupon gives coupon buyers a great deal. It is especially helpful to new businesses without a customer base.[22]

Part of the problem with many online businesses is figuring out how to make a profit. YouTube, founded in 2005 (now owned by Google), still hasn't made a profit, while it only took Groupon seven months to turn a profit.[23] Mason's business model for making money is a three-step process. (1) Its salespeople approach a small business to set up a coupon promotion. (2) Groupon offers, sells, and collects the coupon money online. People buy the coupon from Groupon, which usually gets them around 50 percent off the regular price. (3) The business and Groupon share the profits. Groupon typically gives 50 percent, minus a small credit card fee, to the local business.[24] Plus, Groupon has a steady flow of quick cash to continually grow the business.

1.1 *Is Leadership Really Important?*

Scott Adams is the creator of the cartoon character Dilbert. Adams makes fun of managers, in part because he distrusts top-level managers, saying that leadership is really a crock. Leadership is about manipulating people to get them to do something they don't want to do, and there may not be anything in it for them. CEOs basically run the same scam as fortune-tellers, who make up a bunch of guesses and when by chance one is correct, they hope you forget the other errors. First, CEOs blame their predecessors for anything that is bad, then they shuffle everything around, start a new strategic program, and wait. When things go well, despite the CEO, the CEO takes the credit and moves on to the next job. Adams says we may be hung up on leadership as part of our DNA. It seems we have always sought to put somebody above everybody else.[25]

1. Do you agree with Scott Adams that leadership is a crock?

2. Do we really need to have someone in the leadership role?

Learning Outcome 1 | *Briefly describe the five key elements of leadership.*

Defining Leadership

The topic of leadership has generated excitement and interest since ancient times. When people think about leadership, images come to mind of powerful dynamic individuals who command victorious armies, shape the events of nations, develop religions, or direct corporate empires. How did certain leaders build such great armies, countries, religions, and companies? Why do certain leaders have dedicated followers while others do not? Why were Gandhi, Mother Theresa, Martin Luther King, and Nelson Mandela such influential leaders? How did Adolf Hitler rise to a position of great power? In this book, you will learn the major leadership theories and research findings regarding leadership effectiveness.

There is no universal definition of leadership because leadership is complex, and because leadership is studied in different ways that require different definitions. As in leadership research studies, we will use a single definition that meets our purpose in writing this book. Before you read our definition of leadership, complete Self-Assessment 1 to get a better idea of your leadership potential. In the following section, we will discuss each question as it relates to the elements of our leadership definition and to your leadership potential.

SELF-ASSESSMENT 1 **Leadership Potential**

As with all of the self-assessment exercises in this book, there are no right or wrong answers, so don't try to pick what you think is the right answer. Be honest in answering the questions, so that you can better understand yourself and your behavior as it relates to leadership.

For each pair of statements distribute 5 points, based on how characteristic each statement is of you. If the first statement is totally like you and the second is not like you at all, give 5 points to the first and 0 to the second. If it is the opposite, use 0 and 5. If the statement is usually like you, then the distribution can be 4 and 1, or 1 and 4.

(continued)

(Self-Assessment 1 continued)

If both statements tend to be like you, the distribution should be 3 and 2, or 2 and 3. Again, the combined score for each pair of statements must equal 5.

Here are the scoring distributions for each pair of statements:

0–5 or 5–0	One of the statements is totally like you, the other not like you at all.
1–4 or 4–1	One statement is usually like you, the other not.
2–3 or 3–2	Both statements are like you, although one is slightly more like you.

1. _____ I'm interested in and willing to take charge of a group of people.

   _____ I want someone else to be in charge of the group.

2. _____ When I'm not in charge, I'm willing to give input to the leader to improve performance.

   _____ When I'm not in charge, I do things the leader's way, rather than offer my suggestions.

3. _____ I'm interested in and willing to get people to listen to my suggestions and to implement them.

   _____ I'm not interested in influencing other people.

4. _____ When I'm in charge, I want to share the management responsibilities with group members.

_____ When I'm in charge, I want to perform the management functions for the group.

5. _____ I want to have clear goals and to develop and implement plans to achieve them.

   _____ I like to have very general goals and take things as they come.

6. _____ I like to change the way my job is done and to learn and do new things.

   _____ I like stability, or to do my job the same way; I don't like learning and doing new things.

7. _____ I enjoy working with people and helping them succeed.

   _____ I don't really like working with people and helping them succeed.

To determine your leadership potential score, add up the numbers (0–5) for the first statement in each pair; don't bother adding the numbers for the second statement. The total should be between 0 and 35. Place your score on the continuum at the end of this assessment. Generally, the higher your score, the greater your potential to be an effective leader. However, the key to success is not simply potential, but persistence and hard work. You can develop your leadership ability through this course by applying the principles and theories to your personal and professional lives.

0 — 5 — 10 — 15 — 20 — 25 — 30 — 35
Lower leadership potential   Higher leadership potential

Leadership *is the influencing process of leaders and followers to achieve organizational objectives through change.* Let's discuss the five key elements of our definition; see Exhibit 1.1 for a list.

EXHIBIT **1.1** **Leadership Definition Key Elements**

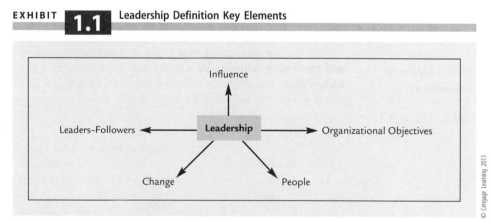

© Cengage Learning 2013

Leaders–Followers

Question 1 of Self-Assessment 1 is meant to get you thinking about whether you want to be a leader or a follower. If you are not interested and not willing to be in charge, you are better suited to be a follower. However, as you will learn in this section, good followers also perform leadership roles when needed.[26] And followers influence leaders. Thus, in our definition of leadership, the influencing process is *between* leaders and followers, not just a leader influencing followers; it's a two-way street.[27] Knowing how to lead and developing leadership skills will make you a better leader and follower.[28] So whether you want to be a leader or a follower, you will benefit from this book.

Throughout this book, leadership is referred to in the context of formal organizational settings in business corporations (GE, IBM), government agencies (Department of Motor Vehicles, the Police Department), and nonprofit organizations (Red Cross, Springfield College). Organizations have two major classifications of employees: managers, who have subordinates and formal authority to tell them what to do; and employees, who do not. All managers perform four major functions: planning, organizing, leading, and controlling. Leadership is thus a part of the manager's job. However, there are managers—you may know some—who are not effective leaders. There are also nonmanagers who have great influence on managers and peers.[29]

Therefore, in this book we do not use the terms *manager* and *leader* interchangeably. When we use the word *manager,* we mean a person who has a formal title and authority. When we use the term *leader,* we mean a person who may be either a manager or a nonmanager. A leader always has the ability to influence others; a manager may not. Thus, a leader is not necessarily a person who holds some formal position such as manager.

A *follower* is a person who is being influenced by a leader. A follower can be a manager or a nonmanager. Good followers are not "yes people" who simply follow the leader without giving input that influences the leader. In short, effective leaders influence followers, and their followers influence them.[30] The qualities needed for effective leadership are the same as those needed to be an effective follower. Throughout this book, we use the term *behavior* when referring to the activities of people or the things they do and say as they are influenced. You will learn more about followership in Chapter 7.

As implied in question 2 of Self-Assessment 1, good followers give input and influence leaders. If you want to be an effective follower, you need to share your ideas. Also, as a leader you need to listen to others and implement their ideas to be effective. According to GE CEO Jeff Immelt, GE is not run like a big company; it is run like a big partnership, where every leader can make a contribution not just to their job, but to the entire company.[31]

Influence

Influencing *is the process of a leader communicating ideas, gaining* acceptance of them, and motivating followers to support and implement the ideas through change. Effective leaders have the ability to influence others.[32] Let's face it, we all want to get our way, which is being influential.[33] Question 3 of Self-Assessment 1 asked if you were interested in and willing to influence others, as a leader or follower. When you have a management position, you have more power to influence others. But, effective followers also influence others. Your ability to influence others can be developed. Influencing includes power, politics, and negotiating; you will learn more about how to influence others in Chapter 5.

Influencing is also about the relationship between leaders and followers. Managers may coerce subordinates to influence their behavior, but leaders do not. Leaders gain the commitment and enthusiasm of followers who are willing to be influenced.[34] Most of the leadership research is concerned with the relationship between leaders and followers. Effective managers know when to lead and when to follow. Thus, leaders and followers often change roles throughout the influencing process.[35] Question 4 of Self-Assessment 1 asked if you want to share management responsibility as a leader.

WORK Application **1**

Recall a present or past job. Were you both a leader and a follower? Explain.

———————————

———————————

———————————

———————————

WORK Application **2**

Briefly explain the influencing relationship between the leader and followers where you work(ed).

———————————

———————————

———————————

———————————

Organizational Objectives

WORK Application **3**
State one or more objectives from an organization where you work(ed).

_____
_____
_____
_____

Effective leaders influence followers to think not only of their own interests but also of the interest of the organization through a shared vision. Leadership occurs when followers are influenced to do what is ethical and beneficial for the organization and themselves. Taking advantage of followers for personal gain is not part of leadership. Members of the organization need to work together toward an outcome that the leader and followers both want, a desired future or shared purpose that motivates them toward this more preferable outcome. As implied in question 5 of Self-Assessment 1, effective leaders set clear goals.[36] You will learn how to set objectives in Chapter 3.

Change

WORK Application **4**
Are the managers where you work(ed) effective at influencing their employees to bring about change? Explain.

_____
_____
_____
_____

Influencing and setting objectives is about change. Organizations need to continually change, to adapt to the rapidly changing global environment.[37] GE is the only company listed in the Dow Jones Industrial Index today that was also included in the original index in 1896. The other companies may have become too comfortable with doing business the same old way, perhaps causing these former business stars to fade. Effective leaders realize the need for continual change to improve performance.

Statements like these are not in a successful leader's vocabulary: _We've always done it this way; We've never done it that way before; It can't be done; No one else has done it;_ and _It's not in the budget._ Leadership involves influencing followers to bring about change toward a desired future for the organization. The company Andrew Mason most admires is Netflix because it continues to change its business model.[38]

As implied in question 6 of Self-Assessment 1 and the information in this section, to be an effective leader and follower you must be open to change.[39] The people who advance in organizations are those who are willing to take a risk and try new things.[40] When was the last time you did something new and different? You will learn more about leading change in Chapter 11.

People

WORK Application **5**
Do managers where you work(ed) treat their employees as valuable assets? Explain.

_____
_____
_____
_____

Although the term _people_ is not specifically mentioned in our definition of leadership, after reading about the other elements, you should realize that leadership is about leading people.[41] As implied in question 7 of Self-Assessment 1, to be effective at almost every job today, you must be able to get along with people.[42] Effective leaders and followers enjoy working with people and helping them succeed.[43] You will learn how to develop your people skills throughout this book.

Research, experience, and common sense all point to a direct relationship between a company's financial success and its commitment to leadership practices that treat people as assets.[44] There is little evidence that being a mean, tough manager is associated with leadership success. It is the collective efforts of all people contributing that make things happen.[45]

OPENING CASE APPLICATION

2. **Does Groupon use our definition of leadership ("the influencing process of leaders and followers to achieve organizational objectives through change")?**

Andrew Mason is clearly the _leader_ at Groupon, but he also gets ideas from his _followers_. Mason is also very _influential_. He convinced investors to give him money to start Groupon, gets local businesses to offer coupons, and customers to buy them. Mason has a clear shared vision and _objectives_ for the company. Groupon is fundamentally _changing_ the way

(continued)

(Opening Case Application 2 continued)

that people buy from local businesses and how the firms advertise. Groupon is about *people*. Groupon is a young company hiring young workers at a rapid pace; the average age is just 25.[46] It takes both users and merchants in each city; this is why Groupon has thousands of salespeople, often called Mason's army of sales reps, and they have a "War Room" to discuss strategy to continue growth and to defend its market share from copycats.[47]

Learning Outcome 2   *Identify and define the managerial leadership skills.*

Leadership Skills

In this section, let's start by answering the age-old question—are leaders born or made and can leadership be taught and skills developed—and then we will discuss the three skills managerial leaders need to succeed. But first complete Self-Assessment 2 to determine your managerial leadership skills.

Are Leaders Born or Made?

WORK Application **6**
Do you believe that you are a born leader? Do you believe that you can develop your leadership skills to improve job performance?

Are leaders born or made, or what determines leadership—nature or nurture? You may think this is a trick question, because most researchers say the answer is both. Effective leaders are not simply born or made. They are born with some leadership ability and develop it. So both perspectives add to the debate on the origins of leadership skills.[48] You will learn more about leadership traits (nature) in Chapter 2.

Some go so far as to say that leaders are definitely made, not born, and that everyone has equal potential to develop leadership skills (nurture). NFL Greenback Packers legendary football coach Vince Lombardi said, "Leaders are made, they are not born. They are made by hard effort."[49] Whatever your leadership ability is now, you can invest in developing your leadership skills, or you can allow them to remain as they are now. You may never become the CEO of an organization, but you can improve your leadership knowledge, ability, and skill through this course.[50] As Vince Lombardi would put it, you can develop your leadership skills through this course if you put in the effort and work hard at it. We'll talk more about this in the last section of this chapter.

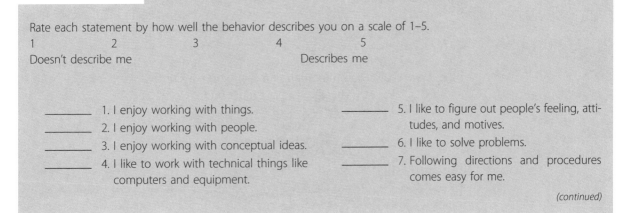

SELF-ASSESSMENT 2   **Managerial Leadership Skills**

Rate each statement by how well the behavior describes you on a scale of 1–5.

| 1 | 2 | 3 | 4 | 5 |
Doesn't describe me   Describes me

_____ 1. I enjoy working with things.

_____ 2. I enjoy working with people.

_____ 3. I enjoy working with conceptual ideas.

_____ 4. I like to work with technical things like computers and equipment.

_____ 5. I like to figure out people's feeling, attitudes, and motives.

_____ 6. I like to solve problems.

_____ 7. Following directions and procedures comes easy for me.

(continued)

_____ 8. Getting along with a variety of people comes easy for me.

_____ 9. Analytical and quantitative reasoning comes easy for me.

_____ 10. I'm good at getting a task done by the deadline.

_____ 11. I'm good at getting people to overcome conflict and work together.

_____ 12. I'm good at figuring out ways of overcoming barriers to get things done.

To determine your score, add up the numbers (1–5) for each skill and place them on the lines below. Each skill score should be between 5 and 20.

_____ **Technical skill** (items 1, 4, 7 10)

_____ **Interpersonal skill** (items 2, 5, 8, 11)

_____ **Decision-making skill** (items 3, 6, 9, 12)

Your score for each skill is essentially a measure of your preference. As the first three questions ask, do you prefer working with things, people, or conceptual ideas, or are they equal? In this section, you will learn about these three skills and throughout the book you will be given the opportunity to develop your managerial leadership skills.

Can Leadership Be Taught and Skills Developed?

Another question to answer is: Can leadership be taught and skills developed?[51] Everyone has potential to lead, and leadership skills can be developed.[52] If leaders are born and skills could not be developed, leading business schools would not be teaching leadership and you would not be taking this course.[53] Also, major corporations would not spend millions of dollars on leadership training each year. A survey found that 54 percent of large companies are developing the leadership skills of internal executives with the goal of one day becoming a CEO successor.[54] GE has a reputation for developing leaders, and for having managers who leave to become executives and CEOs of other companies.[55]

Leadership development is a multibillion industry including both in-house and consulting services.[56] The Center for Creative Leadership (http://www.ccl.org) is one of the world's most respected nonprofit consulting organizations that conducts research and develops leaders in all sectors of the global economy. Clearly, it would not be in business if its global client organizations did not believe it can develop leadership skills.

Managerial Leadership Skills

When we combine our knowledge, skills, and ability (KSAs), they are often referred to as "human capital"[57] and "competencies."[58] Leadership effectiveness stems from managerial competence and support.[59] Now let's discuss the three management skills that all leaders need to be successful—technical, interpersonal, and decision-making skills—and the differences in the skills needed based on the level of management.

But first, are they these skills really all that important? According to a survey of recruiters, the most important attributes they seek in a new employee, out of the 26 they listed, were: (1) communication and interpersonal skills, 89%); (2) ability to work well within a team (which takes interpersonal and decision making skills, 87%; and (3) analytical and problem-solving skills (which is part of decision-making skills, 85%.[60] All employees today need good management skills.[61] Because managerial leadership skills are so important, the focus of this book is on developing our skills.

Technical Skills

Technical skills *involve the ability to use methods and techniques to perform a task.* This includes knowledge about methods, processes, procedures and techniques, and the ability to use tools and equipment to perform a task. Technical skills can also be called *business skills*, or can include them.[62] When managers are working on budgets, for example, they may need computer skills in order to use spreadsheet software such as Microsoft® Excel®. Most employees are promoted to their first management position primarily because of their technical skills. As we know, there is rapid, continual technological change in the global economy.[63] So to be successful, we need to keep up with the latest technology in our field.[64]

Technical skills vary widely from job to job, and they are the easiest of the three management skills to develop.[65] This is why recruiters don't place technical skills high on their list of skills they seek in new employees. Therefore, we do not focus on developing technical skills.

Interpersonal Skills

Interpersonal skills *involve the ability to understand, communicate, and work well with individuals and groups through developing effective relationships.* Interpersonal skills are also called human, people, and soft skills.[66] Our interpersonal relationships lead to gaining influence.[67] Our interpersonal skills are important and they can be developed.[68]

We get our jobs done through our relationships with coworkers, supervisors, teams, and the organization in general.[69] The resources you need to get the job done are made available through relationships, both inside (employees) and outside (customers, suppliers, others) the firm.[70] Organizations are seeking employees with good interpersonal skills,[71] and business schools are placing more emphasis on people skills.[72] However, students have been found to have weak interpersonal skills.[73] So we should develop our interpersonal skills.[74]

Interpersonal skills are based on several other skills including communicating, teamwork, power, politics, negotiating, networking, motivating, conflict, diversity, and ethical skills. We will discuss these interpersonal skills throughout the book and you will have the opportunity to develop your interpersonal skills through this course.

Decision-Making Skills

Decision-making skills *are based on the ability to conceptualize situations and select alternatives to solve problems and take advantage of opportunities.* It's about understanding "What is going on."[75] Because decisions are based on conceptual ability, decision-making skills are often referred to as *conceptual skills*. Clearly, the decisions you have made over your lifetime have affected you today. Leadership decisions determine the success or failure of organizations,[76] so organizations are including employees in decision making,[77] and they are training their people to improve their decision-making skills.[78]

Decision-making skills are based on several other skills, including conceptual, diagnostic, analytical, critical-thinking, quantitative reasoning, and time management skills, as well as the ability to be creative, perceive trends, anticipate changes, and recognize problems and opportunities. We will discuss decision-making skills throughout the book and you will have the opportunity to develop your decision-making skills through this course.

Skills Needed Based on Management Level

Although managers need all three skills, the need for each skill does vary based on the level of management. Top-level managers have a greater need for interpersonal and decision-making skills than technical skills. Middle-level managers have a balanced need for all three skills. First-level managers have a greater need for technical and interpersonal skills than decision-making skills.[79]

To summarize, review the management skills in Exhibit 1.2; then complete Concept Application 1.

WORK Application 7
Select a manager, preferably one who is or was your boss, and state the specific management skills he or she uses on the job.

_____

_____

_____

_____

EXHIBIT **1.2**   Management Skills

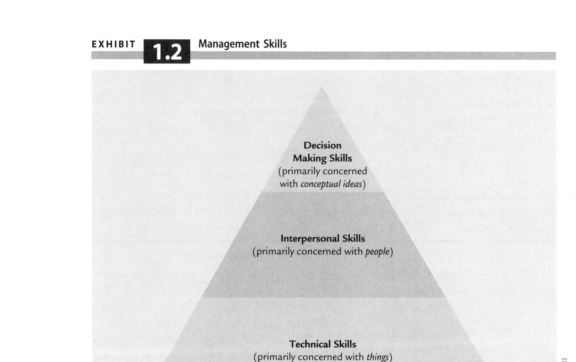

© Cengage Learning 2013

CONCEPT APPLICATION 1
Managerial Leadership Skills

Identify each activity as being one of the following types of management skills:

a. technical
b. interpersonal
c. decision-making

_____ 1. A manager is giving an employee sincere thanks for finishing the job ahead of schedule.

_____ 2. A manager is scheduling employee work hours for next week.

_____ 3. A manager is writing an e-mail.

_____ 4. A manager is running a machine for an employee who is out sick.

_____ 5. A manager is trying to figure out why the department is behind schedule.

OPENING CASE *APPLICATION*

3. **What managerial leadership skills does CEO Andrew Mason use at Groupon? Can leadership skills be developed, and can you develop your leadership skills through this course?**

Mason did develop skills as he earned his college degree. As discussed in this section, you can develop your leadership skills through this course if you put in the effort and work hard at it.

(continued)

(Opening Case Application 3 continued)

Andrew Mason has technical skills as he developed two online businesses. He also has interpersonal skills as he motivates employees to continually grow the business. Mason clearly has decision-making skills as he is the one who had the conceptual ability to develop the successful business model discussed in this chapter. Google made Mason a $6 billion buyout offer, but Mason made the decision to turn it down.[80]

Mason didn't start out as the leader of a successful company. Excited by the power of technology to change the world, Mason developed Policy Tree, a policy debate visualization tool, and won a scholarship to attend the University of Chicago Harris School of Public Policy in 2006. In school for only three months, Mason dropped out after receiving an unexpected offer to fund the idea that would become The Point, in 2007, a ground-breaking approach to online collective action and fundraising. The Point was losing money and his sponsor asked about making money, so in 2008 Mason founded Groupon.[81] Through this experience Mason developed managerial leadership skills that helped fuel his success at Groupon.

Learning Outcome 3   *List the ten managerial roles based on their three categories.*

Managerial Leadership Roles

In this section, we discuss what leaders do on the job—the management roles they play.[82] How well managers implement the managerial leadership roles affects their performance.[83] You will notice an overlap between the skills and roles because the leader needs the competencies (knowledge, skills, and ability—KSAs) to enact the managerial roles.[84] So if we want to be successful leaders, we need to develop the interrelated sets of competencies to play the leadership roles.[85]

Henry Mintzberg identified ten managerial roles that leaders perform to accomplish organizational objectives.[86] The roles represent the dominant classes of behavioral activities that managers or their followers perform. Mintzberg defined a *role* as a set of expectations of how a person will behave to perform a job. He grouped these roles into three categories. *The managerial role categories are interpersonal, informational, and decisional.* Mintzberg's management role theory has been supported by research studies. Exhibit 1.3 shows the ten managerial roles, based on the three categories.

EXHIBIT 1.3   Managerial Roles

Interpersonal Roles	Informational Roles	Decisional Roles
Figurehead	Monitor	Entrepreneur
Leader	Disseminator	Disturbance-handler
Liaison	Spokesperson	Resource-allocator
		Negotiator

© Cengage Learning 2013

Interpersonal Roles

The interpersonal leadership roles include figurehead, leader, and liaison. Clearly, interpersonal skills are needed to successfully play interpersonal roles.

Figurehead Role

Leaders perform the *figurehead role* when they represent the organization or department in legal, social, ceremonial, and symbolic activities. Top-level managers are usually viewed as figureheads for their organization, and Steve Jobs of Apple is an excellent example.[87] However, leaders throughout the organization perform the figurehead role.

Here are some of the figurehead activities: signing official documents (expense authorization, checks, vouchers, contracts, and so on); entertaining clients or customers as official representatives and receiving/escorting official visitors; informally talking to people and attending outside meetings as an organizational representative; presiding at meetings and ceremonial events (awards ceremonies, retirement dinners, and so on).

Leader Role

According to Mintzberg, the *leader role* is that of performing the *management functions* to effectively operate the managers' organization unit. Therefore, the leader role pervades all managerial behavior. In other words, the leader role influences how the leader performs other roles. You will learn more about the leadership role throughout this book.

The many leader behaviors that can be performed by managers or followers include hiring and training, giving instructions and coaching, and evaluating performance.

Liaison Role

WORK Application **8**

Give one job example of the specific behavior you or some other leader displayed when performing the figurehead, leader, and liaison roles. For each of the three roles, be sure to identify the leader as you or another, the role by its name, and the specific behavior.

_____

_____

_____

_____

Leaders perform the *liaison role* when they interact with people outside their organizational unit. Liaison behavior includes networking to develop and maintain relationships that lead to power and influence;[88] also called having connections.[89] Organizational politics is an important part of the liaison role, and you will learn more about how to gain and use power, how to conduct politics, and how to network in Chapter 5.

Liaison role behaviors include serving on committees with members from outside the organizational unit, attending professional/trade association meetings, and calling and meeting with people to keep in touch.

Informational Roles

The **informational leadership roles** *include monitor, disseminator, and spokesperson.* With the rapid technology changes, the informational roles become increasing important.[90] Informational role success is also based on interpersonal skills. You will learn more about informational roles in Chapter 6.

Monitor Role

Leaders perform the *monitor role* when they gather information. Most of the information is analyzed to discover problems and opportunities, and to understand events outside the organizational unit. Some of the information is passed on to other people in the organizational unit (disseminator role), or to people outside the unit (spokesperson role). In the past, leaders never had to communicate with so many constituencies.[91]

Information is gathered by behavior, including reading memos, reports, professional/trade publications, newspapers, and so forth; talking to others; attending meetings inside and outside the organization, and so forth; and observing (visiting a competitor's store to compare products, prices, and business processes).

Disseminator Role

Leaders perform the *disseminator role* when they send information to others in the organizational unit. Managers have access to information that is not available to employees. Some of the information that comes from higher levels of management must be passed on to employees, either in its original form or paraphrased. Using information translated into skills that advance the organization is now often being referred to as *knowledge management*.

Information is passed on in one or both of the following forms: orally through voice mail, one-on-one discussions, and group meetings; or written through e-mail and snail mail (U.S. mail). You will learn how to conduct meetings in Chapter 8.

Spokesperson Role

Leaders perform the *spokesperson role* when they provide information to people outside the organizational unit. People must report information to their boss (board of directors, owner, managers) and people outside the organizational unit (other departments, customers, suppliers). Leaders lobby and serve as public relations representatives for their organizational unit.

Some examples of the spokesperson role being performed would include meeting with the boss to discuss performance and with the budget officer to discuss the unit budget, answering letters, or reporting information to the government (the IRS, OSHA).

Decisional Roles

The **decisional leadership roles** *include entrepreneur, disturbance-handler, resource-allocator, and negotiator.* Decision-making skills are important and they are needed to be successful in the decisional roles.[92]

Entrepreneur Role

Leaders perform the *entrepreneur role* when they innovate and initiate improvements. Leaders often get ideas for improvements through the monitor role.

Examples of entrepreneur behavior would include developing new or improved products and services, developing new ways to process products and services, or purchasing new equipment.

Disturbance-Handler Role

Leaders perform the *disturbance-handler role* when they take corrective action during crisis or conflict situations. You will learn more about how to handle conflicts in Chapter 12. Unlike the planned action of the entrepreneur role to take advantage of an opportunity, the disturbance is a reaction to an unexpected event that creates a problem. Leaders typically give this role priority over all other roles.

Examples of emergencies leaders may have to resolve are a union strike, the breakdown of important machines/equipment, needed material arriving late, or a tight schedule to meet.

Resource-Allocator Role

Leaders perform the *resource-allocator role* when they schedule, request authorization, and perform budgeting activities. Deciding who gets the organization's limited resources is an important task and one of the biggest challenges that affects success.[93]

Examples of resource allocation would include deciding what is done now, done later, and not done (time management; priorities); determining who gets overtime or a merit raise (budgeting); or scheduling when employees will use material and equipment.

Negotiator Role

Leaders perform the *negotiator role* when they represent their organizational unit during routine and nonroutine transactions that do not include set boundaries (such as only one price and term of a sale/purchase for a product/service, or pay of an employee). When there are no set prices or pay conditions, leaders can try to negotiate a good deal to get the resources they need. You will be involved in employment negotiations, and you will learn how to negotiate in Chapter 5.

Examples of negotiations would include a pay and benefits package for a new professional employee or manager, labor union contracts, or a contract with a customer (sale) or supplier (purchase).

WORK Application 9
Give one job example of the specific behavior you or some other leader conducted when performing the monitor, disseminator, and spokesperson roles. For each of the three roles, be sure to identify the leader as you or another, the role by its name, and the specific behavior.

_____

_____

_____

_____

WORK Application 10
Give one job example of the specific behavior you or some other leader performed when fulfilling the entrepreneur, disturbance-handler, resource-allocator, and negotiator roles. For each of the four roles, be sure to identify the leader as you or another, the role by its name, and the specific behavior.

_____

_____

_____

_____

Although managers are responsible for all ten roles, which roles are most important—and which roles the manager performs and which are performed by other leaders—will vary based on the manager's job. The relative emphasis placed on these roles will vary as a function of organizational technology, the day-to-day problems faced by leaders, and the task environment of their organizations. After answering Work Applications 8 through 10, you should realize that we perform the leadership roles regardless of management title.

OPENING CASE APPLICATION

4. **What managerial leadership roles does CEO Andrew Mason perform at Groupon?**

Like all managers who are good leaders, Andrew Mason plays all ten roles, and he delegates these roles to his followers. Mason's interpersonal roles include signing documents; entertaining customers; running and attending meetings; leadership development and evaluation of followers; and serving on committees and boards. His informational roles include extensive communications.

In the decisional role category, Mason is a two-time online entrepreneur. His other roles include developing new territories to keep ahead of the competition, dealing with disturbances created by local business laws and regulations. As stated, Mason is a tough negotiator. The local business only gets around 25 percent of their regular price and Groupon typically gets 50 percent of every dollar it collects.[94]

CONCEPT APPLICATION 2
Leadership Managerial Roles

Identify each of the following 15 behaviors by its leadership role. Write the appropriate letter in the blank before each item.

Interpersonal roles	**Informational roles**	**Decisional roles**
a. figurehead	d. monitor	g. entrepreneur
b. leader	e. disseminator	h. disturbance-handler
c. liaison	f. spokesperson	i. resource-allocator
		j. negotiator

_____ 6. A leader is disciplining an employee for being late again.

_____ 7. A leader is visiting another company to watch how it makes its widgets.

_____ 8. A leader of a stock brokerage firm is trying to get the telephones turned back on so brokers can use the phone.

_____ 9. A leader is having new customized software developed for the organizational unit.

_____ 10. A leader is resolving a conflict between two employees who were verbally arguing how to get the job done and refusing to work together.

_____ 11. A leader is holding a meeting with his followers to discuss a new company policy.

_____ 12. A production leader is talking to a maintenance person about fixing a machine.

_____ 13. A leader is conducting a job interview to replace a retiree.

_____ 14. A sales leader is signing an expense reimbursement form for a sales representative.

_____ 15. A leader is holding a press conference with a local newspaper reporter.

_____ 16. A leader is assigning followers to various accounts and giving them the files.

(continued)

(Concept Application 2 continued)

_____ 17. A leader is working to make a deal on the compensation package for a new supervisor.

_____ 18. A leader is presenting organizational pins to employees for five years of service during a special meeting of all organizational unit members.

_____ 19. A leader is reading daily e-mail.

_____ 20. A leader and his manager, who must authorize the funding of the project, are discussing having new customized software developed for the leader's department.

Levels of Analysis of Leadership Theory

One useful way to classify leadership theory and research is by the levels of analysis. *The three* levels of analysis of leadership theory *are individual, group, and organizational.* Most leadership theories are formulated in terms of processes at only one of these three levels. You will briefly learn about each level in this section, and the details of each in Parts One through Three of this book.

Individual Level of Analysis

The individual level of analysis of leadership theory focuses on the individual leader and the relationship with individual followers. The individual level can also be called the *dyadic process.* As discussed in our definition of leadership, dyadic theories view leadership as a reciprocal influencing process between the leader and the follower.[95] There is an implicit assumption that leadership effectiveness cannot be understood without examining how a leader and follower influence each other over time. Recall that influencing is also about the relationships between leaders and followers. As a leader and as a follower, you will influence other individuals and they will influence your behavior at work. You will also have multiple dyadic relationships at work. In Part One, "Individuals as Leaders" (Chapters 1 through 5), the focus is on the individual level of analysis.

Group Level of Analysis

The second level of analysis of leadership theory focuses on the relationship between the leader and the collective group of followers. This level is also called *group process.* Group process theories focus on how a leader contributes to group effectiveness. Extensive research on small groups has identified important determinants of group effectiveness, which you will learn about in Part Two, "Team Leadership" (Chapters 6 through 8). An important part of group process is meetings. In Chapter 8, you will learn how to conduct productive meetings.

Organizational Level of Analysis

The third level of analysis focuses on the organization. This level is also called *organizational process.* Individuals and teams contribute to organizational success. Organizational performance in the long run depends on effectively adapting to the environment and acquiring the necessary resources to survive, and on whether the organization uses an effective transformation process to produce its products and services.

Much of the current research at the organizational level focuses on how top-level managers can influence organizational performance. Successful leaders, like Ursula Burns of Xerox, have had a positive impact on organizational performance.[96] You will learn more about determinants of organizational performance in Part Three, "Organizational Leadership" (Chapters 9 through 12).

1.2 *Executive Compensation*

Executive compensation is a complex and controversial subject. On one side of the debate, executive management skill has a direct impact on the success of the firm. Top executives should be paid multimillion-dollar compensation packages; after all, if it weren't for some effective CEOs, companies would not be making the millions of dollars of profits they make each year. They deserve a piece of the pie they helped create.[97]

On the other side, top executives have been criticized for being overpaid, especially as CEO pay rose while employees were getting laid off during the recession. In 2010, the economic recovery remained frail, unemployment was high, and corporate profits were roughly flat, up 1.5 percent from where the stock market peaked. However, CEO compensation jumped 27 percent in 2010 as employees pay went up only 2.1 percent. The median pay in 2010 was $9 million. Philippe Dauman of Viacom was the highest paid with total compensation of $84.5 million, followed by Ray Irani of Occidental Petroleum with $76.1 million, and Michael White of DirectTV was third with $32.9 million in compensation.[98]

1. Do executives deserve to make around 200 times as much as the average worker?

2. Is it ethical for managers to take large pay increases while laying off employees and when giving them only small raises?

3. Are companies being socially responsible when paying executives premium compensation?

Learning Outcome 4 Explain the interrelationships among the levels of leadership analysis.

Interrelationships among the Levels of Analysis

Exhibit 1.4 illustrates the interrelationships among the levels of analysis of leadership theory. Note that the individual is placed at the bottom of the triangle because group and organizational performance are based on individual performance. It has been said that an organization is the sum of all of its individual transactions. Depending on the size of the group and organization you work for, your individual performance may influence the performance of the group and organization positively or negatively.

EXHIBIT 1.4 Interrelationships Among the Levels of Analysis of Leadership Theory

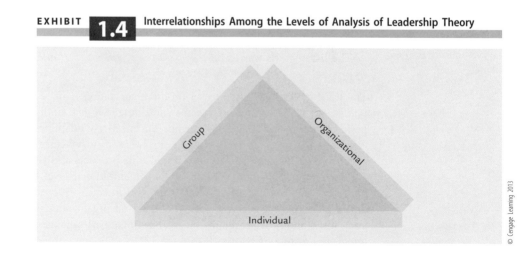

If individual performance is low throughout the organization, the triangle will fall because it will not have a firm foundation, or performance will be low. The group part of the triangle supports the organizational side. So if the groups are not effective, the triangle will fall or organizational performance will be low. At the same time, both group and organizational performance affect the performance of the individual. If groups are highly motivated and productive (or not productive), chances are the individual will be productive (or not) as well. Success tends to be contagious. Working for a winning organization, like Google, tends to motivate individuals to perform at their best to stay on top. However, an organization and its performance are more than the simple sum of its individuals and groups.

Leadership Theory Paradigms

The first thing we need to do is define the important concepts of this section. *A **leadership theory** is an explanation of some aspect of leadership; theories have practical value because they are used to better understand, predict, and control successful leadership.* So, the main purpose of a theory is to inform practice. It has been said that there is nothing as practical as a good theory. There are four major classifications of leadership theory, also called *research approaches,* used to explain leadership. **Leadership theory classifications** *include trait, behavioral, contingency, and integrative.* In this section, we discuss each classification and indicate where it is covered in more detail later in this book.

*A **leadership paradigm** is a shared mindset that represents a fundamental way of thinking about, perceiving, studying, researching, and understanding leadership.* The leadership paradigm has changed in the 60 years during which it has been studied. The four major classifications of leadership theory all represent a change in leadership paradigm. You will also learn about the change in paradigm from management to leadership in this section.

| Learning Outcome 5 | *Describe the major similarity and difference between the trait and behavioral leadership theories.* |

The Trait Theory Paradigm

Early leadership studies were based on the assumption that leaders are born, not made. Researchers wanted to identify a set of characteristics or traits that distinguished leaders from followers, or effective leaders from ineffective leaders. **Leadership trait theories** *attempt to explain distinctive characteristics accounting for leadership effectiveness.* Researchers analyzed physical and psychological traits, or qualities, such as high energy level, appearance, aggressiveness, self-reliance, persuasiveness, and dominance in an effort to identify a set of traits that all successful leaders possessed.

The list of traits was to be used as a prerequisite for promoting candidates to leadership positions. Only candidates possessing all the identified traits would be given leadership positions. Hundreds of trait studies were conducted during the 1930s and 1940s to discover a list of qualities. However, no one has come up with a universal list of traits that all successful leaders possess, or traits that will guarantee leadership success. On the positive side, although there is no list of traits that guarantees leadership success, traits that are related to leadership success have been identified. You will learn more about trait theory in the next chapter.

WORK Application **11**
Give examples of traits and behaviors that helped make your past or present manager a successful leader.

_____

_____

_____

_____

The Behavioral Leadership Theory Paradigm

By the 1950s, most of the leadership research had changed its paradigm, going from trait theory to focusing on what the leader actually did on the job (behavior). In the continuing quest to find the one best leadership style in all situations, researchers attempted to identify differences in the behavior of effective leaders versus ineffective leaders. Another subcategory of behavioral leadership focuses on the nature of management work. Thus, **behavioral leadership theories** *attempt to explain distinctive styles used by effective leaders, or to define the nature of their work*. Mintzberg's ten managerial roles are an example of behavioral leadership theory. Behavioral research focuses on finding ways to classify behavior that will facilitate our understanding of leadership.

Hundreds of studies examined the relationship between leadership behavior and measures of leadership effectiveness. However, there was no agreement on one best leadership style for all management situations. On the positive side, organizations develop leadership skills. And researchers did identify two generic dimensions of leader behavior: task- and people-oriented leadership, both of which have importance in accounting for leadership effectiveness. You will learn about some of the most popular behavioral leadership theories in Chapter 3 and about applications in Chapter 4.

Learning Outcome 6	*Discuss the interrelationships between trait and behavioral leadership theories and contingency theories.*

The Contingency Leadership Theory Paradigm

Both the trait and behavioral leadership theories were attempts to find the one best leadership style in all situations; thus they are called *universal theories*. In the 1960s, it became apparent that there is no one best leadership style in all situations; the right answer often depends on the situation.[99] Thus, the leadership paradigm shifted to contingency theory. **Contingency leadership theories** *attempt to explain the appropriate leadership style based on the leader, followers, and situation*.

In other words, which traits and/or behaviors will result in leadership success given the situational variables? The contingency theory paradigm emphasizes the importance of situational factors, including the nature of the work performed, the external environment, and the characteristics of followers. One aspect of this research is to discover the extent to which managerial work is the same or different across different types of organizations, levels of management, and cultures. Some cultures prefer autocratic leaders while others prefer participative leaders. You will learn about the major contingency leadership theories in Chapter 4.

The Integrative Leadership Theory Paradigm

More recently, theorists have conceptualized leadership more broadly with a mutual influence process.[100] In the mid-to-late 1970s, the paradigm began to shift to the integrative, to tie the theories together, or neo-charismatic theory. As the name implies, **integrative leadership theories** *attempt to combine the trait, behavioral, and contingency theories to explain successful, influencing leader–follower relationships*. Researchers try to explain why the followers of some leaders are willing to work so hard and make personal sacrifices to achieve the group and organizational objectives, or how effective leaders influence the behavior of their followers.[101] Theories identify behaviors and traits that facilitate the leader's effectiveness, and explore why the same behavior by the leader may have a different effect on followers, depending on the situation. The integrative leadership theory paradigm is emphasized in our definition of leadership and thus influences this entire book, especially Chapters 6 through 12.

From the Management to the Leadership Theory Paradigm

In the first section, we talked about some of the differences between a manager (formal position of authority) and a leader (has the ability to influence others), because the overarching paradigm has shifted from management to leadership. Successful managers use a truly participative form of leadership as they share the responsibility of management with employees, or as leadership responsibilities are transitioned from managers to team members.

Some of the differences identified between managers and leaders are as follows. Managers focus on doing things right, and leaders focus on doing the right thing. Managers are concerned with stability and the best way to get the job done, and leaders place greater concern on innovation and change. The old command-and-control model of management just doesn't work in today's global economy.[102] The old-style autocratic managers are not climbing today's corporate ladder. Today, managers must be able to lead through motivating others and creating favorable conditions for success, as well as manage. So, going from the **management to the leadership theory paradigm** *is a shift from the older autocratic management style to the newer participative leadership style of management.*

Although we have made a comparison between managers and leaders, you should realize that successful leaders are also good at managing, and successful managers are good leaders. There is overlap between the two paradigms—a successful organization needs both managers and leaders. The focus is on how to integrate management and leadership, or on developing leadership skills of managers and employees, which we do in this book. To simplistically stereotype people as either managers or leaders does little to advance our understanding of leadership. Also, because the term *manager* is an occupational title, to foster an inaccurate, negative stereotype of managers is certainly not our intent.

WORK Application 12

Does your present or past manager focus more on management or leadership? Explain, using examples.

_____

_____

_____

_____

CONCEPT APPLICATION 3
Leadership Theories

Identify each research approach by its leadership theory paradigm. Write the appropriate letter in the blank before each item.

a. trait

b. behavioral

c. contingency

d. integrative

e. management to leadership

_____ 21. A researcher is attempting to understand how leaders who are charismatic influence followers to achieve high levels of performance.

_____ 22. A researcher is attempting to determine if there is a relationship between how a manager dresses and leadership effectiveness.

_____ 23. A researcher is investigating the specific company, work environment, and followers to determine which leadership style is most appropriate.

_____ 24. A researcher is teaching managers to understand when to include employees in their decision making.

_____ 25. A researcher is observing managers' actions to determine how much time they spend giving employees praise for doing a good job versus criticism for poor performance.

Objectives of the Book

The overarching objectives of this book are reflected in its subtitle: *Theory, Application, and Skill Development.* We call it a three-pronged approach, with these objectives:

- To teach you the theory and concepts of leadership
- To develop your ability to apply leadership theory through critical thinking
- To develop your leadership skills in your personal and professional life

There has been a call to bridge the gap between research and practice,[103] to make education more relevant to practice,[104] and to offer different teaching methods and approaches.[105] To meet these calls, unlike most other books, ever since our first edition, we don't simply teach you leadership theory; we develop your ability to apply the theory and actually develop skills. This book offers some unique features relating to each of the three objectives (see Exhibit 1.5). So that you can get the most from this book, we encourage you to turn back to the preface and read our goals in writing this book, and the descriptions of the features.

EXHIBIT 1.5   The Three-Pronged Approach: Features of the Book

Theory	Application	Skill Development
Research	Opening cases	Self-assessment exercises
References	Work applications	Case role-playing exercises
Learning outcomes	Concept applications	Step-by-step behavior models
	Critical thinking questions	Behavior model videos
Key terms	Cases	Developing your leadership skills exercises
Summary	Video cases	
Review questions	You make the ethical call	Behavior modeling training

© Cengage Learning 2013

Leadership Theory

Throughout this book, you will learn about several leadership theories and the concepts on which they are based. As shown in Exhibit 1.5, this book offers six features to help you learn the leadership theory. The theories and concepts you will learn are based on research (EBM) and are considered important (AACSB), as discussed below.

Evidence-Based Management

Research-based knowledge is relevant and useful to practice, and evidence-based management translates theory into practice.[106] **Evidence-based management (EBM)** *means that decisions and organizational practices are based on the best available scientific evidence.* Faculty have been prompted to use evidence-based management in their courses.[107] The theories and concepts you will learn in this book are based on scientific research (not opinions, outdated research, or myths). If you look at the references at the end of this book, you will see that a majority of the journal articles are published by the premier professional association, the Academy of Management (AoM), and what it publishes is relevant to practicing leaders. However, unlike the AoM journals, we write about the theory and concepts at a level that is easy to read and understand.

Published research influences what people do in organizations; however, many organizations do not practice EBM.[108] As suggested by the past AoM president, our objective is to move you away from making decisions based on personal preference and unsystematic experience toward EBM. If you go to the next level and apply EBM theory and concepts, you can develop your leadership skills.

AACSB Assurance of Learning Standards

It is important to develop managerial leadership competencies. So how do we know what leadership competencies are important to your career success? For the answer, we turned to the Association to Advance Collegiate Schools of Business (AACSB), which gives accreditation to business schools. Below is a list of competencies taken from the AACSB assurance of learning standards. Normally, the curriculum management process will include learning experiences in such general knowledge and skill areas as:[109]

- **Communication abilities** (Chapter 6 covers communication skills)
- **Ethical understanding and reasoning abilities** (Chapters 2 and 10 cover ethics, and each chapter includes "You Make the Ethical Call" situations)
- **Analytic skills** (This general skill is developed throughout the book through multiple applications and skill development exercises)
- **Use of information technology** (This is not normally a topic of a leadership course)
- **Dynamics of the global economy** (Chapters 10–12 include global issues)
- **Multicultural and diversity understanding** (Chapter 10 covers these topics)
- **Reflective thinking skills** (This general skill is developed throughout the book through multiple applications and skill development exercises especially the self-assessment exercises)

All of the Developing Your Leadership Skills exercises state which AACSB assurance of learning standard skills are developed through completing the exercise.

Application of Leadership Theory

Brian Tracy said, "I believe through learning and application of what you learn, you can solve any problem, overcome any obstacle and achieve any goal that you can set for yourself." However, one of the most common criticisms of management education is the tendency to focus on teaching of theory, but not on the application of theory to practice.[110] Building on John Dewey's notion of learning-by-doing, students need to be given the opportunity to properly apply what they learn.[111] To this end, this book offers you seven features (see Exhibit 1.5, the Application column) to practice applying the concepts and theory.

Leadership Skill Development

To be successful, knowledge must be translated into skills.[112] The third and highest-level book objective is to develop leadership skills that can be used in your personal and professional life as a leader and as a follower. AACSB standards include developing managerial leadership skills.[113] To this end, this book offers you six features (see Exhibit 1.5, the Skill Development column) to help you develop your leadership skills. We also discuss a model vs. an exhibit, behavior modeling, and the need to practice the skills next.

Models versus Exhibits

All of the behavioral "models" in this book provide specific, step-by-step instructions, and they are labeled as models. They are "prescriptive models." When we offer general advice without a specific instruction, we label the guidelines "exhibits." However, the purpose of both models and exhibits is to help you improve your performance.

Behavior Modeling Leadership Skills Training

Behavior modeling is the only multiple leadership skills training that has been empirically validated by rigorous procedures.[114] In some of the chapters, the features listed in Exhibit 1.5 are combined in behavior modeling skills training. For these exercises you may do a self-assessment. In any case, follow this procedure: (1) read the step-by-step models, (2) watch a behavior modeling video, and (3) practice the skill (which may include role-playing) through a skill-development exercise. The last step in this training is using the skill in your personal and/or professional life for further development of the leadership skill.

Practice

We need to be more mindful of our own skill development and take more control over our own leadership development.[115] As with just about everything in life, you cannot become skilled by simply reading or trying something once. Recall that Vince Lombardi said that leaders are made by effort and hard work. If we want to develop our leadership skill, we need to learn the leadership concepts, apply the concepts, and do the preparation and skill-development exercises. But most important, to be successful, we need to be disciplined to practice using our leadership skills in our personal and professional lives. Think of leadership development like a sport. If you don't practice, you will not be good at it, and you will lose the skill you do have over time.

Flexibility

This book has so many features that they most likely cannot all be covered during a one-semester course. Your instructor will select the features to be covered that best meet the course objectives and the amount of class time available. You may do some or all of the features not covered in the course on your own, or do some exercises with the assistance of others outside of class.

Organization of the Book

This book is organized by level of leadership analysis and leadership theory paradigm. See Exhibit 1.6 for an illustration of the organization of this book.

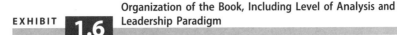

EXHIBIT **1.6** Organization of the Book, Including Level of Analysis and Leadership Paradigm

PART ONE. INDIVIDUALS AS LEADERS (individual-level analysis of leadership theory——Trait, Behavioral, and Contingency Leadership Theories)

1. Who Is a Leader and What Skills Do Leaders Need?
2. Leadership Traits and Ethics
3. Leadership Behavior and Motivation
4. Contingency Leadership Theories
5. Influencing: Power, Politics, Networking, and Negotiation

PART TWO. TEAM LEADERSHIP (group-level analysis of leadership theory——Integrative Leadership Theory Applications)

6. Communication, Coaching, and Conflict Skills
7. Leader–Member Relations and Followership Correct
8. Team Leadership and Self-Managed Teams

PART THREE. ORGANIZATIONAL LEADERSHIP (organizational-level analysis——Integrative Leadership Theory Applications)

9. Charismatic and Transformational Leadership
10. Leadership of Culture, Ethics, and Diversity
11. Strategic Leadership and Change Management
12. Crises Leadership and the Learning Organization

© Cengage Learning 2013

Chapter Summary

The chapter summary is organized to answer the six learning outcomes for Chapter 1.

1. **Briefly describe the five key elements of leadership.**

Leader–Follower—leaders influence the behavior of followers, and vice versa. *Influencing*—the relationship between leaders and followers, who change roles. *Organizational objectives*—outcomes that leaders and followers want to accomplish. *Change*—needed to achieve objectives. *People*—leadership is about leading people.

2. **Identify and define the managerial leadership skills.**

The three skills are technical, interpersonal, and decision-making. *Technical skills* involve the ability to use methods and techniques to perform a task. *Interpersonal skills* involve the ability to understand, communicate, and work well with individuals and groups through developing effective relationships. *Decision-making skills* are based on the ability to conceptualize situations and select alternatives to solve problems and take advantage of opportunities.

3. **List the ten managerial roles based on their three categories.**

Leaders perform the interpersonal role when they act as figurehead, leader, and liaison. Leaders perform the informational role when they act as monitor, disseminator, and spokesperson. Leaders perform the decisional role when they act as entrepreneur, disturbance-handler, resource-allocator, and negotiator.

4. **Explain the interrelationships among the levels of leadership analysis.**

The three levels of leadership analysis are individual, group, and organizational. The individual performance affects the group and organizational performance. The group performance affects the organizational performance. And both the group and organization affect the performance of the individual.

5. **Describe the major similarity and difference between the trait and behavioral leadership theories.**

The similarity between the trait and behavioral leadership theories is that they are both universal theories, or they are seeking one best leadership style for all situations. The difference is the approach to determining leadership effectiveness. Trait theory attempts to explain personal characteristics of effective leaders, whereas behavioral theory attempts to explain what leaders actually do on the job.

6. **Discuss the interrelationships between trait and behavioral leadership theories and contingency theories.**

The contingency theory is interrelated with the trait and behavioral leadership theories because it uses these two theories as the foundation for determining which leadership style is most appropriate—based on the leader, followers, and situation.

7. **Define the following key terms (in order of appearance in the chapter).**

Select one or more methods: (1) fill in the missing key terms from memory; (2) match the key terms from the following list with their definitions below; (3) copy the key terms in order from the list at the beginning of the chapter.

_____ is the influencing process of leaders and followers to achieve organizational objectives through change.

_____ is the process of a leader communicating ideas, gaining acceptance of them, and motivating followers to support and implement the ideas through change.

_____ involve the ability to use methods and techniques to perform a task.

_____ involve the ability to understand, communicate, and work well with individuals and groups through developing effective relationships.

_____ are based on the ability to conceptualize situations and select alternatives to solve problems and take advantage of opportunities

_____ are interpersonal, informational, and decisional.

_____ include figurehead, leader, and liaison.

_____ include monitor, disseminator, and spokesperson.

_____ include entrepreneur, disturbance-handler, resource-allocator, and negotiator.

_____ are individual, group, and organizational.

_____ is an explanation of some aspect of leadership; theories have practical value because they are used to better understand, predict, and control successful leadership.

_____ include trait, behavioral, contingency, and integrative.

_____ is a shared mindset that represents a fundamental way of thinking about, perceiving, studying, researching, and understanding leadership.

_____ attempt to explain distinctive characteristics accounting for leadership effectiveness.

_____ attempt to explain distinctive styles used by effective leaders, or to define the nature of their work.

_____ attempt to explain the appropriate leadership style based on the leader, followers, and situation.

_____ attempt to combine the trait, behavioral, and contingency theories to explain successful, influencing leader–follower relationships.

_____ is a shift from the older autocratic management style to the newer participative leadership style of management.

_____ means that decisions and organizational practices are based on the best available scientific evidence.

Key Terms

behavioral leadership theories, 20

contingency leadership theories, 20

decisional leadership roles, 15

decision-making skills, 11

evidence-based management (EBM), 22

influencing, 7

informational leadership roles, 14

integrative leadership theories, 20

interpersonal leadership roles, 13

interpersonal skills, 11

leadership, 6

leadership paradigm, 19

leadership theory, 19

leadership theory classifications, 19

leadership trait theories, 19

levels of analysis of leadership theory, 17

management to the leadership theory paradigm, 21

managerial role categories, 13

technical skills, 10

Review Questions

1. Why is leadership important?

2. What are the five key elements in our leadership definition? How do the elements interrelate to form this definition?

3. Are leaders born or made, and can leadership skills be developed?

4. List and define the interpersonal managerial leadership roles.

5. List and define the informational managerial leadership roles.

6. List and define the decisional managerial leadership roles.

7. List and define the levels of analysis of leadership theory.

8. List and define the leadership theory paradigms.

9. How can the shift in paradigm from management to leadership possibly help—and hurt—the management profession?

10. What are the three-pronged approach objectives to this book?

Critical Thinking Questions

The following critical-thinking questions can be used for class discussion and/or as written assignments to develop communication skills. Be sure to give complete explanations for all questions.

1. Should leadership be the manager's job, or should leadership be a shared process?

2. Are you interested in sharing leadership, or do you prefer to be a follower?

3. Some people say the hard skills (finance, quantitative analysis) are more important for managers than soft skills (interpersonal skills), and some say the opposite is true. What is your view?

4. Should leadership courses focus on teaching students about leadership or on teaching students to be leaders?

5. Can college students really develop their leadership skills through a college course? Why or why not?

6. Is leadership ability universal, or is a good leader in one environment also effective in another? For example, can a leader in one industry (e.g., a hospital) be successful in another industry (e.g., a bank)?

CASE

Steve Jobs—Apple

At age 21 Steven Jobs coproduced the first PC and Apple Computer, at 25 Jobs was running Apple with a net worth of $25 million, and at age 26 he made the cover of *Time* magazine. More recently, Steven Jobs was given the title CEO of the decade,[116] ranked #1 by *Fortune* on its list of "Smartest People in Tech," calling him the smartest CEO,[117] and he consistently ranks high on its list of "Business-Person of the Year."[118] He is also ranked by *Forbes* in the top 50 of "The Richest People in America."[119] Jobs cofounded Apple Computer with Steven Wozniak back in 1976. Today, Apple is ranked #1 on *Fortune's* "The World's Most Admired Companies,"[120] #1 on *Business Week's* "The 50 Most Innovative Companies,"[121] it pulled ahead of its arch rival Microsoft to become the most valuable tech company,[122] and its revenue growth rate is near three times that

of Microsoft and more than triple that of IBM, HP, and Intel.[123]

Most of us never have any real influence over any industry, but Jobs is ranked #1 for his leadership and power in influencing five industries: computers, Hollywood, music, retailing, and wireless phones/telcom. So far, no one has had more influence over a broader range of businesses than Jobs.[124] Some say that his influence actually transformed these industries.[125] Let's trace his business success, and failure, along the way to his earning these titles for himself and Apple as he influenced these five industries.

Together with Steve Wozniak, Jobs developed and built the personal computer (PC) in 1976 in Jobs's family garage. The Apple II kicked off the PC era in 1977, and in 1984 the Macintosh altered the direction of the computer industry. Jobs is also credited with desktop publishing, laser printers, and for pioneering personal computer networks. So Jobs was an influential founder of the PC industry. However, as Apple grew through selling stock, Jobs lost controlling ownership of his company. In 1985, Jobs was fired by the board of directors because he was controlling and unmanageable.[126] Although considered a failure at this point, Jobs didn't give up and bounced back very quickly.

In 1985, Jobs started NeXT (a computer platform development company specializing in the higher education and business markets). In 1986, he started what became Pixar Animated Studios and became its CEO. Jobs contracted with Disney to produce a number of computer-animated feature films, which Disney would cofinance and distribute. Films included *Toy Story*, *A Bug's Life*, *Monsters, Inc.*, *The Incredibles*, and *Cars*. In 2006, Jobs sold Pixar to Disney and remains on its board as its largest shareholder. In fact, Jobs's shares in Disney are worth more than five times the value of his Apple stock. So Jobs clearly influenced Hollywood films.

In 1997, Apple acquired NeXT to use its technology in its Apple computers and Jobs returned to Apple after a 12-year exile. Apple was close to bankruptcy so the board appointed Jobs to his earlier position as CEO. Jobs changed its culture back to a more entrepreneurial atmosphere. Jobs is a visionary, and Apple's success is born of continual and artful innovation in every aspect of its business. According to Jobs, Apple's success comes from simply trying to make great products that we want for ourselves, and then hope that customers love them as much as we do.

You are most likely aware of Apple's innovations under Jobs's leadership. Through the iPod and iTunes and Apple Stores Jobs has clearly influenced music and retailing. The iPhone has clearly influenced wireless phones/telecom. Its new iTunes App Store is also set to be very profitable as Apple plans to take a 30 percent cut on any media sales, and if they don't agree, they can be thrown off the devices,[127] and its iTunes Match should be a success as well.[128] The iPad was months ahead of the largely absent competition in the tablet market. And by the way, Apple never shortchanged its very profitable PC business. The PC market share has increase from 3 percent to 9.7 percent during the last decade,[129] and its MacBook Air is transitioning from disk-drive-based laptop computers to the radical flash-memory.[130] So PC founder Jobs continues to influence the computer industry.

Although Jobs has been so influential in five industries and has been called perhaps the most charismatic CEO in business history,[131] Jobs is also among the most controversial figures in business. People who have worked for Jobs over the years have mixed reactions to his leadership style. Some call him temperamental, aggressive, tough, intimidating, and very demanding. He has been known to verbally attack people who make mistakes and are not meeting goals and expectations. He is known as a control freak with a compulsive attention to details. He routinely sends products back to the lab, kills new products in their crib, demands new features or euthanizes old ones.[132] He is outspoken and not afraid to anger employees and customers. Even many who feared him also had great respect for him as he did inspire loyalty, enthusiasm, and high levels of performance through continuous innovation. Even people who left Apple say it's often brutal and Jobs hogs the credit, but they've never done better work.[133]

Jobs dictator-like control can cause havoc for Apple partners too.[134] Jobs has publicly criticized Adobe and Microsoft even though they supply Apple with the software for Apple's operating systems. In a combative mood, Jobs launched a public fight with Adobe over Apple's refusal to support Adobe's popular Flash software.[135] He has also attracted Samsung, even though it makes some of the most important components Apple buys, including memory chips and displays. Samsung makes the brains inside the iPhone and IPad.[136]

In his 50s, Jobs has had health problems. In 2009, he took a six-month leave and underwent a liver transplant. In early 2011 he took another leave without saying when he would return or why he was leaving, but stated: "I love Apple so much and hope to be back as soon as I can."[137] Although on leave, showman Jobs unexpectedly presented the iPad 2 in San Francisco in March 2011,[138] and Jobs still calls the shots from home.[139] In June 2011, Jobs took a break from his medical leave again to show off a new online music service called iTunes Match.[140] Jobs also attended a Cupertino, California City Council Meeting to personally present the plans for a new massive headquarters to be built by 2015 on 150 acres of land, which he said will look a little like a spaceship.[141] On August 24, 2011, Jobs resigned as CEO naming Tim Cook as his successor. Jobs died in October 2011. Many people question, can Apple succeed without Jobs?[142] Only time will tell. In any case, Jobs found the secret to career fulfillment—he discovered something he was good at and loved to do. We can't all be another Steve Jobs, but we can find career fulfillment.

GO TO THE INTERNET: To learn more about Steve Jobs and Apple, visit its Web site **(http://www.apple.com)**.

Support your answers to the following questions with specific information from the case and text or with information you get from the Web or another source.

1. Explain how each of the five elements of our definition of leadership applies to Steve Jobs leading Apple.

2. Identify leadership skills Jobs has that lead to his and Apple's success. Which skill is his strongest?

3. Identify managerial leadership roles played by Jobs as CEO of Apple. Which role was the most important?

4. Which level of analysis is the primary focus of this case?

5. Explain how each of the leadership theory classifications applies to this case, and which one is most relevant.

6. Without Steve Jobs, will Apple's performance deteriorate and go back into a crisis of near bankruptcy again? Why or why not?

CASE EXERCISE AND ROLE-PLAY

Preparation: Assume that you were a powerful board member of Apple in the 1980s. You were involved in helping Jobs select the new CEO, John Sculley, and that you have worked with Jobs on the board for five years. The board has disagreed with Jobs's recommendation to replace Sculley as CEO, so Sculley stays in power and Jobs is out of power. You have to tell Jobs the bad news, which you know he will not want to hear.

Your instructor may elect to let you break into small groups to share ideas and develop a plan for your meeting with Jobs. If you develop a group plan, select one leader to present the meeting with Jobs.

Role-Play: One person (representing him- or herself or their group) conducts the meeting with Steve Jobs (to notify him that Sculley stays as CEO and he is removed from power) before the entire class. Or, multiple role-plays may take place in small groups of five to six; however, role-players can't conduct the meeting in front of the team that developed the meeting plan. They must present to a group that did not develop the plan for the meeting. The people role-playing Jobs should put themselves in his place. How would you feel about being thrown out of the company you cofounded and led? Don't forget that Jobs is rather hot tempered and very outspoken.

VIDEO ▶❙❙ CASE

Leadership at P.F. Chang's

Rick Federico is chairman and CEO of P.F. Chang's, which owns and operates a chain of Asian restaurants across the country. During the time he has been head of the company, Federico has taken on the huge tasks of taking the company public and launching Pei Wei, the firm's chain of diners. In addition, he has developed management teams and laid out clear expectations for his employees. He has earned the respect of his managers, his workers, his customers, and even his competitors.

Rick Federico knows the restaurant industry. He began his career as a dishwasher for a steak house and worked his way up the management chain. So he understands everyone's job, from busboy to chef to manager. Federico expects results from every team, manager, and worker. But he expects no less from himself. He believes his greatest tasks as a leader involve remaining focused on his customers, his workers, and the food they serve. As P.F. Chang's grows Federico wants to be sure that the quality of service, atmosphere, and food are always at their highest.

1. Describe some of Rick Federico's personal leadership traits.

2. Choose three of the leadership managerial roles and explain how Rick Federico might use them as head of P.F. Chang's.

Developing Your Leadership Skills **1**

Getting to Know You by Name

Preparing for This Exercise

Complete Self-Assessment 2 on page 9, and read the accompanying information before class.

Objectives

1. To get acquainted with some of your classmates

2. To get to know your instructor

The primary AACSB learning standard skill developed through this exercise is communication ability.

To develop your skill at remembering and calling people by their name

In this chapter you learned about the importance of leader–follower relationships. An important part of leadership relations is making people feel important. It has been said that the sweetest sound people can hear is their own name. Have you ever had a person whom you don't know (or hardly know) call you by name? Have you ever had a person whom you believe should be able to call you by name not be able to—or call you by the wrong name? How did these two situations make you feel? Being able to call people by name will improve your leadership effectiveness.

Tips for Remembering People's Names

- The first thing you need to do is make a conscious effort to improve your skill at calling people by name. If you say you are no good at remembering names, you won't be. If you say "I can be good at it," and work at it, you can.

- When you are introduced to a person, consciously greet them by name. For example, say, "Hi, Juan, glad to meet you." Then, during your conversation, say the name a few more times until it sticks with you. Use the person's name when you ask and answer questions.

- When you meet a person whom you will see again, without being introduced by someone else, introduce yourself by name—and get the other person to say their name. Then, as before, call them by name during your conversation. For example, if you get to class early and want to talk, introduce yourself to someone rather than just talking without learning the person's name. If someone you don't know just starts talking to you, introduce yourself.

- When you are in a small group being introduced to people, don't just say hi and ignore the names. Depending on the number of people, you can say hello and repeat each name as you look at the person. If you don't remember a name, ask. Just say, "I'm sorry, I didn't get your name." You may also want to mentally repeat the person's name several times. As you talk to the people in the group, use their names. If you forget a name, listen for others to say it as the discussion continues.

- If you have been introduced to a person and forget their name the next time you meet them, you have two choices. You can apologetically ask them their name. Or, before talking to the person, you can ask someone else for the person's name, and then greet them by name. Again, use the person's name during the conversation.

- Use association to help you remember. For example, if you meet John Higby you could picture him hugging a bee. If the person's name is Ted, picture him with the body of a teddy bear. If you know the person likes something, say tennis, picture them with a tennis ball on their head. Think of other people you know who have the same name and make an association.

- Ask for a business card, or ask for the person's telephone number so you can write it down; this will help you remember the name.

- Write down the person's name and some information about them after you meet them. Sales representatives use this technique very effectively to recall personal information they may forget. If you are on a committee with people you don't know and don't see very often, use the membership list of names (or write them yourself). Then write an association for each person, so that you can identify all members (this may be done during the meeting without drawing attention). Your notes might include personal characteristics (tall, thin, dark hair) or something about their work (marketing, engineer). Then, before the next meeting, review the list of names and characteristics so you can make the association and greet each person by name.

Doing This Exercise in Class

Procedure 1 *(5–8 minutes)* Break into groups of five or six, preferably with people you do not know. In the group, have each member give his or her name and two or three significant things about himself or herself. After all the members have finished, ask each other questions to get to know each other better.

Procedure 2 *(2–4 minutes)* Can anyone in the group call the others by name? If so, he or she should do so. If not, have each member repeat his or her name. Follow with each member calling all members by name. Be sure that each person has a turn to call everyone by name.

Procedure 3 *(5–8 minutes)* Select a person to play the spokesperson role for your group. Remember, this is a leadership course. The spokesperson writes down questions in the following two areas:

- *Course:* Is there anything more that you want to know about the course, such as any expectations or concerns that you have?
- *Instructor:* Make a list of questions for the instructor in order to get to know him or her better.

Procedure 4 *(10–20 minutes)* Each spokesperson asks the instructor one question at a time, until all questions are asked. If time permits, people who are not the spokesperson may ask questions.

Conclusion

The instructor may make concluding remarks.

Apply It *(2–4 minutes)* What did I learn from this experience? How will I use this knowledge in the future? Specifically state which tip for remembering names you will use in the future. Identify precisely when you will practice this skill: e.g., on "x" day/date when I go to class—or to work, or to a party—I will introduce myself to someone I don't know.

_____
_____
_____

Sharing

In the group, or to the entire class, volunteers may give their answers to the "Apply It" questions.

SELF-ASSESSMENT 3   Names

On the line before each statement, write Y for yes, or N for no.

_____ 1. I enjoy meeting new people.

_____ 2. I'm good at remembering people's names.

_____ 3. When I meet new people, I learn their names and call them by name.

_____ 4. I'm interested in and willing to improve my ability to remember and use names.

If you answered yes to questions 1–3, you have developed some skill in this area. Your answer to question 4 indicates whether you intend to further develop your skill. The choice is yours.

Developing Your Leadership Skills **2**

Identifying Leadership Traits and Behaviors

Objective

To gain a better understanding of leadership traits and behavior

The primary AACSB learning standard skill developed through this exercise is analytic skills.

Preparing for This Exercise

Read and understand the trait and behavioral leadership theories. On the following lines, list specific traits and behaviors that you believe effective leaders have or should have. Your answers may or may not be based on your observation of successful leaders.

Traits: _____
_____

Behaviors: _____
_____

Doing This Exercise in Class

Option 1 *(5–15 minutes)* Students give their answers to the instructor, who writes them on the board under the heading of Traits or Behaviors. During or after the answers are listed, the class may discuss them.

Option 2 *(10–20 minutes)* Break into groups of five or six, and select a leader to perform the spokesperson role (remember, this is a leadership class). The spokesperson records the answers of the group, and then writes them on the board (5–10 minutes). The instructor leads a class discussion (5–10 minutes).

2

Leadership Traits and Ethics

Learning Outcomes

After studying this chapter, you should be able to:

1 Explain the universality of traits of effective leaders. p. 36

2 Describe the Big Five personality dimensions. p. 37

3 Discuss why the trait of dominance is so important for managers to have. p. 37

4 State how the Achievement Motivation Theory and the Leader Motive Profile are related and different. p. 43

5 Identify similarities and differences among Theory X and Theory Y, the Pygmalion effect, and self-concept. p. 49

6 Describe how attitudes are used to develop four leadership styles. p. 52

7 Compare the three levels of moral development. p. 55

8 Explain the stakeholder approach to ethics. p. 60

9 Define the following **key terms** (in order of appearance in the chapter):

traits

personality

personality profiles

Big Five Model of Personality

surgency personality dimension

agreeableness personality dimension

adjustment personality dimension

conscientiousness personality dimension

openness-to-experience personality
    dimension

Achievement Motivation Theory

Leader Motive Profile Theory

Leader Motive Profile (LMP)

attitudes

Theory X and Theory Y

Pygmalion effect

self-concept

ethics

moral justification

stakeholder approach to ethics

OPENING CASE *APPLICATION*

A native of Wilmington, Delaware, Ellen Kullman received a BS in mechanical engineering from Tufts University, and later a masters degree in management from Northwestern University, and she began her career at GE. She started at DuPont (E. I. du Pont de Nemours and Company) in 1988 as a marketing manager. Kullman climbed the corporate ladder and in 2008 she was appointed president to lead the company's focus on growth in emerging international markets. In 2009, Kullman became chair of the board and chief executive officer (CEO) of DuPont. As CEO, Ellen has championed market-driven science to take innovation across the company's businesses.

DuPont was founded over 200 years ago and has the slogan "the miracles of science." DuPont puts science to work by creating sustainable solutions essential to a better, safer, healthier life for people everywhere. DuPont offers a wide range of innovative products and services for markets including agriculture, food and nutrition, health care, electronics, communications, safety and protection, home and construction, transportation and apparel. Look closely at the things around your home and workplace, and chances are, you'll find dozens of items made with DuPont materials.[1]

DuPont operates in approximately 90 countries, with over 60,000 employees, with revenues in excess of $30 billion. DuPont is in the top 100 on the Fortune 500 company list,[2] and in the top 300 on the Global 500.[3] It is ranked second in its industry of natural resources, chemicals, and in the top 50 on the World's Most Admired Companies.[4]

OPENING CASE QUESTIONS:

1. What Big Five personality traits does Ellen Kullman possess?

2. Does Ellen Kullman have the personality profile of an effective leader?

3. How did "attitude" help improve the performance of DuPont?

4. How did Ellen Kullman's self-concept affect her leadership?

5. What role does ethics play at DuPont?

Can you answer any of these questions? You'll find answers to these questions and learn more about DuPont and its leadership throughout the chapter.

To learn more about Ellen Kullman and DuPont, visit its Web site at **http://www.dupont.com**.

Ellen Kullman is an effective leader. The focus of this chapter is on leadership traits, which includes ethics. We begin by learning about personality traits of leaders and the personality profile of effective leaders. Next we learn how attitudes affect leadership. We end with a discussion of ethics in leadership.

Personality Traits and Leadership

Recall that trait theory of leadership was the foundation for the field of leadership studies. Leadership has been conceptualized as a function of personality traits.[5] In this section, we discuss traits and personality, personality profiles, and applying trait theory. But before you learn about personality traits, complete Self-Assessment 1 to determine your personality profile. Throughout this chapter, you will gain a better understanding of personality traits, which help explain why people do the things they do (behavior).

SELF-ASSESSMENT 1   Big Five Personality Profile

There are no right or wrong answers, so be honest and you will really increase your self-awareness. We suggest doing this exercise in pencil or making a copy before you write on it. We will explain why later.

Using the scale below, rate each of the 25 statements according to how accurately it describes you. Place a number from 1 to 7 on the line before each statement.

(continued)

(Self-Assessment 2 continued)

Like me	Somewhat like me			Not like me	
7	6	5	4	3	2	1

_____ 1. I step forward and take charge in leaderless situations.

_____ 2. I am concerned about getting along well with others.

_____ 3. I have good self-control; I don't get emotional, angry, or yell.

_____ 4. I'm dependable; when I say I will do something, it's done well and on time.

_____ 5. I try to do things differently to improve my performance.

_____ 6. I don't give up very easily, and push myself to achieve my objectives.

_____ 7. I enjoy having lots of friends.

_____ 8. I think positively about the outcomes of situations and perform well under pressure.

_____ 9. I work hard to be successful.

_____ 10. I'm flexible and go with the flow when things change.

_____ 11. I am outgoing and willing to be assertive when in conflict.

_____ 12. I try to see things from other people's points of view.

_____ 13. I have confidence in my judgments, decision making, ideas, and capabilities.

_____ 14. I am loyal to my boss, coworkers, and the organizations.

_____ 15. I'm good at problem solving and making decisions.

_____ 16. I want to climb the corporate ladder to as high a level of management as I can.

_____ 17. I want other people to like me and to view me as very friendly.

_____ 18. I give people lots of praise and encouragement; I don't put people down and criticize.

_____ 19. I follow the policies and rules of an organization.

_____ 20. I volunteer to be the first to learn and do new tasks at work.

_____ 21. I try to influence other people to get my way.

_____ 22. I enjoy working with others more than working alone.

_____ 23. I am relaxed and secure, rather than nervous and insecure.

_____ 24. I am considered to be trustworthy because I do a good job and support others.

_____ 25. I believe that my successful performance depends on me, not others or good luck.

To determine your Big Five personality profile: (1) In the blanks, place the number from 1 to 7 that represents your score for each statement. (2) Add up each column; your total should be a number from 5 to 35. (3) On the number scale, circle the number that is closest to your total score. Each column in the chart represents a specific personality dimension.

Surgency		Agreeableness		Adjustment		Conscientiousness		Openness to Experiencee	
	35		35		35		35		35
	30		30		30		30		30
____ 1.	25	____ 2.	25	____ 3.	25	____ 4.	25	____ 5.	25
____ 6.	20	____ 7.	20	____ 8.	20	____ 9.	20	____ 10.	20
____ 11.	15	____ 12.	15	____ 13.	15	____ 14.	15	____ 15.	15
____ 16.	10	____ 17.	10	____ 18.	10	____ 19.	10	____ 20.	10
____ 21.	5	____ 22.	5	____ 23.	5	____ 24.	5	____ 25.	5
____ Total Scale		____ Total Scale		____ Total Scale		____ Total Scale		____ Total Scale	

The higher the total number, the stronger is the personality dimension that describes your personality. What is your strongest dimension? Your weakest dimension? Continue reading the chapter for specifics about your personality in each of the five dimensions.

You may visit **http://ipip.ori.org** for a more complete 50-or 100-item Big Five Personality Assessment.

Personality and Traits

Why are some people outgoing and others shy, loud and quiet, warm and cold, aggressive and passive? This list of behaviors is made up of individual traits. **Traits** *are distinguishing personal characteristics.* **Personality** *is a combination of traits that classifies* *an individual's behavior.* It is the system that organizes our emotions, motives, and capacities to think.[6] Personality is an important topic,[7] as it influences our behavior, relationships, and how we make decisions.[8]

Personality is developed based on genetics and environmental factors. The genes you received before you were born influence your personality traits today. Your family, friends, school, and work also influence your personality. So our personality is partly innate, partly learned, and we can change them a bit, but it isn't easy.[9]

Although it is not easy, we can change our personality and there are executive coaches helping managers assess their personality so that they can change their behavior to be more effective leaders.[10] For example, if you are an introvert, you can work at being more of an extrovert by intentionally putting yourself in situations where you have to meet and interact with new people. With time and practice, you will become more comfortable and more outgoing.

WORK Application 1
Based on your personality profile, identify which dimensions are stronger, moderate, and weaker.

Personality Profiles

Personality profiles *identify individual stronger and weaker traits.* Completing Self-Assessment 1 gives us our personality profile. Student profiles tend to have a range of scores for the five dimensions. Review your personality profile. Do you have higher scores (stronger traits) on some dimensions and lower scores (weaker traits) on others? There are many personality tests, such as the Myers-Briggs Type Indicator and the Minnesota Multiphasic Personality Inventory.

When we take personality tests, our self-awareness goes up as we figure out our stronger and weaker traits. But we have to make a realistic assessment and acceptance of our strengths and weaknesses and work to improve our behavior.[11] We realize that we are different from other people, and as stated above, we can change our behavior to improve our relationships and develop leadership skills.[12]

Job Performance

Many organizations (including the National Football League) give personality tests to ensure a proper match between the worker and the job. Personality profiles are also used to categorize people as a means of predicting job success, and high conscientiousness is a good predictor of job performance, whereas people who are unstable tend to have poor job performance. When we change our behavior based on the personality profile of others, it allows more effective relationships.[13] People who are high in openness to experience tend to lead innovation to improve organizational performance.

The Big Five Correlates with Leadership

Researchers conducted a major meta-analysis combining 73 prior studies to correlate the Big Five personality dimensions with leadership. The highest correlation with leadership was surgency (.31), followed by conscientiousness (.28) and openness to experience (.24). Agreeableness was weakly correlated (.08), and adjustment was negatively correlated with leadership (−.24).[14] In other words, people high in surgency are perceived as leaderlike—they work hard, and they bring about change. They are not too concerned about being well-liked and trying to please everyone, and they are stable or not overly emotional.

Applying Trait Theory

Why Understanding Personality Is Important

Understanding people's personalities is important because personality affects behavior as well as perceptions and attitudes. Certain personality traits, such as ambivalence, play a role in why some people procrastinate or avoid making decisions if possible.[15] Understanding personalities helps us to explain and predict others' behavior and job performance. For a simple example, if you know a person is very shy, you can better understand why he or she is quiet when meeting new people. You can also predict that the person will be quiet when going places and meeting new people. You can also better understand why the person would not seek a job as a salesperson; and if he or she did, you could predict that the person might not be very successful.

Learning Outcome 1

Explain the universality of traits of effective leaders.

There Are Important Leadership Traits, but All Have Exceptions

In applying trait theory, we need to remember that there are traits that many successful leaders have, and we will discuss them in the next major section with the Big Five, but there is no agreed-upon list of traits that leaders need to be successful. So you don't need to have all of them to be a successful leader.

There are always exceptions to all the traits. For example, in Fortune 500 companies, 30 percent of the CEOs are 6 feet 2 inches or taller, compared to only 4 percent of the general U.S. population, and the taller candidate usually wins the U.S. presidency. However, there are lots of CEOs who are less than 6 feet tall and George W. Bush beat taller John Kerry to become president.[16] Successful leaders are commonly extroverts, but 40 percent of CEOs describe themselves as introverts, including Microsoft's Bill Gates, investors Warren Buffet and Charles Schwab, and Avon's Andrea Jung.[17] Also, certain personality traits have been shown to be important in some team settings, but not in others.[18]

How does your Big Five personality correlate with leadership? If it is not a perfect match, don't be too concerned because there are always exceptions to the norm.[19] For another example, Apple CEO Steve Jobs (Chapter 1 case) sometimes gets highly emotional and yells at employees. But we do need to remember that we can improve our leadership traits and we must continually strive to improve.

We Can Improve

As stated, we can change our behavior to be more effective. Although Gates, Buffet, and Jung say they are introverts, clearly they do well in social settings because they make the effort to succeed. The key to success is to assess our personality strengths and weaknesses and to plan how to change our behavior to improve our relationships and leadership skills.[20] Once we determine the behavior we want to improve, it takes deliberate practice to succeed.[21] You are given the opportunity to apply what you learn throughout this book in your personal and professional lives.

Leadership and Neuroscience

WORK Application 2
Select a present or past manager, and state whether he or she has any of the six traits of derailment. Give specific examples of weaknesses.

Although it was the first leadership paradigm, trait theory is still being studied today.[22] A new cutting-edge approach to leadership traits is through the use of neuroscience.[23] There is research being done to study the human brain and the field of neuroscience to better predict inspirational leaders and to understand effective leadership, its assessment, and its development. Understanding the role of the brain in producing effective leadership behavior and how the brain itself might be used to better develop exemplary leadership potential can be useful to improving leadership skills and behaviors. But being a new field of study, it needs further research before we can apply leadership and neuroscience.

Derailed Leadership Traits

Before we go on to the next section and discuss the traits of effective leaders, let's identify traits that led to leadership failure. A study was conducted that compared 21 derailed executives with 20 executives who had successfully climbed the corporate ladder to the top. The derailed executives had prior success and were expected to go far, but they were passed over for promotion again, were fired, or were forced to retire early. See Exhibit 2.1 for a list of the six major reasons for derailment.[24] Overall, the problem of derailed managers is poor human relations skills.

EXHIBIT 2.1   Why Executives Are Derailed

- They used a bullying style viewed as intimidating, insensitive, and abrasive.
- They were viewed as being cold, aloof, and arrogant.
- They betrayed personal trust.
- They were self-centered and viewed as overly ambitious and thinking of the next job.
- They had specific performance problems with the business.
- They overmanaged and were unable to delegate or build a team.

© Cengage Learning 2013

Learning Outcome 2   *Describe the Big Five personality dimensions.*

The Big Five Including Traits of Effective Leaders

There are many personality classification methods. However, the Big Five Model of Personality traits is the most widely accepted way to classify personalities because of its strong research support and its reliability across age, sex, race, and language groups.

The purpose of the Big Five is to reliably categorize, into one of five dimensions, most if not all of the traits you would use to describe someone. Thus, each dimension includes multiple traits. *The* Big Five Model of Personality *categorizes traits into the dimensions of surgency, agreeableness, adjustment, conscientiousness, and openness to experience.* The dimensions are listed in Exhibit 2.2 and described in this section.

Note that some researchers have slightly different names for the five dimensions, and not all will agree under which dimension each leadership trait should be classified; there is some overlap. We include traits of effective leaders under each dimension based on their strong research support, and our definitions of each of the Big Five include the effective leadership traits in that category. However, again we should realize that there is no one list of traits accepted by all researchers, and that not all effective leaders have all these traits and, like all of us, are higher and lower in some than others.

Surgency

The surgency personality dimension *includes dominance, extraversion, and high energy with determination.* Review Self-Assessment 1 statements 1, 6, 11, 16, and 21 for examples of surgency traits. Let's discuss the three important dimensions of surgency here.

Learning Outcome 3   *Discuss why the trait of dominance is so important for managers to have.*

Dominance. Successful leaders assert themselves and want to be managers and to take charge. Their dominant behavior ranges from interest in getting ahead and leading

EXHIBIT **2.2** The Big Five Including Traits of Effective Leaders

The Big Five Model of Personality	Leadership Traits within the Big Five
Surgency	a. Dominance b. Extroversion c. Energy/Determination
Agreeableness	d. Sociability/Sensitivity e. Emotional intelligence
Adjustment	f. Emotional Stability and Narcissism g. Self-confidence
Conscientiousness	h. Dependability i. Integrity
Openness	j. Flexibility k. Intelligence l. Locus of control

© Cengage Learning 2013

through competing and influencing. If a person does not want to be a leader, chances are he or she will not be an effective manager. Thus, the dominance trait affects all the other traits related to effective leaders. To reach full leadership potential, we've got to want to be a leader, work to develop our skills, and enjoy it. Do you want to be a leader?

Extraversion. It is on a continuum between extravert and introvert. Extraverts are outgoing, like to meet new people, and are assertive and willing to confront others, whereas introverts are shy. When we deal with people who are the opposite of us, we need to understand the need to adjust our level of extraversion to create good relationships.[25] Recall that although the majority of CEOs are extraverts, some say they are introverts. How outgoing are you?

High energy with determination. Leaders tend to have high energy with a positive drive to work hard to achieve goals. Their positive attitude and optimism influences their high tolerance for frustration as they strive to overcome obstacles through being persistent; they don't give up easily.[26] Leaders take initiative to bring about improvements rather than ask permission; they don't have to be told what to do. Do you have a high energy level with determination?

Agreeableness

The **agreeableness personality dimension** *includes traits of sociability and emotional intelligence.* Review Self-Assessment 1 statements 2, 7, 12, 17, and 22 for examples of agreeableness traits. Let's discuss the two important dimensions of agreeableness next.

Sociability/Sensitivity. Socialization affects our behavior and performance.[27] Sociable people have an inclination to seek out enjoyable social relationships. Strong sociability personality types spend more time with people than things, and tend to have lots of friends. They are friendly, courteous, easy to get along with, and diplomatic. How important is having good social relationships to you?

Sensitivity is part of being sociable. It refers to understanding group members as individuals, what their positions on issues are, and how best to communicate with and influence them. Sensitivity means not focusing on putting yourself first and remembering that the more you help others, the more you get in return. Recall that being insensitive is one of

WORK Application **3**
Select a present or past manager and assess his or her surgency traits of effective leaders. Give an example of the manager's strong or weak dominance, extroversion, and energy/determination in a typical specific situation.

the reasons why executives are derailed. Sensitivity is critical when playing the negotiator leadership role. If you are concerned only about yourself and don't understand what the other party wants, you probably will not be very successful. Are you sensitive to others?

Emotional Intelligence. An offshoot of IQ is EQ (emotional quotient—EQ or emotional intelligence—EI). EI is the ability to work well with people and it influences our assessment of people.[28] Leaders high in EI outperform the managers with average people skills.[29] There are four components of EQ:[30]

- *Self-awareness* relates to being conscious of your emotions and how they affect your personal and professional life. Self-awareness is the cornerstone of all insight. Use your self-awareness (the exercises in this book help) to accurately assess your strengths and limitations; this leads to higher self-confidence.

- *Social awareness* relates to the ability to understand others. Empathy is an ability to put yourself in other people's situations, sense their emotions, and understand things from their perspective. Social awareness also includes the ability to develop networks and play organizational politics, which we discuss in Chapter 5.

- *Self-management* relates to the ability to control disruptive emotions, ours and others. Successful leaders don't let negative emotions (worry, anxiety, fear, anger) interfere with getting things done. Characteristics of self-management include self-motivation, integrity, conscientiousness, adaptability, and optimism.

- *Relationship management* relates to the ability to work well with others, which is dependent on the other three EI components. Successful leaders build effective relationships by communicating, responding to emotions, handling conflict, and influencing others. Most of this book focuses on developing relationship management skills. Do you have high EI skills in all four areas?

WORK Application **4**
Using the same manager from Work Application 3, assess his or her agreeableness traits of effective leaders. Give an example of the manager's strong or weak sociability/ sensitivity and emotional intelligence in a typical specific situation.

_____

_____

_____

_____

Adjustment

The adjustment personality dimension *includes traits of emotional stability and self-confidence.* Review Self-Assessment 1 statements 3, 8, 13, 18, and 23 for examples of adjustment traits. Let's discuss the two important dimensions of adjustment here.

Emotional stability/self-control and narssisim. We all have emotions in leader–follower interactions.[31] The question is how do we handle them? Adjustment is on a continuum between being emotionally stable and unstable. *Stable* refers to self-control, being calm—good under pressure, relaxed, secure, and positive—praising others. *Unstable* is out of control—poor under pressure, nervous, insecure, negative, and hostile—criticizing others without helping them improve. Note the overlap between EI and stability as self-management is about self-control of our emotions. How emotionally stable are you?

Narcissism is related to being unstable, and it is on the increase. Narcissists are preoccupied with themselves, ignoring the needs of others, and have a sense of entitlement. They have an exaggerated sense of their own self-importance with expectations of special treatment that is not earned. They have an unrealistic assessment of their actual capabilities,[32] which also relates to self-confidence. Are you just looking out for yourself as #1 as a narcissist?

Self-confidence. It is on a continuum from strong to weak, indicating whether we are self-assured in our judgments, decision making, ideas, and capabilities. How can we succeed at anything if we don't believe we can? Our self-confidence builds with our success at setting and achieving our goals. Effective self-confidence is based on an accurate awareness of our strengths and weaknesses, with an orientation to self-improvement.

This relates to effective leaders knowing when to lead and when to follow; they compensate for weaknesses by letting others with the strength lead in those areas.

Effective leaders are less self-centered, are not defensive, are receptive to criticism, and are willing to learn from mistakes to continually improve. People lacking effective self-confidence are self-centered narcissists having an unrealistic view of their capabilities, are defensive, don't take criticism well, and repeat their mistakes without self-improvement. Do you have effective self-confidence?

Conscientiousness

The **conscientiousness personality dimension** _includes traits of dependability and integrity._ Review Self-Assessment 1 statements 4, 9, 14, 19, and 24 for examples of conscientiousness. How strong is your desire to be successful?

Dependability. It is on a continuum between responsible/dependable to irresponsible/undependable. People low on the trait of dependability have low commitment and tend to have counterproductive work behavior.[33] Highly dependable people get the job done and are characterized as loyal, committed to their coworkers and the organization.[34] Are you dependable?

Highly conscientious people are willing to work hard and put in extra time and effort to accomplish goals to achieve success—also called _organization citizenship behavior._[35] The price of top-level achievement is extraordinarily high.[36] How hard are you willing to work to succeed?

Integrity. It is on a continuum between being honest and ethical or not. Integrity is the foundation for trustworthiness. We focus on honesty here and will discuss ethics in more detail in the last section of this chapter. Behavior that is honest and ethical makes a person trustworthy. Integrity is about being honest—no lying, cheating (manipulating), or stealing. People want honest communications.[37] To be viewed as trustworthy, we need to be honest, be loyal in supporting others, keep confidences, and do what we say we are going to do (promises). If others find out we have been dishonest or in some way manipulated them for personal gain, we will lose their trust. Clearly, to be effective, leaders need integrity. Do you have integrity?

YOU Make the **ETHICAL** Call

2.1   _Downsizing and Part-Time Workers_

As firms struggle to compete in the global economy, many have downsized. _Downsizing_ is the process of cutting resources to increase productivity. The primary area of cutting is human resources, which has led to layoffs. Another method of keeping costs down is using part-time employees who do not receive benefits (e.g., health care) rather than full-time employees who receive benefits.

Walmart is known for having a heavy ratio of part- to full-time employees to keep costs down. Walmart is expanding its sales of grocery items, competing directly with supermarket chains. One of the reasons Walmart has lower prices is because it uses mostly part-time workers at or close to minimum wage and without benefits. Most supermarket chain employees are unionized and get higher wages and more benefits, and they want better pay and benefits. But supermarket chains state that they can't afford to pay more; they must compete with Walmart.

1. Do you view Walmart as a company with integrity?

2. Is downsizing ethical and socially responsible?

3. Is using part-time employees, rather than full-time, ethical and socially responsible?

Openness

The **openness-to-experience personality dimension** *includes traits of flexibility, intelligence, and internal locus of control.* Review Self-Assessment 1 statements 5, 10, 15, 20, and 25 for examples of openness-to-experience traits.

Flexibility. It refers to the ability to adjust to different situations and change. Recall that leaders who set objectives and possess the ability to influence others bring about change. Leaders need to stay ahead of the immense number of changes in the world; the pace of change will only continue to increase. Without flexibility, you will not be successful. Flexible people are generally more creative and innovative—willing to try new things and change. How willing are you to change and try new things? Are you flexible?

Intelligence. It refers to cognitive ability to think critically, to solve problems, and to make decisions. It is also referred to as general mental ability intelligence quotient (IQ). Contemporary research suggests going beyond conventional IQ measures to multiple intelligence. Simply, multiple intelligence means that people are better at some things than others. What are intelligent competencies?

Intelligence is the best predictor of job performance, but not the only one as conscientiousness is also important. The founders of Microsoft (Bill Gates), Google (Sergey Brin and Larry Page), and Facebook (Mark Zucherberg) all have 150-plus IQs and math SAT skills at the 800 level, and they tend to have a bias for IQ when hiring.[38] Being in college implies that you most likely have above-average intelligence. This is one reason why most college graduates get better jobs and are paid more than those who do not go to (or finish) college.

IQ, EQ, and I got a clue. It has been said that to be successful a high IQ is not enough. We also need strong interpersonal skills, or a high EQ (leading). Plus, we have to have a clue of what we are trying to accomplish (objectives) and how we will get the job done (planning, organizing, and controlling). Can you think of any people who are intelligent, but lack people skills or don't seem to have a clue about what to do or how to get things done?

Locus of control. It is on a continuum between external and internal belief in control over one's destiny/performance. *Externalizers* believe that they have no control over their fate and that their behavior has little to do with their performance. They generally lack self-confidence, and have lower levels of performance but it is never their fault as they blame others or just bad luck when they fail.

Internalizers believe that they control their fate and that their behavior directly affects their performance. Effective internalizer leaders take responsibility for who they are, for their behavior and performance, and for the performance of their organizational unit. They tend to be future oriented, setting objectives and developing plans to accomplish them. Are you more of an internalizer or an externalizer?

WORK Application 7

Using the same manager from Work Application 3, assess his or her openness to experience traits of effective leaders. Give an example of the manager's strong or weak flexibility, intelligence, and locus of control in a typical specific situation.

WORK Application 8

How can you improve your leadership skills by understanding your manager's (and other people's) personality profile?

OPENING CASE APPLICATION

1. What Big Five and leadership personality traits does Ellen Kullman possess?

To a large extent, Ellen Kullman is a successful leader because of her strong personality in the Big Five.

She has a strong need for *surgency* that helped her climb the corporate ladder at DuPont, which is dominated by men. It took energy and determination to become the first woman CEO of DuPont. Further evidence of her being powerful follows: *Forbes* listed Kullman number 18 on its list of the World's 100 Most Powerful Women.[39] *Fortune* ranked Kullman seventh on its list of 50 Most Powerful Women,[40] and fifth on its Businessperson of the Year list.[41]

(continued)

(Opening Case Application 1 continued)

Kullman has *agreeableness*. She gets along well with people having strong interpersonal skills with EI. Kullman relies more on her personal relationships than her power as CEO to get the job done. She is also sociable and sensitive to others, but she will dominate when it comes to meeting the goals of DuPont.

She is *conscientious* at getting the job done. Being very dependable by achieving great success was a cornerstone of her climbing the corporate ladder at DuPont. Plus she is viewed has having a high level of integrity. Under her leadership, decision making has moved closer to customers around the world, resulting in greater partnering, collaboration, and solutions attuned to local needs.[42]

Kullman is well *adjusted*. Competing in a company and industry dominated by men, she has self-control and self-confidence. She is calm, good under pressure, relaxed, secure, and positive. She praises the accomplishments of her employees at all levels.

She is *open* to new experience because of her innovating and bringing to market new products at a faster clip. Nearly 40 percent of DuPont's 2009 revenues came from products introduced in the past five years—double the rate of just a few years before.[43] Kullman is highly intelligent, has an internal locus of control as she takes charge to bring changes, and is flexible.

CONCEPT APPLICATION 1
Big Five Personality Dimensions

Identify each of these seven traits/behaviors by its personality dimension. Write the appropriate letter in the blank before each item.

a. surgency
b. agreeableness
c. affiliation

d. conscientiousness
e. openness to experience

_____ 1. A leader is being very quiet when meeting some unexpected visitors in the work unit.

_____ 2. A leader is giving in to a follower to avoid a conflict.

_____ 3. A manager is influencing the follower to do the job the way the leader wants it done.

_____ 4. A sales representative submitted the monthly expense report on time as usual.

_____ 5. A leader is saying a warm, friendly good morning to followers as they arrive at work.

_____ 6. A leader is seeking ideas from followers on how to speed up the flow of work.

_____ 7. As a follower is yelling a complaint, a leader calmly explains what went wrong.

CONCEPT APPLICATION 2
Personality Traits of Effective Leaders

Identify each of the following eight behaviors by its trait. The leader may be behaving effectively, or the behavior may be the opposite of the effective trait behavior. Refer to Exhibit 2.2 and use the "leadership traits within the Big Five." Write the appropriate letter a–l in the blank before each item.

(continued)

(Concept Application 2 continued)

_____ 8. A leader assigns a task to one follower, giving him very specific instructions. Then the leader gives another assignment to a different follower, telling her to complete the task any way she wants to.

_____ 9. A leader is engaged in getting the production line working.

_____ 10. A leader is acting very nervous while she is disciplining an employee.

_____ 11. A leader tells a follower that he can have Tuesday off next week. But the next day, the leader tells the follower that he has changed his mind.

_____ 12. A leader very attentively listens to the follower complain, then paraphrases the complaint back to the follower.

_____ 13. A leader in situation 8 above is still working to solve the problem; it's her fifth attempt.

_____ 14. A leader is telling her manager that her unit's poor performance is not her fault; she says that the employees are lazy and there is nothing she can do to improve performance.

_____ 15. A leader is telling his manager that his department is right on schedule to meet the deadline, hoping that he can catch up before the boss finds out otherwise.

The Personality Profile of Effective Leaders

Effective leaders have a common personality profile. McClelland's trait theories of Achievement Motivation Theory and Leader Motive Profile Theory have strong research support and a great deal of relevance to the practice of leadership. Achievement Motivation Theory identifies three major traits, which McClelland calls *needs*. Leader Motive Profile Theory identifies the personality profile of effective leaders.[44] You will learn about both of these theories in this section.

Learning Outcome 4   *State how the Achievement Motivation Theory and the Leader Motive Profile are related and different*

Achievement Motivation Theory

Achievement Motivation Theory *attempts to explain and predict behavior and performance based on a person's need for achievement, power, and affiliation.* The late David McClelland originally developed Achievement Motivation Theory in the 1940s. He believed that we have needs and that our needs motivate us to satisfy them. Our behavior is thus motivated by our needs. However, McClelland says this is an unconscious process. He further stated that needs are based on personality and are developed as we interact with the environment. All people possess the need for achievement, power, and affiliation, but to varying degrees. One of the three needs tends to be dominant in each one of us and motivates our behavior.

The Need for Achievement (n Ach)

The *need for achievement* is the unconscious concern for excellence in accomplishments through individual efforts. People with strong n Ach tend to have an internal locus of control, self-confidence, and high energy with determination traits. High n Ach is categorized as the Big Five dimension of *conscientiousness* with dependability, but the person is not necessarily being high in integrity.

People with high n Ach tend to be characterized as wanting to take personal responsibility for solving problems. They are goal oriented and set moderate, realistic, attainable goals. They seek challenge, excellence, and individuality; take calculated, moderate risk; desire concrete feedback on their performance; and work hard. People with high n Ach think about ways to do a better job, how to accomplish something unusual or important, and career progression. They perform well in nonroutine, challenging, and competitive situations, while people low in n Ach do not.

McClelland's research showed that only about 10 percent of the U.S. population has a "strong" dominant need for achievement. There is evidence of a correlation between high achievement need and high performance in the general population. People with high n Ach tend to enjoy entrepreneurial-type positions where they are in control over what they do and how they do it.

The Need for Power (n Pow)

The *need for power* is the unconscious concern for influencing others and seeking positions of authority. High n Pow is categorized as the Big Five dimension of *surgency*. People with strong n Pow have the dominance trait and tend to be self-confident with high energy with determination.

People with a high need for power tend to be characterized as wanting to control the situation, wanting influence or control over others, enjoying competition in which they can win (they don't like to lose), being willing to confront others, and seeking positions of authority and status. They tend to be ambitious and have a lower need for affiliation and agreeableness. Those with n Pow are more concerned about getting the job done, often their own way (influencing others) than about what others think of them. They are attuned to power and politics as essential for successful leadership, and they tend to seek management positions.

The Need for Affiliation (n Aff)

The *need for affiliation* is the unconscious concern for developing, maintaining, and restoring close personal relationships. High n Aff is categorized as the Big Five dimension of *agreeableness*. People with strong n Aff have the trait of sociability/sensitivity and often high EI. People with high n Aff tend to be characterized as seeking close relationships with others, wanting to be liked by others, enjoying lots of social activities, and seeking to belong; so they join groups and organizations. People with high n Aff think about friends and relationships. They tend to enjoy developing, helping, and teaching others. They tend to seek jobs as teachers, in human resource management, and in other helping professions. People with high n Aff are more concerned about what others think of them than about getting their own way (influencing others). This need is negatively related to leadership. Those with a high n Aff tend to have a low n Pow; they tend to avoid management because they like to be one of the group rather than its leader.

CONCEPT APPLICATION 3
Achievement Motivation Theory

Identify each of the five behaviors below by its need, writing the appropriate letter in the blank before each item. The person may be behaving based on a strong need, or the behavior may be the opposite, indicating a weak need. Also state how the behavior meets the need and predict the performance.

(continued)

(Concept Application 3 continued)

a. achievement   b. power   c. affiliation

_____ 16. A person is working hard to meet a difficult deadline.

_____ 17. A person is refusing to step forward and represent the group as its spokesperson.

_____ 18. A person is going to talk to a fellow employee, with whom she had a disagreement earlier in the day, to peacefully resolve the conflict.

_____ 19. A fellow employee in situation 18 above has made up his mind that he will not be the first one to make a move to resolve the conflict with the other person because he does not want to appear weak; but when the other party comes to him, he will be receptive.

_____ 20. An accounting major has volunteered to calculate the financial analysis for the group's case and to make the presentation to the class.

Your Motive Profile

Note that McClelland does not have a classification for the *adjustment* and *openness-to-experience* Big Five personality dimensions; they are not needs. A person can have a high or low need for achievement, power, and affiliation and be either well adjusted or not, and either open or closed to new experiences. So these two dimensions of personality are ignored in determining the Achievement Motivation Theory personality profile. Complete Self-Assessment 2 to determine your motive profile now.

SELF-ASSESSMENT 2   Motive Profile

Return to Self-Assessment 1 on page 33 and place the scores from your Big Five personality profile in the following blanks, next to their corresponding needs. On the number scale, circle your total score for each need.

Need for Achievement (conscientiousness)	Need for Power (surgency)	Need for Affiliation (agreeableness)
35	35	35
30	30	30
25	25	25
20	20	20
15	15	15
10	10	10
5	5	5
Total Score_____	Total Score_____	Total Score _____

There is no right or wrong score for this profile. To interpret your score, check to see if there is much difference between the three need scores. If all three are about the same, one need is not stronger than the others are. If scores vary, one need is higher than the others and is called the stronger or dominant need, and the lower score is the weaker need. You can also have other combinations, such as two stronger and one weaker, or vice versa. Do you have stronger and weaker needs?

WORK Application **9**
Explain how your need for achievement, power, and/or affiliation has affected your behavior and performance, or that of someone you work with or have worked with. Give an example of the behavior and performance, and list your predicted motive need.

_____

_____

_____

_____

Knowing a motive profile is useful, because it can explain and predict behavior and performance. For example, if you know people have a high need for affiliation, you can understand why they tend to have friends and get along well with people. You can predict that if they are assigned a job as a mentor, they will enjoy the tasks and display helpful, supportive behavior toward the mentoree and will do a good job. Complete Work Application 9, then read on to determine if you have the motive profile of an effective leader.

Leader Motive Profile Theory

Leader Motive Profile Theory *attempts to explain and predict leadership success based on a person's need for achievement, power, and affiliation.* McClelland found that effective leaders consistently have the same motive profile, and that Leader Motive Profile has been found to be a reliable predictor of leader effectiveness.[45] Let's first define the profile of effective leaders and then discuss why it results in success. *The* **Leader Motive Profile (LMP)** *includes a high need for power, which is socialized; that is greater than the need for affiliation and with a moderate need for achievement.* The achievement score is usually somewhere between the power and affiliation score, and the reason is described below.

Power

Power is essential to leaders because it is a means of influencing followers. Without power, there is no leadership. To be successful, leaders need to want to be in charge and enjoy dominance in the leadership role with high energy and determination to succeed. We will need power to influence our followers, peers, and higher-level managers. We will discuss how to gain power and be successful in organizational politics in Chapter 5.

Socialized Power

McClelland further identified power as neither good nor bad. It can be used for personal gain at the expense of others (personalized power), or it can be used to help oneself and others (socialized power).[46] Social power is discussed again later, with ethics. Effective leaders use socialized power, which includes the traits of sensitivity to others and stability with good EI, and is the Big Five *adjustment* dimension. Thus a person with a low need for affiliation can have a high sensitivity to others. McClelland's research supports the reasons for executive derailment, because these negative traits are personalized power. Socialized power is not included in the motive profile, so complete Self-Assessment 3 to determine your motive profile with socialized power.

Achievement

To be effective, leaders generally need to have a moderate need for achievement. They have high energy, self-confidence, and openness-to-experience traits, and they are dependable—*conscientious* (Big Five dimension). The reason for a moderate rather than a high need for achievement, which would include a lower need for power, is the danger of personalized power. People with a high need for achievement tend to seek individual achievement, and when they are not interested in being a leader, there is the chance for personalized power and derailment.

Affiliation

Effective leaders have a lower need for affiliation than power, so that relationships don't get in the way of influencing followers. If the achievement score is lower than that for affiliation, the probability of the following problems occurring may be increased. Leaders with high n Aff tend to have a lower need for power and are thus reluctant to play the bad-guy role, such as disciplining and influencing followers to do things they would rather not do—like change. They have been found to show favoritism behavior toward their friends. However, recall that effective leaders do have concern for followers—socialized power.

SELF-ASSESSMENT 3   Motive Profile with Socialized Power

Return to Self-Assessment 1 on page 33 and place the scores from Self-Assessment 2 (your motive profile) in the following blanks. On the number scale, circle your total score.

Need for Achievement (conscientiousness)	Need for Power (surgency)	Socialized Power (adjustment)	Need for Affiliation (agreeableness)
35	35	35	35
30	30	30	30
25	25	25	25
20	20	20	20
15	15	15	15
10	10	10	10
5	5	5	5
Total Score _____	Total Score _____	Total Score _____	Total Score _____

Again, there is no right or wrong score. The adjustment score will give you an idea if your power is more social or personal. Also realize that the questions in Self-Assessment 1 (3, 8, 13, 18, and 23) are not totally focused on social power. Thus, if you believe you have higher sensitivity to others, your score on McClelland's LMP socialized power could be higher.

WORK Application **10**
Make an intelligent guess about your present or past manager's motive profile. Is it an LMP? Explain.

_____

_____

_____

_____

The Leader Motive Profile is included in the definition of leadership. Our definition of leadership includes the five key elements of leadership (see Exhibit 1.1 on page 6) in the LMP. Our definition of leadership includes *influencing* and *leaders–followers* (power) and getting along with *people* (social power with EI). It also includes *organizational objectives* (which achievers set and accomplish well) and *change* (which achievers are open to).

OPENING CASE *APPLICATION*

2. **Does Ellen Kullman have the personality profile of an effective leader?**

Ellen Kullman has an LMP. Her need for power is illustrated through climbing the corporate ladder in a male-dominated industry and company. She has a socialized need for power since she relies more on relationships than simply her power as CEO, and she uses participative management and does allow others to make decisions in local issues. Kullman has a need for achievement that leads to continued success. She also has a lower need for affiliation as she sets objectives and standards for improving performance and uses her power when needed. Kullman set the goal of increasing earnings over the next three years by an annual compound rate of 20 percent, and is on pace to shatter that goal with an estimated 50 percent.[47]

Do you have an LMP? Complete Self-Assessment 4 now to find out.

Select the option that best describes your interest in leadership now.

_____ 1. I am, or want to become, a manager and leader.

_____ 2. I am, or want to become, a leader without being a manager.

_____ 3. I am not interested in being a leader; I want to be a follower.

If you want to be a leader, recall that research has shown that you can develop your leadership skills.

If you selected option 1, do you have an LMP? If you answered yes, it does not guarantee that you will climb the corporate ladder. However, having an LMP does increase your chances, because it is a predictor of leadership success. On the other hand, an LMP is not enough; you need leadership skills to be successful. If your Self-Assessment 3 score doesn't indicate that you have an LMP, go back to Self-Assessment 1 on page 33 and review questions 1, 6, 11, 16, and 21. Did you score them accurately? The most important question is 16. If you believe you have an LMP, be aware that your profile could be different using McClelland's LMP questionnaire. Also recall that not all successful leaders have an LMP;

you can still be successful. Developing your leadership skills, through effort, will increase your chances of leadership success.

If you selected option 2, don't be concerned about your LMP. Focus on developing your leadership skills. However, your personality profile can help you to better understand your strengths and weaknesses to identify areas to improve upon. This also holds true for people who selected option 1.

If you selected option 3, that's fine. Most people in the general population probably would select this option. Many professionals who have great jobs and incomes are followers, and they have no interest in becoming managers. However, recall that research has shown that leaders and followers need the same skills, that organizations are looking for employees with leadership skills, and that organizations conduct skills training with employees at all levels. To increase your chances of having a successful and satisfying career, you may want to develop your leadership skills. You may someday change your mind about becoming a leader and manager.

Your need for power and LMP can change over time, along with your interest in leadership and management and your skill level, regardless of which option you selected.

EXHIBIT 2.3   Combing the Big Five with Traits and Needs

The Big Five Model of Personality	Leadership Traits within the Big Five	Achievement Motivation Theory and Leader Motive Profile (LMP)
Surgency	a. Dominance b. Extroversion c. Energy/Determination	Need for power
Agreeableness	d. Sociability/Sensitivity e. Emotional intelligence	Need for affiliation
Adjustment	f. Emotional Stability and Narcissism g. Self-confidence	Socialized power (LMP)
Conscientiousness	h. Dependability i. Integrity	Need for achievement
Openness	j. Flexibility k. Intelligence l. Locus of control	No separate need; it is included in the other needs

Before we go on to discuss leadership attitudes, let's review what we've covered so far in Exhibit 2.3 by putting together the Big Five Model of Personality, the nine traits of effective leaders, and Achievement Motivation Theory and LMP.

Leadership Attitudes

Researchers concluded that personality traits play a role in attitudes, which in turn affect our behavior.[48] So what are they? **Attitudes** *are positive or negative feelings about people, things, and issues.* We all have favorable or positive attitudes, and unfavorable or negative attitudes about life, work, school, leadership, and everything else. Employees with positive attitudinal states are generally more willing to work hard,[49] and attitudes help to explain and predict job performance and turnover.[50]

W. Marriott, Jr., president of Marriott Corporation, stated that the company's success depends more upon employee attitudes than any other single factor. Legendary football coach Lou Holtz says that attitude is the most important thing in this world and that we each choose the attitude we have. So, being a positive or negative person is your choice. Successful leaders have positive, optimistic attitudes. Do you?

In this section, we'll discuss how leadership attitudes relate to Theory X and Theory Y, and how the Pygmalion effect influences followers' behavior and performance. Then we will discuss self-concept and how it affects the leader's behavior and performance. Lastly, we will consider how the leader's attitudes about followers, and about his or her self-concept, affect the leadership style of the leader.

Learning Outcome 5 | *Identify similarities and differences among Theory X and Theory Y, the Pygmalion effect, and self-concept.*

Theory X and Theory Y

Today, **Theory X and Theory Y** *attempt to explain and predict leadership behavior and performance based on the leader's attitude about followers.* Before you read about Theory X and Y, complete Self-Assessment 5.

SELF-ASSESSMENT 5   Theory X and Theory Y Attitudes

For each pair of statements distribute 5 points, based on how characteristic each statement is of your belief system. The combined score for each pair of the ten statements must equal 5.

Here are the scoring distributions for each pair of statements:

0–5 or 5–0	I believe one statement and not the other.
1–4 or 4–1	I believe one statement much more than the other.
2–3 or 3–2	I believe both statements, although one more than the other.

_____ 1. People enjoy working.
_____ People do not like to work.

_____ 2. Employees don't have to be closely supervised to do their job well.
_____ Employees will not do a good job unless you closely supervise them.

_____ 3. If the manager is not around, the employees will work just as hard.
_____ If the manager is not around, the employees will take it easier than they will when being watched.

_____ 4. Employees will do a task well for you if you ask them to.
_____ If you want something done right, you need to do it yourself.

(continued)

(Self-Assessment 5 continued)

———— 5. Interesting, challenging work is the best motivator of employee.

———— Money is the best motivator of employees.

———— 6. Employees want to be involved in making decisions.

———— Employees want the managers to make the decisions.

———— 7. Employees will do their best work if you allow them to do the job their own way.

———— Employees will do their best work if they are taught how to do it the one best way.

———— 8. Managers should share the management responsibilities with group members.

———— Managers should perform the management functions for the group.

———— 9. Managers should let employees have full access to information that is not confidential.

———— Managers should give employees only the information they need to know to do their job.

———— 10. The participative management style is the best leadership style.

———— The autocratic management style is the best leadership style.

To determine your attitude about people at work, add up the numbers (0–5) for the first statement in each pair; don't bother adding the numbers for the second statements. The total should be between 0 and 50. Place your score on the continuum below.

Theory X 0——5——10——15——20——25——30——35——40——45——50 *Theory Y*

Generally, the higher your score, the greater are your Theory Y beliefs, and the lower the score, the greater your Theory X attitudes.

Douglas McGregor classified attitudes or belief systems, which he called *assumptions*, as *Theory X* and *Theory Y*.[51] People with Theory X attitudes hold that employees dislike work and must be closely supervised in order to do their work. Theory Y attitudes hold that employees like to work and do not need to be closely supervised in order to do their work. In each of the ten pairs of statements in Self-Assessment 5, the first lines are Theory Y attitudes and the second lines are Theory X attitudes.

Managers with Theory X attitudes tend to have a negative, pessimistic view of employees and display more coercive, autocratic leadership styles using external means of controls, such as threats and punishment. Managers with Theory Y attitudes tend to have a positive, optimistic view of employees and display more participative leadership styles using internal motivation and rewards. In 1966, when McGregor published his Theory X and Theory Y, most managers had Theory X attitudes, and he was calling for a change to Theory Y attitudes. More recently, the paradigm shift from management to leadership also reflects this change in attitudes, as more managers use participative leadership styles.

It is widely accepted that managers with Theory Y attitudes are generally more productive than Theory X attitudes.[52] The six derailed executive traits reflect Theory X behaviors. If you scored higher in Theory X for Self-Assessment 5, it does not mean that you cannot be an effective leader. There are some situations, such as large-scale production and unskilled workers where a more autocratic style works well.[53] As with personality traits, we can change our attitudes, with effort. We don't have to be autocratic leaders.

WORK Application 11
Give an example of when a person (parent, friend, teacher, coach, manager) really expected you either to perform well or to fail, and treated you like you would, which resulted in your success or failure.

————————————

————————————

————————————

The Pygmalion Effect

The **Pygmalion effect** *proposes that leaders' attitudes toward and expectations of followers, and their treatment of them, explain and predict followers' behavior and performance.* Research by J. Sterling Livingston[54] popularized this theory, and others have supported it because supervisors do affect employee performance.[55] We have already talked about attitudes and how they affect behavior (how to treat others) and performance, so let's add expectations. In business, expectations are stated as objectives and standards.

Lou Holtz advises setting a higher standard; the worst disservice you can do as a coach, teacher, parent, or leader is to say to your followers, "I don't think you are capable of doing very much—so I'm going to lower the standard," or just lower standards without saying anything. Holtz says there are two kinds of leaders: those who are optimists and lift others up to higher levels of performance, and those who pull everybody down. If we are in a leadership role, we shouldn't worry about being popular; work at raising the self-image and productivity of our followers.

OPENING CASE APPLICATION

3. How did "attitude" help improve the performance of DuPont?

A major factor in Ellen Kullman's improving the performance of DuPont is in her positive attitude with a Theory Y attitude towards her employees. She has a positive optimistic view of employees and uses a participative leadership style. Kullman has faith in her employees and expects them to succeed, and they do. Recall that nearly 40 percent of DuPont's 2009 revenues came from products introduced in the past five years—double the rate of just a few years before she became CEO. Since Kullman took over as CEO, DuPont stock is up by more than all but one other Dow Jones industrial average company at more than 50 percent.[56]

Self-Concept

So far, we have discussed the leaders' attitudes about followers. Now we will examine leaders' attitudes about themselves. **Self-concept** *refers to the positive or negative attitudes people have about themselves.* If you have a positive view of yourself as being a capable person, you will tend to have the positive self-confidence trait. A related concept, *self-efficacy*, is the belief in your own capability to perform in a specific situation.[57] Self-efficacy is based on self-concept and is closely related to the self-confidence trait, because if you believe you can be successful, you will often have self-confidence. Unfortunately, as discussed, there is a rise in the number on narcissists with unrealistic self-concepts.

There is a lot of truth in the saying Henry Ford used, "if you think you can, you can; if you think you can't, you can't." Recall times when you had positive self-efficacy and were successful, or negative self-efficacy and failed. Successful leaders have positive attitudes with strong self-concepts, are optimistic, and with an internal locus of control believe they can make a positive difference. If we don't believe we can be successful leaders, we probably won't be.

OPENING CASE APPLICATION

4. How did Ellen Kullman's self-concept affect her leadership?

Ellen Kullman rarely doubted that she could do whatever she applied herself to accomplish. Back when she went to Tufts to major in engineering, there were not many women entering the male dominated field, but she knew she would graduate and go on to a successful career. Without a positive self-attitude, she would not have had the confidence, especially being in a male-dominated company, that she could climb the corporate ladder at DuPont all the way to the top. Kullman has self-efficacy as CEO, as she knew she could improve the performance at DuPont, and she is doing that.

Developing a More Positive Attitude and Self-Concept

Our behavior and performance will be consistent with the way we see ourselves. Think and act like a winner, and you may become one. Following are some ideas to help you change your attitudes and develop a more positive self-concept:

1. *Realize that there are few, if any, benefits to negative, pessimistic attitudes about others and yourself.* Do holding a grudge, worrying, and being afraid of failure help you to succeed?

2. *Consciously try to have and maintain a positive, optimistic attitude.* If you don't have a positive attitude, it may be caused by your unconscious thoughts and behavior. Only with conscious effort can you improve your self-concept.

3. *Cultivate optimistic thoughts.* Scientific evidence suggests that your thoughts affect every cell in your body. Every time you think positive thoughts, your body, mind, and spirit respond. You will likely feel more motivated and energetic. Use positive self-talk—I will do a good job; it will be done on time; and so on. Also use mental imagery—picture yourself achieving your goal.

4. *If you catch yourself complaining or being negative in any way, stop and change to a positive attitude.* With time, you will catch yourself less often as you become more positive about yourself.

5. *Avoid negative people, especially any that make you feel negative about yourself.* Associate with people who have a positive self-concept, and use their positive behavior.

6. *Set and achieve goals.* Set short-term goals (daily, weekly, monthly) that you can achieve. Achieving specific goals will improve your self-concept, helping you to view yourself as successful.

7. *Focus on your success; don't dwell on failure.* If you achieve five of six goals, dwell on the five and forget the one you missed. We are all going to make mistakes and experience failure. Effective leaders bounce back from disappointment and don't let it affect them negatively in the future. Lou Holtz says happiness is nothing more than a poor memory for the bad things that happen to you.

8. *Don't belittle accomplishments or compare yourself to others.* If you meet a goal and say it was easy anyway, you are being negative. If you compare yourself to someone else and say they are better, you are being negative. No matter how good you are, there is almost always someone better. So focus on being the best that you can be, rather than putting yourself down for not being the best.

9. *Accept compliments.* When someone compliments you, say thank you; it builds self-concept. Don't say things like it was nothing, or anyone could have done it, because you lose the opportunity for a buildup.

10. *Be a positive role model.* If the leader has a positive attitude, the followers usually do too. We can choose to be optimistic or pessimistic—and we usually find what we are looking for. If you look for the positive, you are likely to be happier and get more out of life; why look for the negative and be unhappy?

11. *When things go wrong and you're feeling down, do something to help someone who is worse off than you.* You will realize that you don't have it so bad, and you will realize that the more you give, the more you get. Volunteering at a hospital, soup kitchen, or becoming a Big Brother or Sister can help change your attitude. This is also a great cure for loneliness.

WORK Application 12

Recall a present or past manager. Using Exhibit 2.4, which combinations of attitudes best describe your manager's leadership style? Give examples of the manager's behavior that illustrate his or her attitudes.

_____

_____

_____

_____

Learning Outcome 6 *Describe how attitudes are used to develop four leadership styles.*

How Attitudes Develop Leadership Styles

We now put together the leader's attitudes toward others, using Theory X and Theory Y, and the leader's attitude toward self, using self-concept, to illustrate how these two sets of attitudes develop into four leadership styles. Combining attitudes with the Leader Motive Profile (LMP), an effective leader tends to have Theory Y attitudes with a positive self-concept. See Exhibit 2.4 to understand how attitudes toward self and others affect leadership styles.

EXHIBIT **2.4**   Leadership Styles Based on Attitudes

	Theory Y Attitudes	Theory X Attitudes
Positive self-concept	The leader typically gives and accepts positive feedback, expects others to succeed, and lets others do the job their way.	The leader typically is bossy, pushy, and impatient; does much criticizing with little praising; and is very autocratic.
Negative self-concept	The leader typically is afraid to make decisions, is unassertive, and is self-blaming when things go wrong.	The leader typically blames others when things go wrong, is pessimistic about resolving personal or organizational problems, and promotes a feeling of hopelessness among followers.

© Cengage Learning 2013

Ethical Leadership

Before we discuss ethical behavior, complete Self-Assessment 6 to find out how ethical your behavior is.

SELF-ASSESSMENT 6   How Ethical Is Your Behavior?

For this exercise, you will be using the same set of statements twice. The first time you answer them, focus on your own behavior and the frequency with which you use it for each question. On the line before the question number, place the number 1–4 that represents how often you "did do" the behavior in the past, if you "do the behavior now," or if you "would do" the behavior if you had the chance.

These numbers will allow you to determine your level of ethics. You can be honest without fear of having to tell others your score in class. *Sharing ethics scores is not part of the exercise.*

Frequently			Never
1	2	3	4

The second time you use the same statements, focus on other people in an organization that you work/worked for. Place an "O" on the line after the number if you observed someone doing this behavior. Also place

an "R" on the line if you reported (whistle-blowing) this behavior within the organization or externally.

O—observed R—reported

1–4   O–R

College

_____ 1. _____ Cheating on homework assignments.

_____ 2. _____ Cheating on exams.

_____ 3. _____ Passing in papers that were completed by someone else, as your own work.

Workplace

_____ 4. _____ Lying to others to get what you want or stay out of trouble.

_____ 5. _____ Coming to work late, leaving work early, taking long breaks/lunches and getting paid for it.

(continued)

(Self-Assessment 6 continued)

_____ 6. _____ Socializing, goofing off, or doing personal work rather than doing the work that should be done and getting paid for it.

_____ 7. _____ Calling in sick to get a day off, when not sick.

_____ 8. _____ Using the organization's phone, computer, Internet, copier, mail, car, and so on for personal use.

_____ 9. _____ Taking home company tools/equipment for personal use without permission and then returning them/it.

_____ 10. _____ Taking home organizational supplies or merchandise and keeping it.

_____ 11. _____ Giving company supplies or merchandise to friends or allowing them to take them without saying anything.

_____ 12. _____ Putting in for reimbursement for meals and travel or other expenses that weren't actually eaten or taken.

_____ 13. _____ Taking spouse/friends out to eat or on business trips and charging it to the organizational expense account.

_____ 14. _____ Accepting gifts from customers/suppliers in exchange for giving them business.

_____ 15. _____ Cheating on your taxes.

_____ 16. _____ Misleading customers to make a sale, such as short delivery dates.

_____ 17. _____ Misleading competitors to get information to use to compete against them, such as saying/pretending to be a customer/supplier.

_____ 18. _____ Manipulating data to make you look good, or others bad.

_____ 19. _____ Selling more of the product than the customer needs, to get the commission.

_____ 20. _____ Spreading false rumors about coworkers or competitors to make yourself look better for advancement or to make more sales.

_____ 21. _____ Lying for your boss when asked/told to do so.

_____ 22. _____ Deleting information that makes you look bad or changing information to look better than actual results—false information.

_____ 23. _____ Being pressured, or pressuring others, to sign off on documents with false information.

_____ 24. _____ Being pressured, or pressuring others, to sign off on documents you haven't read, knowing they may contain information or decisions that might be considered inappropriate.

_____ 25. _____ If you were to give this assessment to a person you work with and with whom you do not get along very well, would she agree with your answers? Use a scale of yes 4–1 on the line before the number 25 and skip O or R.

Other Unethical Behavior:

Add other unethical behaviors you observed. Identify if you reported the behavior by using R.

26. _____
27. _____
28. _____

Note: This self-assessment is not meant to be a precise measure of your ethical behavior. It is designed to get you thinking about ethics and your behavior and that of others from an ethical perspective. There is no right or wrong score; however, each of these actions is considered unethical behavior in most organizations. Another ethical issue of this exercise is your honesty when rating the frequencies of your behavior. How honest were you?

Scoring: To determine your ethics score, add the numbers 1–4. Your total will be between 25 and 100. Place the number here and on the continuum below that represents your score. The higher your score, the more ethical is your behavior, and vice versa for lower scores.

25—30—40—50—60—70—80—90—100
Unethical   *Ethical*

Today, business ethics is a major concern in business schools, in businesses them-selves, and among the public.[58] Recall that AACSB (Chapter 1) lists ethical understand-ing as an important competency.[59] Thus, business schools are focusing on ethics.[60] **Ethics** *are the standards of right and wrong that influence behavior*. Right behavior is considered ethical, and wrong behavior is considered unethical.

Government laws and regulations are designed to help keep business honest. How-ever, it has been said that a culture of lying is infecting American business. After the unethical and illegal business practices of WorldCom, Enron, and Arthur Andersen, Congress passed the *Sarbanes-Oxley Act of 2002* to help ensure that complaints about financial irregularities would surface and be swiftly acted upon, without retaliation against the person who exposed the unethical behavior ("whistle-blower"). However, the government can't make people be ethical.

In this section, we will discuss that ethical behavior does pay; how personality traits and attitudes, moral development, and the situation affect ethical behavior; how people justify unethical behavior; some simple guides to ethical behavior; and being an ethical leader.

Does Ethical Behavior Pay?

Generally, the answer is yes. Ethics is so important that some large organizations have ethics officers who are responsible for developing and implementing ethics codes to help guide employees to ethical behavior. Research studies have reported a positive rela-tionship between ethical behavior and leadership effectiveness.[61] From the societal level of analysis, the public has a negative image of big business. Enron's unethical behavior cost many organizations and people a great deal of money directly, but it also hurt every-one in the stock market, and the general economy.

From the organizational level, ethics scandals hurt the company's performance, access to important resources, and reputation.[62] Enron is no longer the company it was, and its auditor Arthur Andersen lost many of its clients and had to sell most of its business due to unethical behavior.

From the individual level, you may say that people like former Enron executives made millions for their unethical behavior; but they were making millions anyway. However, some went to prison, and they may never hold high-level positions again. With all the negative media coverage, unethical leaders' lives will never be the same. If you are uneth-ical, people will not trust you and you will not be an effective leader.[63]

Unethical employees have helped ruin organizations and the lives of countless stake-holders.[64] Employee deviant behavior (theft, abuse of privileges, lack of regard for cost control or quality) costs businesses more than $20 billion annually, and is the cause of 30 percent of business failures.[65] Thus, corporate recruiters are seeking ethical job candi-dates, and graduates are applying to organizations that have ethical products, ethical practices, and reputations for being ethical.[66]

Learning Outcome 7   *Compare the three levels of moral development.*

Factors Influencing Ethical Behavior

In this subsection, we discuss three related concepts: how personality traits and attitudes, moral development, and the situation affect ethical behavior.

Personality Traits and Attitudes

Our ethical behavior is related to our individual needs and personality traits. But per-sonality alone is not a good predictor of unethical behavior. Leaders with surgency (dominance) personality traits have two choices: to use power for personal benefit or to use socialized power. To gain power and to be conscientious with high achievement, some people will use unethical behavior; also, irresponsible people often do not perform to standard by cutting corners and by other behavior which may be considered unethical.

An agreeableness personality sensitive to others can lead to following the crowd in either ethical or unethical behavior; having a high self-concept tends to lead to doing what the person believes is right and not following the crowd's unethical behavior. Emotionally unstable people and those with external locus of control (they do not take personal responsibility for their behavior—it is not their fault) are more likely to use unethical behavior. Being ethical is part of integrity. People open to new experiences are often ethical. People with positive attitudes about ethics tend to be more ethical than those with negative or weak attitudes about ethics.

Moral Development

A second factor affecting ethical behavior is *moral development*, which refers to understanding right from wrong and choosing to do the right thing. Our ability to make ethical choices is related to our level of moral development. Lack of moral development is considered to be one of the many reasons for unethical behavior.[67] There are three levels of personal moral development, as discussed in Exhibit 2.5.

EXHIBIT 2.5   Levels of Moral Development

3. Postconventional

Behavior is motivated by universal principles of right and wrong, regardless of the expectations of the leader or group. One seeks to balance the concerns for self with those of others and the common good. He or she will follow ethical principles even if they violate the law at the risk of social rejection, economic loss, and physical punishment (Martin Luther King, Jr., broke what he considered unjust laws and spent time in jail seeking universal dignity and justice).

"I don't lie to customers because it is wrong."

The common leadership style is visionary and committed to serving others and a higher cause while empowering followers to reach this level.

2. Conventional

Living up to expectations of acceptable behavior defined by others motivates behavior to fulfill duties and obligations. It is common for followers to copy the behavior of the leaders and group. If the group (can be society/organization/department) accepts lying, cheating, stealing, and so on, when dealing with customers/suppliers/government/ competitors, so will the individual. On the other hand, if these behaviors are not accepted, the individual will not do them either. Peer pressure is used to enforce group norms.

"I lie to customers because the other sales reps do it too."

It is common for lower-level managers to use a similar leadership style of the higher-level managers.

1. Preconventional

Self-interest motivates behavior to meet one's own needs to gain rewards while following rules and being obedient to authority to avoid punishment.

"I lie to customers to sell more products and get higher commission checks."

The common leadership style is autocratic toward others while using one's position for personal advantage.

Source: Adapted from Lawrence Kohlberg, "Moral Stages and Moralization: The Cognitive-Development Approach." In Thomas Likona (ed.), *Moral Development and Behavior: Theory, Research, and Social Issues (Austin, TX: Holt, Rinehart and Winston, 1976), 31–53.*

WORK Application 13

Give an organizational example of behavior at each of the three levels of moral development.

———————————

———————————

———————————

———————————

At the first level, preconventional, we choose right and wrong behavior based on our self-interest and the consequences (reward and punishment). With ethical reasoning at the second level, conventional, we seek to maintain expected standards and live up to the expectations of others. One does what the others do. At the third level, postconventional, we make an effort to define moral principles regardless of leader or group ethics. Although most of us have the ability to reach the third level of moral development, postconventional, only about 20 percent of people reach this level.

Most people behave at the second level, conventional, while some have not advanced beyond the first level, preconventional. How do you handle peer pressure to be unethical? What level of moral development are you on? What can you do to further develop your ethical behavior? We will discuss how to be an ethical leader.

The Situation

Our third factor affecting ethical behavior is the situation. People consider the situational forces in determining ethical behavior. Highly competitive and unsupervised situations increase the odds of unethical behavior. Unethical behavior occurs more often when there is no formal ethics policy or code of ethics, and when unethical behavior is not punished, and it is especially prevalent when it is rewarded. People are also less likely to report unethical behavior (blow the whistle) when they perceive the violation as not being serious and when the offenders are their friends.

Integration. To tie the three factors affecting ethical behavior together, we need to realize that personality traits and attitudes and moral development interact with the situation to determine if a person will use ethical or unethical behavior. In this chapter we use the individual level of analysis: Am I ethical, and how can I improve my ethical behavior? At the organizational level, many firms offer training programs and develop codes of ethics to help employees behave ethically. The organizational level of analysis is examined in Part Three of this book; therefore, ethics and whistle-blowing will be further discussed in Chapter 10.

OPENING CASE *APPLICATION*

5. **What role does ethics play at DuPont?**

It always has been and continues to be the intent of DuPont that its employees maintain the highest ethical standards in their conduct of Company affairs. DuPont has been named among the world's leaders in ethics reputation, earning first place in its industry sector and tenth overall among more than 500 multinational companies, according to the annual global Covalence Ethical Ranking Report. Here are some of its ethical principles. In living up to its ethical philosophy, DuPont will: Be fair and honest in all dealings on behalf of the company; do what is right rather than what is expedient; conduct all dealings with suppliers, customers and others in a manner that excludes consideration of personal advantage.[68]

How People Justify Unethical Behavior

Most people understand right and wrong behavior and have a conscience. So why do good people do bad things? When most people use unethical behavior, it is not due to some type of character flaw or being born a bad person. Few people see themselves as unethical. We all want to view ourselves in a positive manner. Therefore, when we do use unethical behavior, we often justify the behavior to protect our self-concept so that we don't have a guilty conscience or feel remorse. **Moral justification** *is the thinking process of rationalizing why unethical behavior is used*. We *rationalize* with statements like "this is a widespread business practice,"[69] "everybody does it," "I deserve it." Let's discuss several thinking processes used to justify unethical behavior.

- **Higher purpose** is rationalizing immoral behavior in terms of a higher purpose. People state that they have conducted unethical behavior (lie about a competitor to hurt its reputation, fix prices, steal confidential information, and so on) for the good of the organization, department, or employees.

- **Displacement of responsibility** is the process of blaming one's unethical behavior on others. "I was only following orders; my boss told me to inflate the figures."

- **Diffusion of responsibility** is the process of the group using the unethical behavior with no one person being held responsible. "We all take bribes/kickbacks; it's the way we do business," or "We all take merchandise home (steal)." As related to conventional morality, peer pressure is used to enforce group norms.

- **Advantageous comparison** is the process of comparing oneself to others who are worse. "I call in sick when I'm not sick only a few times a year; Tom and Ellen do it all the time." "We pollute less than our competitors do."

- **Disregard or distortion of consequences** is the process of minimizing the harm caused by the unethical behavior. "If I inflate the figures, no one will be hurt and I will not get caught. And if I do, I'll just get a slap on the wrist anyway." Was this the case at Enron? Generally, the greater the negative consequence and the chances of getting caught, the less likely we are to be unethical.[70]

- **Attribution of blame** is the process of claiming the unethical behavior was caused by someone else's behavior. "It's my coworker's fault that I hit him. He called me/did xxx, so I had to hit him."

- **Euphemistic labeling** is the process of using "cosmetic" words to make the behavior sound acceptable. *Terrorist group* sounds bad but *freedom fighter* sounds justifiable. *Misleading* or *covering up* sounds better than *lying to others*.

Which justification processes have you used? How can you improve your ethical behavior by not using justification?

CONCEPT APPLICATION 4
Justifying Unethical Behavior

Identify each thinking process used to justify the unethical behavior below.

a. moral justification
b. displacement of responsibility
c. diffusion of responsibility
d. advantageous comparison
e. disregard or distortion of consequences
f. attribution of blame
g. euphemistic labeling

_____ 21. Let's keep the money. We found it and the company will never miss it.

_____ 22. What else could I do; the president asked me to shred the documents.

_____ 23. They are both married, but they are having an affair.

_____ 24. Yes soldier. We have to kill the boys because they shoot at us and they will grow up and continue the fighting.

(continued)

(Concept Application 4 continued)

_____ 25. I only take around one quart of ice cream a week. Joel takes one every day.

_____ 26. Don't worry about paying. Everyone drinks the soda without paying for it.

_____ 27. It's not my fault. Jean started swearing at me first, so I swore back at her.

2.2 *Sex and Violence*

Over the years, various social activist groups, including the Parents Television Council, the National Viewers and Listeners Association, and the National Coalition Against Censorship, have taken a stance for and against censorship of sex and violence on TV and in the movies. People call for more censorship to protect children from seeing sex and violence (many children watch as many as five hours of TV per day), while others don't want censorship, stating it violates free speech laws.

Advocates for less regulation state that major network TV shows for mature audiences are shown late at night while children should not be watching. However, advocates of regulation state the fact than many daytime soap operas are sexual and that cable stations show reruns of major network shows in the daytime and early evening when children are watching. For example, *Sex and the City* is aired in different areas at all hours of the day and night.

1. Does the media (TV, movies, and music) influence societal values?

2. Does the media, with sex and violence, reflect current religious and societal values?

3. The Federal Communications Commission (FCC) has the power to regulate television. Should the FCC regulate the media, and if yes, how far should it go? Should it require toning down the sex and violence, airing the shows only later at night, or should it take shows like *Sex and the City* off the air?

4. Is it ethical and socially responsible to show sex and violence against women, and to portray women as sex objects?

5. Which of the seven justifications of unethical behavior does the media use to defend sex and violence?

Guides to Ethical Behavior

Every day in our personal and professional life, we face situations in which we can make ethical or unethical choices. As discussed, you make these choices based on your personality traits and attitudes, level of moral development, and the situation. Ethical guidelines can have a positive influence on our making ethical decisions.[71] Following are some guides that can help us make ethical decisions.

Golden Rule

Following the golden rule will help you to use ethical behavior. The golden rule is: "Do unto others as you want them to do unto you." Or, put other ways, "Don't do anything to other people that you would not want them to do to you." "Lead others as you want to be led."

Four-Way Test

Rotary International developed the four-way test of the things we think and do to guide business transactions. The four questions are (1) Is it the truth? (2) Is it fair to all concerned? (3) Will it build goodwill and better friendship? (4) Will it be beneficial to all concerned? When making your decision, if you can answer yes to these four questions, it is probably ethical.

Learning Outcome 8 *Explain the stakeholder approach to ethics.*

Stakeholder Approach to Ethics

Under the stakeholder approach to ethics, *one creates a win–win situation for relevant parties affected by the decision.* A win–win situation meets the needs of the organization and employees as well as those of other stakeholders, so that everyone benefits from the decision. The effective leader uses the moral exercise of power—socialized power, rather than personalized. Stakeholders include everyone affected by the decision, which may include followers, governments, customers, suppliers, society, stockholders, and so on. The higher up in management we go, the more stakeholders we have to deal with. You can ask yourself one simple question to help you determine if your decision is ethical from a stakeholder approach:

"Am I proud to tell relevant stakeholders my decision?"

If you are proud to tell relevant stakeholders your decision, it is probably ethical. If you are not proud to tell others your decision, or you keep justifying it, the decision may not be ethical. Justifying by saying everybody else does it is usually a cop-out. Everybody does *not* do it, and even if many others do it, that doesn't make it right. If you are not sure whether a decision is ethical, talk to your manager, higher-level managers, ethics committee members, and other people with high ethical standards. If you are reluctant to talk to others for advice on an ethical decision because you think you may not like their answers, the decision may not be ethical.

Unfortunately, managers can't always create a win–win situation and have to make decisions that do hurt some stakeholders. For example, sales and revenues may be down and we have to cut cost and the only way to do so is to have a layoff. The layoff will have a negative effect on most of these employees, but the decision may be needed for the company to survive. In this situation, many companies will be ethical and socially responsible and provide some extended pay and benefits and help employees find new jobs.

Being an Ethical Leader

Now let's focus on how to be an ethical leader, not necessarily an ethical manager. We should use guides to aid in our ethical decision making. Most of us are followers when it comes to ethics, and to some degree, silence means we are a follower despite our own personal conduct. So we have to lead by example from the postconventional level. Be one of the 20 percent by doing the right thing even when no one is looking. It is okay to blow the whistle. In doing so, one person has the power to get the government to require businesses to change their illegal and unethical practices.

Ethical leadership requires *courage*—the ability to do the right thing at the risk of rejection and loss. Courage is difficult in an organization that focuses on getting along and fitting in without rocking the boat in order to get approval, promotions, and raises. It is difficult to say no when most others are saying yes, to go against the status quo and offer new alternatives to the group. Courage doesn't mean that we don't have doubt or fear rejection, ridicule, and loss; it means we do the right thing in spite of fear. We need to take risks to make change by speaking our mind and fighting for what we believe is right. Courage also requires taking responsibility for mistakes and failures, rather than trying to cover them up or blaming others.

We should remember that moral values are important and that business is not just about making money; it's also about meeting the needs of all stakeholders. It's not okay to lie. Any lie has hidden costs, not only in teamwork and productivity, but also in our own self-respect. One lie often leads to a trail of lies as we try to cover up the first lie. Once we start to lie, it's easy to continue on to bigger lies. It can take years to develop trust, but it can only take one lie to destroy trust and relationships.

Chapter Summary

The chapter summary is organized to answer the ten learning outcomes for Chapter 2.

1. Explain the universality of traits of effective leaders.

Traits are universal in the sense that there are certain traits that most effective leaders have. However, traits are not universal in the sense that there is no one list of traits that is clearly accepted by all researchers, and not all effective leaders have all the traits.

2. Describe the Big Five personality dimensions.

The surgency personality dimension includes leadership and extraversion traits. The agreeableness personality dimension includes traits related to getting along with people. The adjustment personality dimension includes traits related to emotional stability. The conscientiousness personality dimension includes traits related to achievement. The openness-to-experience personality dimension includes traits related to being willing to change and try new things.

3. Discuss why the trait of dominance is so important for managers to have.

Because the dominance trait is based on the desire to be a leader, this trait affects the other traits in a positive or negative way based on that desire.

4. State how the Achievement Motivation Theory and the Leader Motive Profile are related and different.

Achievement Motivation and Leader Motive Profile theories are related because both are based on the need for achievement, power, and affiliation. They are different because the Achievement Motivation Theory is a general motive profile for explaining and predicting behavior and performance, while the LMP is the one profile that specifically explains and predicts leadership success.

5. Identify similarities and differences among Theory X and Theory Y, the Pygmalion effect, and self-concept.

The concept of Theory X and Theory Y is similar to the Pygmalion effect, because both theories focus on the leader's attitude about the followers. The Pygmalion effect extends Theory X and Theory Y attitudes by including the leader's expectations and how he or she treats the followers, using this information to explain and predict followers' behavior and performance. In contrast, Theory X and Theory Y focus on the leader's behavior and performance. Both approaches are different from self-concept because they examine the leader's attitudes about others, whereas self-concept relates to the leader's attitude about him- or herself. Self-concept is also different because it focuses on how the leader's attitude about him- or herself affects his or her behavior and performance.

6. Describe how attitudes are used to develop four leadership styles.

The leader's attitude about others includes Theory Y (positive) and Theory X (negative) attitudes. The leader's attitude about him- or herself includes a positive self-concept or a negative self-concept. Combinations of these variables are used to identify four leadership styles: Theory Y positive self-concept, Theory Y negative self-concept, Theory X positive self-concept, and Theory X negative self-concept.

7. Compare the three levels of moral development.

At the lowest level of moral development, preconventional, behavior is motivated by self-interest, seeking rewards, and avoiding punishment. At the second level, conventional, behavior is motivated by meeting the group's expectations to fit in by copying others' behavior. At the highest level, postconventional, behavior is motivated to do the right thing, at the risk of alienating the group. The higher the level of moral development, the more ethical is the behavior.

8. Explain the stakeholder approach to ethics.

Under the stakeholder approach to ethics, the leader (or follower) creates a win–win situation for relevant parties affected by the decision. If you are proud to tell relevant stakeholders your decision, it is probably ethical. If you are not proud to tell others your decision, or you keep justifying it, the decision may not be ethical.

9. Define the following key terms (in order of appearance in the chapter).

Select one or more methods: (1) fill in the missing key terms from memory; (2) match the key terms from the following list with their definitions below; (3) copy the key terms in order from the list at the beginning of the chapter.

_____ are distinguishing personal characteristics.

_____ is a combination of traits that classifies an individual's behavior.

_____ identify individual stronger and weaker traits.

_____ categorizes traits into the dimensions of surgency, agreeableness, adjustment, conscientiousness, and openness to experience.

_____ includes traits of dominance, extraversion, and high energy with determination.

_____ includes traits of sociability and emotional intelligence.

_____ includes traits of emotional stability and self-confidence.

_____ includes traits of dependability and integrity.

_____ includes traits of flexibility, intelligence, and internal locus of control.

_____ attempts to explain and predict behavior and performance based on a person's need for achievement, power, and affiliation.

_____ attempts to explain and predict leadership success based on a person's need for achievement, power, and affiliation.

_____ includes a high need for power, which is socialized, that is, greater than the need for affiliation and with a moderate need for achievement.

_____ are positive or negative feelings about people, things, and issues.

_____ attempt to explain and predict leadership behavior and performance based on the leader's attitude about followers.

_____ proposes that leaders' attitudes toward and expectations of followers, and their treatment of them, explain and predict followers' behavior and performance.

_____ refers to the positive or negative attitudes people have about themselves.

_____ are the standards of right and wrong that influence behavior.

_____ is the thinking process of rationalizing why unethical behavior is used.

_____ creates a win–win situation for relevant parties affected by the decision.

Key Terms

Achievement Motivation Theory, 43

adjustment personality dimension, 39

agreeableness personality dimension, 38

attitudes, 49

Big Five Model of Personality, 37

conscientiousness personality dimension, 40

ethics, 55

Leader Motive Profile (LMP), 46

Leader Motive Profile Theory, 46

moral justification, 57

openness-to-experience personality dimension, 41

personality, 34

personality profiles, 35

Pygmalion effect, 50

self-concept, 51

stakeholder approach to ethics, 60

surgency personality dimension, 37

Theory X and Theory Y, 49

traits, 34

Review Questions

1. What are the Big Five dimensions of traits?

2. What is the primary use of personality profiles?

3. What are some of the traits that describe the high-energy trait?

4. Is locus of control important to leaders? Why?

5. What does intelligence have to do with leadership?

6. Does sensitivity to others mean that the leader does what the followers want to do?

7. Does McClelland believe that power is good or bad? Why?

8. Should a leader have a dominant need for achievement to be successful? Why or why not?

9. How do attitudes develop leadership styles?

10. Which personality traits are more closely related to ethical and unethical behavior?

11. Do people change their level of moral development based on the situation?

12. Why do people justify their unethical behavior?

Critical Thinking Questions

The following critical-thinking questions can be used for class discussion and/or as written assignments to develop communication skills. Be sure to give complete explanations for all questions.

1. Would you predict that a person with a strong agreeableness personality dimension would be a successful computer programmer? Why or why not?

2. McGregor published Theory X and Theory Y over 30 years ago. Do we still have Theory X managers? Why?

3. In text examples related to the Pygmalion effect, Lou Holtz calls for setting a higher standard. Have the standards in school, society, and work increased or decreased over the last five years?

4. Do you believe that if you use ethical behavior it will pay off in the long run?

5. Can ethics be taught and learned?

6. Which justification do you think is used most often?

7. As related to the simple guide to ethical behavior, how do you want to be led?

CASE

The Bill & Melinda Gates Foundation

The Bill & Melinda Gates Foundation is guided by the belief that every life has equal value. The Foundation essentially gives money (grants) to other organizations (business, nonprofits, and governments) to support them in implementing the Foundation's work to help all people lead healthy, productive lives. It has three grant-making areas: Global Development Program, Global Health Program, and United States Program. In developing countries, it focuses on improving people's health and giving them the chance to lift themselves out of hunger and extreme poverty. In the United States, it seeks to ensure that all people—especially those with the fewest resources—have access to the opportunities they need to succeed in school and life.

The Foundation is headquartered in Seattle, Washington, with offices in Washington, D.C.; Delhi, India; Beijing, China; and London, United Kingdom. It has more than 900 employees, with an asset trust endowment of $37.1 billion, with total grant commitments since inception of $24.81 billion.

The Foundation is led by CEO Jeff Raikes and Co-chair William H. Gates Sr., under the direction of Co-chairs and Trustees Bill and Melinda Gates and Trustee Warren Buffett. Bill and Melinda Gates are the founders and together they shape and approve foundation strategies, review results, advocate for the foundation's issues, and help set the overall direction of the organization.[72]

Before Bill and Melinda were even married, they talked about giving away 95 percent of their wealth during their lifetime. That is why they cofounded and cochair their foundation. They agreed to focus on a few areas of giving,

choosing where to place their money by asking two questions: Which problems affect the most people? and Which problems have been neglected in the past? They give where they can effect the greatest change. They have pumped billions into easing the suffering of those plagued by some of the world's deadliest diseases (AIDS, malaria, and tuberculosis) and revitalized failing public high schools in the United States with their financial support. Bill and Melinda will very likely give away more than $100 billion in their lifetime, and they are truly world leaders together. But let's discuss them separately so we can get to know them a bit more.

William (Bill) H. Gates, III, was born in 1955 and began programming mainframe computers at age 13. While attending Harvard University, Gates developed a version of the programming language BASIC for the first microcomputer—the MITS Altair. In 1975, Gates and his childhood friend Paul Allen founded Microsoft as a partnership, and it was incorporated in 1981. He invented the software industry, masterminded the rise of the PC, and has hung in there as a force on the Internet. Bill Gates is consistently ranked as the richest man in America valued at $54 billion in 2010 by *Forbes*,[73] and as one of the richest men in the world. He remains Chairman of the Board at Microsoft but retired from day-to-say operations in 2008 to devote most of his time to the Bill & Melinda Gates Foundation. With more time for family, when home, Bill makes time to drop off or pick up his three kids from school every day.[74]

Bill Gates has an extraordinary capacity for work, having slept under his desk rather than lose minutes away from the office while building Microsoft into the software king it is today.[75] He can be abrasive and is known as a demanding boss who encourages creativity and recognizes employee achievements. Several of his early employees are now million-aires. Employees are expected to be well-informed, logical, vocal, and thick-skinned. Teams must present their ideas at "Bill" meetings. During the meetings, Gates often interrupts presentations to question facts and assumptions. He shouts criticisms and challenges team members. Team members are expected to stand up to Gates, giving good logical answers to his questions. He has a personal Web site www.thegatesnotes.com that catalogs his activities and interests. You can also read his tweets on Twitter at *twitter.com/BillGates*.

Melinda French grew up in Dallas in a hard-working, middle-class family. Unlike Bill, she graduated from college, earning a BA (double major in computer science and economics) and an MBA from Duke University. She went to work for Microsoft in 1987; at age 22 she was the youngest recruit and the only woman among ten MBAs. For nine years she was a hotshot who climbed the corporate ladder to become general manager of information products, managing 300 employees. Along the way, Bill asked her out (in the parking lot), which led to their wedding on January 1, 1994. Melinda stopped working at Microsoft after having the first of their three children (Jennifer, Rory, and Phoebe), but she continued to serve on corporate boards, including that of Duke University.

Melinda Gates is a total systems thinker who constantly sets and achieves goals. She is known as a strong team builder, who strives for collaboration in decision making. Melinda is loving and charming; she wins people over by being persuasive. She is compassionate and not afraid to get involved as she travels the world to help solve its prob-lems. She held AIDS babies with dirty pants and comforted patients when she visited Mother Teresa's Home for the Dying in India. She has more influence than Bill when it comes to investing their assets in philanthropic projects. She is ranked in the top 30 on The World's 100 Most Power-ful Women by *Forbes*.[76]

GO TO THE INTERNET: To learn more about Bill and Melinda Gates and their foundation, visit their Web site (**http://www.gatesfoundation.org**).

Support your answers to the following questions with specific information from the case and text or with other information you get from the Web or other sources.

1. What do you think Bill and Melinda Gates's personality traits are for each of the Big Five dimensions? Compare the two.

2. Which of the traits of effective leaders would you say has had the greatest impact on Bill and Melinda Gates's success? Compare the two.

3. Which motivation would McClelland say was the major need driving Bill and Melinda Gates to continue to work so hard despite being worth many billions of dollars?

4. Do Bill and Melinda Gates have an LMP? Compare the two.

5. What type of self-concept do Bill and Melinda Gates have, and how does it affect their success?

6. Is Bill Gates ethical in business at Microsoft? Which level of moral development is he on?

CUMULATIVE CASE QUESTION

7. Which leadership managerial role(s) played by Bill and Melinda Gates have an important part in the success of their foundation (Chapter 1)?

CASE EXERCISE AND ROLE-PLAY

Preparation: Think of a business that you would like to start some day and answer these questions, which will help you develop your plan. (1) What would be your company's name? (2) What would be its mission (purpose or reason for being)? (3) What would your major products and/or ser-vices be? (4) Who would be your major competitors? (5) What would be your competitive advantage? (What makes you different from your competitors? Why would anyone buy your product or service rather than the competition's?) Your instructor may elect to let you break into groups to develop a group business idea. If you do a group business, select one leader with a thick skin who can handle a "Bill" meeting to present the proposal to the entire class. An alter-native is to have a student(s) who has an actual business idea/project/proposal of any type present it for feedback.

Role-Play "Bill" Meeting: One person (representing one-self or a group) may give the business proposal idea to the entire class; or break into groups of five or six and, one at a time, deliver proposals. The members of the class that listen play the role of Bill Gates during the "Bill" meeting, or they chal-lenge presenters and offer suggestions for improvement.

VIDEO ▶❚ CASE

"P.F." Chang's Serves Its Workers Well

Founded in 1993, P.F. Chang's owns and operates over 120 full-service, casual dining Asian bistros and contemporary Chinese diners across the country. P.F. Chang's strives to create an exceptional dining experience for every customer—-and that includes a friendly, knowledgeable staff. By treating employees with respect, restaurant managers find that they can expect more from their staffs—-and get it. Unlike many hourly restaurant employees, those at P.F. Chang's have the authority to make decisions that benefit customers. Giving employees the freedom to make decisions has had a huge impact on their attitudes and performance. Managers at P.F. Chang's receive extensive training on how to create and nurture a positive attitude among their employees, and all workers receive an employee handbook, which clearly spells out exactly what is expected of them.

1. In what ways does P.F. Chang's create organizational commitment among its workers?

2. How might a manager at P.F. Chang's use the Big Five personality factors to assess whether a candidate for a position on the wait staff would be suitable?

Developing Your Leadership Skills **1**

Improving Attitudes and Personality Traits

Preparing for This Exercise

You should have read and now understand attitudes and personality traits. Effective leaders know themselves and work to maximize their strengths and minimize their weaknesses. As the name of this exercise implies, you can improve your attitudes and personality traits through this exercise by following these steps.

1. **Identify strengths and weaknesses**. Review the six self-assessment exercises in this chapter. List your three major strengths and areas that can be improved:

Strengths: 1. _____
                2. _____
                3. _____
Areas to Improve: 1. _____
                2. _____
                3. _____

We don't always see ourselves as others do. Research has shown that many people are not accurate in describing their own personalities, and that others can describe them more objectively. Before going on with this exercise, you may want to ask someone you know well to complete your personality profile (see Self-Assessment 1 on page 33), rate your attitude as positive or negative, and list your strengths and areas for improvement.

2. **Develop a plan for improving**. Start with your Number One area to improve on. Write down specific things that you can do to improve. List specific times, dates, and places that you will implement your plans. You may want to review the 11 tips for developing a more positive attitude and self-concept for ideas. Use additional paper if you need more space.

_____

_____

_____

_____

3. **Work on other areas for improvement**. After you see improvement in your first area, develop a new plan for your second area, and proceed through the steps again.

Optional: If you have a negative attitude toward yourself or others—or you would like to improve your behavior with others (family, coworkers), things, or issues (disliking school or work)—try following the internationally known motivational speaker and trainer Zig Ziglar's system.[77] Thousands of people have used this system successfully. This system can also be used for changing personality traits as well.

Here are the steps to follow, with an example plan for a person who has a negative self-concept and also wants to be more sensitive to others. Use this example as a guide for developing your own plan.

1. *Self-concept*. Write down everything you like about yourself. List all your strengths. Then go on and list all your weaknesses. Get a good friend to help you.

2. Make a clean new list, and using positive affirmations, write all your strengths. Example: "I am sensitive to others' needs."

3. *On another sheet of paper, again using positive affirmations, list all your weaknesses.* For example, don't write "I need to lose weight." Write, "I am a slim (whatever you realistically can weigh in 30 days) pounds." Don't write, "I have to stop criticizing myself." Write, "I positively praise myself often, every day." Write "I have good communications skills," not "I am a weak communicator." The following list gives example affirmations for improving sensitivity to others. Note the repetition; you can use a thesaurus to help.

I am sensitive to others.

My behavior with others conveys my warmth for them.

I convey my concern for others.

My behavior conveys kindness toward others.

My behavior helps others build their self-esteem.

People find me easy to talk to.

I give others my full attention.

I patiently listen to others talk.

I answer others slowly and in a polite manner.

I answer questions and make comments with useful information.

My comments to others help them feel good about themselves.

I compliment others regularly.

4. *Practice.* Every morning and night for at least the next 30 days, look at yourself in the mirror and read your list of positive affirmations. Be sure to look at yourself between each affirmation as you read. Or, record the list on a tape recorder and listen to it while looking at yourself in the mirror. If you are really motivated, you can repeat this step at other times of the day. Start with your areas for improvement. If it takes five minutes or more, don't bother with the list of your strengths. Or stop at five minutes; this exercise is effective in short sessions. Although miracles won't happen overnight, you may become more aware of your behavior in the first week. In the second or third week, you may become aware of yourself using new behavior successfully. You may still see some negatives, but the number will decrease in time as the positive increases.

Psychological research has shown that if a person hears something believable repeated for 30 days, he or she will tend to believe it. Ziglar says that you cannot consistently perform in a manner that is inconsistent with the way you see yourself. So, as you listen to your positive affirmations, you will believe them, and you will behave in a manner that is consistent with your belief. Put simply, your behavior will change with your thoughts without a

lot of hard work. For example, if you listen to the affirmation, "I am an honest person" (not, "I have to stop lying"), in time—without having to work at it—you will tell the truth. At first you may feel uncomfortable reading or listening to positive affirmations that you don't really believe you have. But keep looking at yourself in the mirror and reading or listening, and with time you will feel comfortable and believe it and live it.

Are you thinking you don't need to improve, or that this method will not work? Yes, this system often does work. Zig Ziglar has trained thousands of satisfied people. One of this book's authors tried the system himself, and within two or three weeks, he could see improvement in his behavior. The question isn't will the system work for you, but rather will you work the system to improve?

5. *When you slip, and we all do, don't get down on yourself.* In the sensitivity-to-others example, if you are rude to someone and catch yourself, apologize and change to a positive tone. Effective leaders admit when they are wrong and apologize. If you have a hard time admitting you are wrong and saying you are sorry, at least be obviously nice so that the other person realizes you are saying you are sorry indirectly. Then forget about it and keep trying. Focus on your successes, not your slips. Don't let ten good discussions be ruined by one insensitive comment. If you were a baseball player and got nine out of ten hits, you'd be the best in the world.

6. *Set another goal.* After 30 days, select a new topic, such as developing a positive attitude toward work, school, or trying a specific leadership style that you want to develop. You can also include more than one area to work on.

Doing This Exercise in Class

Objective

To develop your skill at improving your attitudes and personality traits. As a leader, you can also use this skill to help your followers improve.

The primary AACSB competencies developed through this exercise are analytic and reflective thinking skills.

Preparation

You should have identified at least one area for improvement and developed a plan to improve.

Procedure 1 *(1–2 minutes)* Break into groups of two or preferably three; be sure the others in your group are people you feel comfortable sharing with.

Procedure 2 *(4–6 minutes)* Have one of the group members volunteer to go first. The first volunteer states the attitude or personality trait they want to work on and describes the plan. The other group members give feedback on how to improve the plan. Try to give other plan ideas that can be helpful and/

or provide some specific help. You can also make an agreement to ask each other how you are progressing at set class intervals. Don't change roles until you're asked to do so.

Procedure 3 *(4–6 minutes)* A second group member volunteers to go next. Follow the same procedure as above.

Procedure 4 *(4–6 minutes)* The third group member goes last. Follow the same procedure as above.

Conclusion

The instructor may lead a class discussion and/or make concluding remarks.

Apply It *(2–4 minutes)* What did I learn from this exercise? Will I really try to improve my attitude and personality by implementing my plan?

_____

_____

_____

Sharing

In the group, or to the entire class, volunteers may give their answers to the "Apply It" questions.

Developing Your Leadership Skills 2

Personality Perceptions

Preparing for This Exercise

Read the section on "Personality Traits and Leadership," and complete Self-Assessment 1 on page 33. From that exercise, rank yourself below from the highest score (1) to lowest (5) for each of the Big Five traits. Do not tell anyone your ranking until asked to do so.

_ surgency   _ agreeableness
_ adjustment   _ conscientiousness
_ openness to experience

Doing This Exercise in Class

Objective

To develop your skill at perceiving personality traits of other people. With this skill, you can better understand and predict people's behavior, which is helpful to leaders in influencing followers.

The primary AACSB competencies developed through this exercise are analytic and reflective thinking skills.

Procedure 1 *(2–4 minutes)* Break into groups of three. This group should be with people you know the best in the class. You may need some groups of two. If you don't know people in the class, and you did Skill-Development Exercise 1 in Chapter 1, "Getting to Know You by Name," get in a group with those people.

Procedure 2 *(4–6 minutes)* Each person in the group writes down their perception of each of the other two group members. Simply rank which trait you believe to be the highest and lowest (put the Big Five dimension name on the line) for each person. Write a short reason for your perception, including some behavior you observed that leads you to your perception.

Name _____ Highest personality score
_____ Lowest score _____
Reason for ranking _____

_____

Name _____ Highest personality score _____ Lowest score _____

Reason for ranking _____

_____

Procedure 3 *(4–6 minutes)* One of the group members volunteers to go first to hear the other group members' perceptions.

1. One person tells the volunteer which Big Five dimension he or she selected as the person's highest and lowest score, and why these dimensions were selected. Do not discuss this information yet.

2. The other person also tells the volunteer the same information.

3. The volunteer gives the two others his or her actual highest and lowest scores. The three group members discuss the accuracy of the perceptions.

Procedure 4 *(4–6 minutes)* A second group member volunteers to go next to receive perceptions. Follow the same procedure as above.

Procedure 5 *(4–6 minutes)* The third group member goes last. Follow the same procedure as above.

Conclusion The instructor may lead a class discussion and/or make concluding remarks.

Apply It *(2–4 minutes)* What did I learn from this exercise? How will I use this knowledge in the future?

_____

_____

_____

Sharing

In the group, or to the entire class, volunteers may give their answers to the "Apply It" questions.

Developing Your Leadership Skills 3

Ethics and Whistle-blowing

Preparing for This Exercise

Now that you have completed Self-Assessment 6 on pages 53–54 regarding ethical behavior, answer the discussion questions based on that assessment.

Discussion Questions

1. For the "College" section, items 1–3, who is harmed and who benefits from these unethical behaviors?

2. For the "Workplace" section, items 4–24, select the three items (circle their numbers) you consider the most seriously unethical behavior. Who is harmed and who benefits by these unethical behaviors?

3. If you observed unethical behavior but didn't report it, why didn't you report the behavior? If you did blow the whistle, why did you report the unethical behavior? What was the result?

4. As a manager, it is your responsibility to uphold ethical behavior. If you know employees are using any of these unethical behaviors, will you take action to enforce compliance with ethical standards?

Doing This Exercise in Class

Objective
To better understand ethics and whistle-blowing, and decide what you will do about unethical behavior.

The primary AACSB compentencies developed through this exercise are ethical understanding, analytic, and reflective thinking skills.

Preparation
You should have completed the preparation for this exercise.

Experience
You will share your answers to the preparation questions, but are not requested to share your ethics score.

Procedure 1 *(5–10 minutes)* The instructor writes the numbers 1–24 on the board. For each statement, students first raise their hands if they have observed this behavior, then if they have reported the behavior. The instructor writes the numbers on the board. (Note: Procedure 1 and Procedure 2A can be combined.)

Procedure 2 *(10–20 minutes)* Option A: As the instructor takes a count of the students who have observed and reported unethical behavior, he or she leads a discussion on the statements.

Option B: Break into groups of four to six, and share your answers to the four discussion questions at the end of the preparation part of this exercise. The groups may be asked to report the general consensus of the group to the entire class. If so, select a spokesperson before the discussion begins.

Option C: The instructor leads a class discussion on the four discussion questions at the end of the preparation part of this exercise.

Conclusion
The instructor may make concluding remarks.

Apply It *(2–4 minutes)* What did I learn from this exercise? How will I use this knowledge in the future to be ethical? When will I use a simple guide to ethics?

_____

_____

_____

Sharing
Volunteers may give their answers to the "Apply It" questions.

Leadership Behavior and Motivation

Learning Outcomes

After studying this chapter, you should be able to:

1. List the University of Iowa leadership styles. p. 71

2. Describe similarities and differences between the University of Michigan and Ohio State University leadership models. p. 73

3. Discuss similarities and differences between the Ohio State University Leadership Model and the Leadership Grid. p. 77

4. Discuss similarities and differences among the three content motivation theories. p. 82

5. Discuss the major similarities and differences among the three process motivation theories. p. 89

6. Explain the four types of reinforcement. p. 96

7. State the major differences among content, process, and reinforcement theories. p. 103

8. Define the following **key terms** (in order of appearance in the chapter):

leadership style

Ohio State University Leadership
    Model

Leadership Grid

motivation

motivation process

content motivation theories

hierarchy of needs theory

two-factor theory

acquired needs theory

process motivation theories

equity theory

expectancy theory

University of Michigan Leadership Model

goal setting theory

writing objectives model

reinforcement theory

giving praise model

OPENING CASE *APPLICATION*

Trader Joe's mission is to bring you the best-quality products at the best prices. It's not complicated; it just focuses on what matters—great food + great prices = Value. Joe Coulombe named the store Trader Joe's to evoke images of the South Seas. As part of its unique culture, employees wear Hawaiian shirts because they're traders on the culinary seas, searching the world over for cool items to bring home to its customers. They sail those seven seas, so customers can have some fun with its finds at their neighborhood Trader Joe's.[1]

Joe Coulombe opened the first Trader Joe's over 40 years ago in Pasadena, California, with a quirky in-store culture with a different business model to make shopping at Trader Joe's different from what people were used to in a supermarket—it's an adventure. It's an offbeat, fun discovery zone that elevates food shopping from being a chore to a cultural experience. Trader Joe's stocks its shelves with a winning combination of low-cost, yuppie-friendly staples and exotic affordable luxuries.[2]

It offers low prices, every day. No coupons, no membership cards, no specials, no discounts. At Trader Joe's, you won't find a lot of branded items, instead, you'll find unconventional and interesting products in the Trader Joe's label as well as everyday basics. It stocks fewer items than grocery stores, allowing high volume and lower prices, and about 80 percent of the products bear the Trader Joes' brand. Because the focus is on in-store fun shopping, there are no online sales.[3]

Joe Coulombe founded Trader Joe's in 1967 and sold the chain to Germany's Albrecht family (the people behind the Aldi Nord supermarket empire) in 1979, but he continued to run the company for Albrecht for another 10 years under a management contract. Trader Joe's is still family-owned, not having any publicly owned stock. The Albrecht family essentially lets current CEO Dan Bane run the company. They visit the U.S. operation about once a year. Although he moved on, Joe's fingerprints are still all over the company that bears his name, from the business model, robust selection of products, and culture to the Hawaiian-print shirts that employees wear.[4]

OPENING CASE QUESTIONS:

1. Which Ohio State University, University of Michigan, and Leadership Grid leadership style is emphasized at Trader Joe's?

2. What does Trader Joe's do to motivate its employees, and how does it affect performance?

3. (a–c). How does Trader Joe's meet its employees' content motivation needs?

4. (a–c). How does Trader Joe's meet its employees' process motivation needs?

5. How does Trader Joe's use reinforcement theory to motivate its employees?

Can you answer any of these questions? You'll find answers to these questions and learn more about Trader Joe's and its leadership throughout the chapter.

To learn more about Trader Joe's, visit the company's Web site at **http://www.traderjoes.com**.

Your leadership style, and your ability to motivate yourself and others will affect your career success and the organization's performance.[5] So how can you, as a leader, motivate followers to go beyond mediocrity to become committed organizational citizens?[6] That is what this chapter is all about. We will discuss four behavioral leadership models and seven motivation theories.

Leadership Behavior and Styles

Leadership Behavior

By the late 1940s, most of the leadership research had shifted from the trait theory paradigm (Chapter 2) to the behavioral theory paradigm, which focuses on what the leader says and does. In the continuing quest to find the one best leadership style in all situations, researchers attempted to identify the differences in the behavior of effective leaders versus ineffective leaders. Although the behavioral leadership theory made major contributions to leadership research, which we will discuss more fully in the Leadership Grid section later, it never achieved its goal of finding one best style. Unfortunately, no leadership behaviors were found to be consistently associated with leadership effectiveness.[7] The leadership behavior theory paradigm lasted nearly 30 years. Today, research continues to seek a better understanding of behavior, and more importantly, to predict behavior.[8]

Leadership Behavior Is Based on Traits

Although the behavioral theorists focus on behavior, it's important to realize that leaders' behavior is based on their traits and skills. The manager's leadership personality traits and attitudes directly affect his or her behavior and relationship with employees.[9] Recall that the Pygmalion effect is based on traits, attitude expectations, and the manager's behavioral treatment of employees, which in turn determines the followers' behavior and performance. Thus, developing skill at behavioral change is an important topic of leadership,[10] and it continues to be studied today.[11]

Leading by example is important to managers. In fact, as Albert Einstein said, "Setting an example is not the main means of influencing another; it is the only means." Leading by example takes place as followers observe the leader's behavior and copy it. And the leader's behavior is based on his or her traits. Thus, traits and behavior go hand-in-hand. However, behavior is easier to learn and change than traits. We need to condition ourselves to new behavior.[12]

| **Learning Outcome 1** | List the University of Iowa leadership styles. |

Leadership Styles and the University of Iowa Research

Leadership style *is the combination of traits, skills, and behaviors leaders use as they interact with followers.* Although a leadership style is based on traits and skills, the important component is the behavior, because it is a relatively consistent pattern of behavior that characterizes a leader.

WORK Application 1
Recall a present or past manager. Which of the University of Iowa leadership styles does or did your manager use most often? Describe the behavior of your manager.

_____

_____

_____

_____

University of Iowa Leadership Styles

In the 1930s, before behavioral theory became popular, Kurt Lewin and associates conducted studies at the University of Iowa that concentrated on the leadership style of the manager.[13] Their studies identified two basic leadership styles:

- *Autocratic leadership style.* The autocratic leader makes the decisions, tells employees what to do, and closely supervises workers.

- *Democratic leadership style.* The democratic leader encourages participation in decisions, works with employees to determine what to do, and does not closely supervise employees.

The autocratic and democratic leadership styles are often placed at opposite ends of a continuum, as shown in Exhibit 3.1; thus a leader's style usually falls somewhere between the two styles. The Iowa studies contributed to the behavioral movement and led to an era of behavioral rather than trait research. With the shift in paradigm from management to leadership, the leadership style of effective managers is no longer autocratic, but more democratic.[14]

EXHIBIT **3.1** University of Iowa Leadership Styles

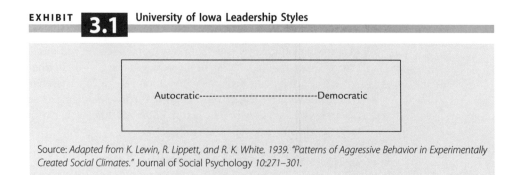

Autocratic---------------------------------------Democratic

Source: *Adapted from K. Lewin, R. Lippett, and R. K. White. 1939. "Patterns of Aggressive Behavior in Experimentally Created Social Climates."* Journal of Social Psychology *10:271–301.*

University of Michigan and Ohio State University Studies

Leadership research was conducted at Ohio State and the University of Michigan at about the same time during the mid-1940s to mid-1950s. These studies were not based on prior autocratic and democratic leadership styles, but rather sought to determine the behavior of effective leaders. Although these two studies used the term *leadership behavior* rather than *leadership styles,* the behaviors identified are actually more commonly called leadership styles today. In this section, we discuss leadership styles identified by these two universities. Before reading about these studies, complete Self-Assessment 1 to determine your behavioral leadership style.

SELF-ASSESSMENT 1 Your Behavioral Leadership Style

For each of the following statements, select one of the following:

1– "I **would not** tend to do this."

0– "I **would** tend to do this."

as a manager of a work unit. There are no right or wrong answers, so don't try to select correctly.

_____ 1. I (would or would not) let my employees know that they should not be doing things during work hours that are not directly related to getting their jobs done.

_____ 2. I (would or would not) spend time talking to my employees to get to know them personally during work hours.

_____ 3. I (would or would not) have a clearly written agenda of things to accomplish during department meetings.

_____ 4. I (would or would not) allow employees to come in late or leave early to take care of personal issues.

_____ 5. I (would or would not) set clear goals so employees know what needs to be done.

_____ 6. I (would or would not) get involved with employee conflicts to help resolve them.

_____ 7. I (would or would not) spend much of my time directing employees to ensure that they meet department goals.

_____ 8. I (would or would not) encourage employees to solve problems related to their work without having to get my permission to do so.

_____ 9. I (would or would not) make sure that employees do their work according to the standard method to be sure it is done correctly.

_____ 10. I (would or would not) seek the advice of my employees when making decisions.

_____ 11. I (would or would not) keep good, frequent records of my department's productivity and let employees know how they are doing.

(continued)

(Self-Assessment 1 continued)

_____ 12. I (would or would not) work to develop trust between my employees and me, and among the department members.

_____ 13. I (would or would not) be quick to take corrective action with employees who are not meeting the standards or goals.

_____ 14. I (would or would not) personally thank employees for doing their job to standard and meeting goals.

_____ 15. I (would or would not) continue to set higher standards and goals and challenge my employees to meet them.

_____ 16. I (would or would not) be open to employees to discuss personal issues during work time.

_____ 17. I (would or would not) schedule my employees' work hours and tasks to be completed.

_____ 18. I (would or would not) encourage my employees to cooperate with rather than compete against each other.

_____ 19. I (would or would not) focus on continually trying to improve the productivity of my department with activities like cutting costs.

_____ 20. I (would or would not) defend good employees of mine if my manager or peers criticized their work, rather than agree or say nothing.

Add up the number of **would do** this for all *odd-* numbered items and place it here _____ and on the continuum below.

10 — 9 — 8 — 7 — 6 — 5 — 4 — 3 — 2 — 1
High Task Leadership Style   Low Task Leadership Style

Add up the number of **would do** this for all *even-* numbered items and place it here _____ and on the continuum below.

10 — 9 — 8 — 7 — 6 — 5 — 4 — 3 — 2 — 1
High People Leadership Style   Low People Leadership Style

The higher your score for task leadership, the stronger is your tendency to focus on getting the job done. The higher your score for people leadership, the stronger is your tendency to focus on meeting people's needs and developing supportive relationships. Read on to better understand these leadership styles.

Learning Outcome 2	*Describe similarities and differences between the University of Michigan and Ohio State University leadership models.*

University of Michigan: Job-Centered and Employee-Centered Behavior

The University of Michigan's Survey Research Center, under the principal direction of Rensis Likert, conducted studies to determine how leaders functioned in small groups. Researchers created a questionnaire called the *Survey of Organizations* and conducted interviews to gather data on leadership styles. They gave the survey, similar to the one in Self-Assessment Exercise 1, to employees to complete based on their managers behavior. You can give Self-Assessment 1 to others to determine if they perceive your leadership style the same as you assessed it.

The researchers' goals were to (1) classify the leaders as effective and ineffective by comparing the behavior of leaders from high-producing units and low-producing units and (2) determine reasons for effective leadership.[15] The researchers identified two styles of leadership behavior, which they called *job-centered* and *employee-centered*. The University of Michigan model stated that a leader is either more job-centered or more employee-centered. *The* University of Michigan Leadership Model *thus identifies two leadership styles: job-centered and employee-centered.* See Exhibit 3.2 for the University of Michigan Leadership Model: it is a one-dimensional continuum between two leadership styles.

EXHIBIT **3.2**   The University of Michigan Leadership Model: Two Leadership Styles, One Dimension

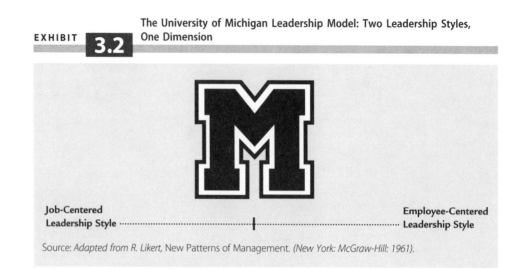

**Job-Centered
Leadership Style** ··|·· **Employee-Centered
Leadership Style**

Source: *Adapted from R. Likert,* New Patterns of Management. *(New York: McGraw-Hill: 1961).*

Job-Centered Leadership Style

The job-centered style has scales measuring two job-oriented behaviors of goal emphasis and work facilitation. Job-centered behavior refers to the extent to which the leader takes charge to get the job done. The leader closely directs subordinates with clear roles and goals, while the manager tells them what to do and how to do it as they work toward goal achievement. Review the odd-numbered items in Self-Assessment 1 for examples of job-(task-)oriented leadership behavior.

Employee-Centered Leadership Style

The employee-centered style has scales measuring two employee-oriented behaviors of supportive leadership and interaction facilitation. Employee-centered behavior refers to the extent to which the leader focuses on meeting the human needs of employees while developing relationships. The leader is sensitive to subordinates and communicates to develop trust, support, and respect while looking out for their welfare. Review the even-numbered items in Self-Assessment 1 for examples of employee-(people-)oriented leadership behavior.

Based on Self-Assessment 1, is your leadership style more job-(task-) or employee-(people-) centered?

CONCEPT APPLICATION 1
University of Michigan Leadership Styles

Identify each of these five behaviors by its leadership style. Write the appropriate letter in the blank before each item.

a. job-centered   b. employee-centered

_____ 1. A manager is saying a friendly good morning to followers as they arrive at work.

_____ 2. A manager is the office developing a plan for the team.

_____ 3. A manager is asking followers for ideas on a decision to be made.

(continued)

(Concept Application 1 continued)

_____ 4. A manager is instructing the follower to do the job the way the leader wants it done.

_____ 5. A manager just calculated the monthly sales report and is sending it to all the sales representatives so they know if they met their quota.

Ohio State University: Initiating Structure and Consideration Behavior

The Personnel Research Board of Ohio State University, under the principal direction of Ralph Stogdill, began a study to determine effective leadership styles. In the attempt to measure leadership styles, these researchers developed an instrument known as the *Leader Behavior Description Questionnaire (LBDQ)*. The LBDQ had 150 examples of definitive leader behaviors, which were narrowed down from 1,800 leadership functions. Respondents to the questionnaire perceived their manager's behavior toward them on two distinct dimensions or leadership types, which they eventually called *initiating structure* and *consideration:*[16]

- *Initiating structure behavior.* The initiating structure leadership style is essentially the same as the job-centered leadership style; it focuses on getting the task done.

- *Consideration behavior.* The consideration leadership style is essentially the same as the employee-centered leadership style; it focuses on meeting people's needs and developing relationships.

Because a leader can be high or low on initiating structure and/or consideration, four leadership styles are developed. *The Ohio State University Leadership Model identifies four leadership styles: low structure and high consideration, high structure and high consideration, low structure and low consideration, and high structure and low consideration.* Exhibit 3.3 illustrates the four leadership styles and their two dimensions.

Leaders with high structure and low consideration behavior use one-way communications, and decisions are made by the managers, whereas leaders with high consideration and low structure use two-way communications and tend to share decision making. To determine your two-dimensional leadership style from Self-Assessment 1, put your two separate ("task" and "people") scores together and determine which of the four styles in Exhibit 3.3 is the closest match.

WORK Application **2**
Recall a present or past manager. Which of the four Ohio State leadership styles does or did your manager use most often? Describe the behavior of your manager.

_____

_____

_____

_____

Differences, Contributions, and Applications of Leadership Models

Differences between the Models

The Ohio State and University of Michigan leadership models are different in that the University of Michigan places the two leadership behaviors at opposite ends of the same continuum, making it one-dimensional. The Ohio State University model considers the two behaviors independent of one another, making it two-dimensional; thus this model has four leadership styles.

EXHIBIT **3.3**   The Ohio State University Leadership Model: Four Leadership Styles, Two Dimensions

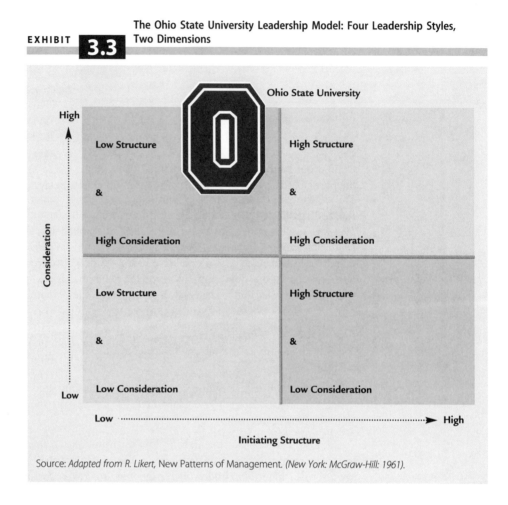

Source: *Adapted from R. Likert,* New Patterns of Management. *(New York: McGraw-Hill: 1961).*

Contributions of the Models

The two leadership behaviors on which the models of both universities are based have strong research support. Leadership behaviors were developed, and repeatedly tested, using statistical factor analysis to narrow the dimensions down to structure/job-centered and consideration/employee-centered. The LBDQ and modified versions have been used in hundreds of past studies by many different researchers.

Research efforts to determine the one best leadership style have been weak and inconsistent for most criteria of leadership effectiveness. In other words, there is no one best leadership style in all situations; this is the first contribution to leadership theory, because it has helped lead researchers to the next paradigm—that of contingency leadership theory (the topic of our next chapter). Thus, the contribution of the behavioral leadership paradigm was to identify two generic dimensions of leadership behavior that continue to have importance in accounting for leader effectiveness today.

Although there is no one best leadership style in all situations, there has been a consistent finding that employees are more satisfied with a leader who is high in consideration. Prior to the two university leadership studies, many organizations had focused on getting the job done with little, if any, concern for meeting employee needs. So, along with other behavioral theory research, there was a shift to place more emphasis on the human side of the organization to increase productivity; this is a second contribution. The saying that a happy worker is a productive worker comes from this period of research, and this relationship is still being studied today.[17]

Another important research finding was that most leadership functions can be carried out by someone besides the designated leader of a group. Thus, due to behavioral leadership research, more organizations began training managers to use participative leadership styles. In fact, Rensis Likert proposed three types of leadership behavior: job-centered behavior, employee-centered behavior, and participative leadership. Thus, as a third contribution of these leadership models, Likert has been credited as being the first to identify the participative leadership style that is commonly used today.

Applications of the Models

The two models don't tell the leader how to behave, but they do provide a classification system reminding us that our behavior affects others through the "task" we perform as well as the "relationships" we develop. Many leadership development programs are structured along the behavioral styles approach, and almost all give managers a questionnaire that in some way assesses their task and relationship behavior toward followers. Managers use the assessment to improve their overall leadership style.[18]

The behavioral styles approach is easily applied to leadership by assessing our behavioral style. It helps us answer the question, "How am I doing as a leader?" Through our ongoing self-assessment, we can determine how we are coming across to others and how we could change our behavior to be more effective in performing our task and in developing our relations.[19]

The Leadership Grid

In this section, we discuss the Leadership Grid theory, including research and contributions of the high-concern-for-people and high-concern-for-production (team leader) leadership styles.

Learning Outcome 3   *Discuss similarities and differences between the Ohio State University Leadership Model and the Leadership Grid.*

Leadership Grid Theory

Behavior leadership theory did not end in the mid-1950s with the University of Michigan and Ohio State University studies. Robert Blake and Jane Mouton, from the University of Texas, developed the Managerial Grid® and published it in 1964, updated it in 1978 and 1985, and in 1991 it became the Leadership Grid® with Anne Adams McCanse replacing Mouton, who died in 1987. Blake and Mouton published numerous articles and around 40 books describing their theories.[20]

The Leadership Grid builds on the Ohio State and Michigan studies; it is based on the same two leadership dimensions, which Blake and Mouton called *concern for production* and *concern for people*. The concern for both people and production is measured through a questionnaire on a scale from 1 to 9. Therefore, the grid has 81 possible combinations of concern for production and people. However, *the* Leadership Grid *identifies five leadership styles: 1,1 impoverished; 9,1 authority compliance; 1,9 country club; 5,5 middle of the road; and 9,9 team leader.* See Exhibit 3.4 for an adaptation of the Leadership Grid.

Following are descriptions of leadership styles in the Leadership Grid:

- The *impoverished leader* (1,1) has low concern for both production and people. The leader does the minimum required to remain employed in the position.

- The *authority-compliance leader* (9,1) has a high concern for production and a low concern for people. The leader focuses on getting the job done while people are treated like machines.

- The *country-club leader* (1,9) has a high concern for people and a low concern for production. The leader strives to maintain a friendly atmosphere without regard for production.

- The *middle-of-the-road leader* (5,5) has balanced, medium concern for both production and people. The leader strives to maintain satisfactory performance and morale.

- The *team leader* (9,9) has a high concern for both production and people. This leader strives for maximum performance and employee satisfaction. According to Blake, Mouton, and McCanse, the team leadership style is generally the most appropriate for use in all situations.

To estimate your Leadership Grid leadership style, using Self-Assessment 1, use your task score as your concern for production and your people score, and plot them on the Leadership Grid in Exhibit 3.4. Then select the closest of the five leadership styles.

WORK Application **3**

Recall a present or past manager. Which of the five Leadership Grid styles does or did your manager use most often? Describe the behavior of your manager.

_____

_____

_____

_____

EXHIBIT 3.4   Blake, Mouton, and McCanse Leadership Grid

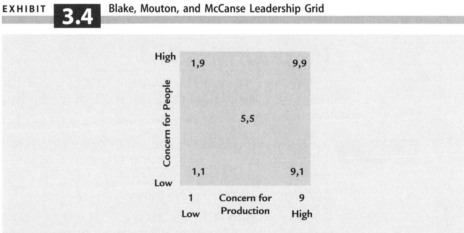

Source: *Adapted from Robert R. Blake and Jane S. Mouton,* The Managerial Grid III *(Houston: Gulf, 1985); and Robert R. Blake and Anna Adams McCanse,* Leadership Dilemmas-Grid Solutions *(Houston: Gulf, 1991), 29.*

OPENING CASE *APPLICATION*

1. **Which Ohio State University and Leadership Grid leadership style is emphasized at Trader Joe's?**

Trader Joe's emphasizes the Ohio State University high structure and high consideration style, which is called the Leadership Grid team leader's high concern for people and high concern for production (9,9) leadership style. Trader Joe's treats its employees well, but at the same time stresses high levels of performance. We will provide more detail with the answers to the other case application answers.

CONCEPT APPLICATION 2
The Leadership Grid

Identify the five statements by their leader's style. Write the appropriate letter in the blank before each item.

a. 1,1 (impoverished)   c. 9,1 (authority compliance)   e. 9,9 (team)

b. 1,9 (country club)   d. 5,5 (middle of the road)

_____ 6. A group has one of the lowest levels of morale in the company; most employees do not like the manager. It is one of the top performers compared to other departments.

_____ 7. A group is one of the lowest producers in the company; employees don't seem to care about doing a good job. It has a low level of morale, because the employees generally don't like the manager.

_____ 8. A group is one of the top performers; the manager challenges employees to continue to meet and exceed goals. Employees have high morale because they like the manager.

_____ 9. A group has very high morale; members enjoy their work. Productivity in the department is one of the lowest in the company. The manager is one of the best liked in the company.

_____ 10. A group has adequate morale; the employees are satisfied with their manager. They have an average productivity level compared to the other departments in the company.

Leadership Grid and High-High Leader Research

The *high-high leader* has concern for both production and people; this is the *team* leadership style. However, authors of the Leadership Grid were not the only ones to conduct research to determine if the high-high style was the most effective leadership style in all situations. Blake and Mouton did conduct an extensive empirical research study that measured profitability before and after a 10-year period. In the study, one company subsidiary used an extensive Grid Organizational Development program designed to teach managers how to be 9,9 team leaders (experimental group), while another subsidiary did not use the program (control group). The subsidiary using the team leadership style increased its profits four times more than the control subsidiary. Thus, the researchers claimed that team leadership usually results in improved performance, low absenteeism and turnover, and high employee satisfaction.

However, another researcher disagreed with these findings, calling high-high leadership a myth. A more objective meta-analysis (a study combining the results of many prior studies) found that although task and relationship behavior tends to correlate positively with subordinate performance, the correlation is usually weak.[21] In conclusion, although there is some support for the universal theory, the high-high leadership style is not accepted as the one best style in all situations.

Behavioral Theory Contributions and Applications

Critics of behavioral theories suggested that different leadership styles are more effective in different situations. Thus, a contribution of behavioral research is that it led to the shift in paradigm to contingency leadership theory. As you will learn in Chapter 4, contingency leadership theory is based on the behavioral theory of production and people leadership styles. Situational leadership models don't agree with using the same leadership style in all situations, but rather prescribe using the existing behavioral leadership style that best meets the situation.

A second contribution of behavioral leadership theory was the recognition that organizations need both production and people leadership. A generic set of production-oriented and people-oriented leadership functions must be performed to ensure effective organizational performance.

A third related contribution of behavioral leadership theory supports coleadership. The manager does not have to perform both production and people functions. Thus, strong production-oriented leaders can be successful if they have coleaders to provide the people-oriented functions for them, and vice versa. So, if you tend to be more production- or people-oriented, seek coleaders to complement your weaker area.

Before we go on to motivation, let's tie personality traits from Chapter 2 together with what we've covered so far. Complete Self-Assessment 2 now.

SELF-ASSESSMENT 2   Your Personality Traits and Leadership Styles

We stated in the first section that *traits affect leadership behavior*. How does this relate to you? For the University of Michigan Leadership Model, generally, if you had a high personality score for the Big Five surgency dimension in Self-Assessment 1 in Chapter 2 (dominance trait, high need for power), you most likely have a high score for the task (job-centered) leadership style. If you had a high score for agreeableness (sensitivity to others trait, high need for affiliation), you most likely have a high score for the people (employee-centered) leadership style. My U of M leadership style is primarily _____

_____.

For the Ohio State University Leadership Model, you need to score your personality for surgency and agreeableness as high or low. Then you combine them, and these personality scores should generally provide the same two-dimensional behaviors corresponding to one of the four leadership styles. My OSU leadership style is primarily _____

_____.

For the Leadership Grid, you need to score your personality for surgency and agreeableness on a scale of 1 to 9. Then you combine them on the grid, and these personality scores should generally provide about the same score as Self-Assessment 1. My Leadership Grid style is primarily _____

_____.

If you scored a Leader Motive Profile, your score for tasks should generally be higher than your score for people, because you have a greater need for power than affiliation. However, your leadership style on the Ohio State model could be high structure and high consideration, because this implies socialized power. You could also have a 9,9 team leader score on the Leadership Grid. My LMP is primarily

_____

_____.

Leadership and Major Motivation Theories

In this section we discuss motivation and leadership, the motivation process (which explains how motivation affects behavior), and three classifications of motivation theories (content, process, and reinforcement).

Motivation and Leadership

Motivation *is anything that affects behavior in pursuing a certain outcome.* Outcomes in business are usually organizational goals or objectives, and it takes motivation to reach our goals.[22] Success is about motivation that includes effort,[23] commitment,[24] being engaged,[25] practice,[26] and persistent.[27] Motivation is an important leadership topic because leadership competencies include the ability to motivate employees.[28] Thus, as leaders, an important part of our job is to motivate our followers.[29]

The pursuit of happiness and satisfaction is fundamental to motivation.[30] In general, satisfied employees outperform those that are not motivated.[31] Unfortunately, in today's complex organizations most employees are not really satisfied and motivated in their work.[32]

So what motivates us? We tend to seek to satisfy our self-interest. So, if we want to motivate others, we should answer their often-unasked question, "What's in it for me?"[33] If we give people what they want, they will in turn tend to give us what we want.[34] Unfortunately, it's easier said than done, but you will learn how in the rest of this chapter.

The Motivation Process

Through the **motivation process**, *people go from need to motive to behavior to consequence to satisfaction or dissatisfaction.* For example, you are thirsty (need) and have a drive (motive) to get a drink. You get a drink (behavior) that quenches (consequence and satisfaction) your thirst. However, if you could not get a drink, or a drink of what you really wanted, you would be dissatisfied. Satisfaction is usually short-lived. Getting that drink satisfied you, but sooner or later you will need another drink. For this reason, the motivation process has a feedback loop. See Exhibit 3.5 for an illustration of the motivation process.

EXHIBIT 3.5 The Motivation Process

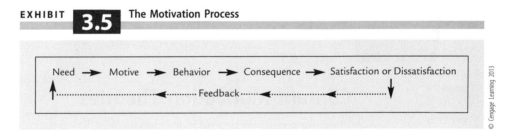

© Cengage Learning 2013

Some need or want motivates all behavior. However, needs and motives are complex: We don't always know what our needs are, or why we do the things we do. Have you ever done something and not known why you did it? Understanding needs will help you to better understand motivation and behavior, or you will gain a better understanding of why people do the things they do.

Like traits, motives cannot be observed; but you can observe behavior and infer what the person's motive is (*attribution theory*). However, it is not easy to know why people behave the way they do, because people do the same things for different reasons. Also, people often attempt to satisfy several needs at once.

OPENING CASE APPLICATION

2. What does Trader Joe's do to motivate its employees, and how does it affect performance?

Trader Joe's primary motivator is creating an innovative fun environment to work in with good pay and benefits. Providing good compensation allows Trader Joe's to hire highly self-motivated crew members. Full-time crew members can start in the $40,000 to $60,000 range and store management (mates, commanders, captains) can make more than $100,000.[35]

At Trader Joe's, quality benefits play a vital role in promoting the health and well-being of crew members and their families. It offers medical, dental, and vision coverage to eligible full-time and part-time crew members. Most crew members qualify after a couple of months. Trader Joe's also has a great paid time-off plan, and a fabulous 10 percent crew member discount on everything in the store. It also contributes 15.4 percent of employees' gross income annually to tax-deferred retirement accounts.[36]

Employees are motivated and provide a high-quality customer experience. The results are more than $8 billion in sales with more than 345 stores in 25 states. Sales are estimated at $1,750 in merchandise per square foot, more than double Whole Foods. Trader Joe's has no debt and funds all growth from its own profits.[37]

An Overview of Three Major Classifications of Motivation Theories

There is no single, universally accepted theory of how to motivate people, or how to classify the theories. We will discuss motivation theories and how we can use them to motivate ourselves and others. In the following sections, you will learn about content motivation theories, process motivation theories, and reinforcement theory. See Exhibit 3.6 for this classification, which is commonly used, with a listing of major motivation theories you will learn.

After studying all of the theories separately, we can put them back together using the unifying motivation process to see the relationship between the theories. You can select one theory to use, or take from several to make your own theory, or apply the theory that best fits the specific situation.

*Learning
Outcome 4*   *Discuss similarities and differences among the three content motivation theories.*

Content Motivation Theories

Before we present the content motivation theories, let's discuss content motivation theories in general. Content motivation theories *focus on explaining and predicting behavior based on people's needs.* The primary reason people do what they do is to meet their needs or wants—to be satisfied. Thus, it is important to understand needs (content motivation) theory. People want job satisfaction, and they will leave one organization for another to meet this need. The key to successful leadership is to meet the needs of employees while achieving organizational objectives.

Hierarchy of Needs Theory

In the 1940s, Abraham Maslow developed his hierarchy of needs theory, which is based on four major assumptions. (1) Only unmet needs motivate. (2) People's needs are arranged in order of importance (hierarchy) going from basic to complex needs.

EXHIBIT 3.6   Major Motivation Theories

CLASSIFICATION OF MOTIVATION THEORIES	SPECIFIC MOTIVATION THEORY
1. *Content motivation theories* focus on explaining and predicting behavior based on employee need motivation.	A. *Hierarchy of needs theory* proposes that employees are motivated through five levels of need—physiological, safety, social, esteem, and self-actualization. B. *Two-factor theory* proposes that employees are motivated by motivators (higher-level needs) rather than maintenance (lower-level needs) factors. C. *Acquired needs theory* proposes that employees are motivated by their need for achievement, power, and affiliation.
2. *Process motivation theories* focus on understanding how employees choose behaviors to fulfill their needs.	A. *Equity theory* proposes that employees will be motivated when their perceived inputs equal outputs. B. *Expectancy theory* proposes that employees are motivated when they believe they can accomplish the task, they will be rewarded, and the rewards for doing so are worth the effort. C. *Goal-setting theory* proposes that achievable but difficult goals motivate employees.
3. *Reinforcement theory* proposes that behavior can be explained, predicted, and controlled through the consequences for behavior.	Types of Reinforcement · Positive · Avoidance · Extinction · Punishment

© Cengage Learning 2013

(3) People will not be motivated to satisfy a higher-level need unless the lower-level need(s) has been at least minimally satisfied. (4) Maslow assumed that people have five classifications of needs, which are presented here in hierarchical order from low to high level of need.[38]

Hierarchy of Needs

The hierarchy of needs theory proposes that people are motivated through five levels of needs—physiological, safety, belongingness, esteem, and self-actualization:

1. *Physiological needs:* These are people's primary or basic needs: air, food, shelter, sex, and relief from or avoidance of pain.
2. *Safety needs:* Once the physiological needs are met, the individual is concerned with safety and security.
3. *Belongingness needs:* After establishing safety, people look for love, friendship, acceptance, and affection. Belongingness is also called *social needs*.
4. *Esteem needs:* After the social needs are met, the individual focuses on ego, status, self-respect, recognition for accomplishments, and a feeling of self-confidence and prestige.
5. *Self-actualization needs:* The highest level of need is to develop one's full potential. To do so, one seeks growth, achievement, and advancement.

Maslow's hierarchy of needs is commonly taught in psychology and business courses, because it offers a very rich theory of human motivation and its determinants at the individual level. However, Maslow's work was criticized because it did not take into consideration that people can be at different levels of needs based on different aspects of their lives. Nor did he mention that people can revert back to lower-level needs. Today, Maslow's followers and others realize that needs are not on a simple five-step hierarchy. Maslow's assumptions have recently been updated to reflect this insight, and many organizations today are using a some of the management methods he proposed 30 years ago. Maslow has also been credited with influencing many management authors, including Douglas McGregor, Rensis Likert, and Peter Drucker.

WORK Application **4**
On what level of the hierarchy of needs are you at this time for a specific aspect of your life (professional or personal)? Be sure to specify the level by name, and explain why you are at that level.

_____

_____

_____

_____

Motivating Employees with Hierarchy of Needs Theory

An important contribution of this theory is that we realize that people have a need for more than just pay. Secondly, even if we don't have much money to give raises, we can have inexpensive socials, like barbecues, and there is no cost to giving compliments.[39] Also, employees are more motivated when they perceive the organization supports them,[40] which again does not have to be costly.

The major recommendation to leaders is to meet employees' lower-level needs so that they will not dominate the employees' motivational process. You should get to know and understand people's needs and meet them as a means of increasing performance. See Exhibit 3.7 for a list of ways in which managers attempt to meet all five needs.

OPENING CASE *APPLICATION*

3-a. **How does Trader Joe's meet its employees' content motivation needs?**

Trader Joe's allows people to climb the *hierarchy of needs.* As stated opening case answer to question 2, it pays well with great working conditions (*physiological*), with great benefits (*safety*). There is continual employee and customer contact (*social*). The job itself is interesting and challenging, with participation in decision making, and employee development with opportunity for advancement through the Career Adventure path (*esteem and self-actualization*).[41]

Two-Factor Theory

In the 1960s, Frederick Herzberg published his two-factor theory.[42] Herzberg combined lower-level needs into one classification he called *hygiene* or *maintenance*; and higher-level needs into one classification he called *motivators. The* two-factor theory *proposes that people are motivated by motivators rather than maintenance factors.* Before you learn about two-factor theory, complete Self-Assessment 3.

Maintenance—Extrinsic Factors

Maintenance factors are also called *extrinsic motivators* because motivation comes from outside the person and the job itself.[43] Extrinsic motivators include pay, job security, working conditions, fringe benefits, and relationships.[44] These factors are related to meeting lower-level needs. Review Self-Assessment 3, the even-numbered questions, for a list of extrinsic job factors.

Motivators—Intrinsic Factors

Motivators are called *intrinsic motivators* because motivation comes from within the person through the work itself.[45] Intrinsic motivators include achievement, recognition, challenge, and advancement.[46] These factors are related to meeting higher-level needs, and are better at motivating than extrinsic factors.[47] Doing something we want to do and doing it well can be its own reward.[48] Review Self-Assessment 3, the odd-numbered questions, for a list of intrinsic job factors.

EXHIBIT How Organizations Motivate With Hierarchy of Needs Theory

Self-Actualization Needs

Organizations meet these needs by the development of employees' skills, the chance to be creative, achievement and promotions, and the ability to have complete control over their jobs.

Esteem Needs

Organizations meet these needs through titles, the satisfaction of completing the job itself, merit pay raises, recognition, challenging tasks, participation in decision making, and change for advancement.

Social Needs

Organizations meet these needs through the opportunity to interact with others, to be accepted, to have friends. Activities include parties, picnics, trips, and sports teams.

Safety Needs

Organizations meet these needs through safe working conditions, salary increases to meet inflation, job security, and fringe benefits (medical insurance/sick pay/pensions) that protect the physiological needs.

Physiological Needs

Organizations meet these needs through adequate salary, breaks, and working conditions.

© Cengage Learning 2013

SELF-ASSESSMENT 3   Job Motivators and Maintenance Factors

Here are 12 job factors that contribute to job satisfaction. Rate each according to how important it is to you by placing a number from 1 to 5 on the line before each factor.

Very important		Somewhat important		Not important
5	4	3	2	1

_____ 1. An interesting job I enjoy doing

_____ 2. A boss who treats everyone the same regardless of the circumstances

_____ 3. Getting praise and other recognition and appreciation for the work that I do

_____ 4. A job that is routine without much change from day-to-day

_____ 5. The opportunity for advancement

_____ 6. A nice title regardless of pay

_____ 7. Job responsibility that gives me freedom to do things my way

_____ 8. Good working conditions (safe environment, cafeteria, etc.)

_____ 9. The opportunity to learn new things

_____ 10. An emphasis on following the rules, regulations, procedures, and policies

(continued)

(Self-Assessment 3 continued)

——— 11. A job I can do well and succeed at

——— 12. Job security; a career with one company

For each factor, write the number from 1 to 5 that represents your answer. Total each column (should be between 6 and 30 points).

Motivating factors   Maintenance factors

1. ———   2. ———
3. ———   4. ———
5. ———   6. ———

7. ———		8. ———
9. ———		10. ———
11. ———		12. ———
Totals ———		———

Did you select motivators or maintenance factors as being more important to you? The closer to 30 (6) each score is, the more (less) important it is to you. Continue reading to understand the difference between motivators and maintenance factors.

Herzberg's Two-Factor Motivation Model

Based on research, Herzberg and associates disagreed with the traditional view that satisfaction and dissatisfaction were at opposite ends of one continuum (a one-dimensional model). There are two continuums: not dissatisfied with the environment (maintenance) to dissatisfied, and satisfied with the job itself (motivators) to not satisfied (a two-dimensional model). See Exhibit 3.8 for Herzberg's motivation model.

Employees are on a continuum from dissatisfied to not dissatisfied with their environment. Herzberg contends that providing maintenance factors will keep employees from being dissatisfied, but it will not make them satisfied or motivate them. For example,

EXHIBIT **3.8** **Two-Factor Motivation Theory**

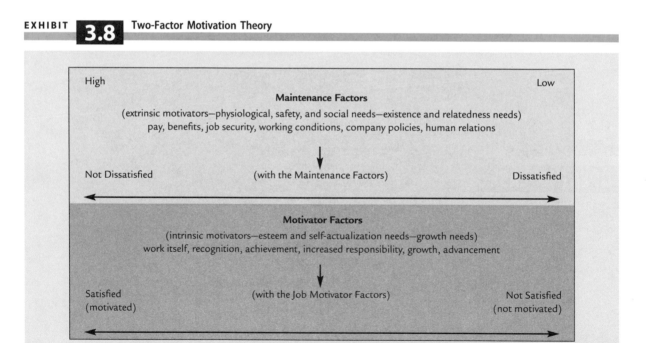

Source: *Adapted from F. Herzberg. "The Motivation-Hygiene Concept and Problems of Manpower."* Personnel Administrator: *3–7 (1964); and F. Herzberg. "One More Time: How Do You Motivate Employees?"* Harvard Business Review *(January–February 1967):53.*

Herzberg believes that if employees are dissatisfied with their pay and they get a raise, they will no longer be dissatisfied. However, before long people get accustomed to the new standard of living and will become dissatisfied again. Employees will need another raise to not be dissatisfied again. The vicious cycle goes on. So, Herzberg says you have to focus on motivators.

Money as a Motivator

Some research supports that education and income does buy happiness.[49] However, the connection between pay and motivation and job satisfaction has produced inconclusive, if not contradictory, findings.[50] Money can buy things, but there are lots of rich and famous people who are unhappy and make poor choices as a result. The current view of money as a motivator is that money matters more to some people than others, and that it may motivate some employees but not others.

Money, however, does not necessarily motivate employees to work harder. Have you ever gotten a raise? Were you more motivated and more productive? Money also is limited in its ability to motivate. For example, many commissioned workers get to a comfortable point and don't push to make extra money; and some employees get to the point where they don't want overtime work, even though they are paid two or three times their normal wage for overtime.

Motivating Employees with Two-Factor Theory

WORK Application 5
Recall a present or past job; are you or were you dissatisfied or not dissatisfied with the maintenance factors? Are or were you satisfied or not satisfied with the motivators? Be sure to identify and explain your satisfaction with the specific maintenance and motivator factors.

Under the old management paradigm, money (and other extrinsic motivators) was considered the best motivator. Under the new leadership paradigm, pay is important, but it is not the best motivator; intrinsic motivators are. Herzberg's theory has been criticized for having limited research support. However, current research does support that giving more responsibility increases motivational engagement and performance.[51]

Herzberg fits the new paradigm: He said that managers must first ensure that the employees' level of pay and other maintenance factors are adequate. Once employees are not dissatisfied with their pay (and other maintenance factors), they can be motivated through their jobs. Herzberg also developed *job enrichment,* the process of building motivators into the job itself by making it more interesting and challenging. Job enrichment methods are commonly used today.[52] Job enrichment has been used successfully to motivate employees to higher levels of performance at many organizations, including AT&T, GM, IBM, Maytag, Monsanto, Motorola, Polaroid, and the Traveler's Life Insurance Company.

OPENING CASE APPLICATION

3-b. How does Trader Joe's meet its employees' content motivation needs?

Related to *two-factor theory,* although Trader Joe's offers great pay and benefits (*maintenance*), its focus is really more on *motivators* so employees can grow and meet their high-level needs of esteem and self-actualization. Its motto is "Where fun, food and opportunity align." The Trader Joe's Career Adventure (career path) has three levels.[53]

1. *Store Crew* members do a little of everything—run registers, stock shelves, merchandise products, and chat up terrific customers; there is never a dull moment. They have the opportunity to advance.
2. *Store Leadership.* They don't spend their days in an office. Leaders are out on the store floor with their customers and crew creating a WOW! experience. Store leadership begins at the Novitiate level (entry-level supervisor). They participate in all aspects of managing a Trader Joe's—from stocking shelves, running a register and merchandising to leading teams and, perhaps most importantly, providing customers with knowledgeable assistance.

(continued)

(Opening Case Application 3-b continued)

3. *Store Management* includes working up to becoming a 2nd and 1st Mate (assistant store managers) to Commander and Captain (store managers). There is also a Regional Mobile Thriver (RMT) Training Program for fast-tracking *experienced* and *relocatable* retail store managers through its promote-from-within structure. The RMT Program is not an entry-level management training program. Rather, the RMT Program is designed to train senior-level retail, restaurant, and hospitality managers to apply their proven leadership skills in Trader Joe's stores.

Acquired Needs Theory

Acquired needs theory proposes that people are motivated by their need for achievement, power, and affiliation. This is essentially the same definition given for achievement motivation theory in Chapter 2. It is now called *acquired needs theory* because David McClelland was not the first to study these needs. Because other management writers call McClelland's theory *acquired needs theory*, a general needs theory was developed by Henry Murray, then adapted by John Atkinson, and David McClelland.[54] You have already learned about McClelland's work, so we will be brief here.

Acquired needs theory says that all people have the need for achievement, power, and affiliation, but to varying degrees. It's important to realize how closely linked traits, behavior, and motivation are as our acquired needs lead to varying characteristics in what we do and say.[55] Acquired need is also widely classified as both a trait and a motivation, since McClelland and others believe that needs are based on personality traits. McClelland's affiliation need is essentially the same as Maslow's belongingness need; and power and achievement are related to esteem, self-actualization, and growth. McClelland's motivation theory does not include lower-level needs for safety and physiological needs. Here are some ideas for motivating employees based on their dominant needs:

WORK Application 6
Explain how your need for achievement, power, and/or affiliation has affected your behavior, or that of someone you work with or have worked with. What were the consequences of the behavior, and was the need satisfied?

_____
_____
_____
_____

- *Motivating employees with a high n Ach.* Give them nonroutine, challenging tasks with clear, attainable objectives. Give them fast and frequent feedback on their performance. Continually give them increased responsibility for doing new things. Keep out of their way.

- *Motivating employees with a high n Pow.* Let them plan and control their jobs as much as possible. Try to include them in decision making, especially when they are affected by the decision. They tend to perform best alone rather than as team members. Try to assign them to a whole task rather than just part of a task.

- *Motivating employees with a high n Aff.* Be sure to let them work as part of a team. They derive satisfaction from the people they work with rather than the task itself. Give them lots of praise and recognition. Delegate responsibility for orienting and training new employees to them. They make great buddies and mentors.

OPENING CASE *APPLICATION*

3-c. How does Trader Joe's meet its employees' content motivation needs?

Trader Joe's does help employees meet all three *acquired needs*. It provides support they can do a good job, and it has a career path so that employees can *achieve* their goal of advancing. They have the *power* to be in control at the crew, leader, and manager positions. Employees are also encouraged to develop an *affiliation* with employees and customers.[56]

Before we discuss the need to balance professional and personal needs, see Exhibit 3.9 for a comparison of the three content theories of motivation.

EXHIBIT 3.9   A Comparison of Content Motivation Theories

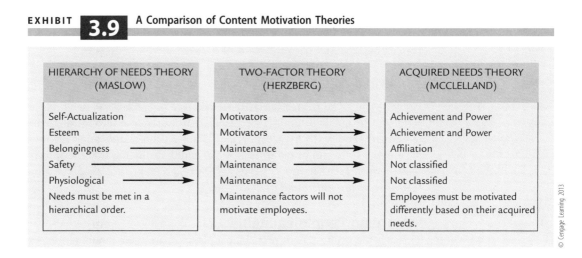

HIERARCHY OF NEEDS THEORY (MASLOW)	TWO-FACTOR THEORY (HERZBERG)	ACQUIRED NEEDS THEORY (MCCLELLAND)
Self-Actualization ⟶	Motivators ⟶	Achievement and Power
Esteem ⟶	Motivators ⟶	Achievement and Power
Belongingness ⟶	Maintenance ⟶	Affiliation
Safety ⟶	Maintenance ⟶	Not classified
Physiological ⟶	Maintenance ⟶	Not classified
Needs must be met in a hierarchical order.	Maintenance factors will not motivate employees.	Employees must be motivated differently based on their acquired needs.

© Cengage Learning 2013

Balancing Work-Life Needs

Work–life balance is also called work–home and work–family balance. As discussed, we all have personal life needs and we have work needs, and both needs overlap and influence each other. We need a healthy balance between our life and our work.[57] However, with organizations working around the clock competing in a global marketplace, with a focus on getting more done with fewer people, and with technology making it easy to check our cellphones and work all hours of the day and night from anywhere, life and work are blurring together for many people. Negative consequences of imbalance (often called work–life conflict) include stress, burnout, absenteeism, turnover, and dissatisfaction with job, family, and life. Balance is a much sought-after but rarely claimed state of being.[58]

Two major things organizations are doing to help employees meet their personal needs are providing on-site day care centers—or giving employees information to help them find good day and elder care—and offering flextime. Some leaders are also telling employees to go home and "get a life" before it is too late. Author Jack Welch says work–life balance is a personal decision, so choose what you want to do, be good at it, and live with the consequences.

Learning Outcome 5   *Discuss the major similarities and differences among the three process motivation theories.*

Process Motivation Theories

Process motivation theories *focus on understanding how people choose behavior to fulfill their needs.* Process motivation theories are more complex than content motivation theories. Content motivation theories simply focus on identifying and understanding people's needs. Process motivation theories go a step further by attempting to understand

• why people have different needs,

• why their needs change,

- how and why people choose to try to satisfy needs in different ways,
- the mental processes people go through as they understand situations, and
- how they evaluate their need satisfaction.

In this section you will learn about three process motivation theories: equity theory, expectancy theory, and goal setting theory.

Equity Theory

Do you want to be treated fairly? If we perceive organizational decisions and managerial actions to be unfair or unjust, we are likely to experience feelings of anger, outrage, and resentment. Equity theory is primarily J. Stacy Adams's motivation theory, in which people are said to be motivated to seek social equity in the rewards they receive (output) for their performance (input).[59] **Equity theory** *proposes that people are motivated when their perceived inputs equal outputs.*

Rewarding People Equitably

Through the equity theory process, people compare their inputs (effort, experience, loyalty, commitment, seniority, and so forth) and outputs (financial compensation and intangibles of praise, recognition, and so forth) to that of relevant others.[60] A relevant other could be a coworker or group of employees from the same or different organizations, or even from a hypothetical situation. Notice that our definition says *perceived* and not *actual* inputs to outputs. Others may perceive that equity actually exists, and that the person complaining about inequity is wrong.

Equitable distribution of pay is crucial to organizations. Unfortunately, many employees tend to inflate their own efforts or performance when comparing themselves to others. Employees also tend to overestimate what others earn.[61] Employees may be very satisfied and motivated until they find out that a relevant other is earning more for the same job, or earning the same for doing less work. A comparison with relevant others leads to one of three conclusions: The employee is under-rewarded, over-rewarded, or equitably rewarded. When inequity is perceived, employees attempt to correct the balance by reducing input (e.g., put forth less effort) or increasing output (e.g., get a raise).

Motivating with Equity Theory

People who believe they are over-rewarded usually don't change their behavior. Instead, they often rationalize that they deserve the outputs. One view of equity is that it is like Herzberg's maintenance factors. When employees are not dissatisfied, they are not actively motivated; but maintenance factors do demotivate when employees are dissatisfied. According to equity theory, when employees believe they are equitably rewarded they are not actively motivated. However, when employees believe they are under-rewarded, they are demotivated.

Using equity theory in practice can be difficult, because you don't always know who the employee's reference group is, nor his or her view of inputs and outcomes. However, this theory does offer some useful general recommendations:

1. Managers should be aware that equity is based on perception, which may not be correct. It is possible for the manager to create equity or inequity. Some managers have favorite subordinates who get special treatment; others don't. So don't play favorites; treat employees equally but in unique ways.

WORK Application 7
Give an example of how equity theory has affected your motivation, or that of someone else you work with or have worked with. Be sure to specify if you were under-rewarded, over-rewarded, or equitably rewarded.

2. Rewards should be equitable. When employees perceive that they are not treated fairly, morale and performance problems occur. Employees producing at the same level should be given equal rewards. Those producing less should get less.

3. High performance should be rewarded, but employees must understand the inputs needed to attain certain outputs. When incentive pay is used, there should be clear standards specifying the exact requirements to achieve the incentive. A manager should be able to objectively tell others why one person got a higher merit raise than another did.

OPENING CASE *APPLICATION*

4-a. How does Trader Joe's meet its employees' process motivation needs?

Trader Joe's treats all employees with *equity*. The management style is participative so everyone shares in the management at each store. Employees who put in the effort (*inputs*) to climb the corporate ladder have potential rewards (*outputs*). However, not everyone is expected to move to leadership and store management. But even the part-time crew get good pay and benefits—yes, health insurance for all.[62]

Expectancy Theory

Expectancy theory is based on Victor Vroom's formula: motivation = expectancy × instrumentality × valence.[63] **Expectancy theory** *proposes that people are motivated when they believe they can accomplish the task, they will get the reward, and the rewards for doing the task are worth the effort.* The theory is based on the following assumptions: Both internal (needs) and external (environment) factors affect behavior; behavior is the individual's decision; people have different needs, desires, and goals; and people make behavior decisions based on their perception of the outcome. Expectancy theory continues to be popular in the motivation literature today.[64]

Three Variables

All three variable conditions must be met in Vroom's formula for motivation to take place:

- *Expectancy* refers to the person's perception of his or her ability (probability) to accomplish an objective. Generally, the higher one's expectancy, the better the chance for motivation. When we do not believe that we can accomplish objectives, we will not be motivated to try.

- *Instrumentality* refers to belief that the performance will result in getting the reward. Generally, the higher one's instrumentality, the greater the chance for motivation. If employees are certain to get the reward, they probably will be motivated. When not sure, employees may not be motivated. For example, Dan believes he would be a good manager and wants to get promoted. However, Dan has an external locus of control and believes that working hard will not result in a promotion anyway. Therefore, he will not be motivated to work for the promotion.

- *Valence* refers to the value a person places on the outcome or reward. Generally, the higher the value (importance) of the outcome or reward, the better the chance of motivation. For example, the supervisor, Jean, wants an employee, Sim, to work harder. Jean talks to Sim and tells him that working hard will result in a promotion. If Sim wants a promotion, he will probably be motivated. However, if a promotion is not of importance to Sim, it will not motivate him.

Motivating with Expectancy Theory

One study found that expectancy theory can accurately predict a person's work effort, satisfaction level, and performance—but only if the correct values are plugged into the formula. A meta-analysis (a study using the data of 77 other prior studies) had inconsistent findings with some positive correlations. A more recent study found that expectancy theory can be used to determine if leaders can be trained to use ethical considerations in decision making.[65]

Therefore, this theory works in certain contexts but not in others. Expectancy theory also works best with employees who have an internal locus of control, because if they believe they control their destiny, their efforts will result in success. The following conditions should be implemented to make the theory result in motivation:

WORK Application **8**
Give an example of how expectancy theory has affected your motivation, or that of someone else you work with or have worked with. Be sure to specify the expectancy and valence.

1. Clearly define objectives and the performance necessary to achieve them.[66]
2. Incentives are important.[67] Tie performance to rewards. High performance should be rewarded. When one employee works harder to produce more than other employees and is not rewarded, he or she may slow down productivity.
3. Be sure rewards are of value to the employee. Managers should get to know employees as individuals. Develop good human relations as a people developer.
4. Make sure our employees believe we will do what we say we will do. For example, employees must believe we will give them a merit raise if they do work hard. So that employees will believe us, follow through and show them we do what we say we'll do.
5. Founder of Walmart Sam Walton said "High expectations are the key to everything." So use the Pygmalion effect (Chapter 2) to increase expectations. Your high expectation can result in follower self-fulfilling prophecy. As the level of expectation increases, so will performance.

OPENING CASE *APPLICATION*

4-b.   How does Trader Joe's meet its employees' process motivation needs?

Trader Joe's focuses on attracting people who have the *expectancy* that they can be successful at the level of their choice, and it provides the training to help them succeed as store crew, leader, and manager. Employees know that if they do a good job they will get rewarded (*instrumentality*). The *valence* of employees does vary, but as discussed, Trader Joe's offers good pay and benefits.

Goal Setting Theory

Goal setting theory *proposes that specific, difficult goals motivate people.* Our behavior has a purpose, which is usually to fulfill a need. Goals give us a sense of purpose as to why we are working to accomplish a given task.[68] We all can become goal oriented and develop this skill,[69] and that is what this subsection is all about.

Writing Objectives

To help you to write effective objectives that meet the criteria you will learn next, use the model. The parts of the **writing objectives model** *are (1) To + (2) action verb + (3) singular, specific, and measurable result to be achieved + (4) target date.* This is shown in Model 3.1, with objectives, that is adapted from Max E. Douglas's model.

MODEL **3.1** Writing Effective Objectives Model

	1	2	3	4
KFC				
	To	double	the number of outlets in Africa to 1,200	by 2014[70]
GM				
	To	double	sales in China to 5 million vehicles	by 2015[71]
VW				
	To	increase	sales in the U.S. to 1 million vehicles	by 2018[72]
	To	become	the world's largest car maker	by 2018[73]
China Government				
	To	build	27 new nuclear power plants	by 2020[74]

Criteria for Objectives

For an objective to be effective, it should include the four criteria listed in steps 3 and 4 of the writing objectives model:

1. *Singular result.* To avoid confusion, each objective should contain only one end result. When multiple objectives are listed together, one may be met but the other(s) may not.
2. *Specific.* The objective should not be vague,[75] such as to learn a lot in this leadership course. It should state the exact level of performance expected,[76] such as to get an A.
3. *Measurable.* The saying, "what gets measured gets done," is true. If people are to achieve objectives, they must be able to observe and measure their progress regularly to monitor progress and to determine if the objective has been met.[77]
4. *Target date.* A specific date should be set for accomplishing the objective. When people have a deadline, they usually try harder to get the task done on time. If people are simply told to do it when they can, they don't tend to "get around to it" until they have to. It is also more effective to set a specific date, such as October 29, 2015, rather than a set time, such as in two weeks, because you can forget when the time began and should end. However, some objectives are ongoing and do not require a stated date. The target date is indefinite until it is changed, such as the Domino's objective to deliver pizza within 30 minutes.

In addition to the four criteria from the model, there are three other criteria that do not always fit within the model:

1. *Difficult but achievable.* Research shows that individuals perform better with challenging objectives rather than (1) easy objectives, (2) objectives that are too difficult, or (3) simply told "do your best."[78] Challenging goals can also lead to creativity.[79] How bad do you want it (success)? To continuously improve, we need to push ourselves just beyond our current abilities.[80]
2. *Participatively set.* People that participate in setting their objectives generally out perform those that are assigned objectives, because it helps gain commitment.[81]

WORK Application 9

1. Using the writing objectives model, write one or more objectives for an organization you work for or have worked for that meet the criteria for objectives.

2. Give an example of how a goal(s) affected your motivation and performance, or those of someone else you work with or have worked with.

3. *Commitment.* For objectives to be met, employees must accept them.[82] If employees are not committed to striving for the objective, even if they meet the other criteria, they may not meet the objective.[83]

Microsoft has a long tradition of having individuals set goals as part of its high performance-based culture. All employees are trained to set "SMART" (Specific, Measurable, Achievable, Results-based, and Time-specific) written goals. Managers are trained to assist in the goal-setting process, including how to provide relevant performance feedback during the review process.

3.1   *Academic Standards*

Lou Holtz, former successful Notre Dame football coach, said that the power of goal setting is an incredible motivator for high performance; to be successful we need to set a higher goal. Have colleges followed his advice? Have academic standards dropped, maintained, or increased over the years?

The academic credit-hour system was set many years ago to establish some formal standardization across colleges throughout the country so that academics and employers had the same expectations of the workload that a college student carried to earn a degree. This also allowed students to transfer credit from one university to another, assuming the same standards were met.

The credit-hour system was set at students doing two hours of preparation for each hour of in-class time. So, a student taking five classes should spend 15 hours in class and 30 hours preparing for class, or a total of 40+ hours per week—which is a full-time schedule.

1. How many hours outside of class, on average, do you and other students use to prepare for class each week?

2. Are college professors throughout the country assigning students two hours of preparation for every hour in class today? If not, why have they dropped the standard?

3. Are students who are putting in part-time hours (20–30 hours) during college being well prepared for a career after graduation (40–60 hours)?

4. Is it ethical and socially responsible for professors to drop standards and for colleges to award degrees for doing less work today than 5, 10, or 20 years ago?

Using Goal Setting to Motivate Employees

Goal setting is an important leadership competency,[84] it has been studied for more than 40 years,[85] and it is one of the most replicated and influential management theories.[86] The research conducted by Edwin Locke and others has revealed that setting objectives, which utilize the model and meet the criteria, has a positive effect on motivation and performance.[87] High-achievement motivated individuals, including the super-rich, consistently engage in goal setting.[88]

Need we say anything more about it besides to follow the guidelines above? Yes. Setting a goal is just the first step; the next step is just as important as we need to plan how we will accomplish it.[89] Relying on willpower is a horrible strategy; it's doomed to fail, and this is why so few people keep their new year's resolutions.[90] We will provide details on tying goals and plans in the subsection "Changing Behavior."

CONCEPT APPLICATION 3
Objectives

For each objective, state which "must" criteria is not met.

a. singular result   c. measurable

b. specific   d. target date

_____ 11. To write the department's objectives within a month

_____ 12. To double the sales of PCs in Africa

_____ 13. To sell 5 percent more furniture and 7 percent more rugs in 2012

_____ 14. To increase revenue in 2013

_____ 15. To be perceived as the best car dealer in the Springfield area by the end of 2014

OPENING CASE *APPLICATION*

4-c. **How does Trader Joe's meet its employees' process motivation needs?**

Trader Joe's does use *goal setting* theory. One of its ongoing goals is to introduce 10–15 new products a week. Some of the new products are sold nationally and some are selected by the store to take advantage of local products, such as farm fresh produce.

Reinforcement Theory

B. F. Skinner, reinforcement motivation theorist, contended that to motivate employees it is really not necessary to identify and understand needs (content motivation theories), nor to understand how employees choose behaviors to fulfill them (process motivation theories). All the manager needs to do is understand the relationship between behaviors and their consequences, and then arrange contingencies that reinforce desirable behaviors and discourage undesirable behaviors.[91] **Reinforcement theory** *proposes that through the consequences for behavior, people will be motivated to behave in predetermined ways.*

Let's face it, all organizations develop systems to control employee behavior, and that is what reinforcement theory is all about.[92] Reinforcement theory uses behavior modification (apply reinforcement theory to get employees to do what you want them to do) and operant conditioning (types and schedules of reinforcement). Skinner stated that behavior is learned through experiences of positive and negative consequences. The three components of Skinner's framework are shown with an example in Exhibit 3.10.

A recent meta-analysis of empirical research over the past 20 years found that reinforcement theory does in fact increase performance.[93] As illustrated in the example in Exhibit 3.10, behavior is a function of its consequences. Employees learn what is, and is not, desired behavior as a result of the consequences for specific behavior. In this section, we have five subsections, as we discuss the two important concepts used to modify behavior (1 the types of reinforcement and 2 the schedules of reinforcement): 3 that

EXHIBIT 3.10   Components of Reinforcement Theory

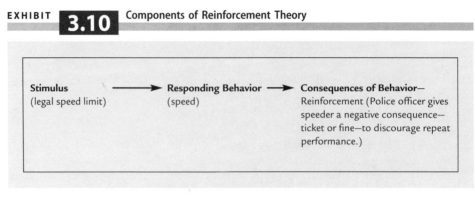

Stimulus ⟶ Responding Behavior ⟶ Consequences of Behavior—
(legal speed limit)   (speed)   Reinforcement (Police officer gives speeder a negative consequence—ticket or fine—to discourage repeat performance.)

you get what you reinforce, 4 how to motivate using reinforcement, and 5 how to give praise.

Learning Outcome 6   *Explain the four types of reinforcement.*

Types of Reinforcement

The four types of reinforcement are positive, avoidance, punishment, and extinction. Exhibit 3.11 illustrates the four types of reinforcement.

Positive Reinforcement

A method of encouraging continued behavior is to offer attractive consequences (rewards) for desirable performance. Positive reinforcements are pay, promotions, time off, increased status, and so forth. Giving praise is a positive reinforcement, and you will learn how to give praise at the end of this section.

Motivating with rewards.   There has been an ongoing debate about using the carrot (reward) or the stick (punishment), and the general consensus is to use rewards (be positive not negative) when possible.[94] Positive reinforcement is generally the most effective motivator.[95] Ever heard of the *Angry Birds* game that has sold more than 12 million copies? A big part of its success is that the game gives lots of positive reinforcement, and doesn't punish players.[96] So when possible, use rewards to motivate yourself and others.

Avoidance Reinforcement

Avoidance is also called *negative reinforcement*. *Rules* with punishment for violations are designed to get employees to avoid certain behavior. Employees don't necessarily want to follow the rules, but they usually do to avoid the negative consequence of punishment.

Motivating with avoidance.   Organizational leaders do need to develop rules, but rules in and of themselves are not a punishment. Punishment is given only if the rule is broken, which we hope will not happen. So note that with avoidance there is no actual punishment; it's the "threat" of the punishment that controls behavior. So when needed, set rules that will contribute to performance.

Punishment

Punishment is used to provide an undesirable consequence for undesirable behavior. Methods of punishment include harassing, taking away privileges, probation, fining, demoting, firing, and so forth.

Motivating with punishment. Punishment is the most controversial and the least effective method in motivating employees to do a good job. Punishment may reduce the undesirable behavior; but its overuse may cause other undesirable behaviors, such as poor morale, lower productivity, and acts of theft or sabotage. However, leaders need to enforce the rules, so there are times when only punishment will do.[97] So punish when rules are broken.

Extinction

Rather than encourage desirable behavior, extinction (and punishment) attempts to reduce or eliminate undesirable behavior by withholding reinforcement when the behavior occurs. Extinction also includes ignoring the behavior to get the employee to stop it. From another perspective, managers who do not reward good performance can cause its extinction. In other words, if you ignore good employee performance, good performance may stop because employees think, "Why should I do a good job if I'm not rewarded in some way?"

Motivating with extinction. When employees don't earn rewards, withhold them. For example, the manager may withhold a reward of value, such as a pay raise, until the employee performs to set standards. Also, don't ignore good performance.

3.2 *Airlines*

An airline often charges higher fares for one-way tickets than round-trip tickets, and for direct flight tickets to its hub than for flight connections from its hub to another destination. So some travelers buy round-trip tickets and only go one way, and some end their travel at the hub instead of taking the connection (a "hidden city" itinerary), to save money. The airlines call this breach of contract: They have *punished* travel agencies for tickets that aren't properly used, they sometimes demand higher fares from travelers caught, and they have seized some travelers' frequent-flier miles, saying they were fraudulently obtained.

1. Not using the full travel of a ticket breaks airline rules but not the law, so it's not illegal, unless travelers lie about what they are doing. But is it ethical and socially responsible behavior of travelers?
2. Is it ethical and socially responsible for airlines to charge more for less travel?
3. Is it ethical and socially responsible to punish people who break the ticket rules?
4. Is reinforcement theory effective (does it motivate you and others) in today's global economy?
5. Is reinforcement theory ethical and socially responsible, or is it manipulative?

WORK Application 10

Give one or more examples of the types of reinforcement, and the schedules used, on a present or past job.

_____

_____

_____

_____

Schedules of Reinforcement

The second reinforcement consideration in controlling behavior is determining when to reinforce performance. The two major classifications are *continuous* and *intermittent*.

Continuous Reinforcement

With a continuous method, each and every desired behavior is reinforced. Examples of this method would be a machine with an automatic counter that lets the employee know (at any given moment) exactly how many units have been produced, and a manager who comments on every budget report.

EXHIBIT **3.11** Types of Reinforcement

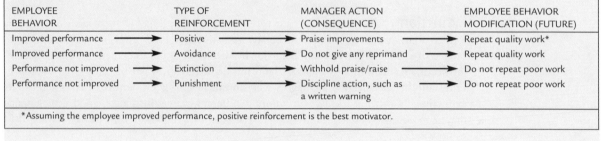

As a manager, you have an assistant who makes many errors when completing correspondence. Your objective, which you discussed with the assistant, is to decrease the error rate by 50 percent by Friday, June 4, 2010. Based on the assistant's performance at that time, you have four types of reinforcement that you can use with her when you next review her work.

EMPLOYEE BEHAVIOR	TYPE OF REINFORCEMENT	MANAGER ACTION (CONSEQUENCE)	EMPLOYEE BEHAVIOR MODIFICATION (FUTURE)
Improved performance	Positive	Praise improvements	Repeat quality work*
Improved performance	Avoidance	Do not give any reprimand	Repeat quality work
Performance not improved	Extinction	Withhold praise/raise	Do not repeat poor work
Performance not improved	Punishment	Discipline action, such as a written warning	Do not repeat poor work

*Assuming the employee improved performance, positive reinforcement is the best motivator.

Motivating with a continuous schedule. Continuous reinforcement is generally better at sustaining desired behavior. It works well as an incentive to produce. For example, a piece rate reward of $1 for each unit produced or a 10 percent commission on every sale.

Intermittent Reinforcement

With the intermittent reinforcement, the reward is given based on the passage of time or output. When the reward is based on the passage of time, it is called an *interval* schedule. When it is based on output, it is called a *ratio* schedule. When electing to use intermittent reinforcement, you have four alternatives:

1. *Fixed interval schedule.* Giving a salary paycheck every week, or breaks and meals at the same time every day
2. *Variable interval schedule.* Giving praise only now and then, a surprise inspection, or a pop quiz
3. *Fixed ratio schedule.* Giving a piece rate or bonus after producing a standard rate
4. *Variable ratio schedule.* Giving praise for excellent work, or a lottery for employees who have not been absent for a set amount of time

Motivating with an intermittent schedule. Continuous reinforcement is not always possible or practical, such as with giving praise. To be more effective, praise is generally only given for exceptional, not routine, performance. Otherwise, it becomes routine and tends to lose its effect. Ratios are generally better motivators than intervals. The variable ratio tends to be the most powerful schedule for sustaining behavior.

You Get What You Reinforce

One of the important things you should learn in this course is that people will do what they are reinforced for doing. People seek information concerning what activities are reinforced, and then seek to do (or at least pretend to do) those things, often to the exclusion of activities not reinforced. The extent to which this occurs, of course, depends on the attractiveness of the rewards offered and the punishment for the behavior.

For example, if a professor gives a class a reading list of several sources, but tells students that they will not discuss them in class or be tested on them, how many students will read them? Or, if the professor says, "A, B, and C from this chapter are important and I'll test you on them, but X, Y, and Z will not be on the test," will students spend equal time studying both groups of material?

In the business setting, if the manager repeatedly says quality is important, but the standard of evaluation includes only quantity and meeting scheduled shipments, how many employees will ship poor-quality products to meet the scheduled shipment? How many will miss the scheduled shipment, take a reprimand for missing the scheduled shipment, and get a poor performance review in order to do a quality job? An incomplete standard measuring only quantitative output that is highly visible and easy to measure is a common problem.

The Folly of Rewarding A, While Hoping for B

Reward systems are often fouled up when the types of behavior being rewarded are those that the manager is trying to discourage, while the desired behavior is not being rewarded at all. This problem is called the folly of rewarding A, while hoping for B.[98] Exhibit 3.12 presents a couple of examples.

EXHIBIT 3.12   **Common Management Reward Follies**

MANAGERS HOPE FOR:	BUT MANAGERS FREQUENTLY REWARD:
Long-term growth and environmental social responsibility	Quarterly earnings
Innovative thinking and risk-taking	Proven methods and not making mistakes
Teamwork and collaboration	The best competitive individual performers
Employee involvement and empowerment	Tight control over operations and resources
High achievement	Another year's effort
Candor such as telling of bad news early	Reporting good new not, and agreeing with the boss, whether the boss is right or wrong

Source: *Adapted from S. Kerr. "On the Folly of Rewarding A, While Hoping for B." Academy of Management Executive 9 (February 1995): 32–40.*

Motivating with Reinforcement

General Guides

Here are some general guidelines for using reinforcement:

1. Make sure employees know exactly what is expected of them. Set clear objectives— goal setting theory.
2. Select the appropriate type of reinforcement. A reward may work better for some, and avoidance, punishment, or extinction for others. Know your employees' needs.
3. Select the appropriate reinforcement schedule—continuous in some situations and intermittence in others.
4. Do not reward mediocre or poor performance (use extinction), and punish rule violators.

5. Look for the positive and give praise, rather than focus on the negative and criticize. Listen to people and make them feel good about themselves (Pygmalion effect).
6. Never go a day without giving sincere praise.
7. Do things for your employees, instead of to them, and you will see productivity increase.

Changing Behavior

If we are going to change our behavior—as already stated willpower doesn't work—we need to retrain our brain to form new habits by conditioning ourselves to new behavior. Here are some tips on using reinforcement to change our behavior.[99] The tips include a personal example, which is the same process as for professional behavior changes.

1. Begin by setting an objective using goal setting theory. For example, to get into shape by working out three days a week for 30 minutes starting (list a specific date).
2. Specify the who, what, when, where, and how of your plan. I will go to the gym (or walk from my home) every Monday, Wednesday, and Friday at 6:00am before going to school/work.
3. Next, further develop the plan by implementing the following ideas within your overall plan.

   - Reduce other life stress, if possible, so you can focus on your new behavior without distractions. I'm going to stop my relationship with Chris.
   - Think in advance about what might cause you to slip and plan how you can avoid those things. Why would you skip a workout?
   - Expect setbacks and slips and how you will bounce back as part of your plan. The next tip can help.
   - Plan your reinforcement. Have punishments for undesirable behavior. If I skip a workout, I will not watch TV that day, or I will make it up on another day. Have rewards for desired behavior. After working out for the three days of the week, I will treat myself to an ice cream.

Giving Praise

Pay is not the only, nor necessarily the best, reinforcer for performance. Empirical research studies have found that feedback and social reinforcers (praise) may have as strong an impact on performance as pay. Praise actually works by boosting levels of dopamine in the brain, a chemical linked to joy. In the 1940s, a survey revealed that what employees want most from a job is full appreciation for work done. Similar studies have been performed over the years with little change in results. Employees want to know that their organization values their contributions and cares about their well-being.[100]

Giving praise develops a positive self-concept in employees and leads to better performance—the Pygmalion effect and self-fulfilling prophecy. Praise is a motivator (not maintenance) because it meets employees' needs for esteem and self-actualization, growth, and achievement. Giving praise creates a win–win situation, only takes a minute, and doesn't cost anything.[101] It is probably the most powerful, simplest, least costly, and yet most underused motivational technique there is.

Ken Blanchard and Spencer Johnson popularized giving praise back in the 1980s through their best-selling book, *The One-Minute Manager*. They developed a technique that involves giving one-minute feedback of praise. Model 3.2, Giving Praise, is an adaptation. *The steps in the* giving praise model *are (1) Tell the employee exactly what was done correctly. (2) Tell the employee why the behavior is important. (3) Stop for a moment of silence. (4) Encourage repeat performance.* Blanchard calls it one-minute praise because it should not take more than one minute to give the praise. It is not necessary for the employee to say anything. The four steps are described below and illustrated in Model 3.2.

MODEL 3.2   **Giving Praise**

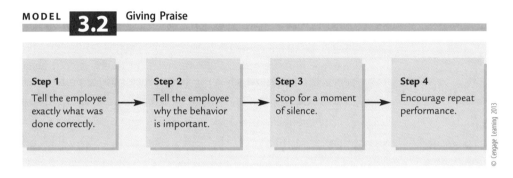

Step 1	Step 2	Step 3	Step 4
Tell the employee exactly what was done correctly.	Tell the employee why the behavior is important.	Stop for a moment of silence.	Encourage repeat performance.

© Cengage Learning 2013

Step 1.   **Tell the employee exactly what was done correctly.** When giving praise, look the person in the eye. Eye contact shows sincerity and concern. It is important to be very specific and descriptive. General statements, like "you're a good worker," are not as effective. On the other hand, don't talk for too long or the praise loses its effectiveness.

Step 2.   **Tell the employee why the behavior is important.** Briefly state how the organization and/or person benefits from the action. It is also helpful to tell the employee how you feel about the behavior. Be specific and descriptive.

Step 3.   **Stop for a moment of silence.** Being silent is tough for many managers. The rationale for the silence is to give the employee the chance to "feel" the impact of the praise. It's like "the pause that refreshes." When you are thirsty and take the first sip or gulp of a refreshing drink, it's not until you stop, and maybe say, "Ah," that you feel your thirst quenched.

Step 4.   **Encourage repeat performance.** This is the reinforcement that motivates the employee to continue the desired behavior. Blanchard recommends touching the employee. Touching has a powerful impact. However, he recommends it only if both parties feel comfortable. Others say don't touch employees; it could lead to a sexual harassment charge.

As you can see, giving praise is easy, and it doesn't cost a penny. Managers trained to give praise say it works wonders. It's a much better motivator than giving a raise or other monetary reward. One supermarket manager stated that an employee was taking his time stacking cans on a display. He gave the employee praise for stacking the cans so straight. The employee was so pleased with the praise that the display went up with about a 100 percent increase in productivity.

   Note that the manager looked for the positive, and used positive reinforcement rather than punishment. The manager could have given a reprimand comment such as, "Quit goofing off and get the display up faster." That statement would not have motivated the employee to increase productivity. All it would have done was hurt human relations, and could have ended in an argument. The cans were straight. The employee was not praised for the slow work pace. However, if the praise had not worked, the manager should have used another reinforcement method.

In this global environment, it is not always possible to give praise in person, so when you don't see people face-to-face, use written communication, including e-mail, instead. The personal handwritten note is considered to be special.[102] Disney CEO Bob Iger writes personal, handwritten notes on Disney stationery to praise employees, even those he has never met. He says that writing a simple note goes a long way with people.

OPENING CASE *APPLICATION*

1. How does Trader Joe's use reinforcement theory to motivate its employees?

Trader Joe's uses *positive reinforcement* with good pay and benefits and its career path opportunities. Sales are on a *continuous reinforcement schedule* as managers know the sales volume throughout the day. Paychecks are given on a *fixed interval schedule*. Praise and other recognition for accomplishments are given on a *variable interval and ratio schedule*.

CONCEPT APPLICATION 4
Motivation Theories

Identify each supervisor's statement of how to motivate employees by the theory behind the statement. Write the appropriate letter in the blank before each item.

a. hierarchy of needs d. equity f. expectancy
b. two-factor e. goal setting g. reinforcement
c. acquired needs

_____ 16. Jays Manufacturing now offers good working conditions, salaries, and benefits, so Jay is working at meeting socialization needs by having monthly barbecues in the summer so employees can get to know each other better.

_____ 17. A manager thanks at least one employee for doing a good job everyday by using a four-step model.

_____ 18. A manager used to try to improve working conditions to motivate employees. But he stopped and now focuses on giving employees more responsibility so they can grow and develop new skills.

_____ 19. A manager tells employees exactly what she want them to do, with a tough deadline that they can achieve.

_____ 20. A manager now realizes that he tends to be an autocratic manager because it helps fill his needs. But now he is giving some of his employees more autonomy on how they do their jobs.

_____ 21. A manager motivates employees by making their jobs interesting and challenging.

_____ 22. A manager makes sure she treats everyone fairly to motivate them.

_____ 23. A manager knows Kate likes people, so he gives her jobs in which she works with other employees.

_____ 24. Carl would often yell in the halls because he knew it bothered the manager. So the manager decided to ignore his yelling, and he stopped.

_____ 25. A manager got to know all of her employees' values. Now she can offer rewards that will motivate them when they achieve attainable task performance.

State the major differences among content, process, and reinforcement theories.

EXHIBIT 3.13   The Motivation Process with the Motivation Theories

1. Need

(Unmet need or want to be satisfied at work)
Content Motivation Theories
Hierarchy of Needs Theory
Two-Factor Theory
Acquired Needs Theory

2. Motive

(Selecting behavior to satisfy need)
Process Motivation Theories
Equity Theory
Expectancy Theory
Goal-Setting Theory

3. Behavior

(Employee action to satisfy need)

4. Consequence

(Manager behavior and/or natural outcome of employee action)
Reinforcement Theory

5. Satisfaction or Dissatisfaction

(Degree to which the need is met— and for how long—before dissatisfaction recurs, creating an unmet need)

© Cengage Learning 2013

Putting the Motivation Theories Together within the Motivation Process

Goal setting theory gurus Edwin Locke and Gary Latham stated that there is an urgent need to tie motivational theories and processes together into an overall model, insofar as it is possible. Others have attempted to do so. That is exactly what we do in this last section of the chapter.

Motivation is important because it helps to explain why employees behave the way they do. At this point you may be wondering: How do these theories fit together? Is one the best? Should I try to pick the correct theory for a given situation? Actually, the groups of theories are complementary; each group of theories refers to a different stage in the motivation process. Each group of theories answers a different question. Content motivation theories answer the question: What needs do employees have that should be met on the job? Process motivation theories answer the question: How do employees choose behavior to fulfill their needs? Reinforcement theory answers the question: What can managers do to get employees to behave in ways that meet the organizational objectives?

In this chapter you learned that the motivation process went from need to motive to behavior to consequence to satisfaction or dissatisfaction. Now let's make the motivation process a little more complex by incorporating the motivation theories, or answers to the preceding questions, into the process. See Exhibit 3.13 for an illustration.

Note that step 4 loops back to step 3 because, according to reinforcement theory, behavior is learned through consequences. Step 4 does not loop back to steps 1 or 2 because reinforcement theory is not concerned about needs, motives, or satisfaction; it focuses on getting employees to behave in predetermined ways, through consequences provided by managers. Also note that step 5 loops back to step 1 because meeting needs is ongoing; meeting our needs is a never-ending process. Finally, be aware that according to two-factor theory, step 5 (satisfaction or dissatisfaction) is not on one continuum but on two separate continuums (satisfied to not satisfied, or dissatisfied to not dissatisfied), based on the level of need being met (motivator or maintenance).

Chapter Summary

The chapter summary is organized to answer the eight learning outcomes for Chapter 3.

1. **List the University of Iowa leadership styles.**

The University of Iowa leadership styles are autocratic and democratic.

2. **Describe similarities and differences between the University of Michigan and Ohio State University leadership models.**

The University of Michigan and Ohio State University leadership models are similar because they are both based on the same two distinct leadership behaviors, although the models use different names for the two behaviors. The models are different because the University of Michigan model identifies two leadership styles based on either job- or employee-centered behavior. The Ohio State University model states that a leader uses high or low structure and consideration, resulting in four leadership style combinations of these two behaviors.

3. **Discuss similarities and differences between the Ohio State University Leadership Model and the Leadership Grid.**

Both theories are based on the same two leadership behaviors, but they use different names for the two dimensions. The theories are different because the Leadership Grid identifies five leadership styles, with one being middle of the road, while the Ohio State model identifies four leadership styles. The Leadership Grid also gives each combination of the two-dimensional behaviors one leadership style name. Authors of the Leadership Grid were strong supporters of the high-high team leadership style as the best.

4. **Discuss similarities and differences among the three content motivation theories.**

Similarities among the content motivation theories include their focus on identifying and understanding employee needs. The theories identify similar needs, but are different in the way they classify the needs. Hierarchy of needs theory includes physiological, safety, belongingness, esteem, and self-actualization needs. Two-factor theory includes motivators and maintenance factors. Acquired needs theory includes achievement, power, and affiliation needs and includes no lower-level needs, as the other two theories do.

5. **Discuss the major similarities and differences among the three process motivation theories.**

The similarity among the three process motivation theories includes their focus on understanding how employees choose behaviors to fulfill their needs. However, they are very different in their perceptions of how employees are motivated. Equity theory proposes that employees are motivated when their perceived inputs equal outputs. Expectancy theory proposes that employees are motivated when they believe they can accomplish the task and the rewards for doing so are worth the effort. Goal setting theory proposes that achievable, difficult goals motivate employees.

6. **Explain the four types of reinforcement.**

(1) Positive reinforcement provides the employee with a reward consequence for performing the desired behavior. (2) Avoidance reinforcement encourages employees to perform the desired behavior in order to avoid a negative consequence. (3) Extinction reinforcement withholds a positive consequence to get the employee to stop performing undesirable behavior. (4) Punishment reinforcement gives the employee a negative consequence to get the employee to stop performing undesirable behavior.

7. **State the major differences among content, process, and reinforcement theories.**

Content motivation theories focus on identifying and understanding employees' needs. Process motivation goes a step farther to understand how employees choose behavior to fulfill their needs. Reinforcement theory is not as concerned about employee needs; it focuses on getting employees to do what managers want them to do through the consequences provided by managers for their behavior. The use of rewards is the means of motivating employees.

8. **Define the following key terms (in order of appearance in the chapter).**

Select one or more methods: (1) fill in the missing key terms from memory; (2) match the key terms from the following list with their definitions below; (3) copy the key terms in order from the list at the beginning of the chapter.

_____ is the combination of traits, skills, and behaviors leaders use as they interact with followers.

_____ identifies two leadership styles: job-centered and employee-centered.

_____ identifies four leadership styles: low structure and high consideration, high structure and high consideration, low structure and low consideration, and high structure and low consideration.

_____ identifies five leadership styles: 1,1 impoverished; 9,1 authority-compliance; 1,9 country club; 5,5 middle of the road; and 9,9 team leader.

_____ is anything that affects behavior in pursuing a certain outcome.

_____ is when people go from need to motive to behavior to consequence to satisfaction or dissatisfaction.

_____ focus on explaining and predicting behavior based on people's needs.

_____ proposes that people are motivated through five levels of needs—physiological, safety, belongingness, esteem, and self-actualization.

_____ proposes that people are motivated by motivators rather than maintenance factors.

_____ proposes that people are motivated by their need for achievement, power, and affiliation.

_____ focus on understanding how people choose behavior to fulfill their needs.

_____ proposes that people are motivated when their perceived inputs equal outputs.

_____ proposes that people are motivated when they believe they can accomplish the task, they will get the reward, and the rewards for doing the task are worth the effort.

_____ proposes that specific, difficult goals motivate people.

_____ includes (1) To + (2) action verb + (3) singular, specific, and measurable result to be achieved + (4) target date.

_____ proposes that through the consequences for behavior, people will be motivated to behave in predetermined ways.

_____ includes four steps: (1) Tell the employee exactly what was done correctly. (2) Tell the employee why the behavior is important. (3) Stop for a moment of silence. (4) Encourage repeat performance.

Key Terms

acquired needs theory, 88

content motivation theories, 82

equity theory, 90

expectancy theory, 91

giving praise model, 100

goal setting theory, 92

hierarchy of needs theory, 83

Leadership Grid, 77

leadership style, 71

motivation, 81

motivation process, 81

Ohio State University Leadership Model, 75

process motivation theories, 89

reinforcement theory, 95

two-factor theory, 84

University of Michigan Leadership Model, 73

writing objectives model, 92

Review Questions

1. Why was there a shift from the trait to the behavioral theory paradigm?

2. How is leadership behavior based on traits?

3. What are the University of Iowa leadership styles?

4. What are the University of Michigan leadership styles?

5. What are the Ohio State University leadership styles?

6. What are three important contributions of the University of Michigan and Ohio State University studies?

7. What are the Leadership Grid leadership styles?

8. What are the three important contributions of the Leadership Grid and high-high research?

9. What is motivation, and why is it important to know how to motivate employees?

10. What are the content motivation theories?

11. What are the process motivation theories?

12. What are the types and schedules of reinforcement theory?

Critical Thinking Questions

The following critical-thinking questions can be used for class discussion and/or as written assignments to develop communication skills. Be sure to give complete explanations for all questions.

1. Which leadership model do you prefer?

2. Do you agree with the University of Michigan model (with two leadership styles) or with the Ohio State model (with four leadership styles)?

3. Do you agree with the Leadership Grid's claim that the one best leadership style is the team leader (9,9)?

4. Which of the three content motivation theories do you prefer? Why?

5. Which of the three process motivation theories do you prefer? Why?

6. What is your motivation theory? What major methods, techniques, and so on, do you plan to use on the job as a manager to increase motivation and performance?

7. Reinforcement theory is unethical because it is used to manipulate employees. Do you agree with this statement? Explain your answer.

8. Which type and schedule of reinforcement do you plan to use most often as a leader?

9. Do you really get what you reinforce? Explain.

CASE

Art Friedman—Friedmans Appliance

Art Friedman started his business in 1970 as Friedmans Appliance, selling all types of major appliances. In 1976, Friedman changed the company name to Friedmans Microwave Ovens to match his new strategy of focusing only on microwave ovens, which was the new thing back then. His goal was to be the absolute best place to buy a microwave oven and its accessories. Friedmans sold more than two million microwaves. His third strategic move was to franchise his microwave business, using Art Friedman's motivational technique of making everyone a boss. Friedmans also went online. For more than 35 years, Friedmans has been accomplishing its goal by providing superior service, good prices, and unconditional satisfaction guarantees.

The company name changed back to Friedmans Appliances. Today it is still a family-owned and -operated appliance dealer with a new strategy specializing in built-in appliances and kitchen remodelling. Friedmans Appliance combines the best of online convenience with traditional face-to-face customer service in a 24,000-square-foot showroom, which is located in Pleasant Hill, California. It features fully functioning appliance vignettes that allow a unique opportunity to experience firsthand many of the amazing products it offers. Pay a visit to the showroom, or call its friendly and professional staff at 925-808-2950. It's a great way to discover why Friedmans Appliance genuinely is your one true appliance authority in Northern California.[103]

Today, Art Friedman is retired. But if you visit the company Web site home page, you will find a link to an animated video titled "A Few Words from Art Friedman." The original Friedmans store employed 15 people in Oakland, California. Friedman believed that his employees were not motivated, so he implemented the following changes to motivate his employees. The following conversation took place between Bob Lussier and founder Art Friedman.

Bob: What is the reason for your success in business?
Art: My business technique.
Bob: What is it? How did you implement it?
Art: I called my 15 employees together and told them, "From now on I want you to feel as though the company is ours, not mine. We are all bosses. From now on you decide what you're worth and tell the accountant to put it in your pay envelope. You decide which days and hours you work and when to take time off. We will have an open petty cash system that will allow anyone to go into the box and borrow money when they need it."
Bob: You're kidding, right?
Art: No, it's true. I really do these things.
Bob: Did anyone ask for a raise?
Art: Yes, several people did. Charlie asked for and received a $100-a-week raise.
Bob: Did he and the others increase their productivity to earn their raises?
Art: Yes, they all did.
Bob: How could you run an appliance store with employees coming and going as they pleased?
Art: The employees made up schedules that were satisfactory to everyone. We had no problems of under- or overstaffing.
Bob: Did anyone steal from the petty cash box?
Art: No.
Bob: Would this technique work in any business?
Art: It did work, it still works, and it will always work!

GO TO THE INTERNET: To learn more about Art Friedman and Friedmans, visit their Web site (**http://www. friedmansappliance.com**).

Support your answers to the following questions with specific information from the case and text or with other information you get from the Web or other sources.

1. Which University—Iowa, Michigan, and Ohio State— leadership styles did Art Friedman use?

2. Which specific motivation level, factor, and need (from the content motivation theories) applies to Friedmans Appliance?

3. Do equity and expectancy theory apply to this case? Explain.

4. Which type of reinforcement did Friedman use?

5. Do you know of any organizations that use any of Friedman's or other unusual techniques? If yes, what is the organization's name? What does it do?

6. Could Friedman's techniques work in all organizations? Explain your answer.

7. In a position of authority, would you use Friedman's techniques? Which ones?

CUMULATIVE CASE QUESTIONS

8. Which of the Big Five personality dimensions is best illustrated in this case by Art Friedman (Chapter 2)?

9. Does Friedman have a Theory X or Theory Y attitude (Chapter 2)?

CASE EXERCISE AND ROLE-PLAY

Preparation: From Case question 7, which of Friedman's motivational techniques would you use to motivate franchisees? Which techniques of your own or from other organizations would you use? Justify your choice of motivation techniques.

In-Class Groups: Break into groups of four to six members and develop a list of motivational techniques group members would use, with justification. Select a spokesperson to record the techniques with justification and present them to the class.

Role-Play: One person (representing him- or herself or a group) may give the speech to the entire class, stating which new motivational techniques will be used and explaining each technique.

VIDEO ▸❚❚ CASE

Motivation at Washburn Guitars

Founded in the late 1800s in Chicago, Washburn Guitars boasts a rich tradition of fine instrument making. Today the company sells more than 50,000 guitars annually, totaling about $40 million in revenue. Washburn Guitars produces a variety of acoustic and electric guitars. Washburn craftsmen also enjoy making custom guitars. In recent years, custom shop production has grown dramatically from 20 to 300 guitars per month. Having a motivated workforce is essential because guitar making is labor intensive and requires attention to detail.

Quality materials combined with quality craftsmanship are necessary to produce quality guitars. Washburn Guitars' workforce is motivated because they love music and care about the instruments.

1. What motivates most employees at Washburn Guitars?

2. What kinds of guitars do employees most like to produce?

3. What is the connection between quality guitars and workforce motivation?

Developing Your Management Skills **1**

Writing Objectives

Preparing for This Exercise

For this exercise, you will first work at improving objectives that do not meet the criteria for objectives. Then you will write nine objectives for yourself.

Part 1. For each objective below, identify the missing criteria and rewrite the objective so that it meets all essential criteria. When writing objectives, use the model:

To + action verb + singular, specific, and
measurable result + target date

1. To improve our company image by year-end 2013.

Criteria missing: _____

Improved objective: _____

_____

_____

2. To increase the number of customers by 10 percent.

Criteria missing: _____

Improved objective: _____

_____

_____

3. To increase profits during 2014.

Criteria missing: _____

Improved objective: _____

_____

_____

4. To sell 5 percent more hot dogs and soda at the baseball game on Sunday, June 13, 2012.

Criteria missing: _____

Improved objective: _____

_____

_____

Part 2. Write three educational, personal, and career objectives you want to accomplish. Your objectives can be as short term as something you want to accomplish today, or as long term as 20 years from now. Be sure your objectives meet the criteria for effective objectives.

Educational objectives:

5. _____

6. _____

7. _____

Personal objectives:

8. _____

9. _____

10. _____

Career objectives:

11. _____

12. _____

13. _____

Doing This Exercise in Class

Objective

To develop your skill at writing objectives.

The primary AACSB learning standard skill developed through this exercise is analytic skills—students learn to set goals.

Preparation

You should have corrected the objectives in Part 1 and have written objectives in Part 2 during the preparation for this exercise.

Experience

You will get feedback on how well you corrected the four objectives and share your written objectives with others.

Options (8–20 minutes)

A. The instructor goes over suggested corrections for the four objectives in part 1 of the preparation, and then calls on class members to share their written objectives with the class in part 2.

B. The instructor goes over suggested corrections for the four objectives in part 1 of the preparation, and then the class breaks into groups of four to six to share their written objectives.

C. Break into groups of four to six and go over the corrections for the four objectives in part 1. Tell the instructor when your group is done, but go on to part 2, sharing your written objectives, until all groups are finished with the four corrections. The instructor goes over the corrections and may allow more time for sharing objectives. Give each other feedback for improving your written objectives during part 2.

Conclusion

The instructor may lead a class discussion and/or make concluding remarks.

Apply It *(2–4 minutes)* What did I learn from this experience? How will I use the knowledge in the future?

_____

_____

_____

Behavior Model Skills Training 1

Giving Praise

This training for leadership behavior modeling skills has four parts, as follows:

1. First, read how to use the model.

2. Then, view the behavior model video that illustrates how to give praise, following the four steps in the model.

3. Develop the skill in class by doing Developing Your Leadership Skills Exercise 2.

4. Further develop this skill by using the model in your personal and professional life.

Giving Praise Model

Review Model 3.2, "Giving Praise," in the text.

Behavior Model Video 1

Giving Praise

Objective

To assist you in giving praise that motivates others to high levels of performance.

Video (4½ minutes) Overview

You will watch a bank branch manager give praise to an employee for two different jobs well done.

Developing Your Leadership Skills 2

Giving Praise

Preparing for This Exercise

Think of a job situation in which you did something well-deserving of praise and recognition. For example, you may have saved the company some money, you may have turned a dissatisfied customer into a happy one, and so forth. If you have never worked, interview someone who has. Put yourself

in a management position and write out the praise you would give to an employee for doing what you did. Briefly describe the situation:

_____

_____

_____

Step 1. Tell the employee exactly what was done correctly.

_____

_____

_____

Step 2. Tell the employee why the behavior is important.

_____

_____

_____

Step 3. Stop for a moment of silence. (Count to five silently to yourself.)

Step 4. Encourage repeat performance.

_____

_____

_____

Doing This Exercise in Class

Objective

To develop your skill at giving praise.

The primary AACSB learning standard skill developed through this exercise is communication ability—motivating others.

Preparation

You will need your prepared praise.

Experience

You will give and receive praise.

Procedure *(10–15 minutes)* Break into groups of four to six. One at a time, give the praise you prepared.

1. Explain the situation.

2. Select a group member to receive the praise.

3. Give the praise. (Talk; don't read it off the paper.) Try to select the position you would use if you were actually giving the praise on the job (both standing, both sitting, etc.).

4. Integration. The group gives the praise-giver feedback on how he or she did:

Step 1. Was the praise very specific and descriptive? Did the giver look the employee in the eye?

Step 2. Was the importance of the behavior clearly stated?

Step 3. Did the giver stop for a moment of silence?

Step 4. Did the giver encourage repeat performance? Did the giver of praise touch the receiver (optional)?

Step 5. Did the praise take less than one minute? Was the praise sincere?

Conclusion

The instructor may lead a class discussion and/or make concluding remarks.

Apply It *(2–4 minutes)* What did I learn from this experience? How will I use this knowledge in the future? When will I practice?

_____

_____

_____

Sharing

In the group, or to the entire class, volunteers may give their answers to the "Apply It" questions.

4

Contingency Leadership Theories

Learning Outcomes

After studying this chapter, you should be able to:

1. State the major difference between behavioral and contingency leadership theories, and explain the behavioral contribution to contingency theories. p. 112

2. Describe the contingency leadership theory variables. p. 113

3. Identify the contingency leadership model styles and variables. p. 115

4. State the leadership continuum model major styles and variables. p. 122

5. Identify the path-goal leadership model styles and variables. p. 122

6. State the normative leadership model styles and the number of variables. p. 126

7. Discuss the major similarities and differences between the behavioral and contingency leadership theories. p. 133

8. Compare and contrast four major differences among the four contingency leadership models. p. 133

9. List which leadership models are prescriptive and descriptive, and explain why they are classified as such. p. 133

10. Explain substitutes and neutralizers of leadership. p. 135

11. Define the following **key terms** (in order of appearance in the chapter):

contingency leadership model

descriptive leadership models

leadership continuum model

leadership model

normative leadership model

path–goal leadership model

prescriptive leadership models

substitutes for leadership

OPENING CASE APPLICATION

PepsiCo's three primary lines of business with five brands are snack foods (Frito-Lay—its largest unit), beverages (Pepsi, Tropicana, Gatorade), and Quaker foods (such as Quaker Oats cereals, Quaker Rice Cakes, Chewy Granola Bars, Rice-A-Roni, and its Aunt Jemima brand).[1] PepsiCo is a $60 billion company getting 50 percent of its revenues from overseas, and it commands about 40 percent of the global market in salty snacks.[2] PepsiCo ranks in the top 50 on the Fortune 500 list and is number 1 in the Food and Consumer Products category,[3] and it is in the top 175 of the Fortune Global 500[4] (Coca-Cola is #70 and #404). It was ranked 26th on the Fortune World's Most Admired Companies list.[5]

Indra K. Nooyi is Chairman and Chief Executive Officer of PepsiCo, and according to *Fortune*, Nooyi is ranked as the most powerful woman in business five years running, with an annual pay of more than $14.2 million.[6] She is also ranked sixth on the Forbes World's 100 Most Powerful Women.[7] Beginning in the mid-1990s, Nooyi was the chief strategist that dramatically reshaped PepsiCo. The company got out of the restaurant business by selling Pizza Hut, Taco Bell, and KFC in 1997. It got into the juice business by buying the world's largest brand juice producer Tropicana in 1998. PepsiCo entered the sports drink business in 2001 by acquiring the best seller Gatorade, through the purchase of its maker Quaker Oats, which also gave PepsiCo a line of cereal and other food products. PepsiCo also acquired Izze sparkling juice drinks in 2006 and Naked Juice smoothies and other fruit drinks in 2007. PepsiCo also has joint ventures with partners, including Lipton (ice teas) and Starbucks (frappuccino). Nooyi acquired PepsiCo's two largest bottlers in 2010 to save an estimated $400 million a year.[8]

Nooyi is a different kind of CEO. She says her approach boils down to balancing the profit motive with making healthier snacks (in a speech to the food industry, she pushed the group to tackle obesity), striving for a net-zero impact on the environment, and taking care of your workforce. She was one of the first executives to realize that the health and green movements were not just fads, and she demanded true innovation. PepsiCo is gradually shifting its percentage of "better for you" and "good for you" snacks and widening its product portfolio with whole grains, nuts, and fruits. The company was one of the first to invest in green capital expenditures for water- and heat-related conservation projects for sustainability.[9] Her mottos, "Growth Through Innovation" and "Performance with Purpose," are both a means of herding the organization and of presenting PepsiCo globally.[10] Every two weeks she sends e-mails to 285,000 staffers about what's on her mind.[11] So far Nooyi has been a great success at PepsiCo, but cola wars, higher energy costs, and rising ingredient costs will test her leadership.

OPENING CASE QUESTIONS:

1. What does climbing the corporate ladder to CEO of PepsiCo have to do with contingency leadership? What life, educational, and job experiences qualified Indra Nooyi for her job as CEO?

2. What do colleagues say about Indra Nooyi's leadership—is it task or relationship, does she have a life outside of PepsiCo, and does she have any future career plans?

3. Which continuum leadership style does Indra Nooyi tend to use in making acquisitions at PepsiCo?

4. Which path-goal leadership styles does Indra Nooyi tend to use at PepsiCo?

5. Which normative leadership styles does Indra Nooyi tend to use at PepsiCo?

Can you answer any of these questions? You'll find answers to these questions about PepsiCo and Indra Nooyi throughout the chapter.

To learn more about Indra Nooyi and PepsiCo, visit the company's Web site at **http://www.pepsico.com**.

| Learning Outcome 1 | *State the major difference between behavioral and contingency leadership theories, and explain the behavioral contribution to contingency theories.* |

Contingency Leadership Theories and Models

Both the trait and behavioral leadership theories were attempts to find the one best leadership style in all situations. In the late 1960s, it became apparent that there is no one best leadership style in all situations. Managers need to adapt different leadership styles,[12] as leadership success requires adapting leadership styles to meet the situation.[13] Thus, contingency leadership theory became the third major leadership paradigm (Chapter 1), and the leadership styles used in its models are based on the behavioral leadership theories. Although there are no new leadership models, researchers continue to try to better understand and predict which leadership styles are the most appropriate in a given situation.[14] In this section, we discuss theories versus models, the contingency theory factors, and the need for global contingency leadership.

Leadership Theories versus Leadership Models

As defined in Chapter 1, a *leadership theory* is an explanation of some aspect of leadership; theories have practical value because they are used to better understand, predict, and control successful leadership. A leadership model *is an example for emulation or use in a given situation*. In earlier chapters, we talked about leading by example, which is emulation or the hope that followers will imitate the leader's behavior.[15] In this chapter, we discuss using models in a given situation to improve performance of leaders, followers, or both.

All of the contingency leadership theories in this chapter have leadership models. The leadership theory is the longer text that explains the variables and leadership styles to be used in a given contingency situation.[16] The leadership model is the short (one page or less) summary of the theory to be used when selecting the appropriate leadership style for a given situation. Models have been compared to baseball in this way. A model can't teach you to get a hit every time at bat, but if you use the model, it will improve your batting average.

Learning Outcome 2   *Describe the contingency leadership theory variables.*

Contingency Theory and Model Variables

Contingency means "it depends." One thing depends on other things, and for a leader to be effective there must be an appropriate fit between the leader's behavior and style and the followers and the situation.[17] Recall from Chapter 1 that *contingency leadership theories* attempt to explain the appropriate leadership style based on the leader, followers, and situation.[18]

See Exhibit 4.1 for a list of general contingency leadership variables that can be used as a framework in which to place all the contingency leadership model variables for analyzing leadership. Throughout this chapter, each contingency leadership model's variables are described in terms of this framework. For each model, the *leader* variable also includes the leadership styles of each model.

EXHIBIT 4.1   Framework for Contingency Leadership Variables

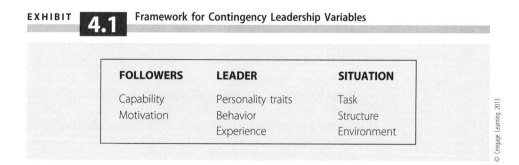

FOLLOWERS	LEADER	SITUATION
Capability	Personality traits	Task
Motivation	Behavior	Structure
	Experience	Environment

© Cengage Learning 2013

YOU Make the ETHICAL Call

4.1 *Leadership Gender*

Should gender be a contingency variable in leadership? Are there differences in the leadership of men and women? Some researchers say that women tend to be more participative, relationship-oriented leaders and men are more assertive and task oriented. However, others say that men and women leaders are more alike than different because they do the same things. Thus, there currently is no consensus in the literature that men and women lead differently or the same as men.[19]

1. Do you think that men and women lead the same or differently?

2. Are men or women more ethical and socially responsible leaders?

3. Would you prefer to have a man or woman for a boss?

4. Is it ethical and socially responsible to say that one gender makes better leaders?

5. Should global companies appoint women as managers in countries that believe in equal rights for women, but not allow women to be managers in countries that don't have these beliefs?

Global Contingency Leadership

Before we get into all the theories, let's take a minute to quickly realize how important contingency leadership is in the global economy of today.[20] Global companies like McDonald's, with restaurants all over the world, realize that successful leadership styles can vary greatly from place to place. In Europe and other parts of the world, managers have more cultural than technical variables to deal with as they encounter diverse value systems and religious backgrounds among employees. Employees in some countries prefer domineering, self-centered, autocratic leaders, whereas other countries prefer a more democratic and participative leadership style. More companies are now looking for graduates with an international openness and flexibility who can master the complexity of the global economy.[21] The focus of Chapter 10 is on organizational culture, ethics and diversity. With respect to the discussion on diversity, we emphasize that the growing cultural diversity of the workforce and the increasing globalization of the marketplace, creates the need for leaders with multicultural backgrounds and experiences. This reinforces the message of global contingency leadership.

National culture has a major impact on employees' work-related values and attitudes and thus should affect the way organizations manage.[22] To be successful in the global village, it is important to understand and be able to work with people from different cultures.[23] Companies, including IBM, are training their managers to work with a variety of foreigners to become successful global players.[24] In countries that are more like the United States (such as Australia, Canada, and England), American managers have fewer adjustments to make, whereas countries with cultures that are quite different from that of the United States (such as China, India, and Japan) require greater adjustment.

GLOBE stands for *Global Leadership and Organizational Behavior Effectiveness*, which is an ongoing cross-cultural investigation of leadership and national culture. The GLOBE research team used data from 825 organizations, with 18,000 managers, in 62 countries to identify nine dimensions in which national cultures are diverse.[25] For more information on GLOBE Research Project, visit **www.thunderbird.edu/sites/globe**. Also, see Chapter 10 for an expanded discussion of national culture identities using Hofstede's Model of five dimensions that he used to distinguish a nation's culture from other nations.

OPENING CASE APPLICATION

1. **What does climbing the corporate ladder to CEO of PepsiCo have to do with contingency leadership? What life, educational, and job experiences qualified Indra Nooyi for her job as CEO?**

Contingency theory is about using the right style in the right situation to succeed, which Indra Nooyi continues to do. Growing up in India, Nooyi was the right person to continue to take PepsiCo global, as 50 percent of its total revenue now comes from international sales.[26] On special occasions, Nooyi wears a traditional Indian sari. Her South Asian heritage gives her a wide-angle view on the world. She grew up in Chennai (formerly Madras), on the southeast coast of India, the daughter of a stay-at-home mom and an accountant father. Although her family is Hindu, Nooyi attended a Catholic school, was an avid debater, played cricket and the guitar, and formed an all-girl rock band. She earned a BS degree from Madras Christian College, an MBA from the Indian Institute of Management in Calcutta, and a Masters of Public and Private Management from Yale University. Before coming to PepsiCo, Nooyi was Senior VP and Director of Corporate Strategy and Planning at Motorola from 1986 to 1990 and Senior VP of Strategy and Strategic Marketing at Asea Brown Bovri from 1990 to 1994. She spent 12 years climbing the corporate ladder at PepsiCo. Nooyi started as Senior VP of Strategic Planning in 1994, was promoted to Senior VP of Corporate Strategy and Development in 1996, was promoted to President and CFO in 2001, and was promoted to CEO in 2006.

Learning Outcome 3   *Identify the contingency leadership model styles and variables.*

Contingency Leadership Theory and Model

In 1951, Fred E. Fiedler began to develop the first situational leadership theory. It was the first theory to specify how situational variables interact with leader personality and behavior. He called the theory "Contingency Theory of Leader Effectiveness."[27] Contingency suggests that a leader's effectiveness depends on how well the leader's style fits the context of the job. So he was the first to develop a model to match the leadership style to the job.

Fiedler believed that leadership style is a reflection of personality (trait theory–oriented) and behavior (behavioral theory–oriented), and that leadership styles are basically constant. Leaders should not change styles; they should change the context of their job. So he was the first research to match the leader's style to the situation. Because he was the first, today his term "Contingency Theory" is used in other contexts that have nothing to do with Fiedler's theory and model.[28] You may have noticed that the title of this chapter is "Contingency Leadership Theories." The objective of all four contingency theories we present is to choose the leadership style that matches the situation to maximize performance.[29]

*The **contingency leadership model** is used to determine if a person's leadership style is task- or relationship-oriented, and if the situation (leader–member relationship, task structure, and position power) matches the leader's style to maximize performance.* In this section, we discuss Fiedler's leadership styles, situational favorableness, determining the appropriate leadership style for the situation, and research by Fiedler and others. See Exhibit 4.2 to see how Fiedler's model fits into the framework of contingency leadership variables.

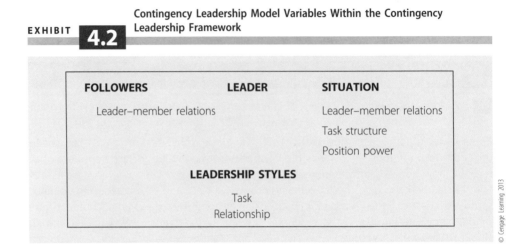

EXHIBIT 4.2 Contingency Leadership Model Variables Within the Contingency Leadership Framework

FOLLOWERS	LEADER	SITUATION
Leader–member relations		Leader–member relations
		Task structure
		Position power

LEADERSHIP STYLES

Task
Relationship

© Cengage Learning 2013

Leadership Style and the LPC

Although we may be able to change your behavior with different followers (although Fiedler didn't think we can), we also have a dominant leadership style. The first major factor in using Fiedler's model is to determine whether your dominant leadership style is task-motivated or relationship-motivated. People primarily gain satisfaction either from task accomplishment or from forming and maintaining relationships with followers.[30] To determine leadership style, using Fiedler's model, you must complete the *least-preferred coworker (LPC)* scales. The LPC essentially answers the question, "Are you more task-oriented or relationship-oriented?" The two leadership styles are (1) *task* and (2) *relationship*.

Note that Fiedler developed two leadership styles, which is a one-dimensional model. The leadership styles part of Fiedler's model is similar to the University of Michigan Leadership Model, in that it is based on only two leadership styles: one focusing on the task (job-centered leadership) and the other focusing on relationship (employee-centered). To determine your Fiedler leadership style, complete Self-Assessment 1.

SELF-ASSESSMENT 1   **Leadership Style**

Your Fiedler LPC

Return to Chapter 3, Self-Assessment 1 on pages 72–73, and place your score for tasks on the following Task line and your score for people on the Relationship line.

10 — 9 — 8 — 7 — 6 — 5 — 4 — 3 — 2 — 1
High Task Leadership Style

10 — 9 — 8 — 7 — 6 — 5 — 4 — 3 — 2 — 1
High Relationship Leadership Style

According to Fiedler, you are primarily either a task- or relationship-oriented leader. Your highest score is your primary leadership style. Neither leadership style is the one best style. The one appropriate leadership style to use is based on the situation—our next topic.

Situational Favorableness

After determining your leadership style, determine the situational favorableness. *Situational favorableness* refers to the degree to which a situation enables the leader to exert influence over the followers. The more control the leader has over the followers, the more favorable the situation is for the leader. The three variables, in order of importance, are as follows.

1. *Leader–member relations.* This is the most powerful determinant of overall situational favorableness. Is the relationship good (cooperative and friendly) or poor (antagonistic and difficult)?[31] Do the followers trust, respect, accept, and have confidence in the leader (good)? Leaders with good relations have more influence. The better the relations, the more favorable the situation.
2. *Task structure.* This is second in importance: Is the task structured or unstructured? Do employees perform repetitive, routine, unambiguous, standard tasks that are easily understood? Leaders in a structured situation have more influence. The more structured the jobs are, the more favorable the situation.
3. *Position power.* This is the weakest factor: Is position power strong or weak? Does the leader have the power to assign work, reward and punish, hire and fire, give raises and promotions? The leader with position power has more influence. The more power, the more favorable the situation.

The relative weights of these three factors together create a continuum of situational favorableness of the leader. Fiedler developed eight levels of favorableness, going from 1 (highly favorable) to 8 (very unfavorable). See Exhibit 4.3 for an adapted model.

Determining the Appropriate Leadership Style

To determine whether task or relationship leadership is appropriate, the user answers the three questions pertaining to situational favorableness, using the Fiedler contingency theory model (Exhibit 4.3). The user starts with question 1 and follows the decision tree to Good or Poor depending on the relations. The user then answers question 2 and follows the decision tree to Repetitive or Nonrepetitive. When answering question 3, the user ends up in one of eight possible situations. If the LPC leadership style matches, the user does nothing, since they may be successful in that situation.

Changing the Situation

However, if the leadership style does not match the situation, the leader may be ineffective. One option is to change to a job that matches the leadership style. Fiedler recommends (and trained people to) change the situation, rather than their leadership styles. Here are a few general examples of how to change the situation variables to make a more favorable match for the leader's style:

- If relations are poor, the leader can work to improve them by showing interest in followers, listening to them, and spending more time getting to know them personally.

- The *task* can be more or less structured by stating more or less specific standards and procedures for completing the task, and giving or not giving clear deadlines.

- Leaders with strong *position power* do not have to use it; they can downplay it. Leaders with weak power can try to get more power from their manager and play up the power by being more autocratic.

EXHIBIT **4.3** Fiedler Contingency Leadership Model

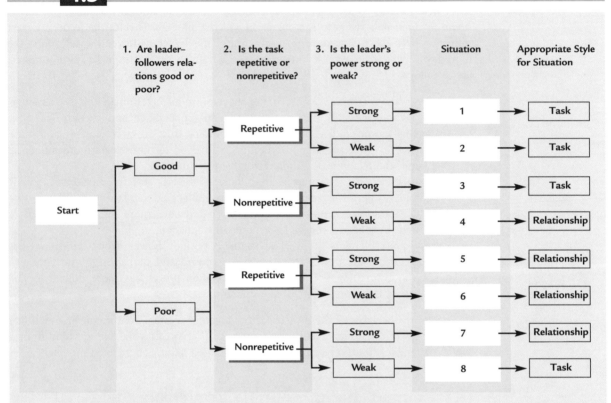

If the manager's LPC leadership style matches the situation, the manager does nothing. If the LPC leadership style does not match the situation, the manager changes the situation to match his or her LPC leadership style.

Source: Adapted from Fred E. Fiedler, *A Theory of Leadership Effectiveness (New York: McGraw-Hill, 1967).*

CONCEPT APPLICATION 1
Contingency Leadership Theory

Using the contingency model in Exhibit 4.3, answer the three questions at the top of the model to get to the situation (numbered 1–8). Follow the situation to the appropriate style in the last column of the model to determine the situation number with its corresponding appropriate leadership style (task or relationship). Select two answers below based on the answers you get from the model, writing the appropriate two letters in the blanks before each item.

Situation number   a. 1   b. 2   c. 3   d. 4   e. 5   f. 6   g. 7   h. 8
Leadership style   A. task-oriented   B. relationship-oriented

_____ 1. Carlos, the manager, oversees the processing of cancelled checks for the bank. He is well liked by the employees. Carlo's manager enjoys hiring and evaluating his employees' performance.

_____ 2. Tania, the principal of a school, assigns teachers to classes and has various other duties. She hires and decides on tenure appointments. The school atmosphere is tense.

(continued)

(Concept Application 1 continued)

_____ 3. Juan, the chairperson of the committee, is highly regarded by its volunteer members from a variety of departments. The committee members are charged with recommending ways to increase organizational performance.

_____ 4. Sally, the manager, oversees the assembly of mass-produced containers. She has the power to reward and punish. Sally is viewed as a hard-nosed manager.

_____ 5. Chet, the manager, is from the corporate planning staff. Chet helps the other departments plan. He is viewed as being a dreamer; he doesn't understand the various departments. Employees tend to be rude in their dealings with Chet.

Research, Criticism, and Applications

In the course of 20 years, numerous studies have tested the Contingency Leadership Model. Two meta-analyses concluded that the research tends to support the model, although not for every situation and not as strongly for field studies as for laboratory studies.[32] Despite its groundbreaking start to contingency theories, Fiedler's work was criticized in the 1970s for conceptual reasons, and because of inconsistent empirical finding and inability to account for substantial variance in group performance. Fiedler disagreed with some of the criticism and published two rejoinders.[33] Thus, the debate continues over the validity and usefulness of the model.

Another major criticism is of Fiedler's view that we leaders should not change our style, but rather the context of our job should be changed. It is generally agreed that it is much easier to change our style to meet the context of the job than to change the job context. Fiedler's model also doesn't really teach us how to change our job context. The other situational writers in this chapter suggest changing leadership styles, not our job context.

Despite the critics, Fiedler has helped contribute to the other contingency theories. It has application as it can be used to answer questions about the leadership of individuals in different types of organizations. It can help with recruiting managers based on their style and the job context. For example, the theory can help predict if a manager in one department will also be effective in another different type of department. It can also help explain why a hard-working manager is not effective in a specific job—no match of style to context.

OPENING CASE *APPLICATION*

2. What do colleagues say about Indra Nooyi's leadership—-is it task or relationship, does she have a life outside of PepsiCo, and does she have any future career plans?

Her colleagues say Indra Nooyi is intense, decisive, an excellent negotiator, very open and very direct, demanding, and she challenges you. Nooyi is charismatic. She can rouse an audience and rally them around any project. Although she is task oriented, Nooyi also has strong relationships with her colleagues. She insists that everybody's birthday is celebrated with a cake. She has a supportive husband (Raj) and two daughters (Preetha and Tara), and she enjoys being a soccer mom. Nooyi is a karaoke fan, and her karaoke machine is the ubiquitous party game at every PepsiCo gathering. Being CEO of PepsiCo will not be Nooyi's last job. She said that she eventually wants to give back by going to Washington to work for the government.

Learning Outcome 4   *State the leadership continuum model major styles and variables.*

Leadership Continuum Theory and Model

Robert Tannenbaum and Warren Schmidt also developed a contingency theory in the 1950s.[34] They stated that leadership behavior is on a continuum from boss-centered to subordinate-centered leadership. Their model focuses on who makes the decisions. They noted that a leader's choice of a leadership pattern should be based on forces in the boss, forces in the subordinates, and forces in the situation. Look at Exhibit 4.4 to see how Tannenbaum and Schmidt's variables fit within the framework of contingency leadership variables.

EXHIBIT 4.4   Leadership Continuum Model Variables Within the Contingency Leadership Framework

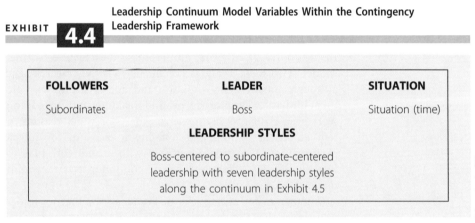

FOLLOWERS	LEADER	SITUATION
Subordinates	Boss	Situation (time)

LEADERSHIP STYLES

Boss-centered to subordinate-centered
leadership with seven leadership styles
along the continuum in Exhibit 4.5

© Cengage Learning 2013

WORK Application 1
Select a present or past manager. Which LPC leadership style is or was dominant for that manager? Using the Fiedler model (see Exhibit 4.3 on page 118), which situation number is the manager in? What is the appropriate leadership style for the manager in this situation? Does it match his or her style? How successful a leader is your manager? Do you think there is a relationship between the manager's leadership style and the situation?

If you are a manager, you may want to repeat this work application, using yourself as the manager.

Tannenbaum and Schmidt identify seven major styles the leader can choose from. Exhibit 4.5 is an adaptation of their model, which lists the seven styles. *The leadership continuum model is used to determine which one of seven styles to select, based on the use of boss-centered versus subordinate-centered leadership, to meet the situation (boss, subordinates, situation/time) in order to maximize performance.*

Before selecting one of the seven leadership styles, the leader must consider the following three forces or variables:

- *Boss.* The leader's personality and behavioral preferred style—based on experience, expectation, values, background, knowledge, feeling of security, and confidence in the subordinates—is considered in selecting a leadership style. Based on personality and behavior, some leaders tend to be more autocratic and others more participative.

- *Subordinates.* The followers' preferred style for the leader is based on personality and behavior, as with the leader. Generally, the more willing and able the followers are to participate, the more freedom of participation should be used, and vice versa.

- *Situation (time).* The environmental considerations, such as the organization's size, structure, climate, goals, and technology, are considered in selecting a leadership style. Upper-level managers also influence leadership styles. For example, if a middle manager uses an autocratic leadership style, the leader may tend to use it too.

The *time* available is another consideration. It takes more time to make participative decisions. Thus, when there is no time to include followers in decision making, the leader uses an autocratic leadership style.

In a 1986 follow-up by Tannenbaum and Schmidt to their original 1958 and 1973 articles, they recommended that (1) the leader become a group member when allowing the group to make decisions; (2) the leader clearly state the style (follower's authority) being used; (3) the leader not try to trick the followers into thinking they made a decision that was actually made by the leader; and (4) it's not the number of decisions the followers make, but their significance that counts.[35]

EXHIBIT 4.5 Tennenbaum and Schmidt's Leadership Continuum Model

Autocratic	1. State the decision that is not open to discussion
	2. Make the decision and convince employees that it is a good idea
	3. Present decision and ask if there are any questions
	4. Present a decision that is subject to change based on input
	5. State the situation, ask for a recommended decision, then makes the decision
	6. Lets employees make a decision within set limits
Participative	7. Let employees make ongoing decisions

Source: Adapted from "How to Choose a Leadership Pattern" by Robert Tannenbaum and Warren H. Schmidt, May-June 1973.

CONCEPT APPLICATION 2
Leadership Continuum

Using the continuum model in Exhibit 4.5, *identify these five statements by their leadership style (numbered 1–7 in the model). Select each answer, writing the appropriate letters in the blank before each item.*

a. 1   b. 2   c. 3   d. 4   e. 5   f. 6   g. 7

_____ 6. "John, go bring this letter to the mailroom right away."

_____ 7. "This is the way we will complete orders from now on. Does anyone have any questions about the new process?"

_____ 8. "Here is list of holidays you can get paid for. Fred, you get five paid, so pick the ones you want."

_____ 9. "I'd like your ideas on how to stop the bottleneck on the production line. But I have the final say on the solution we implement."

_____ 10. "Heather, I selected you to take on the new assignment of training the new person; let me know how you feel about this assignment."

WORK Application 2

Using the leadership continuum model (Exhibit 4.5), identify your manager's most commonly used leadership style by number and description. Would you say this is the most appropriate leadership style based on the leader, the followers, and the situation? Explain.

_____

_____

_____

_____

Note that Tannenbaum and Schmidt developed two major leadership styles, with seven continuum styles, which is a one-dimensional model. The leadership styles part of their model is similar to the University of Michigan Leadership Model in that it is based on two major leadership styles: one focusing on boss-centered behavior (job-centered leadership) and the other focusing on subordinate-centered behavior (employee-centered).

Although the leadership continuum model was very popular, it did not undergo research testing like the contingency leadership model. One major criticism of this model is that the three factors to consider when selecting a leadership style are very subjective. In other words, determining which style to use, and when, is not clear in the model. The Situational Leadership® Model and Normative Leadership Model (to be discussed later in this chapter) thus took over in popularity, most likely because they clearly identified which leadership style to use in a given, clearly defined situation.

You will determine your major leadership continuum style later in Self-Assessment 4 on page 146, which puts together three of the contingency leadership styles (continuum, path–goal, and normative).

OPENING CASE APPLICATION

3. **Which continuum leadership style does Indra Nooyi tend to use in making acquisitions at PepsiCo?**

Nooyi tends to use #5—-the leader presents the problem, gets suggested solutions, and makes the decision. She has others look into possible acquisition targets and gets recommendations from them, but Nooyi has the final say on which companies will be acquired.

Learning Outcome 5   *Identify the path–goal leadership model styles and variables.*

Path–Goal Leadership Theory and Model

The path–goal leadership theory was developed by Robert House, based on an early version of the theory by M. G. Evans, and published in 1971 and other articles over years.[36] House intended to reconcile prior conflicting findings concerning task- and relationship-oriented leader behavior. His theory specified a number of situational moderators of relationships between task- and person-oriented leadership and their effects. House attempted to explain how the behavior of a leader influences the performance and satisfaction of the followers (subordinates). Look at Exhibit 4.6 to see how House's model fits into the framework of contingency leadership variables. Note that unlike the earlier contingency leadership models, House's model does not have a leader trait and behavior variable. The leader is supposed to use the appropriate leadership style (one of four), regardless of preferred traits and behavior to motivate employees to enhance their performance.

The **path–goal leadership model** *is used to select the leadership style (directive, supportive, participative, or achievement-oriented) appropriate to the situation (subordinate and environment) to maximize both performance and job satisfaction.* Note that path–goal leadership theory is based on motivation theories of goal setting and expectancy theory. The leader is responsible for increasing followers' motivation to attain personal and organizational goals. Motivation is increased by (1) clarifying the follower's path to the rewards that are available, or (2) increasing the rewards that the follower values and desires. *Path clarification* means that the leader works with followers to help them identify and learn the behaviors that will lead to successful task accomplishment and organizational rewards.

EXHIBIT 4.6 Path–Goal Leadership Model Variables within the Contingency Leadership Framework

FOLLOWERS	LEADER	SITUATION
Subordinates	None	Environment
(authoritarianism, locus of control, ability)		(task structure, formal authority, and work group)
	LEADERSHIP STYLES	
	Directive	
	Supportive	
	Participative	
	Achievement-oriented	

© Cengage Learning 2013

The path–goal model is used to determine employee objectives and to clarify how to achieve them using one of four leadership styles. It focuses on how leaders influence employees' perceptions of their goals and the paths they follow toward goal attainment. As shown in Exhibit 4.7 (an adaptation of the model), the situational factors are used to determine the leadership style that affects goal achievement through performance and satisfaction.

EXHIBIT 4.7 House Path–Goal Leadership Model

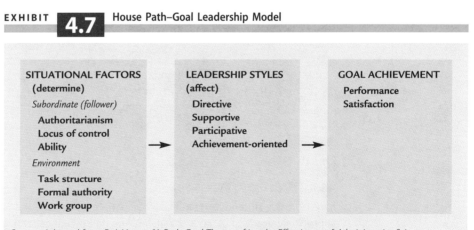

SITUATIONAL FACTORS (determine)	LEADERSHIP STYLES (affect)	GOAL ACHIEVEMENT
Subordinate (follower)	Directive	Performance
Authoritarianism	Supportive	Satisfaction
Locus of control	Participative	
Ability	Achievement-oriented	
Environment		
Task structure		
Formal authority		
Work group		

Source: Adapted from R. J. House, "A Path-Goal Theory of Leader Effectiveness," *Administrative Science Quarterly 16 (2), 1971: 321–329.*

Situational Factors

Subordinate

Subordinate situational characteristics are:

1. *Authoritarianism* is the degree to which employees defer to others, and want to be told what to do and how to do the job.
2. *Locus of control* (Chapter 2) is the extent to which employees believe they control goal achievement (internal) or if goal achievement is controlled by others (external).
3. *Ability* is the extent of the employees' ability to perform tasks to achieve goals.

Environment

Environment situational factors are:

1. *Task structure* is the extent of repetitiveness of the job.
2. *Formal authority* is the extent of the leader's position power. Note that task structure and formal authority are essentially the same as Fiedler's.
3. *Work group* is the extent to which coworkers contribute to job satisfaction or the relationship between followers. Note that House identifies work group as a situational variable. However, under the contingency framework, it would be considered a follower variable.

YOU Make the ETHICAL Call

4.2 *Drug Research*

Several drug companies, including Glaxo-SmithKline and Merck, have been accused of situationally favorable research reporting. When results support the use of the drug, they are reported; when they don't, results are not reported. Although all medications have side effects, some drug users have died because of medication. As a result, the Food and Drug Administration (FDA) has been criticized for its process of approving drugs and monitoring their safety.

1. Is it ethical and socially responsible to report only the results that help gain FDA approval of drugs?

2. If you worked for a drug company and knew that the results of a study showed negative effects, but were not included in a report, what would you do?

3. If you worked for a drug company and your boss asked you to change negative results into positive results, or to make results even better, what would you do?

4. What would you do if you gave your boss a negative report on a drug and found out the results were changed to positive results?

5. Is the FDA doing a good job of monitoring the safety of drugs? If not, what else should it do?

Leadership Styles

Based on the situational factors in the path–goal model, the leader can select the most appropriate leadership style by using the following general guidelines for each style. The original model included only the directive (based on initiating structure, job-centered style) and supportive (based on consideration and employee style) leadership styles (from the Ohio State and University of Michigan behavioral leadership studies).

The participative and achievement-oriented leadership styles were added in a 1974 publication by House and Mitchell.

Directive

The leader provides high structure. Directive leadership is appropriate when the followers want authority leadership and have external locus of control, and when the follower ability is low. Directive leadership is also appropriate when the environmental task is complex or ambiguous, formal authority is strong, and the work group provides job satisfaction.

Supportive

The leader provides high consideration. Supportive leadership is appropriate when the followers do not want autocratic leadership and have internal locus of control, and when follower ability is high. Supportive leadership is also appropriate when the environmental tasks are simple, formal authority is weak, and the work group does not provide job satisfaction.

Participative

The leader includes employee input into decision making. Participative leadership is appropriate when followers want to be involved and have internal locus of control, and when follower ability is high; when the environmental task is complex, authority is either strong or weak, and job satisfaction from coworkers is either high or low.

Achievement-Oriented

The leader sets difficult but achievable goals, expects followers to perform at their highest level, and rewards them for doing so. In essence, the leader provides both high directive (structure) and high supportive (consideration) behavior. Recall that achievement is motivational acquired need[37] and goal setting is also a motivational technique.[38] Achievement-oriented leadership is appropriate when followers are open to autocratic leadership and have external locus of control, and when follower ability is high; when the environmental task is simple, authority is strong, and job satisfaction from coworkers is either high or low.

CONCEPT APPLICATION 3
Path-Goal Leadership

Using Exhibit 4.7 on page 123 and text descriptions, identify the appropriate leadership style for the five situations. Write the appropriate letter in the blank before each item.

a. directive   c. participative

b. supportive   d. achievement-oriented

_____ 11. A manager has an employee who has been coming in late for work, with no apparent good reason. The manager has decided to take some corrective action to get the employee to come in on time.

_____ 12. A manager has a new, complex task for her department, and she is not sure how it should be done. Her employees are experienced and like to be involved in decision making.

_____ 13. A manager is putting together a new task force that will have an ambiguous task to complete. The members all know each other and get along well.

(continued)

(Concept Application 3 continued)

_____ 14. A manager has decided to delegate a new task to an employee who has been doing a good job. The employee, however, tends to be insecure and may feel threatened by taking on a new task, even though it is fairly easy and the manager is confident that the employee can do the job easily.

_____ 15. Department members just finished the production quarter and easily met the quota. The manager has strong position power and has decided to increase the quota to make the job more challenging.

Research, Criticism, and Applications

A meta-analysis based on 120 studies examined directive and supportive behavior and showed that support for path–goal theory was significantly greater than chance, but results were quite mixed. An extensive review of the research on moderator variables in leaders also had inconclusive findings.[39] Recent reviews of the history of path–goal theory have concluded that it has not been adequately tested, possibly because it is such a complex model.

Although path–goal theory is more complex and specific than leadership continuum, it is also criticized by managers because it is difficult to know which style to use when. As you can see, there are many situations in which not all six situational factors are exactly as presented in the guidelines for when to use the style. Judgment calls are required to select the appropriate style as necessary. Plus, House suggests adding your own variables to the model.

Despite its limitations, the path–goal model has already made an important contribution to the study of leadership by providing a conceptual framework to guide researchers in identifying potentially relevant situational variables. Path–goal leadership theory led to the development of the theory of *charismatic leadership* in 1976. Path–goal theory was considerably broadened in scope, and in 1996 House referred to it as *value-based leadership theory*. You will learn about charismatic and values-based leadership in Chapter 9.

Path–goal theory also provides a useful way for leaders to think about motivating followers. It provides a set of general recommendation based on the characteristics of subordinates and tasks for how leadership should behave in different situations if they want to be effective. It informs us as to when to use each of its four leadership styles: directive, supportive, participative, or achievement-oriented. You will determine your path–goal leadership style in Self-Assessment 4 on page 146, which puts together the contingency leadership styles.

WORK Application **3**

Identify your manager's most commonly used path-goal leadership style. Would you say this is the most appropriate leadership style based on the situational factors? Explain.

_____

_____

_____

_____

OPENING CASE *APPLICATION*

4. **Which path–goal leadership styles does Indra Nooyi tend to use at PepsiCo?**

Nooyi tends to use the achievement-oriented and participative styles. She sets high standards and expects everyone around her to measure up. She has red, green, and purple pens and uses them liberally to mark up everything that crosses her desk. Her scribbles are legendary, and include the following, "I have never seen such gross incompetence," and "This is unacceptable," with "unacceptable" underlined three times. Nooyi believes in people; you give them an objective and get them all to buy into it, and they can move mountains. She uses input from others, including her second in command, whom she treats like a partner, and her "Team Pepsi" members.

 Learning Outcome 6   *State the normative leadership model styles and the number of variables.*

Normative Leadership Theory and Models

An important leadership question today is, "When should the manager take charge and when should the manager let the group make the decision?" In 1973, Victor Vroom (yes, the same guy who developed expectancy theory) and Philip Yetton published a decision-making model to answer this question while improving decision-making effectiveness. Vroom and Arthur Jago refined the model and expanded it to four models in 1988. The four models are based on two factors: individual or group decisions and time-driven or development-driven decisions. In 2000, Victor Vroom published a revised version entitled "Leadership and the Decision-Making Process." We present the latest version with a focus on time- and development-driven decisions.[40]

The **normative leadership model** *has a time-driven and development-driven decision tree that enables the user to select one of five leadership styles (decide, consult individually, consult group, facilitate, and delegate) appropriate for the situation (seven questions/variables) to maximize decisions.* See Exhibit 4.8 to see how the normative leadership model fits into the contingency leadership framework variables. It is called a *normative model* because it provides a sequential set of questions that are rules (norms) to follow to determine the best leadership style for the given situation.

EXHIBIT 4.8   **Normative Leadership Model Variables within the Contingency Leadership Framework**

FOLLOWERS	LEADER	SITUATION
Development-Driven Decision Model	3. Leader expertise	*Time-Driven Decision Model*
2. Importance of commitment	**LEADERSHIP STYLES**	1. Decision significance
4. Likelihood of commitment	Decide	
5. Group support for objectives	Consult individually	
6. Group expertise	Consult group	
7. Team competence	Facilitate	
	Delegate	

© Cengage Learning 2013

To use the normative model, you must have a specific decision to make, have the authority to make the decision, and have specific potential followers to participate in the decision.

Leadership Participation Styles

Vroom identified five leadership styles based on the level of participation in the decision by the followers. Vroom adapted them from Tannenbaum and Schmidt's leadership continuum model (see Exhibit 4.5 on page 121, ranging from autocratic to participative styles. Vroom's five leadership styles follow.

Decide

The leader makes the decision alone and announces it, or sells it, to the followers. The leader may get information from others outside the group and within the group without specifying the problem.

Consult Individually

The leader tells followers individually about the problem, gets information and suggestions, and then makes the decision.

Consult Group

The leader holds a group meeting and tells followers the problem, gets information and suggestions, and then makes the decision.

Facilitate

The leader holds a group meeting and acts as a facilitator to define the problem and the limits within which a decision must be made. Leaders seek participation and concurrence on the decision without pushing their ideas. The style is essentially the same as the path–goal participative style.

Delegate

The leader lets the group diagnose the problem and make the decision within stated limits. The role of the leader is to answer questions and provide encouragement and resources.

Model Questions to Determine the Appropriate Leadership Style

To determine which of the five leadership styles is the most appropriate for a given situation, we answer a series of diagnostic questions based on seven variables. The seven variables presented in Exhibit 4.8 are repeated in Exhibit 4.9 and in Exhibit 4.10.

We now explain how to answer the questions, based on the variables, when using the two models.

1. *Decision Significance.* How important is the decision to the success of the project or organization? Is the decision of high (H) importance or low (L) importance to the success? When making highly important decisions, leaders need to be involved.

2. *Importance of Commitment.* How important is follower commitment to implement the decision? If acceptance of the decision is critical to effective implementation, importance is high (H). If commitment is not important, it's low (L). When making highly important commitment decisions that followers may not like and may not implement, followers generally need to be involved in making the decision.

3. *Leader Expertise.* How much knowledge and expertise does the leader have with this specific decision? Is expertise high (H) or low (L)? The more expertise the leader has, the less need there is for follower participation.

4. *Likelihood of Commitment.* If the leader were to make the decision alone, is the certainty that the followers would be committed to the decision high (H) or low (L)? When making decisions that followers will like and want to implement, there is less need to involve them in the decision.

5. *Group Support for Objectives.* Do followers have high (H) or low (L) support for the team or organizational goals to be attained in solving the problem? Higher levels of participation are acceptable with high levels of support.

EXHIBIT 4.9   Normative Leadership Time-Driven Model

Instructions: The model is a decision tree that works like a funnel. Define the problem statement, then answer the questions from left to right as high (H) or low (L), skipping questions when not appropriate to the situation and avoiding crossing any horizontal lines. The last column you come to contains the appropriate leadership participation decision-making style for the situation.

	1. Decision Significance?	2. Importance of Commitment?	3. Leader Expertise?	4. Likelihood of Commitment?	5. Group Support?	6. Group Expertise?	7. Team Competence?	Leadership Style
P R O B L E M S T A T E M E N T	H	H	H	H	-	-	-	Decide
				L	H	H	H	Delegate
							L	Consult (Group)
						L	-	Consult (Group)
					L	-	-	Consult (Group)
			L	H	H	H	H	Facilitate
							L	Consult (Individually)
						L	-	Consult (Individually)
					L	-	-	Consult (Individually)
				L	H	H	H	Facilitate
							L	Consult (Group)
						L	-	Consult (Group)
					L	-	-	Consult (Group)
		L	H	-	-	-	-	Decide
			L	-	H	H	H	Facilitate
							L	Consult (Individually)
						L	-	Consult (Individually)
					L	-	-	Consult (Individually)
	L	H	-	H	-	-	-	Decide
				L	-	-	H	Delegate
							L	Facilitate
		L	-	-	-	-	-	Decide

Source: Adapted from *Organizational Dynamics 28*, Victor H. Vroom, *"Leadership and the Decision-Making Process,"* p. 87, Copyright © 2000 with permission from Elsevier.

EXHIBIT **4.10** Normative Leadership Development-Driven Model

Instructions: The model is a decision tree that works like a funnel. Define the problem statement, then answer the questions from left to right as high (H) or low (L), skipping questions when not appropriate to the situation and avoiding crossing any horizontal lines. The last column you come to contains the appropriate leadership participation decision-making style for the situation.

	1. Decision Significance?	2. Importance of Commitment?	3. Leader Expertise?	4. Likelihood of Commitment?	5. Group Support?	6. Group Expertise?	7. Team Competence?	Leadership Style
P R O B L E M S T A T E M E N T	H	H	–	H	H	H	H	Delegate
							L	Facilitate
						L	–	Consult (Group)
					L	–	–	Consult (Group)
				L	H	H	H	Delegate
						H	L	Facilitate
						L	–	Facilitate
					L	–	–	Consult (Group)
		L	–	–	H	H	H	Delegate
						H	L	Facilitate
						L	–	Consult (Group)
					L	–	–	Consult (Group)
	L	H	–	H	–	–	–	Decide
				L	–	–	–	Delegate
		L	–	–	–	–	–	Decide

Source: Adapted from *Organizational Dynamics 28*, Victor H. Vroom, "Leadership and the Decision-Making Process," p. 88, Copyright © 2000 with the permission from Elsevier.

6. *Group Expertise.* How much knowledge and expertise do the individual followers have with this specific decision? Is expertise high (H) or low (L)? The more expertise the followers have, the greater the individual or group participation can be.

7. *Team Competence.* Is the ability of the individuals to work together as a team to solve the problem high (H) or low (L)? With high team competence, more participation can be used.

Not all seven variables/questions are relevant to all decisions. All seven or as few as two questions are needed to select the most appropriate leadership style in a given situation. Tying questions 1, 3, and 6 together, when making important decisions it is critical to include the leader and/or followers with the expertise to solve the problem.

Then, the issue of commitment (questions 2 and 4) becomes relevant. Tying questions 5, 6, and 7 together in decision making, the leader should not delegate decisions to groups with low support for objectives, low group expertise, and low team competence. The great thing about the models is that they tie the relevant variables together for us as we answer the questions to determine the most appropriate leadership style for the given situation.

Selecting the Time-Driven or Development-Driven Model for the Situation

The first step is actually to select one of the two models, based on whether the situation is driven by the importance of time or development of followers. The characteristics of the decision are focus, value, and orientation.

The Time-Driven Model

See Exhibit 4.9 on page 129 for the three characteristics:

1. *Focus.* The model is concerned with making effective decisions with minimum cost. Time is costly, as it takes longer for groups to make decisions than the leader alone.
2. *Value.* Value is placed on time, and no value is placed on follower development.
3. *Orientation.* The model has a short-term horizon.

The Development-Driven Model

See Exhibit 4.10 for these three characteristics:

1. *Focus.* The model is concerned with making effective decisions with maximum development of followers. Follower development is worth the cost.
2. *Value.* Value is placed on follower development, and no value is placed on time.
3. *Orientation.* The model has a long-term horizon, as development takes time.

Computerized Normative Model

Vroom has developed a computerized CD-ROM model that is more complex and more precise, yet easier to use. It combines the time-driven and development-driven models into one model, includes 11 variables/questions (rather than seven), and has five variable measures (rather than H or L). It guides users through the process of analyzing the situation with definitions, examples, and other forms of help as they progress through the use of the model. The computerized model is beyond the scope of this course, but you will learn how to use the time-driven and development-driven models presented here in Exhibits 4.9 and 4.10 and used with Developing Your Leadership Skills Exercise 2.

Determining the Appropriate Leadership Style

To determine the appropriate style for a specific situation, use the best model (time-driven or development-driven) for the situation and answer the questions, some of which may be skipped based on the model used and answers to prior questions. The questions are sequential and are presented in a decision-tree format similar to the Fiedler model, in which you end up with the appropriate style to use. If we use both models for the same situations, for some decisions the appropriate style will be the same, and different for others.

WORK Application 4
Recall a specific decision you or your boss has or had to make. Is or was the decision time-driven or development-driven? Using Exhibit 4.9 on page 129 or 4.10 on page 130, select the appropriate participation style for the situation. Be sure to state the questions you answered and how (H or L) you answered each.

_____

_____

_____

_____

Research, Criticism, and Applications

The current normative model is based on the research of Vroom and colleagues at Yale University on leadership and decision-making processes, with more than 100,000 managers making decisions.[41] Numerous studies conducted by others have tested the normative leadership model. In general, the results found in the empirical research have supported the model.[42] In a summary of prior research based on six separate studies conducted in three different countries, managers—contrary to Fiedler—do change their style to meet the situation. Managers using the decision style recommended by the normative model were almost twice as likely to be successful as were managers using decisions not recommended by the model. Higher-level managers use more participation in decision making. Women managers tend to use more participation than men. Almost all managers view themselves as using a higher level of participation than do their followers. Over the 25 years of research, there has been a move toward higher levels of participation, greater empowerment, and use of teams.

Although the normative model is, of the contingency theories, the one best supported by research, the model is not without its critics. Vroom treats decisions as a single, discrete episode that occurs at one point in time, but most important decisions are not made that way. Important decisions often involve multiple meetings with various people. Thus, the leader may have to use a sequence of different decision procedures with different people at different times before the final decision is made. Also, the leader is assumed to have the skills needed to use each of the five leadership styles, and the leader's skills are not included in the model.

The Vroom and Vroom Yetton/Jago model tends to be popular in the academic community because it is based on research and it is complex. It is not very popular with managers because they find it cumbersome to select models and to pull out the model and follow a 7-question decision tree every time they have to make a decision.

In his defense of the application of his model, Vroom states that his models are not tools to be slavishly embraced and used in all decisions. Besides, once you learn how to use the model, you can better mentally judge the most appropriate style for the situation without the model. Thus, Vroom agrees with other researchers who state that leadership styles evolve, and that leaders can develop their leadership skill by using his normative leadership models. Vroom and Jago conducted research concluding that the model does work. Managers using the style recommended in the model have a 62 percent probability of a successful decision; not using the recommended style allows only a 37 percent probability of a successful decision.[43]

You will determine your major normative leadership style in Self-Assessment 3 on pages 141–143, and you will learn how to use the models in Developing Your Leadership Skills Exercise 1 and 2.

OPENING CASE *APPLICATION*

5. Which normative leadership styles does Indra Nooyi tend to use at PepsiCo?

Based on the decision to be made, Nooyi consults and facilitates others. As chairman and CEO, she has the final say in major decisions affecting PepsiCo. However, she also delegates some decisions down the chain of command that involve specific products in American and international markets.

Learning Outcomes 7 and 8

Discuss the major similarities and differences between the behavioral and contingency leadership theories.

Compare and contrast four major differences among the four contingency leadership models.

WORK Application 5

1. Identify the one contingency leadership model you prefer to use on the job, and state why.

2. Describe the type of leader that you want to be on the job. Identify specific behavior you plan to use as a leader. You may also want to identify behavior you will not use.

_____

_____

_____

_____

Putting the Behavioral and Contingency Leadership Theories Together

Today in the global economy, we need different kinds of leaders.[44] We need leaders who are flexible and can change quickly,[45] leaders who can integrate and implement theories to succeed.[46] Exhibit 4.11 is a review of different words that are used to describe the same two leadership behavior concepts. It includes the number of leadership styles based on the two behavior concepts and the different names given to the leadership styles. We should realize that all the leadership styles are based on the same two behavior concepts. We developed Exhibit 4.11 and Exhibit 4.12 to put all these contingency leadership theories together with behavioral leadership styles. These exhibits should help us to better understand the similarities and differences between these theories.

Learning Outcome 9

List which leadership models are prescriptive and descriptive, and explain why they are classified as such.

Prescriptive and Descriptive Models

One last difference between models, not shown in any exhibits, is the difference between prescriptive and descriptive models. The contingency leadership model and the normative leadership model are **prescriptive leadership models**: *They tell the user exactly which style to use in a given situation.* However, the continuum and path-goal leadership models are **descriptive leadership models**: *They identify contingency variables and*

EXHIBIT 4.11   Names Given to the Same Two Leadership Behavior Concepts

	Leadership & Behavior/Style		Number of Leadership Styles Based on Behavior Concepts
Behavioral Theories			
University of Iowa	Autocratic	Democratic	2
University of Michigan	Job-centered	Employee-centered	2
Ohio State University	Structure	Consideration	4
Leadership Grid®	Concern for production	Concern for people	5
Contingency Theories			
Contingency model	Task	Relationship	2
Leadership continuum	Boss-centered	Subordinate-centered	7
Path-goal model	Directive	Supportive	4
Normative model	Autocratic	Group	5

EXHIBIT 4.12 Putting the Behavioral and Contingency Leadership Theories Together

BEHAVIORAL THEORIES	LEADERSHIP STYLES				CONTINGENCY VARIABLES	CONTINGENCY CHANGE	DESIRED OUTCOME
	Job-Centered		Employee-Centered				
U of Michigan	High Structure/ Low Consideration	High Structure/ High Consideration	Low Structure/ High Consideration	Low Structure/ Low Consideration			
Ohio State U							
CONTINGENCY THEORIES							
Contingency Leadership Model	Task		Relationship		Leader/Follower Relations; Task Structure; Position Power	Situation	Performance
Leadership Continuum Model	1	2 & 3	4 & 5	6 & 7	Manager; Subordinates; Situation/time	Leadership Style	Performance
Path-Goal Model	Directive	Achievement	Supportive	Participative	Subordinate (authoritarianism, locus of control, ability); Environment (task structure, formal authority, work group)	Leadership Style	Performance Job Satisfaction
Normative Leadership Model	Decide	Consult Individual or Group	Facilitate	Delegate	Development-Driven or Time-Driven Models: (1) Decision significance (2) Importance of commitment (3) Leader expertise (4) Likelihood of commitment (5) Group support for objectives (6) Group expertise (7) Team competence	Leadership Style	Decisions

leadership styles without specifying which style to use in a given situation. In other words, users of the descriptive model select the appropriate style based more on their own judgment. Look at all the leadership models and you will see what we mean.

Many managers prefer prescriptive models; this is a reason why they are more commonly used in organizational leadership training programs than the descriptive leadership models. On the other hand, many academic researchers scoff at prescriptive models, especially simple ones, and prefer the more complex descriptive models based on solid theoretical foundations.

Learning Outcome 10   *Explain substitutes and neutralizers of leadership.*

Leadership Substitutes Theory

The four leadership theories presented assume that some leadership style will be effective in each situation. However, in keeping with contingency theory, there are factors outside the leader's control that have a larger impact on outcomes than do leadership actions. Contingency factors provide guidance and incentives to perform, making the leader's role unnecessary in some situations. Steven Kerr and John Jermier argued that certain situational variables prevent leaders from affecting subordinates' (followers') attitudes and behaviors.[47] **Substitutes for leadership** include characteristics of the subordinate, task, and organization that replace the need for a leader or neutralize the leader's behavior. This is the motivation for some organizations adopting self-managed teams. Self-managed teams are discussed in Chapter 8.

Substitutes and Neutralizers

Thus, *substitutes* for leadership make a leadership style unnecessary or redundant. Highly skilled workers do not need a leader's task behavior to tell them how to do their job. *Neutralizers* reduce or limit the effectiveness of a leader's behavior. For example, managers who are not near an employee cannot readily give task-directive behavior. See Exhibit 4.13 to see how the substitutes for leadership fit into the framework of contingency leadership variables. Then, read a description of each substitute.

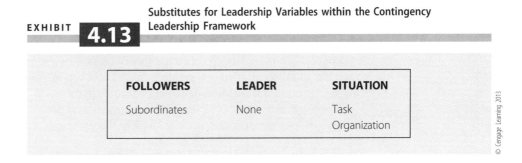

EXHIBIT 4.13 Substitutes for Leadership Variables within the Contingency Leadership Framework

FOLLOWERS	LEADER	SITUATION
Subordinates	None	Task
		Organization

© Cengage Learning 2013

The following variables may substitute or neutralize leadership by providing task-oriented direction and/or people-oriented support rather than a leader.

1. *Characteristics of followers.* Ability, knowledge, experience, training. Need for independence. Professional orientation. Indifference toward organizational rewards.

2. *Characteristics of the task.* Clarity and routine. Invariant methodology. Provision of own feedback concerning accomplishment. Intrinsic satisfaction. This characteristic is similar to Fiedler's and others' task behavior.

3. *Characteristics of the organization.* Formalization (explicit plans, goals, and areas of responsibility). Inflexibility (rigid, unbending rules and procedures). Highly specified and active advisory and staff functions. Closely knit, cohesive work groups. Organizational rewards not within the leader's control. Spatial distance between leader and followers.

Leadership Style

Leaders can analyze their situation and better understand how these three characteristics substitute or neutralize their leadership style and thus can provide the leadership and followership most appropriate for the situation. The leader role is to provide the direction and support not already being provided by the task, group, or organization. The leader fills the gaps in leadership.

Changing the Situation

Like Fiedler suggested, leaders can change the situation rather than their leadership style. Thus, substitutes for leadership can be designed in organizations in ways to complement existing leadership, to act in leadership absence, and to otherwise provide more comprehensive leadership alternatives. After all, organizations have cut middle-management numbers, and something has to provide the leadership in their absence. One approach is to make the situation more favorable for the leader by removing neutralizers. Another way is to make leadership less important by increasing substitutes such as job enrichment, self-managing teams, and automation.

WORK Application **6**
Identify your present or past manager. Can the characteristics of followers, task, and/or the organization substitute for this leader? In other words, is his or her leadership necessary? Explain.

Research, Criticism, and Applications

A meta-analysis was conducted to estimate bivariate relationships among leadership behaviors, substitutes for leadership, followers' attitudes, and role perceptions and performance, and to examine the relative strengths of the relationships among these variables. It was based on 435 relationships obtained from 22 studies containing 36 independent samples. Overall, the theory was supported.[48]

However, the theory does have its critics. As with the other theories, results are mixed. Research has found support for some aspects of the theory, but other aspects have not been tested or supported. Critics point out that for many of the substitutes, the behavior of the formal leader is merely replaced by similar leadership behavior carried out by peers or other informal leaders—so leadership still exits anyway.

Applications of leadership substitute theory include its strong evidence that situational variables can directly affect job satisfaction and motivation. As already discussed, changing the situation is a major application of substitute theory.

To close this chapter, complete Self-Assessment 2 to determine how your personality influences your use of contingency leadership theory.

SELF-ASSESSMENT 2   **Your Personality and Contingency Leadership Theories**

In Self-Assessment 1 on page 116 were you more task or relationship oriented? Your being more task or relationship oriented is based very much on your personality.

Based on surgency, if you have a high need for power, you may tend to be more task oriented. Based on agreeableness, if you are a real "people" person with a high

(continued)

(Self-Assessment 2 continued)

need for affiliation, you may tend to be more relationship oriented. Based on conscientiousness, if you have a high need for achievement, you may tend to be more task oriented to make sure the job gets done, and done your way.

Based on your personality profile, does it match Fiedler's contingency leadership theory, as presented in Self-Assessment 1? If you have a higher need for power, do you tend to use the autocratic (1–3) leadership continuum styles, the directive and achievement path-goal leadership styles, and then decide and consult normative leadership styles?

If you have a higher need for affiliation, do you tend to use more participative leadership continuum

styles, the supportive and participative path-goal styles, and the facilitate and delegate normative leadership styles?

You will better be able to understand which leadership style you do tend to use when you complete Self-Assessment 3 on page 141, "Determining Your Preferred Normative Leadership Style." The leadership continuum and path-goal styles are explored in Self-Assessment 4 on page 146. It is important to realize that your personality does affect your leadership style. However, you can use the leadership style that is most appropriate for the situation. You will learn how in Developing Your Leadership Skills Exercises 1 and 2.

Chapter Summary

The chapter summary is organized to answer the 11 learning outcomes for Chapter 4.

1. **State the major difference between behavioral and contingency leadership theories, and explain the behavioral contribution to contingency theories.**

Behavioral theories attempt to determine the one best leadership style for all situations. Contingency leadership theories contend that there is no one best leadership style for all situations. Behavioral theories contributed to contingency theories because their basic leadership styles are used in contingency leadership models.

2. **Describe the contingency leadership theory variables.**

The contingency leadership variables used to explain the appropriate leadership style are the leader, followers, and situation. The leader factor is based on personality traits, behavior, and experience. The followers factor is based on capability and motivation. The situational factor is based on task, structure, and environment.

3. **Identify the contingency leadership model styles and variables.**

The contingency leadership model styles are task and relationship. The variables include (1) the leader–follower relationship, (2) the leadership styles—task or relationship, and (3) the situation—task structure and position power.

4. **State the leadership continuum model major styles and variables.**

The two major continuum leadership model styles are boss centered and subordinate centered. The variables

include (1) the boss, (2) the subordinates, and (3) the situation (time).

5. **Identify the path–goal leadership model styles and variables.**

The path–goal leadership model styles include directive, supportive, participative, and achievement-oriented. Variables used to determine the leadership style are the subordinate and the environment.

6. **State the normative leadership model styles and the number of variables.**

The five normative leadership model styles are decide, consult individually, consult group, facilitate, and delegate. The model has seven variables.

7. **Discuss the major similarities and differences between the behavioral and contingency leadership theories.**

The primary similarity between these theories is that their leadership styles are all based on the same two leadership concepts, although they have different names. The major difference is that the contingency leadership models identify contingency variables on which to select the most appropriate behavioral leadership style for a given situation.

8. **Compare and contrast four major differences among the four contingency leadership models.**

Using Exhibit 4.12 on page 134, note that the first difference is in the number of leadership styles used in the four models, which ranges from 2 (contingency) to 7 (continuum). The second difference is in the number of contingency variables used to select the appropriate leadership style, which ranges from 2 (path-goal) to 7 (normative). The third difference is what is changed when using the model. When using the contingency model, the leader changes the situation; with the other three models, the leader changes behavior (leadership style). The last difference is the desired outcome. Contingency and continuum leadership models focus on performance, and the path-goal model adds job satisfaction. The normative model focuses on decisions.

9. List which leadership models are prescriptive and descriptive, and explain why they are classified as such.

The contingency and normative leadership models are prescriptive models, because they specify exactly which leadership style to use in a given situation. The continuum and path-goal leadership models are descriptive models, because users select the appropriate leadership style for a given situation based on their own judgment.

10. Explain substitutes and neutralizers of leadership.

Substitutes for leadership include characteristics of the subordinate, task, and organization that make leadership behavior unnecessary or redundant; neutralizers reduce or limit the effectiveness of a leader's behavior.

11. Define the following key terms (in order of appearance in the chapter).

Select one or more methods: (1) fill in the missing key terms from memory; (2) match the key terms from the following list with their definitions below; (3) copy the key terms in order from the list at the beginning of the chapter.

_____ is an example for emulation or use in a given situation.

_____ determines if a person's leadership style is task- or relationship-oriented, and if the situation (leader–member relationship, task structure, and position power) matches the leader's style to maximize performance.

_____ determines which one of seven styles to select, based on the use of boss-centered versus subordinate-centered leadership, to meet the situation (boss, subordinates, situation/time) in order to maximize performance.

_____ determines the leadership style (directive, supportive, participative, or achievement-oriented) appropriate to the situation (subordinate and environment) to maximize both performance and job satisfaction.

_____ has a time-driven and development-driven decision tree that enables the user to select one of five leadership styles (decide, consult individually, consult group, facilitate, and delegate) appropriate for the situation.

_____ tell the user exactly which style to use in a given situation.

_____ identify contingency variables and leadership styles without specifying which style to use in a given situation.

_____ include characteristics of the subordinate, task, and organization that replace the need for a leader or neutralize the leader's behavior.

Key Terms

Review Questions

1. What is the difference between a theory and a model?
2. What contingency leadership variables are common to all of the theories?
3. How does the global economy relate to contingency leadership?
4. What are the two contingency leadership theory leadership styles?
5. Do the three situational favorableness factors of the contingency leadership model (see Exhibit 4.3 on page 118) fit in only one of the three variables (follower, leader, situation) or all contingency leadership variables (see Exhibit 4.1 on page 113)? Explain.
6. What is the difference in the outcomes of the contingency leadership and the continuum leadership models and that of the path–goal model?
7. What are the three subordinate and environment situational factors of the path–goal model?
8. What are the path–goal theory leadership styles?
9. What are the normative leadership theory leadership styles?
10. What is the primary difference between the contingency leadership model and the other leadership models (leadership continuum, path–goal, and normative leadership)?
11. What are the three substitutes for leadership?

Critical Thinking Questions

The following critical-thinking questions can be used for class discussion and/or as written assignments to develop communication skills. Be sure to give complete explanations for all questions.

1. Do you agree with Fiedler's belief that people have one dominant leadership style and cannot change styles? Explain.

2. Do you believe that managers today are using more boss- or more subordinate-centered leadership styles?

3. Do you agree that time is an important situational factor to consider in selecting a leadership style for the situation? Explain.

4. The normative leadership model is the most complex. Do more variables improve the model?

5. One group of authors believes that Fiedler's contingency leadership model is the model best supported by research. However, a different author believes that it is the normative leadership model. Which model do you believe is best supported by research? Why?

6. Which contingency leadership theory do you think is the best?

7. Which contingency leadership theory do you actually plan to use, and how? If you don't plan to use any, give a detailed reason for not wanting to use any of the models.

CASE

Terry Gou—Foxconn Technology Group

Have you ever heard of Foxconn Technology Group and its founder and CEO Terry Gou? It is the largest exporter out of China. Foxconn is a Taiwanese contract manufacturer employing 920,000 Chinese workers across more than 20 mainland factories.[49] Its business is fueled by the United States' and the world's hunger for high-tech gadgets and toys at rock-bottom prices, shareholders demanding solid profit margins, and workers eager to move up the economic ladder.[50]

Foxconn has been the most trusted name in contract manufacturing services.[51] Some of the major companies Foxconn makes contracted products for include IBM, Cisco, Microsoft, Nokia, Sony, Dell, Hewlett-Packard, and Apple.[52] If you have a PlayStation, computer, or smart phone there is a good chance that all or part of it was made by Foxconn. It is the only manufacturer that makes the iPad and one of two producer of the iPhone.[53]

Foxconn has a plant in Houston, Texas, that employs around 1,000 workers, specializing in high-end servers for corporate clients. Gou plans to move additional automated production to the United States and ship its goods to China.[54] Foxconn is the second largest exporter in the Czech Republic,[55] and it also plans to expand to Slovakia and Turkey and may lead a plan to expand Brazil's electronics industry.[56]

Gou started Hon Hai Precision Industry Company, the anchor company of Foxconn Technology Group, in 1974 at age 23 with a $7,500 loan from his mother.[57] He has been characterized as always thinking about a way to shave another nickel off the cost of a product, as a charming salesman, as a daring strategist, as a ruthless taskmaster, and as a reincarnated Henry Ford.[58] Gou was ranked sixth on the Fortune Asia's 25 Most Powerful list.[59] *Forbes* estimated Gou's personal fortune at $5.9 billion, but he says, "I think for me, I am not interested in knowing how much I have. I don't care. I am working not for the money at this moment, I am working for society, I am working for my employees."[60]

Although Terry Gou's story is interesting, in this case we focus on lower-level manager Li Chang. (Please note: Foxconn is an existing company. However, Chang and Jackie Lee are not the names of actual managers at Foxconn; they are used to illustrate contingency leadership.)

Li Chang worked her way up to become the manager in a department making parts for the iPad. Chang's job was to supervise the production of one part that is used as a component in other products. Running the machines to make the standard parts is not complicated, and her employees generally find the job to be boring with low pay. Chang closely supervised the employees to make sure they kept production on schedule. She believed that if she did not watch the employees closely and keep them informed of their output, they would slack off and miss production goals. Chang's employees viewed her as an okay boss to work for, as she did take a personal interest in them, and employees were productive. Chang did discipline employees who did not meet standard productivity, and she ended up firing some workers.

Jackie Lee, the manager of a larger department that made instruments to customer specifications, retired, and Chang was given a promotion to manage this department because she did a good job running her old department. Chang never did any design work, nor supervised it. The designers are all engineers who are paid well and who were doing a good job according to their prior supervisor Lee. As Chang observed workers in her usual manner, she realized that all of the designers did their work differently. So she closely observed their work and looked for good ideas that all her employees could follow. It wasn't long before Chang was telling employees how to do a better job of designing the custom specifications. Things were not going too well, however, as employees told Chang that she did not know what she was talking about. Chang tried to rely on her authority, which worked while she was watching employees. However, once she left one employee to observe another, the workers went back to doing things their own way. Chang's employees were complaining about her being a poor manager behind her back.

The complaints about Chang being a poor manager got to Terry Gou. Gou also realized that performance in the design department had gone down since Chang took over as manager. Gou decided to call Chang into his office to discuss how things are going.

GO TO THE INTERNET: To learn more about Terry Gou and Foxconn, visit its Web site **(http://www.foxconn.com)**.

Support your answers to the following questions with specific information from the case and text or with other information you get from the Web or other sources.

1. Which leadership style would Fiedler say Li Chang uses?

2. Using Exhibit 4.3 on page 118, Fiedler's contingency leadership model, what situation and leadership style are appropriate for the production department and for the custom design department?

3. Why isn't Chang doing an effective job in the design department?

4. What would Fiedler and Kerr and Jermier recommend that Chang do to improve performance?

5. Which of the two basic continuum leadership styles would Tannenbaum and Schmidt recommend for Chang and other managers of the design department?

6. Which path–goal leadership style would House recommend for Chang and other managers of the design department?

CUMULATIVE CASE QUESTIONS

7. Describe Chang's personality based on the Big Five model of personality (Chapter 2). How does Chang's personality influence her leadership style?

8. How is Chang's leadership style and behavior affecting employee needs and motivation (Chapter 3)?

9. Which source and type of power does Chang use? Is she using the appropriate power? If not, which power should Chang use (Chapter 4)?

CASE EXERCISE AND ROLE-PLAY

Preparation: Put yourself in the role of Terry Gou. (1) Which normative leadership style would you use with Chang during the meeting? (2) How would you handle the meeting with Chang? (3) What will you say to her?

In-Class Meeting: Break into groups of four to six members, and discuss the three preparation questions.

Role-Play: One person (representing themselves or a group) meets with Chang to role-play the meeting for the class to observe. The person does not identify which normative leadership style they are using. You can discuss the role-play, as discussed next. More than one role-play may also take place.

Observer Role: As the rest of the class members watch the role-play, they should: (1) Identify the leadership style used by the person playing the role of Gou. (2) State if it is the appropriate leadership style for this situation. (3) Look for things that Gou does well, and does not do so well. For your suggested improvements, be sure to have alternative behaviors that are coaching.

Discussion: After the first role-play, the class (1) votes for the leadership style used by the person role-playing Gou, (2) determines the appropriate leadership style, and (3) discusses good behavior and better behavior that could be used. If additional role-plays are used, skip step 2.

VIDEO ►❚ CASE

Leadership at McDonald's

McDonald's has achieved the status of one of the most recognizable franchises across the globe through a mixture of successful marketing, consistent service and products, and strong leadership. Ray Kroc was a visionary leader who inspired others through his charisma. He saw the potential for standardizing an efficient, systematized restaurant model and replicating it across the country. Kroc is quoted as saying, "If you've got time to lean, you've got time to clean," which highlights his goal-oriented and task-focused leadership style that still exists in the corporation today. McDonald's espouses a commitment to investing in the growth and job satisfaction of its employees so they can realize their full potential.

1. What kind of normative leadership style do you think Ray Kroc, as a leader in the first years of McDonald's, likely used? Explain your answer.

2. What are the benefits of a corporate leadership strategy?

SELF-ASSESSMENT 3   Determining Your Preferred Normative Leadership Style

Following are 12 situations. Select the one alternative that most closely describes what you would do in each situation. Don't be concerned with trying to pick the right answer; select the alternative you would really use. Circle a, b, c, or d. Ignore the S _____ part, which will be explained later in Developing Your Leadership Skills Exercise 1.

1. Your rookie crew seems to be developing well. Their need for direction and close supervision is diminishing. What do you do?

   a. Stop directing and overseeing performance unless there is a problem. S _____
   b. Spend time getting to know them personally, but make sure they maintain performance levels. S _____
   c. Make sure things keep going well; continue to direct and oversee closely. S _____
   d. Begin to discuss new tasks of interest to them. S _____

2. You assigned Jill a task, specifying exactly how you wanted it done. Jill deliberately ignored your directions and did it her way. The job will not meet the customer's standards. This is not the first problem you've had with Jill. What do you decide to do?

   a. Listen to Jill's side, but be sure the job gets done right. S _____
   b. Tell Jill to do it again the right way, and closely supervise the job. S _____

   c. Tell her the customer will not accept the job, and let Jill handle it her way. S _____
   d. Discuss the problem and possible solutions to it. S _____

3. Your employees work well together; the department is a real team. It's the top performer in the organization. Because of traffic problems, the president okayed staggered hours for departments. As a result, you can change your department's hours. Several of your workers have suggested changing. You take what action?

   a. Allow the group to decide its hours. S _____
   b. Decide on new hours, explain why you chose them, and invite questions. S _____
   c. Conduct a meeting to get the group members' ideas. Select new hours together, with your approval. S _____
   d. Send around a memo stating the hours you want. S _____

4. You hired Bill, a new employee. He is not performing at the level expected after one month's training. Bill is trying, but he seems to be a slow learner. What do you decide to do?

   a. Clearly explain what needs to be done and oversee his work. Discuss why the procedures are important; support and encourage him. S _____
   b. Tell Bill that his training is over and it's time to pull his own weight. S _____

(continued)

(Self-Assessment 3 continued)

c. Review task procedures and supervise Bill's work closely. S _____

d. Inform Bill that his training is over, and tell him to feel free to come to you if he has any problems. S _____

5. Helen has had an excellent performance record for the last five years. Recently you have noticed a drop in the quality and quantity of her work. She has a family problem. What do you do?

   a. Tell Helen to get back on track and closely supervise her. S _____

   b. Discuss the problem with Helen. Help her realize that her personal problem is affecting her work. Discuss ways to improve the situation. Be supportive and encourage her. S _____

   c. Tell Helen you're aware of her productivity slip, and that you're sure she'll work it out soon. S _____

   d. Discuss the problem and solution with Helen, and supervise her closely. S _____

6. Your organization does not allow smoking in certain areas. You just walked by a restricted area and saw Joan smoking. She has been with the organization for 10 years and is a very productive worker. Joan has never been caught smoking before. What action do you take?

   a. Ask her to put it out, and then leave. S _____

   b. Discuss why she is smoking, and ask what she intends to do about it. S _____

   c. Give her a lecture about not smoking, and check up on her in the future. S _____

   d. Tell her to put it out, watch her do it, and tell her you will check on her in the future. S _____

7. Your department usually works well together with little direction. Recently a conflict between Sue and Tom has caused problems. As a result, you take what action?

   a. Call Sue and Tom together and make them realize how this conflict is affecting the department. Discuss how to resolve it and how you will check to make sure the problem is solved. S _____

   b. Let the group resolve the conflict. S _____

   c. Have Sue and Tom sit down and discuss their conflict and how to resolve it. Support their efforts to implement a solution. S _____

   d. Tell Sue and Tom how to resolve their conflict and closely supervise them. S _____

8. Jim usually does his share of the work with some encouragement and direction. However, he has migraine headaches occasionally and doesn't pull his weight when this happens. The others resent doing Jim's work. What do you decide to do?

   a. Discuss his problem and help him come up with ideas for maintaining his work; be supportive. S _____

   b. Tell Jim to do his share of the work and closely watch his output. S _____

   c. Inform Jim that he is creating a hardship for the others and should resolve the problem by himself. S _____

   d. Be supportive, but set minimum performance levels and ensure compliance. S _____

9. Barbara, your most experienced and productive worker, came to you with a detailed idea that could increase your department's productivity at a very low cost. She can do her present job and this new assignment. You think it's an excellent idea; what do you do?

   a. Set some goals together. Encourage and support her efforts. S _____

   b. Set up goals for Barbara. Be sure she agrees with them and sees you as being supportive of her efforts. S _____

   c. Tell Barbara to keep you informed and to come to you if she needs any help. S _____

   d. Have Barbara check in with you frequently, so that you can direct and supervise her activities. S _____

10. Your boss asked you for a special report. Frank, a very capable worker who usually needs no direction or support, has all the necessary skills to do the job. However, Frank is reluctant because he has never done a report. What do you do?

    a. Tell Frank he has to do it. Give him direction and supervise him closely. S _____

    b. Describe the project to Frank and let him do it his own way. S _____

    c. Describe the benefits to Frank. Get his ideas on how to do it and check his progress. S _____

    d. Discuss possible ways of doing the job. Be supportive; encourage Frank. S _____

11. Jean is the top producer in your department. However, her monthly reports are constantly late and contain errors. You are puzzled because she does everything else with no direction or support. What do you decide to do?

    a. Go over past reports with Jean, explaining exactly what is expected of her. Schedule a meeting so

(continued)

(Self-Assessment 3 continued)

that you can review the next report with her. S ____

b. Discuss the problem with Jean, and ask her what can be done about it; be supportive. S ____

c. Explain the importance of the report. Ask her what the problem is. Tell her that you expect the next report to be on time and error free. S ____

d. Remind Jean to get the next report in on time without errors. S ____

12. Your workers are very effective and like to participate in decision making. A consultant was hired to develop a new method for your department using the latest technology in the field. What do you do?

a. Explain the consultant's method and let the group decide how to implement it. S ____

b. Teach them the new method and closely supervise them. S ____

c. Explain the new method and the reasons that it is important. Teach them the method and make sure the procedure is followed. Answer questions. S ____

d. Explain the new method and get the group's input on ways to improve and implement it. S ____

To determine your preferred normative leadership style, follow these steps:

1. In this chart, circle the letter you selected for each situation.

The column headings (S1 through S4) represent the style you selected.

S1 = Decide, S2 = Consult (Individually or Group), S3 = Facilitate, S4 = Delegate

	S1 D	S2 C	S3 F	S4 DL
1	c	b	d	a
2	b	a	d	c
3	d	b	c	a
4	c	a	d	b
5	a	d	b	c
6	d	c	b	a
7	d	a	c	b
8	b	d	a	c
9	d	b	a	c
10	a	c	d	b
11	a	c	b	d
12	b	c	d	a
Totals	____	____	____	____

2. Add up the number of circled items per column. The column with the highest total is your preferred leadership style. There is no correct or best normative leadership style. Below is an explanation about each style.

S1 Decide Leadership Style. The decide style includes making the decision alone. As a decider, you autocratically tell people how to implement your decision and follow up to make sure performance is maintained, or you tell people what to do and make sure they continue to do it.

S2 Consult (Individually or Group) Leadership Style. As they are both consult styles, we combine individual and group styles for this exercise. The consult style includes talking to individuals or groups for input in a supportive way before you make the decision. As a consulter, after making the decision, you also tell people how to implement your decision and follow up to make sure performance is maintained, while you support and encourage them as they implement your decision.

S3 Facilitate Leadership Style. The facilitate style includes having a group meeting to get input from members as you attempt to support the group to agree on a decision within boundaries set by you; in other words, you still have the final say on the decision. As a facilitator, you are supportive and encouraging to the group members to both make the decision and implement the decision.

S4 Delegate Leadership Style. The delegate style includes letting the group make the decision within limits. As a delegator, you don't tell the group what to do or facilitate the group during the decision making and its implementation.

To determine your flexibility to change styles, do the following. Look at your total score for each column leadership style. The more evenly distributed the totals (for example 4, 4, 4, 4), the more flexible you appear to be at changing your leadership style. Having high numbers in some columns and low in others indicates a strong preference to use or avoid using one or more leadership styles.

Note: There is no right, correct, or best normative leadership style. What this self-assessment exercise does is allow you to know your preferred leadership style and your flexibility at changing styles. In Developing Your Leadership Skills Exercise 1, you will develop your skill to identify the normative leadership styles. In Skill-Development Exercise 2, you will learn to use the normative leadership models to select the most appropriate leadership style for a given situation.

Developing Your Leadership Skills 1

Identifying Normative Leadership Styles

Preparing for This Exercise

Return to the 12 situations in Self-Assessment 3. This time, instead of selecting one of the four options, a–d, identify the normative leadership style used in each option, with the aid of the leadership style definitions in Self-Assessment 3 above. Let's do the following example.

Example

Your rookie crew seems to be developing well. Their need for direction and close supervision is diminishing. What do you do?

1. Stop directing and overseeing performance unless there is a problem. S__DL__

2. Spend time getting to know them personally, but make sure they maintain performance levels. S__C__

3. Make sure things keep going well; continue to direct and oversee closely. S__D__

4. Begin to discuss new tasks of interest to them. S__F__

Answers

5. As indicated on the S__DL__ line, this is the delegate leadership style. As in the definition of delegate, you are leaving the group alone—unless there is a problem (limits)—to make and implement its own decisions about work.

6. As indicated on the S__C__ line, this is the consult leadership style. As in the definition of consult, you are being supportive by getting to know them, yet you are still following up to make sure they get the job done.

7. As indicated on the S__D__ line, this is the decide leadership style. As in the definition of decide, you are following up to make sure performance is maintained.

8. As indicated on the S__F__ line, this is the facilitate leadership style. As in the definition of facilitate, you are facilitating a group decision on possible new tasks for the group to perform.

Now, complete situation numbers 2–12 by determining the leadership style and placing the letters D, C, F, and DL on each of the a–d S__ lines as illustrated above. All four alternative behaviors do represent a different normative leadership style.

Doing This Exercise in Class

Objective

To develop the skill of identifying normative leadership styles.

The primary AACSB competencies developed through this exercise are communication and analytic skills.

Procedure (5–30 minutes) Select an option:

9. The instructor goes over the answers.

10. The instructor calls on students and goes over the answers.

Developing Your Leadership Skills 2

Using the Normative Leadership Models

Preparing for This Exercise

You should have studied the normative leadership model text material. Using Exhibits 4.9 and 4.10 on pages 129 and 130, determine the appropriate leadership style for the given problem statements below. Follow these steps:

1. Determine which normative leadership model to use for the given situation.

2. Answer the variable questions (between 2 and 7) for the problem.

3. Select the appropriate leadership style from the model.

1. Production department manager. You are the manager of a mass-produced manufactured product. You have two major machines in your department with 10 people working on each. You have an important order that needs to be shipped first thing tomorrow morning. Your boss has made it very clear that you must meet this deadline. It's 2:00 and you are right on schedule to meet the order deadline. At 2:15 an employee comes to tell you that one of the machines is smoking a little and making a noise. If you keep running the machine, it may make it until the end of the day and you will deliver the important shipment on time. If you shut down the machine, the manufacturer will not be able to check the machine until tomorrow and you will miss the deadline. You call your boss and there is no answer, and you don't know how else to contact the boss or how long it will be before the boss gets back to you if you leave a message. There are no higher-level managers than you or anyone with more knowledge of the machine than you. Which leadership style should you use?

Step 1   Which model should you use? (_____ time-driven _____ development-driven)

Step 2   Which questions on the normative model Exhibit 4.9 or 4.10 did you answer and how? (H = high, L = low, NA = not answered/skipped)

1. H L or NA   3. H L or NA   5. H L or NA   7. H L or NA
2. H L or NA   4. H L or NA   6. H L or NA

Step 3   Which leadership style is the most appropriate?

_____ decide _____ consult individually _____ consult group _____ facilitate _____ delegate

2. Religious leader. You are the top religious leader of your church with 125 families and 200 members. You have a Doctor of Religious Studies degree with just two years' experience as the head of a church, and no business courses. The church has one paid secretary, three part-time program directors for religious instruction, music, and social activities, plus many volunteers. Your paid staff serves on your advisory board with 10 other church members who are primarily top-level business leaders in the community. You make a yearly budget with the board's approval. The church source of income is weekly member donations. The board doesn't want to operate in the red, and the church has very modest surplus funds. Your volunteer accountant (CPA), who is a board member, asked to meet with you. During the meeting, she informed you that weekly collections are 20 percent below budget and the cost of utilities has increased 25 percent over the yearly budget figure. You are running a large deficit, and at this rate your surplus will be gone in two months. Which leadership style will you use in this crisis?

Step 1   Which model should you use? (_____ time-driven _____ development-driven)

Step 2   Which questions did you answer and how? (H = high, L = low, NA = not answered/skipped)

1. H L or NA   3. H L or NA   5. H L or NA   7. H L or NA
2. H L or NA   4. H L or NA   6. H L or NA

Step 3   Which leadership style is the most appropriate?

_____ decide _____ consult individually _____ consult group _____ facilitate _____ delegate

3. School of business dean. You are the new dean of the school of business at a small private university. Your faculty includes around 20 professors, only two of whom are nontenured, and the average length of employment at the school is 12 years. Upon taking the job, you expect to leave for a larger school in three years. Your primary goal is to start a business school faculty advisory board to improve community relations and school alumni relations, and to raise money for financial aid scholarships. You have already done this in your last job as dean. However, you are new to the area and have no business contacts. You need help to develop a network of alumni and other community leaders fairly quickly if you are to show achieved results on your resume in two-and-a-half years. Your faculty gets along well and is talkative, but when you approach small groups of them they tend to become quiet and disperse. Which primary leadership style would you use to achieve your objective?

Step 1   Which model should you use? (_____ time-driven _____ development-driven)

Step 2   Which questions did you answer and how? (H = high, L = low, NA = not answered/skipped)

1. H L or NA   3. H L or NA   5. H L or NA   7. H L or NA
2. H L or NA   4. H L or NA   6. H L or NA

Step 3   Which leadership style is the most appropriate?

_____ decide _____ consult individually _____ consult group _____ facilitate _____ delegate

4. Dot.com president. You are the president of a dot.com company that has been having financial problems for a few years. As a result, your top two managers left for other jobs. One left four months ago and the other two months ago. With your networking contacts you replaced both managers within a month; thus, they don't have a lot of time on the job and haven't worked together for very long. Plus, they currently do their own thing to get their jobs done. However, they are both very bright, hard-working, and dedicated to your vision of what the company can be. You know how to turn the company around and so do your two key managers. To turn the company around, you and your two managers will have to work together, with the help of all your employees. Virtually all the employees are high-tech specialists who want to be included in decision making. Your business partners have no more money to invest. If you cannot turn a profit in four to five months, you will most likely go bankrupt. Which primary leadership style would you use to achieve your objective?

Step 1   Which model should you use? (_____ time-driven _____ development-driven)

Step 2   Which questions did you answer and how? (H = high, L = low, NA = not answered/skipped)

1. H L or NA   3. H L or NA   5. H L or NA   7. H L or NA
2. H L or NA   4. H L or NA   6. H L or NA

Step 3   Which leadership style is the most appropriate?

_____ decide _____ consult individually _____ consult group _____ facilitate _____ delegate

Doing This Exercise in Class

Objective

To develop your skill at determining the appropriate leadership style to use in a given situation using the normative leadership models, Exhibits 4.9 and 4.10.

The primary AACSB competencies developed through this exercise are communications and analytic skills.

Experience

You will use the normative leadership models in four given problem situations.

Procedure 1 *(10–15 minutes)* The instructor goes over the normative leadership models and uses the models to illustrate how to select the appropriate leadership style for problem situation 1.

Procedure 2 *(10–20 minutes)* Break into groups of two or three and use the models to determine the appropriate leadership style for situations 2–4 in the preparation above. This is followed by the instructor going over or just stating the answers to situations 2–4.

Conclusion

The instructor may lead a class discussion and/or make concluding remarks.

Apply It *(2–4 minutes)* What did I learn from this experience? How will I apply normative leadership in the future?

_____

_____

_____

Sharing

In the group, or to the entire class, volunteers may give their answers to the "Apply It" questions.

SELF-ASSESSMENT 4   Your Leadership Continuum and Path-Goal Leadership Styles

You have already determined your preferred LPC contingency leadership style (Self-Assessment 1 on page 116) and your preferred normative leadership style (Self-Assessment 3 on pages 141–143). Using Self-Assessment 4, you can determine your other preferred styles by checking your preferred normative leadership style in the first column. In the same row, the columns to the right show your continuum and path-goal preferred leadership styles. Does your preferred leadership style match your personality for Self-Assessment 2 on page 136?

NORMATIVE LEADERSHIP STYLE	LEADERSHIP CONTINUUM STYLE	PATH-GOAL LEADERSHIP STYLE
Decide	1 Boss-centered	Directive
Consult (individually or group)	2 or 3	Achievement-oriented
Facilitate	4 or 5	Supportive
Delegate	6 or 7 Subordinate-centered	Participative

Influencing: Power, Politics, Networking, and Negotiation

Learning Outcomes

After studying this chapter, you should be able to:

1. Explain the differences between position power and personal power. p. 149

2. Discuss the differences among legitimate, reward, coercive, and referent power. p. 149

3. Discuss how power and politics are related. p. 161

4. Describe how money and politics have a similar use. p. 161

5. List and explain the steps in the networking process. p. 167

6. List the steps in the negotiation process. p. 174

7. Explain the relationships among negotiation and conflict, influencing tactics, power, and politics. p. 174

8. Define the following **key terms** (in order of appearance in the chapter):

power	connection power
legitimate power	politics
reward power	networking
coercive power	reciprocity
referent power	one-minute self-sell
expert power	negotiating
information power	

OPENING CASE *APPLICATION*

You may have heard that the NBA Dallas Mavericks won their first national basketball championship title in 2011. But did you know that the team is owned by the controversial Mark Cuban. He is known as the billionaire entrepreneur now focusing on the sports and entertainment industries. Cuban's holdings also include ownership stakes in Landmark Theatres, Magnolia Pictures, and the HDTV cable network HDNet. He is worth $2.5 billion and is ranked in the top 150 on the Forbes 400 Richest Americans list.[1]

But Mark Cuban didn't start at the top. Truth be told, Mark Cuban was the last guy anyone would have expected to become a billionaire. Here is Cuban's entrepreneurial story. His family's last name, Cuban, was shortened from Chabenisky when his grandparents, Russian Jews, arrived at Ellis Island. Cuban grew up in Mt. Lebanon, Pennsylvania, a suburb of Pittsburgh, in a working-class family. Cuban's first step into the business world occurred at age 12, when he sold garbage bags door-to-door. Soon after, he was selling stamps, coins, and baseball cards, which paid for his business degree at Indiana University. While attending IU, Cuban bought a Bloomington bar and named it Motley's, raising the money by selling shares to his friends.

After college, he moved to Dallas, Texas, and went into computer sales. Cuban and Martin Woodall founded Micro-Solutions, and they sold the company for $6 million; Cuban

netted approximately $2 million after taxes on the deal. Cuban moved to Los Angeles for a time; there he day-traded and took acting lessons. Todd Wagner proposed starting AudioNet, which later became Broadcast.com, and Cuban leapt at the chance. Broadcast.com's initial public offering (IPO) stock price was $18, but it climbed to $62 at the end of the first day; Cuban was suddenly $85 million richer. They sold Broadcast.com to Yahoo!, and Cuban became worth more than $1 billion in Yahoo! stock. With this fortune, he entered the sports and entertainment industries with his partner Wagner.[2]

OPENING CASE QUESTIONS:

1. What sources and types of power does Mark Cuban have, and why has he had problems with power?

2. Why are organizational politics important to Mark Cuban's enterprises?

3. How has Mark Cuban used networking?

4. What types of negotiations does Mark Cuban engage in?

5. Is Mark Cuban ethical in influencing others?

Can you answer any of these questions? You'll find answers to these questions and learn more about Mark Cuban's businesses and leadership style throughout the chapter.

B esides excellent work, what does it take to get ahead in an organization? To climb the corporate ladder, you will have to influence people[3]—to gain power, play organizational politics, network, and negotiate to get what you want. These related concepts are the topics of this chapter. Recall from our definition of leadership (Chapter 1) that leadership is the "*influencing*" process of leaders and followers to achieve organizational objectives through change. Leaders and followers influence each other, because we are all potential leaders. Influencing is so important that it is called the essence of leadership. Influence has a direct effect on organizational performance and your career success.[4] In essence, this chapter is a continuation of Chapter 3; it focuses on leadership behavior by explaining how leaders influence others at the individual level of analysis. Let's begin with power.

Power

If we want to understand why organizations do the things they do, we must consider the power of top executives. Power is about achieving influence over others.[5] However, *power is the leader's potential influence over followers*. Because power is the *potential* to influence, you do not actually have to use power to influence others. Often, it is the perception of power, rather than the actual use of power, that influences others. Power is based on certain qualities or capabilities, but power itself is transactional and flows out of relationships, real or perceived.[6] So understanding power is an important leadership topic.[7] In this section, we discuss sources of power, types of power, influencing tactics, ways to increase your power, and how power is acquired and lost.

Learning Outcome 1 *Explain the differences between position power and personal power.*

Sources of Power

There are two sources of power: position power and personal power.

Position Power

Position power is derived from top management, and it is delegated down the chain of command. Thus, a person who is in a management position has more potential power to influence than an employee who is not a manager. Power is used to get people to do something they otherwise would not have done. Some people view power as the ability to make people do what they want them to do or the ability to do something to people or for people. These definitions may be true, but they tend to give power a manipulative, negative connotation, as does the old saying by Lord Acton, "Power corrupts. Absolute power corrupts absolutely."

Within an organization, power should be viewed in a positive sense. Without power, managers could not achieve organizational objectives. Leadership and power go hand-in-hand. Leadership is the art of persuading others to want to do what you want them to do. Martin Luther King, Jr. said, "Power properly understood is nothing but the ability to achieve purpose. It is the strength to bring about change." Employees are not influenced without a reason, and the reason is often the power a manager has over them. Managers rely on position power to get the job done.

Personal Power

Personal power is derived from the followers based on the leader's behavior. Charismatic leaders have personal power. Again, followers do have some power over leaders. Followers must consent to the governing influence of managers for the organization to be successful. Unions are often the result of follower dissatisfaction with management behavior and the desire to balance power. Followers can restrict performance, sabotage operations, initiate grievances, hold demonstrations, make complaints to higher managers, and hurt the leader's reputation. Power can be gained or lost—we will discuss how later.

The two sources of power are relatively independent, yet they have some overlap. For example, a manager can have only position power or both position and personal power, but a nonmanager can have only personal power. Today companies are looking for a different kind of leadership.[8] Unlike the autocratic leaders of the past, leaders share power (*empowerment*) by pushing power and decision making down the organization.[9] Therefore, as a manager, it is best to have both position power and personal power.

Learning Outcome 2 *Discuss the differences among legitimate, reward, coercive, and referent power.*

Types of Power and Influencing Tactics, and Ways to Increase Your Power

Seven types of power are illustrated, along with their source of power and influencing tactics, in Exhibit 5.1. In the late 1950s, French and Raven distinguished five types of power (reward, coercive, legitimate, expert, and referent).[10] Connection (politics) and information power have been added to update the important types of power. We will discuss these seven types of power, and explore ways to increase each type with *influencing tactics.* You can acquire power, without taking it away from others. Generally, power is given to those who get results and have good human relations skills.

Legitimate Power

Legitimate power *is based on the user's position power, given by the organization.* It is also called the *legitimization influencing tactic.* Managers assign work, coaches decide who plays, and teachers award grades. These three positions have formal authority from the organization. Without this legitimate authority, they could not influence followers in the same way.[11] Employees tend to feel that they ought to do what their manager says within the scope of the job.

Appropriate Use of Legitimate Power   Employees agree to comply with management authority in return for the benefits of membership. The use of legitimate power is appropriate when asking people to do something that is within the scope of their job. Most day-to-day manager–employee interactions are based on legitimate power.

When using legitimate power, it is also helpful to use the *consultation influencing tactic.* With consultation, you seek others' input about achieving an objective and are open to developing a plan together to achieve the objective. This process is also known as *participative management* and *empowering employees.* We will talk more about participative management throughout the book.

Legitimate Use of Rational Persuasion. When we as managers are meeting objectives through our employees, or dealing with higher-level managers and people over whom we have no authority, it is often helpful to use the *rational persuasion influencing tactic.* Rational persuasion includes logical arguments with factual evidence to persuade others to implement your recommended action.

When we use rational persuasion, we need to develop a persuasive case based on the other party's needs, not ours. What seems logical and reasonable to you may not be to others. With multiple parties, a different logical argument may be made to meet individual needs. Logical arguments generally work well with people whose behavior is more influenced by thinking than by emotions. It works well when the leader and follower have the same shared interest and objectives.

When trying to persuade others to do something for us, it is helpful to put forth our request when they are in a good mood. To get people in a good mood, the *ingratiation influencing tactic* may be used by being friendly and praising others before you ask them for what you want. The initial compliment must be sincere (use the giving praise model in Chapter 3), and it helps to determine if the other party is in a good mood or not. If not, it is generally a good idea to wait to ask no matter how rational your request.

EXHIBIT **5.1**   Sources and Types of Power with Influencing Tactics

Source	Position Power ———————————————→			←——————————————— Personal Power			
Types	Legitimate	Reward	Coercive	Connection	Information	Expert	Referent
Tactics	Legitimization Consultation Rational persuasion Ingratiation	Exchange	Pressure	Coalitions	Rational persuasion Inspirational appeal	Rational persuasion	Personal appeal Inspirational appeal

Ingratiation is discussed in Chapter 7 as one of the tactics available to followers in influencing the social exchange relationship between leaders and members. This does lead to the creation of high-quality leader–member exchange (LMX).

Using Rational Persuasion   When you develop a rational persuasion, follow these guidelines:

- Explain the reason why the objective needs to be met. Managers cannot simply give orders, since employees want to know the rationale for decisions. Even if we disagree with higher-level managers' decisions, as a manager it is our job to give employees the rationale for their decisions.

- Explain how the other party will benefit by meeting the objective. People respond to incentives.[12] Try to think of the other party's often-unasked question: what's in it for me? Sell the personal benefits to others, rather than focusing on how the organization benefits by achieving the objective.

- Provide evidence that the objective can be met. Remember the importance of expectancy motivation theory (Chapter 3). When possible, demonstrate how to do a task; seeing is believing. Give examples of how others have met the objective. Offer a detailed step-by-step plan. Be supportive and encouraging, showing your confidence in the followers to meet the objective.

- Explain how potential problems and concerns will be handled. Know the potential problems and concerns and deal with them in the rational persuasion. If others bring up problems that you have not anticipated, which is likely, be sure to address them. Do not ignore people's concerns or make simple statements like, "That will not happen, we don't have to worry about that." Get the followers' input on how to resolve any possible problems as they come up. This will help gain their commitment.

- If there are competing plans to meet the objective, explain why one proposal is better than the others. Do your homework. We need to be well-versed about the competition. To simply say "my idea is better than theirs" won't cut it. Be sure to state *how* your plan is superior to the others and the weaknesses and problems with the other plans.

Increasing Legitimate Power   To increase legitimate power, follow these guidelines:

- To have legitimate power, we need management experience, which could also be a part of the job—for example, being in charge of a team project with peers. Work at gaining people's perception that we do have power. Remember that people's perception that we have power gives us power.

- Exercise authority regularly. Follow up to make sure that policies, procedures, and rules are implemented and that objectives are achieved.

- Follow the guidelines for using rational persuasion, especially when authority is questioned.

- Back up your authority with *rewards and punishment,* our next two types of power, which are primarily based on having legitimate power.

Reward Power

Reward power *is based on the user's ability to influence others with something of value to them.* Reward power affects performance expectations and achievement. In a management position, use positive reinforcements to influence behavior, with incentives such as praise, recognition (with pins, badges, hats, or jackets), special assignments or desirable activities, pay raises, bonuses, and promotions. Many organizations, including Kentucky Fried Chicken (KFC), have employee-of-the-month awards. Tupperware holds rallies for its salespeople, and almost everyone gets something—ranging from pins to lucrative prizes for top performers. A leader's power is strong or weak based on ability to punish and reward followers. The more power, the more favorable the situation for the leader (Chapter 4).

An important part of reward power is having control over resources, such as allocating expense and budget funds.[13] This is especially true for scarce resources. Upper- and middle-level managers usually have more discretion in giving rewards (including scarce resources) than do lower-level managers.

Appropriate Use of Reward Power   When employees do a good job, they should be rewarded, as discussed with reinforcement motivation theory (Chapter 3). Catching people doing things right and rewarding them is a great motivator to continue the behavior. When dealing with higher-level managers and people over whom we have no authority, we can use the *exchange influencing tactic* by offering some type of reward for helping meet our objective. The incentive for exchange can be anything of value, such as scarce resources, information, advice or assistance on another task, or career and political support. Exchange is common in reciprocity (you do something for me and I'll do something for you—or you owe me one, for a later reward), which we will discuss in a later section on organizational politics. For example, when Professor Jones is recruiting a student aide, he tells candidates that if they are selected and do a good job, he will recommend them for an MBA fellowship at Suffolk University, where he has connection power. As a result he gets good, qualified help, at minimum wages, while helping both his student aide and his alma mater. The discussion of LMX theory in Chapter 7 emphasizes that exchange influencing tactics differ for followers in the leader's in-group and those in the out-group. In return for their loyalty and commitment to a leader, members of the in-group get rewards such as better assignments, higher positive job evaluations, and greater involvements in decision making. They are more likely to be influenced using tactics such as consultation, rational persuasion, and ingratiation. Out-group members are managed strictly according to the terms of the employment contract.

Increasing Reward Power   To increase reward power, follow these guidelines:

- Gain and maintain control over evaluating employees' performance and determining their raises, promotions, and other rewards.

- Find out what others value, and try to reward people in that way. Using praise can help increase our power. Employees who feel they are appreciated rather than used will give us more power.

- Let people know we control rewards, and state our criteria for giving rewards. However, don't promise more than you can deliver. Reward as promised, and don't use rewards to manipulate or for personal benefit.

Coercive Power

The use of coercive power *involves punishment and withholding of rewards to influence compliance.* It is also called the *pressure influencing tactic*. From fear of reprimands, probation, suspension, or dismissal, employees often do as their manager requests. The fear of lost valued outcomes or rewards—such as receiving poor performance evaluations, losing raises and benefits, being assigned to less-desirable jobs, and hurting a relationship—causes employees to do as requested. Other examples of coercive power include verbal abuse, humiliation, and ostracism. Group members also use coercive power (peer pressure) to enforce group norms. Some managers use coercion to gain resources.[14]

WORK Application **1**

Select a present or past manager who has or had coercive power. Give a specific example of how he or she uses or used reward and punishment to achieve an objective. Overall, how effective is (or was) this manager at using rewards and punishment?

Appropriate Use of Coercive Power   Coercive power is appropriate to use in maintaining discipline and enforcing rules. When employees are not willing to do as requested, coercive power may be the only way to gain compliance. In fact, without it, employees may not take you seriously and ignore your requests. Coercion is effective when applied to a small percentage of followers under conditions considered legitimate by most of them. When leaders use coercion on a large scale against followers, it undermines their authority and creates a hostile opposition that may seek to restrict their power or to remove them from their position.[15] Employees tend to resent managers' use of coercive power. There has been a general decline in use of coercion by all types of leaders. Managers that bully employees are being fired. So keep the use of coercive power to a minimum by using it only as a last resort.

Increasing Coercive Power   To increase coercive power, follow these guidelines.

- Gain authority to use punishment and withhold rewards. However, make sure employees know the rules and penalties, give prior warnings, understand the situation, remain calm and helpful, encourage improvement, use legitimate punishments (withhold rewards) that fit the infraction, and administer punishment in private.

- Don't make rash threats; do not use coercion to manipulate others or to gain personal benefits.

- Be persistent. If we request that followers do something and we don't follow up to make sure it is done, followers will take advantage of the situation and ignore our request. Set specific deadlines for task completion and frequently check progress. Put the deadline and progress checks on the calendar to make sure of persistently following up.

YOU Make the **ETHICAL** Call

5.1 *Following Orders*

The armed forces are hierarchical by rank, based on power. Officers tend to give orders to troops by using legitimate power. When orders are followed, reward power is common. When orders are not followed, coercive power is commonly used to get the troops to implement the order. The conditioning of the military is to respect the power of authority and to follow orders, usually without questioning authority.

1. Is it ethical and socially responsible to teach people to follow orders without questioning authority in the military or any other organization?

2. What would you do if your boss asked you to follow orders that you thought might be unethical? (Some options include: just do it; don't say anything but don't do it; question the motives; look closely at what you are asked to do; go to your boss's boss to make sure it's okay to do it; tell the boss you will not do it; ask the boss to do it him- or herself; blow the whistle to an outside source like the government or media; and so on.)

3. Is following orders a good justification for unethical practices?

Referent Power

Referent power *is based on the user's personal relationships with others.* It is also called the *personal appeals influencing tactic* based on loyalty and friendship. Power stems primarily from relationships with the person using power. Charismatic leaders tend to use referent power.[16] The personal feelings of "liking" or the desire to be liked by the leaders also gives referent power.

Leaders can also use the *inspirational appeals influencing tactic.* The leader appeals to the follower's values, ideals, and aspirations, or increases self-confidence by displaying his or her feelings to appeal to the follower's emotions and enthusiasm. So rational persuasion uses logic, whereas inspirational persuasion appeals to emotions and enthusiasm. Thus, inspirational appeals generally work well with people whose behavior is more influenced by emotions than logical thinking. Great sports coaches, such as Vince Lombardi, are well respected for their inspirational appeals to get the team to win the game. Have you heard the football "win one for the Gipper" saying from Notre Dame?

To be inspirational, we need to understand the values, hopes, fears, and goals of followers. We need to be positive and optimistic and create a vision of how things will be when the objective is achieved. Use nonverbal communication to bring emotions to the verbal message, such as raising and lowering voice tone and pausing to intensify key points, showing moist eyes or a few tears, and maintaining eye contact. Facial expressions, body movement, and gestures like pounding on a table effectively reinforce verbal messages.[17] You can also include the ingratiation influencing tactic within your inspirational appeal.

Appropriate Use of Referent Power   The use of referent power is particularly appropriate for people with weak, or no, position power, such as with peers. Referent power is needed in self-managed teams because leadership should be shared.

Increasing Referent Power   To increase referent power, follow these guidelines:

- Develop people skills, which are covered in all chapters. Remember that we don't have to be a manager to have referent power. The better we get along with more diverse people (good working relationships), the more referent power we will have.[18]

- Work at relationships with managers and peers. Our relationship with our manager will have a direct effect on our job satisfaction. Gain the manager's confidence in order to get more power. Remember that the success of the manager and peers depends to some extent on you and your performance.

Expert Power

Expert power *is based on the user's skill and knowledge.* Being an expert makes other people dependent on you. Employees with expert power have personal power and are often promoted to management positions. People often respect an expert, and the fewer people who possess an expertise, the more power the expert individual has. For example, because so few people have the ability to become the CEO of a large corporation, they have the power to command multimillion-dollar contracts, and superstars at all levels are capable of negotiating distinctive employment conditions.

The more people come to us for advice, the greater is our expert power. In the changing global economy, expert power is becoming more important. It's wise to be sure that our expertise does not become unimportant or obsolete. Experts commonly use the *rational persuasion influencing tactic* because people believe they know what they are saying and that it is correct.

Appropriate Use of Expert Power   Managers, particularly at lower levels, are often—but not always—experts within their departments. New managers frequently depend on employees who have expertise in how the organization runs and know how to get things done politically. Thus, followers can have considerable influence over the leader. Expert power is essential to employees who are working with people from other departments and organizations. Because such employees have no direct position power to use, being seen as an expert gives them credibility and power.

WORK Application 2
Select a past or present job. Who did (or do) you usually go to for expertise and information? Give examples of when you went to someone for expertise and when you went to someone for information.

Increasing Expert Power   To increase expert power, follow these guidelines:

- To become an expert, take all the training and educational programs the organization provides.

- Attend meetings of your trade or professional associations, and read their publications (magazines and journals) to keep up with current trends in your field. Write articles to be published. Become an officer in the organization.

- Keep up with the latest technology. Volunteer to be the first to learn something new.

- Project a positive self-concept (Chapter 2), and let people know about your expertise by developing a reputation for having expertise. You have no expert power unless others perceive that you have an expertise and come to you for advice. You may want to display diplomas, licenses, publications, and awards.

Information Power

Information power *is based on the user's data desired by others.* Information power involves access to vital information and control over its distribution to others. Managers often have access to information that is not available to peers and subordinates. Thus, they have the opportunity to distort information to influence others to meet their objective. Distortion of information includes selective editing to promote only our position, giving a biased interpretation of data and even presenting false information. Managers also rely on employees for information, so followers sometimes have the opportunity to distort information that influences management decisions. Distortion of information is an ethical issue. Some administrative assistants have more information and are more helpful in answering questions than the managers they work for.

Appropriate Use of Information Power   An important part of the manager's job is to convey information. Employees often come to managers for information on what to do and how to do it. Leaders use information power when making *rational persuasion* and often with *inspirational appeals.* Personal computers give organizational members information power, since information flows freely through informal channels.

Increasing Information Power   To increase information power, follow these guidelines:

- Have information flow through you. For example, if customer leads come in to the company and all sales representatives have direct access to them, the sales manager has weak information power. However, if all sales leads go directly to the manager, who then assigns the leads to sales representatives, the manager has strong information power. Having control of information makes it easier to cover up failures and mistakes (another ethical question), and to let others know of your accomplishments, which can also increase expertise.

- Know what is going on in the organization. Provide service and information to other departments. Serve on committees because it gives both information and a chance to increase connection power.

- Develop a network of information sources, and gather information from them.[19] You will learn how to network later in this chapter.

Connection Power

Connection power *is based on the user's relationships with influential people.* Connection power is also a form of politics, the topic of our next major section, but first we discuss how power is acquired and lost. You rely on the use of contacts or friends who can influence the person you are dealing with. The right connections can give power, or

WORK Application 3
1. Think of a present or past manager. Which type of power does (or did) the manager use most often? Explain.

2. Which one or two suggestions for increasing your power base are the most relevant to you? Explain.

at least the perception of having power. If people know you are friendly with people in power, they are more apt to do as you request. For example, if the owner's son has no position power but wants something done, he may gain compliance by making a comment about speaking to his father or mother about the lack of cooperation.

Sometimes it is difficult to influence others all alone. With a *coalition influencing tactic* you use influential people to help persuade others to meet your objective. There is power and safety in numbers. The more people you can get on your side, the more influence you can have on others. Superiors, peers, subordinates, and outsiders can help you influence others. We can tell others who support our idea, have the supporters with us when we make a request, have supporters follow up, or ask a higher authority to get what we need done. Coalitions are also a political strategy—a tactic that will be discussed again later in this chapter.

Appropriate Use of Connection Power   When you are looking for a job or promotions, connections can help. There is a lot of truth in the statement, "It's not what you know; it's who you know." Connection power can also help you to get resources you need and increase business.[20]

Increasing Connection Power   To increase connection power, follow these guidelines:

- Expand your network of contacts with important managers who have power.

- Join the "in-crowd" and the "right" associations and clubs. Participating in sports like golf may help you meet influential people.

- Follow the guidelines for using the coalition influencing tactic. When you want something, identify the people who can help you attain it, make coalitions, and win them over to your side.

- Get people to know your name. Get all the publicity you can. Have your accomplishments known by the people in power; send them notices without sounding like a bragger.

In Chapter 9, we discuss charismatic and transformational leadership models. Effective charismatic and transformational leaders are more likely to rely on connection, information, expert, and referent power to influence followers. They are less likely to employ coercive power. Transformational and transactional leaders rely heavily on legitimate and reward power. It is not always the case that charismatic leaders have position power and thus their legitimate power is tied to the power of their cause and not to any formal authority.

Now that you have read about nine influencing tactics within seven types of power, see Exhibit 5.1 for a review, and test your ability to apply them in Concept Applications 1 and 2. Then, complete Self-Assessment 1 to better understand how your personality traits relate to how you use power and influencing tactics to get what you want.

WORK Application 4

Give three different influencing tactics you or someone else used to achieve an objective in an organization you have worked for.

_____

_____

_____

_____

CONCEPT APPLICATION 1
Influencing Tactics

For each situation, select the most appropriate individual tactic that will enhance your chances of getting a desired outcome. Write the appropriate letter in the blank before each item.

a. rational persuasion	d. ingratiation	g. coalition
b. inspirational appeals	e. personal appeals	h. legitimization
c. consultation	f. exchange	i. pressure

(continued)

(Concept Application 1 continued)

_____ 1. You believe you deserve a pay raise, and have ideas about why you should get a raise. So you decide to talk to your manager about it.

_____ 2. You serve on a committee, and next week the committee members will elect officers. Nominations and elections will be done at the same time. You are interested in being the president. But you don't want to nominate yourself and you certainly don't want to run and lose.

_____ 3. You have an employee who regularly passes in assignments late. The assignment you are giving the person now is very important; it must be done on time.

_____ 4. You are the manager and have an idea about how to increase performance of your department. You are not too sure if it will work, or if the employees will like the idea.

_____ 5. You are in sales and want some information about a new product that has not yet been produced, nor has it been announced inside or outside the company. You know a person in the production department who has been working on the new product, so you decide to contact that person.

_____ 6. The production person from situation 5 has given you the information you were looking for. She calls a week later to ask you for some information.

_____ 7. Five of your 15 crew workers did not come in to work today. You have a large order that should be shipped out at the end of the day. It will be tough for the small crew to meet the deadline.

_____ 8. Although the crew members in situation 7 have agreed to push to meet the deadline, you would like to give them some help. You have an employee whose job is to perform routine maintenance and cleaning. She is not one of your 15 crew workers. However, you realize that she could be of some help filling in for the five missing workers. You decide to talk to this nonunion employee about working with the crew for two hours today.

_____ 9. The nonunion employee in situation 8 is resisting helping the other workers. She is basically asking the unasked question, "What's in it for me?"

_____ 10. You have an employee who is very moody at times. You want this employee, who has a big ego, to complete an assignment before the established due date.

CONCEPT APPLICATION 2
Using Power

Identify the relevant type of power to use in each situation to get the best results. Write the appropriate letter in the blank before each item.

a. coercive

b. connection

c. reward or legitimate

d. referent

e. information or expert

_____ 11. Once again, Hal, one of your worst employees, has ignored one of your directives.

_____ 12. Aden, who needs some direction and encouragement from you to maintain production, is not working to standard today. As occasionally happens, he claims that he does not feel well but cannot afford to take time off. You have to get an important customer order shipped today.

(continued)

(Concept Application 2 continued)

_____ 13. Juan, one of your best workers, who needs little direction from you, recently hit a performance slump. You're quite sure that a personal problem is affecting his work.

_____ 14. Money for resources is allocated by a committee, which is very political in nature. You want a new computerized machine for production to help your department do a better job.

_____ 15. Jeff, one of your best workers, wants a promotion. He has talked to you about getting ahead and has asked you to help prepare him for when the opportunity comes.

SELF-ASSESSMENT 1   Influencing Tactics, Power, and Personality Traits

Review the nine influencing tactics. Which ones do you tend to use most often to help you get what you want? Also review your personality profile self-assessment exercises in Chapter 2.

Surgency/High Need for Power

If you have n Pow, you are apt to try to influence others, and you enjoy it. You tend to hate to lose, and when you don't get what you want, it bothers you. Thus, you are more likely to use harder methods of influence and power, such as pressure, exchange, coalitions, and legitimization, than other personality types. You probably also like to use rational persuasion and don't understand why people don't think or see things the way you do. Be careful; use socialized rather than personalized power to influence others.

Agreeableness/High Need for Affiliation

If you have a high n Aff, you are apt to be less concerned about influencing others and gaining power than about getting along with them. Thus, you are more likely to use softer methods of influence, such as personal and inspirational appeals and ingratiation, as well as rational appeals. You may tend not to seek power, and even avoid it.

Conscientiousness/High Need for Achievement

If you have a high n Ach, you tend to be between the other two approaches to influencing others. You tend to have clear goals and work hard to get what you want, which often requires influencing others to help you. So, you don't want power for its own sake, only to get what you want. But you like to play by the rules and may tend to use rational persuasion frequently.

Based on the preceding information, briefly describe how your personality affects the ways you attempt to influence others.

_____

_____

_____

Acquiring and Losing Power

Power is needed to bring about organizational change. Power and organizations can affect each other. Research supports that managers and employees can find it advantageous to change their firms to acquire more power, just as organizations limit what they can do. Managers can create and acquire the resources that expand their authority.[21] However, power imbalances can lead to overt conflict and a struggle for power (some management union situations for example) that impede individual, group, and organizational performance.[22]

Personal power is more easily gained and lost than position power. *Social exchange theory* explains how power is gained and lost as reciprocal influence processes occur over time between leaders and followers in small groups. Social interaction is an exchange of benefits or favors. Friendship is a social exchange, and some people place a higher value on the friendships they have at work than on the work itself. Group members especially watch managers, because they each have expectations of the leader. If the leader meets follower expectations, power is acquired and maintained. If not, the leader loses status and expert power with followers, and they may undermine the leader's legitimate authority as well. Power can change over time as followers may fight to gain the upper hand in a battle for power.[23]

OPENING CASE *APPLICATION*

1. What sources and types of power does Mark Cuban have, and why has he had problems with power?

Mark Cuban is used to getting his own way, and he wants to be famous and influential as he attempts to reorder the landscape of professional sports and entertainment. He has position power as an owner of four businesses. Because of his great success, many people as followers look up to him. As a business owner, Cuban has legitimate power, and he rewards his employees for doing a good job. He has used coercive power (he fired the Mavericks' coach), he has some referent power, and he is viewed as an expert in business. He also has information power and has connections with some influential people.

On the dark side, Cuban's behavior has cost him money and respect. Cuban is not your typical pro sports team owner who watches the games from the owner's box. He sits next to the Mavericks team bench and yells at the players. He is also known to go out on the court during games and listen in on team huddles. Cuban has stormed into the locker room and cursed out the players when they lost. He has berated the referees and even gone after them on the court, which has led to fines and problems with the NBA. Some players and other owners view Cuban as being out of control and question when he will grow up.

Cuban admits that his behavior has worked against him in multiple situations. He'd like to own more pro sports teams, but other professional sports leagues turned him down, partly because of his NBA behavior. He has also alienated key strategic partners while trying to get HDNet off the ground. Three of the largest cable operators—Comcast, Cox, and Cablevision—refused to carry the channel or its sister network, HDNet Movies, although ultimately HDNet reached an agreement with Comcast.[24]

Organizational Politics

Management has a political dimension. Just as the nine influencing tactics (see Exhibit 5.1) are used within the seven types of power, these tactics are also used in organizational politics. For example, to develop a successful rational persuasion, you need to base it within organizational politics. In this section, we discuss the nature of organizational politics, political behavior, and guidelines for developing political skills. But first, determine your own use of political behavior by completing Self-Assessment 2.

SELF-ASSESSMENT 2   Use of Political Behavior

Select the response that best describes your actual or planned use of the following behavior on the job. Place a number from 1 to 5 on the line before each statement.

1 — 2 — 3 — 4 — 5
Rarely   Occasionally   Usually

_____ 1. I use my personal contacts to get a job and promotions.

_____ 2. I try to find out what is going on in all the organizational departments.

_____ 3. I dress the same way as the people in power and take on the same interests (watch or play sports, join the same clubs, and so forth).

_____ 4. I purposely seek contacts and network with higher-level managers.

_____ 5. If upper management offered me a raise and promotion requiring me to move to a new location, I'd say yes even if I did not want to move.

_____ 6. I get along with everyone, even those considered to be difficult to get along with.

_____ 7. I try to make people feel important by complimenting them.

_____ 8. I do favors for others and use their favors in return, and I thank people and send them thank-you notes.

_____ 9. I work at developing a good working relationship with my manager.

_____ 10. I ask my manager and other people for their advice.

_____ 11. When a person opposes me, I still work to maintain a positive working relationship with that person.

_____ 12. I'm courteous, pleasant, and positive with others.

_____ 13. When my manager makes a mistake, I never publicly point out the error.

_____ 14. I am more cooperative (I compromise) than competitive (I seek to get my own way).

_____ 15. I tell the truth.

_____ 16. I avoid saying negative things about my manager and others behind their backs.

_____ 17. I work at getting people to know me by name and face by continually introducing myself.

_____ 18. I ask some satisfied customers and people who know my work to let my manager know how good a job I'm doing.

_____ 19. I try to win contests and get prizes, pins, and other awards.

_____ 20. I send notices of my accomplishments to higher-level managers and company newsletters.

To determine your overall political behavior, add the 20 numbers you selected as your answers. The number will range from 20 to 100. The higher your score, the more political behavior you use. Place your score here _____ and on the continuum below.

20 — 30 — 40 — 50 — 60 — 70 — 80 — 90 — 100
Nonpolitical   Political

To determine your use of political behavior in four areas, add the numbers for the following questions and divide by the number of questions to get the average score in each area.

A. *Learning the organizational culture and power players*

Questions 1–5 total: _____ divided by 5 = _____

B. *Developing good working relationships, especially with your boss*

Questions 6–12 total: _____ divided by 7 = _____

C. *Being a loyal, honest team player*

Questions 13–16 total: _____ divided by 4 = _____

D. *Gaining recognition*

Questions 17–20 total: _____ divided by 4 = _____

The higher the average score of items A–D, the more you use this type of political behavior. Do you tend to use them all equally, or do you use some more than others?

Learning Outcome 3 *Discuss how power and politics are related.*

The Nature of Organizational Politics

There is a relationship between power and organizational politics, as executives with political skills have greater power and influence.[25] *Politics* is the process of gaining and using power. Most executives believe that organizations are, at least to an extent, political arenas. Consequently, you must possess both political will and political skill to survive, and to be a successful leader.[26] The amount and importance of politics vary from organization to organization. However, larger organizations tend to be more political; and the higher the level of management, the more important politics becomes.

Learning Outcome 4 *Describe how money and politics have a similar use.*

Politics Is a Medium of Exchange

Like power, politics often has a negative connotation due to people who abuse political power. Organizational politics is ever-present and has widespread effects on critical processes (e.g., performance evaluation, resource allocation, and decision making) that influence organizational effectiveness and efficiency, and it can be beneficial to groups and organizations.[27]

A positive way to view politics is to realize that it is simply a social medium of exchange. *Social Exchange Theory* regards exchanges between people as "social," as opposed to economic, in nature.[28] Like money, politics in and of itself is inherently neither good nor bad. Politics is simply a system of getting what we want. In our economy, money is the medium of exchange (tangible currency); in an organization, social politics is the medium of exchange (political behavior). Favors are the currency by which productivity is purchased and goodwill is gained. You cannot really do a job well without political skills. Politically effective leaders marshal resources to accomplish personal and professional goals through the power and influence of their relationships. So political skill is not about taking advantage of others or backstabbing to enhance self-interest at the expense of others, it's about building relationships to help you meet your objectives.[29] Leaders in organizations use political behavior to meet organizational objectives, our next topic.

Political Behavior

How well you play politics directly affects your success. Networking, reciprocity, and coalitions are common organizational political behaviors.

Networking

Networking is a critical facet of political skills. *Networking* is the process of developing relationships for the purpose of socializing and politicking. The activities managers engage in and the time spent on each area have been studied. The activities have been categorized into four areas: traditional management, communication, human resource management, and networking. Of these four activities, networking has the highest relative contribution to successful management advancement. Successful managers spend around twice as much time networking as average managers, so reach out to establish an ongoing network of contacts.[30] Because networking is so important to career success, we are going to discuss it as our next major section, after we finish our other political skills discussions.

Reciprocity

Using reciprocity *involves creating obligations and developing alliances, and using them to accomplish objectives.* Notice that the exchange influencing tactic is used with reciprocity. When people do something for you, you incur an obligation that they may expect to be repaid. When you do something for people, you create a debt that you may be able to collect at a later date when you need a favor. Isn't part of relationships doing things for each other? Thus, ongoing reciprocal relationships are needed to meet your objectives,[31] and reciprocity builds trust in social exchange relationships.[32]

Here is a tip to increase your chances of getting help from others. When asking for help, use the word *favor*, because the mere mention of that word can persuade people to help you. People have a modal, rote response to a favor request, which is, "Yeah, sure, what is it?" So start with the phrase, "Will you please do me a favor?"

Coalitions

Using coalitions as an influencing tactic is political behavior.[33] Each party helps the others get what they want. Reciprocity and networking are commonly used to achieve ongoing objectives, whereas coalitions are developed for achieving a specific objective. A political tactic when developing coalitions is to use co-optation. *Co-optation is the process of getting a person whose support you need to join your coalition rather than compete.*

WORK Application 5
Give a job example of how networking, reciprocity, or a coalition was used to achieve an organizational objective.

_____

_____

_____

_____

The reality of organizational life is that most important decisions are made by coalitions outside of the formal meeting in which the decision is made. For example, let's say you are on a team and the captain is selected by a nomination and vote of the team members. If you want to be captain, you can politic by asking close teammates who they will vote for to try to get their votes; and if they are supportive, you can ask them to promote you for captain to others. If the majority of the team says they will vote for you, you have basically won the election before the coach even starts the meeting, nominating, and voting by building a coalition. If you don't get any support from your close teammates and others, you can drop the effort to build a coalition, knowing that you will lose. This same coalition-building process is used to influence all types of decisions.

We have not discussed how to increase your political skills with each type of political behavior, because all three may be used at the same time. As you will see, the upcoming guidelines can be used with any of the three political behaviors. Before considering how to develop political skills, review Exhibit 5.2 for a list of political behaviors and guidelines.

OPENING CASE *APPLICATION*

2. Why are organizational politics important to Mark Cuban's enterprises?

Mark Cuban has clearly used politics to gain and use power in creating his business empire. For the owner of multiple businesses, organizational politics is not as important as using political skills outside the organization. The NBA is an organization of multiple team owners, so politics is important for making changes in the league. Because of Cuban's behavior, the NBA owners voted to pass rules of conduct that were really meant for Cuban. The NBA commissioner said the more stringent rules were called for to prevent individual owners from overshadowing the games. Cuban was so upset that he walked out of the meeting before the vote. So Cuban can improve on his organizational politics skills.

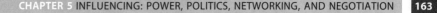

EXHIBIT 5.2   Political Behavior and Guidelines for Developing Political Skills

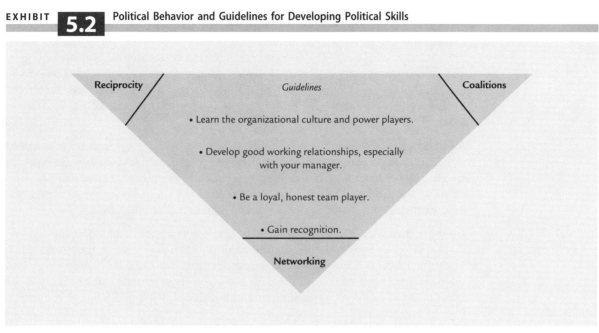

Guidelines for Developing Political Skills

If you want to climb the corporate ladder, or at least avoid getting thrown off it, you should develop your political skills. Researchers have found that women and minorities tend to have weak political skills and will have many more opportunities for advancement if they expand and exercise their political skills.[34] Carly Fiorina stated that she lost her job as CEO of HP due to politics. Successfully implementing the behavior guidelines presented here can result in increased political skills. However, if you don't agree with a particular political behavior, don't use it. You do not have to use all of the political behaviors to be successful. Learn what it takes in the organization where you work as you follow the guidelines.

Understand the Organizational Culture and Power Players

Develop your connection power through politicking. It is natural, especially for young people, to take a purely rational approach to a job without considering politics. But many business decisions are not very rational; they are based on power and politics. Learn the cultural (Chapter 10) shared values and beliefs and how business and politics operate where you work. Learn to read between the lines.

In all organizations, there are some powerful key players. Your manager is a key player to you. Don't just find out who the managers are; gain an understanding of what makes each of them tick. By understanding them, you can tailor the presentation of your ideas and style to fit each person's needs. For example, some managers want to see detailed financial numbers and statistics, while others don't. Some managers expect you to continually follow up with them, while others will think you are bugging them.

Review Self-Assessment 2, questions 1 through 5   You can use these tactics to increase your political skills. Network with power players. Try to do favors for power players. When developing coalitions, get key players on your side. When selecting a mentor, try to get one who is good at organizational politics. Your mentor can help you learn how to play politics. Also try to observe people who are good at politics, and copy their behavior.

Develop Good Working Relationships, Especially with Your Manager

The ability to work well with others is critical to your career success, and it's an important foundation of politics. The more people like and respect you, the more power you will gain. Managers often promote informal leaders to supervise their peers. Let's focus on the relationship with our boss because it is a major indicator of job satisfaction today.

Advancement   If we want to get ahead, we need to have a good working relationship with our manager. Your boss usually gives you formal performance appraisals, which are the primary bases for raises and promotions. Fair or not, many evaluations are influenced by the manager's relationship with the employee. If your manager likes you, you have a better chance of getting a good review, raises, and promotions.

Do more than what is required   Supervisors also give higher ratings to employees who share their goals (goal congruence) and priorities than they give to those who don't. Thus, get to know what your manager expects from you, and do it. Beat or at least meet deadlines, and don't miss them. Impress your boss by doing more than you are asked to do. If you don't agree with your boss's way of doing things, ask if you can do it your way, but don't go against your boss.

Share bad news   It's common to put off telling the manager bad news. But if you are having a problem on the job, don't put off letting your manager know about it. Most managers, and peers, like to be asked for advice. If you are behind schedule to meet an important deadline and your manager finds out about it from others, it is embarrassing, especially if your manager finds out from his or her manager. Also avoid showing up your manager in public, such as during a meeting. If you do, don't be surprised if the next time you open your mouth at a meeting, your manager embarrasses you.

Don't go to your boss's manager   If you cannot get along with your manager and are in conflict, avoid going to his or her manager to resolve the conflict. There are two dangers in going over the manager's head. First, chances are your manager has a good working relationship with his or her manager, who will side with your manager. Even if the higher-level manager agrees with you, you will most likely hurt your relationship with your manager. He or she may consciously or unconsciously take some form of retaliation, such as giving you a lower performance review, which can hurt you in the long run.

Review Self-Assessment 2, questions 6 through 12   You can use these tactics to increase your political skills. Include your manager in your network, try to do favors for your manager, and include your manager in your coalitions. Use the ingratiation tactic with everyone. When was the last time you gave anyone, including your manager, a compliment? When was the last time you sent a thank-you or congratulations note?

Be a Loyal, Honest Team Player

Ethical behavior is important in organizational politics. The Indian leader Mohandas Gandhi called business without morality and politics without principle a sin. Some back-stabbing gossips may get short-term benefits from such behavior, but in the long run they are generally unsuccessful because others gun them down in return. In any organization, you must earn others' respect, confidence, and trust.

Once you are caught in a lie, it's difficult to regain trust. There are very few, if any, jobs in which organizational objectives can be achieved without the support of a group or team of individuals. Even lone-wolf salespeople are subject to the systems effect, and they need the help of production to make the product, transportation to deliver it, and service to maintain it. The trend is toward teamwork, so if you're not a team player, work at it.

WORK Application 6

Which one or two suggestions for developing political skills are the most relevant to you? Explain.

_____

_____

_____

_____

Review Self-Assessment 2, questions 13 through 16 You can use these tactics to increase your political skills. Be a loyal, honest team player in your network, in your reciprocity, and with your coalition members.

Gain Recognition

Doing a great job does not help you to get ahead in an organization if no one knows about it, or doesn't know who you are. Author Ken Blanchard says, "It's not who you know that counts; it's who knows you and what they think of you."[35] Recognition and knowing the power players go hand in hand; you want the power players to know who you are and what you can do. You want people higher in the organization to know your expertise and the contributions you are making to the organization.

Review Self-Assessment 2, questions 17 through 20 You can use these tactics to increase your political skills. Let people in your network and coalitions, and people you reciprocate with, know of your accomplishments. You can also serve on committees and try to become an officer, which gives you name recognition. A committee job many people tend to avoid is that of secretary. But when the meeting minutes are sent to higher management and throughout the organization with your name on it as secretary, you increase your name recognition.

CONCEPT APPLICATION 3
Political Behavior

Identify the behavior in each situation as effective or ineffective political behavior. Write the appropriate letter in the blank before each item.

a. effective   b. ineffective

_____ 16. John tells his boss's manager about mistakes his boss makes.

_____ 17. Juan avoids spending time socializing, so that he can be more productive on the job.

_____ 18. Sonia sent a very positive performance report to three higher-level managers to whom she does not report. They did not request copies.

_____ 19. Julio has to drop off a daily report by noon. He delivers the report at around 10:00 a.m. on Tuesday and Thursday, so that he can run into some higher-level managers who meet at that time near the office where the report goes. On the other days, Julio drops the report off at around noon on his way to lunch.

_____ 20. Latoya is taking golf lessons so she can join the Saturday golf group, which includes some higher-level managers.

Networking

Recall that networking is part of politics, and through networking you can develop your power and influence.[36] Research has shown the importance of networking in career success.[37] The topic is also covered extensively in the popular press.[38]

You have most likely heard things like, "It's not what you know, it's who you know that is important," or "It's who you know, not what, that's responsible for the big things in your professional life."[39] More people find jobs through networking than all the other

SELF-ASSESSMENT 3   Networking

Identify each of the 16 statements according to how accurately it describes your behavior. Place a number from 1–5 on the line before each statement.

5 — 4 — 3 — 2 — 1
Describes me   *Does not describe me*

_____ 1. When I start something (a new project, a career move, a major purchase), I seek help from people I know and seek new contacts for help.

_____ 2. I view networking as a way to create win–win situations.

_____ 3. I like to meet new people; I can easily strike up a conversation with people I don't know.

_____ 4. I can quickly state two or three of my most important accomplishments.

_____ 5. When I contact business people who can help me (such as with career information), I have goals for the communication.

_____ 6. When I contact business people who can help me, I have a planned short opening statement.

_____ 7. When I contact business people who can help me, I praise their accomplishments.

_____ 8. When I contact people who can help me, I have a set of questions to ask.

_____ 9. I know contact information for at least 100 people who can potentially help me.

_____ 10. I have a file/database with contact information of people who can help me in my career, and I keep it updated and continue to add new names.

_____ 11. During communications with people who can help me, I ask them for names of others I can contact for more information.

_____ 12. When seeking help from others, I ask them how I might help them.

_____ 13. When people help me, I thank them at the time and for big favors with a follow-up thanks.

_____ 14. I keep in touch with people who have helped or can potentially help me in my career at least once a year, and I update them on my career progress.

_____ 15. I have regular communications with people in my industry who work for different organizations, such as members of trade/professional organizations.

_____ 16. I attend trade/professional/career types of meetings to maintain relationships and to make new contacts.

Add up your score and place it here _____ and on the continuum below.

80 — 70 — 60 — 50 — 40 — 30 — 16
Effective Networking   *Ineffective Networking*

If you are a full-time student, you may not score high on networking effectiveness, but that's okay as you can develop networking skills by following the steps and guidelines in this chapter.

methods combined. But networking produces a number of other positive outcomes including friendships, information benefits, heightened control, and power.[40] Assess your networking skills now in Self-Assessment 3 before reading on.

Networking is about building relationships.[41] It's not about asking everyone you know for a job (or whatever you need assistance with). How would you react if someone directly said, "Can you give me a job?" Although the same networking process applies to broad career development, we focus more on the job search. Whenever you start something—a new project, a career move, a car or house purchase—use your networks.

You may have a social networking account, like Facebook, to communicate with your friends, but "career" networking is more than this. Networking skills can be developed.[42] This section provides a how-to network process that can enhance career development.[43] As you read, you will find out that networking is work, but that it can pay off.[44] The process is summarized in Exhibit 5.3.

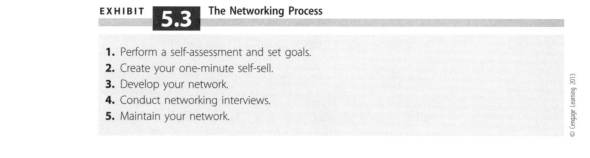

EXHIBIT **5.3**   The Networking Process

1. Perform a self-assessment and set goals.
2. Create your one-minute self-sell.
3. Develop your network.
4. Conduct networking interviews.
5. Maintain your network.

© Cengage Learning 2013

*Learning
Outcome 5*   *List and explain the steps in the networking process.*

Perform a Self-Assessment and Set Goals

The self-assessment includes writing down your skills, competencies, and knowledge. Self-assessment gives you insight into your transferable skills and the criteria that are important to you in a new job. Listing the major criteria that are most important to you in the new job and prioritizing these can help to clarify your ideal next position.

Factors to consider are: industry, company size and growth, location, travel and commuting requirements, compensation package/benefits, job requirements, and promotion potential. Other factors to assess are the style of management, culture, and work style of the organization. Critical to career satisfaction is the ability to use your talents, grow in your field, and do what you do best in your job. Although many tools exist to assess skills and preferences, a simple list with priorities can suffice to clarify your talents and the characteristics of an ideal new career or job.

Accomplishments

After completing a self-assessment, you are ready to translate your talents into accomplishments. The results you achieved in your jobs and/or college are the best evidence of your skills. Your future employer knows that your past behavior predicts your future behavior and that if you achieved results in the past, you will likely produce similar results again. Accomplishments are what set you apart and provide evidence of your skills and abilities. To be an effective networker, we must articulate what we have accomplished in our past in a way that is clear, concise, and compelling. Write down your accomplishments (at least two or three) and include them in your resume. Whether you are looking for a job or not, you should always have an updated resume handy.

Tie Your Accomplishments to the Job Interview

You want to be sure to state your accomplishments that are based on your skill during the job interview. Many interviews begin with a broad question such as, "Tell me about yourself." Oftentimes candidates do not reveal anything compelling. The second step after listing key results you have achieved is to elaborate on a problem that was solved or an opportunity taken and how you achieved it using your skills. These simple result statements should be transferred from your resume as critical results achieved. Thus, if you are asked to tell the interviewer about yourself, use your accomplishment statements as answers.

WORK Application 7

Write a networking goal.

_____

_____

_____

_____

Set Networking Goals

After a self-assessment focusing on your accomplishments, you need to clearly state your goal.[45] For example: to get a mentor; to determine the expertise, skills, and requirements needed for XYZ position; to get feedback on my resume and job and/or career preparation for a career move into XYZ; or to attain a job as XYZ. Be sure to write objectives using the setting objectives Model 3.1 from Chapter 3.

Create Your One-Minute Self-Sell

We need a networking plan, so based on a goal, our next step is to create a one-minute sell to help accomplish that goal. *The one-minute self-sell is an opening statement used in networking that quickly summarizes your history and career plan and asks a question.* It is also referred to as an elevator pitch. To take 60 seconds or less, your message must be concise, but it also needs to be clear and compelling. It gives the listener a sense of your background, identifies your career field and a key result you've achieved, plus provides the direction of your next job. It tells the listener what you plan to do next and why. It also stimulates conversation by asking your network for help in the area of support, coaching, contacts, or knowledge of the industry.

Part 1. History: Start with a career summary, the highlights of your career to date. Include your most recent career or school history and a description of the type of work/internship or courses you have taken. Also include the industry and type of organization.

Part 2. Plans: Next, state the target career you are seeking, the industry you prefer, and a specific function or role. You can also mention names of organizations you are targeting as well as let the acquaintance know why you are looking for work.

Part 3. Question: Last, ask a question to encourage two-way communication. The question will vary depending on the person and your goal or the reason you are using the one-minute self-sell, for example:

- In what areas might there be opportunities for a person with my experience?
- In what other fields can I use these skills or this degree?
- In what other positions in your organization could my skills be used?
- How does my targeted future career sound to you? Is it a match with my education and skills?
- Do you know of any job openings in my field?

Write and Practice Your One-Minute Self-Sell

WORK Application 8
Write a one-minute self-sell to achieve your networking goal from Work Application 7.

Write out your one-minute self-sell. Be sure to clearly separate your history, plans, and question, and customize your question based on the contact with whom you are talking. For example, *Hello, my name is Will Smith. I am a junior at Springfield College majoring in marketing, and I have completed an internship in the marketing department at the Big Y supermarket. I am seeking a job in sales in the food industry. Can you give me some ideas on the types of sales positions available in the food industry?* Practice delivering it with family and friends and get feedback to improve it. The more opportunities you find to use this brief introduction, the easier it becomes.

Develop Your Network

Networking is often structured.[46] Begin with who you know. Everyone can create a written network list of about 200 people consisting of professional and personal contacts. You may already have a network on an online social networking site, such as Facebook or MySpace, and you most likely have an e-mail account with an address book. Address books and rolodexes are written network lists, but you need to continually develop and expand them. An e-mail or Facebook account is a good place to store your network list and information on each person because you can easily contact one or more people.

One word of caution regarding social networking and other Web sites: Be careful with what is online. If a potentially helpful person or employer looks you up online, and finds unflattering pictures of you (under the influence of drugs or alcohol, not fully dressed, doing embarrassing things, and so forth), it may cost you a contact or potential job.[47] You may want to do a search on yourself to make sure that others don't have unflattering pictures or other things of you posted.

Professional contacts include colleagues (past and present), professional organizations, alumni associations, vendors, suppliers, managers, mentors, and many other professional acquaintances. On a personal level, your network includes family, neighbors, friends, religious groups, and other personal service providers (doctor, dentist, insurance agent, stock broker, accountant, hairstylist, politician). Compose a list of your network using the above categories, and continually update and add to your list with referrals from others. You will discover that your network grows exponentially and can get you closer to the decision makers in a hiring position. In today's job market, it is critical to engage in a "passive job hunt" using your network and having your resume ready.

Now expand your list to people you don't know. Who do you want to build a tie to?[48] Where should you go to develop your network? Anywhere people gather. Talk to everyone because you never know who's connected to whom. To be more specific, get more involved with professional associations. Many have special student memberships, and some even have college chapters. If you really want to develop your career reputation, become a leader in your associations and not just a member. Volunteer to be on committees and boards, to give presentations, and so on. Other opportunities to network with people you don't know include the Chamber of Commerce, college alumni clubs/reunions, civic organizations (Rotary, Lions, Kiwanis, Elks, Moose, Knights of Columbus, and so on), courses of any type, trade shows and career fairs, community groups, charities and religious groups (Goodwill, American Cancer Society, your local church), and social clubs (exercise, boating, golf, tennis, and so on).

Another important point is to work at developing your ability to remember people by name. If you want to impress people you have never met or hardly know, call them by their name. Ask others who they are, then go up and call them by name and introduce yourself with your one-minute self-sell. When you are introduced to people, call them by name during the conversation two or three times. If you think the person can help you, don't stop with casual conversation; make an appointment at a later time for a phone conversation, personal meeting, coffee, or lunch. Get their business cards to add to your network list, and give your business card and/or resume when appropriate.

Conduct Networking Interviews

Even though the trend is toward more online communications, networking in person is important.[49] Based on your goal, use your network list of people to set up a networking interview to meet your goal. It may take many interviews to meet a goal, such as to get a job. An informational interview is a phone call or preferably a meeting that you initiate to meet a goal, such as to gain information from a contact with hands-on experience in your field of interest.

You are the interviewer (in contrast to a job interview) and need to be prepared with specific questions to ask the contact regarding your targeted career or industry based on your self-assessment and goal. Keep your agenda short, focus on what is most important. Ask for a 20-minute meeting, and, as a result, many people will talk to you.

These meetings can be most helpful when you have accessed someone who is in an organization you'd like to join, or has a contact in an industry you are targeting. A face-to-face meeting of 20 minutes can have many benefits. Your contact will remember you after a personal meeting, and the likelihood of getting a job lead increases. Keeping the person posted on your job search progress as well as a thank-you note after the meeting also solidifies the relationship. The interviewing steps are:

Step 1. **Establish Rapport:** Provide a brief introduction and thank the contact for his or her time. Clearly state the purpose of the meeting; be clear that you are not asking for a job. Don't start selling yourself; project an interest in the other person. Do some research and impress the person by stating an accomplishment, such as, "I enjoyed your presentation at the Rotary meeting on…."

Step 2. **Deliver Your One-Minute Self-Sell:** Even if the person has already heard it, say it again. This enables you to quickly summarize your background and career direction.

Step 3. **Ask Prepared Questions:** As stated above, do your homework before the meeting and compose a series of questions to ask during the interview. Your questions should vary depending on your goal, the contact, and how he or she may help you with your job search. Sample questions include the following:

- What do you think of my qualifications for this field?
- With your knowledge of the industry, what career opportunities do you see in the future?
- What advice do you have for me as I begin/advance in my career?
- If you were exploring this field, who else would you talk with?

During the interview, if the interviewee mentions anything that could hinder your search, ask how such obstacles could be overcome. Take notes during the interview.

Step 4. **Get Additional Contacts for Your Network:** As mentioned previously, always ask who else you should speak with. Most people can give you three names, so if you are only offered one, ask for others. Add the new contacts to your network list; be sure to write them down. When contacting new people, be sure to use your network person's name. Be sure not to linger beyond the time you have been offered, unless invited to stay. Leave a business card and/or resume so the person can contact you in case something comes up.

Step 5. **Ask Your Contacts How You Might Help Them:** Offer a copy of a recent journal article or any additional information that came up in your conversation. Remember, it's all about building relationships, and making yourself a resource for other people.[50]

Step 6. **Follow Up with a Thank-You Note and Status Report:** By sending a thank-you note, along with another business card/resume, and following up with your progress, you are continuing the networking relationship and maintaining a contact for the future.

Be sure to assess the effectiveness of your networking meetings using the five steps as your criteria. Did you establish rapport and were you clear about the intent of the meeting? Did you deliver your one-minute self-sell, including a question? Did you follow with additional prepared questions? Did you get additional names to contact? And finally, did you send a follow-up thank-you note? It is always helpful to create a log of calls, meetings, and contacts in order to maintain your network as it expands.

Maintain Your Network

It is important to keep your network informed of your career progress. Get a mentor in your current or new role who can help you to focus on results that matter to your employer and guide your assimilation process. If an individual was helpful in finding your new job, be sure to let him or her know the outcome. Saying thank you to those who helped in your transition will encourage the business relationship; providing this information will increase the likelihood of getting help in the future.

It is also a good idea to notify everyone in your network that you are in a new position and provide contact information. Networking doesn't stop once you've made a career change. Make a personal commitment to continue networking in order to be in charge of your career development. Go to trade shows and conventions, make business friends, and continue to update, correct, and add to your network list. Always thank others for their time.

Networking is also about helping others, especially your network. Give before you take.[51] As you have been helped, you should help others. You will be amazed at how helping others comes back to you. Jack Gherty, former CEO of Land O' Lakes, said that he got ahead by helping other people win. Connect other people together who can help each other.[52]

Try to contact everyone on your network list at least once a year (calls, e-mail, and cards are good), and find out what you can do for them. Send congratulations on recent achievements. By contacting everyone, we don't mean sending a note to your 500 friends at the same time. You need to maintain regular personal contact, which is generally limited to around 150 people.[53]

After you have read this section on networking, you have at least two choices. One is to do nothing with it. The other choice is to begin developing your networking skills. Schedule the time to sit down and do one or all of the steps in the networking process: do a self-assessment and set a goal(s), create your one-minute self-sell to meet your goal, develop your network to meet the goal, set up and conduct network interviews, and maintain your network. What's it going to be? Developing Your Leadership Skills Exercise 3 can help get you started.

Social Networking at Work

With increasing technology advances, people are blurring the differences between their personal and professional lives, including the use of social networking media.[54] Established rules of communicating are unraveling, driven by a shift in how we use the Internet. E-mails and corporate Web sites are fast being replaced by Facebook and Twitter.[55] For example, a sales agent sets up a Facebook page to attract new clients; an employee forwards work e-mails to a personal iPhone; a manager responds to customer complaints from a personal Twitter account; an executive merges business and personal calendars on an iPad.[56] IBM, Salesforce.com, Yammer, and others offer corporate social networking software.[57]

Although many companies are encouraging employees to use social networking media on the job, it brings a host of new challenges. Here is the question constantly lurking: "Is it business, or is it personal?"[58] But there are greater challenges: for example, how does the firm measure communications and keep employees on track, without running into legal problems?[59] Anything any employee says in social media can get the business into legal problems. To deal with potential problems, many companies are developing new social media policies and rules, and they are monitoring for legal compliance as many heavily regulated industries, such as banking, treat social media messages the same as e-mail for the purposes of archiving and financial reporting.[60] It's not easy to control and keep track of what thousands of employees are doing and saying in social media.

OPENING CASE *APPLICATION*

3. How has Mark Cuban used networking?

Mark Cuban first started networking by selling garbage bags door-to-door and then by selling stamps and baseball cards before the Internet was available. As the owner of Motley's, between bartending and spinning records, he schmoozed customers. In fact, people came to see him; and when he wasn't there, business wasn't as good. When Cuban was selling computers, he was constantly socializing and trading business cards. To be successful in the entertainment business, you have to network with the right people to get productions from HDNet and HDNet Movies, 2929 Productions, and Magnolia Pictures viewed.[61]

Negotiation

Let's face it, whether you realize it or not, and whether you like it or not, we are all negotiators because we attempt to get what we want everyday. When we and another person both want something from each other, we are in conflict and can negotiate to get what we want.[62] Thus, **negotiating** *is a process in which two or more parties are in conflict and attempt to come to an agreement.* Are negotiation skills really important? Yes. It is listed as an important competency by the AACSB,[63] and in research studies.[64] Your negotiating ability directly affects your success in your personal and professional lives.[65]

Influence tactics, power, and politics are commonly used during the negotiation process.[66] Walmart keeps its everyday low prices because it is such a good negotiator. In this section, we focus on getting what we want by influencing others through negotiation. Before we get into the details of negotiating, complete Self-Assessment 4.

SELF-ASSESSMENT 4 | Negotiating

Identify each of the 16 statements according to how accurately it describes your behavior. Place a number from 1–5 on the line before each statement.

5 — 4 — 3 — 2 — 1
Describes me   *Does not describe me*

_____ 1. Before I negotiate, if possible, I find out about the person I will negotiate with to determine what they want and will be willing to give up.

_____ 2. Before I negotiate, I set objectives.

_____ 3. When planning my negotiating presentation, I focus on how the other party will benefit.

_____ 4. Before I negotiate, I have a target price I want to pay, a lowest price I will pay, and an opening offer.

_____ 5. Before I negotiate, I think through options and trade-offs in case I don't get my target price.

_____ 6. Before I negotiate, I think of the questions and objections the other party might have, and I prepare answers.

_____ 7. At the beginning of negotiations, I develop rapport and read the person.

_____ 8. I let the other party make the first offer.

_____ 9. I listen to what the other parties are saying and focus on helping them get what they want, rather than focusing on what I want.

_____ 10. I don't give in too quickly to others' offers.

_____ 11. When I compromise and give up something, I ask for something in return.

(continued)

(Self-Assessment 4 continued)

_____ 12. If the other party tries to postpone the negotiation, I try to create urgency and tell them what they might lose.

_____ 13. If I want to postpone negotiation, I don't let the other party pressure me into making a decision.

_____ 14. When I make a deal, I don't second-guess, wonder whether I got the best price, and check prices.

_____ 15. If I can't make an agreement, I ask for advice to help me with future negotiations.

_____ 16. During the entire business negotiating process, I'm trying to develop a relationship, not just a one-time deal.

Add up your score and place it here _____ and on the continuum below.

80 — 70 — 60 — 50 — 40 — 30 — 16
Effective Negotiating   *Ineffective Negotiating*

If you did not score high on negotiating effectiveness, that's okay, as you can develop negotiating skills by following the steps and guidelines in this chapter.

Negotiating

At certain times, negotiations are appropriate, such as when conducting management–union collective bargaining, buying and selling goods and services, accepting a new job and compensation offer, getting a raise, or setting the boundaries between work and home life[67]—all situations without a fixed price or deal. If there's a set, take-it-or-leave-it deal, there is no negotiation. For example, in most all U.S. retail stores, you must buy the product for the price listed; you don't negotiate price. But car dealers are known for negotiating.

All Parties Should Believe They Got a Good Deal

Negotiation is often a *zero–sum game* in which one party's gain is the other party's loss. For example, every dollar less that we pay for a car is our gain and the seller's loss. But it doesn't have to be an "I win and you lose" negotiation.[68] Like power and politics, negotiating is not about taking advantage of others, it's about building relationships and helping each other get what we want.[69]

To get what we want, we have to sell our ideas and convince the other party to give us what we want. However, negotiation should be viewed by all parties as an opportunity for everyone to win. When possible, make the pie larger rather than fight over how to split it. In other words, all parties should believe they got a good deal. If union employees believe they lost and management won, employees may experience job dissatisfaction, resulting in lower performance in the long run. If customers believe they got a bad deal, they may not give repeat business.

Negotiation Skills Can Be Developed

Not everyone is born a great negotiator. In fact, most people don't have a clue about how to get what they want, other than making demands and digging in their heels. Taking the time to learn how to negotiate before entering a deal is the best way to arrive at a successful conclusion. Learning to negotiate the right way will not only help us get what we want, it will also improve our personal and professional relationships.[70] Following the steps in the negotiation process can help develop negotiation skills.

Learning Outcomes 6 and 7

List the steps in the negotiation process.

Explain the relationships among negotiation and conflict, influencing tactics, power, and politics.

The Negotiation Process

The negotiation process has three, and possibly four, steps: plan, negotiations, possibly a postponement, and an agreement or no agreement. These steps are summarized in Model 5.1 and discussed in this section. Like the other models in this book, Model 5.1 is meant to give us step-by-step guidelines. However, in making it apply to varying types of negotiation, you may have to make slight adjustments.

Plan

The key to any negotiation is preparation, so develop a plan. Know what's negotiable and what's not. Be clear about what it is you are negotiating over. Is it price, options, delivery time, sales quantity, or all four? Ask yourself, "What exactly do I want?"[71] Planning has four steps.

Step 1.   Research the other party(ies). Put yourself in the other party's shoes. Be a detective.[72] Try to find out what the other parties want, and what they will and will not be willing to give up, before you negotiate. Find out their personality traits and negotiation style by networking with people who have negotiated with the other party before. If possible, establish a personal relationship before the negotiation. If you have experience working with the other party (e.g., your manager or a potential customer), what worked and did not work in the past?

Step 2.   Set objectives. Based on your research, what can you expect from the negotiation—what is your objective? Set a lower limit, a target objective, and an opening objective. The objective may be price, but it could be working

MODEL 5.1   The Negotiation Process

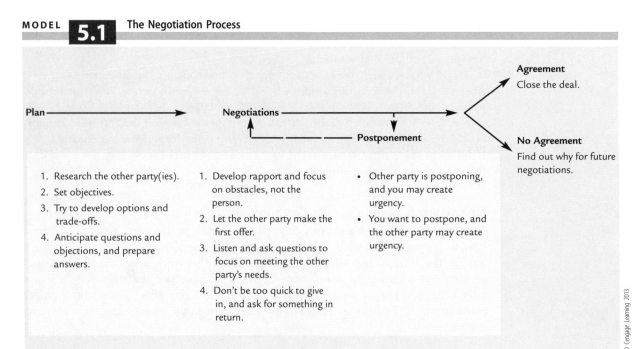

conditions, longer vacation, job security, and so on. Follow steps a, b, and c: (a) Set a specific lower limit and be willing to walk away; do not come to an agreement unless you get it. You need to be willing to walk away from a bad deal. (b) Set a target objective of what you believe is a fair deal. (c) Set an opening objective offer that is higher than you expect; you might get it. Remember that the other party is probably also setting three objectives. So don't view their opening offer as final. The key to successful negotiations is for all parties to get between their minimum and target objective. This creates a win–win; everyone got a good deal situation.

Step 3.   **Try to develop options and trade-offs.** In purchasing something as well as in looking for a job, if you have multiple sellers and job offers, you are in a stronger power position to get your target price. It is common practice to quote other offers and to ask if the other party can beat them.

   If you have to give up something, or cannot get exactly what you want, be prepared to ask for something else in return. If you cannot get the higher raise you want, maybe you can get more days off, more in your retirement account, a nicer office, an assistant, and so on. When some companies were having financial difficulty, they asked employees to take a pay cut. Rather than simply accept a cut, they asked for a trade-off and got company stock. Based on your research, what trade-offs do you expect from the other party?

Step 4.   **Anticipate questions and objections, and prepare answers.** The other party may want to know why you are selling something, looking for a job, how the product or service works, or what are the features and benefits. You need to be prepared to answer the unasked question, "What's in it for me?" Don't focus on what you want, but on how your deal will benefit the other party.

   There is a good chance that you will face some objection—reasons why the negotiations will not result in agreement or sale. Be prepared to overcome the no's you are bound to encounter.[73] When a union asks for a raise, management typically says the organization can't afford it. However, the union has done its research and quotes the specific profits to overcome the objection. Unfortunately, not everyone comes out to state their real objections. So we need to listen and ask open-ended questions to get them talking so we can find out what is preventing the agreement.

   We need to fully understand our product or deal, and project positive self-esteem, enthusiasm, and confidence. If the other party does not trust us and believes the deal is not a good one, we will not reach an agreement.[74]

Negotiations

After we have planned, we are now ready to negotiate the deal. Face-to-face negotiations are generally preferred because you can see the other person's nonverbal behavior and better understand objections. However, telephone and written negotiations (e-mail) work too. Again, know the other party's preference. Handling negotiations also has four steps.

Step 1.   **Develop rapport and focus on obstacles, not the person.** The first thing we sell in any negotiation is ourselves. The other party needs to trust us.[75] People look for four things: inclusion, control, safety, and respect. Most people, if they perceive that you are trying to push them into something, threaten them in some way, or belittle them, will not trust you and will not make an agreement.

   Smile and call the other party by name as you greet them. A smile tells people you like them and are interested in them. Open with some small talk, like the weather, to get to know them. Deciding on how much time to wait until you get down to business depends on the other party's style. Some people like to get right down to business; others, want to get to know you first. However, you want the other party to make the first offer, so don't wait too long or you may lose your chance.

"Focus on the obstacle, not the person" means never to attack the other's personality or put others down with negative statements like, "You are being unfair to ask for such a price cut." If we do so, the other party will become defensive, we may end up arguing, and it will be harder to reach an agreement. So even if the other person starts it, refuse to fight on a name-calling level. Make statements like, "You think my price is too high" to calm them down.

Step 2.   Let the other party make the first offer. This gives you the advantage, because if the other party offers you more than your target objective, you can close the agreement. For example, if you are expecting to be paid $35,000 a year (your target objective) and the other party offers you $40,000, are you going to reject it? On the other hand, if you are offered $30,000 you can realize that it may be low and work at increasing the compensation. Ask questions like, "What is the salary range?" or "What do you expect to pay for such a fine product?"

Try to avoid negotiating simply on price. When others pressure you to make the first offer with a common question like, "Give us your best price, and we'll tell you whether we'll take it," try asking them a question such as, "What do you expect to pay?" or "What is a reasonable price?" When this does not work, say something like, "Our usual (or list) price is *xxx*. However, if you make me a proposal, I'll see what I can do for you."

If things go well during steps 1 and 2, you may skip to closing the agreement. If you are not ready to agree, proceed to the next step or two.

Step 3.   Listen and ask questions to focus on meeting the other party's needs. Create an opportunity for the other party to disclose reservations and objections. When you speak you give out information, but when you ask questions and listen, you receive information that will help you to overcome the other party's objections.[76]

If you go on and on about the features you have to offer, without finding out what features the other party is really interested in, you may be killing the deal. Ask questions such as, "Is the price out of the ballpark?" or "Is it fast enough for you?" or "Is any feature you wanted missing?" If the objection is a "want" criteria, such as two years of work experience and you have only one, play up the features you know they want and that you do have, and you may reach an agreement.

If the objection is something you cannot meet, at least you found out and don't waste time chasing a deal that will not happen. However, be sure the objection is really a "must" criteria: What if the employer gets no applicants with two years' experience and you apply? You may get the job offer.

Step 4.   Don't be too quick to give in, and ask for something in return. Those who ask for more get more. Be persistent, don't just give up.[77] If our competitive advantage is service, and during negotiation we quickly give in for a lower price, we lose all the value in a minute. We want to satisfy the other party without giving up too much during the negotiation. Remember not to go below your minimum objective. If it is realistic, be prepared to walk away.

When we are not getting what we want, having other planned options can help give us bargaining power. If we do walk away, we may be called back; and if not, we may be able to come back for the same low price—but not always. If other parties know we are desperate, or just weak and will accept a low agreement, they will likely take advantage of us. Have you ever seen a sign on a product saying, "must sell—need cash"? What type of price do you think that seller gets? You also need to avoid being intimidated by comments such as this said in a loud voice: "Are you kidding me, that's too much." Many people will quickly drop the price, but you don't have to be intimidated.

However, when you are dealing with a complex deal, such as a management–union contract negotiation with trade-offs, be willing to be the first to make a concession. The other party tends to feel obligated, and then we can come back with a counter trade-off that is larger than the one we gave up.

Avoid giving unilateral concessions. Recall your planned trade-offs. If the other party asks for a lower price, ask for a trade-off such as a large-volume sale to get it, or a longer delivery time, a less popular color, and so on. We need to send the message that we don't just give things away.

Postponement

Take your time. When there doesn't seem to be any progress, it may be wise to postpone the negotiations.

The Other Party Is Postponing, and You May Create Urgency   The other party says, "I'll get back to you." When we are not getting what we want, we may try to create urgency. For example, "This product is on sale, and the sale ends today." However, honesty is the best policy. The primary reason people will negotiate with you is that they trust and respect you. Again, establishing a relationship of trust is the necessary first step in closing a deal.[78] If we do have other options, we can use them to create urgency, such as saying, "I have another job offer pending; when will you let me know if you want to offer me the job?"

But what if urgency does not apply—or does not work—and the other party says, "I'll think about it?" You might say, "That's a good idea." Then at least review the major features the other party liked about our proposed deal and ask if it meets their needs. The other party may decide to come to an agreement or sale. If not, and they don't tell you when they will get back to you, ask, for example, "When can I expect to hear if I got the job?" Try to pin the other party down for a specific time; tell the person that if you don't hear from them by then, you will call them. If you are really interested, follow up with a letter (mail, e-mail, or fax) of thanks for their time, and again highlight the features you think they liked. If you forgot to include any specific points during the negotiation, add them in the letter.

One thing to remember when the other party becomes resistant to making the agreement is that the hard sell will not work. Take the pressure off. Ask something like, "Where do you want to go from here?" If we press for an answer, it may be no agreement; however, if we wait we may have a better chance. To your manager, you might say, "Why don't we think about it and discuss it some more later?" (then pick an advantageous time to meet with your manager).

We also need to learn to read between the lines, especially when working with people from different cultures. Some people will not come right out and tell us there is no deal. We should be persistent in trying to come to an agreement,[79] but we also don't want to waste our time chasing a deal that will not happen.

You Want to Postpone, and the Other Party May Create Urgency   Don't be hurried by others, and don't hurry yourself. If we are not satisfied with the deal, or want to shop around, tell the other party you want to think about it. You may also need to check with your manager or someone else, which simply may be for advice, before you can finalize the deal. If the other party is creating urgency, be sure it really is urgent. In many cases, we can get the same deal at a later date; don't be pressured into making a deal you are not satisfied with or may regret later. If we do want to postpone, give the other party a specific time that we will get back to them, and do so with more prepared negotiations or simply to tell them we cannot make an agreement.

Agreement

Once the agreement has been made, restate it and/or put it in writing when appropriate. It is common to follow up an agreement with a letter of thanks, restating the agreement to ensure the other parties have not changed their mind about what they agreed to. Also, after the deal is made, stop selling it. Change the subject to a personal one and/or leave, depending on the other person's preferred negotiations. If they want a personal relationship, stick around; if not, leave.

No Agreement

Our goal is to come to an agreement,[80] but rejection, refusal, and failure happen to us all, even the superstars. The difference between the also-rans and the superstars lies in how they respond to the failure. The successful people keep trying, learn from their mistakes, and continue to work hard; failures usually don't persevere. When there is no agreement, analyze the situation and try to determine what went wrong to improve in the future. We may also ask the other party for advice, such as, "I realize I did not get the job; thanks for your time. Can you offer me any suggestions for improving my resume and interview skills, or other ideas to help me to get a job in this field?"

OPENING CASE *APPLICATION*

4.   **What types of negotiations does Mark Cuban engage in?**

A large part of Mark Cuban's job is negotiating. He had to negotiate to buy the Dallas Mavericks and to get HDNet and HDNet Movies on DirecTV. Some believe that Cuban is asking way too much money for his network to be viewed on cable. Cuban still needs to negotiate to distribute his 2929 Productions and Magnolia Pictures through big studios. The Mavericks won the championship in 2011, and the fans like Mark Cuban, who has bought the first $2,000 worth of drinks after winning games.

Ethics and Influencing

Recall that leadership is the *influencing* process of leaders and followers to achieve organizational objectives through change (Chapter 1). We usually influence others to get what we want. Power, politics, networking, and negotiating are all forms of influencing that can be used by leaders and followers. When influencing, recall that it pays to be ethical[81] (Chapter 2); with deception comes loss of trust and influence.[82]

People respond to incentives and can usually be motivated for good or bad if we find the right levers.[83] So influence is neither good nor bad; it's what we do with it. *Power* is ethical when it is used to help meet organizational objectives and those of its members, as well as to get what we want (socialized power, Chapters 2 and 9). Power is unethical when used to promote self-interest and manipulate others at their expense (personalized power). This misuse of power is further illustrated in Chapter 9 where we described the difference between socialized charismatic leadership and personalized charismatic leadership.

5.2 *Facebook Hired Firm to Target Google*

The social networking company secretly hired the public-relations firm Burson-Marsteller to push stories critical of Google's privacy practices to shift the online privacy spotlight away from itself, and onto rival Google. But the controversial strategy backfired when bloggers and journalists disclosed Facebook's behind-the-scenes role, forcing the company to explain its tactic.

Facebook said that it didn't authorize or intend to run a "smear campaign" but wanted to highlight that Facebook didn't approve of Google's data collection from its social-network accounts.

The nonprofit Public Relations Society of America said that Burson-Marsteller's lack of disclosure of Facebook is "deceptive" and violated its ethical standards.

Burson-Marsteller said that Facebook requested that its name be withheld because it was merely asking to bring publicly available information to light. But withholding Facebook's name was against its policy and the assignment on those terms should have been declined.

Google did not respond to a request for a comment on the newspaper story.[84]

1. Was Facebook's hiring of Burson-Marsteller to shift the online privacy spotlight away from itself, and onto rival Google ethical and socially responsible? Do you believe that Facebook was or was not really trying to run a "smear campaign" to get itself out of the headline and Google into the news for lack of privacy? If your boss asked you to be the one to hire Burson-Marsteller, what would you have done?

2. Do you agree with the Public Relations Society of America statement that Burson-Marsteller's lack of disclosure of Facebook is "deceptive" and is an unethical business tactic?

3. Was Burson-Marsteller ethical and socially responsible in taking the job from Facebook? Do you believe that the company simply made a mistake in taking the job or that it took the job knowing it was against company policy? If your boss asked you to be the one to smear Facebook against company policy, what would you have done?

4. Was it ethical and socially responsible of Google not to respond on this story when asked to do so? If you were the CEO of Google, what would your comment be about the behavior or your rival Facebook and Burson-Marsteller?

When playing *organizational politics* (and to a lesser extent *networking*), it can be tempting to be unethical, but don't do it. Even if others are using unethical behavior, don't stoop to their level. Talking negatively about people behind their back or stabbing them in the back is usually destructive in the long run. We should confront others if we believe they are being unethical and try to resolve the issues. You will learn how to resolve conflict in the next chapter.

An ethical challenge in *negotiation* is telling the truth, or not lying to the other party or being lied to. There is a difference between not giving extra information that is not asked for and lying to the other party. The person who caught us lying may tell others, and we can lose even more friends and business.

So when influencing others, try to use the stakeholders' approach to ethics by creating a win–win situation for relevant parties.

OPENING CASE APPLICATION

5. Is Mark Cuban ethical in influencing others?

As discussed, Mark Cuban's behavior has not always been appropriate, and thus has gotten him into some trouble in sports and entertainment. Cuban is aware of this shortcoming, and only time will tell if he will earn the respect he believes he deserves as he strives to be famous and influential.

Chapter Summary

The chapter summary is organized to answer the eight learning outcomes for Chapter 5.

1. **Explain the differences between position power and personal power.**

Position power is derived from top management and is delegated down the chain of command. Thus, people at the top of the organization have more power than those at the bottom of the organization. Personal power is derived from the followers based on the leader's behavior. All managers have position power, but they may or may not have personal power. Nonmanagers do not have position power, but they may have personal power.

2. **Discuss the differences among legitimate, reward, coercive, and referent power.**

Legitimate, reward, and coercive power are all related. A leader with position power usually has the power to reward and punish (coercive). However, a person with referent power may or may not have position power to reward and punish, and the leader influences followers based on relationships.

3. **Discuss how power and politics are related.**

Power is the ability to influence others' behavior. Politics is the process of gaining and using power. Therefore, political skills are a part of power.

4. **Describe how money and politics have a similar use.**

Money and politics have a similar use, because they are mediums of exchange. In our economy, money is the medium of exchange. In an organization, politics is the medium of exchange.

5. **List and explain the steps in the networking process.**

The first step in the networking process is to perform a self-assessment to determine accomplishments and to set goals. Second, create a one-minute self-sell that quickly summarizes history and career plans and asks a question. Third, develop a written network list. Fourth, conduct networking interviews to meet your goals. Finally, maintain your network for meeting future goals.

6. **List the steps in the negotiation process.**

The first step in the negotiation process is to plan for the negotiation. The second step is to conduct the actual negotiation, which can be postponed, and results in an agreement or no agreement.

7. **Explain the relationships among negotiation and conflict, influencing tactics, power, and politics.**

Negotiations take place when there is a conflict; and influencing tactics, power, and politics can be used during the negotiation process.

8. **Define the following key terms (in order of appearance in the chapter).**

Select one or more methods: (1) fill in the missing key terms from memory; (2) match the key terms from the following list with their definitions below; (3) copy the key terms in order from the list at the beginning of the chapter.

_____ is the leader's potential influence over followers.

_____ is based on the user's position power, given by the organization.

_____ is based on the user's ability to influence others with something of value to them.

_____ involves punishment and withholding of rewards to influence compliance.

_____ is based on the user's personal relationships with others.

_____ is based on the user's skill and knowledge.

_____ is based on the user's data desired by others.

_____ is based on the user's relationships with influential people.

_____ is the process of gaining and using power.

_____ is the process of developing relationships for the purpose of socializing and politicking.

_____ involves creating obligations and developing alliances, and using them to accomplish objectives.

_____ is an opening statement used in networking that quickly summarizes your history and career plan and asks a question.

_____ is a process in which two or more parties are in conflict and attempt to come to an agreement.

Key Terms

coercive power, 152

connection power, 155

expert power, 154

information power, 155

legitimate power, 150

negotiating, 172

networking, 161

one-minute self-sell, 168

politics, 161

power, 148

reciprocity, 162

referent power, 153

reward power, 151

Review Questions

1. What are the seven types of power?
2. What are the nine influencing tactics?
3. What is ingratiation influencing?
4. What is the difference between inspirational appeal and personal appeal influencing?
5. What are the three political behaviors and four guidelines for developing political skills?
6. How many interview questions should you bring to a networking interview?
7. Which step of "conduct networking interviews" involves getting additional contacts for your network?
8. What type of situation (win/lose) is the goal of negotiation?
9. What are the steps in negotiations?
10. What are the steps in planning a negotiation?

Critical Thinking Questions

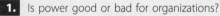

The following critical-thinking questions can be used for class discussion and/or as written assignments to develop communication skills. Be sure to give complete explanations for all questions.

1. Is power good or bad for organizations?
2. Which influencing tactics do you tend to use most and least? How will you change and develop the ability to influence using influencing tactics?
3. How would you rate your political skills, and which political behavior do you use most often? How will you change and develop your political skills?
4. How would you rate your relationship with your current or past boss? What will you do differently in the future to improve your relationship with your boss?
5. Can management stop the use of power and politics in their organizations?
6. Should people be judged based on their social skills?
7. How would you rate your networking skills? What will you do differently in the future to improve your networking skills?
8. Do people really need a written networking list?
9. How would you rate your negotiation skills? What will you do differently in the future to improve your negotiation skills?
10. Do you believe that most managers use influencing (power, politics, networking, and negotiating) for the good of the organization, or for their own personal benefit? What can be done to help managers be more ethical in influencing others?

Latoya Washington—Department of Marketing

Latoya Washington, an African-American woman, was highly sought after receiving her PhD in marketing. Today, she is a tenured professor of marketing at a small teaching college in the Midwest.[85] The Department of Marketing (DM) has nine faculty members; it is one of five departments in the School of Business (SB). The marketing department chair is John Carl, who is in his first year as chair. Six faculty members, including Latoya, have been in the department longer than Carl. Carl likes to have policies in place, so that faculty members have guides for their behavior. On the college-wide level, however, there is no policy about the job of graduate assistant. Carl has asked the dean of the SB about the policy. After a discussion with the vice president for academic affairs, the dean told Carl that there is no policy. The vice president and dean suggested letting the individual departments develop their own policy regarding what graduate assistants can and cannot do in their position. So, Carl has made developing a policy for graduate assistants an agenda item for the department meeting.

During the DM meeting, Carl asks for members' views on what graduate assistants should and should not be allowed to do. He was hoping that the department can come to a consensus on a policy. It turns out that Washington is the only faculty member using graduate assistants to grade exams. Two other faculty members speak out against having graduate assistants grade exams. They believe it is the professor's job to grade exams. Washington makes a few statements in hopes of not having to correct her own exams. Because her exams are objective, requiring a correct answer, Washington believes it's not necessary for her to personally grade the exams. She also points out that across the campus, and across the country, other faculty members are using graduate assistants to teach entire courses and to correct subjective papers and exams. Washington states that she does not think it fair that she can no longer use graduate assistants to grade objective exams when others are doing so. She also states that the department does not need to have a policy, and requests that the department not set a policy. However, Carl states that he wants a policy. Washington is the only one to speak in favor of allowing grad assistance to grade exams, although three others made no comments either way. But, after the meeting, one other member, Eddie Accorsi, who said nothing during the meeting, tells Washington he agrees that it is not fair to deny her this use of a graduate assistant.

There was no department consensus, as Carl hoped there would be. Carl says that he will draft a department policy,

which will be discussed at a future DM meeting. The next day, Washington sends a memo to department members asking if it is ethical and legal to deny her the same resources as others are using across the campus. She also states that if the department sets a policy stating that she can no longer use graduate assistants to correct objective exams, she will appeal the policy decision to the dean, vice president, and president.

Support your answers to the following questions with specific information from the case and text, or with other information you get from the Web or other sources.

1. (a) What source of power does Carl have, and (b) what type of power is he using? (c) Which influencing tactic is Carl using during the meeting? (d) Is negotiation and/or the (e) exchange tactic appropriate in this situation?

2. (a) What source of power does Washington have, and (b) what type of power is she using during the meeting? (c) Which two influencing tactics is Washington primarily using during the meeting? (d) Which influencing tactic is Washington using with the memo? (e) Is the memo a wise political move for Washington? What might she gain and lose by sending it?

3. What would you do if you were Carl? (a) Would you talk to the dean, letting him know that Washington said she would appeal the policy decision? (b) Which influencing tactic would this discussion involve? (c) Which political behavior would the discussion represent? (d) Would you draft a policy directly stating that graduate assistants cannot be used to grade objective exams? (e) Would your answer to (d) be influenced by your answer to (a)?

4. (a) If you were Washington, knowing you had no verbal supporters during the meeting, would you have continued to defend your position or agreed to stop using a graduate assistant? (b) What do you think of Washington sending the memo? (c) As a tenured full professor, Washington is secure in her job. Would your answer change if you (as Washington) had not received tenure or promotion to the top rank?

5. (a) If you were Washington, and Carl drafted a policy and department members agreed with it, what would you do? Would you appeal the decision to the dean? (b) Again, would your answer change if you had not received tenure or promotion to the top rank?

6. If you were the dean of the School of Business (SB), knowing that the vice president does not want to set a college-wide policy, and Washington appealed to you,

what would you do? Would you develop a school-wide policy for SB?

7. At what level (college-wide, by schools, or by departments within each school) should a graduate assistant policy be set?

8. (a) Should Eddie Accorsi have spoken up in defense of Washington during the meeting? (b) If you were Accorsi, would you have taken Washington's side against the other seven members? (c) Would your answer change if you were or were not friends with Washington, and if you were or were not a tenured full professor?

CUMULATIVE CASE QUESTIONS

9. Which level(s) of analysis of leadership theory is (are) presented in this case (Chapter 1)?

10. Is it ethical for graduate students to correct undergraduate exams (Chapter 2)?

11. Which of the four Ohio State University leadership styles did Carl use during the department meeting (Chapter 3)?

CASE EXERCISE AND ROLE-PLAY

Preparation: Read the case and think about whether you agree or disagree with using graduate assistants to correct objective exams. If you do this exercise, we recommend that you complete it before discussing the questions and answers to the case.

In-Class DM Meeting: A person who strongly agrees with Washington's position volunteers to play this role (can

be male) during a department of marketing (DM) meeting. A second person who also agrees with the use of graduate assistants correcting exams plays the role of Eddie (or Freddie). However, recall that Eddie/Freddie cannot say anything during the meeting to support Washington. One person who strongly disagrees with Washington—who doesn't want graduate assistants to correct exams, and who also feels strongly that there should be a policy stating what graduate assistants can and cannot do—volunteers to play the role of the department chair (Carl) who runs the DM meeting. Six others who are neutral or disagree with graduate assistants grading exams play the roles of other department members.

The ten role-players sit in a circle in the center of the room, with the other class members sitting around the outside of the circle. Observers just quietly watch and listen to the meeting discussion.

Role-Play: (about 15 minutes) Carl opens the meeting by simply stating that the agenda item is to set a graduate assistants policy stating what they can and cannot do, and that he or she hopes the department can come to a consensus on a policy. Carl states his or her position on why graduate students should not be allowed to correct exams, and then asks for other views. Washington and the others, except Eddie/Freddie, jump in anytime with their opinions.

Discussion: After the role-play is over, or when time runs out, the person playing the role of Washington expresses to the class how it felt to have everyone against him or her. Other department members state how they felt about the discussion, followed by observers' statements as time permits. A discussion of the case questions and answers may follow.

VIDEO ⏸ CASE

Employee Networks at Whirlpool Corporation

Since 1911, Whirlpool Corporation has grown from a small company to a global corporation with manufacturing locations on every major continent and over 68,000 employees worldwide. Like many organizations, one of Whirlpool's strategies for creating a culture of pluralism is encouraging the formation of employee network groups. These are voluntary groups formed around primary dimensions such as gender and ethnicity, and which meet regularly to focus on business issues. The groups are also a resource to the employees by providing a supportive community, decreasing social isolation, and promoting career development. Further, they help retain employees by providing them a forum for expressing ideas. These discussions often spark new ideas that benefit the company as a whole.

1. Using the Whirlpool Corporation Web site (**http://www.whirlpoolcorp.com**), identify the employee network groups at Whirlpool and the mission of each.

2. Do you think Whirlpool's encouragement of employee networks works for or against creating a culture of diversity? Explain your answer.

Developing Your Leadership Skills **1**

Influencing Tactics

Preparing for This Exercise

Below are three situations. For each situation, select the most appropriate influencing tactic(s) to use. Write the tactic(s) on the lines following the situation. At this time, don't write out how you would behave (what you would say and do).

1. You are doing a college internship, which is going well. You would like to become a full-time employee in a few weeks, after you graduate.

Which influencing tactic(s) would you use? _____

_____

Who would you try to influence? _____

_____

How would you do so (behavior)? _____

_____

2. You have been working at your job for six months, and you are approaching the elevator. You see a powerful person who could potentially help you advance in your career waiting for the elevator. You have never met her, but you do know that her committee has recently completed a new five-year strategic plan for the company and that she plays tennis and is active at the same religious organization (church, synagogue, mosque) as you. Although you only have a couple of minutes, you decide to try to develop a connection.

Which influencing tactic(s) would you use? _____

_____

How would you strike up a conversation? What topic(s) do you raise? _____

_____

3. You are the manager of the production department. Some of the sales staff has been scheduling deliveries for your product that your department can't meet. Customers are blaming you for late delivery. This is not good for the company, so you decide to talk to the sales staff manager about it over lunch.

Which influencing tactic(s) would you use? _____

_____

How would you handle the situation (behavior)? _____

_____

Now select one of the three situations that seems real to you—you can imagine yourself in the situation. Or briefly

write in a real-life situation that you can quickly explain to a small group. Now, briefly write out the behavior (what you would do and say) that you would use in the situation to influence the person to do what you want.

Situation # _____ Or, my situation: _____

_____

Influencing tactic(s) to use: _____

Behavior: _____

_____

_____

Doing This Exercise in Class

Objective

To develop your persuasion skills by using influencing tactics

The primary AACSB learning standard skills developed through this exercise are analytic skills—students learn to achieve their goals by influencing others.

Experience

You will discuss which influencing tactics are most appropriate for the preparation situations. You may also be given the opportunity to role-play how you would handle the one situation you selected; you will also play the role of the person to be influenced, and observer.

Procedure 1 *(10–20 minutes)*

Break up into groups of three, with one or two groups of two if needed. Try not to have two members in a group who selected the same situation; use people who selected their own situation. First, try to quickly agree on which influencing tactics are most appropriate in each situation. Select a spokesperson to give group answers to the class. In preparation to role-play, have each person state the behavior selected to handle the situation. The others give feedback for improvement: suggestions to delete, change, and/or add to the behavior (e.g., I would not say … , I'd say it this way … , I'd add … to what you have now).

Procedure 2 *(5–10 minutes)*

One situation at a time, each group spokesperson tells the class which influencing styles it would use, followed by brief remarks from the professor. The professor may also ask people who selected their own situation to tell the class the situation.

Conclusion

The instructor may lead a class discussion and/or make concluding remarks.

Apply It *(2–4 minutes)*

What did I learn from this exercise? How will I use this knowledge in the future?

_____

_____

_____

Sharing

In the group, or to the entire class, volunteers may give their answers to the "Apply It" questions.

Developing Your Leadership Skills 2

Influencing, Power, and Politics

Preparing for This Exercise

Your instructor will tell you to select one, two, or all three of the following topics (influencing, power, and/or politics) for this preparation.

To get what you want, you need to develop your ability to influence others and gain power through politics. It is helpful to read about these topics and how to improve your skills, but unless you apply the concepts in your personal and professional life, you will not develop these skills.

This preparation covers three skills, each with two activities. The first activity is to develop a general guide to daily actions you can take to increase your influence, power, and/or understanding of politics. The second is to think of a specific situation in the future, and develop a plan to get what you want. Use additional paper if you need more space to write your plan.

Influencing

Write down the influencing tactic that you are the strongest at using: _____. The weakest: _____. The one you would like to improve on: _____ (it does not have to be your weakest). Review the ideas for using this tactic, and write down a few ways in which you will work at developing your skill.

_____

_____

_____

Think of a specific situation in the near future in which you can use this tactic to help you get what you want. Briefly describe the situation, and explain how you will use this tactic—what you will say and do, and so on.

_____

_____

_____

Power

Write down the one type of your power you would like to improve on: _____. Review the ideas for increasing this type of power, and write down a few ways in which you will work at developing your power.

_____

_____

_____

Think of a specific situation in the near future in which you can use this type of power to help you get what you want. Briefly describe the situation, and explain how you will use this tactic—what you will say and do, and so on.

_____

_____

_____

Politics

Write down the one area of politics you would like to improve on: _____. Review the ideas for using this type of politics, and write down a few ways in which you will work at developing your skill.

_____

_____

_____

Think of a specific situation in the near future in which you can use this type of politicking to help you get what you want. Briefly describe the situation, and explain how you will use this tactic—what you will say and do, and so on.

Doing This Exercise in Class

Objective

To develop your ability to influence others and gain power through politics

The primary AACSB learning standard skills developed through this exercise are analytic skills—students learn to achieve their goals by influencing others.

Experience

You will develop a general guide to daily actions you can take to increase your influence, power, and/or understanding of politics. You'll also develop a plan to get what you want.

Preparation

You should have completed the preparation for this exercise, unless told not to do so by your instructor.

Procedure 1 *(10–20 minutes)*

Break into groups of three, with some groups of two if necessary. If group members developed plans for more than one skill area, select only one to start with. One group member volunteers to share first and states his or her preparation for influencing, power, or politics. The other members give input into how effective they think the plan is and offer ideas on how to improve the plan. After the first member shares, the other two have their turn, changing roles with each round. If there is time remaining after all have shared, go on to another skill area until the time is up.

Procedure 2 *(2–3 minutes)*

Each member commits to implementing his or her plan by a set time, and to telling the others how well the influence,

power, or politics went by a specific date—before or after the class ends.

Name _____

Date of implementation _____

Date to report results _____

Name _____

Date of implementation _____

Date to report results _____

Name _____

Date of implementation _____

Date to report results _____

Conclusion

The instructor may make concluding remarks.

Apply It *(2–4 minutes)*

What did I learn from this experience? How will I use this knowledge in the future?

_____

_____

_____

Sharing

In the group, or to the entire class, volunteers may give their answers to the "Apply It" questions.

Developing Your Leadership Skills **3**

Networking Skills*

Preparing for This Exercise

Based on the section "Networking" and the subsection on the networking process, complete the following steps.

1. Perform a self-assessment and set goals. List two or three of your accomplishments and set a goal. The goal can be to learn more about career opportunities in your major; to get an internship, part-time, summer, or full-time job; and so on.

_____

_____

_____

2. Create your one-minute self-sell. Write it out. See page 168 for a written example.

History: _____

Plan: _____

Question: _____

3. Develop your network. List at least five people to be included in your network, preferably people who can help you achieve your goal.

_____

_____

_____

4. Conduct networking interviews. To help meet your goal, select one person for a personal 20-minute interview or to interview by phone if it is difficult to meet in person. List the person and write questions to ask during the interview. This person can be a person in your college career center or a professor in your major.

_____

_____

_____

Source: This exercise was developed by Andra Gumbus, assistant professor, College of Business, Sacred Heart University. © Andra Gumbus, 2002. It is used with Dr. Gumbus's permission.

Doing This Exercise in Class

Objective

To develop networking skills by implementing the steps in the networking process

The primary AACSB learning standard skills developed through this exercise are analytic skills—students learn to achieve their goals by networking.

Experience

You will deliver your one-minute self-sell from the preparation and get feedback for improvement. You will also share your network list and interview questions and get feedback for improvement.

Procedure 1 *(7–10 minutes)*

A. Break into groups of two. Show each other your written one-minute self-sell. Is the history, plan, and question clear (do you understand it), concise (60 seconds or less to say), and compelling (does it promote interest to help)? Offer suggestions for improvement.

B. After perfected, each person states (no reading) the one-minute self-sell. Was it stated clearly, concisely, and with confidence? Offer improvements. State it a second and third time, or until told to go on to the next procedure.

Procedure 2 *(7–10 minutes)*

Break into groups of three with people you did not work with during procedure 1. Follow procedures A and B above in your triad. Repeating your self-sell should improve your delivery and confidence.

Procedure 3 *(10–20 minutes)*

Break into groups of four with people you did not work with during procedures 1 and 2, if possible. Share your answers from steps 3 (your network list) and 4 (your interview questions). Offer each other improvements to the questions and new questions. You should also get ideas for writing new questions for your own interview.

Applications (done outside of class)

Expand your written network list to at least 25 names. Conduct the networking interview using the questions developed through this exercise.

Conclusion

The instructor may make concluding remarks, including requiring the network lists and/or networking interview in the "Applications" section. Written network lists and/or interview questions and answers (following the name, title, and organization of interviewee; date, time, and type of interview—phone or in person) may be passed in.

Apply It *(2–4 minutes)*

What did I learn from this experience? How will I use this knowledge in the future?

_____

_____

_____

Sharing

In groups, or to the entire class, volunteers may give their answers to the "Apply It" questions.

Source: This exercise was developed by Andra Gumbus, Associate Professor of Management, College of Business, Sacred Heart University. © Andra Gumbus, 2002. It is used with Dr. Gumbus's permission.

Developing Your Leadership Skills **4**

Car Dealer Negotiation*

Preparing for This Exercise

You should have read and should understand the negotiation process.

Doing This Exercise in Class

Objective

To develop your negotiation skills

The primary AACSB learning standard skills developed through this exercise are analytic skills—students learn to achieve their goals through negotiating.

Experience

You will be the buyer or seller of a used car.

Procedure 1 *(1–2 minutes)*

Break up into groups of two and sit facing each other, so that you cannot read each other's confidential sheet. Each group should be as far away from other groups as possible, to avoid overhearing each other's conversations. If there is an odd number of students in the class, one student will be an observer or work with the instructor. Select who will be the buyer and who will be the seller of the used car.

Procedure 2 *(1–2 minutes)*

The instructor goes to each group and gives each buyer and seller their confidential sheet.

Procedure 3 *(5–6 minutes)*

Buyers and sellers read their confidential sheets and write down some plans (what will be your basic approach, what will you say) for the lunch meeting.

Procedure 4 *(3–7 minutes)*

Negotiate the sale of the car. Try not to overhear your classmates' conversations. You do not have to buy or sell the car. After you make the sale, or agree not to sell, read the confidential sheet of your partner in this exercise and discuss the experience.

Integration *(3–7 minutes)*

Answer the following questions:

1. Which of the nine influencing tactics (see Exhibit 5.1) did you use during the negotiations?

2. Which of the seven types of power (Exhibit 5.1) did you use during the negotiations? Did both parties believe that they got a good deal?

3. During your planning, did you (1) research the other party, (2) set an objective (price to pay or accept), (3) develop options and trade-offs, and (4) anticipate questions and objections and prepare answers?

4. During the negotiations, did you (1) develop a rapport and focus on obstacles, not the person; (2) let the other party make the first offer; (3) listen and ask questions to focus on meeting the other party's needs; and (4) did you refuse to give in too quickly, and did you remember to ask for something in return?

5. Did you reach an agreement to sell/buy the car? If yes, did you get exactly, more than, or less than your target price?

6. When negotiating, is it a good practice to ask for more than you expect to receive, or to offer less than you expect to pay?

7. When negotiating, is it better to be the one to give or receive the initial offer?

8. When negotiating, is it better to appear to be dealing with strong or weak power? In other words, should you try to portray that you have other options and don't really need to make a deal with this person? Or, should you appear to be in need of the deal?

9. Can having the power to intimidate others be helpful in negotiations?

Conclusion

The instructor leads a class discussion, or simply gives the answers to the "Integration" questions, and makes concluding remarks.

Apply It *(2–4 minutes)*

What did I learn from this experience? How will I use this knowledge in the future? What will I do differently?

_____

_____

_____

Sharing

In the group, or to the entire class, volunteers may give their answers to the "Apply It" questions.

Source: The car dealer negotiation confidential information is from Arch G. Woodside, Tulane University. The Car Dealer Game is part of a paper, "Bargaining Behavior in Personal Selling and Buying Exchanges," that was presented at the 1980 *Eighth Annual Conference of the Association for Business Simulation and Experiential Learning (ABSEL)*. It is used with Dr. Woodside's permission.

PART TWO

TEAM LEADERSHIP

6

Communication, Coaching, and Conflict Skills

Learning Outcomes

After studying this chapter, you should be able to:

1. List the steps in the oral message-sending process. p. 193

2. List and explain the three parts of the message-receiving process. p. 197

3. Describe paraphrasing and state why it is used. p. 199

4. Identify two common approaches to getting feedback, and explain why they don't work. p. 200

5. Describe the difference between criticism and coaching feedback. p. 207

6. Discuss the relationship between the performance formula and the coaching model. p. 207

7. Define the five conflict management styles. p. 211

8. List the steps in the initiating conflict resolution model. p. 215

9. Define the following **key terms** (in order of appearance in the chapter):

communication

oral message-sending process

message-receiving process

feedback

paraphrasing

360-degree feedback

coaching

job instructional training

coaching feedback

attribution theory

performance formula

mentoring

conflict

initiating conflict resolution model

BCF model

mediator

arbitrator

OPENING CASE *APPLICATION*

The Ranch Golf Club, where every player is a special guest for the day, opened in 2001 in Southwick, Massachusetts, so it was 10 years old in July 2011. The Ranch's competitive advantage is its upscale public course with links, woods, and a variety of elevations with unsurpassed service in New England. From the start, The Ranch strived to be the best golf club in New England. In less than a year, The Ranch earned a 4-star course rating, one of only four in New England. In the January 2003 issue of *Golf Digest*, The Ranch was rated number 3 in the country in the new upscale public golf course category, and it was ranked as the best public golf course in Massachusetts in 2007–2008. In *GolfWorld's* 2010 Readers' Choice Awards, The Ranch was voted in the top 50 of all public golf courses; one of only two courses in all of New England who made the list.

So how did The Ranch get started? Prior to being a golf club, it was a dairy farm owned by the Hall family. The Hall family wanted to turn the farm into a golf club with the help of Rowland Bates as project coordinator. The Halls were to provide the land, and investors would provide the capital.

Peter and Korby Clark were part owners of nearly 50 Jiffy Lubes, selling most to Pennzoil in 1991. Through the 1990s, the Clarks had a variety of opportunities to invest in new and ongoing businesses. Nothing interested the Clarks until the late 1990s. They were not simply offered a business looking for investors; Bates offered Peter Clark the opportunity to create and help manage a new golf club. Although Clark played golf, it was not so much the golf but the challenge of creating a new course and also playing an ongoing part in its management that interested him. Bates found two more investors, Bernard Chiu and Ronald Izen, to provide the additional funding, creating a one-third ownership by the Halls, Clarks, and Chiu and Izen.

The Clarks were happy to have the professional golf management team of Willowbend. First, they realized that they could not create and run a successful golf club business without expertise. Neither of them had ever worked for a golf club, and they only played recreational golf. Secondly, they would not have to manage The Ranch full time. However, in 2005 Willowbend stopped managing golf courses and sold its business. By then the Clarks had gained enough experience running The Ranch and no longer needed professional management. Peter Clark stopped his part-time coaching of football and baseball and increased his management role to become the managing partner, overseeing day-to-day operations, and Korby works full time too.[1]

OPENING CASE QUESTIONS:

1. Why is communication important to the management of The Ranch?

2. How does management use feedback at The Ranch?

3. Is there a difference in managing an oil change business, a golf course, and a sports team; and how does Peter Clark use coaching at The Ranch?

4. Which conflict management style does Peter Clark tend to use at The Ranch?

5. What types of conflict resolutions do the Clarks deal with at The Ranch?

Can you answer any of these questions? You'll find answers to these questions and learn more about The Ranch Golf Club and its leadership throughout the chapter.

To learn more about The Ranch Golf Club, or take a virtual tour of the course, visit its Web site at **http://www.theranchgolfclub.com**.

nterpersonal skills are as important as technical skills.[2] Leadership success is based on interpersonal skills,[3] and the focus of this chapter is on three important interrelated parts of interpersonal skills.[4] They are communication, coaching, and conflict skills. Interpersonal skills can be developed.[5] We begin with sending and receiving *communications*, because it is the foundation for coaching and managing conflict. We also discuss feedback as it relates to both communication and coaching. Based on this foundation, you will learn how to *coach followers*, and then how to *manage conflicts*.

Communication

In this section, we discuss the importance of communication in leadership and examine the communication process of sending and receiving messages. **Communication** *is the* *process of conveying information and meaning.* True communication takes place only when all parties understand the message (information) from the same perspective (meaning).

Communication and Leadership

Communication is a rich process underlying all information exchanges, decision making, and cooperative efforts.[6] Thus, organizations can't run successfully without effective communications,[7] and honesty is needed.[8] On a list of 26 attributes identified by company recruiters, the most important for new hires to have is communication and interpersonal skills.[9] This supports the known link between knowledge, skills, and communication ability and leadership competency.[10] Leadership is about influencing others, which we do through communications, and it comes through relationships, which are also based on communications.[11] Because communications is so important, there are hundreds of books on the topic.[12]

With changing technology, how we communicate has changed over the years. To a large extent, we moved from face-to-face, to the phone call, to e-mail, instant messaging, texting, and now to Twitter and Facebook. Teens send and receive an average of 3,339 texts per month.[13] Facebook introduced an in-box that stresses instant communications by mashing together e-mail with instant messages and cell phone text into a single stream of chatter, customized for the Age of Urgency.[14] But no matter which technology we use to communicate, two important parts of communication remain: sending and receiving messages.

Sending Messages and Giving Instructions

Leaders send a variety of messages orally, in writing, and nonverbally. An important part of a manager's job is to give instructions, which is sending a message. Have you ever heard a manager say, "This isn't what I asked for"? As managers, how well we give instructions directly affects our ability to motivate employees, as well as their satisfaction with our supervisory leadership.

Planning the Message

Before sending a message, we should plan it, remembering that brevity rules.[15] Answer these questions while planning. *What* is the goal of my message? *Who* should receive my message? *When* will my message be transmitted? *Where* will my message be transmitted? *How* will I send the message?

With the receivers in mind, plan how you will convey the message so that it will be understood. Select the appropriate method for the audience and situation (see Concept Application 1 for a list). As a general guide, use rich oral channels for sending difficult and unusual messages, less rich written channels for transmitting simple and routine messages to several people, and combined channels for important messages that employees need to attend to and understand.

CONCEPT APPLICATION 1
Methods of Sending Messages

For each of these ten communication situations, select the most appropriate channel for transmitting the message. Write the most appropriate letter in the blank before each item.

(continued)

(Concept Application 1 continued)

Oral communication	**Written communication (includes e-mail/ texting and traditional methods)**	
a. face-to-face	e. memo	h. bulletin board
b. meeting	f. letter	i. poster
c. presentation	g. report	j. newsletter
d. telephone		

_____ 1. You write well and want to become better known by more people throughout the organization.

_____ 2. You have been given a written complaint from a customer and asked to take care of it.

_____ 3. You are waiting for an important document to arrive, and you want to know if it is in the mail room yet.

_____ 4. You want employees to start saving electricity by shutting off the lights in the storage room when no one is in it.

_____ 5. You have three guys who will be working on a new project as a team. You need to explain the project to them.

_____ 6. You want an employee of yours to stop coming in late for work.

_____ 7. You have exceeded your departmental goals and you want your manager to know about it, because it should have a positive influence on your upcoming performance appraisal.

_____ 8. Your significant other wants you to help her sell Super Spectrum vitamin supplements where you work. However, you don't want to ask anyone directly to buy it.

_____ 9. You have been asked by people in another department for some numbers relating to your work.

_____ 10. You have been asked to be the speaker for the local Rotary Club meeting.

Learning Outcome 1 *List the steps in the oral message-sending process.*

The Oral Message-Sending Process

Oral face-to-face communication is the richest channel because it allows for a maximum amount of information to be transmitted through dialogue between the parties. The big advantage over the other channels is that it allows us to read the person's nonverbal communication.[16] When using electronics, we lose the personal touch that is important to building and maintaining relationships.[17]

Be careful not to talk too fast when giving instructions in person, or over the phone. It is helpful to follow these steps in the oral message-sending process: (1) *develop rapport*; (2) *state your communication objective*; (3) *transmit your message*; (4) *check the receiver's understanding*; and (5) *get a commitment and follow up*. Model 6.1 lists these steps.

Step 1. **Develop rapport.** Put the receiver at ease. It is usually appropriate to begin communications with small talk correlated to the message. It helps prepare the person to receive the message.

MODEL **6.1**   The Oral Message-Sending Process

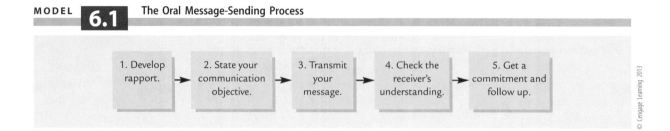

© Cengage Learning 2013

Step 2.   **State your communication objective.** The common business communication objective is to influence followers.[18] When influencing, it is helpful for the receiver to know the desired end result of the communication before covering all the details.

Step 3.   **Transmit your message.** When the objective is to influence, tell the people what you want them to do—give instructions. Be sure to set deadlines for completing tasks. We will discuss how to delegate task in the next chapter.

Step 4.   **Check the receiver's understanding.** When communicating, we should ask direct questions and/or use paraphrasing.[19] To simply ask, "Do you have any questions?" does not check understanding. In the next section of this chapter, you will learn how to check understanding by using feedback.

WORK Application **1**
Recall a specific task that your manager assigned to you. Identify which steps the manager did and did not use in the oral message-sending process.

_____

_____

_____

_____

Step 5.   **Get a commitment and follow up.** When giving instructions, it is important to get a commitment to the action. We need to make sure that followers can do the task and have it done by a certain time or date. For situations in which the follower does not intend to get the task done, it is better to know this when sending the message, rather than to wait until the deadline before finding out. When followers are reluctant to commit to the necessary action, leaders can use persuasive power within their authority. When giving instructions, we should follow up to ensure that the necessary action has been taken.

Written Communication and Writing Tips

With information technology and the Internet, you can communicate with anyone in the world—in real time. Because the use of will continue to increase, your written communication skills are more important than ever. Even if people aren't telling you that you're using incorrect grammar, they are evaluating you and may conclude you're not intelligent. So we have included some simple but important tips that can help you to improve your writing.

WORK Application **2**
Select two or three of the tips that you can use to improve your written communication. Explain how using the tip will improve your writing.

_____

_____

_____

_____

• Lack of organization is a major writing problem. Before you begin writing, set an objective for your communication. Keep the audience in mind. What do you want them to do? Make an outline, using letters and/or numbers, of the major points you want to get across. Now put the outline into written form. The first paragraph states the purpose of the communication. The middle paragraphs support the purpose of the communication: facts, figures, and so forth. The last paragraph summarizes the major points and clearly states the action, if any, to be taken by you and other people.

• Write to communicate, not to impress. Keep the message short and simple.[20] Follow the 1-5-15 rule. Limit each paragraph to a single topic and an average of five sentences. Sentences should average 15 words. Vary paragraph and sentence length. Write in the active voice (I recommend…) rather than the passive voice (it is recommended…). If it's more than 200 words, it shouldn't be an e-mail; it should be a document attachment or a phone call or even a face-to-face visit.[21]

- Edit your work and rewrite where necessary. To improve sentences and paragraphs, add to them to convey full meaning, cut out unnecessary words and phrases, and/or rearrange the words. Check your work with the computer spelling and grammar checkers. Have others edit your important work as well.

YOU Make the **ETHICAL** Call

6.1   *Advertising*

Companies use oral, nonverbal, and written communications to advertise their products in order to increase sales. Selecting the best words to sell a product or service is important. However, some of the terms used in ads are misleading and even deceptive, although in some cases the words are legal.

For example, some companies use the word "natural" on foods that are highly processed, such as products including white sugar. So, some question the use of the term "natural." Bags of chips are advertised as being "all natural," which leads people to think they are healthy, when in fact others classify them as junk food. Because obesity has become such a major health problem, the Food and Drug Administration (FDA) obesity task force is trying to crack down on misleading labels and ads, and is calling for warnings and fines for violators.

1. Is it ethical and socially responsible for food companies to use terms (like "natural") that can be misleading to increase sales and profits?

2. Should companies use terms that are considered misleading by some but are not illegal?

3. How would you define "natural"?

4. How should the FDA define "natural" so that it is not used to mislead people to buy food thinking that it is healthy, when in fact it is not?

Receiving Messages

The second communication process that leaders are involved in is receiving messages. With oral communications, the key to successfully understanding the message is listening. Let's begin by completing the Self-Assessment to determine the level and quality of your listening skills, and be honest.

SELF-ASSESSMENT 1   **Listening Skills**

Select the response that best describes the frequency of your actual behavior. Write the letter A, U, F, O, or S on the line before each of the 15 statements.

A—almost always   U—usually   F—frequently

O—occasionally   S—seldom

———— 1. I like to listen to people talk. I encourage others to talk by showing interest, smiling, nodding, and so forth.

———— 2. I pay closer attention to people who are more similar to me than I do to people who are different from me.

(continued)

(Self-Assessment 1 continued)

_____ 3. I evaluate people's words and their nonverbal communication ability as they talk.

_____ 4. I avoid distractions; if it's noisy, I suggest moving to a quiet spot.

_____ 5. When people come to me and interrupt me when I'm doing something, I put what I was doing out of my mind and give them my complete attention.

_____ 6. When people are talking, I allow them time to finish. I do not interrupt, anticipate what they are going to say, or jump to conclusions.

_____ 7. I tune people out who do not agree with my views.

_____ 8. While the other person is talking, or professors are lecturing, my mind wanders to personal topics.

_____ 9. While the other person is talking, I pay close attention to the nonverbal communication to help me fully understand what they are trying to communicate.

_____ 10. I tune out and pretend I understand when the topic is difficult for me to understand.

_____ 11. When the other person is talking, I think about and prepare what I am going to say in reply.

_____ 12. When I think there is something missing or contradictory, I ask direct questions to get the person to explain the idea more fully.

_____ 13. When I don't understand something, I let the other person know I don't understand.

_____ 14. When listening to other people, I try to put myself in their position and to see things from their perspective.

_____ 15. During conversations I repeat back to the other person what has been said in my own words to be sure I correctly understand what has been said.

If people you talk to regularly were to answer these questions about you, would they have the same responses that you selected? To find out, have friends fill out the questions with you in mind rather than themselves. Then compare answers.

To determine your score, give yourself 5 points for each A, 4 for each U, 3 for each F, 2 for each O, and 1 for each S for statements 1, 4, 5, 6, 9, 12, 13, 14, and 15. Place the numbers on the line next to your response letter. For items 2, 3, 7, 8, 10, and 11 the score reverses: 5 points for each S, 4 for each O, 3 for each F, 2 for each U, and 1 for each A. Place these score numbers on the lines next to the response letters. Now add your total number of points. Your score should be between 15 and 75. Place your score on the continuum below. Generally, the higher your score, the better your listening skills.

15–20–25–30–35–40–45–50–55–60–65–70–75
Poor listener   *Good listener*

Any leader aspiring to greatness must do two things that matter the most: listening and telling the truth.[22] People talk and we need to listen to them to improve.[23] In fact, failure to listen is one of the top five reasons leaders fail, and Warren Bennis said it is the most common reason CEOs fail. Thus, we need to improve our communication skills by listening to others.[24]

If someone asks us, are you a good listener, most likely we would say yes. What was your score on the self-assessment? Unfortunately, a recent survey found that the number 1 thing lacking in new college grads is listening skills.[25] All the screens we pay attention to are robbing our ability to focus.[26] Constant multitasking is deteriorating our ability to pay attention for long and listen.[27] For how long can you pay attention and listen effectively at school and work? Next time you begin reading a textbook, time how long you can go before you "have" to stop and do something else. By using the message-receiving process below, we can become better listeners.

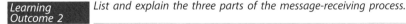

Learning
Outcome 2
List and explain the three parts of the message-receiving process.

The Message-Receiving Process

The **message-receiving process** *includes listening, analyzing, and checking understanding.* To improve your listening skills, spend one week focusing your attention on listening by concentrating on what other people say and the nonverbal communications they send when they speak. Notice if their verbal and nonverbal communication are consistent. Talk only when necessary, so that you can listen and "see" what others are saying. If you apply the following tips, you will improve your listening skills. The tips are presented in the depiction of the message-receiving process (Exhibit 6.1): We should listen, analyze, and then check understanding.

EXHIBIT 6.1   The Message-Receiving Process

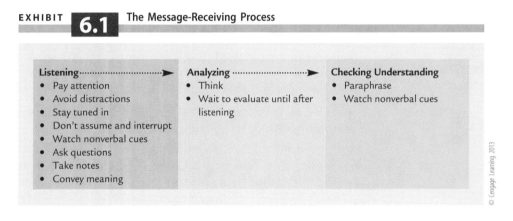

Listening	Analyzing	Checking Understanding
• Pay attention	• Think	• Paraphrase
• Avoid distractions	• Wait to evaluate until after	• Watch nonverbal cues
• Stay tuned in	listening	
• Don't assume and interrupt		
• Watch nonverbal cues		
• Ask questions		
• Take notes		
• Convey meaning		

© Cengage Learning 2013

Listening

Listening is the process of giving the speaker your undivided attention. As the speaker sends the message, you should listen by:

- *Paying attention.* When people interrupt, stop what you are doing and give them your complete attention before you begin the conversation.

- *Avoiding distractions.* Keep your eye on the speaker. Do not fiddle with pens or other distractions; let your phone "take a message."[28] If you are in a noisy or distracting place, suggest moving to a quiet spot.

- *Staying tuned in.* Do not let your mind wander. If it does, gently bring it back or repeat in your mind what the person is saying to force yourself to pay attention. Do not think about what you are going to say in reply; just listen.

- *Not assuming and interrupting.* Do not assume you know what the speaker is going to say, or listen to the beginning and jump to conclusions. Most listening mistakes are made when people hear the first few words of a sentence, finish it in their own minds, and miss the second half. Listen to the entire message without interrupting the speaker.

- *Watching nonverbal cues.* Understand both the feelings and the content of the message. People sometimes say one thing and mean something else. So watch as you listen to be sure that the speaker's eyes, body, and face are sending the same message as the verbal message. If something seems out of sync, get it cleared up by asking questions.

- *Asking questions.* When you feel there is something missing, contradictory, or you just do not understand, ask direct questions to get the person to explain the idea more fully.

- *Taking notes.* Part of listening is writing important things down so you can remember them later, and document them when necessary. This is especially true when you're listening to instructions. You should always have something to take notes with, such as a pen and a notebook or some index cards.

- *Conveying meaning.* The way to let the speaker know you are listening to the message is to use verbal clues, such as, "you feel …," "uh huh," "I see," and "I understand." Use nonverbal communication such as eye contact, appropriate facial expressions, nodding of the head, or leaning slightly forward in your chair to indicate interest and listening.

Analyzing

Analyzing is the process of thinking about, decoding, and evaluating the message. Poor listening occurs in part because people speak at an average rate of 120 words per minute, while they are capable of listening at a rate of over 500 words per minute. The ability to comprehend words more than four times faster than the speaker can talk often results in minds wandering. As the speaker sends the message, we should analyze by:

- *Thinking.* Use the speed of the brain positively. Listen actively by organizing, summarizing, reviewing, interpreting, and critiquing often. These activities will help to do an effective job of decoding the message.

- *Waiting to evaluate until after listening.* When we try to listen and evaluate what is said at the same time, we tend to miss part or the entire message. Just listen to the entire message, and then come to a conclusion.

Checking Understanding

Checking understanding is the process of giving feedback. After we have listened to the message—or during the message, if it's a long one—check understanding of the message by:

WORK Application **3**
Refer to Self-Assessment 1 and the listening tips. What is your weakest listening skill area on the job? How will you improve your listening ability?

——————————

——————————

——————————

——————————

- *Paraphrasing.* Begin speaking by giving feedback, using paraphrasing to repeat the message to the sender in your own words. When you can paraphrase the message correctly, you convey that you have listened and understood the other person.[29]

- *Watching nonverbal cues.* As you speak, watch the other person's nonverbal cues. If the person does not seem to understand what you are talking about, clarify the message before finishing the conversation.

Work to change your behavior to become a better listener. Review the 15 statements in Self-Assessment 1. To improve your listening skills, practice doing items 1, 4, 5, 6, 9, 12, 13, 14, and 15; and avoid doing items 2, 3, 7, 8, 10, and 11.

OPENING CASE APPLICATION

1. Why is communication important to the management of The Ranch?

The key to success at The Ranch is clear, open communications of expectations. Peter Clark has to continually communicate with his partners and department heads, and nothing takes the place of sitting down face-to-face during regular

(continued)

(Opening Case Application 2 continued)

weekly meetings and listening to each other to continually improve operations. Meetings of department managers with employees continually focus on the importance of communicating the philosophy of unsurpassed professional service. To communicate professionalism, all employees wear The Ranch uniforms and name tags, and they are trained with instructions on how to perform high-quality service. Even the words used are chosen to communicate professionalism. For example, The Ranch has player assistants (PAs), not rangers; golf cars, not golf carts; and it has a golf shop, not a pro shop.

Learning Outcome 3	*Describe paraphrasing and state why it is used.*

Feedback

In this section, we discuss the importance of feedback, the common approaches to getting feedback (and why they don't work), and how to get feedback. We end with formal 360-degree feedback. In the next section we discuss how to give feedback as part of coaching.

The Importance of Feedback

Feedback motivates employees to achieve high levels of performance **Feedback** *is the process of verifying messages and determining if objectives are being met.* In Chapter 7, we discuss leader–follower performance feedback. Effective leader–follower feedback focuses on the leader's assessment of a follower's job performance on assigned tasks and responsibilities. A common name for this activity is job or employee evaluation. Effective communication during this process is critical for both the leader and follower.

The Role of Feedback in Verifying Messages

Recall that checking receiver understanding is the fourth step in the oral message-sending process. The best way to make sure communication has taken place is to get feedback from the receiver of the message through questioning and paraphrasing. **Paraphrasing** *is the process of having the receiver restate the message in his or her own words.* If the receiver of the message can answer the questions or paraphrase the message, communication has taken place.

The Role of Feedback in Meeting Objectives

Feedback is also essential to knowing how the leader and organization are progressing to meet objectives.[30] Giving and receiving feedback must be an ongoing or continuous process to be effective.[31] Thus, leaders should set specific measurable objectives (Chapter 3) and monitor the process through ongoing feedback.[32] See Guidelines for Effective Leader Feedback in Chapter 7.

The Need to Be Open to Feedback—Criticism

To improve our performance and get ahead in an organization, we have to be open to feedback commonly called *criticism*.[33] We should actually solicit feedback. However, if we're asking for personal feedback, remember that we are asking to hear things that may surprise, upset, or insult us, and even hurt our feelings. If we become defensive and emotional—and it is tough not to when we feel attacked—feedback will stop.

We do not really enjoy being criticized by our manager, peers, or others, even when it is constructive, because it tends to be painful. But keep the phrase, "no pain, no gain" in

WORK Application 4

Are you really open to feedback or criticism from others at work? How can you improve on accepting criticism?

_____

_____

_____

_____

mind when it comes to criticism. When criticized, whether you asked for it or not, stay calm (even when the other person is emotional), don't get defensive, and don't blame others. View it as an opportunity to improve. If the feedback is vague, ask what specific behavior they want that will improve performance.[34] Although it is difficult to change our behavior, is the only way we will improve.[35]

YOU Make the **ETHICAL** Call

6.2 *Academic Grades*

Grades are a form of feedback and are often criticized. (Recall Ethical Call "Academic Standards" in Chapter 3.) Successful managers set and maintain high expectations for all their employees, and as Lou Holtz said, we need to set a higher standard. While students are doing less work than in prior years, grades continue to increase, which is called grade inflation. At one time, most colleges had a set grade point average (GPA) to determine honors. But today, most colleges use a ranking system of GPA, because of grade inflation, to limit the number of students graduating with honors.

1. How do you react when you get a grade that is lower than you wanted or expected?
2. Do you use the feedback of correcting and grades to help you improve? Why or why not, and if yes, how?
3. Why are professors giving higher grades today than were given 5, 10, or 20 years ago?
4. Are students who are putting in less time and getting higher grades being well prepared for a career with high standards after graduation?
5. Is it ethical and socially responsible for professors to drop standards and for colleges to award degrees with higher grades today than 5, 10, or 20 years ago?

Learning Outcome 4

Identify two common approaches to getting feedback, and explain why they don't work.

Common Approaches to Getting Feedback on Messages—and Why They Don't Work

One common approach that ignores feedback is to send the entire message and then assume that the message has been conveyed with mutual understanding. A second approach is to give the entire message and then ask "Do you have any questions?" Feedback usually does not follow, because people have a tendency "not" to ask questions. There are at least four good reasons why people do not ask questions:

1. *Receivers feel ignorant.* Asking questions, especially if no one else does, is often considered an admission of not paying attention or not being bright enough to understand.
2. *Receivers are ignorant.* Sometimes people do not know enough about the message to know whether it is incomplete, incorrect, or subject to interpretation. There are no questions, because what was said sounds right. The receiver does not understand the message or does not know what to ask.
3. *Receivers are reluctant to point out the sender's ignorance.* Employees often fear that asking a question suggests that the manager has done a poor job of preparing and sending the message. Or it suggests that the manager is wrong.
4. *Receivers have cultural barriers.* For example, in many Asian countries it is considered impolite to disagree with the manager, so the employee would answer yes when asked by the manager if the message was understood.

After managers send a message and ask if there are questions, they then proceed to make another common error: Managers assume that no questions means communication is complete, that there is mutual understanding of the message. In reality, the message is often misunderstood. When "this isn't what I asked for" happens, the task often has to be done all over again. The end result is often wasted time, materials, and effort.

The most common cause of messages not resulting in communication is the lack of getting feedback that ensures mutual understanding. The proper use of questioning and paraphrasing can help you ensure that your messages are communicated.

How to Get Feedback on Messages

Here are four guidelines we can use to ensure getting feedback on messages:

- *Be open to feedback.* There are no dumb questions. When someone asks a question, we need to be responsive, patiently answer questions, and explain things clearly. If people sense that we get upset if they ask questions, they will not ask questions.

- *Be aware of nonverbal communication.* Be sure nonverbal communications encourage feedback. For example, if you say, "I encourage questions," but when people ask questions you look at them as though they are stupid, or you act impatient, people will learn not to ask questions. You must also be aware of, and read, people's nonverbal communications.[36] For example, if you are explaining a task to Larry and he has a puzzled look on his face, he is probably confused but may not be willing to say so. In such a case, you should stop and clarify things before going on.

- *Ask questions.* When sending messages, it is better to know whether the messages are understood before action is taken, so that the action will not have to be changed or repeated. Ask questions to check understanding, rather than simply asking, "Do you have any questions?" Direct questions dealing with the *specific information* you have given will indicate if the receiver has been listening, and whether he or she understands enough to give a direct reply. If the response is not accurate, try repeating, giving more examples, or elaborating further on the message.

- *Use paraphrasing.* The most accurate indicator of understanding is paraphrasing. How we ask the receiver to paraphrase will affect attitudes. For example, if we say "Joan, tell me what I just said so that I can be sure you will not make a mistake as usual," this will probably result in defensive behavior on Joan's part. Joan will probably make a mistake. Here are two examples of proper requests for paraphrasing:

  "Now tell me what you are going to do, so we will be sure that we are in agreement."

  "Would you tell me what you are going to do, so that I can be sure that I explained myself clearly?"

  Notice that the second statement takes the pressure off the employee. The sender is asking for a check on *his or her* ability, not that of the employee. These types of requests for paraphrasing should result in a positive attitude toward the message and the sender. They show concern for the employee and for communicating effectively.

360-Degree Multi-Rater Feedback

The use of feedback from multiple sources has become popular as a means of improving performance.[37] So far, we have discussed the informal methods of getting feedback. We now turn to a formal evaluation process using 360-degree multi-rater feedback.[38] As the

WORK Application 5

Recall a past or present manager. Did or does your manager use the common approach to getting feedback on messages regularly? Was or is he or she open to feedback and aware of nonverbal communication on a regular basis? Did the manager regularly ask questions and ask you to paraphrase?

_____

_____

_____

_____

name implies, 360-degree feedback *is based on receiving performance evaluations from many people.* Usually a 360-degree evaluation form is completed by the person being evaluated, his or her manager, peers, and subordinates when applicable. Customers, suppliers, and other outside people are also asked for an evaluation when applicable. See Exhibit 6.2 for an illustration of the 360-degree feedback process.

EXHIBIT 6.2   360-Degree Feedback Sources

may be customers

Manager

Peers   360-degree multirater
feedback form results   Self

Employees

may be suppliers

© Cengage Learning 2013

If you are serious about getting ahead, it is critical to focus on feedback from your manager and any other evaluators and do what it takes to receive a good formal performance evaluation. You should work together with your manager to develop and implement a plan for improvement during the next evaluation period.

OPENING CASE *APPLICATION*

2.   How does management use feedback at The Ranch?

Feedback is critical to success at The Ranch, because it is how the Clarks and the managers know if the players are getting quality service and learn how to improve service. The Clarks, managers, and employees are open to player criticism because they realize that the only way to improve is to listen and make changes to improve performance. In fact, Peter and Korby Clark spend much of their time at The Ranch talking to players about their experience, with the focus on listening for ways to make improvements. The Clarks and managers set clear objectives and have regular meetings with employees to get and give feedback on how The Ranch is progressing toward meeting its objectives.

Although it is a small business, during the summer 80 people work at The Ranch, and it has a sophisticated information system for its three departments—golf (greens and practice, tournaments/outings, golf shop), maintenance (the course and other facilities), and food and beverage (The Ranch Grille, bar, and functions)—that include many performance measures. The Ranch does not have a formal 360-degree feedback system. However, managers who evaluate employee performance do interact regularly with each employee, and with employee peers, the players, and other managers at The Ranch; and they use the feedback from others in their performance appraisals.

Coaching

Coaching is an important leadership competency.[39] Research supports that providing coaching in addition to giving feedback increases the amount of performance improvement.[40] Thus, coaching is on the rise.[41] Coaching is based on feedback and communications. Coaching *is the process of giving motivational feedback to maintain and improve performance.* Coaching is designed to maximize strengths and minimize weaknesses.

In this section, we discuss how to give coaching feedback, and what criticism is—and why that doesn't work. We then present a coaching model you can use on the job, and we end by briefly discussing mentoring, which may be considered a form of coaching.

How to Give Coaching Feedback

When people hear the word *coaching*, they often think of athletes, but managers should also be looking for steady performance and continual improvement. Athlete-coaching skills are being used successfully in the business world. If you have ever had a good coach, think about the behavior he or she used that helped to maintain and improve your performance and that of other team members. The next time you watch a sporting event, keep an eye on the coaches and learn some ways to coach employees. Here we discuss some guidelines that will help us to be effective coaches; the guidelines are also shown in Exhibit 6.3. The guidelines are designed primarily for use with employees who are doing a good job.

EXHIBIT 6.3 Coaching Guidelines

1. Develop a supportive working relationship.
2. Give praise and recognition.
3. Avoid blame and embarrassment.
4. Focus on the behavior, not the person.
5. Have employees assess their own performance.
6. Give specific and descriptive feedback.
7. Give coaching feedback.
8. Provide modeling and training.
9. Make feedback timely, but flexible.
10. Don't criticize.

© Cengage Learning 2013

Develop a Supportive Working Relationship

Manager and employee do not have to be personal friends and socialize together—it's about having a good working relationship. Our relationship with followers needs to convey concern for them as individuals and our commitment to coach them to success. A supportive working relationship can build enthusiasm and commitment to continual performance improvement.

We should periodically ask employees if there is anything we can do to help them do a better job. Take the time to listen to them. There will seldom be big problems. Problems are often caused by petty annoyances that an employee believes are too trivial to bother the manager with. Our job as a manager is to run interference and to remove the stumbling blocks for the employees to improve their performance and that of the business unit.

Give Praise and Recognition

Why should you give recognition to employees for doing their job? The reason is simple: It motivates employees to maintain and increase performance. In Chapter 3 you learned the importance of giving praise, and how to use the giving praise model. We cannot overemphasize the importance of giving praise and recognition. Recognition includes praise, awards, and recognition ceremonies. Awards include certificates of achievement, a letter of commendation, a pin, a plaque, a trophy, a medal, a ribbon, clothing, cash, trips, meals, employee of the month, and so on.

WORK Application 6
Recall the best and worst manager you ever had. With which manager did you have the best working relationship? Which one gave you the most encouragement, praise, and recognition for a job well done? Which one gave you the most negative criticism? Was your performance at a higher level for your best or worst manager?

_____

_____

_____

_____

Avoid Blame and Embarrassment

The objective of coaching is to develop employees' knowledge, skills, and abilities (KSA).[42] Thus, any leadership behavior that focuses on making the person feel bad does not help to develop the employee. Some things are best not said. For example, if an employee makes a mistake and realizes it, verbalizing it is not needed; doing so only makes them feel bad. Statements like, "I'm surprised that you did XYZ," or "I'm disappointed in you" should be avoided. Besides, effective leaders treat mistakes as learning experiences.

Focus on the Behavior, Not the Person

The purpose of coaching is to achieve desirable behavior, not to belittle the person. Let's use examples to illustrate the difference between coaching by focusing on changing behavior and coaching by focusing on the person.[43] Notice that the statements focusing on the person place blame and embarrassment—or belittle the person:

- *Situation 1.* The employee is dominating the discussion at a meeting.
  Focus on person—You talk too much; give others a chance.
  Focus on behavior—I'd like to hear what some of the other group members have to say.

- *Situation 2.* The employee is late for a meeting again.
  Focus on person—You are always late for meetings; why can't you be on time like the rest of us?
  Focus on behavior—This is the second time in a row that you arrived late for our meeting. The group needs your input right from the start of the meeting.

Have Employees Assess Their Own Performance

Here are some examples of criticism and of self-evaluation coaching feedback to help explain the difference:

- *Situation 3.* The employee has been making more errors lately.
  Criticism—You haven't been working up to par lately; get on the ball.
  Self-evaluation—How would you assess the number of errors you have been making this week?

- *Situation 4.* The employee is working on a few reports, and one is due in two days. The manager believes the employee may not meet the deadline.
  Criticism—Are you going to meet the deadline for the report?
  Self-evaluation—How are you progressing on the cost-cutting report that's due this Thursday? Is there something I can do to help?

Can the criticism statements result in defensive behavior, not listening, feeling bad about oneself, and disliking the task and the manager? Do the self-evaluation statements create different feelings and behavior?

Give Specific and Descriptive Feedback

Specific feedback is needed to avoid confusion over which particular behavior needs to be improved.[44] Compare the preceding criticism statements, which are not specific, to the self-evaluation statements, which are specific. Can you understand how the person being criticized may not understand specifically what the manager is talking about, and therefore may be unable to change even if willing to do so?

Descriptive feedback can be based on *facts* or *inferences*. Facts can be observed and proven; inferences cannot. In situation 3, the manager can observe and prove that the employee made more errors this week than in prior weeks. However, the manager cannot observe or prove why. The manager may infer many reasons for the changed behavior, such as laziness, illness, a personal problem, and so on. In situation 4, the manager cannot prove that the report will be late; the manager is inferring that it will be and attempting to coach the employee to make sure it is completed on time. Give factual rather than inferential feedback, because factual feedback tends to be specific and more positive, while inferential feedback tends to be more negative criticism.

Give Coaching Feedback

Self-assessment can work well, especially when performance needs to be maintained rather than improved. However, it is not always appropriate; if overused, it can have limited success. There are often times when you will want to offer coaching feedback without self-assessment. It is important to respond positively to negative behavior and outcomes, and the way to do this is not by pointing out mistakes but by selling the benefits of positive behavior. Here are some examples of how to coach versus criticize:

- *Situation 5.* The manager just saw an employee, who knows how it should be done, incorrectly pick up a fairly heavy box.
  Criticism—You just picked up the box wrong. Don't let me catch you again.
  Coaching feedback—If you don't want to injure your back, use your legs—not your back.

- *Situation 6.* A student sees a fellow student going to the Yahoo! Web site by typing in the entire address, **http://www.yahoo.com**.
  Criticism—You just wasted time typing in the entire Yahoo! Web site address. Don't use the entire address, or make it a favorite address.
  Coaching feedback—Would you like me to show you a faster way to get to the Yahoo! home page?

- *Situation 7.* A worker is completing a task by following an inefficient, step-by-step procedure.
  Criticism—You're not doing that the best way. Do X, Y, then Z from now on.
  Coaching feedback—Have you given any thought to changing the sequence of steps for completing that task to X, Y, then Z?

Provide Modeling and Training

A good manager leads by example. If employees see the manager doing things in an effective manner, they will tend to copy the manager. As illustrated in situations 4 and 5, coaching often requires some training.[45] The job instructional training method is widely used (see Model 6.2). *The job instructional training (JIT) steps include (1) trainee receives preparation; (2) trainer presents the task; (3) trainee performs the task; and (4) trainer follows up.* Remember that tasks we know well seem very simple, but they are usually difficult for the new trainee. We can also use coleadership and have others do the training, especially if they are better at training than we are.

Step 1. Trainee receives preparation. Put the trainee at ease as you create interest in the job and encourage questions. Explain the quantity and quality requirements and why they are important.

MODEL **6.2** Job Instructional Training Steps

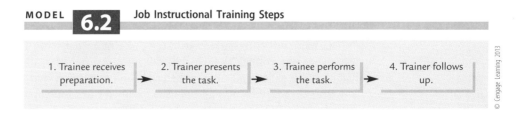

1. Trainee receives preparation. → 2. Trainer presents the task. → 3. Trainee performs the task. → 4. Trainer follows up.

Step 2. **Trainer presents the task.** Perform the task yourself at a slow pace, explaining each step several times. Once the trainee seems to have the steps memorized, have the trainee explain each step as you slowly perform the task again. For complex tasks with multiple steps, it is helpful to write them out and to give a copy to the trainee.

Step 3. **Trainee performs the task.** Have the trainee perform the task at a slow pace, while explaining each step to you. Correct any errors and be patiently willing to help the trainee perform any difficult steps. Continue until the trainee is proficient at performing the task.

Step 4. **Trainer follows up.** Tell the trainee whom to ask for help with any questions or problems. Gradually leave the trainee alone. Begin by checking quality and quantity frequently, and decrease checks based on the trainee's skill level. Observe the trainee performing the task, and be sure to correct any errors or faulty work procedures before they become a habit. As you follow up, be sure to be patient and encouraging. Praise a good effort at first, and good performance as skills develop.

WORK Application **7**

Recall a present or past manager. Which of the ten guidelines does or did the manager use most frequently and least frequently?

_____

_____

_____

_____

Make Feedback Timely, but Flexible

Feedback should be given *as soon as possible* after the behavior has been observed. For example, in situation 5 you will want to give the coaching feedback as soon as you see the employee lift the box incorrectly. To tell the employee about it a few days later will have less impact on changing the behavior, and the employee could be injured by then. The *flexibility* part comes into play in two ways: (1) When you don't have the time to do the full coaching job, make an appointment to do so; (2) when emotions are high, wait until everyone calms down to discuss the issue.

Don't Criticize

Jack Falvey, management consultant and author, takes the positive versus negative feedback to the point of recommending only positive feedback:

> *Criticism is to be avoided at all costs (there is no such thing as constructive criticism; all criticism is destructive). If you must correct someone, never do it after the fact. Bite your tongue and hold off until the person is about to do the same thing again and then challenge the person to make a more positive contribution.*[46]

Remember that you can be a good coach by following the simple guidelines presented here. These general guidelines apply to any leadership situation. So start coaching—today.

What Is Criticism—and Why Doesn't It Work?

Falvey's statement may seem a bit extreme, but it is true. Placing blame and embarrassment and focusing on the person are types of criticism. Criticism is rarely effective. Criticism involves a judgment, which is that either the person is right or wrong. Criticism is also the process of pointing out mistakes, which places blame and is embarrassing.

Once we tell people they are wrong or made a mistake, directly or indirectly, four things usually happen. (1) They become defensive and justify their behavior, or they blame it on someone or something. (2) They don't really listen to so-called constructive feedback. (3) They are embarrassed and feel bad about themselves, or they view themselves as losers. (4) They begin to dislike the task or job, as well as the critic.

The more criticism employees receive the more defensive they become. They listen less; they are in conflict as their self-concept is threatened or diminished; they eventually hate the task or job and usually the critic; and they often quit the job, get a transfer, or are fired. Giving praise has an opposite, positive effect on employees, their behavior, and their performance.

Demotivating

Employees with overly critical managers tend to develop a negative attitude: "My manager doesn't care about me or appreciate my work, so why should I work hard to do a good job?" They play it safe by doing the minimum, taking no risks, focusing on not making errors, and covering up any errors so they aren't criticized. They avoid contact with the manager and they feel stress just seeing the manager approach them. They think, "What did I do this time?"

| Learning Outcome 5 | Describe the difference between criticism and coaching feedback. |

The Difference between Criticism and Coaching Feedback

By now you probably agree that criticism usually does not work; in fact, it often makes the behavior worse. But you may be thinking that you can't always catch an employee in the act and challenge them to perform better. What do you do? The major difference between criticism and coaching feedback is that **coaching feedback** *is based on a good, supportive relationship; it is specific and descriptive; and it is not judgmental criticism.* And coaching is often based on the employee doing a self-assessment of performance. Criticism makes employees feel like losers; praise and coaching feedback makes them feel like winners. And nothing breeds success like good coaches.

CONCEPT APPLICATION 2
Criticism or Coaching Feedback

Identify each of these five statements as criticism or coaching feedback. For each criticism only, write a coaching feedback statement to replace it.

a. criticism   b. coaching feedback

_____ 11. I couldn't help overhearing your conflict with Joel. Would you like me to tell you how you can minimize this problem in the future?

_____ 12. You are a poor speller. Make sure you don't forget to use the spell check before you pass in your work.

_____ 13. *In a loud, angry voice*: Why did you do it that way?

_____ 14. Why did you drop it on the floor?

_____ 15. This is still dirty. You are going to have to clean it again.

| Learning Outcome 6 | Discuss the relationship between the performance formula and the coaching model. |

The Coaching Model for Employees Who Are Performing Below Standard

Coaching is needed when performance falls below expected levels.[47] When managers are giving feedback to employees who are performing below standard, all ten of the coaching guidelines are important. However, most managers are more apt to use embarrassment, to focus on the person, and to criticize the person who is performing below standard than to focus on the person who is doing a good job. Avoid this temptation, because it doesn't really work. They need your one-on-one coaching at its best. Be patient but persistent; don't give up on them. Before getting into the coaching model, let's discuss attribution theory and the performance formula because they affect the coaching model.

Attribution Theory

Attribution theory *is used to explain the process managers go through in determining the reasons for effective or ineffective performance and deciding what to do about it.* The reaction of a manager to poor performance has two stages. First, we try to determine the cause of the poor performance, and then to select an appropriate corrective action. To help determine the cause of poor performance, we provide the performance formula; and to take corrective action, the coaching model.

Determining the Cause of Poor Performance and Corrective Coaching Action

The **performance formula** *explains performance as a function of ability, motivation, and resources.* Model 6.3 is a simple model that can help us determine the cause of poor performance and the corrective action to take based on the cause. When ability, motivation, or resources are low, performance will be lower.

When the employee's *ability* is the reason for keeping performance from being optimal, the corrective coaching action is training (JIT). When *motivation* is lacking, motivational techniques (discussed in Chapter 3) such as giving praise might help. Coach the employee, and work together to develop a plan to improve performance.[48] When *resources* (tools, material, equipment, and so on) are the problem, look at getting the needed resources. When obstacles are getting in the way of performance, we need to overcome them.

MODEL 6.3   The Performance Formula

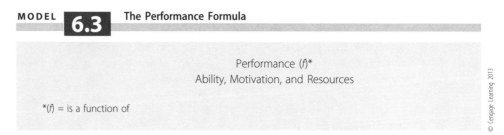

Performance (*f*)*
Ability, Motivation, and Resources

*(*f*) = is a function of

© Cengage Learning 2013

Improving Performance with the Coaching Model

The steps in the coaching model are (1) describe current performance; (2) describe desired performance; (3) get a commitment to the change; and (4) follow up. Use all ten guidelines to coaching within the framework of the coaching model.

Step 1.   **Describe current performance.** In detail, using specific examples, describe the current behavior that needs to be changed.

For example, for an ability or motivation problem, say something like, "There is a way to lift boxes without straining our back that will decrease chances of getting injured."

Step 2.   **Describe desired performance.** Tell the employee exactly what the desired performance is, in detail. If *ability* is the reason for poor performance, modeling and training the employee with JIT are very appropriate. If the employee knows the proper way, the reason for poor performance is *motivational*. Demonstration is not needed; just describe desired performance as you ask the employee to state why the performance is important.

For example: *Ability*—"If you squat down and pick up the box using your legs instead of your back, it is easier and there is less chance of injuring yourself. Let me demonstrate for you." *Motivation*—"Why should you squat and use your legs rather than your back to pick up boxes?"

Step 3.   **Get a commitment to the change.** When dealing with an *ability* performance issue, it is not necessary to get employees to verbally commit to the change if they seem willing to make it. However, if employees defend their way, and you're sure it's not as effective, explain why your proposed way is better. If you cannot get the employee to understand and agree based on rational persuasion, get a verbal commitment through coercive power, such as a threat of discipline. For *motivation* performance issues, this is important because, if employees are not willing to commit to the change, they will most likely not make the change.

For example: *Ability*—the employee will most likely be willing to do it correctly, so skip the step. *Motivation*—"Will you squat rather than use your back from now on?"

Step 4.   **Follow up.** Remember, some employees do what managers inspect, not what they expect. We should follow up to ensure that the employee is behaving as desired.

When we are dealing with an *ability* performance issue, the person is receptive, and we skip step 3, say nothing. But watch to be sure the task is done correctly in the future. Coach again, if necessary. For a *motivation* problem, make a statement that you will follow up, and describe possible consequences for repeated poor performance.

For example: *Ability*—say nothing, but observe. *Motivation*—"You know that picking up boxes with your back is dangerous; if I catch you doing it again, I will take disciplinary action."

See Model 6.4 for a review of the steps in the coaching model.

MODEL **6.4**   **Coaching Model**

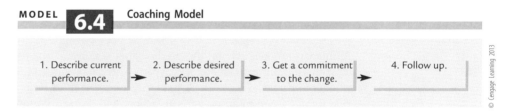

1. Describe current performance. → 2. Describe desired performance. → 3. Get a commitment to the change. → 4. Follow up.

© Cengage Learning 2013

Mentoring

Mentoring *is a form of coaching in which a more experienced manager helps a less experienced protégé.* Thus, the ten tips for coaching apply to mentoring. However, mentoring includes more than coaching, and it is more involved and personal than coaching. The formal mentor is usually at a higher level of management and is not the protégé's immediate manager. Family, friends, and peers can also be mentors.

WORK Application 8

Recall a person who is or was a mentor to you. Briefly describe the relationship and type of advice you got from your mentor.

The primary responsibility is to coach the protégé by providing good, sound career advice and to help develop leadership skills necessary for a successful management career. Mentoring is especially important in progressing from middle management to upper level management, especially for women because only 26 percent of vice presidents and other senior managers of Fortune 500 companies are women.[49] However, the protégé should not try to become just like the mentor; we all need to learn from others, yet we need to be ourselves to be effective.[50]

We all need mentors, so don't wait for someone to ask you. Seek out a good mentor.[51] If your organization has a formal mentoring program, try to sign up for it. If it is informal, ask around about getting a mentor, and remember that a mentor can be from another organization. Whenever you have job- or career-related questions and would like advice, contact your mentor.

3. Is there a difference in managing an oil change business, a golf course, and a sports team; and how does Peter Clark use coaching at The Ranch?

Peter Clark says there are more similarities than differences in running a Jiffy Lube business and a golf club and coaching sports. The focus is the same—high-quality service. You have to treat the customer or player right. Clark uses the same 3 I's coaching philosophy for all three: You need Intensity to be prepared to do the job right, Integrity to do the right thing when no one is watching, and Intimacy to be a team player. If one person does not do the job right, everyone is negatively affected. In business and sports, you need to strive to be the best. You need to set and meet challenging goals.

Clark strongly believes in being positive and in the need to develop a supportive working relationship, which includes sitting down to talk and really listening to the other person. He also strongly believes in the need for good training. Employees at The Ranch give high-quality service because they are thoroughly trained to do so, and they are continually coached to maintain and improve performance. Although The Ranch does not have a formal mentoring program, Clark clearly sees mentoring as an important role he plays at The Ranch.

Managing Conflict

Poor communications, feedback, and coaching can lead to conflict.[52] A **conflict** *exists whenever people are in disagreement and opposition*. In this section, we discuss the psychological contract, conflict and leadership, and the five conflict management styles we can use to resolve conflicts.

The Psychological Contract

All human relations rely on the psychological contract.[53] The *psychological contract* is the unwritten implicit expectations of each party in a relationship. At work, you have a set of expectations of what you will contribute to the organization (effort, time, skills) and what it will provide to you (compensation, job satisfaction, and so on). We are often not aware of our expectations until they have not been met[54] (for example, how we are treated by a manager).

Conflict Arises by Breaking the Psychological Contract

The psychological contract is broken for two primary reasons: (1) We fail to make explicit our own expectations and fail to inquire into the expectations of the other parties; and/or (2) we further assume that the other party(ies) has the same expectations that we hold. So as long as people meet our expectations, everything is fine; when they don't meet our expectations, we are in conflict.[55] Thus, it is important to share information and negotiate expectations assertively.[56] After all, how can you expect others to meet your expectations when they don't know what they are?

Conflict and Leadership

Many leaders are constantly exposed to conflict. Executives say their managers spend an average of more than seven hours a week sorting out conflicts among their staff members.[57] Conflict management resolution is an important leadership skill[58] because conflict affects performance.[59] Thus, ability to resolve conflicts will have a direct effect on your leadership success. With the trend toward teamwork, conflict skills are increasingly important to team decision making.[60]

Conflict Can Be Dysfunctional or Functional

People often think of conflict as fighting and view it as disruptive. When conflict is not resolved effectively, negative consequences occur.[61] When conflict prevents the achievement of organizational objectives, it is negative or *dysfunctional conflict*. However, some say conflict is not only inevitable, it's good.[62] *Functional conflict* exists when disagreement and opposition supports the achievement of organizational objectives. The real question today is not whether conflict is negative or positive, but how to manage conflict to benefit the organization.[63]

Learning Outcome 7

Define the five conflict management styles.

Conflict Management Styles

When we are in conflict, we have five conflict management styles to choose from. The five styles are based on two dimensions of concern: concern for others' needs and concern for our own needs. These concerns result in three types of behavior:

- A low concern for your own needs and a high concern for others' needs results in passive behavior.

- A high concern for your own needs and a low concern for others' needs results in aggressive behavior.

- A moderate or high concern for your own needs and others' needs results in assertive behavior.

Each conflict style of behavior results in a different combination of win–lose situations. The five styles, along with concern for needs and win–lose combinations, are presented in Exhibit 6.4 and discussed here in order of passive, aggressive, and assertive behavior. The conflict style that we tend to use the most is based on our personality and leadership style. There is no one best conflict management style for all situations. In this section, we present the advantages and disadvantages and the appropriate use of each of the five conflict management styles.

EXHIBIT 6.4 Conflict Management Styles

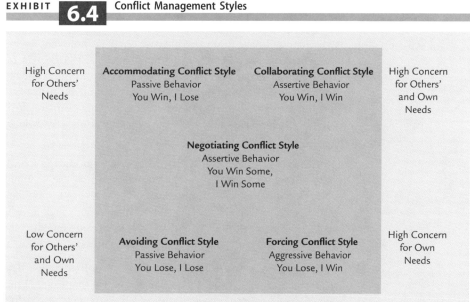

© Cengage Learning 2013

Avoiding Conflict Style

The *avoiding conflict style* user attempts to passively ignore the conflict rather than resolve it. When we avoid a conflict, we are being unassertive and uncooperative. People avoid conflict by refusing to take a stance, or escape conflict by mentally withdrawing and physically leaving. A lose–lose situation is created because the conflict is not resolved.

Advantages and Disadvantages of the Avoiding Conflict Style   The advantage of the avoiding style is that it may maintain relationships that would be hurt through conflict resolution. The disadvantage of this style is that conflicts do not get resolved, so avoiding is often not the best option.[64] An overuse of this style leads to conflict within the individual. People tend to walk all over the consistent avoider. Some managers allow employees to break rules without confronting them. Avoiding problems usually does not make them go away; the problems usually get worse. And the longer you wait to confront others, the more difficult the confrontation usually is.

Appropriate Use of the Avoiding Conflict Style   The avoiding style is appropriate to use when (1) the conflict is trivial; (2) our stake in the issue is not high; (3) confrontation will damage an important relationship; (4) we don't have time to resolve the conflict; or (5) emotions are high. When we don't have time to resolve the conflict or people are emotional, we should confront the person(s) later. However, it is inappropriate to repeatedly avoid confrontation until you get so upset that you end up yelling at the other person(s). This passive–aggressive behavior tends to make the situation worse by hurting human relations. Often people do not realize they are doing something that bothers us (that we are in conflict), and when approached properly, they are willing to change.

Accommodating Conflict Style

The *accommodating conflict style* user attempts to resolve the conflict by passively giving in to the other party. When we use the accommodating style, we are being unassertive but cooperative. We attempt to satisfy the other party, neglecting our own needs by letting others get their own way. A win–lose situation is created, as we try to please everyone.

Differences between the Avoiding Accommodating Style   A common difference between the avoiding and accommodating styles is based on behavior. With the avoiding style, we don't have to do anything we really do not want to do; with the accommodating style, we do. For example, if you are talking to someone who makes a statement that you disagree with, to avoid a conflict you can say nothing, change the subject, or stop the conversation. However, suppose you have to put up a display with someone who says, "Let's put up the display this way." If you don't want to do it the other person's way, but say nothing and put it up the other person's way, you have done something you really did not want to do.

Advantages and Disadvantages of the Accommodating Conflict Style   The advantage of the accommodating style is that relationships are maintained by doing things the other person's way. The disadvantage is that giving in may be counterproductive.[65] The accommodating person may have a better solution, such as a better way to put up a display. An overuse of this style tends to lead to people taking advantage of the accommodator, and the type of relationship the accommodator tries to maintain is usually lost.

Appropriate Use of the Accommodating Conflict Style   The accommodating style is appropriate when (1) the person enjoys being a follower; (2) maintaining the relationship outweighs all other considerations; (3) the changes agreed to are not important to the accommodator, but are to the other party; or (4) the time to resolve the conflict is limited. This is often the only style that can be used with an autocratic manager who uses the forcing style.

Forcing Conflict Style

The *forcing conflict style* user attempts to resolve the conflict by using aggressive behavior to get his or her own way. When we use the forcing style, we are uncooperative and *aggressive*, doing whatever it takes to satisfy our own needs—at the expense of others, if necessary. Forcers use authority, threaten, intimidate, and call for majority rule when they know they will win. Forcers commonly enjoy dealing with avoiders and accommodators. If you try to get others to change without being willing to change yourself, regardless of the means, then you use the forcing style. A win–lose situation is created.

Advantages and Disadvantages of the Forcing Style   The advantage of the forcing style is that better organizational decisions will be made, when the forcer is correct, rather than less-effective compromised decisions. The disadvantage is that overuse of this style leads to hostility and resentment toward its user. Forcers tend to have poor human relations.

Appropriate Use of the Forcing Style   Some managers commonly use their position power to force others to do what they want them to do. The forcing style is appropriate to use when (1) unpopular action must be taken on important issues; (2) commitment by others to proposed action is not crucial to its implementation—in other words, people will not resist doing what we want them to do; (3) maintaining relationships is not critical; or (4) the conflict resolution is urgent.

Negotiating Conflict Style

The *negotiating conflict style* user attempts to resolve the conflict through assertive, give-and-take concessions. This is also called the *compromising style*. When you use the compromising approach, you are moderate in assertiveness and cooperation. An "I win some, you win some" situation is created through compromise. As discussed in Chapter 5, negotiation skills are important in both your personal and your professional life.

Advantages and Disadvantages of the Negotiating Conflict Style   The advantage of the negotiating style is that the conflict is resolved relatively quickly and working relationships are maintained. The disadvantage is that the compromise may lead to counterproductive results, such as suboptimum decisions. An overuse of this style leads to people playing games such as asking for twice as much as they need in order to get what they want. It is commonly used during management and labor collective bargaining.

Appropriate Use of the Negotiating Conflict Style   The negotiating style is appropriate to use when (1) the issues are complex and critical, and there is no simple and clear solution; (2) parties have about equal power and are interested in different solutions; (3) a solution will be only temporary; or (4) time is short. Note that we are being assertive, not aggressive, to get what we want without being taken advantage of.[66]

Collaborating Conflict Style

The *collaborating conflict style* user assertively attempts to jointly resolve the conflict with the best solution agreeable to all parties. It is also called the *problem-solving style*. When we use the collaborating approach, we are being assertive and cooperative. Although avoiders and accommodators are concerned about others' needs, and forcers are concerned about their own needs, the collaborator is concerned about finding the best solution to the problem that is satisfactory to all parties. Unlike the forcer, the collaborator is willing to change if a better solution is presented. While negotiating is often based on secret information, collaboration is based on open and honest communication. This is the only style that creates a true win–win situation.

Differences between the Negotiation and Collaborating Style   A common difference between negotiating and collaborating is the solution. Let's continue with the example of putting up a display. With negotiation, the two people may trade off by putting up one display one person's way and the next display the other person's way. This way they each win and lose. With collaboration, the two people work together to develop one display method that they both like. It may be a combination of both, or simply one person's idea if, after an explanation, the other person really agrees that the method is better. The key to collaboration is agreeing that the solution is the best possible one.

Advantages and Disadvantages of the Collaborating Style   The advantage of the collaborating style is that it tends to lead to the best solution to the conflict, using assertive behavior. Again, assertiveness, not aggression, is often a good option.[67] The disadvantage is that the skill, effort, and time it takes to resolve the conflict are usually greater and longer than the other styles. There are situations, mentioned under "Negotiating Conflict Style," when collaboration is difficult, and when a forcer prevents its use. The collaborating style offers the most benefit to the individual, group, and organization.

WORK Application 9

Select a present or past manager. Which conflict management style did that manager use most often? Explain by giving a typical example. Which one of the five conflict management styles do you tend to use most often? Explain your answer.

_____

_____

_____

_____

CONCEPT APPLICATION 3
Selecting Conflict Management Styles

For each of these five conflict situations, identify the most appropriate conflict management style. Write the appropriate letter in the blank before each item.

a. avoiding   c. forcing   e. collaborating

b. accommodating   d. negotiating

_____ 16.   You are on a task force that has to select a new machine to make your smart phones. The four alternatives will all do the job. It's the brand, price, and service that people disagree on.

_____ 17.   You are a sales manager. Bob, one of your competent salespeople, is trying to close a big sale. The two of you are discussing the next sales call he will make. You disagree on the strategy to use to close the sale.

_____ 18.   You're late and on your way to an important meeting. As you leave your office, at the other end of the work area you see Johns, one of your average employees, goofing off instead of working.

_____ 19.   You're over budget for labor this month. It's slow, so you ask Sonia, a part-time employee, to leave work early. Sonia tells you she doesn't want to go because she needs the money.

_____ 20.   You have joined a committee in order to meet people. Your interest in what the committee does is low. While serving on the committee, you make a recommendation that is opposed by another member. You realize that you have the better idea. The other party is using a forcing style.

Appropriate Use of the Collaborating Conflict Style   The collaborating style is appropriate when (1) you are dealing with an important issue that requires an optimal solution, and compromise would result in suboptimizing; (2) people are willing to place the group goal before self-interest, and members will truly collaborate; (3) maintaining relationships is important; (4) time is available; and (5) it is a peer conflict.

Of the five styles, the relatively easiest to use are the avoiding and accommodating styles. We generally want to avoid using the forcing style. The most difficult to implement successfully, due to the complexity and level of skill needed, is the collaborative style. It is most likely to be underutilized when it would have been appropriate. Therefore, in order to develop your conflict skills, the collaborative style is the only one that we cover in detail in the next section. Recall that you learned how to negotiate in Chapter 5.

OPENING CASE *APPLICATION*

4. Which conflict management style does Peter Clark tend to use at The Ranch?

At The Ranch, with partners and managers, conflict is inevitable. Peter Clark prefers to use the collaborating conflict style, which goes back to the importance he places on open communications and a good supportive working relationship. He prefers to sit down and work through problem issues together and agree on solutions. He believes that when you have a conflict problem, ignoring it using the avoiding conflict style usually does not solve the problem. When Clark is in conflict with a manager, he does not like to simply accommodate when he does not agree with what the manager wants to do, but he has accommodated, such as in the case of building a waterfall on the course

Clark does not like to use the forcing conflict style, but there are times when he says no to managers, such as operating an expensive waterfall on the course—he stopped it based on his guiding question: Will spending the money clearly improve player satisfaction enough to pay for itself? Having a waterfall is attractive, but it will not be a deciding factor in playing golf at The Ranch. Clark also has to negotiate with outside organizations.

Collaborating Conflict Management Style Models

It is challenging to get along with everyone. But we can develop our skill to assertively confront (or be confronted by) people we are in conflict with, and in a manner that resolves the conflict without damaging interpersonal relationships.[68] If done correctly, conflict resolution takes only a few minutes in most cases.[69] In this last section, we provide a model with the steps we can follow when initiating, responding to, and mediating a conflict resolution in or out of work.

Learning Outcome 8   *List the steps in the initiating conflict resolution model.*

Initiating Conflict Resolution

We are the initiators when we confront the other person(s) to resolve the conflict. Confronting others that we are in conflict with is usually the better solution to conflict, rather than avoiding or accommodating.[70] If we did or said something that was wrong and hurt the other person or when we make a mistake, placing us in conflict, we should apologize. Telling others we are sorry is very beneficial for building and maintaining relationship. Apologizing to our boss, rather than trying to defend our action when we were wrong or made a mistake, can help our performance reviews.[71]

When initiating a conflict resolution using the collaborating style, there is a model to use. *The* **initiating conflict resolution model** *steps are (1) plan a BCF statement that* *maintains ownership of the problem; (2) present your BCF statement and agree on the conflict; (3) ask for, and/or give, alternative conflict resolutions; and (4) make an agreement for change.*

Step 1.   **Plan a Behavior, Consequence, and Feeling (BCF) statement that maintains ownership of the problem.** Planning is the starting point of initiating a conflict resolution. Let's begin by stating what *maintains ownership of the problem* means. Assume you don't smoke, and someone visits you while smoking. Is it you or the smoker who has a problem? The smoke bothers you, not the smoker. It's your problem. So we should open the confrontation with a request for the respondent to help us solve our problem. This approach reduces defensiveness and establishes an atmosphere of problem solving that will maintain the relationship.

There are three things we *should NOT do in the BCF statement:*

Don't make judgments that evaluate others' behavior ("You are wrong"). Avoid trying to determine who is to blame for something or who is right and wrong. Fixing blame or correctness only makes people defensive and argue about who is right as opposed to resolving the conflict.

Don't make threats ("I'm going to tell the boss on you"). This can hurt your relationship. Using threats should be our last, not first option.

Don't give solutions. This is done step 3, so don't start with a solution.

Don't make statements like, You are inconsiderate of others, You shouldn't smoke, (judgmental evaluation), You are going to get cancer, I'm going to tell on you and you will get in trouble (threats), Just quit smoking (solution).

The **BCF model** *describes a conflict in terms of behavior, consequences, and feelings.* When you do B (behavior), C (consequences) happens, and I feel F (feelings). The longer the statement, the longer it will take to resolve the conflict, so keep the opening BCF statement short. For example, when you smoke in my room (behavior), I have trouble breathing and become nauseous (consequence), and I feel uncomfortable and irritated (feeling). You can vary the BCF sequence. For example, I fear (feeling) that the advertisement is not going to work (behavior), and that we will lose money (consequences).

Try to put yourself in the other person's position. If you were the other person, would you like the BCF presented? Would it make you defensive?I If so, change it. After planning our BCF statement, we should practice saying it before confronting the other party. In addition, think of some possible alternatives we can offer to resolve the conflict.

Step 2.   **Present your BCF statement and agree on the conflict.** After making the short, planned BCF statement, let the other party respond. If the other party does not understand or avoids acknowledgment of the problem, repeat the planned statement by explaining it in different terms until getting an acknowledgment or realizing it's hopeless. But don't give up too easily; be assertive.[72] If you cannot agree on a conflict, you may have to change our approach and use one of the other four conflict management styles.

Step 3.   **Ask for, and/or give, alternative conflict resolutions.** Begin by asking the other party what can be done to resolve the conflict. If both agree, great; if not, offer your resolution. However, remember that you are collaborating, not simply trying to change others. When the other party acknowledges the problem, but is not responsive to resolving it, appeal to common goals. Make others realize the benefits to them in resolving the conflict.

Step 4.   **Make an agreement for change.** Our goal is not to win but to agree on a plan of action so that the same error, mistake, or problem doesn't occur again.[73] Try to

WORK Application **10**
Use the BCF model to describe a conflict you face or have faced on the job.

_____

_____

_____

_____

come to an agreement on specific action you will both take to resolve the conflict. Clearly state—or better yet for complex change, write down—the specific behavior changes necessary by all parties to resolve the conflict. Again, remember that you are collaborating, not forcing. The steps are also listed in Model 6.5.

Responding to Conflict Resolution

As the responder, an initiator has confronted you. Here's how to handle the role of the responder to a conflict. Most initiators do not follow the model. Therefore, we must take responsibility for successful conflict resolution by following the conflict resolution model steps, which are also listed in Model 6.5:

1. Listen to and paraphrase the conflict using the BCF model. You need to state the conflict in your own words to make sure you get it and agree to the conflict.[74]
2. Agree with some aspect of the complaint. Rarely is only one part the problem. So even if you don't think you are wrong, at least agree with something so the conflict can be resolved.
3. Ask for, and/or give, alternative conflict resolutions. This is the same as step 3 of initiating conflict discussed above.
4. Make an agreement for change. This is the same as step 4 of initiating conflict.

Mediating Conflict Resolution

Frequently, conflicting parties cannot resolve their dispute alone.[75] In these cases, a mediator should be used. A **mediator** *is a neutral third party who helps resolve a conflict.* In nonunionized organizations, managers are commonly the mediators. But some organizations have trained and designated employees as mediators. In unionized organizations, the mediator is usually a professional from outside the organization. However, a conflict resolution should be sought internally first. As leaders, we should mediate conflicts to keep the peace that maintains relationships and resolves problems.

Before bringing the conflicting parties together, we should decide whether to start with a joint meeting or conduct individual meetings. If one employee comes to complain, but has not confronted the other party, or if there is a serious discrepancy in employee perceptions, meet one-on-one with each party before bringing them together. On the other hand, when both parties have a similar awareness of the problem and

MODEL 6.5   The Collaborating Conflict Style

Initiating Conflict Resolution	Responding to Conflict Resolution	Mediating Conflict Resolution
Step 1. Plan a BCF statement that maintains ownership of the problem.	Step 1. Listen to and paraphrase the conflict using the BCF model.	Step 1. Have each party state his or her complaint using the BCF model.
Step 2. Present your BCF statement and agree on the conflict.	Step 2. Agree with some aspect of the complaint.	Step 2. Agree on the conflict problem(s).
Step 3. Ask for, and/or give, alternative conflict resolutions.	Step 3. Ask for, and/or give, alternative conflict resolutions.	Step 3. Develop alternative conflict resolutions.
Step 4. Make an agreement for change.	Step 4. Make an agreement for change.	Step 4. Make an agreement for change.
		Step 5. Follow up to make sure the conflict is resolved.

motivation to solve it, you can begin with a joint meeting when all parties are calm. The leader should be a mediator, not a judge. Get the employees to resolve the conflict, if possible. Remain impartial, unless one party is violating company policies. Do a good job of coaching. Avoid blame and embarrassment. Don't make comments such as, "I'm disappointed in you two," or "you're acting like babies."

When bringing conflicting parties together, follow the mediating conflict model steps. These steps are listed in Model 6.5.

If either party blames the other, make a statement such as, "We are here to resolve the conflict; placing blame is not productive." Focus on how the conflict is affecting their work. Discuss the issues by addressing specific behavior, not personalities. If a person says, "We cannot work together because of a personality conflict," ask the parties to state the specific behavior that is bothering them. The discussion should make the parties aware of their behavior and the consequences of their behavior. The mediator may ask questions or make statements to clarify what is being said. The mediator should develop one problem statement that is agreeable to all parties, if possible.

If the conflict has not been resolved, an arbitrator may be used. *An* arbitrator *is a neutral third party who makes a binding decision to resolve a conflict*. The arbitrator is like a judge; the decision must be followed. However, the use of arbitration should be kept to a minimum because it is not a collaborative conflict style. Arbitrators commonly use a negotiating style in which each party wins some and loses some. Mediation and then arbitration tend to be used in management–labor negotiations, when collective bargaining breaks down and the contract deadline is near.

OPENING CASE *APPLICATION*

5. What types of conflict resolutions do the Clarks deal with at The Ranch?

At The Ranch, Peter Clark more often responds to conflict than initiating conflict resolutions since, when problems arise, he is asked for solutions or to approve actions. Clark also has to occasionally mediate a conflict between partners or between managers and employees.

As we end this chapter, you should understand how important communication, feedback, coaching, and conflict resolution are to leadership effectiveness in all organizations. Self-Assessment 2 will help you to understand how your personality traits affect your communication, feedback, coaching, and conflict management style.

SELF-ASSESSMENT 2 | **Your Personality Traits and Communication, Feedback, Coaching, and Conflict Management Style**

Let's tie personality traits from Chapter 2 together with what we've covered in this chapter. We are going to present some general statements about how your personality may affect your communication, feedback, coaching, and conflict management styles. For each area, determine how the information relates to you. This will help you better understand your behavior strengths and weaknesses, and identify areas you may want to improve.

Communication

If you have a high *surgency* personality, you most likely are an extrovert and have no difficulty initiating and communicating with others. However, you may be dominating during communication and may not listen well and be open to others' ideas. Be careful not to use communications simply as a means of getting what you

(continued)

(Self-Assessment 2 continued)

want; be concerned about others and what they want. If you are low in surgency, you may be quiet and reserved in your communications. You may want to be more vocal.

If you are high in *agreeableness* personality trait, you are most likely a good listener and communicator. Your *adjustment* level affects the emotional tone of your communications. If you tend to get emotional during communications, you may want to work to keep your emotions under control. We cannot control our feelings, but we can control our behavior. If you are high in *conscientiousness*, you tend to have reliable communications. If you are not conscientious, you may want to work at returning messages quickly. People who are *open to new experience* often initiate communication, because communicating is often part of the new experience.

Feedback and Coaching

If you have a high *surgency* personality, you have a need to be in control. Watch the tendency to give feedback, but not listen to it. You may need to work at *not* criticizing. If you have low surgency, you may want to give more feedback and do more coaching. If you have a high *agreeableness* personality, you are a people person and probably enjoy coaching others. However, as a manager, you must also discipline when needed, which may be difficult for you.

If you are high on the *adjustment* personality trait, you may tend to give positive coaching; people with low *adjustment* need to watch the negative criticism. If you have a high *conscientiousness* with a high need for achievement, you may tend to be more concerned about your own success. This is also true of people with a high *surgency* personality. Remember that an important part of leadership is coaching others. If you have a low *conscientiousness*, you may need to put forth effort to be a good coach. Your *openness to experience* personality affects whether you are willing to listen to others' feedback and make changes.

Conflict Styles

Generally, the best conflict style is collaboration. If you have a high *surgency* personality, you most likely have no problem confronting others when in conflict. However, be careful not to use the forcing style with others; remember to use social, not personal power. If you have a high *agreeableness* personality, you tend to get along well with others. However, be careful not to use the avoiding and accommodating styles to get out of confronting others; you need to satisfy your needs too.

Adjustment will affect how to handle a conflict situation. Try not to be low in adjustment and get too emotional. If you are *conscientious*, you may be good at conflict resolution; but again, be careful to meet others' needs too. *Openness to experience* affects conflicts, because their resolution often requires change; be open to new things.

Action Plan

Based on your personality, what specific things will you do to improve your communication, feedback, coaching, and conflict management style?

_____

_____

_____

Chapter Summary

This chapter summary is organized to answer the nine learning outcomes for Chapter 6.

1. List the steps in the oral message-sending process.

The five steps in the oral message-sending process are (1) develop rapport; (2) state your communication objective; (3) transmit your message; (4) check the receiver's understanding; (5) get a commitment and follow up.

2. List and explain the three parts of the message-receiving process.

The three parts of the message-receiving process are listening, analyzing, and checking understanding.

Listening is the process of giving the speaker your undivided attention. Analyzing is the process of thinking about, decoding, and evaluating the message. Checking understanding is the process of giving feedback.

3. Describe paraphrasing and state why it is used.

Paraphrasing is the process of having the receiver restate the message in his or her own words. Paraphrasing is used to check understanding of the transmitted message. If the receiver can paraphrase the message accurately, communication has taken place. If not, communication is not complete.

4. Identify two common approaches to getting feedback, and explain why they don't work.

The first common approach to getting feedback is to send the entire message and to assume that the message has been conveyed with mutual understanding. The second approach is to give the entire message followed by asking, "Do you have any questions?" Feedback usually does not follow because people have a tendency not to ask questions. There are at least four good reasons why people do not ask questions: receivers feel ignorant, receivers are ignorant, receivers are reluctant to point out the sender's ignorance, and receivers have cultural barriers.

5. Describe the difference between criticism and coaching feedback.

Criticism is feedback that makes a judgment about behavior being wrong. Coaching feedback is based on a supportive relationship and offers specific and descriptive ways to improve performance. Criticism focuses on pointing out mistakes, while coaching feedback focuses on the benefits of positive behavior.

6. Discuss the relationship between the performance formula and the coaching model.

The performance formula is used to determine the reason for poor performance and the corrective action needed. The coaching model is then used to improve performance.

7. Define the five conflict management styles.

(1) The *avoiding conflict style* user attempts to passively ignore the conflict rather than resolve it. (2) The accommodating conflict style user attempts to resolve the conflict by passively giving in to the other party. (3) The forcing conflict style user attempts to resolve the conflict by using aggressive behavior to get his or her own way. (4) The negotiating conflict style user attempts to resolve the conflict through assertive, give-and-take concessions. (5) The *collaborating conflict style* user assertively attempts to jointly resolve the conflict with the best solution agreeable to all parties.

8. List the steps in the initiating conflict resolution model.

The initiating conflict resolution model steps are (1) plan a BCF statement that maintains ownership of the problem; (2) present your BCF statement and agree on the conflict; (3) ask for, and/or give, alternative conflict resolutions; and (4) make an agreement for change.

9. Define the following key terms (in order of appearance in the chapter).

Select one or more methods: (1) fill in the missing key terms from memory; (2) match the key terms from the following list with their definitions below; (3) copy the key terms in order from the list at the beginning of the chapter.

_____ is the process of conveying information and meaning.

_____ steps include (1) develop rapport; (2) state your communication objective; (3) transmit your message; (4) check the receiver's understanding; and (5) get a commitment and follow up.

_____ includes listening, analyzing, and checking understanding.

_____ is the process of verifying messages and determining if objectives are being met.

_____ is the process of having the receiver restate the message in his or her own words.

_____ is a formal evaluation process based on receiving performance evaluations from many people.

_____ is the process of giving motivational feedback to maintain and improve performance.

_____ steps include (1) trainee receives preparation; (2) trainer presents the task; (3) trainee performs the task; and (4) trainer follows up.

_____ is (1) based on a good, supportive relationship; (2) specific and descriptive; and (3) not judgmental criticism.

_____ is used to explain the process managers go through in determining the reasons for effective or ineffective performance and deciding what to do about it.

_____ explains performance as a function of ability, motivation, and resources.

_____ is a form of coaching in which a more experienced manager helps a less experienced protégé.

_____ exists whenever people are in disagreement and opposition.

_____ steps are (1) plan a BCF statement that maintains ownership of the problem; (2) present your BCF statement and agree on the conflict; (3) ask for, and/or give, alternative conflict resolutions; (4) make an agreement for change.

_____ describes a conflict in terms of behavior, consequences, and feelings.

_____ is a neutral third party who helps resolve a conflict.

_____ is a neutral third party who makes a binding decision to resolve a conflict.

Key Terms

arbitrator, 218

attribution theory, 208

BCF model, 216

coaching, 202

coaching feedback, 207

communication, 191

conflict, 210

feedback, 199

initiating conflict resolution model, 215

job instructional training, 205

mediator, 217

mentoring, 209

message-receiving process, 197

oral message-sending process, 193

paraphrasing, 199

performance formula, 208

360-degree feedback, 202

Review Questions

1. What should be included in your plan to send a message?

2. What are the three parts of a written outline?

3. As an average, how many words should a sentence have, and how many sentences should there be in a paragraph?

4. Which personality traits are associated with being closed to feedback?

5. What are the four guidelines to getting feedback on messages?

6. What is 360-degree feedback, and are many organizations using it?

7. Should a supportive working relationship be a true friendship?

8. Why doesn't criticism work?

9. Are all managers mentors?

10. How do you know when you are in conflict?

11. What is the difference between functional and dysfunctional conflict, and how does each affect performance?

12. What is meant by *maintaining ownership of the problem?*

13. How is the BCF model used?

14. What is the difference between a mediator and an arbitrator?

Critical Thinking Questions

The following critical-thinking questions can be used for class discussion and/or as written assignments to develop communication skills. Be sure to give complete explanations for all questions.

1. How would you assess communications in organizations? Give examples of good and poor communications in organizations.

2. How did you score on Self-Assessment 1, "Listening Skills"? State your plan for improving your listening skills.

3. How would you assess managers at giving feedback? Specifically, what should managers do to improve?

4. Is 360-degree multi-rater feedback really better than a boss-based assessment? As a manager, would you elect to use 360?

5. Do you agree with the statement, "Don't criticize"? Do managers tend to give criticism or coaching feedback? How can managers improve?

6. Women and minorities are less likely to have mentors, so should they get mentors? Will you seek out career mentors?

7. What are your psychological contract expectations of your boss and coworkers? Give examples of conflicts you have had at work, listing the expectation that was not met.

8. What percentage of the time do you think a manager can actually use the collaborating conflict management style? Give detailed examples of when managers have used collaboration at work.

Reed Hastings—Netflix

In January 2005, Wedbush Securities stock analysts Michael Pachter called Netflix a "worthless piece of crap." He put a price target of $3 on the stock that was trading at around $11. Doubters thought Blockbuster, Wal-mart, or Amazon.com, with their economies of scale and established customer bases would simply destroy Netflix. Founder and CEO Reed Hastings wasn't supposed to be *Fortune*'s Businessperson of the Year in 2010, five years after his demise was predicted. Not only did Hasting earn the No. 1 spot, he and Netflix also killed it. Netflix was the stock of the year, up more than 200 percent in 2010, while the S&P 500 was up only 7 percent. Netflix shares ran laps around even Apple's.[76] In July 2011, the stock was selling in the $280–290 range.[77] Don't you wish you bought it back in 2005 when it was selling for $11?

So how did Hastings do it? A lot of his success is based on how he built his company on a hard-driving and risk-taking culture, and Hastings never stops looking over his shoulder to stay one step ahead of the competition. Unlike Blockbuster, which went into bankruptcy, Netflix wasn't afraid to change its business model by cannibalizing its own customers. His strategy is paying off as 66 percent of Netflix subscribers are doing some streaming of video content.[78] Compare this to Blockbuster; they were too slow to offer mail order service, which led to Netflix taking its customers away. But the surprising thing is that mail DVD subscriptions continued to increase into 2011, so the two services together helped make Netflix so successful.[79]

Let's talk about Hastings's leadership style that led to success. It has changed over the years between the two companies he created. As a young founding CEO of Pure Software, Hastings was considered as hard headed as they come and couldn't take criticism. He used the autocratic style to push for his ways of doing things, and he sometimes embarrassed employees with nonverbal eye rolling and critical comments about dumb ideas. So much so that Hastings earned the nickname "Animal." Hastings sold Pure for $750 million, and it made him realize he had helped build a company he didn't want to be part of.[80]

So when he used the money to start Netflix, as CEO Hastings was determined to create a culture in which people enjoyed coming to every day. He wanted the company to be run differently, so he changed his style to be participative. He is more honest and direct with employees, but not confrontational, but he still has a Steve Jobs–like perfectionist streak. Instead of simply telling others what to do, he actively seeks out ideas and advice from his employees. Now when he hears ideas that seem silly, he doesn't roll his eyes and humiliate employees by making critical comments about the idea or person being dumb. Hastings digs deeper by responding with comments like, "I don't understand how your idea will work, so help me to understand how it will solve the problem."[81]

Hastings was ahead of the technology curve. Even back in 1997 when Hastings cofounded Netflix, he anticipated that consumers would eventually prefer to get movies instantly delivered via the Internet. This is actually amazing foresight because back then less than 7 percent of U.S. homes even had broadband. Hastings actually had a team working on the technology to bring movies to the home via the Internet back in 2000. They even developed a Netflix-branded box with a hard drive that connected to your movie queue, but it took six hours to download a movie back in the early 2000s. Once Hastings saw YouTube videos, he killed the hard-drive device and put this team to work on a streaming machine, a sort of YouTube-in-a-box. This again was meant to be a branded piece of hardware produced and sold by Netflix. However, even though they built the technology, once again Hasting killed the idea in favor of software that could be embedded in all kinds of devices—the software today is known as apps.[82]

No. This wasn't wasted time. Netflix built on this base to be able to come out streaming a year and a half, in 2007, after YouTube showed the world instant viewing over the Internet.[83] Also, it spun off the hardware technology into an existing company called Roku, which today makes a digital device that plays content via software from Netflix, as well as Hulu, Amazon and others. Netflix's cost to roundtrip a video by mail, including labor fees, is $1 versus 5 cents for streaming the same movie.[84]

A major reason for the jump in stock prices was the fact that Netflix cut a deal with Epix, a three-studio joint venture, to stream relatively new movies from Paramount, Lions Gate, and MGM. The deal is valued at $1 billion over five years. Viacom owns a majority stake in Epix, and its CEO was involved in making the deal.[85]

With streaming, Netflix is now stealing customers from cable and pay movie channels HBO, Showtime, and Starz as their customer numbers are down or level while Netflix continues to increase.[86] Netflix subscribers are reaching 25 million in 2011. It has more subscribers than the Comcast cable company. In fact, it is the world's leading Internet subscription service for enjoying movies and TV shows.[87] Plus, it is growing fast. It went international in 2010 by expanding its streaming first in Canada, where it had no present customer DVD mail service base. It was a great success, so it plans to launch streaming-only around the world.[88] Next it went to 43 countries in Latin America and the Caribbean.[89] It takes one to three years for a new country to be profitable, and Canada took only a year, which is extraordinary.[90]

Netflix TV-everywhere model is clearly working.[91] You can instantly watch TV episodes and movies and Netflix is even working on offering original content.[92] Watch right on your TV with Wii™, PS3™, and Xbox 360. You can also stream instantly from certain Internet-connected HDTVs, Blu-ray players, and more. Of course, watch on your computer, and your Apple *iPhone*, *iPad* or selected Android phones. In all, more than 200 devices that stream from Netflix are available in the United States and a growing number are available in Canada.[93] Customers get all these options with a free one month trial and then for just $7.99 per month.[94] To push its members to stop using the more expensive mail and only use streaming, Netflix raised its combined mail and stream by 60 percent to $15.98 in July 2011, double the cost of streaming only.[95] This strategic move angered customers and around 1 million dropped Netflix, resulting in a 19 percent drop in its stock price.[96] Hastings renamed the DVD business Qwikster, and made the snail mail a separate subsidiary with its own billing system, website, and list of movies.[97]

Does this mean that Netflix doesn't face any future threats? As Hastings admits, there are plenty of challenges ahead. Pundits and analysts like Pachter now are warning that Netflix could be crushed or acquired by the likes of Google or Apple. Amazon.com was developing a Netflix-like subscription in 2010.[98] Anyone can come after Netflix by streaming bits via contracts with data-delivery companies like Level 3, Limelight, and Akamai. Who knows what Facebook will come up with? Also, Netflix has to pay the studios for contents, which can be locked up in "windows" for years following theatrical and DVD release. Content acquisition costs could go through the roof. But Hastings is confident, as he enjoys solving subtle yet tough problems alongside the smartest people he can find. He said, "For me the thrill is making a contribution by solving hard problems."[99] Only time will tell if he can stay ahead of the competition and technology curve.

Go to the Internet: To learn more about Reed Hastings and Netflix, visit their Web site **(http://www.netflix.com).**

Support your answers to the following questions with specific information from the case and text or with other information you get from the Web or other sources.

1. How did Hastings change his use of communications in sending and receiving messages from Pure Software to Netflix?

2. How did Hastings change his use of feedback from Pure Software to Netflix?

3. How did Hastings change his use of coaching guidelines (Exhibit 6.3) from Pure Software to Netflix?

4. Which conflict management style did Hastings tend to use at Pure and Netflix?

5. In making a deal with Epix, which conflict management style was most likely used by Netflix?

6. How would you improve Netflix's product offerings (i.e., what things can't you watch that you would like to watch) or processes (i.e., how can it improve its delivery or service)?

CUMULATIVE CASE QUESTIONS

7. Which level or levels of analysis and leadership paradigm are presented in this case, and did Hastings use the management or leadership paradigm (Chapter 1)?

8. How did Hastings's Big Five model of personality leadership traits change from Pure Software to Netflix (Chapter 2)?

9. Which University of Iowa leadership styles did Hastings use at Pure Software and Netflix (Chapter 3)?

10. Explain how power, organizational politics, networking, and negotiation are, or are not, discussed in the case (Chapter 5)?

CASE EXERCISE AND ROLE-PLAY

Preparation: An important part of success is to continually improve products and processes. So we are going to use answers to case question 6.

In-Class Groups: Break into groups of four to six members, and develop a list of improvements for Netflix. Select a spokesperson to record the ideas and then present them to Hastings in front of the class.

Role-Play: One person from each group at a time presents the group's suggested improvements to Hastings (played by the professor or one or more students as a committee). During, and/or after the presentation, Hastings and/or committee members ask questions and make comments on the ideas. Are the ideas practical? Would you consider implementing the ideas? What research would you need to make a decision?

VIDEO ▶❚❚ CASE

Communication at Navistar International

The decision to dedicate the resources needed to fund and support the Department of Communications within Navistar International sends a signal that corporate communication is seen as vital to the health of this $12 billion truck and engine manufacturing and financial services corporation. The Department of Communications functions as a business partner with the company's three major business units. Each plant has a communications manager who reports to both the plant manager and the corporate director of the Department of Communications. The role of the communications manager is to drive the message to the target audience. The manager uses different approaches depending on the audience and the direction of the message, whether it's heading up or down the corporate ladder or across business units.

1. Explain why the communication skills and techniques used within a business unit (department) are not always effective in communicating across business units or up and down the corporate ladder.

2. Explain why conflict resolution communication skills are not always present in everyday workplace situations and how a skilled communications professional would add value to that workplace.

Developing Your Leadership Skills **1**

Giving Instructions

Doing This Exercise in Class

Objective

To develop your ability to give and receive messages (communication skills)

The primary AACSB learning standard skill developed through this exercise is communication abilities.

Preparation

No preparation is necessary except reading and understanding the chapter. The instructor will provide the original drawings that must be drawn.

Experience

You will plan, give, and receive instructions for completing a drawing of three objects.

Procedure 1 *(3–7 minutes)* Read all of procedure 1 twice. The task is for the manager to give an employee instructions for completing a drawing of four objects. The objects must be drawn to scale and look like photocopies of the originals. You will have up to 15 minutes to complete the task.

The exercise has four separate parts or steps:

1. The manager plans.

2. The manager gives the instructions.

3. The employee does the drawing.

4. Evaluation of the results takes place.

Rules: The rules are numbered to correlate with the four parts of the exercise.

1. *Planning.* While planning, the manager may write out instructions for the employee, but may not do any drawing of any kind.

2. *Instructions.* While giving instructions, the manager may not show the original drawing to the employee. (The instructor will give it to you.) The instructions may be given orally, and/or in writing, but no nonverbal hand gestures are allowed. The employee may take notes while the instructions are being given, but cannot do any drawing with or without a pen. The manager must give the instructions for all four objects before drawing begins.

3. *Drawing.* Once the employee begins the drawing, the manager should watch but no longer communicate in any way.

4. *Evaluation.* When the employee is finished or the time is up, the manager shows the employee the original drawing. Discuss how you did. Turn to the "Integration" section of this exercise, and answer the questions. The manager writes the answers, not the employee. The employee will write when playing the manager role.

Procedure 2 *(2–5 minutes)* Half of the class members will act as the manager first and give instructions. Managers move their seats to one of the four walls (spread out). They should be facing the center of the room with their backs close to the wall.

Employees sit in the middle of the room until called on by a manager. When called on, bring a seat to the manager. Sit facing the manager so that you cannot see any managers' drawing.

Procedure 3 (*Up to 15 minutes for drawing and integration*) The instructor gives each manager a copy of the drawing, being careful not to let any employees see it. The manager plans the instructions. When a manager is ready, she or he calls an employee and gives the instructions. It is helpful to use the message-sending process. Be sure to follow the rules. The employee should do the drawing on an 8½" by 11" sheet of paper, not in this book. If you use written instructions, they may be on the reverse side of the page that the employee draws on or on a different sheet of paper. You have up to 15 minutes to complete the drawing and about 5 minutes for integration (evaluation). When you finish the drawing, turn to the evaluation questions in the "Integration" section.

Procedure 4 (*Up to 15 minutes*) The employees are now the managers, and they sit in the seats facing the center of the room. New employees go to the center of the room until called for.

Follow procedure 3, with the instructor giving a different drawing. Do not work with the same person; change partners.

Integration

Evaluating Questions: You may select more than one answer. The manager and employee discuss each question; and the manager, not the employee, writes the answers to the questions.

1. The goal of communication was to:

   a. influence   b. inform
   c. express feelings

2. The manager transmitted the message through _____ communication channel(s).

   a. oral   b. written
   c. nonverbal   d. combined

3. The manager spent _____ time planning.

   a. too much   b. too little
   c. the right amount of

Questions 4 through 8 relate to the steps in the message-sending process.

4. The manager developed rapport. (Step 1)

   a. true   b. false

5. The manager stated the communication objective. (Step 2)

   a. true   b. false

6. The manager transmitted the message _____. (Step 3)

   a. effectively   b. ineffectively

7. The manager checked understanding by using _____. (Step 4)

   a. direct questions   b. paraphrasing
   c. both   d. neither

   The amount of checking was _____.

   a. too frequent   b. too infrequent
   c. about right

9. The manager got a commitment and followed up. (Step 5)

   a. true   b. false

10. The employee did an _____ job of listening, an job of analyzing, and an _____ job of checking understanding through the receiving message process.

    a. effective   b. ineffective

11. When going over this integration, the manager was _____ and the employee was _____ to criticism that can help improve communication skills.

    a. open   b. closed

12. Were the objects drawn to approximate scale (same size)? If not, why not?

13. Did you follow the rules? If not, why not?

14. If you could do this exercise again, what would you do differently to improve communications?

Conclusion
The instructor leads a class discussion and/or makes concluding remarks.

Apply It (*2–4 minutes*) What did I learn from this experience? How will I use this knowledge in the future? When will I practice?

_____

_____

_____

Behavior Model Skills Training **1**

Session 1

In this behavior model skills training session, you will perform four activities:

1. Complete Self-Assessment 3 (to determine your preferred communication style).

2. Read "The Situational Communications Model."

3. Watch Behavior Model Video 6.1, "Situational Communications."

4. Complete Developing Your Leadership Skills Exercise 2 (to apply the model to various situations).

For practice, use the situational communications model in your personal and professional communication.

SELF-ASSESSMENT 3   **Determining Your Preferred Communication Style**

To determine your preferred communication style, select the one alternative that most closely describes what you would do in each of the 12 situations described. Do not be concerned with trying to pick the correct answer; select the alternative that best describes what you would actually do. Circle the letter a, b, c, or d.

For now, ignore these three types of lines:
1. (before each number)

_____ time _____ information
_____ acceptance _____ capability
_____ communication style
- S_____ (following each letter)

They are explained later, and will be used during the in-class part of Developing Your Leadership Skills Exercise 2.

1. Wendy, a knowledgeable person from another department, comes to you, the engineering supervisor, and requests that you design a special product to her specifications. You would:

_____ time _____ information
_____ acceptance _____ capability
_____ communication style

a. Control the conversation and tell Wendy what you will do for her. S _____
b. Ask Wendy to describe the product. Once you understand it, you would present your ideas. Let her realize that you are concerned and want to help by offering your ideas. S _____
c. Respond to Wendy's request by conveying understanding and support. Help clarify what is

to be done by you. Offer ideas, but do it her way. S _____
d. Find out what you need to know. Let Wendy know you will do it her way. S _____

2. Your department has designed a product that is to be fabricated by Saul's department. Saul has been with the company longer than you have; he knows his department. Saul comes to you to change the product design. You decide to:

_____ time _____ information
_____ acceptance _____ capability
_____ communication style

a. Listen to the change and why it would be beneficial. If you believe Saul's way is better, change it; if not, explain why the original design is superior. If necessary, insist that it be done your way. S _____
b. Tell Saul to fabricate it any way he wants to. S _____
c. You are busy; tell Saul to do it your way. You don't have time to listen and argue with him. S _____
d. Be supportive; make changes together as a team. S _____

3. Upper management has a decision to make. They call you to a meeting and tell you they need some information to solve a problem they describe to you. You:

_____ time _____ information
_____ acceptance _____ capability
_____ communication style

(continued)

(Self-Assessment 3 continued)

a. Respond in a manner that conveys personal support and offer alternative ways to solve the problem. S _____
b. Just answer their questions. S _____
c. Explain how to solve the problem. S _____
d. Show your concern by explaining how to solve the problem and why it is an effective solution. S _____

4. You have a routine work order. The work order is to be placed verbally and completed in three days. Sue, the receiver, is very experienced and willing to be of service to you. You decide to:

_____ time _____ information
_____ acceptance _____ capability
_____ communication style

a. Explain your needs, but let Sue make the order decision. S _____
b. Tell Sue what you want and why you need it. S _____
c. Decide together what to order. S _____
d. Simply give Sue the order. S _____

5. Work orders from the staff department normally take three days; however, you have an emergency and need the job today. Your colleague Jim, the department supervisor, is knowledgeable and somewhat cooperative. You decide to:

_____ time _____ information
_____ acceptance _____ capability
_____ communication style

a. Tell Jim that you need it by three o'clock and will return at that time to pick it up. S _____
b. Explain the situation and how the organization will benefit by expediting the order. Volunteer to help in any way you can. S _____
c. Explain the situation and ask Jim when the order will be ready. S _____
d. Explain the situation and together come to a solution to your problem. S _____

6. Danielle, a peer with a record of high performance, has recently had a drop in productivity. Her problem is affecting your performance. You know Danielle has a family problem. You:

_____ time _____ information

_____ acceptance _____ capability
_____ communication style

a. Discuss the problem; help Danielle realize the problem is affecting her work and yours. Supportively discuss ways to improve the situation. S _____
b. Tell the manager about it and let him decide what to do about it. S _____
c. Tell Danielle to get back on the job. S _____
d. Discuss the problem and tell Danielle how to solve the work situation; be supportive. S _____

7. You are a knowledgeable supervisor. You buy supplies from Peter regularly. He is an excellent salesperson and very knowledgeable about your situation. You are placing your weekly order. You decide to:

_____ time _____ information
_____ acceptance _____ capability
_____ communication style

a. Explain what you want and why. Develop a supportive relationship. S _____
b. Explain what you want, and ask Peter to recommend products. S _____
c. Give Peter the order. S _____
d. Explain your situation and allow Peter to make the order. S _____

8. Jean, a knowledgeable person from another department, has asked you to perform a routine staff function to her specifications. You decide to:

_____ time _____ information
_____ acceptance _____ capability
_____ communication style

a. Perform the task to her specifications without questioning her. S _____
b. Tell her that you will do it the usual way. S _____
c. Explain what you will do and why. S _____
d. Show your willingness to help; offer alternative ways to do it. S _____

9. Tom, a salesperson, has requested an order for your department's services with a short delivery date. As usual, Tom claims it is a take-it-or-leave-it offer. He

(continued)

(Self-Assessment 3 continued)

wants your decision now, or within a few minutes, because he is in the customer's office. Your action is to:

_____ time _____ information
_____ acceptance _____ capability
_____ communication style

a. Convince Tom to work together to come up with a later date. S _____
b. Give Tom a yes or no answer. S _____
c. Explain your situation, and let Tom decide if you should take the order. S _____
d. Offer an alternative delivery date. Work on your relationship; show your support. S _____

10. As a time-and-motion expert, you have been called regarding a complaint about the standard time it takes to perform a job. As you analyze the entire job, you realize that one element of the job should take longer, but other elements should take less time. The end result is a shorter total standard time for the job. You decide to:

_____ time _____ information
_____ acceptance _____ capability
_____ communication style

a. Tell the operator and foreman that the total time must be decreased and why. S _____
b. Agree with the operator and increase the standard time. S _____
c. Explain your findings. Deal with the operator and/or foreman's concerns, but ensure compliance with your new standard. S _____
d. Together with the operator, develop a standard time. S _____

11. You approve budget allocations for projects. Marie, who is very competent in developing budgets, has come to you. You:

_____ time _____ information
_____ acceptance _____ capability
_____ communication style

a. Review the budget, make revisions, and explain them in a supportive way. Deal with concerns, but insist on your changes. S _____

b. Review the proposal and suggest areas where changes may be needed. Make changes together, if needed. S _____
c. Review the proposed budget, make revisions, and explain them. S _____
d. Answer any questions or concerns Marie has and approve the budget as is. S _____

12. You are a sales manager. A customer has offered you a contract for your product, but the contract has a short delivery date—only two days. The contract would be profitable for you and the organization. The cooperation of the production department is essential to meet the deadline. Tim, the production manager, and you do not get along very well because of your repeated request for quick delivery. Your action is to:

_____ time _____ information
_____ acceptance _____ capability
_____ communication style

a. Contact Tim and try to work together to complete the contract. S _____
b. Accept the contract and convince Tim in a supportive way to meet the obligation. S _____
c. Contact Tim and explain the situation. Ask him if he and you should accept the contract, but let him decide. S _____
d. Accept the contract. Contact Tim and tell him to meet the obligation. If he resists, tell him you will go to his manager. S _____

To determine your preferred communication style, do the following. (1) Circle the letter you selected as the alternative you chose in situations 1 through 12. The column headings indicate the style you selected. (2) Add up the number of circled items per column. The total for all the columns should not be more than 12. The column with the highest number represents your preferred communication style. There is no one best style in all situations. The more evenly distributed the numbers are between the four styles, the more flexible are your communications. A total of 0 or 1 in any column may indicate a reluctance to use the style(s). You could have problems in situations calling for the use of this style.

(continued)

(Self-Assessment 3 continued)

	Autocratic (S1A)	Consultative (S2C)	Participative (S3P)	Empowerment (S4E)
1.	a	b	c	d
2.	c	a	d	b
3.	c	d	a	b
4.	d	b	c	a
5.	a	b	d	c
6.	c	d	a	b
7.	c	a	b	d
8.	b	c	d	a
9.	b	d	a	c
10.	a	c	d	b
11.	c	a	b	d
12.	d	b	a	c
	Totals			

The Situational Communications Model

The Interactive Process System

Communication has the following five dimensions, which are each on a continuum:

Initiation _____ **Response**

- *Initiation*. The sender starts, or initiates, the communication. The sender may or may not expect a response to the initiated message.
- *Response*. The receiver's reply or action taken to the sender's message. In responding, the receiver can become an initiator. As two-way communication takes place, the role of initiator (sender) and responder (receiver) may change.

Presentation _____ **Elicitation**

- *Presentation*. The sender's message is structured, directive, or informative. A response may not be needed, although action may be called for. ("We are meeting to develop next year's budget." "Please open the door.")

- *Elicitation*. The sender invites a response to the message. Action may or may not be needed. ("How large a budget do we need?" "Do you think we should leave the door open?")

Closed _____ **Open**

- *Closed*. The sender expects the receiver to follow the message. ("This is a new form to fill out and return with each order.")
- *Open*. The sender is eliciting a response as a means of considering the receiver's input. ("Should we use this new form with each order?")

Rejection _____ **Acceptance**

- *Rejection*. The receiver does not accept the sender's message. ("I will not fill out this new form for each order!")
- *Acceptance*. The receiver agrees with the sender's message. ("I will fill out the new form for each order!")

Strong ———————————————— **Mild**

- *Strong.* The sender will use force or power to have the message acted upon as directed. ("Fill in the form or you're fired.")
- *Mild.* The sender will not use force or power to have the message acted upon as directed. ("Please fill in the form when you can.")

Situational Communication Styles

Following is the interactive process. Acceptance or rejection can come from any of the styles because, to a large extent, it is out of the sender's control.

The Autocratic Communication Style (S1A). This style demonstrates high task/low relationship behavior (HT-LR), initiating a closed presentation. The other party has little, if any, information and is low in capability.

- *Initiation/Response.* You initiate and control the communication with minimal, if any, response.
- *Presentation/Elicitation.* You make a presentation letting the other parties know they are expected to comply with your message; there is little, if any, elicitation.
- *Closed/Open.* You use a closed presentation; you will not consider the receiver's input.

The Consultative Communication Style (S2C). This style demonstrates high task/high relationship behavior (HT-HR), using a closed presentation for the task with an open elicitation for the relationship. The other party has moderate information and capability.

- *Initiation/Response.* You initiate the communication by letting the other party know that you want him or her to buy into your influence. You desire some response.
- *Presentation/Elicitation.* Both are used. You use elicitation to determine the goal of the communication. For example, you may ask questions to determine the situation and follow up with a presentation. When the communication goal is known, little task elicitation is needed. Relationship communication is elicited in order to determine the interest of the other party and acceptance of the message. The open elicitation should show your concern for the other party's point of view and motivate him or her to follow your influence.
- *Closed/Open.* You are closed to having the message accepted (task), but open to the person's feelings (relationship). Be empathetic.

The Participative Communication Style (S3P). This style demonstrates low task/high relationship behavior (LT-HR), responding with open elicitation, some initiation, and little

presentation. The other party is high in information and capability.

- *Initiation/Response.* You respond with some initiation. You want to help the other party solve a problem or get him or her to help you solve one. You are helpful and convey personal support.
- *Presentation/Elicitation.* Elicitation can occur with little presentation. Your role is to elicit the other party's ideas on how to reach objectives.
- *Closed/Open.* Open communication is used. If you participate well, the other party will come to a solution you can accept. If not, you may have to reject the other party's message.

The Empowerment Communication Style (S4E). This style demonstrates low task/low relationship behavior (LT-LR), responding with the necessary open presentation. The other party is outstanding in information and capability.

- *Initiation/Response.* You respond to the other party with little, if any, initiation.
- *Presentation/Elicitation.* You present the other party with information, structure, and so forth, which the sender wants.
- *Closed/Open.* Open, you convey that the other party is in charge; you will accept the message.

Situational Variables

When selecting the appropriate communication style, you should consider four variables: time, information, acceptance, and capability. Answering the questions related to each of these variables can help you select the appropriate style for the situation.

Time. Do I have enough time to use two-way communication—yes or no? When there is no time, the other three variables are not considered; the autocratic style is appropriate. When time is available, any of the other styles may be appropriate, depending on the other variables. Time is a relative term; in one situation, a few minutes may be considered a short time—in another situation, a month may be a short time.

Information. Do I have the necessary information to communicate my message, make a decision, or take action? When you have all the information you need, the autocratic style may be appropriate. When you have some of the information, the consultative style may be appropriate. When you have little information, the participative or empowerment style may be appropriate.

Acceptance. Will the other party accept my message without any input? If the receiver will accept the message, the autocratic style may be appropriate. If the receiver will be reluctant to accept it, the consultative style may be appropriate. If the receiver will reject the message, the participative or empowerment style may be appropriate to gain acceptance. There are situations in which acceptance is critical to success, such as in the area of implementing changes.

Capability. Capability has two parts. *Ability:* Does the other party have the experience or knowledge to participate in two-way communications? Will the receiver put the organization's goals ahead of personal needs or goals? *Motivation:* Does the other party want to participate? When the other party is low in capability, the autocratic style may be appropriate; moderate in capability, the consultative style may be appropriate; high in capability, the participative style may be appropriate; outstanding in capability, the empowerment style may be appropriate. In addition, capability levels can change from one task to another. For example, a professor may have outstanding capability in classroom teaching but be low in capability for advising students.

Selecting Communication Styles

Successful managers rely on different communication styles according to the situation. There are three steps to follow when selecting the appropriate communication style in a given situation. After reading these steps and looking at Model 6.6, you will get to practice this selection process in the section, "Determining the Appropriate Communications Style for Situation 1."

Step 1. **Diagnose the situation.** Answer the questions for each of the four situational variables (time, information, acceptance, and capability). In Self-Assessment 3 at the beginning of this training session, you were asked to select an alternative to 12 situations. You were told to ignore certain lines. When completing the in-class part of Developing Your Leadership Skills Exercise 2, you will place the style letters (S1A, S2C, S3P, S4E) on the lines provided for each of the 12 situations.

Step 2. **Select the appropriate communication style for the situation.** After analyzing the four variables, you select the appropriate communication style for the situation. In some situations, variables may have conflicting styles; you should select the style of the most important variable for the situation. For example, capability may be

MODEL 6.6   Situational Communication

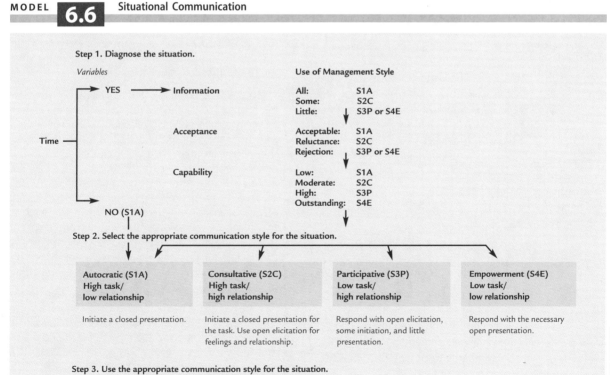

outstanding (S4E) but you have all the information needed (S1A). If the information is more important, use the autocratic style even though the capability is outstanding. When doing the in-class part of Developing Your Leadership Skills Exercise 2, place the letters (S1A, S2C, S3P, S4E) for the appropriate communication styles on the style lines (S _____).

Step 3.   Use the appropriate communication style for the situation. During the in-class part of Developing Your Leadership Skills Exercise 2, you will identify one of the four communication styles for each alternative action; place the S1A, S2C, S3P, or S4E on the S _____ lines. Select the alternative (a, b, c, or d) that represents the appropriate communication style for each of the 12 situations, and place it on the line before the number of the situation.

Model 6.6 summarizes the material in this preparation for the exercise. Use it to determine the appropriate communication style in situation 1 and during the in-class part of Developing Your Leadership Skills Exercise 2.

Determining the Appropriate Communication Style for Situation 1

Step 1.   Diagnose the situation. Answer the four variable questions from the model, and place the letters on the four variable lines for situation 1.

_____   1.   Wendy, a knowledgeable person from another department, comes to you, the engineering supervisor, and requests that you design a special product to her specifications. You would:
_____ time _____ information
_____ acceptance _____ capability
_____ communication style

  a. Control the conversation and tell Wendy what you will do for her. S _____
  b. Ask Wendy to describe the product. Once you understand it, you would present your ideas. Let her realize that you are concerned and want to help by offering your ideas. S _____
  c. Respond to Wendy's request by conveying understanding and support. Help clarify what is to be done by you. Offer ideas, but do it her way. S _____

  d. Find out what you need to know. Let Wendy know you will do it her way. S _____

Step 2.   Select the appropriate communication style for the situation. Review the four variables. If they are all consistent, select one style. If they are conflicting, select the most important variable as the style to use. Place its letters (S1A, S2C, S3P, or S4E) on the style line.

Step 3.   Use the appropriate communication style for the situation. Review the four alternative actions. Identify the communication style for each, placing its letters on the S _____ line, then place the appropriate match (a, b, c, d) on the line before the number.

Let's See How You Did

1.   *Time:* Time is available (or yes, you have time); it can be any style. *Information:* You have little information, so you need to use a participative or empowerment style to find out what Wendy wants done (S3P or S4E). *Acceptance:* If you try to do it your way rather than Wendy's way, she will most likely reject it. You need to use a participative or empowerment style (S3P or S4E). *Capability:* Wendy is knowledgeable and has a high level of capability (S3P).

2.   Reviewing the four variables, you see that there is a mixture of S3P and S4E. Because you are an engineer, it is appropriate to participate with Wendy to give her what she needs. Therefore, the choice is S3P.

3.   Alternative (a) is S1A; this is the autocratic style, high task/low relationship. Alternative (b) is S2C; this is the consultative style, high task/high relationship. Alternative (c) is S3P; this is the participative style, low task/high relationship. Alternative (d) is S4E; this is empowerment style, low task/low relationship behavior. If you selected (c) as your action, you chose the most appropriate action for the situation. This was a three-point answer. If you selected (d) as your answer, this is also a good alternative; it scores two points. If you selected (b), you get one point for overdirecting. If you selected (a), you get zero points; this is too much directing and will most likely hurt communications.

The better you match your communication style to the situation, the more effective you will be at communicating. In the in-class part of Developing Your Leadership Skills Exercise 3, you will apply the model to the other 11 situations in Self-Assessment 3 to develop your ability to communicate as a situational communicator.

Behavior Model Video **6.1**

Situational Communications

Objectives

To better understand the four situational communication styles and which style to use in a given situation

Video *(12 minutes)* Overview

You will first listen to a lecture to understand how to use the situational communications model. Then, you will view two managers, Steve and Darius, meeting to discuss faulty parts. You are asked to identify the communication style

Darius uses in four different scenes. Write the letters of the style on the scene line after each scene. This may be completed as part of Developing Your Leadership Skills Exercise 2.

Scene 1. _____ Autocratic (S1A)

Scene 2. _____ Consultative (S2C)

Scene 3. _____ Participative (S3P)

Scene 4. _____ Empowerment (S4E)

Developing Your Leadership Skills **2**

Situational Communications

Doing This Exercise in Class

Objectives

To develop your ability to communicate using the appropriate style for the situation

The primary AACSB learning standard skill developed through this exercise is analytic skills and communication abilities.

Preparation

You should have competed Self-Assessment 3, and finished the reading about situational communications. You may also want to view Behavior Model Video 6.1.

Experience

You will select the appropriate style for the 12 situations in Self-Assessment 3. On the *time* line, place Y (yes); on the *information*, *acceptance*, and *capability* lines, place the letters S1A, S2C, S3P, or S4E that are appropriate for the situation. Based on your diagnoses, select the one style you would use by placing its letters (S1A, S2C, S3P, or S4E) on the *communication style* line. On the four S lines, write the letters S1A, S2C, S3P, or S4E to identify each style being used. Place the letter a, b, c, or d on the line before the exercise number that represents the most appropriate communication style for the situation.

Procedure 1 *(10–20 minutes)* The instructor shows the video and then reviews the situational communications model,

explaining how to apply it to determine the appropriate style for situation 2.

Procedure 2 *(4–8 minutes)* Students, working alone, complete situation 3 of Self-Assessment 3 using the model. The instructor then goes over the recommended answers.

Procedure 3 *(20–50 minutes)*

A. Break into groups of two or three. As a team, apply the model to situations 4 through 8. The instructor will go over the appropriate answers when all teams are finished, or the time is up.

B. Break into new groups of two or three and do situations 9 through 12. The instructor will go over the appropriate answers.

Conclusion

The instructor leads a class discussion and/or makes concluding remarks.

Apply It *(2–4 minutes)* What did I learn from this experience? How will I use this knowledge in the future? When will I practice using the model?

_____

_____

_____

Behavior Model Skills Training 2

Session 2

In this behavior model skills training session, you will perform three activities:

1. Read "Improving Performance with the Coaching Model" (to review how to use the model).

2. Watch Behavior Model Video 6.2, "Coaching."

3. Complete Developing Your Leadership Skills Exercise 3 (to develop your coaching skills).

For further practice, use the coaching model in your personal and professional life.

The Coaching Model

In the text, read about the coaching model and review Model 6.4.

Behavior Model Video 6.2

Coaching

Objective

To assist you in coaching to improve performance of employees who are not performing to standard

Video (3½ minutes) Overview

You will watch a Web development manager coach an employee who has missed deadlines for completing Web sites.

Developing Your Leadership Skills 3

Coaching

Preparing for This Exercise

You should have read and understood the text material on coaching. You may also view Behavior Model Video 6.2.

Doing This Exercise in Class

Objective

To develop your skill at improving performance through coaching

The primary AACSB learning standard skill developed through this exercise is communication abilities.

Experience

You will coach, be coached, and be observed coaching using Model 6.4 from the text.

Procedure 1 *(2–4 minutes)* Break into groups of three. Make some groups of two, if necessary. Each member selects one of the following three situations in which to be the manager, and a different one in which to be the employee. In each situation, the employee knows the standing plans, but is not

motivated to follow them. You will take turns coaching and being coached.

Three Employee-Coaching Situations

1. *Employee 1 is a clerical worker.* The person uses paper medical files, as do the other three employees in the department. The employees all know that they are supposed to return the files when they are finished so that others can find the files when they need them. Employees should have only one file out at a time. The supervisor notices that employee 1 has five files on the desk, and another employee is looking for one of them. The supervisor thinks that employee 1 will complain about the heavy workload as an excuse for having more than one file out at a time.

2. *Employee 2 is a server in an ice cream shop.* The person knows that the tables should be cleaned up quickly after customers leave so that new customers do not have to sit at dirty tables. It's a busy night. The supervisor finds dirty dishes on two of this employee's occupied tables. Employee 2 is socializing with some friends at one of the tables. Employees are supposed to be friendly; employee 2 will probably use this as an excuse for the dirty tables.

3. *Employee 3 is an auto technician.* All employees at the garage where this person works know that they are supposed to put a paper mat on the floor of each car so that the carpets don't get dirty. When the service supervisor got into a car repaired by employee 3, the car did not have a mat and there was grease on the carpet. Employee 3 does excellent work and will probably mention this fact when coached.

Procedure 2 *(3–7 minutes)* Prepare for coaching to improve performance. On the following lines, each group member writes an outline of what he or she will say when coaching employee 1, 2, or 3, following the coaching steps listed:

1. Describe current performance. _____

_____

_____

2. Describe the desired behavior. _____

_____

_____

3. Get a commitment to the change. _____

_____

_____

4. Follow up. _____

_____

_____

Procedure 3 *(5–8 minutes)*

· Role-playing. The manager of employee 1, the clerical worker, coaches him or her as planned. (Use the actual name of the group member playing employee 1. Talk— do not read your written plan.) Employee 1, put yourself in the worker's position. You work hard; there is a lot of pressure to work fast. It's easier when you have more than one file. Refer to the workload while being coached. Both the manager and the employee will have to improvise their roles.

The person not playing a role is the observer. He or she takes notes using the observer form. Try to make positive coaching feedback comments for improvement. Give the manager alternative suggestions for what he or she could have said to improve the coaching session.

Observer Form

1. How well did the manager describe current behavior?

_____

_____

_____

2. How well did the manager describe desired behavior?

_____

_____

_____

3. How successful was the manager at getting a commitment to the change? Do you think the employee would change?

_____

_____

_____

4. How well did the manager describe how he or she was going to follow up to ensure that the employee performed the desired behavior?

_____

_____

_____

· Feedback. The observer leads a discussion on how well the manager coached the employee. (This should be a coaching discussion, not a lecture.) Focus on what the manager did well, and on how the manager could improve. The employee should also give feedback on how he or she felt, and what might have been more effective in getting him or her to change.

Do not go on to the next interview until you are told to do so. If you finish early, wait for the others to finish.

Procedure 4 *(5–8 minutes)* Same as procedure 3, but change roles so that employee 2, the server, is coached. Employee 2 should make a comment about the importance of talking to customers to make them feel welcome. The job is not much fun if you can't talk to your friends.

Procedure 5 *(5–8 minutes)* Same as procedure 3, but change roles so that employee 3, the auto technician, is coached. Employee 3 should comment on the excellent work he or she does.

Conclusion

The instructor leads a class discussion and makes concluding remarks.

Apply It *(2–4 minutes)* What did I learn from this experience? How will I use this knowledge in the future? When will I practice?

_____

_____

_____

Behavior Model Skills Training 3

Session 3

In this behavior model skills training session, you will perform three activities:

1. Read "Initiating Conflict Resolution" to review how to use the model.

2. Watch Behavior Model Video 6.3, "Initiating Conflict Resolution."

3. Complete Developing Your Leadership Skills Exercise 4 (to develop your conflict resolution skills).

For further practice, use the conflict resolution model in your personal and professional life.

The Initiating Conflict Resolution Model 6.5

In the text, read the initiating conflict resolution model and review Model 6.5.

Behavior Model Video 6.3

Initiating Conflict Resolution

Objective

To assist you in resolving conflicts

Video *(4½ minutes)* Overview

You will watch an advertising agency's employees. Alex initiates a conflict resolution with Catherine to resolve a conflict over a client.

Developing Your Leadership Skills 4

Initiating Conflict Resolution

Preparing for This Exercise

During class you will be given the opportunity to role-play a conflict you face, or have faced, in order to develop your conflict skills. Students and workers have reported that this exercise helped prepare them for a successful initiation of a conflict resolution with roommates and coworkers. Fill in the following information.

Other party(ies) (You may use fictitious names.)

_____

Describe the conflict situation:

_____

_____

_____

List pertinent information about the other party (i.e., relationship with you, knowledge of the situation, age, background, and so on).

_____

_____

_____

Identify the other party's possible reaction to your confrontation. (How receptive will they be to collaborating? What might they say or do during the discussion to resist change?)

_____

_____

_____

How will you overcome this resistance to change?

_____

_____

_____

Following the initiating conflict resolution model steps, write out your planned opening BCF statement that maintains ownership of the problem.

_____

_____

_____

Doing This Exercise in Class

Objective

To experience and develop skills in resolving a conflict.

The primary AACSB learning standard skill developed through this exercise is communication abilities.

Preparation

You should have completed the questionnaire in Developing Your Leadership Skills Exercise 4.

Experience

You will initiate, respond to, and observe a conflict role-play, and then evaluate the effectiveness of its resolution.

Procedure 1 (*2–3 minutes*) Break into as many groups of three as possible. If there are any people not in a triad, make one or two groups of two. Each member selects the number 1, 2, or 3. Number 1 will be the first to initiate a conflict role-play, then 2, followed by 3.

Procedure 2 (*8–15 minutes*)

1. Initiator number 1 gives his or her information from the preparation to number 2 (the responder) to read. Once number 2 understands, proceed with role-play (see item B). Number 3 is the observer.

2. Role-play the conflict resolution. Number 3, the observer, writes his or her observations on the feedback form at the end of this exercise.

3. Integration. When the role-play is over, the observer leads a discussion on the effectiveness of the conflict resolution. All three should discuss the effectiveness. Number 3 is not a lecturer. Do not go on until told to do so.

Procedure 3 (*8–15 minutes*) Same as procedure 2, only number 2 is now the initiator, number 3 is the responder, and number 1 is the observer.

Procedure 4 (*8–15 minutes*) Same as procedure 2, only number 3 is the initiator, number 1 is the responder, and number 2 is the observer.

Conclusion

The instructor leads a class discussion and/or makes concluding remarks.

Apply It (*2–4 minutes*) What did I learn from this experience? How will I use this knowledge in the future? When will I practice?

_____

_____

_____

Feedback Form

Try to have positive coaching improvement feedback comments for each step in initiating conflict resolution. Remember to be *specific* and *descriptive*, and for all improvements have an alternative positive behavior (APB). (For example: "If you would have said/done …, it would have improved the conflict resolution by…")

Initiating Conflict Resolution Model Steps

Step 1.   Plan a BCF statement that maintains ownership of the problem. (Did the initiator have a well-planned, effective BCF statement?)

_____

_____

_____

Step 2.   Present your BCF statement and agree on the conflict. (Did the initiator present the BCF statement effectively? Did the two agree on the conflict?)

_____

_____

_____

Step 3.   Ask for, and/or give, alternative conflict resolutions. (Who suggested alternative solutions? Was it done effectively?)

_____

_____

_____

Step 4.   Make an agreement for change. (Was there an agreement for change?)

_____

_____

_____

_____

Behavior Model Video **6.4**

Mediating Conflict Resolution

Objective

To view the process of mediating a conflict resolution between employees.

Video *(6½ minutes)* Overview

This is a follow-up to the advertising agency conflict (Video 6.3). The two employees end up in conflict again. Their manager, Peter, brings them together to resolve the conflict by following the steps in "Mediating Conflict Resolution" (Model 6.5 in text).

Note: There is no skill-development exercise.

Leader–Member Exchange and Followership

Learning Outcomes

After studying this chapter, you should be able to:

1. Describe the evolution of dyadic theory. p. 242

2. Define the two kinds of relationships that can occur among leaders and followers under the vertical dyadic linkage model. p. 242

3. Describe the main focus of team building from a leader–follower perspective. p. 245

4. Describe the three factors whose combined effect influences LMX relationships. p. 246

5. Discuss a strength and a limitation of LMX theory. p. 250

6. Explain how LMX relationships can lead to unintended consequences. p. 251

7. Describe the two behaviors used in the Kelley Model and identify the resulting follower types. p. 252

8. Discuss the three determinants of follower influence. p. 258

9. List five things a leader should delegate. p. 262

10. Effective leader evaluation and feedback involves before, during, and after steps in the process. Identify some recommended activities during each step. p. 266

11. Define the following **key terms** (in order of appearance in the chapter):

dyadic theory	impressions management	passive follower
dyad	ingratiation	effective follower
in-group	self-promotion	pragmatic follower
out-group	social capital	self-efficacy
leader–member exchange (LMX)	followership	locus of control
	follower	delegation
team-member exchange (TMX)	alienated follower	delegation model
organizational citizenship behavior	conformist follower	

OPENING CASE *APPLICATION*

For connecting more than half a billion people and mapping the social relations among them (something that has never been done before); for creating a new system of exchanging information that has become both indispensable and sometimes a little scary; and finally, for changing how we all live our lives in ways that are innovative and even optimistic, Mark Elliot Zuckerberg is *Time*'s 2010 Person of the Year.

The interview that provided information for the *Time* magazine article is one of the few occasions that Mark Zuckerberg allowed the media into his world. The *Time* interview revealed information about Mr. Zuckerberg's interpersonal relationship with his coworkers and the dynamic between them. According to the interviewer, upon meeting Mark Zuckerberg, the first thing that comes across is that he is very warm, with a quick smile and does not shy away from eye contact. His best friends are his staff; there are no separate offices. Zuckerberg, it is said, loves being around people. A far cry from the shy recluse that he has been portrayed to be. Zuckerberg's coworkers are adamant in their declarations of affection for him. "He has great EQ," says Naomi Gleit, Facebook's product manager for growth and internationalization.

Facebook has been able to recruit and hire some of the best minds in the industry. According to one analyst, everyone at Facebook was a star in their previous employment. In 2008, Zuckerberg hired Sheryl Sandberg, a veteran of Google who was the chief of staff for former Treasury Secretary Lawrence Summers. She joined Facebook as the company's chief operating officer (COO). Former Google employees soon followed. This did not stop with Google; other companies like eBay, Genentech, and Mozilla also saw an exodus of some of their best talents to Facebook. "You don't get a lot of shy, retiring types at Facebook," said one writer. These are intelligent, experienced, productive and highly-sought-after talents, "power nerds" for sure. Zuckerberg has a compelling vision for Facebook and has been able to communicate it to his followers in such a way that they have become totally committed to it. Chris Cox, Facebook's vice president of product, was doing a master's in artificial intelligence at Stanford before he quit to join Facebook. As he puts it, "the interview completely changed my mind. I saw the vision."

Zuckerberg does not have one of those plush executive suites typical of corporate CEOs. His desk is near the middle of the office, within arm's length of his most senior employees. He is said to be a hands-on type leader. Debate is the hallmark of staff meetings at Facebook and employees describe what an intense listener Zuckerberg is during these debates. It is said that he is often one of the last persons to leave the office.[1]

OPENING CASE QUESTIONS:

1. According to the evolution of dyadic theory, where would you put Mark Zuckerberg's relationship with his followers?

2. What evidence is there that LMX relationships at Facebook might have created in-groups and out-groups?

3. What leadership qualities does Mark Zuckerberg possess, and how have these qualities influenced the quality of LMX relationships at Facebook?

4. According to the followership model of follower types, what types of followers has Facebook generally attracted?

5. The text discusses factors that can determine follower influence; when applied to Facebook employees, which factor(s) in your opinion stands out?

Can you answer any of these questions? You'll find answers to these questions and learn more about Mark Zuckerberg and his leadership approach throughout the chapter.

To learn more about Mark Zuckerberg and Facebook, visit the company's Web site at **http://www.facebook.com**

In this chapter, you will explore the intricate nature of work-based relationships, in particular the relationship that forms between a leader and a follower. The relationship that develops between a follower and the leader does influence the follower's job satisfaction, commitment, and performance.[2] Often one of the reasons given for why employees quit their jobs is the lack of a good working relationship with the leader. In fact, there is ample evidence from the literature showing that a high leader–member exchange (LMX) relationship does indeed enhance follower organizational commitment and decreases their likelihood of quitting the job.[3,4]

This focus on the dyadic relationship between a leader and a follower is significant because early theories of leadership focused on leaders and ignored followers or members of the work unit, as if leaders did it alone. We will discuss the evolution of dyadic theory, from vertical dyadic linkage (VDL) theory to leader–member exchange (LMX) theory and to team–member exchange (TMX) theory. Then we will turn our attention to followership, an often ignored but relevant component of the leadership process. The last section of the chapter covers delegation, including a model that can help you develop your delegation skills.

Evolution of Dyadic Theory

Dyadic theory approaches leadership as an exchange relationship which develops between a leader and a follower over time during role-making activities. This pairing that takes place between a leader and a follower is called a dyad and, given the power/authority gap between the two, some have called it a vertical dyad.[5] A *dyad* is defined as *the individualized relationship between a leader and each follower in a work unit.* Over the years, dyadic theory has evolved. As shown in Exhibit 7.1, the three stages of evolution in the dyadic approach are vertical dyadic linkage theory (VDL), leader–member exchange theory (LMX), and team-member exchange theory. These three evolutionary stages of dyadic theory are presented below.

EXHIBIT 7.1 Dyadic Theory: Stages of Evolution

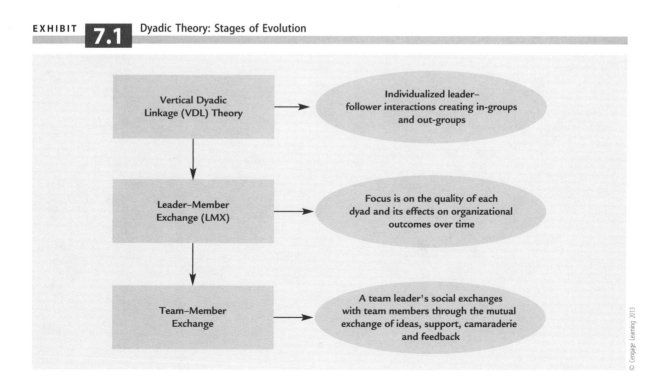

© Cengage Learning 2013

OPENING CASE *APPLICATION*

1. According to the evolution of dyadic theory, where would you put Mark Zuckerberg's relationship with his followers?

It is evident from the case that Zuckerberg's relationship with his coworkers has evolved beyond VDL and LMX to the team-building stage. Mark Zuckerberg seems committed to building a team rather than a collection of varied dyadic relationships. As mentioned in the article, his best friends are his staff. It is said that he loves being around people. His desk is near the middle of the office, within arm's length of his most senior employees. He is said to be a hands-on type leader. Debate is the hallmark of staff meetings at Facebook and employees describe what an intense listener Zuckerberg is during these debates.

Learning Outcome 1 — *Describe the evolution of dyadic theory.*

Vertical Dyadic Linkage (VDL) Theory

Before we begin, determine the dyadic relationship with your manager by completing Self-Assessment 1.

SELF-ASSESSMENT 1　　**Dyadic Relationship with Your Manager**

Select a present or past manager and answer each question describing your relationship using the following scale:

1 　—　 2 　—　 3 　—　 4 　—　 5

Is descriptive of our relationship　　　　*Is not descriptive of our relationship*

_____ 1. I have quick, easy access to talk with my manager anytime I want to.

_____ 2. I get along well with my manager.

_____ 3. I can influence my manager to get things done my way—to get what I want.

_____ 4. When I interact with my manager, our conversation is often relationship-oriented (we talk on a personal level), rather than just task-oriented (we talk only about the job).

_____ 5. We have a loyal, trusting relationship. We look out for each other's interest.

_____ 6. My manager understands my job and the problems that I face; he or she appreciates the work I do.

_____ 7. My manager recognizes my potential and gives me opportunities to grow on the job.

_____ 8. My manager listens carefully to what I have to say and seeks my advice.

_____ 9. My manager gives me good performance evaluations.

_____ 10. My manager gives me rewards (raises and other perks) in excess of the minimum.

Add up the numbers on lines 1 through 10 and place your score here and on the continuum below.

10 　—　 20 　—　 30 　—　 40 　—　 50
In-group　　　　　　　　　　　　*Out-group*

The lower your score, the more characteristic your relationship is of the in-group. Read on to better understand the in-group and the out-group.

Learning Outcome 2 — *Define the two kinds of relationships that can occur among leaders and followers under the vertical dyadic linkage model.*

The vertical dyadic theory evolved from individualized leadership research. Early studies on individualized leadership focused on average leadership style (ALS), in which a leader applies the same style of leadership toward a group as a whole.[6] As the name implies, the leader finds a middle ground approach to leadership that treats everyone the same.

Vertical dyadic linkage (VDL) theory takes a different approach. It focuses on the heterogeneity of dyadic relationships, arguing that a single leader will form different relationships with different followers. According to dyadic theorists, the degree of latitude that a leader grants to a follower to negotiate his or her role, often influences subsequent behavior on the part of both the leader and the follower. The theory proposes that leaders typically employ different influencing tactics for different followers within the same work unit. With a select subset of their members, leaders develop positive social exchanges (influence without authority), and with others, leaders developed only formal authority relationships (influence based primarily upon authority). These relationships do lead to the formation of in-groups and out-groups.

The in-group includes followers with strong social ties to their leader in a supportive relationship characterized by high mutual trust, respect, loyalty, and influence. Leaders primarily use expert, referent, and reward power to influence members of the in-group. *The out-group includes followers with few or no social ties to their leader, in a strictly task-centered relationship characterized by low exchange and top-down influence.* Leaders mostly use reward, as well as legitimate and coercive power, to influence out-group members. (These types of power were discussed in Chapter 5) To satisfy the terms of the exchange relationship, out-group followers need only comply with formal role requirements (such as duties, rules, standard procedures, and legitimate direction from the leader). As long as such compliance is forthcoming, the out-group follower receives the standard benefits for the job (such as a salary) and no more.[7]

There is a reciprocal exchange between the leader and the followers in the in-group. For example, the leader pays close attention, offers support, feedback, and consideration to a follower. The follower in turn renders exceptional performance to the leader, often the one willing to go the extra mile for the leader. It is conceivable that members of the in-group will be those invited to participate in important decision making, given added responsibility, and with greater access to the leader. The governing principle for in-group members is expanded to include a social contract. Meanwhile, members of the out-group are more likely to be managed according to the requirements of the employment contract. They receive little inspiration, encouragement, or recognition.

WORK Application 1
Recall a work unit or organization you worked at that had both in-groups and out-groups. Describe some of the ways in which the manager's behavior and actions toward in-group and out-group members varied.

_____

_____

_____

_____

OPENING CASE *APPLICATION*

2. What evidence is there that LMX relationships at Facebook might have created in-groups and out-groups?

The Time magazine article did mention that some of Zuckerberg's close friends, who worked for Facebook at the start, have left. These departures could in part reflect the status that former Facebook employees have in the industry; but it could also point to the difficulty some people have working for Zuckerberg. As one close associate said, it's hard to have a friend for a boss." According to this associate, "Ultimately, it's the Mark show." The literature does point out that out-group members tend to have a higher turnover than in-group members. The statement that "ultimately, it's the Mark show," may be indicative of the fact that some followers felt left out.

CONCEPT APPLICATION 1
In-Groups versus Out-Groups

From each of the following statements from a subordinate, identify the group to which he or she belongs. Write the appropriate letter in the blank before each item.

a. in-group   b. out-group

_____ 1. I seldom have any direct contact with my boss unless something is wrong with the way I have done my job.

_____ 2. As far as my feelings toward my boss go, we relate to each other strictly along professional lines and work.

_____ 3. My boss and I are similar in a lot of ways; as such we get along well.

_____ 4. When I am not sure what is going on, I can count on my boss to tell me the truth even if it will hurt my feelings.

_____ 5. When I have a major problem at work or in my personal life, my boss would do only that which is required of him or her as my manager without going out of his or her way.

Leader–Member Exchange (LMX) Theory

Vertical dyadic linkage theory evolved into leader–member exchange (LMX) theory. The focus of LMX is on the quality of the dyadic exchange that develops between leaders and followers. For decades, the nature of the relationship between a leader and a follower has a topic of much interest for scholar and practitioners alike.[8,9,10] Some have suggested that it is one of the most important relationships for followers, arguing that the quality of the social exchange between a leader and a follower would be more predictive of follower performance than traits or behaviors of leaders.[11,12,13] Therefore, **leader–member exchange (LMX)** *is defined as the quality of the exchange relationship between a leader and a follower.*[14]

LMX theory offers an alternative way of examining organizational leadership. The underlying assumption of LMX theory is that leaders or superiors have limited amounts of social, personal, and organizational resources (such as energy, time, attention, and discretion) and as a result tend to distribute them among followers selectively.[15,16,17] Leaders do not interact with all followers equally, which ultimately results in the formation of LMX exchanges that vary in quality. LMX is discussed in greater detail later in this chapter.

YOU
Make the
ETHICAL
Call

7.1   *LMX at Work*

Leader–member exchange theory states that in each work group some employees belong to the in-group and others belong to the out-group. Think about your present or past employment. Can you identify members of the in-group and the out-group? Which group were you in?

1. Is it ethical to exclude employees from the in-group?

2. Do you think people in the in-group tend to think exclusion is ethical and those in the out-group tend to think it is unethical?

3. Is your answer to question 1 based on whether you were a member of the in-group or the out-group?

4. Is it possible for all employees to be in the in-group?

5. Should managers work to overcome LMX theory by including all employees in the in-group?

Learning
Outcome 3 *Describe the main focus of team–member exchange (TMX) theory.*

Team-Member Exchange Theory

The third evolutionary phase of dyadic theory is team–member exchange. Many organizations have adopted the team structure as a way of getting work done.[18,19] As a result, employers are requiring new hires to show evidence of teamwork skills and knowledge.[20] In a team working environment, each team member is going to form an exchange relationship with the team leader and/or other team members. The former is what we have referred to as leader-member exchange (LMX), and the later is defined as **team-member exchange (TMX)**, defined as *a team member's social exchanges with peers in terms of the mutual exchange of ideas, support, camaraderie, and feedback.* Some have argued that the creation of in-groups and out-groups brought on by differentiated leadership (a leader treating individuals within a group differently) at best creates a divergence in leader identification and member self-efficacy and at worst lowers group collective efficacy. On the other hand, team-focused leadership facilitates group identification and collective efficacy, which positively contributes to team effectiveness.[21,22] In order words, there is poor team dynamics brought on by the fact that some members don't identify with the leader and thus are not too motivated or committed to the team effort.

Differentiated leadership inevitably leads to questions of fairness in team leadership as some members (more than likely those in the out-group) may feel that they are not being treated fairly. *Procedural fairness* is the perception among team members that they are treated fairly, and *distributive fairness* is the perception that they have been rewarded fairly. When team members question whether they are is being treated fairly by other teammates or whether the leader is treating team members equally when he or she assigns tasks, evaluates performance, or shares information, they are driving at the issue of procedural fairness. On the other hand, questions about fairness in the distribution of rewards and recognition go to the issue of distributive fairness.[23] Team effectiveness and cohesion is affected when team members feel that they are unfairly treated either by the team leader or by other teammates. Effective team leadership is about ensuring that procedures and outcomes are fair to all members.

Studies have shown that when leaders are trained to develop and nurture high-quality relationships with all of their followers, the results on follower performance are dramatic. Followers who feel they have developed a positive one-on-one relationship with the leader tend to show higher creativity, organizational citizenship behavior and performance gains.[24] Through the leader's support, encouragement, and training, followers feel a sense of self-worth, appreciation, and value for their work, and they respond with high performance.[25] As these relationships mature, the entire work group becomes more cohesive, and the payoffs only increase. In essence, partnership building enables a leader to meet both the personal and work-related needs of each group member, one at a time. The concept of leading teams is covered in detail in Chapter 8.

OPENING CASE *APPLICATION*

3. What leadership qualities does Mark Zuckerberg possess, and how have these qualities influenced the quality of LMX relationship at Facebook?

Zuckerberg is close to all his employees. He has created a work environment that does not reflect rankings in the organizational hierarchy. He does not have one of those plush executive suites typical of Corporate CEO offices. He maintains an office location that keeps him physically close to his most senior employees. This symbolic gestures

(continued)

(Opening Case Apllication 3 continued)

conveys a sense of camaraderie and teamwork to his associates. Facebook employees get treated well—three free, good meals a day; unlimited snacks; free dry cleaning. He has earned the trust and respect of his coworkers, so much so that they they're adamant in their avowals of affection for him and in their insistence that you not misconstrue his odd personality. It seems the quality of the exchange relationship between Zuckerberg and his followers is quite high.

CONCEPT APPLICATION 2
Stages of Evolution in Dyadic Theory

Which stage is described by the following statements? Write the appropriate letter in the blank before each item.

a. vertical dyadic linkage theory
c. team–member exchange theory
b. leader–member exchange theory

_____ 6. A relationship in which leader–follower interactions lead to the creation of in-groups and out-groups.

_____ 7. A theory that encourages leaders to aspire to the creation of positive relationships with all followers, not just a few special individuals.

_____ 8. The notion that leaders do not interact with all followers equally, but rather focus on the formation of relationships that varies in quality.

_____ 9. A hierarchical relationship in which leader–follower dyads develop.

Leader–Member Exchange Theory

As defined earlier, leadership is the ability to influence others to contribute toward the achievement of organizational goals. Leader–member exchange is one theory that deals with how leaders influence member behaviors.[26] According to this theory, leaders form high-quality social exchanges (based on trust and liking) with some members and low-quality economic exchanges with others that do not extend beyond the employment contract.[27] Such differentiated leadership does affect group effectiveness.[28] Past studies have confirmed that high-quality LMX relationships are associated with positive follower outcomes such as performance, satisfaction, commitment, and organizational citizenship behavior.[29,30] Followers in high-quality exchange relationships tend to reciprocate their leader's trust and liking by showing greater "citizenship behaviors" and excellent performance.[31,32]

This section will examine the following topics related to LMX theory: the factors that influence LMX relationships, how one develops high-quality LMX relations, how LMX relationships influence follower behavior, and the strengths and limitations of LMX theory.

Learning Outcome 4

Describe the three factors whose combined effect influences LMX relationships.

Factors That Influence LMX Relationships

LMX relationships are based on social exchanges, meaning that there is reciprocity. Each party must contribute something that is valued by the other party. According to LMX theory, a leader varies his or her behavior according to the quality of the interpersonal relationship with each individual. Therefore, within the same work group, the quality of each dyadic relationship will likely differ between followers of the same leader.[33] It takes at least two parties to form a relationship, and for our purpose the two parties will be the leader and the follower. Each plays a role in influencing the relationship that ensues between them. A third factor that can influence the LMX relationship is the situation surrounding the leader and follower. This will be internal and external environmental factors. We therefore propose that the quality of each dyadic relationship can be influenced by the combined effects of the following factors: follower behavior and attributes, leader–follower perceptions and self-identities and situational factors. Each is briefly discussed.

Follower Behavior and Attributes

The difference between traditional leadership theories and LMX is that while the former focused on the leader primarily, the latter was one of the first attempts in leadership studies to formally recognize the role of the follower in the leadership process. A follower's behavior and attributes influences how the leader and other members see such a follower. For example, a follower's feedback-seeking behavior and self-promoting personality can have a positive or negative effect on the LMX relationship. A proactive follower who takes the time to actively seek information and feedback about his or her role expectations and how to successfully perform them, sets the right tone for forming not just a relationship, but a high-quality relationship with the leader. Such followers show initiative even in areas outside their immediate responsibility, possess a strong sense of commitment to work unit goals, and show a greater sense of responsibility for unit success. In short, they have the right attitude.[34] As the saying goes, "attitude affects altitude."

Also, followers who are good at self-promotion will use this attribute to adjust their attitudes and behaviors to align with the expectations of the leader. This in turn influences the leader to show support, delegate more, allow greater discretion and engage in open communication with the follower.[35] This reciprocation strengthens the LMX relationship.

Leader–Follower Perceptions and Self-Identities

The leader's first impressions of the follower can influence the leader's behavior toward the follower. A positive relationship is more likely when the follower is perceived to be competent and dependable, and when the follower's values and ideals are similar to those of the leader. When this happens, followers are more likely to be supported, encounter fewer pressure tactics (for example, threats and demands), experience greater involvement and mentoring, and receive more honest input from the leader. The same is true for the follower's perceptions of the leader. One study's findings confirmed that followers' identification and satisfaction with their leaders are stronger, the more leaders match followers' ideal.[36]

Also, the leader and the follower self-concept can influence the LMX relationship. Self-concept or self-identity has the potential to influence behavior in interpersonal relationships. Social psychologists have broken down self-identity into three dimensions: individual, relational, and collective.[37,38] These three dimensions are said to be mutually exclusive and thus cannot be simultaneously activated. An individual self-identity is about being self-centered and unique. A relational self-identity is dyad-centered, forming relationships with others. A collective self-identity is defined in terms of the broader group.[39] A leader or a follower who has an individual self-identity, and is perceived by other team members as such, may have a difficult time forming high-quality LMX relationships compared to someone with a relational or collective self-identity.

WORK Application 2

Based on your current job or a past job you held for some time, how did your relationship with the leader/boss change as you progressed from the stranger to the acquaintance and finally to the mature stages as described in the life-cycle model?

_____

_____

_____

_____

Situational Factors

Any number of situational factors can influence the exchange relationship that develops between a leader and a follower. We offer five such factors here. The first of these is the stage of the relationship according to the life-cycle model. According to this model, both task and social working relationships develop from the initial stage of strangers to the middle stage of acquaintances and finally to the mature stage of sharing and mutual commitment to the work group or team. From a behavioral perspective, actions taken by a follower during the stranger stage to gather information about their role expectations as well as how they are meeting such expectations will influence the quality of the LMX relationship that ultimately develops between the leader and member. As the leader and follower become acquainted, they engage in further refining the roles they will play together. The relationship transitions from an economic-based exchange, which is contractual in nature to a social-exchange characterized by mutual trust, loyalty, and respect between the leader and the follower. There is a greater likelihood that followers will exhibit greater organizational citizenship behavior (OCB). **Organizational citizenship behavior** is defined as *individual behavior that is discretionary, not directly or explicitly recognized by the formal reward system, and that in the aggregate promotes the effective functioning of the organization.*[40] It is behavior that *goes above and beyond the expected* duties of an employee. Followers perceived to be hard working and willing to go the extra mile for the leader have a higher-quality exchange relationship with the leader than those who are perceived to be lazy or unwilling to go the extra mile for the leader.

A second situational factor is managerial resource strength. An underline assumption of LMX is that due to limited time and social resources, a leader cannot form close positive LMX relationships with all followers. Therefore, a leader is more likely to form high-quality LMX relationships with some members (in-group) and low-quality LMX relationships with others (out-group). This situation may be exacerbated by a third situational factor: the leader's span of control. A leader's *span of control* is the number of direct followers to a particular leader. The wider the span of control and the fewer the resources the leader possesses, the greater the disparity in the quality of LMX.

A fourth situational factor is the work group climate. A work climate of trust, respect, and openness may provide a setting for positive LMX relationships to develop. A fifth situational factor would be one's social identity. Social identity is the degree to which members form close social ties with the group based on relevant characteristics such as ethnicity, gender, personalities, and age and how it subsequently influences interactions within and between groups.[41] Within the work group, members who show a positive social identity to the group are more likely to develop high-quality LMX relationships than members with a negative social identity or a lack of it.

WORK Application 3

Recall a work situation in which you were required to do something that was beyond your employment contract. How did you respond to your manager's request, and what consequences did it have on your relationship with him or her?

_____

_____

_____

_____

Developing High-Quality LMX Relationships

Proactive followers who want to form positive relationships with their leaders can employ any number of options. Here we discuss three such options: impressions management, ingratiation, and self-promotion. **Impressions management** *is a follower's effort to project a favorable image in order to gain an immediate benefit or improve a long-term relationship with the leader.* Employees seeking to form a positive relationship with the leader will often be the ones seeking feedback on how to improve their work performance. Researchers have identified two kinds of motives associated with follower feedback-seeking behavior: performance-driven motive and impressions-driven motive. The *performance-driven motive* is the follower's genuine attempt to seek information from the leader that will help improve work performance, while the *impressions-driven motive* refers to the desire to control how one appears to the leader.[42]

WORK Application 4

Recall an occasion when you had the opportunity to make a positive first impression on your manager. Describe what tactics you employed and their effects on your manager.

_____

_____

_____

_____

Ingratiation *is the effort to appear supportive, appreciative, and respectful.* Ingratiatory influence tactics include favor rendering, self-promotion, and behavioral conformity. In this instance, followers go beyond the call of duty to render services to the leader and to conform their behavior to the expectations of the leader. Self-promotion *is the effort to appear competent and dependable.* Studies have found a positive correlation between ingratiation by a follower and affection (or liking) of the leader for the follower. Affection, in turn, is positively related to the quality of the exchange relationship and the leader's assessment of the follower's competence, loyalty, commitment, and work ethic. These tactics are valuable tools that can enhance the visibility of the follower's strengths and performance. However, there is the possibility that these tactics can have a negative effect on the LMX relationship in that leaders may discount or devalue the follower's attempts, if deemed to be self-serving.

The Benefits of High-Quality LMX Relationships

LMX takes a relationship-based approach to leadership, focusing on social dimensions of trust, loyalty, honesty, support, and respect that help define the nature of the dyadic relationship between a leader and a follower. As discussed earlier, followers with strong social ties to the leader (high-quality LMX) are said to belong to the in-group, while those with no social ties to the leader (low-quality LMX) are said to belong to the out-group. Being a member of the in-group puts you in a very favorable position. For example, in-group followers routinely receive higher performance ratings than out-group followers; out-group followers routinely show higher levels of turnover than in-group followers. When asked to evaluate organizational climate, in-group followers give more positive ratings than out-group followers.[43,44]

The benefits of establishing a deeper exchange relationship with in-group members is the leader's control over outcomes that are desirable to the followers. These outcomes include such benefits as helping with a follower's career (for example, recommending advancement), giving special favors (bigger office, better work schedule), allowing participation in decision making, delegating greater responsibility and authority, more sharing of information, assigning in-group members to interesting and desirable tasks, and giving tangible rewards such as a pay increase.[45,46] In return for these benefits, in-group members have certain obligations and expectations beyond those required of out-group members. In-group members are expected to be loyal to the leader, to be more committed to task objectives, to work harder, and to share some of the leader's administrative duties.[47,48] This reciprocal exchange between the leader and the follower is such that the greater the perceived value of the tangible and intangible benefits exchanged, the higher the quality of LMX. There is even empirical evidence that LMX and TMX quality does affect individual creativity in work teams.[49]

The special relationship with in-group followers creates certain obligations and constraints for the leader.[50] To maintain the relationship, the leader must continuously pay attention to in-group members, remain responsive to their needs and feelings, and rely more on time-consuming influence methods such as persuasion and consultation. The leader cannot resort to coercion or heavy-handed use of authority without endangering the quality of the relationship. The followers are therefore said to possess social capital, defined as *the set of resources that inheres in the structure of relations between members of the group, which helps them get ahead.*[51,52]

Unless this cycle of reciprocal reinforcement of leader and member behavior is interrupted, the relationship is likely to develop to a point where there is a high degree of mutual dependence, support, and loyalty. Organizational culture, and more specifically perceptions of fairness, trust, and respect for people, plays a key role in protecting the cycle and strengthening the relationship.[53,54]

The positive relationship between LMX and follower job satisfaction is stronger when leaders have high perceived organizational support (POS) because these leaders feel they have more resources to exchange with followers.[55] Compared to employees in

WORK Application 5

Think of a leader you've had or now have a very positive high-quality relationship with. Describe some of the work related benefits you received that can be directly or indirectly tied to your relationship with this leader/ supervisor.

_____

_____

_____

_____

low-quality LMXs, high-quality LMX employees exhibit greater organizational citizenship behavior.[56,57,58]

Now that you understand LMX, complete Self-Assessment 2.

SELF-ASSESSMENT 2   In-Group and Out-Group

Based on Self-Assessment 1 on page 242 and your reading of VDL and LMX theory, place the people who work or have worked for your present or past manager in the in-group or out-group. Be sure to include yourself.

In-Group Members	Out-Group Members
_____	_____
_____	_____
_____	_____

Learning Outcome 5   *Discuss the strengths and limitations of LMX theory.*

Strengths and Limitations of LMX Theory

From a strength perspective, the fact that LMX focuses on the relationship between the leader and each follower is important; early leadership studies (such as the Great Man Theory of leadership) focused on the leader and ignored the follower, as if leaders alone were responsible for organizational success. LMX emphasizes the importance of forming positive relationships with followers and how this in turn influences their behavior. Many empirical studies have revealed that high-quality LMX and TMX relationships do influence followers' organizational commitment, organizational citizenship behavior, job performance, and creativity.[59] Also, underlying LMX theory is the fact that leaders and followers have to learn to communicate with each other for any kind of exchange to occur.

A limitation of LMX is measurement difficulty. Too often, LMX is measured only from the followers' perspective prompted by the assumption that the leader's view of the quality of the exchange relationship will match that of the follower. Some scholars argue that this may not necessarily be the case and thus question the accuracy of what may be seen as a high-quality LMX.[60] An example of this will be the LMX-7 questionnaire that focuses solely on the follower's evaluation of the exchange relationship with the leader.[61]

The LMX-7 questionnaire is viewed as one of the best and most commonly used instruments for measuring the quality of LMX relationships.[62] It assesses the extent to which leaders and followers share similar or different viewpoints on such dimensions as mutual respect for each other's abilities, personal understanding, trust, and commitment to one another. Questions featured on the LMX-7 scale include structured questions, such as the following:

- How well does your leader understand your job problems and needs? (Not a bit, a little, a fair amount, quite a bit, and a great deal)

- How well does your leader recognize your potential? (Not at all, a little, moderately, mostly, and fully)

- How would you characterize your working relationship with your leader? (Extremely ineffective, worse than average, average, better than average, and extremely effective)

Another limitation of LMX is its inherent bias in favor of in-group members. Given the variability in a leader's treatment of in-group and out-group members, it is worth asking to what extent this bias ultimately enhances or hurts the future career aspirations of followers? It is often the case that a leader's liking for an in-group member will then translate into a favorable performance evaluation even when actual performance of the in-group member may be comparable or even less than that of an out-group member. This kind of favorable treatment is not given to members of the out-group. These positive ratings often then become a part of an individual's employment record. The ratings may ultimately be used—formally or informally—in future selection, development, and promotion decisions. Generally, employees with a history of high performance ratings are those who get promoted to higher-level positions. Job satisfaction among members of the in-group is much higher, which then leads to lower attrition rates compared to that of out-group members.

Complete Self-Assessment 3 to determine your LMX relationship with your manager.

SELF-ASSESSMENT 3   Your LMX Relationship with Your Manager

Self-Assessment 1 determined your status in terms of your relationship with your manager – whether you were part of the in-group or out-group. Your score in Self-Assessment 1 also indicates the quality of the relationship that you have with your manager. Place your score from Self-Assessment 1 here _____ and on the following continuum. Note that some of the questions in Self-Assessment 1 are similar to the LMX-7 questions.

10   —   20   —   30   —   40   —   50

High-quality LMX relationship   *Low-quality LMX relationship*

The lower your score, generally, the better is your relationship with your manager. We say generally, because you could have a manager who does not have a good relationship with any employee. Thus, a good LMX can be a relative measure.

Learning Outcome 6   *Explain how LMX relationships can lead to unintended consequences.*

On its face, the idea of promoting those who consistently score high in their performance evaluations seems harmless and even rational were it not for the possibility that some positive evaluations are earned strictly for being in the in-group and not because of actual work performance. As it turns out, those who often get the promotions are also those who show consistently higher scores in performance evaluations. Therefore, the development and career advancement of other group members who (regardless of their performance) are not similar to, familiar to, or well liked by their leader may be jeopardized. The out-group members may be paying a price for not having the same social standing with their leaders as in-group members.

Therefore, managers and human resource management specialists need to be made aware of the potential biasing effects inherent in high-quality LMX relationships. Procedural checks and controls need to be applied to minimize such biases—if indeed this is possible. Otherwise, the development of high-quality LMX relations could result in unintended consequences such as discrimination against out-group members. A necessary first step may be simply to train and encourage leaders to maintain high-quality LMX relationships with all followers, not just a few.

Followership

Most scholars would agree that there is increasing use of the words *follower* and *followership* in discussions of organizational leadership. Past leadership research has focused on leaders and ignored the role of followers in explaining organizational successes or failures. This has led to criticism of extant leadership theories for being too "leader-centric."[63] The focus of these theories has been almost exclusively on the impact of leader traits and behaviors on follower attitudes and behaviors. However, there is increasing recognition of the reality that leadership is a relationship that is jointly produced by leaders and followers, and that to adequately understand it, we must know more about the often-nameless persons who comprise the followers of leaders.[64] Robert Kelley, a pioneer and early proponent of followership stated that "without followers, leadership is meaningless and leaders don't exist."[65] To adequately understand the cognitions, attributes, behaviors, and contexts of followership, we organize this section according to the following topics: defining followership, followership types, follower influencing characteristics, suggested guidelines to become an effective follower, and the dual role of being a leader and follower.

Defining Followership

Followership refers to *the behavior of followers that result from the leader-follower mutual influencing relationship.* Not much has been done to advance understanding of the follower and the psychological processes and mechanisms that connect leaders and followers.[66] To a large extent, societal views about followers have contributed to our limited understanding of followership. From an early age we are taught that organizations succeed because of the leader, with very little or no mention of the role of followers. The follower is seen as someone who carries out the instructions of the leader. From this perspective, the **follower** is defined as *someone who is being influenced by a leader.* There is increasing recognition that leaders are just one part of a duality, because there can be no leaders without followers. Effective leadership requires effective followership. Kelley (1988) and Chaleff (2003) are two early pioneers who brought focus to the role of followers in the leadership process. No work unit or organized effort can succeed and be sustained without followers; this, according to Kelley, is the power of followership.[67] Chaleff discussed the fact that effective followers are also courageous followers who tend to demonstrate certain behaviors. He identifies the five behaviors as courage to accept responsibility, courage to serve, courage to question, courage to be part of necessary change and courage to take a moral stand when necessary.[68]

Effective followers do more than fulfill the vision laid out by their leader; they are partners in creating the vision. They take responsibility for getting their jobs done, take the initiative in fixing problems, and question leaders when they think they are wrong.

Learning Outcome 7   *Describe the two behaviors used in the Kelley Model and identify the resulting follower types.*

Types of Followers

As in the case of leaders, there are different types of followers. Based on individual characteristics, motivations, and behaviors, some followers may be more active and involved than others. Some of the names that have been used to describe different types of followers include *isolates, bystanders, participants, activists,* and *diehards.*[69] The best conceptualization of follower types is Kelley's model.[70] Using a combination of two types of behavior—independent critical thinking and level of involvement in organizational affairs—Kelley groups followers into five categories based on their specific behavioral mix.

Exhibit 7.2 depicts these two behavioral dimensions, where level of independent critical thinking is on a continuum from low to high and the level of involvement is on a continuum from low to high as well. The high independent critical thinker refers to the follower who is able to examine, analyze, and evaluate matters of significance in the organization's life. Conversely, the opposite of this person is someone who is low in ability to think critically. The second behavior variable—level of involvement—refers to the follower who takes a visible and active role in organizational affairs. The opposite of this person is someone who prefers to be in the background and take a passive role in organizational affairs.

EXHIBIT 7.2   Follower Types

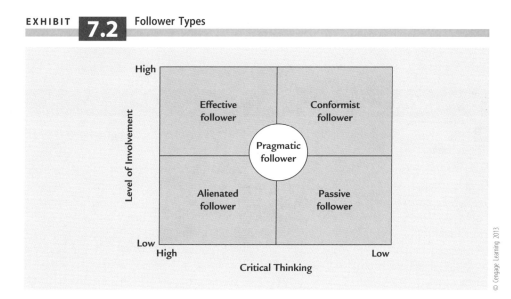

© Cengage Learning 2013

According to Kelley, combining these dimensions results in five basic follower types, identified as: alienated, passive, conformist, pragmatic, and effective follower (see Exhibit 7.3):[71]

- *The alienated follower is someone who is low on involvement yet is high on critical thinking.* The alienated follower is someone who feels cheated, or unappreciated, by his or her organization for exemplary work. Often cynical in their behavior, alienated followers are capable but unwilling to participate in developing solutions to problems. They are just happy to dwell on the negatives and ignore the positives as far as organizational life goes.

- *The conformist follower is someone who is high on involvement but low on critical thinking.* In other words, conformists are the "yes people" of the organization. They carry out all orders without considering the consequences of such orders. A conformist would do anything to avoid conflict. Authoritarian leaders prefer conformist followers.

- *The passive follower is someone who is neither high on critical thinking nor involvement.* The passive follower looks to the leader or others to do all the thinking and does not get involved. Lacking in initiative and commitment to the team, the invisible follower requires constant supervision and never goes beyond the job description. They are often described by their leaders as lazy, unmotivated, and incompetent.

- *The* **effective follower** *is someone who is high on critical thinking and involvement.* Effective followers are not risk-averse nor do they shy from conflict. They have the courage to initiate change and put themselves at risk or in conflict with others, even their leaders, to serve the best interest of the organization. As such, they are often described as proactive. Effective followers tend to function very well in self-managed teams. They are a manager's best asset in that they complement the leader and can be relied upon to relieve the leader of many tasks.

- *The* **pragmatic follower** *exhibits a little of all four styles—depending on which style fits the prevailing situation.* Pragmatic followers are "stuck in the middle" most of the time. Because it is difficult to discern just where they stand on issues, they present an ambiguous image, with positive and negative sides. On the positive side, when an organization is going through desperate times, the pragmatic follower knows how to "work the system to get things done." On the negative side, this same behavior can be interpreted as "playing political games," or adjusting to maximize self-interest.

OPENING CASE *APPLICATION*

4. According to the followership model of follower types, what types of followers has Facebook generally attracted?

Facebook has been able to recruit and hire some of the best minds in the industry. According to one analyst, everyone at Facebook was a star in their previous employment. Sheryl Sandberg, a veteran of Google, was the chief of staff for former Treasury Secretary Lawrence Summers. She joined Facebook as the company's chief operating officer (COO). Chris Cox, Facebook's vice president of product, was doing a master's in artificial intelligence at Stanford when Zuckerberg personally convinced him to join Facebook. "You don't get a lot of shy, retiring types at Facebook," said one writer. These are intelligent, experienced, productive and highly-sought after talents, "power nerds" to say the least. Remember, the effective follower is someone who is high on critical thinking and involvement. It is a safe bet that Zuckerberg and Facebook have mostly attracted effective followers. Zuckerberg is close to all his employees. He has created a work environment that does not reflect rankings in the organizational hierarchy. He does not have one of those plush executive suites typical of corporate CEO offices. His desk is near the middle of the office, within arm's length of his most senior employees. Facebook employees get treated well—three free, good meals a day; unlimited snacks; free dry cleaning. He has earned the trust and respect of his coworkers—so much so that they they're adamant in their avowals of affection for him and in their insistence that you not misconstrue his odd personality. It seems the quality of the exchange relationship between Zuckerberg and his followers is quite high.

The Effective Follower

To be effective as a follower, it is important to acquire the skills necessary to combine two opposing follower roles—namely, to execute decisions made by a leader, and to raise issues about those decisions when they are deemed misguided or unethical. Although this is not always easy to do, followers must be willing to risk the leader's displeasure with such feedback. Moral integrity and a willingness to take stands based on principle are distinguishing characteristics of the effective follower. Developing a high level of mutual trust and respect between the leader and follower can mitigate the risk of falling out of favor with the leader. In such a relationship, a leader is likely to view criticism and dissenting views as an honest effort to facilitate achievement of shared objectives, rather than as an intentional expression of personal disagreement or disloyalty.[72,73]

The effective follower has a high self-efficacy compared to the ineffective follower. **Self-efficacy** is defined *as a person's beliefs in his or her capabilities to produce at a* *certain level of performance.*[74] Self-efficacy beliefs determine how people feel, think, motivate themselves and behave, which in turn influences their work ethic.

How followers perceive a leader plays a critical role in their ability to help the leader grow and succeed. Just as leaders make attributions about follower competence, followers make attributions about leader competence and intentions. Followers assess whether the leader's primary motivation is more for his or her personal benefit or career advancement than for their own welfare and the organization's well-being. Credibility is increased and follower commitment is enhanced when the leader makes self-sacrifices to gain support for his or her ideas, rather than imposing on followers. Leaders who appear insincere, or motivated only by personal gain, create an atmosphere in which integrating the two opposing follower roles is impossible. Here, followers would play the passive role of conforming to the leader's expectations without offering any constructive criticism, even when it is called for in a leader's decisions and actions. Complete Self-Assessment 4 to learn how effective you are as a follower.

SELF-ASSESSMENT 4   **Effective Followers**

Select a present or past boss and answer each question describing your behavior using the following scale.

5 — 4 — 3 — 2 — 1
I do this regularly   *I do not do this*

_____ 1. I offer my support and encouragement to my boss when things are not going well.

_____ 2. I take initiative to do more than my normal job without having to be asked to do things.

_____ 3. I counsel and coach my boss when it is appropriate, such as with a new, inexperienced boss, and in a unique situation in which the boss needs help.

_____ 4. When the boss has a bad idea, I raise concerns and try to improve the plans, rather than simply implement a poor decision.

_____ 5. I seek and encourage the boss to give me honest feedback, rather than avoid it and act defensively when it is offered.

_____ 6. I try to clarify my role in tasks by making sure I understand my boss's expectations of me and my performance standards.

_____ 7. I show my appreciation to my boss, such as saying thanks when the boss does something in my interest.

_____ 8. I keep the boss informed; I don't withhold bad news.

_____ 9. I would resist inappropriate influence by the boss; if asked, I would not do anything illegal or unethical.

Add up the numbers on lines 1 through 9 and place your score here _____ and on the continuum below.

9 — 15 — 25 — 35 — 45
Ineffective Follower   *Effective Follower*

The higher your score, generally, the more effective you are as a follower. However, your boss also has an effect on your followership. A poor boss can affect your followership behavior; nevertheless, make sure you do try to be a good follower. Read on to better understand how to be an effective follower.

Guidelines to Becoming an Effective Follower

Research focused on followership has identified certain behaviors that are associated with effective followers.[75,76] These behaviors distinguish followers on top-performing teams from their counterparts on marginally performing teams. Exhibit 7.3 presents nine guidelines for effective followership; note that the nine questions in Self-Assessment 4 are based on these guidelines.

EXHIBIT **7.3** Guidelines to Becoming an Effective Follower

a. Offer support to leader.
b. Take initiative.
c. Play counseling and coaching roles to leader when appropriate.
d. Raise issues and/or concerns when necessary.
e. Seek and encourage honest feedback from the leader.
f. Clarify your role and expectations.
g. Show appreciation.
h. Keep the leader informed.
i. Resist inappropriate influence of leader.

© Cengage Learning 2013

Offer Support to Leader

A good follower looks for ways to express support and encouragement to a leader who is encountering resistance in trying to introduce needed change in his or her organization. Successful organizations are characterized by followers whose work ethic and philosophy are in congruence with those of the organization and the leader.

Take Initiative

Effective followers take the initiative to do what is necessary without being told, including working beyond their normally assigned duties. They look for opportunities to make a positive impact on the organization's objectives. When serious problems arise that impede the organization's ability to accomplish its objectives, effective followers take the risk to initiate corrective action by pointing out the problem to the leader, suggesting alternative solutions, or if necessary, resolving the problem outright. While taking the initiative often involves risks, if done carefully and properly, it can make the follower a valuable part of the team and a member of the leader's trusted circle.

Counsel and Coach the Leader When Appropriate

Contrary to the myth that leaders have all the answers, most people now recognize that followers also have opportunities to coach and counsel leaders, especially when a leader is new and inexperienced. A mutually trusting relationship with a leader facilitates upward coaching and counseling. An effective follower must be alert for opportunities to provide helpful advice, and ask questions, or simply be a good listener when the leader needs someone to confide in. Because some leaders may be reluctant to ask for help, it is the follower's responsibility to recognize such situations and step in when appropriate. For example, a leader whose interpersonal relationship with another follower may be having a different effect than the leader intended could be counseled to see the ineffectiveness of his approach or style by another follower: "I am sure you intended for Bob to see the value of being on time when you said…, but that is not how he took it." When coaching and counseling a leader is done with respect, it is most effective. Respect creates symmetry, empathy, and connection in all kinds of relationships, including that between a leader and a follower.[77]

Raise Issues and/or Concerns When Necessary

When there are potential problems or drawbacks with a leader's plans and proposals, a follower's ability to bring these issues or concerns to light is critical. How the follower raises these issues is crucial, because leaders often get defensive in responding to negative feedback. Followers can minimize such defensiveness by acknowledging the leader's superior status and communicating a sincere desire to be of help in accomplishing the organization's goals, rather than personal interest. When challenging a leader's flawed plans and proposals, it is important for the follower to pinpoint specifics rather than vague generalities, and to avoid personalizing the critique. This guideline is consistent with the prevailing view of the courageous follower as a person who is highly involved and very much an independent thinker with initiative and a well-developed sense of responsibility.

Seek and Encourage Honest Feedback from the Leader

Followers can play a constructive role in how their leaders evaluate them. Some leaders are uncomfortable with expressing negative concerns about a follower's performance, so they tend to focus only on the follower's strengths. One way to overcome this tendency is for the follower to show willingness to accept both positive and negative feedback without being defensive. Encourage the leader to point out the strongest and weakest aspects of your work.

Clarify Your Role and Expectations

Where there is evidence of role ambiguity or uncertainty about job expectations, this must be clarified with the leader. As will be revealed in Chapter 8 on leading effective teams, it is the leader's responsibility to clearly communicate role expectations for followers. Nevertheless, some leaders fail to communicate clear job expectations, scope of authority and responsibility, performance targets, and deadlines. Followers must insist on clarification in these areas by their leaders. In some cases the problem is that of role conflict. The leader directs a follower to perform mutually exclusive tasks and expects results on all of them at the same time. Followers should be assertive but diplomatic about resolving role ambiguity and role conflict.

Show Appreciation

Everyone, including leaders, loves to be appreciated when they perform a good deed that benefits others. When a leader makes a special effort to help a follower, such as helping to protect the follower's interest, or nurturing and promoting the follower's career, it is appropriate for the follower to show appreciation. Even if the leader's actions don't directly benefit a particular follower but represent a significant accomplishment for the organization, it is still an appropriate gesture for followers to express their appreciation and admiration for the leader. Recognition of this kind only reinforces desirable leadership behavior. Although some may argue that praising a leader is a form of ingratiation easily used to influence the leader, when sincere, it can help to build a positive leader–follower exchange relationship.

Keep the Leader Informed

Accurate and timely information enables a leader to make good decisions and to have a complete picture of where things stand in the organization. Leaders who appear not to know what is going on in their organizations do feel and look incompetent in front of their peers and superiors. It is embarrassing for a leader to hear about events or changes taking place within his or her unit from others. This responsibility of relaying information to the leader includes both positive and negative information. Some followers tend to withhold bad news from their leaders; this is just as detrimental as providing no information at all.

Resist Inappropriate Influence from the Leader

A leader may be tempted to use his or her power to influence the follower in ways that are inappropriate (legally or ethically). Despite the power gap between the leader

WORK Application 6

Give examples of how you, or someone you worked with, implemented three of the nine guidelines to effective followership.

_____

_____

_____

_____

and follower, the follower is not required to comply with inappropriate influence attempts, or to be exploited by an abusive leader. Effective followers challenge the leader in a firm, tactful, and diplomatic way. Reminding the leader of his or her ethical responsibilities, insisting on your rights, and pointing out the negative consequences of complying are various ways in which a follower can resist inappropriate influence attempts by a leader. It is important to challenge such behavior early, before it becomes habitual, and to do it without personal hostility. Taking a moral stand may sometimes require the follower to psychologically and/or physically separate from the leader.

CONCEPT APPLICATION 3
Guidelines to Becoming an Effective Follower

Identify each guideline using the letters a–i from Exhibit 7.3 on page 256:

_____ 10. I showed up early for the meeting and the conference room was messy, so I cleaned up.

_____ 11. We have a new boss, and I've been filling her in on how we do things in our department.

_____ 12. My boss and I have short daily meetings.

_____ 13. We only have performance reviews once a year. But I wanted to know what my boss thinks of my work, so we had a meeting to discuss my performance.

_____ 14. Employees have not been following safety rules as they should, and the boss hasn't done anything about it. So I went to talk to my boss about it.

_____ 15. My boss hinted about having a sexual relationship, so I reminded her that I was happily married and clearly told her I was not interested and not to talk about it again.

_____ 16. We started a new project today, and I did not understand what I was supposed to do. So I went to talk to my boss about what to do.

_____ 17. My boss gave me a new assignment that I wanted, so I thanked him

Learning Outcome 8   _Discuss the three determinants of follower influence._

Determinants of Follower Influence

In every organization or work setting, some followers seem to have more influence over their peers (and even their leaders) than others. These are the followers that command respect, trust, and loyalty from everyone, including the leader. They are opinion leaders amongst their peers. It is not uncommon for a follower of such stature to exert greater influence over other followers than even the leader of the group can. Leaders who understand this "follower–follower" dynamic can use it to their advantage.

It is not always the case that influential followers use their influence appropriately. Some may employ their influence in negative ways to make the leader's job difficult. This section examines the factors that determine follower influence. The three determining factors that have been found to distinguish influential followers are: the follower's relative power position, locus of control, and education/experience (see Exhibit 7.4).

EXHIBIT **7.4** Factors That Determine Follower Influence

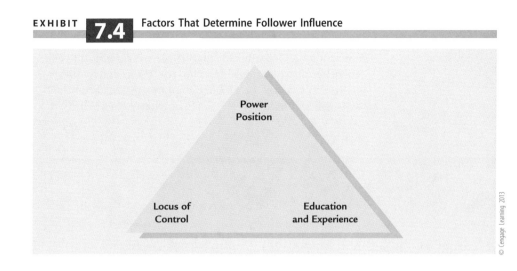

EXHIBIT **7.4** Factors That Determine Follower Influence

© Cengage Learning 2013

Power Position

Leaders need to realize that they are no longer the sole possessors of power and influence in their work units. The new reality is that no matter what position a person holds in the workplace, they can be a force for change. Some followers distinguish themselves as innovators, self-managers, or risk-takers. These are terms that have traditionally been reserved for describing leaders, not followers. Some followers may have personal, referent, expert, information, and connection-based power that can be used to boost upward influence. These power sources are discussed in Chapter 5. Any of these sources of powers can give the follower the ability to influence others at different levels of the organization. As more and more employees come to rely on a particular follower for information, expertise, or simply because of his or her personality, the follower's relative power position increases. These are the followers that can influence other followers to slow down performance, file grievances, stage demonstrations, or even sabotage operations—all actions that can hurt a leader's reputation.

Locus of Control

As discussed in Chapter 2, **locus of control** *is on a continuum between an external and internal belief over who has control of a person's destiny.* People who believe they are "masters of their own destiny" are said to have an *internal locus of control;* they believe that they can influence people and events in their workplace. People who believe they are "pawns of fate" (*external locus of control*) tend to believe they have no influence or control at work. Followers with an internal locus of control prefer a work environment that encourages honest and open communication with leaders, participation in decision making, and opportunities to be creative. They are likely to be more influential with other followers than are those with external locus of control.

WORK Application **7**

Recall a work-related incident when you felt more qualified to do the job than your boss because of your education and experience. Describe how this characteristic enabled you to influence your boss.

Education and Experience

Not all followers have the same level of education and/or experience. These differences can have a major impact on the influential power of different followers. Followers with valuable skills and experience may be able to use their expert power to influence other followers and even the leader. Leaders have to create opportunities to learn from others including followers. This imperative is dictated by the fact that leaders and followers today work in an environment of constant change. Today's workforce is far more educated, mobile, diverse, and younger than the workforce of 30 years ago. The experienced and educated follower can be much more influential with other followers than can the leader.

Leaders have to shift away from the top-down directive style of leading that was common when tasks were highly structured and power tended to be centralized, and move toward a more decentralized, participative style of managing. As workers' education and experience increase, they tend to reject top-down directive leadership. Leaders who ignore this fact will face higher employee dissatisfaction and turnover and miss out on the benefits of utilizing the talents of effective followers.[78]

CONCEPT APPLICATION 4
Determinants of Follower Influence

Identify the specific follower influencing characteristic in each of these statements.

a. power position   b. locus of control   c. education and experience

_____ 18. I am determined to succeed in this organization because I believe I have what it takes to do it.

_____ 19. It is not what you know; it's who you know around here that gets you promoted.

_____ 20. Many of my peers depend on me for technical assistance because I am the only one in the department who has been trained to work with this new machine successfully.

_____ 21. When it comes to selling my points to peers, I easily get them to see things my way rather than the boss's way due to my seniority and popularity in this division.

OPENING CASE APPLICATION

5. The text discusses factors that can determine follower influence, when applied to Facebook employees; which factor(s) in your opinion stands out?

The text discusses three determinants of follower influence: power position, locus of control, and education/experience. It is clear from the case that Facebook employees are highly skilled and experienced software engineers. They are highly sought-after in the tech world. As mentioned in the case, everyone at Facebook was a star somewhere else and you don't find a lot of shy, retiring types there. They are described as "power nerds." Even those who have left Facebook have gone on to create their own ventures. For example, Adam D'Angelo, who has been friends with Zuckerberg since high school, teamed up with another former Facebook employee, Charlie Cheever, to start Quora.com, a social network that aggregates questions and answers on various topics. Chris Hughes, Zuckerberg's Harvard roommate, left to join the Obama campaign and later founded the philanthropic site Jumo.com. This shows that Facebook employees have been very influential because of their education and experience.

Dual Role of Being a Leader and a Follower

As the guidelines for effective followership reveal, good leadership is found in highly effective followers. It is important to recognize that even when someone is identified as a leader, the same person often holds a complementary follower role.[79] It is not at all uncommon to switch between being a leader and being a follower several times over the course of a day's work. For example, within an organization, middle managers answer to vice presidents, who answer to the CEO, who answers to the board of directors; within the school system, teachers answer to the principal, who answers to the school superintendent, who answers to school board members. Regardless of one's position in an organization, we are all in a follower role to someone else.

To execute both roles effectively is a challenge. How to balance these often conflicting demands and perform the dual roles of leader and follower effectively is not an easy challenge.

Delegation

We now focus on developing followers by delegating tasks to them. **Delegation** *is the process of assigning responsibility and authority for accomplishing objectives.* Telling employees to perform the tasks that are part of their job design is issuing orders, not delegating. *Delegating* refers to giving employees new tasks. The new task may become a part of a redesigned job, or it may simply be a one-time task. The true art of delegation lies in a manager's ability to know what cannot be delegated and what should be delegated. Some management experts believe that if there were a top ten list of managerial mistakes, failure to delegate would be one of them.[80] In this section we discuss delegating, delegation decisions, and delegating with a model.

Delegating

Effective delegation requires that a leader should carefully consider several factors relating to the task, time requirement, and follower characteristics before delegating. A leader should delegate work when there is not enough time to attend to priority tasks, when followers desire more challenges and opportunities, and when the tasks match follower skill levels and experiences. Also a leader must find the proper person for the job and provide careful instructions. Effective delegation allows people to prosper in their own uniqueness.

Let's begin by discussing the benefits of delegation, the obstacles to delegation, and signs of delegating too little.

Benefits of Delegation

When managers delegate, they have more time to perform high-priority tasks. Delegation gets tasks accomplished and increases productivity. Delegation can empower followers and give them more confidence. Delegating both responsibility and authority pushes decision-making down the ladder, encourages input from operational employees who are closest to problems, and promotes a participative work environment.[81,82] It enables leaders to mobilize resources and secure better results than they could have gotten alone. Delegation trains employees and improves their self-esteem, as well as eases the stress and burden on managers. By delegating responsibilities, leaders can focus on doing a few tasks well instead of many tasks less effectively. Consequently, they improve their management and leadership potential while training others to succeed them. It is a means of developing followers by enriching their jobs. From the organization's perspective, delegating can result in increased performance and work outcomes. It can also lead to more communication between leaders and followers, thus encouraging followers to voice their opinions on how to improve the work environment.[83]

Obstacles to Delegation

Managers become used to doing things themselves. They forget part of leadership is "getting work done through others."[84] Managers fear that employees will fail to accomplish tasks.[85] You can delegate responsibility and authority, but not your accountability. Managers believe they can perform tasks more efficiently than others. Some managers don't realize that delegation is an important part of their job, others don't know what to delegate, and some don't know how to delegate. Effective delegation greatly improves a leader's time management, without which efficiency and effectiveness suffer. If you let anything keep you from delegating, you could end up like Dr. Rudenstine, former president of Harvard University, who became ill due to job stress by trying to do too much by himself.

Signs of Delegating Too Little

WORK Application **8**

Describe an obstacle to delegation, or sign of delegating too little, that you have observed on the job.

_____

_____

_____

_____

Certain behaviors are associated with leaders who are reluctant to delegate to their subordinates. These behaviors are signs that a leader is delegating too little. Some of these behaviors include taking work home, performing employee tasks, being behind in work, a continual feeling of pressure and stress, rushing to meet deadlines, and requiring that employees seek approval before acting. Leaders who can't disengage from the office and delegate authority and responsibility undermine employees' confidence to make decisions and take responsibility for their actions.[86] Unfortunately, in many of today's cost-cutting environments, you don't always have someone you can delegate some of your tasks to.

Learning Outcome 9

List five things a leader should delegate.

Delegation Decisions

As mentioned earlier, an important part of delegation is knowing which tasks to delegate. Successful delegation is often based on selecting what task to delegate and whom to delegate it to.

What to Delegate

As a general guide, use your prioritized to-do list and delegate anything that you don't have to be personally involved with because of your unique knowledge or skill. Some possibilities include the following:

- *Paperwork.* Have others prepare reports, memos, letters, and so on.
- *Routine tasks.* Delegate checking inventory, scheduling, ordering, and so on.
- *Technical matters.* Have top employees deal with technical questions and problems.
- *Tasks with developmental potential.* Give employees the opportunity to learn new things. Prepare them for advancement by enriching their jobs.
- *Employees' problems.* Train employees to solve their own problems; don't solve problems for them, unless their capability is low.

What Not to Delegate

As a general guide, do not delegate anything that you need to be personally involved with because of your unique knowledge or skill. Here are some typical examples:

- *Personnel matters.* Performance appraisals, counseling, disciplining, firing, resolving conflicts, and so on.

- *Confidential activities.* Unless you have permission to do so.
- *Crises.* There is no time to delegate.
- *Activities delegated to you personally.* For example, if you are assigned to a committee, do not assign someone else without permission.

Determining to Whom to Delegate

Once you have decided what to delegate, you must select an employee to do the task. When selecting an employee to delegate to, be sure that he or she has the capability to get the job done right by the deadline. Consider your employees' talents and interests when making a selection. You may consult with several employees to determine their interests before making the final choice.

Before you learn how to delegate with the use of a model, complete Self-Assessment 5 to learn how your personality may affect your followership and delegation.

SELF-ASSESSMENT 5   Followership and Personality

Personality Differences

Generally, if you have an agreeableness Big Five personality type, which is a high need for affiliation, you will have a good relationship with your manager, because having a good relationship with everyone helps you to meet your needs. If you have a lower need for power, you prefer to be a follower, rather than a leader. Generally, you will be willing to delegate authority.

If you have a surgency/high need for power, you may have some problems getting along with your manager. You prefer to be in control, or to be a leader rather than a follower. However, if you don't get along well with your manager, you will have difficulty climbing the corporate ladder. You may have some reluctance to delegate authority because you like to be in control—and when you delegate, you lose some control.

If you have a conscientiousness/high need for achievement, you may not be concerned about your relationship with your manager, other than getting what you need to get the job done. However, if you don't get along well with your manager, you will have difficulty getting what you want. You may also be reluctant to delegate tasks that you like to do, because you get satisfaction from doing the job itself, rather than having someone else to do it.

Being well adjusted also helps you to have a good relationship with your manager. Being open to experience, which includes an internal locus of control (Chapter 2), helps you to get along with others since you are willing to try new things.

Gender Differences

Although there are exceptions, generally women tend to seek relationships that are on a more personal level than those favored by men. For example, two women who work together are more apt to talk about their family lives than two men. Men do socialize, but it is more frequently about other interests such as sports. It is not unusual for women who have worked together for months to know more about each other's personal and family lives than men who have worked together for years. Men who do enjoy talking about their personal lives tend to talk more about their families in dyads with women than in those with men. One of the reasons men enjoy working with women is because they often bring a personal-level relationship to the job.

How does your personality affect your dyadic relationships, followership, and delegation?

On May 3, 2011, Senator John Ensign of Nevada resigned. Ensign admitted in 2009 to having an affair with Cynthia Hampton—a past campaign aide and the wife of Doug Hampton. During a two-year inquiry into possible violations by Ensign, the Senate Ethics Committee found that he violated campaign finance laws and obscured justice to cover up his affair.

Senator Tom Coburn of Oklahoma, a friend of Ensign's who confronted him about the adultery, became involved as an intermediary in negotiations between Ensign and Doug Hampton. The former aide is said to have sought some kind of financial settlement from Ensign soon after he became aware of the affair. Senator Coburn was the go-between in trying to negotiate settlement terms. According to reports, Ensign's father eventually gave the Hamptons $96,000 as a gift, which the Ethics Committee determined to be in violation of campaign finance laws.[87]

1. Is it ethically responsible for Senator Coburn to be trying to help his friend Senator Ensign pay off the Hamptons in a deal that is seen as a violation of campaign finance laws?

2. What would you do if your boss asked you to cover up evidence of wrongdoing by your organization? (Some options include: just do it, don't say anything but don't do it, question the motives, look closely at what you are asked to destroy, go to your boss's boss to make sure it's okay to do it, tell the boss you will not do it, ask the boss to do it him- or herself, blow the whistle to an outside source like the government or media, and so on.)

3. If you went to court for trying to cover up a violation like Senator Coburn was doing, do you believe you would have a good ethical defence by saying "I was not directly involved?"

Delegating with the Use of a Model

After determining what to delegate and to whom, you must plan for and delegate the tasks. *The* **delegation model** *steps are (1) explain the need for delegating and the reasons for selecting the employee; (2) set objectives that define responsibility, level of authority, and deadline; (3) develop a plan; and (4) establish control checkpoints and hold employees accountable.*[88,89] Following these four steps can increase your chances of successfully delegating. As you read on, you will see how the delegation model is used with the job characteristics model, core job dimensions, and critical psychological states to influence performance and work outcomes.

Step 1. Explain the need for delegating and the reasons for selecting the employee. It is helpful for the employee to understand why the assignment must be completed. In other words, how will the department or organization benefit? Informing employees helps them realize the importance of the task (experienced meaningfulness of work). Telling the employee why he or she was selected should make him or her feel valued. Don't use the "it's a lousy job, but someone has to do it" approach. Be positive; make employees aware of how they will benefit from the assignment. If step 1 is completed successfully, the employee should be motivated, or at least willing, to do the assignment.

Step 2. Set objectives that define responsibility, level of authority, and deadline. The objectives should clearly state the end result the employee is responsible for achieving by a specific deadline. You should also define the level of authority the employee has, as the following choices illustrate:

- Make a list of all supplies on hand, and present it to me each Friday at 2:00 (inform authority).
- Fill out a supply purchase order, and present it to me each Friday at 2:00 (recommend authority).
- Fill out and sign a purchase order for supplies; send it to the purchasing department with a copy put in my in-basket each Friday by 2:00 (report authority).
- Fill out and sign a purchase order for supplies, and send it to the purchasing department each Friday by 2:00, keeping a copy (full authority).

Step 3. Develop a plan. Once the objective is set, a plan is needed to achieve it. It is helpful to write out the objective, specifying the level of authority and the plan. When developing a plan, be sure to identify the resources needed to achieve the objectives, and give the employee the authority necessary to obtain the resources. Inform all parties of the employee's authority and with whom the employee must work. For example, if an employee is doing a marketing report, you should contact the marketing department and tell them the employee must have access to the necessary information.

Step 4. Establish control checkpoints and hold employees accountable. For simple, short tasks, a deadline without control checkpoints is appropriate. However, it is often advisable to check progress at predetermined times (control checkpoints) for tasks that have multiple steps or will take some time to complete. This builds information flow into the delegation system right from the start. You and the employee should agree on the form (phone call, visit, memo, or detailed report) and time frame (daily, weekly, or after specific steps are completed but before going on to the next step) for information regarding the assignment. When establishing control, consider the employee's capability level. The lower the capability, the more frequent the checks; the higher the capability, the less frequent the checks.

WORK Application **9**
Select a manager you work or have worked for, and analyze how well he or she implements the four steps of delegation. Which steps does the manager typically follow and not follow?

It is helpful to list the control checkpoints in writing on an operational planning sheet, making copies of the finished plan so that the parties involved and you as the delegating manager have a record to refer to. In addition, all parties involved should record the control checkpoints on their calendars. If the employee to whom the task was delegated does not report as scheduled, follow up to find out why the person did not report, and get the information. You should evaluate performance at each control checkpoint, and upon completion provide feedback that develops knowledge of the results of work.

Providing praise for progress and completion of the task motivates employees to do a good job. You will recall that Chapter 6 discussed how to give praise.

The four steps of the delegation process are summarized in Model 7.1. In Developing Your Leadership Skills Excercise 2, you will have the opportunity to use the model to delegate a task and to develop your delegation skills.

MODEL **7.1**   Steps in the Delegation Process

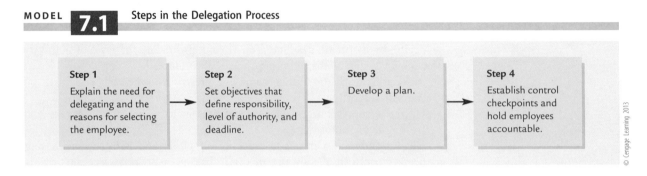

Step 1	Step 2	Step 3	Step 4
Explain the need for delegating and the reasons for selecting the employee.	Set objectives that define responsibility, level of authority, and deadline.	Develop a plan.	Establish control checkpoints and hold employees accountable.

© Cengage Learning 2013

Learning Outcome 10   *Effective leader evaluation and feedback involves before, during, and after steps in the process. Identify some recommended activities during each step.*

Follower Evaluation and Feedback

Followers work with leaders to realize organizational objectives. They are delegated tasks with specific performance targets and deadlines. For a leader, it is always a good practice to perform the task of evaluating how well delegated tasks have been performed. Most leaders will attest that this is an important but difficult managerial responsibility. People in general tend to be defensive when being evaluated, especially when the evaluation is not very positive. To some followers, a negative evaluation questions their abilities and threatens their self-esteem. Some leaders are uncomfortable confronting followers who underperform because of this sentiment and the fear of hurting their relationship with the follower. However, correcting a follower's performance deficiencies is required in order to help the follower address weaknesses; but the way it is done can preserve or strain the leader–follower relationship.[90,91]

Researchers and practitioners generally agree that followers admire and respect leaders who show honesty, caring, understanding and empathy during the evaluation process. Followers also want to be convinced that the evaluation is fair and effective. That's why the 360-degree multi-rater evaluation method is highly recommended. This evaluation tool uses multiple sources (self, peer, superior, customers, suppliers, etc.) to evaluate an individual.[92,93,94,95]

When it comes to providing feedback after an evaluation, leaders must learn to stay calm and professional when followers over-react to a negative evaluation. Leaders must avoid a rush to judgment when followers don't agree with their assessment. The leader must be specific in stating the deficiency, calmly explaining the impact of poor performance on team or organizational objectives, involving the follower in identifying the reasons for negative evaluation, and suggesting remedies for change. At the conclusion of an evaluation session, the follower must come away believing that the leader showed a genuine desire to be of help, and that both parties arrived at a mutual agreement on specific action steps for improvement. The follower's self-confidence should remain intact or be enhanced through evaluation and feedback, rather than being shattered. This is an indication that not only was the evaluation done well, but the feedback between the leader and follower was equally effective.

Exhibit 7.5 presents 12 guidelines for effective leader evaluation and feedback. It should be noted that these 12 guidelines are not in sequential order; however, they have been organized in a three-step approach to underscore the importance of careful planning before, during, and after an evaluation/feedback exercise. We should note here that Chapter 6 has an expanded discussion on feedback. Other approaches for providing feedback are presented as part of coaching.

EXHIBIT **7.5**   Guidelines for Effective Leader Evaluation and Feedback

Pre-Evaluation and Feedback—Leader should:
- Remind self to stay calm and professional
- Gather accurate facts on follower performance
- Remind self to avoid rush to judgment

During Evaluation and Feedback Session—Leader should:
- Be specific in stating performance deficiency
- Explain negative impact of ineffective behavior
- Help follower identify reasons for poor performance
- Ask follower to suggest remedies
- Arrive at mutual agreement on specific action steps

Post-Evaluation and Feedback Session—Leader should:
- Follow up to ensure implementation of action steps
- Show desire to be of help to follower
- Build follower's self-confidence

© Cengage Learning 2013

Chapter Summary

The chapter summary is organized to answer the 11 learning outcomes for Chapter 7.

1. Describe the evolution of dyadic theory.

Dyadic theory has evolved through three stages. The first conception of dyadic theory was the awareness of a hierarchical top-down relationship between a leader and a follower. The second stage of dyadic theory focused on specific nature of the relationship between the leader and the follower that led to the creation of in-groups and out-groups in the same work unit—leader-member exchange (LMX). The third stage of dyadic theory focused on team-member exchange (TMX) that emphasizes team building.

2. Define the two kinds of relationships that can occur among leaders and followers under the vertical dyadic linkage model.

The two types of relationships that can occur among leaders and followers under the VDL model are in-group and out-group members. In-groups include followers with strong social ties to their leader in a people-oriented relationship, characterized by high mutual trust, respect, loyalty, and influence. Out-groups include followers with little or no social ties to their leader in a strictly task-oriented relationship, characterized by low exchange, lack of trust and loyalty, and top-down influence.

3. Describe the main focus of team building from a leader–follower perspective.

The emphasis of the team-building view is the notion that effective leaders should aspire to establish relationships with all followers, not just with a few special individuals. It is about forging a partnership with each group member without alienating anyone.

4. Describe the three factors whose combined effect influences LMX relationships.

LMX relationships can be influenced by the combining effects following three factors: (1) Follower attributes—attributes such as commitment, trust, respect, and loyalty will influence leaders to show support, delegate more, allow followers more discretion in conducting their work, and engage in open communication with followers. (2) Leader/follower perceptions and self-identities—the leader's first impressions of a group member's competency plays an important role in defining the quality of the relationship. (3) Situational factors—factors such as managerial resources, leader's span of control, and relationship life-cycle stage do influence the type of LMX relationship that develops.

5. Discuss a strength and a limitation of LMX theory.

The fact that LMX focuses on the relationship between the leader and each follower is important because early leadership studies (such as the Great Man Theory of leadership) focused on the leader and ignored the follower, as if leaders alone were responsible for organizational success. It emphasizes the importance of forming positive relationships with followers and how this in turn influences their behavior. A major limitation of LMX is measurement difficulty. LMX theory deals with attitudes and perceptions of individuals—two issues that are often difficult to quantify and measure. For this reason, recent research efforts on LMX have focused on instrumentation of the theory. The ways in which the attributes of high-quality LMX relationships have been defined and measured have varied somewhat from study to study.

6. **Explain how LMX relationships can lead to unintended consequences.**

In LMX relationships, leaders develop strong social ties with in-group members. Whether intentionally or unintentionally, this positive relationship has been known to correlate with higher performance ratings for in-group members compared to out-group members. HR decisions regarding promotions, demotions, reassignments, layoffs, and salary increases are often based on information accumulated in employee files. An employee's performance evaluation from his or her manager may influence the decision on who gets promoted, demoted, or worse, laid off. If the evaluation was based on a manager liking or not liking a follower in the first place, rather than on actual job performance, then it may seem unfair to use it as the basis for any action; and yet it happens everyday.

7. **Describe the two behaviors used in the Kelley Model and identify the follower types.**

Using a combination of two types of behavior—independent critical thinking and level of involvement in organizational affairs—Kelley groups followers into five categories. The independent critical thinking variable is on a continuum from low to high and the level of involvement on a continuum from low to high as well. The five basic follower types are: alienated, passive, conformist, pragmatic, and effective follower.

8. **Discuss the three determinants of follower influence.**

The three follower influencing characteristics are: (1) Relative power position—leaders need to realize that followers also have the power to influence them. (2) Locus of control—followers can have an internal or external locus of control, based on their belief about who is the master of their destiny. Thus, leader–member exchanges should be different based on locus of control. (3) Education and experience—leaders need to realize that followers may have different levels of education and experience, and that they need to supervise them differently.

9. **List five things a leader should delegate.**

A leader should delegate paperwork, routine tasks, technical matters, tasks with developmental potential, and employees' own problems.

10. **Effective leader evaluation and feedback involves before, during, and after steps in the process. Identify some recommended activities during each step.**

The leader needs to think very carefully not only about what to say but also how it is going to be said. That's why it is good to break down the process into "before," "during," and "after" steps. We call the before step *pre-feedback*. Here a leader should remind him- or herself to maintain calm and professionalism, even if the subordinate is not, and to get all the facts about the subordinate's performance so the evaluation is not based on inaccurate information. During the evaluation and feedback session itself, the leader should try to establish rapport, state the task expectations and the follower's actual performance, help follower identify reasons for gaps in performance, and involve the follower in suggesting corrective behaviors (feedback). The post-evaluation and feedback session should include activities such as follow-up to ensure adherence to change plan, offering to be of assistance if needed, and helping to build follower's confidence that it can be done.

11. **Define the following key terms (in order of appearance in the chapter).**

Select one or more methods: (1) fill in the missing key terms from memory; (2) match the key terms from the following list with their definitions below; (3) copy the key terms in order from the list at the beginning of the chapter.

_____ refers to the individualized relationship between a leader and each follower in a work unit.

_____ is an approach to leadership that attempts to explain why leaders vary their behavior with different followers.

_____ is defined as individual behavior that is discretionary, not directly or explicitly recognized by the formal reward system, and that in the aggregate promotes the effective functioning of the organization.

_____ is the set of resources that inheres in the structure of relations between members of the group, which helps them get ahead.

_____ is defined as a team member's social exchanges with peers in terms of the mutual exchange of ideas, support, camaraderie, and feedback.

_____ includes followers with strong social ties to their leader in a supportive relationship characterized by high mutual trust, respect, loyalty, and influence.

_____ includes followers with few or no social ties to their leader, in a strictly task-centered relationship characterized by low exchange and top-down influence.

_____ is the quality of the exchange relationship between an employee and his or her superior.

_____ is a follower's effort to project a favorable image in order to gain an immediate benefit or improve a long-term relationship with the leader.

_____ is the effort to appear supportive, appreciative, and respectful.

_____ is the effort to appear competent and dependable.

_____ refers to the behavior of followers that results from the leader–follower influence relationship.

_____ as a person's beliefs in his or her capabilities to produce at a certain level of performance.

_____ is a person who is being influenced by a leader.

_____ is someone who is low on involvement yet is high on critical thinking.

_____ is someone who is high on involvement but low on critical thinking.

_____ is someone who is neither high on critical thinking nor involvement.

_____ is someone who is high on critical thinking and involvement.

_____ exhibits a little of all four styles—depending on which style fits the prevailing situation.

_____ is on a continuum between an external and internal belief over who has control over a person's destiny.

_____ is the process of assigning responsibility and authority for accomplishing objectives.

_____ steps are (1) explain the need for delegating and the reasons for selecting the employee; (2) set objectives that define responsibility, level of authority, and deadline; (3) develop a plan; and (4) establish control checkpoints and hold employees accountable.

_____ is defined as a team member's social exchanges with peers in terms of the mutual exchange of ideas, support, camaraderie and feedback.

Key Terms

alienated follower, 253

conformist follower, 253

delegation, 261

delegation model, 264

dyad, 241

dyadic theory, 241

effective follower, 254

follower, 252

followership, 252

impressions management, 248

ingratiation, 249

in-group, 243

leader–member exchange (LMX), 244

locus of control, 259

organizational citizenship behavior, 248

out-group, 243

passive follower, 253

pragmatic follower, 254

self-efficacy, 254

self-promotion, 249

social capital, 249

team-member exchange (TMX), 245

Review Questions

1. What are the differences between in-groups and out-groups?

2. How do quality leader–member exchange relationships influence follower behavior?

3. How does a leader's first impression and perception of a follower influence the quality of their relationship?

4. The development of a high-quality LMX relationship has been described as a "life-cycle model" that grows and matures over time. Discuss how this works.

5. How can a follower's perception or attribution of a leader influence their relationship?

6. Describe the inherent bias of LMX theory and how it can lead to unintended consequences.

7. How do education and experience, described as follower-influencing characteristics, affect effective followership?

8. What are some of the benefits of delegating?

9. What are some things that a leader should not delegate?

Critical Thinking Questions

The following critical-thinking questions can be used for class discussion and/or as written assignments to develop communication skills. Be sure to give complete explanations for all questions.

1. In your opinion, can a leader maintain a personal friendship with some members of his or her work group or team without creating the perception of

in-groups (those in his or her social circle) and out-groups (those outside his or her social circle)?

2. What should a leader do to dispel any notion or misperception that there are in-groups and out-groups in his or her work unit?

3. High-quality LMX relationships create a circle of reciprocity where followers feel like they should go the extra mile for a leader who supports them and the leader feels like he or she should offer the followers more support and benefits to keep their loyalty. Do you believe this is the case in the real world or is it something different?

4. Movies dealing with the prison or college environment often depict one or two prisoners or students who

seem to have more influence over other prisoners or students than even the guards or administrators. Can you think of one such case and explain why the individual was influential over other prisoners or students?

5. What do you say to those who argue that tactics used by followers to get noticed by their leader (such as impressions management, ingratiation, and self-promotion) are shameful and self-serving and should be avoided?

6. Can someone have a successful career by aspiring to be an effective follower? Explain.

7. As a leader, how will you motivate the alienated follower?

CASE

W. L. Gore & Associates

Founded in 1958, W. L. Gore & Associates has become a modern-day success story as a uniquely managed, privately owned, family business. Founders Bill and Vieve Gore set out to create a business where innovation was a way of life and not a by-product. Today Gore is best known for its Gore-Tex range of high-performance fabrics and Elixir Strings for guitars. Gore is the leading manufacturer of thousands of advanced technology products for the medical, electronics, industrial, and fabrics markets. With annual revenues of $2.5 billion, the company employs approximately 9,000 associates at more than 50 facilities around the world.

Terri Kelly replaced Chuck Carroll as the president and CEO of W. L. Gore & Associates in April 2005. Gore has repeatedly been named among the "100 Best Companies to Work For," in the United States by *Fortune* magazine. In a recent interview, Ms. Kelly was asked what would be the most distinctive elements of the Gore management model to an outsider. She listed four factors: "We don't operate in a hierarchy; we try to resist titles; our associates, who are all owners in the company, self-commit to what they want to do; and our leaders have positions of authority because they have followers." According to CEO Kelly, these four attributes enable Gore to maximize individual potential while cultivating an environment that fosters creativity and also to operate with high integrity. She is quick to remind everyone that all of Gore's practices and ways of doing business reflect the innovative and entrepreneurial spirit of its founders.

CEO Kelly attributes Gore's success to its unique culture. How work is conducted at Gore and how employees relate to one another sets Gore apart. There are no titles, no bosses and no formal hierarchy. Compensation and promotion decisions are determined by peer rankings of each other's performance. To avoid dampening employee creativity, the company has an organizational structure and culture that goes against conventional wisdom. W. L. Gore & Associates has been described as not only unmanaged but also unstructured. Bill Gore (the founder) referred to the company's structure as a "lattice organization." Gore's lattice structure includes the following features:[96]

- Direct lines of communication—person to person—with no intermediary
- No fixed or assigned authority
- Sponsors, not bosses
- Natural leadership as evidenced by the willingness of others to follow
- Objectives set by those who must "make them happen"
- Tasks and functions organized through commitments
- Complete avoidance of the hierarchical command and control structure

The lattice structure as described by the people at Gore encourages hands-on innovation and discourages bureaucratic red tape by involving those closest to a project in decision making. Instead of a pyramid of bosses and managers, Gore has a flat organizational structure. There are no chains of command, no predetermined channels of communication. It sounds very much like a self-managed team at a much broader scale.

Why has Gore achieved such remarkable success? W. L. Gore & Associates prefers to think of the various people who play key roles in the organization as being leaders, not managers. While Bill Gore did not believe in smothering the company in thick layers of formal management, he also knew that as the company grew, he had to find ways to assist new people and to follow their progress. Thus, W. L. Gore & Associates came up with its "sponsor" program. The sponsor program is a dyadic relationship between an incumbent, experienced employee and a newly hired, inexperienced employee. Before a candidate is hired, an associate has to agree to be his or her sponsor or what others refer to as a mentor. The sponsor's role is to take a personal interest in the new associate's contributions, problems, and goals, acting as both a coach and an advocate. The sponsor tracks the new associate's progress, offers help and encouragement, points out weaknesses and suggests ways to correct them, and concentrates on how the associate might better exploit his or her strengths.

Sponsoring is not a short-term commitment. All associates have sponsors, and many have more than one. When individuals are hired, at first they are likely to have a sponsor in their immediate work area. As associates' commitments change or grow, it's normal for them to acquire additional sponsors. For instance, if they move to a new job in another area of the company, they typically gain a sponsor there. Sponsors help associates chart a course in the organization that will offer personal fulfillment while maximizing their contribution to the enterprise. Leaders emerge naturally by demonstrating special knowledge, skill, or experience that advances a business objective.

An internal memo describes the three kinds of sponsorship and how they might work:

- **Starting sponsor**—a sponsor who helps a new associate get started on his or her first job at Gore, or helps a present associate get started on a new job.
- **Advocate sponsor**—a sponsor who sees to it that the associate being sponsored gets credit and recognition for contributions and accomplishments.
- **Compensation sponsor**—a sponsor who sees to it that the associate being sponsored is fairly paid for contributions to the success of the enterprise.

An associate can perform any one or all three kinds of sponsorship. Quite frequently, a sponsoring associate is a good friend, and it's not uncommon for two associates to sponsor each other as advocates.

Being an associate is a natural commitment to four basic principles articulated by Bill Gore and still a key belief of the company: fairness to each other and everyone we come in contact with; freedom to encourage, help, and allow other associates to grow in knowledge, skill, and scope of responsibility; the ability to make one's own commitments and keep them; and consultation with other associates before undertaking actions that could affect the reputation of the company.

Over the years, W. L. Gore & Associates has faced a number of unionization drives. The company neither tries to dissuade associates from attending organizational meetings nor retaliates against associates who pass out union flyers. However, Bill Gore believes there is no need for third-party representation under the lattice structure. He asks, "Why would associates join a union when they own the company? It seems rather absurd."

Commitment is seen as a two-way street at W. L. Gore & Associates—while associates are expected to commit to making a contribution to the company's success, the company is committed to providing a challenging, opportunity-rich work environment, and reasonable job security. The company tries to avoid laying off associates. If a work force reduction becomes necessary, the company uses a system of temporary transfers within a plant or cluster of plants, and requests voluntary layoffs. According to CEO Kelly, Gore's structure, systems, and culture have continued to yield impressive results for the company. In the more than 50 years that Gore has been in business, it has never made a loss.[97]

GO TO THE INTERNET: To learn more about W. L. Gore & Associates, visit its Web site **(http://www.gore.com).**

Support your answers to the following questions with specific information from the case and text or with other information you get from the Web or other sources.

1. What theories from this chapter are revealed through the case?

2. How did Gore's "sponsors" program facilitate the creation of high-quality relationships among leaders, sponsors, and associates?

3. Evaluate followership at W. L. Gore & Associates. What company actions and/or policies account for the quality of followership?

CUMULATIVE CASE QUESTIONS

4. Would you characterize the leadership style at W. L. Gore & Associates as job-centered or employee-centered (Chapter 3)? Support your answer.

5. Based on the types of power discussed in the text, what type(s) of power do sponsors have in their relationships with associates (Chapter 5)?

6. What role, if any, does coaching play in W. L. Gore's lattice structure (Chapter 6)?

CASE EXERCISE AND ROLE-PLAY

Preparation: You are part of an organization that evaluates its employees at the end of each year. The month of the year when evaluations need to be completed by all leaders and managers is approaching. Your task is to play the role of a leader evaluating your followers, and then play the role of follower being evaluated by your own manager. Based on your understanding of the discussion of guidelines for effective leader feedback and guidelines for effective followership, (1) present a scenario of an effective and an ineffective feedback session, applying at least three of the guidelines discussed in the text; and (2) present a scenario of effective and ineffective followership, applying at least three of the guidelines discussed in the text.

Role-Play: The instructor forms students into leader–follower pairs and has each pair dramatize scenarios 1 and 2 in front of the rest of the class. After each scenario, the class is to contrast the two approaches (effective versus ineffective feedback) by identifying the guidelines that the presenters or actors employed in making their points. Different student teams should try the exercise by employing different guidelines to both scenarios.

VIDEO ▶❙❙ CASE

Delegation at Boyne USA Resorts

Detroit native Everett Kircher moved to northern Michigan in 1947 and purchased land (for the price of $1) necessary to start his first ski resort known today as Boyne Mountain. Kircher practiced a traditional chain of command in a vertical organizational structure. Every decision came from his desk. As his company expanded, additional people were needed to manage the different locations. For Kircher, it was the beginning of a partial decentralization and delegation of his leadership and decision making. In 2002, Everett Kircher died at the age of 85, but his legacy lives on. The company's reorganization in 2004 paved the way for the "Boyne Brand" to grow while maintaining organizational integrity. General managers were hired at each resort location to oversee operations. In addition, vice presidents known as "subject matter experts" were hired. The VPs share critical information with the general managers to help each resort operation. The general managers fold these experts into the decision-making process and help provide policy.

1. Describe leader–follower relations at Boyne USA Resorts.

2. Why was decentralization and delegation necessary to Boyne's future despite the success with Everett Kircher at the helm of a vertical structure?

Developing Your Leadership Skills **1**

Improving Dyadic Relationships—Followership

Preparing for This Exercise

Based on your reading of effective leader–member exchange relationships, how can you improve your current or future relationship with your manager?

Be sure to list specific things you plan to do.

_____

_____

Based on Self-Assessment 4 on page 255, "Effective Followers," how can you improve your followership skills with your present or future manager? Be sure to list specific things you plan to do.

_____

_____

Doing This Exercise in Class

Objective

To develop a plan to improve your dyadic relationship with your manager and to improve your followership skills

The primary AACSB learning standard skills developed through this exercise are reflective thinking and analytic skills.

Preparation

You should have completed a plan in the preparation part of this exercise.

Experience

You will share your plan in a small group to provide further development.

Procedure 1 *(8–12 minutes)*

Option A: Break into groups of three or four and share your plans. Offer each other ideas for improving plans.

Option B: Same as Option A, but add a spokesperson to record some of the best ideas from each group member.

Procedure 2 *(10–20 minutes)* Option B, each spokesperson reports to the entire class.

Conclusion

The instructor leads a class discussion and/or makes concluding remarks.

Apply It *(2–4 minutes)* What did I learn from this exercise? When will I implement my plan?

_____

_____

Sharing

In the group, or to the entire class, volunteers may give their answers to the "Apply It" questions.

Behavior Model Skills Training

In this behavior model skills training session, you will perform three activities:

1. Read the section, "Delegation," in this chapter (to learn how to use Model 7.1, page 266).

2. Watch Behavior Model Video 7.1, "Delegating."

3. Complete Developing Your Leadership Skills 2 (to develop your delegating skills).

For further practice, use the delegation model in your personal and professional life.

The Delegation Model

Step 1 Explain the need for delegating and the reasons for selecting the employee.

Step 2 Set objectives that define responsibility, level of authority, and deadline.

Step 3 Develop a plan.

Step 4 Establish control checkpoints and hold employees accountable.

Behavior Model Video **7.1**

Delegating

Objective

To observe a manager delegating a task to an employee

Video *(4½ minutes)* Overview

You will watch a production manager, Steve, delegate the completion of a production output form to Dale.

Developing Your Leadership Skills 2

Delegating

Preparing for This Exercise

You should have read and understood the material on delegation.

Doing This Exercise in Class

Objective

To experience and develop skills in delegating a task

The primary AACSB learning standard skills developed through this exercise are leadership and communication abilities.

Experience

You will delegate, be delegated to, and observe the delegation of a task, and then evaluate the effectiveness of the delegated task. You may also see a video example of how to delegate using the delegation model.

Procedure 1 *(4–8 minutes)* Break into as many groups of three as possible, with the remainder in groups of two. Each person in the group picks a number 1, 2, or 3. Number 1 will be the first to delegate a task, then 2, and then 3. The level of difficulty of the delegation will increase with the number.

Each person then reads his or her delegation situation below (1, 2, or 3) and plans how he or she will delegate the task. If you prefer, you can use an actual delegation from a past or present job. Just be sure to fully explain the situation to the delegatee. Be sure to follow the four delegation steps in this chapter. An observer sheet is included at the end of this exercise for giving feedback on each delegation.

Delegation Situation 1

Delegator 1, you are a college student with a paper due in three days for your 10:00 a.m. class. It must be typed. You don't type well, so you have decided to hire someone to do it for you. The going rate is $1.50 per page. Think of an actual paper you have written in the past or will write in the future. Plan to delegate. Be sure to include the course name, paper title, special typing instructions, and so on. Assume that you are meeting the typist for the first time. He or she doesn't know you and doesn't expect you.

Delegator 2, assume that you do typing and are willing to do the job if the delegation is acceptable to you.

Delegation Situation 2

Delegator 2, you are the manager of a fast-food restaurant. In the past, you have scheduled the workers. Your policy is to keep changing the workers' schedules. You have decided to delegate the scheduling to your assistant manager. This person has never done any scheduling, but appears to be very willing and confident about taking on new responsibility. Plan your delegation.

Delegator 3, assume that you are interested in doing the scheduling if the manager delegates the task effectively.

Delegation Situation 3

Delegator 3, you own and manage your own business. You have eight employees, one of whom is the organization's secretary. The secretary currently uses an old computer, which needs to be replaced. You have not kept up with the latest technology and don't know what to buy. You can spend $1,200. You try to keep costs down and get the most for your money. Because the secretary will use the new machine, you believe that this employee should be involved or maybe even make the decision. The secretary has never purchased equipment, and you believe he or she will be somewhat insecure about the assignment. Plan your delegation.

Delegator 1, assume that you are able to do the job but are somewhat insecure. Accept the task if the delegator "participates" effectively.

Procedure 2 *(7–10 minutes)*

A. *Delegation 1.* Delegator 1 delegates the task (role-play) to number 2. Number 3 is the observer. As the delegation takes place, the observer uses the form at the end of this exercise to provide feedback on the effectiveness of the delegator. Answer the questions on the form.

B. *Integration.* The observer (or number 3) leads a discussion of the effectiveness of the delegation, although all team members should participate. Do not continue until you are told to do so.

Procedure 3 *(7–10 minutes)*

A. *Delegation 2.* Follow procedure 2A, except number 2 is now the delegator, number 3 is the delegatee, and number 1 is the observer.

B. *Integration.* Follow procedure 2B with number 1 as the observer. Do not continue until you are told to do so.

Procedure 4 *(7–10 minutes)*

A. *Delegation 3.* Follow procedure 2A, except number 3 is now the delegator, number 1 is the delegatee, and number 2 is the observer. If you are in a group of two, be an additional observer for another group.

B. *Integration.* Follow procedure 2B with number 2 as the observer.

Conclusion

The instructor may lead a class discussion and make concluding remarks.

Apply It (2–4 minutes) What did I learn from this experience? When will I delegate using the model?

_____

_____

Note: Remember that the process does not end with delegating the task; you must control (check progress at control points and help when needed) to ensure that the task is completed as scheduled.

Sharing

In the group, or to the entire class, volunteers may give their answers to the "Apply It" questions.

OBSERVER FORM

During the delegation process, the observer checks off the items performed by the delegators. Items not checked were not performed. After the delegation, the delegator and delegatee also check off the items.

This sheet is used for all three situations. Use the appropriate column for each situation.

		Situation	
Delegation items for all situations	1	2	3

Did the delegator follow these steps?

Step 1. Explain the need for delegating and the reasons for selecting the person.

Step 2. Set an objective that defines responsibility, level of authority, and deadline.

Step 3. Develop a plan.

Step 4. Establish control checkpoints and hold the person accountable.

Process

Did the delegate clearly understand what was expected of him or her and know how to follow the plan?

_____

_____

Improvements

How could the delegation be improved if done again?

_____

_____

_____

8

Team Leadership and Self-Managed Teams

Learning Outcomes

After studying this chapter, you should be able to:

1. Discuss the advantages and disadvantages of working in teams. p. 280

2. Briefly describe the 10 characteristics of effective teams. p. 284

3. What role can a team leader play in creating an effective team? p. 287

4. Describe how organizational climate can influence team creativity. p. 288

5. Outline the three parts of conducting effective meetings. p. 299

6. Explain the differences between conventional and self-managed teams. p. 302

7. Describe the benefits of using self-managed teams in organizations. p. 303

8. Describe the top management's role in improving the success rate of self-managed teams. p. 304

9. Describe the challenges of implementing effective self-managed teams. p. 307

10. Define the following **key terms** (in order of appearance in the chapter):

group	team creativity
team	functional team
teamwork	cross-functional team
social loafing	virtual team
groupthink	
team effectiveness	self-managed teams (SMTs)
team learning	self-managed team champion
team norms	distributed leadership
team cohesion	self-managed team facilitator

OPENING CASE *APPLICATION*

Southwest Airlines epitomizes the concept of teamwork and a people-centered culture. According to Gary Kelly, its Chairman, President and CEO, "Our people are our single greatest strength and most enduring long-term competitive advantage." At Southwest, each department has a dedicated team working together to create action plans to realize its mission and vision. Mr. Kelly never misses an opportunity to reiterate this mission. As he puts it, at Southwest, "We believe in Living the Southwest Way, which is to have a Warrior Spirit, a Servant's Heart, and a Fun-LUVing Attitude. The culture of Southwest is about keeping its employees happy because happy employees provide great customer service and great customer service leads to satisfied customers and profits for the company.

Southwest has an extensive training and development program for its employees that focuses on building their leadership and teamwork skills. The University for People and the Manager-in-Training (MIT) are two flagship programs that make this possible. According to the company's Web site, the University for People is a state-of-the-art training facility that offers employees training and development for every stage of their careers. Offerings include orientation sessions for hires, leadership for frontline and management-level employees, oral and written communication, performance appraisals, and even a Myers-Briggs personality assessment session to help teams better appreciate individual differences and work more cohesively.

The Manager-in-Training program focuses on employees with high potential for leadership and interest in a long-term career at Southwest Airlines. MIT I is designed for employees at the supervisor, team leader, and manager levels. MIT II is designed for managers and directors who aspire to higher leadership positions. Participants learn how to become strategic leaders.

Asked what he thought of the job Mr. Kelly was doing so far, Herb Kelleher (former Chairman and CEO) said "To be an excellent leader, you have to be a superb follower," referring to the transition period he shared with Kelly

before stepping down. He went on to say, "Gary has provided great leadership."

In his 2009 annual report to shareholders, Mr. Kelly said, "We weathered the stormy, recessionary economy of 2009 by focusing on our triple bottom line—our Performance, our People, and our Planet."[1]

OPENING CASE QUESTIONS:

1. What does it say about Gary Kelly's leadership philosophy when he categorically proclaims, "Our people are our single greatest strength and most enduring long-term competitive advantage?"

2. How can you match our definition of team effectiveness as a multivariable concept involving three components (task performance, group process, and individual satisfaction) to this statement by Mr. Kelly: "We believe in Living the Southwest Way, which is to have a Warrior Spirit, a Servant's Heart, and a Fun-LUVing Attitude?"

3. What is the evidence that there is strong organizational support for teamwork at Southwest?

4. In what way has Southwest shown that it understands the connection between team leadership and team success?

5. Southwest encourages its teams to be creative problem solvers. What are some examples of creative problem solving by Southwest teams?

6. Of the four types of teams discussed, which type(s) do you think Southwest is using?

7. Do you think Gary Kelly is the type of leader who would embrace the self-managed team concept? Explain your answer.

Can you answer any of these questions? You'll find answers to these questions and learn more about Southwest Airlines and team leadership throughout the chapter.

To learn more about Gary Kelly and Southwest Airlines visit Southwest's Web site at **http://www.southwest.com**.

The focus of this chapter is on how organizations can develop and use effective teams to achieve organizational goals. The first half of the chapter focuses on the team concept. We will explore the increasing use of teams into the organization structure, different types of teams, the advantages and disadvantages of teams, characteristics of effective teams, and the role of team leaders. The second half of the chapter focuses on self-managed teams. We discuss the nature of self-managed teams (SMT), the difference between SMTs and conventional teams, the benefits of using SMTs, improving their effectiveness, and the challenges of implementing SMTs.

The Use of Teams in Organizations

Teamwork is a way of life in the postmodern organization.[2] There was a time when the use of teams in production processes made news because few companies were doing it. Today, it's just the opposite. It's the organization that does not use teams that has become newsworthy. Through the years, many studies have heralded the importance of teams for achieving organizational success.[3] The basic message behind teamwork is that teams offer the best opportunity for better organizational performance in the form of increased productivity and profits. In other words, the synergistic benefits of teamwork are such that members of a team working cooperatively with one another can achieve more than working independently. As such, teams have become the basic unit of empowerment—large enough for the collective strength and synergy of diverse talents and small enough for effective participation and bonding.[4]

Since the early 1990s, various studies have reported greater numbers of U.S. corporations using teams to accomplish organizational tasks.[5] The reasons for this trend are obvious. Many companies, large and small, face serious challenges from a dynamic and complex global economy—challenges that have put in question the effectiveness of a functional approach to getting work done. Traditional teams are functionally specialized work groups commonly referred to as departments. Some of the challenges in today's global economy include growing demands from customers for better-quality products and services at lower prices, technological advances, environmental concerns, cheap labor, emerging markets, and pressure from global competitors and suppliers.[6] Because of these trends, many more organizations are seeking leaders who possess team leadership skills. Employers expect colleges and universities to be at the forefront of preparing graduates to effectively work in teams. They are increasingly looking for applicants who possess teamwork knowledge, skills, and abilities.[7]

According to some estimates, over 50 percent of all organizations and 80 percent of organizations with more than 100 employees use some form of teams.[8] Many organizations have reengineered their work processes and procedures to be performed by teams.[9]

However, not all team efforts have resulted in success. In some cases, the use of teams has resulted in such negative outcomes as increased costs, stress, and lower group cohesion.[10] To avoid these negative outcomes, it is recommended that an organization ask critical questions of itself before embracing the team concept. Examples of such questions include:

- Will the use of teams diffuse important organizational capabilities?
- How much infrastructure realignment will be required?
- Will leaders embrace the team concept and change their styles to suit?
- Can teams carry out tasks previously performed by individuals or functional units?
- How difficult it will be to develop team problem-solving capabilities?

This chapter addresses several important issues pertaining to conventional teams and the emerging trend toward self-managed teams. This section will address the definitional question of whether a team is the same as a group and examine the advantages and disadvantages of using teams.

Groups Versus Teams: What Is the Difference?

All teams are groups, but not all groups are teams. A manager can put together a group of people and never build a team. A *group* is a collection of individuals who interact primarily to share information and to make decisions that enable each member to perform within his or *her area of responsibility.* As such, group performance is merely the summation of each group member's individual contribution. There is no synergy. A team creates synergy. That is, the individual efforts of the members result in a level of performance that is greater than the sum of the individual inputs. In other words, the whole is greater than the sum of its parts. A team brings together individuals from varied backgrounds to contribute towards a collective output. Team members have both individual and collective accountability for performance. From these attributes, we define a **team** as *a unit of interdependent individuals with complementary skills who are committed to a common purpose and set of performance goals and to common expectations, for which they hold themselves accountable.*[11]

WORK Application **1**

Think of a past or present job. Based on your knowledge of the distinction between a group and a team, would you say you were part of a team or a group? Explain.

_____

_____

_____

_____

There is some debate about whether a group functions in the same way as a team. We take the view that some differences do indeed exist between teams and groups. The team concept implies a sense of shared mission and collective responsibility. Whereas groups focus on individual performance and goals, and reliance on individual abilities, teams have a collective mentality that focuses on: (1) common objectives; (2) sharing information, insights, and perspectives; (3) making decisions that support each individual to do his or her own job better; and/or (4) reinforcing each other's individual performance standards.[12]

Team members tend to have shared responsibilities, whereas group members sometimes work slightly more independently with greater motivation to achieve personal goals. The leadership style in a group tends to be very hierarchical, while in a team it is more likely to be participative or empowerment-oriented. In a team, performance measures create direct accountability for the team and incentives are team-based; in contrast, a group is more likely to be characterized by individual self-interest, with a mentality of "what's in it for me." A group, some say, is simply a collection of people working together. Teams strive for equality between members; in the best teams, there are no stars, and everyone suppresses individual ego for the good of the whole. From this perspective, it is apparent that the terms *team* and *group* are not exactly interchangeable, although some authors have not distinguished between them. It is important to bear in mind that these distinctions probably reflect matters of degree. One might consider teams to be highly specialized groups.

OPENING CASE *APPLICATION*

1. **What does it say about Gary Kelly's leadership philosophy when he categorically proclaims, "Our people are our single greatest strength and most enduring long-term competitive advantage?"**

It demonstrates his people-centered leadership style. With his strong belief in the value of his followers to the company's success, it is not surprising that his orders are for each department to have a dedicated team working together to create action plans to make Southwest a happy place to work. Teamwork is a way of life at Southwest and this is a direct result of the commitment of the CEO to this approach to structuring tasks.

CONCEPT APPLICATION 1
Group or Team

Based on each statement, identify it as characteristic of a group or a team. Write the appropriate letter in the blank before each item.

a. group   b. team

(continued)

(Concept Application 1 continued)

_____ 1. We all have a common objective that focuses our energies and resources.

_____ 2. Here every individual does his or her tasks separately and we add up our outputs at the end.

_____ 3. My compensation is based primarily on my department's performance and there is shared responsibility.

_____ 4. Our tasks are interconnected and we make decisions that support each individual to do his or her own job better.

_____ 5. We are just a collection of about 30 people working individually on an assigned project.

Learning Outcome 1 *Discuss the advantages and disadvantages of working in teams.*

Advantages and Disadvantages of Teamwork

Teamwork *is an understanding and commitment to a common goal on the part of all team members.* The increased acceptance and use of teams suggests that their usage offers many advantages. However, teams also present organizations with many challenges, including the need for effective communication; resolving personality conflicts and egos; establishing unifying goals, direction, and focus; establishing appropriate rewards and incentives; clarity about team structure; effective leadership; and organizing the team's work to ensure success. Clearly, teamwork skills and knowledge are imperative as organizations learn to compete in the information and knowledge economy.[13,14] Failure to effectively handle these challenges often results in dysfunctional teams.

Advantages of Teamwork

There are several advantages of teamwork:

1. Teams offer synergistic benefits that nonteam arrangements fail to offer. *Synergy* is when a team's total output exceeds the sum of the various members' contributions. It involves the creative cooperation of people working together to achieve something beyond the capacities of individuals working alone.

2. Team members can help each other avoid major errors. This tendency of mutual support and peer review of ideas helps teams make better decisions and can provide immunity for an organization against disruptive surprises.

3. Teams offer more opportunities for new ideas that advance innovation. Besides speeding up decision making and innovation, team members report greater satisfaction with their jobs.[15]

4. Teams present a work environment that encourages people to become self-motivated, empowered, and satisfied with their jobs. Job satisfaction is important because it is associated with other positive organizational outcomes. For example, employees who are satisfied with their jobs are said to be less likely to quit their jobs, are absent less, and are more likely to display organizational citizenship behavior.[16,17]

5. Being a member of a team makes it possible to satisfy more needs than if one worked alone; among these are the needs for affiliation, security, self-esteem, and self-fulfillment. Team members develop trust for each other and come to see the team as a social unit that fulfills other needs.[18]

Research on teamwork does reveal that individuals who are part of an effective team report greater levels of job satisfaction and are less likely leave their jobs. They are more likely to perform well and behave pro-socially.[19]

WORK Application **2**

Identify a team you were or are a part of and describe the advantages that you derived from being a member of the team.

_____

_____

_____

_____

Disadvantages of Teamwork

Teamwork has some potential disadvantages for both organizations and individuals:

1. A common problem may be that members face pressure to conform to group standards of performance and conduct even if it goes against the individual's or organization's interest. For example, a team member may be ostracized for being much more productive than his or her coworkers if the team's goal is to slow down production.[20] This can lead to intrateam conflict.

2. Shirking of individual responsibility, also known as social loafing is another problem frequently noted in groups. **Social loafing** *is the conscious or unconscious tendency by some team members to shirk responsibilities by withholding effort toward group goals when they are not individually accountable for their work.*[21] Many students who have worked on team projects (like group term papers) have encountered a social loafer. Social loafing is likely to result when individual effort is not recognized and assessed.[22,23] Individual performance evaluations can help to discourage social loafing by holding each team member accountable for assigned tasks; however, this goes against the argument that team-based performance measures are necessary for a strong team identity. It's a conundrum in that while instituting individual-level accountability may help reduce social loafing, it risks jeopardizing team accountability for shared goals—a critical characteristic of effective teams.

3. Another well-known disadvantage associated with highly cohesive teams is groupthink. **Groupthink** *is when members of a cohesive group tend to agree on a decision not on the basis of its merit but because they are less willing to risk rejection for questioning a majority viewpoint or presenting a dissenting opinion.* The group values getting along more than getting things done. The group often becomes more concerned with striving for unanimity than with objectively appraising different courses of action. Dissenting views are suppressed in favor of consensus.[24]

4. Though cohesiveness is a desirable quality of teams, teams that are extremely cohesive can also become, at their worst, a source of conflict with other teams. A team may become so cohesive that it resembles a clique. This can lead to interteam conflict if not addressed.[25,26] A clan culture develops with each team (clan) fighting for political dominance. There is pressure for members to stand by their teammates and to achieve the team's goals at any cost.

Effective team leaders find ways to maximize the advantages of teams and to minimize the disadvantages of teams. Complete Self-Assessment 1 to evaluate teamwork from your own work experience.

WORK Application **3**

Based on Self-Assessment 1, list some things that a team could do to improve its level of teamwork. Use experiences associated with a present or past job.

_____

_____

_____

_____

SELF-ASSESSMENT 1   Assessing Teamwork in Your Group

Based on experiences you have or have had with teams, indicate whether your team has (or had) the following characteristics by placing a checkmark in the appropriate column:

In my team:	Mostly True	Mostly False
1. There is a common understanding and commitment to group goals on the part of all team members.	____	____
2. Members support and provide constructive feedback to one another's ideas.	____	____
3. Members do not feel the pressure to conform to group standards of performance and conduct.	____	____
4. Dissenting views are accepted and discussed rather than suppressed in favor of consensus.	____	____

(continued)

(Self-Assessment 1 continued)

In my team:	Mostly True	Mostly False
5. The level of interpersonal interaction among members is high.	——	——
6. Much of the responsibility and authority for making important decisions is turned over to the team.	——	——
7. There is an open communication channel for all members to voice their opinions.	——	——
8. Members are provided with the opportunity for continuous learning and training in appropriate skills.	——	——
9. Every team member is treated equally.	——	——
10. Members are more likely to provide backup and support for one another without the team leader's instruction.	——	——

	Mostly True	Mostly False
11. Rewards and recognition are linked to individual as well as team results.	——	——
12. Roles and responsibilities for performing various tasks are clearly established.	——	——

Scoring

Add up the number of mostly true answers and place the total on the continuum below.

12 — 11 — 10 — 9 — 8 — 7 — 6 — 5 — 4 — 3 — 2 — 1
Effective teamwork   *Ineffective teamwork*

Interpreting the Score

The higher the score, the more effective is the teamwork. Self-assessment exercises like this can be used by groups during team building to improve teamwork. You will learn more about the team leader's role in building effective teams in the next section and about self-managed teams later in the chapter.

YOU Make the **ETHICAL** Call

8.1   *He Is Not a Team Player*

The story is told of a company that took a drastic decision to not interview a candidate for a job because of the feedback from the employee who picked up the candidate from the airport. The company prides itself on a culture that highly values its employees and teamwork attitude. It's a culture that takes the happiness of its employees seriously and everyone feels a sense of being part of a fun-loving team. On her way back to the company headquarters with a prospective candidate for a leadership position, she tried unsuccessfully to get the candidate to acknowledge her or even respond to her attempts at "small talk." The candidate seemed unwilling to acknowledge or engage in conversation with someone much lower in status than himself. Upon arrival back at headquarters, the employee reported her feeling to her leader. She said, she didn't think the candidate will make a good team player or fit in with the open, friendly and fun-loving attitude of the company. Given her reputation as an honest, hardworking, easy-to-get-along with individual and the fact that she has been with the company for more than 20 years, that was all it took for the candidate to be returned to the airport.

1. Is being a team player really necessary to be a successful employee?
2. Is it ethical and socially responsible of the company in this case to reject job candidates because they are considered not to be good team players?
3. Would you act the same way if you were the driver picking up the candidate?

What Is an Effective Team?

Teams vary in terms of their effectiveness. The obvious question then becomes, what makes one team effective and another ineffective? According to one author, there are five dysfunctions that every team must overcome to be effective: lack of trust, fear of conflict, lack of commitment, lack of accountability, and inattention to results.[27] One model of team effectiveness focused on internal team processes such as group learning, team efficacy, self-leadership, interdependency, and team cohesion.[28,29] Another model examined three contextual factors—team design, organizational resources and rewards, and process assistance—as determinants of team effectiveness.[30] With these ideas in mind, we present *team effectiveness as a model consisting of three components: (1) task performance—the degree to which the team's output (product or service) meets the needs and expectations of those who use it; (2) group process—the degree to which members interact or relate in ways that allow the team to work increasingly well together over time; and (3) individual satisfaction—the degree to which the group experience, on balance, is more satisfying than frustrating to team members.*[31]

This definition embodies a number of performance outcomes that others have used as a basis for evaluating team effectiveness. These include innovation, efficiency, quality, and employee satisfaction. Innovative teams are those with the capability to rapidly respond to environmental needs and changes with creative solutions. They are teams that have mastered what some refer to as "team learning." *Team learning is the collective acquisition, combination, creation, and sharing of knowledge.*[32,33,34] Efficient teams enable the organization to attain goals with fewer resources. Quality is the team's ability to produce outputs that meet or exceed customer expectations. Satisfaction measures the team's ability to achieve not only the team's goals (team satisfaction) but also satisfy the personal needs of its members (individual satisfaction).

OPENING CASE *APPLICATION*

2. How can you match our definition of team effectiveness as a multivariable concept involving three components (task performance, group process, and individual satisfaction) to this statement by Mr. Kelly: "We believe in Living the Southwest Way, which is to have a Warrior Spirit, a Servant's Heart, and a Fun-LUVing Attitude?"

The "Southwest way" is the team spirit that every employee of the company shares. Having a "warrior spirit" is the overwhelming desire to succeed at whatever your task requires. Having a "servant's heart" is the way employees treat each other and the customer. It's about everyone working together towards a common end. A good servant is a giver, a selfless and gracious individual. Finally, a "Fun-LUVing Attitude" is about the individual. People should love what they are doing and be satisfied doing it.

WORK Application 4

Interview someone you have worked with or know who is a team leader. Ask him or her to provide specific examples for some of the roles outlined in Exhibit 8.1 that he or she employed.

Characteristics of Effective Teams

Based on the relevant literature on team effectiveness, this section summarizes key characteristic of effective teams. Exhibit 8.1 presents ten characteristics of effective teams that are discussed next. It should be noted that this is not an exhaustive list of characteristics. Others, such as team efficacy, experience working together, team culture, and team structure have also been found to directly or indirectly influence team effectiveness

EXHIBIT 8.1   Ten Characteristics of Effective Teams

1. A highly publicized team charter and team norms
2. Widely shared goals and objectives
3. Strong team cohesion and high task inter-dependence
4. A diversified team mix
5. Clearly define roles and responsibilities
6. Positive interpersonal relationships
7. Clearly stated standard operating procedures
8. Trust and conflict management abilities
9. Effective interpersonal communication skills
10. Strong top management support

Learning Outcome 2 *Briefly describe the ten characteristics of effective teams.*

Highly Publicized Team Charter and Team Norms

A team charter is a document that should be jointly developed by team members and should specify the rules by which they agree to be governed. Norms evolve out of a team charter and become the framework for the decision-making process within the group and provide the underpinnings for group cohesion.[35] Therefore, we define **team norms** as *acceptable standards of behavior that are shared by team members.* For example, a team norm might specify cooperative over competitive behavior. This may be reflected by the level of importance members place on shared pursuits, objectives, and mutual interests rather than personal interests. The reward structure must match this cooperative norm.[36]

YOU
Make the
ETHICAL
Call

8.2 *Norms*

One or a few employees can break the norms and cause disastrous consequences for not only one organization but also entire industries. On the other hand, one or a few people can blow the whistle to disclose illegal and unethical business practices, which can lead to decreasing unethical behavior, such as at Enron. On the microteam level, employees influence each other's behavior through developing and enforcing norms; we can also call it peer pressure.

1. Should employees be able to do their own thing without the group enforcing norms?
2. Is it ethical and socially responsible for groups to develop and enforce norms? If so, what type of ethical standards should a group have?

Widely Shared Goals and Objectives

The most effective teams are committed to team goals as well as individual goals. When team members all share the same goals and objectives and each member clearly understands his or her role in helping to achieve the goals, performance is enhanced. It is often the case that when team goals and objectives conflict, tensions can appear within the team, and the whole will no longer be greater than the sum of its parts. Therefore, setting team goals and objectives should be an inclusive process.[37] The process should allow for open and honest exchange of ideas. Effective teams strive for consensus, consistency, and agreement on team goals and objectives. There is a sense of ownership in the goals and objectives of the team and thus greater accountability for team actions.[38]

Strong Team Cohesion and High Task Interdependence

Members of effective teams are able to collaborate and work well with each other. There is a high level of cohesion and interdependence found in effective teams.[39] **Team cohesion** *is the extent to which team members band together and remain committed to achieving team goals.* Team cohesion is increased when the following takes place.[40]

- Team members agree on a common purpose and direction.
- There is high team efficacy—the shared belief by a team that it can be successful at performing its task.[41,42]

- Top management gives high praise and recognition for the team's success.

- The organization encourages and motivates teams to compete with each other for rewards.

- Members find they have common ground and similar attitudes and values and enjoy being on the team.

- The quality of interpersonal relations is strong and member self-identification with the team is strong.[43]

The degree to which team members depend on each other for information, resources, and other inputs to complete their own tasks determines the level of task interdependence.[44] Researchers have suggested that the impact of group processes on group outcomes is much greater when team tasks require higher levels of interdependence.[45] The higher the level of interdependency, the greater the responsibility members feel towards each other. With interdependence comes the need for coordination to ensure that the team functions as a unified whole. In effective teams, interdependence and coordination are built into the team's goal, reward system, and job structure.

A Diversified Team Mix

An effective team is more than just a bunch of people brought together to accomplish a goal. Team mix focuses on the diversity in knowledge, background, and experiences of team members.[46,47,48] Effective teams must have the right mix of complementary skills, personality, knowledge, and ability to perform the team's job.[49,50,51] Teams that have experience working together tend to demonstrate greater task proficiency and teamwork effectiveness.[52,53]

Another aspect of team composition is the size of the team. Size may affect team members' ability to form close interpersonal relationships with other members. Small teams, typically fewer than 12 people, are generally more effective than larger teams. In small teams, conflicts and differences are more manageable. In larger teams, it is much more difficult for members to interact and share ideas with each other. As a general rule, teams that participants perceive as too small or too large relative to the task at hand are deemed to have failed the size test and are generally less effective.[54,55]

Clearly Defined Roles and Responsibilities

There is a greater chance of realizing team goals and objectives when team members clearly understand their roles and responsibilities.[56] In other words, each team member should know what his or her job is, how it contributes to meeting team goals and objectives, and how performance is measured. As one individual puts it, you know team roles and responsibilities are clearly defined when each team member is able to state, in one sentence, that: "My job on this team is to help us get to our goal of X by doing Y. I know I am doing my job when Z happens."[57] The benefits of having clearly defined roles and responsibilities are that team members are more likely to accept personal responsibility and not assign blame when things go wrong. They are more accountable for their actions. These are the kinds of teams where team members tend to be their own toughest critics.

Positive Interpersonal Relationships

Positive interpersonal relationships exist when there is mutual respect and trust, support, inclusion, collaboration, and open and honest communication between team members. Members of an effective team can show support for each other by being attentive to each others' needs, and by spending the appropriate amount of time together to ensure success.[58] Isolation from your team—such as not getting information, being excluded from team meetings, your work going unnoticed, your suggestions going unanswered, or the team leader playing favorites—is symptomatic of poor or negative interpersonal relationships. This can lead to feelings of insecurity, low self-esteem and even depression. Positive interpersonal relationships give members a sense of belonging in the team.

Clearly Stated Standard Operating Procedures

An effective team starts out by laying down the operating rules and procedures that will govern how the team carries out its work together. Typical areas for setting rules and operating procedures include communicating, meetings, performance evaluation, decision making and problem solving, completing tasks, and managing conflict. Setting and abiding by the team's rules and operating procedures will assure consistency in behavior among team members and reduce the chance of mistakes or conflict that can jeopardize team success.

Trust and Conflict Management Abilities

Trust between team members and the team leader (what some have described as intra-team trust) influences interpersonal relations and ultimately, team performance.[59] As one study's findings revealed, trust among teammates mediates the relationship between trust in the team leader as well as team cohesion in determining team performance.[60]

With respect to conflict management and team effectiveness, it is important to realize that conflict is an inevitable consequence of working with other people; however, it does not have to be dysfunctional.[61] In any given team, differences of goals, needs/aspirations, opinions, values, and personality provide more than enough grounds for disagreement and conflict. Disagreements can have both positive and negative consequences on team effectiveness. On the positive side, constructive disagreement is actually part of the reason why teams can be so effective; the more perspectives that go into a process, the better the end result. On the negative side, allowing disagreements to get out of hand can cause unnecessary disruption and lead to breakdowns in working relationships.[62] Such breakdowns can result in intrateam conflicts, lack of communication, and ultimately lack of any team spirit. Effective teams are proactive both in anticipating the need for conflict resolution and in developing conflict resolution strategies that apply to all team members.

Effective Interpersonal Communication Skills

Effective interpersonal communication is a vital part of a team's life because it determines the efficiency with which everything else is done within the team. According to one source, it is "like the circulatory system in the human body."[63] Effective teams have open and honest communication with each other. Team members of effective teams tend to show a high competency in oral and written communication skills. To enhance interpersonal communication, effective teams make use of the communications model: message encoding (sender), message decoding (receiver), common frame of reference, message channel, noise, and feedback. Effective communication also takes into account how team members communicate with each other. Hurtful and insensitive ways of communicating can damage relations in a team. Other obstructions to effective interpersonal communication—like information overload, filtering, defensiveness, and cultural differences—can be overcome by effective listening, applying feedback, being sensitive to others, and simplifying communication.[64]

WORK Application 5
Recall a team you have worked with that you would characterize as effective. What role(s) did your leader and/or organization play in making the team effective?

Strong Top Management Support

Effective teams are those that have strong support from the top management.[65] After all, team resources and rewards come from top management. Assessing team effectiveness as it relates to the overall organizational mission is an important part of top management's responsibility.[66] When teams are not achieving expected results, top management must determine if all the characteristics of effective teams described above are present. Also, top management must determine if the organizational culture supports teamwork and has reward programs that motivate and reinforce team behavior.[67] For example, recognizing and rewarding team accomplishments helps weave teamwork into the culture.

OPENING CASE *APPLICATION*

3. **What is the evidence that there is strong organizational support for teamwork at Southwest?**

At Southwest, there is the "University for People." The University for People is a state-of-the-art training facility led by Southwest Airlines facilitators and senior leaders as guest professors. Here the company offers training and development for its employees at every stage of their careers. For example, the curriculum includes a Myers-Briggs personality assessment seminar to help teams better appreciate individual differences and work more cohesively.

Learning Outcome 3 — *What role can a team leader play in creating an effective team?*

Team Leadership

There have been studies that have documented the positive relationship between team leadership and team performance.[68,69] Team leaders must manage not just the work but also team member relations across diverse functional and cultural boundaries.[70,71] The team leader's role is critical in motivating team members and creating an effective working environment for them to succeed in today's challenging global economy. Team-based organizations need leaders who are knowledgeable in the team process and are capable of leading a productive and effective team.[72]

Effective team leadership requires a shift in mindset from differentiated leadership (leaders treating individual team members differently) to team-based leadership (leaders treating all team members with equality and fairness). Studies have shown that team-based leadership facilitates group identification and collective efficacy, which positively contributes to team effectiveness.[73] Empowering leadership, for example, has a stronger effect on team members who have a high need for autonomy than directive leadership.[74] Also empowering leadership has been found to positively affect both knowledge sharing and team efficacy, which in turn, positively affect team performance.[75,76]

The team leader must model the behavior that he or she desires. A leader's self-sacrificing behavior and display of self-confidence does influence team members. Self-sacrificing leaders are those who go above and beyond what's expected of them. They don't just issue orders; they get involved in making things happen. The findings of other studies revealed that productivity levels, effectiveness ratings, and charisma were positively affected by a leader's self-sacrificing behavior.[77]

Team leadership is also about creating a team culture that supports the team's goals and operational strategies. A team culture sets standards and values that govern team member behavior. Research focused on college athletics reveals that coaches have regularly identified team culture as key to success because it creates an environment in which team member behaviors are consistent.[78,79]

Being an effective team leader requires social skills.[80] Leaders with strong social skills tend to have greater influencing abilities and interpersonal skills, and they relate well with team members.[81] When a leader or a team member can leverage his social skills to obtain resources for the team, he or she is said to possess social capital.[82] Without effective team leaders, teams can get off course, go too far or not far enough, lose sight of their mission, and become meshed by interpersonal conflict.[83]

While some individuals are skilled in all these areas and appear to have been born to be team leaders, the majority of aspiring leaders can benefit from team leadership development programs designed to assess and improve their effectiveness in this critical area. The team leader's role in influencing team effectiveness[84,85] is summarized in Exhibit 8.2.

EXHIBIT 8.2   The Team Leader's Role in Creating Effective Teams

- Emphasize group recognition and rewards.
- Identify and build on the team's strengths.
- Develop trust and a norm of teamwork.
- Develop the team's capabilities to anticipate and deal with change effectively.
- Empower teams to accomplish their work with minimal interference.
- Inspire and motivate teams toward higher levels of performance.
- Recognize individual and team needs and attend to them in a timely fashion.
- Encourage and support team decisions.
- Provide teams with challenging and motivating work.

© Cengage Learning 2013

OPENING CASE APPLICATION

4. In what way has Southwest shown that it understands the connection between team leadership and team success?

Southwest has a program called "Manager-in-Training" (MIT) aimed at identifying employees with a high potential for leadership and interest in a long-term career with the company. Among the courses offered, there is one specifically designed for team leaders. The first course is called MIT I, designed for employees at the supervisor, team leader, and manager levels. This is a clear indication that top management takes team leadership seriously.

 Learning Outcome 4   *Describe how organizational climate can influence team creativity.*

Organizational Climate and Team Creativity

Creativity feeds innovation, which is fast becoming a critical requirement for success in any type of business (profit or not-for-profit)—particularly for those organizations operating in turbulent and uncertain environments. Today's economy has been rightly described as a "knowledge economy" because more companies are gaining competitive advantages based on knowledge rather than on physical or financial resources. The companies that will survive and thrive may not always be those that have the greatest financial resources. It will take both physical and financial resources and a highly creative workforce to be competitive. Creativity is generally viewed as the actions of individual employees exchanging ideas and information with each other. Harnessing the creativity of a group is what team creativity is all about. Therefore, we define **team creativity** as *the creation of something that is valuable, useful, and novel by individuals working together in a complex social system.*

WORK Application 6

Think of a work situation in which you were required to do a lot of creative thinking, or in which your job required doing a lot of very creative things. In what ways did the organization and your immediate supervisor or leader facilitate or hinder your effectiveness? Use the discussion of top management and the team leader's roles in facilitating creativity as your guide.

_____

_____

_____

_____

Existing literature on team creativity has shown that top management can play a significant role in fostering a culture of creativity. Top management decisions in areas such as team autonomy, performance measurement and incentive systems, team bonuses, team structure, team composition, and a sufficient resource endowment can affect the creative spirit of a team. Creating an organizational culture that supports and encourages creativity provides the protection that team members need to take creative risks.

Encouraging interteam rivalries does stimulate creativity because the competition challenges teams to bring out their best.[86] Interteam rivalries can turn a team into a vortex of creativity. Also, as discussed in Chapter 7, the quality of the social exchange relationship between the leader and followers (leader–member exchange, LMX) and fellow team members (team–member exchange, TMX) enhances creativity in work teams.[87] To summarize, top management can influence team creativity by providing:

1. Appropriate and adequate resources
2. Appropriate recognition and rewards
3. Flexible team structure
4. Supportive organizational culture

Self-Assessment 2 should help you assess the climate for creativity in your organization or institution.

SELF-ASSESSMENT 2   Assessing the Climate for Creativity

Place a checkmark in the appropriate column for each question.

	Mostly Agree	Mostly Disagree
1. Organizational practices generally encourage creativity.	____	____
2. The reward system has been carefully designed to encourage creativity.	____	____
3. People are not restricted by rules and regulations or many layers of approval when they want to try new ideas.	____	____
4. "Doing things the way they have always been done" is not a slogan that applies in this organization.	____	____
5. People are able to experiment and dream outside their regular functional area on company time.	____	____
6. The organization's culture values and appreciates input from members.	____	____
7. People feel they have been properly matched with tasks that fit their skills, interests, and experiences.	____	____

	Mostly Agree	Mostly Disagree
8. Employees have greater autonomy to think and act freely than they would in another organization.	____	____
9. In looking around, it is certain that the work environment has been carefully designed to encourage creativity.	____	____
10. Managerial practices in this organization would lead to the conclusion that creativity and innovation are highly valued at all levels.	____	____

Scoring

Begin by placing a checkmark in the appropriate column for each question. Add up the number of "mostly agree" checkmarks and place the sum on the continuum below.

10 — 9 — 8 — 7 — 6 — 5 — 4 — 3 — 2 — 1
Supportive climate   _Unsupportive climate_

Interpreting the Score

The higher the score, the more supportive the organizational climate is of creativity and innovation. Self-assessment exercises like this can be used to encourage students to relate their work environments to the concepts in ways that others can benefit from their experience.

OPENING CASE *APPLICATION*

5. Southwest encourages its teams to be creative problem solvers. What are some examples of creative problem solving by Southwest teams?

Southwest employees have teamed up to find better ways of performing their task. Working together, Southwest employees found better and faster ways to turn around their planes in just 25 minutes, one of the fastest in the industry. There are also countless customer accounts of Southwest employees going out of their way to help them. In many of the cases, the employees took it upon themselves to find a solution to the customer's problem without waiting for managerial approval. The company definitely encourages its employees to find creative, yet efficient ways to accomplish their tasks and this is showing in the company's bottom line.

CONCEPT APPLICATION 2
Managing Creative Teams

Identify which strategy for creative teams each statement relates to:

a. quality resources   c. flexibility

b. recognition and rewards   d. free time

_____ 6. It is hard to be creative when company policy dictates strict adherence to standard operating procedures.

_____ 7. I wish a certain part of my work day was left up to me to do whatever I chose—like experimenting with new ideas.

_____ 8. There is very little room for thinking "out of the box" in this team.

_____ 9. How does management expect our outputs to be better when our inputs are of such poor quality?

_____ 10. I received a $500 gift certificate for an idea I suggested that helped my team cut cost and improve quality.

Types of Teams

Structural metamorphosis seems to be the one constant in organizational life today. Traditional organizational structures, known for their stable designs, are changing in favor of more fluid designs that can respond to external opportunities and threats. These flexible designs include a flatter and more horizontal structure, a focus on new ways to motivate employees, and the use of teams instead of functional structures. A manufacturing enterprise might, for example, make use of a variety of teams, such as a quality improvement team, customer service team, self-managed team, cross-functional team, technology integration team, virtual team, new product development team, or safety teams instead of relying on the old functional departmental form to get work done. In this section, we will examine four team types that are common across organizations today. They are: the functional team, the cross-functional team, the virtual team, and the self-managed team.

Functional Team

One hundred years ago, Frederick Taylor, called the "father of scientific management," espoused a leadership approach whereby managers made themselves functional experts, divided work processes into simple repetitive tasks, and treated workers as interchangeable parts. The functional team is mostly made up of a functional manager and a small group of frontline employees within that functional area or department. *A **functional team** is a group of employees belonging to the same functional department, such as marketing, R&D, production, human resources, or information systems, who have a common objective.*

Over time, the drawbacks of this approach became evident, as workers suffered from boredom due to the repetitive nature of their jobs. The structure of the functional team is generally more hierarchical, with the functional leader making all the decisions and expecting followers to implement them. Another drawback of the functional team, although unintended, is the tendency for team members to focus on their local area of specialization and ignore or downplay the overall organizational mission. This can lead to a lack of cooperation between functional teams, resulting in poor overall organization performance. In fact, rivalry rather than cooperation is what often happens between functional teams that don't interact with each other.

Over the years, the use of functional teams has been in decline. Cross-functional teams became popular in the late 1980s, when companies started to readjust their organizational structures to make them more flexible and competitive.

Cross-Functional Team

In today's flatter organizations, completing tasks often requires cooperation across functional boundaries. Team leaders are under pressure to dismantle walls separating functional units and form cross-functional teams for the purpose of accomplishing a common objective.[88] By way of definition, a **cross-functional team** *is composed of members from different functional departments of an organization who are brought together to perform unique tasks to create new and nonroutine products or services.*[89] Team members may also include representatives from outside the organization, such as suppliers, clients, and joint-venture partners.

The appeal of the cross-functional team concept is that interaction, cooperation, coordination, information sharing, and cross-fertilization of ideas among people from different functional areas produces better-quality products/services with shorter developmental cycles.[90] This is especially true for cross-functional teams charged with developing innovative products/services or new technologies.[91]

As cross-functional teams have become popular, research interest in their effectiveness has also kept pace. In one study, researchers interviewed 75 current and previous leaders of cross-functional teams in Hewlett-Packard's marketing, R&D, manufacturing, and information systems units. The interviews focused on identifying factors that were critical to the optimal performance of the teams.[92] In another study, a survey of frontline managers regarding the barriers and gateways to management cooperation and teamwork identified five keys or gateways proposed by respondents for getting frontline managers to work effectively in cross-functional teams.[93] Combined, these two studies highlight some of the influencing factors of cross-functional team effectiveness. Exhibit 8.3 presents six guidelines that if followed, can improve cross-functional team effectiveness.

EXHIBIT 8.3   Guidelines for Effective Cross-Functional Teams

1. Develop consensus around a common mission and goals that focus on organizational outcomes.
2. Implement team-based performance measures, feedback, and reward systems.
3. Ensure effective leadership and top management support.
4. Promote the use of team building, skill development, and team training as common practices.
5. Assemble the right skills.
6. Organize at the right size.

© Cengage Learning 2013

Cross-functional teams offer many potential benefits to an organization. For example:

- Bringing together the right mix of people gives the team a rich and diverse base of knowledge and creative potential that far exceeds anything a single functional team could come up with.

- Coordination is improved and many problems are avoided when people from different functions come together to work on a project at the same time, rather than working in separate units.

- The cross-functional makeup of a team offers the benefit of multiple sources of information and perspectives and contacts outside of one's functional specialty; these are critical for success in globally competitive, high-technology markets.[94]

- Members learn new skills that are carried back to their functional units and to subsequent teams.

- Finally, the positive synergy that occurs in effective cross-functional teams can help them achieve a level of performance that far exceeds the sum of the individual performances of members.[95]

Cross-functional teams are often an organization's first step toward greater employee participation and empowerment. These teams may gradually evolve into virtual or self-managed teams, depending on the type of environmental challenges or opportunities the organization faces.

WORK Application 7
Recall any experience you have had or currently have working with individuals from different disciplines or technical specialties outside of yours. How did you get along with these individuals? Describe the positives and negatives of your experience.

Virtual Team

Virtual teams are probably the most recent structural innovation of the 21st century.[96] An increasing number of organizations are using virtual teams to provide human resource flexibility, customer service responsiveness, innovation, and speed in project completion.[97,98] Increasingly, companies are investing in virtual teams to enhance their performance and competitiveness.[99]

Globalization and technological advances are driving organizations to adopt virtual teams. Virtual cross-functional teams are growing at a much faster rate in companies with global operations for obvious reasons. Global virtual team leaders are counseled to employ success strategies, such as building trust-based relationships, encouraging members to show respect for other cultures and languages, and promoting diversity as a team strength and not a weakness.[100,101]

Virtual teams enable organizations to pool the talents and expertise of employees and nonemployees by eliminating time and space barriers. In particular, new and advanced technologies are providing the means for work that is dispersed (carried out in different locations) and asynchronous (carried out at different times) to still be performed in team settings. The virtual team and can be organized along functional or cross-functional lines. We define a virtual team as one *whose members are geographically distributed, requiring them to work together through electronic means with minimal face-to-face interaction.*

In the United States, it is estimated that among companies with 5,000 or more employees, more than half of them use virtual teams.[102] Another survey by the Gartner Group revealed that more than 60 percent of professional employees now work in virtual teams.[103] A recent report revealed that 102,900 federal employees worked in a telecommuting environment in 2008.[104]

Virtual teams present significant collaboration, communication, and leadership challenges that if not handled properly can potentially hinder team cohesion, information sharing, and knowledge integration—all critical to success.[105,106] Recommendations for dealing with these challenges include focusing attention on both technological and interpersonal issues, with team leaders staying alert to relational and communication problems. Leaders of successful virtual teams establish and maintain trust and commitment in their teams by making sure that the necessary technology, support, and reward systems are in place.[107] The fourth type of team is called the self-managed team.

WORK Application **8**
Recall a present or past job. Describe what type of team you are in or have been in—functional, cross-functional, or self-managed.

_____

_____

_____

_____

Self-Managed Team (SMT)

With self-managed (autonomous) work teams, a group of people work together without a leader to plan, coordinate, and evaluate each other's work. We define **self-managed teams (SMTs)** as _relatively autonomous teams whose members share or rotate leadership responsibilities and hold one another mutually responsible for a set of performance targets assigned by top management._ The self-managed team concept is discussed in greater depth later in the chapter.

OPENING CASE _APPLICATION_

6. **Of the four types of teams discussed, which type(s) do you think Southwest is using?**

At Southwest, you get the sense that there are no walls separating the different departments—what some have called "silos." There is evidence of cross-functional teamwork at different levels. The effort to achieve a 25–minute turnaround time for each arriving flight takes a highly integrated and coordinated cross-functional team to accomplish.

CONCEPT APPLICATION 3
Type of Team

Identify each statement as characteristic of the following team types:

a. functional   c. virtual

b. cross-functional   d. self-managed

_____ 11. Members of my team are dispersed all over the country and even overseas, yet we conduct meetings and get our work done using the Internet and videoconferencing technologies.

_____ 12. We are developing a multispecialty work team to speed up processing our orders, and we are including two of our major customers in the mix.

_____ 13. We don't really have a boss in our team.

_____ 14. Our team has been charged with developing a new product within three months, and we get to decide many job-related issues on our own.

_____ 15. The marketing manager is creating a team with three other marketing employees to come up with ideas to increase sales.

Decision Making in Teams

Leadership is about making decisions. In a hierarchical command and control structure, the leader is the key decision maker. The followers are there to implement the leader's decisions. More and more, organizations are finding out that this top-down decision-making model does not work well in a team-oriented organization. For work teams to be effective, leaders must relinquish some of the decision-making responsibilities and allow team members to participate in the process. Exactly how this can be done effectively is the essence of this section. Recall that in Chapter 4, "Contingency Leadership Theories," we discussed the normative leadership model. Also, recall that the normative models (Exhibits 4.9 and 4.10 on pages 129 and 130) and Chapter 4's Developing Your Leadership Skills Exercise 2 (on page 144) apply to group decision making, because the models are used to determine the level of participation in a given decision. Developing Your Leadership Skills Exercise 1 in this chapter (on pages 317–318) presents a contingency leadership decision-making model that is adapted from the normative leadership model. It is a simpler model and uses the same leadership styles as situational communications (Developing Your Leadership Skills Exercise 2 in Chapter 6 on page 233) to help you determine the appropriate level of participation to use in a given situation.

Normative Leadership Model

The Normative Leadership Model has a time-driven and development-driven decision tree that enables the user to select one of five leadership styles (decide, consult individually, consult group, facilitate, and delegate) appropriate for the situation in order to maximize decision outcomes. Each of the five leadership styles affects the level of participation in the decision by followers. Leaders who employ the "facilitate" and "delegation" leadership styles allow greater team participation in decision making.

Team-Centered Decision-Making Model

The team-centered decision-making model is preferred when relevant information and expertise are scattered among different people, when participation is needed to obtain necessary commitment, when concentrating power in a single individual hurts the team, and when unpopular decisions need to be made.[108] The team-centered approach empowers team members to make decisions and follow through.[109] Advocates of the team-centered approach argue that empowerment results in a more dedicated, energetic, and creative workforce. Supporters of the team-centered approach argue that employees can be trusted to make decisions about their work, that they can be trained to acquire the skills and abilities needed to do so, and that organizational effectiveness is enhanced through this approach.

The role of leadership in a team-centered decision-making model is best accomplished by a team leader's ability to do the following:[110,111]

- The leader should listen attentively and observe nonverbal cues to be aware of member needs, feelings, and conflict.
- The role of the leader should be to serve as a consultant, advisor, coach, and facilitator for the team.
- The leader should model appropriate behaviors and encourage members to learn to perform these behaviors themselves.
- The leader should establish a climate of trust and respect for expressions of feelings as well as ideas.
- The leader should relinquish control to the team and allow it to make the final choice in all appropriate decisions.

Advantages and Disadvantages of Team-Centered Decision Making

Some advantages of team-centered decision making include the following:

- It can improve decision quality.

- It shifts much of the decision-making action away from the leader, thereby freeing him or her to focus on more strategic issues.

- It allows responsibility to be diffused among several people, thereby facilitating support for some types of unpopular decisions.

- It results in higher commitment by team members to implement decisions as compared to decisions made alone by a leader.

Some disadvantages of team-centered decision making include the following:

- It can take longer than decisions made alone by a manager.

- It can be self-serving and contrary to the best interests of the organization, if team members have objectives and/or priorities that are different from those of the leader.

- It can end up being a poor compromise rather than an optimal solution, when team members cannot agree among themselves.

WORK Application 9
Recall a team decision that you were a part of, and describe the team leader's role during the process leading up to the final decision. Would you characterize the leader's role as belonging to the leader-centered or team-centered approach to decision making?

_____

_____

_____

_____

Problems can occur when an organization has to transition from a leader-centered to a team-centered decision-making model. Leaders who are accustomed to making most or all team decisions may not want to give up this power or fear that if they do, they will appear weak or incompetent. Also, resistance may come from team members who prefer to avoid assuming more responsibility for leadership functions in the team. Despite these potential problems, empowering team members to make team decisions is a far better approach than concentrating such power in a single individual.

There is general agreement that personality traits of team members affect their effectiveness in decision making. Team members with similar traits and experiences will more likely share a common frame of reference when making decisions.[112] We should note that the characteristics of effective teams discussed earlier will also contribute to effective decision making. Complete Self-Assessment 3 to better understand how your personality will affect your teamwork.

SELF-ASSESSMENT 3   Personality Traits and Teams

Answer the following two questions, and then read how your personality profile can affect your teamwork.

I enjoy being part of a team and working with others more than working alone.

$$7 - 6 - 5 - 4 - 3 - 2 - 1$$
Strongly agree   *Strongly disagree*

I enjoy achieving team goals more than individual accomplishments.

$$7 - 6 - 5 - 4 - 3 - 2 - 1$$
Strongly agree   *Strongly disagree*

The stronger you agree with the two statements, the higher the probability that you will be a good team player. However, lower scores do not mean that you are not a good team player. The following is some information on how Big Five personality dimensions and their related motive needs can affect your teamwork.

Surgency—high need for power. If you have a high need for power, whether you are the team leader or not, you have to be careful not to dominate the group. Seek others' input, and know when to lead and when to follow. Even when you have great ideas, be sensitive to

(continued)

(Self-Assessment 3 continued)

others so they don't feel that you are bullying them, and stay calm (adjustment) as you influence them. Be aware of your motives to make sure you use socialized rather than personalized power. You have the potential to make a positive contribution to the team with your influencing leadership skills. If you have a low need for power, try to be assertive so that others don't take advantage of you, and speak up when you have good ideas.

Agreeableness—high need for affiliation. If you have a high need for affiliation, you tend to be a good team player. However, don't let the fear of hurting relationships get in the way of your influencing the team when you have good ideas. Don't be too quick to give in to others; it doesn't help the performance of the team when you have a better idea that is not implemented. You have the potential to be a valuable asset to the team as you contribute your skills of working well with others and making them feel important. If you have a low need for affiliation, be careful to be sensitive to others.

Conscientiousness—high need for achievement. If you have a high need for achievement, you have to watch your natural tendency to be more individualistic than team oriented. It's good to have your own goals; but if the team and organization fail, so do you. Remember that there is usually more than one good way to do anything; your way is not always the best. In a related issue, don't be a perfectionist, as you can cause problems with team members. Being conscientious, you have the potential to help the team do a good job and reach its full potential. If you have a low need for achievement, push yourself to be a valuable contributor to the group, or pull your own weight.

OPENING CASE APPLICATION

7. **Do you get the sense that decision making at Southwest is leader-centered or team-centered?**

Given the CEO's commitment to his employees and his desire to make Southwest a happy place to work, it will be hard to imagine decision making at Southwest being leader-centered. To say that Southwest Airlines employees are the single greatest strength and most enduring long-term competitive advantage means you value their input. Therefore, it is more likely the case that decision making at Southwest is a team-centered process.

An important part of a leader's job is conducting team meetings. The next section focuses on conducting team meetings.

Leadership Skills for Effective Team Meetings

With a team structure, leaders spend a great deal of time conducting meetings. Most meetings include employees, and it is common for teams to have daily meetings. With the trend toward teams, meetings are taking up an increasing amount of time. Therefore, the need for meeting management skills is stronger than ever.[113] The success of meetings depends on the leader's skill at managing the group process. The most common complaints about meetings are that there are too many of them, they are too long, and they are unproductive. Meeting leadership skills can lead to more productive meetings. A few years back, Ford Motor Company spent $500,000 to send 280 employees to a 3-day training session on developing meeting leadership skills, with three 1-day sessions to follow. After the training, fewer employees complained of meetings being too long or unproductive. Managers had gained the necessary meeting leadership skills and were putting this knowledge into practice. Ford's investment had obviously paid off. In this section, we learn how to plan and conduct a meeting and how to handle problem group members.

Planning Meetings

Leader and member preparations for a meeting have a direct effect on the meeting. Unprepared leaders tend to conduct unproductive meetings. Planning is needed in at least five areas: objectives, selecting participants and making assignments, the agenda, the time and place for the meeting, and leadership. A written copy of the plan should be sent to members prior to the meeting (see Exhibit 8.4).

EXHIBIT 8.4   Meeting Plans

- **Time.** List date, place (if it changes), and time (both beginning and ending).
- **Objective.** State the objectives and/or purpose of the meeting. The objectives can be listed with agenda items, as shown below, rather than as a separate section. However, be sure objectives are specific.
- **Participation and Assignments.** If all members have the same assignment, list it. If different members have different assignments, list their names and assignments. Assignments may be listed as agenda items, as shown below for Ted and Karen.
- **Agenda.** List each item to be covered, in order of priority, with its approximate time limit. Accepting the minutes of the preceding meeting may be an agenda item. Here is an example agenda:

GOLD TEAM MEETING

November 22, 2012, Gold room, 9:00 a.m. to 10:00 a.m.

Participation and Assignments

All members will attend and should have read the six computer brochures enclosed before the meeting. Be ready to discuss your preferences.

Agenda

1. Discussion and selection of two PCs to be presented to the team at a later date by PC representatives—45 minutes. (Note that this is the major objective; the actual selection takes place later.)
2. Ted will give the Venus project report—5 minutes.
3. Karen will present an idea for changing the product process slightly, without discussion—5 minutes. Discussion will take place at the next meeting, after members have given the idea some thought.

© Cengage Learning 2013

Objectives

Probably the single greatest mistake made by those who call meetings is that they often have no clear idea and purpose for the meeting. Before calling a meeting, clearly define its purpose and set objectives to be accomplished during the meeting. The only exceptions may be at regularly scheduled information-dissemination or brainstorming meetings.

Participants and Assignments

Before calling the meeting, decide who should attend. The more members who attend a meeting, the less the chance that any work will get done. Does the full group/team need to attend? Should some nongroup specialist be invited to provide input? On controversial issues, the leader may find it wiser to meet with the key members before the meeting to discuss the issue. Participants should know in advance what is expected of them at the meeting. If any preparation is expected (read material, do some research, make a report, and so forth), they should have adequate advance notice.

Agenda

Before calling the meeting, identify the activities that will take place during the meeting in order to achieve the objective. The agenda tells the members what is expected and how the meeting will progress. Having a set time limit for each agenda item helps keep the group on target; needless discussion and getting off the subject are common at all meetings. However, you need to be flexible and allow more time when really needed. Agenda items may also be submitted from members. If you get agenda items that require action, they should have objectives.

Place agenda items in order of priority. That way, if the group does not have time to cover every item, the least important items carry forward. In meetings in which the agenda items are not prioritized, the tendency is for the leader to put all the so-called quick items first. When this happens, the group gets bogged down and either rushes through the important items or puts them off until later.

Date, Time, and Place

To determine which day(s) and time(s) of the week are best for meetings, get members' input. Members tend to be more alert early in the day. When members are working in the same office or nearby, it is better to have more frequent shorter meetings focusing on one or just a few items. However, when members have to travel, fewer but longer meetings are needed. Be sure to select an appropriate place for the meeting, and plan for the physical comfort of the group. Be sure seating provides eye contact for small discussion groups, and plan enough time so that the members do not have to rush. If reservations are needed for the meeting place, make them far enough in advance to get a proper meeting room.

With advances in technology, telephone conferences are becoming quite common. Videoconferences are also gaining popularity. These techniques have saved travel costs and time and have resulted in better and quicker decisions. The majority of companies (big and small) today use videoconferencing and teleconferencing technologies to conduct meetings. The personal computer has been said to be the most useful tool for running meetings since *Robert's Rules of Order*. The personal computer can be turned into a large-screen "intelligent chalkboard" that can dramatically change meeting results. Minutes (notes on what took place during the last meeting) can be taken on the personal computer and distributed at the end of the meeting.

Leadership

The leader should determine the appropriate leadership style for the meeting. It is recommended that leaders play the role of facilitators, which involves guiding the process of the meeting while not influencing the content.[114] Each agenda item may need to be handled differently. For example, some items may simply call for disseminating information; others require a discussion, vote, or consensus; other items require a simple, quick report from a member, and so forth. An effective way to develop group members' ability is to rotate the role of the group moderator/leader for each meeting.

Conducting Meetings

The First Meeting

At the first meeting, the group is in the orientation stage. The leader should use the high-task role. However, the members should be given the opportunity to spend some time getting to know one another. Introductions set the stage for subsequent interactions. A simple technique is to start with introductions, then move on to the group's purpose and objectives and members' job roles. Sometime during or following this procedure, have a break that enables members to interact informally. If members find that their social needs will not be met, dissatisfaction may occur quickly.

Learning Outcome 5 *Outline the three parts of conducting effective meetings.*

The Three Parts of a Meeting

Each meeting should cover the following:

1. *Identifying objectives.* Begin the meeting on time; waiting for late members penalizes the members who are on time and develops a norm for arriving late. Begin by reviewing progress to date, the group's objectives, and the purpose/objective for the specific meeting. If minutes are recorded, they are usually approved at the beginning of the next meeting. For most meetings it is recommended that a secretary be appointed to take minutes.

2. *Covering agenda items.* Be sure to cover agenda items in priority order. Try to keep to the approximate times, but be flexible. If the discussion is constructive and members need more time, give it to them; however, if the discussion becomes more of a destructive argument, move ahead.

3. *Summarizing and reviewing assignments.* End the meeting on time. The leader should summarize what took place during the meeting. Were the meeting's objectives achieved? Review all of the assignments given during the meeting. Get a commitment to the task that each member should perform for the next or a specific future meeting. The secretary and/or leader should record all assignments. If there is no accountability and follow-up on assignments, members may not complete them.

The team leader needs to focus on group structure, process, and development. As stated, the leadership style needs to change with the group's level of development. The leader must be sure to provide the appropriate task and/or maintenance behavior when it is needed.

Handling Problem Members

As members work together, personality types tend to emerge. Certain personality types can cause the group to be less efficient. Some of the problem members you may have in your group are the following: silent, talker, wanderer, bored, and arguer.

Silent

To have a fully effective meeting, all group members should participate. If members are silent, the group does not get the benefit of their input. It is the leader's responsibility to encourage the silent member to participate without being obvious or overdoing it. One technique the leader can use is the rotation method, in which all members take turns giving their input. This method is generally less threatening than directly calling on people. However, the rotation method is not always appropriate. To build up the silent members' confidence, call on them with questions they can easily answer. When you believe they have convictions, ask them to express them. Watch their nonverbal communication as indicators of when to call on them. If you are a silent type, try to participate more often. Know when to stand up for your views and be assertive. Silent types generally do not make good leaders.

Talker

Talkers have something to say about everything. They like to dominate the discussion. However, if they do dominate, the other members do not get to participate. The talker can cause intragroup problems, such as low cohesiveness and conflicts. It is the leader's responsibility to slow talkers down, not to shut them up. Do not let them dominate the group. The rotation technique is also effective with talkers. They have to wait their turn. When not using a rotation method, gently interrupt the talker and present your own ideas or call on other members to present their ideas. Prefacing questions with statements like "let's give those who have not answered yet a chance" can also slow the talker down. If you tend to be a talker, try to slow down. Give others a chance to talk and do things for themselves. Good leaders develop others' abilities in these areas.

Wanderer

Wanderers distract the group from the agenda items; they tend to change the subject and often like to complain. The leader is responsible for keeping the group on track. If the wanderer wants to socialize, cut it off. Be kind; thank the member for the contribution, then throw a question out to the group to get it back on track. If the wanderer has a complaint that is legitimate and solvable, allow the group to discuss it. Group structure issues should be addressed and resolved. However, if an issue is not resolvable, get the group back on track. Griping without resolving anything tends to reduce morale and commitment to task accomplishment. If the wanderer complains about irresolvable issues, make statements like, "We may be underpaid, but we have no control over our pay. Complaining will not get us a raise; let's get back to the issue at hand." If you tend to be a wanderer, try to be aware of your behavior and stay on the subject at hand.

Bored

Your group may have one or more members who are not interested in the job. The bored person may be preoccupied with other issues and not pay attention or participate in the group meeting. The bored member may also feel superior and wonder why the group is spending so much time on the obvious.

The leader is responsible for keeping members motivated. Assign the bored member a task like recording ideas on the board and recording the minutes. Call on bored members; bring them into the group. If you allow them to sit back, things may get worse and others may decide not to participate either. If you tend to be bored, try to find ways to help motivate yourself. Work at becoming more patient and in control of behavior that can have negative effects on other members.

Arguer

Like the talker, the arguer likes to be the center of attention. This behavior can occur when you use the devil's advocate approach, which is helpful in developing and selecting alternative courses of action. However, arguers enjoy arguing for the sake of arguing, rather than helping the group. They turn things into a win–lose situation, and they cannot stand losing.

The leader should resolve conflict, but not in an argumentative way. Do not get into an argument with arguers; that is exactly what they want to happen. If an argument starts, bring others into the discussion. If it is personal, cut it off. Personal attacks only hurt the group. Keep the discussion moving on target. If you tend to be an arguer, strive to convey your views in an assertive debate format, not as an aggressive argument. Listen to others' views and be willing to change if they have better ideas.

CONCEPT APPLICATION 4
Group Problem People

Identify the problem type as:

a. silent   b. talker   c. wanderer   d. bored   e. arguer

_____ 16. As the group is trying to resolve crisis, Paul's focus was on trying to inform everyone about the company owner and the mailroom clerk.

_____ 17. Greg enjoys challenging members' ideas even if he does not have a strong case. When a group member does not agree with Greg, he makes wisecracks about the member's prior mistakes.

_____ 18. Richard is always first or second to give his ideas. He endlessly elaborates on his ideas. Other members are whispering about his "pushy" attitude.

_____ 19. Zora is usually reluctant to share her ideas. When asked to explain her position, Zora often changes her answers to agree with others in the group.

_____ 20. One of the usually active group members is sitting back quietly today and looking very absent-minded for the first time. The other members are doing all the discussing and volunteering for assignments.

WORK Application 10

Recall a meeting you attended. Did you receive an agenda prior to the meeting? How well did the leader conduct the meeting? Give ideas on how the meeting could have been improved. Did the group have any problem members? How well did the leader handle them?

_____

_____

_____

_____

Working with Group Members

Whenever you work in a group, do not embarrass, intimidate, or argue with any members, no matter how they provoke you. If you do, the result will make a martyr of them and a bully of you to the group. If you have serious problem members who do not respond to the above techniques, confront them individually outside of the group. Get them to agree to work in a cooperative way.

The remainder of this chapter will focus on the concept of self-managed teams, an innovative extension of the team concept.

Self-Managed Teams

As work increases in complexity and domestic economies become part of the global economy, the desire to find new and more effective ways of organizing employees grows accordingly. During the latter part of the 20th century to the present, the use of teams has been the competitive weapon of choice for many organizations (for-profit and not-for-profit). Lately, many of these organizations are experimenting with an innovative extension of the team concept called the *self-managed team (SMT)*. The proponents of the self-managed team concept argue that autonomy in the form of shared control over critical task-related decisions does enable SMTs to perform better than conventional teams.[115] It is the belief that team members who have such autonomy are more likely to feel invested in the process and be dedicated to accomplishing the stated goals. Self-managed teams go by many different names: self-directed, autonomous, self-leading, self-maintaining, or self-regulating.

This section examines the nature of self-managed teams by highlighting the differences between self-managed teams and conventional teams, the benefits of using SMTs, guidelines for improving their effectiveness, the role of leadership in the SMT concept, and the challenges of incorporating SMTs into an organization's structure.

The Nature of Self-Managed Teams

In the quest to remain competitive in new product/service development, companies are finding out that effectively managing human interactions and the rapid transfer of technology/ideas among individuals and functional units is key to staying competitive. Selecting, training, and rewarding employees as well as giving them autonomy in the form of collective control over critical task-related decisions can enable self-managed teams to perform more effectively.[116] To understand the nature of SMTs, we focus on the key differences between SMTs and traditional teams.

Explain the differences between conventional and self-managed teams.

How Are SMTs Different from Conventional Teams?

Self-managed teams differ from conventional teams in a number of ways. In conventional teams, decision making resides in the hands of a leader who provides the team with direction and maintains control over work-related decisions. In contrast, self-managed teams have a significant amount of decision-making authority. Members are charged with duties such as managing themselves, self-appraisals, planning and scheduling work, making production- or service-related decisions, peer evaluation, and conflict resolution. Members take responsibility for outlining how they will achieve the team's objectives.[117]

The leadership function in a self-managed team is different from that in a conventional team. Self-managed team members share or rotate leadership responsibilities and hold themselves mutually responsible for meeting team goals. Roles interchange frequently as members learn to be followers as well as leaders. Rather than being specialized, SMT members develop multiskilled capabilities that make them very flexible in performing various tasks within the team. Self-managed teams give all team members a voice in making decisions about the design of work, as well as greater autonomy and discretion in task accomplishment. Members operate without direct managerial supervision—an idea almost unthinkable a generation ago.[118]

The nature of self-managed teams is one of team rather than individual empowerment and accountability. Team accountability is a significant responsibility, since SMT members are responsible not only for their own performance but for that of other team members as well. In successful SMTs, members have come to see that what they collectively gain is greater than what they could achieve individually. A key part of any SMT is who is on the team. Team members of effective SMTs generally share the following characteristics:

- A strong belief in personal accountability
- An internal locus of control coupled with emotional stability
- Openness to new ideas/viewpoints
- Effective communication
- Good problem-solving skills
- Ability to engender trust
- Good conflict-resolution skills

Depending on the types of decisions, the amount of authority vested in a self-managed team varies greatly from one organization to another. For instance, in some organizations, SMTs are given the primary responsibility for personnel decisions such as hiring and firing team members, conducting performance appraisals, and determining compensation (within specified limits); in other organizations, such decisions are left to top management. Teams are usually allowed to make small expenditures for supplies and equipment without prior approval, but like in most organizations, any action involving large purchases must be approved by top management. Exhibit 8.5 summarizes the key differences between conventional and self-managed teams.

EXHIBIT **8.5** Differences between Conventional and Self-Managed Teams

Characteristics	Self-Managed Teams	Conventional Teams
Leadership	Within the team	Outside the team
Team member role	Interchangeable	Fixed
Accountability	Team	Individual
Work effort	Cohesive	Divided
Task design	Flexible	Fixed
Skills	Multiskilled	Specialized

© Cengage Learning 2013

CONCEPT APPLICATION 5
Types of Teams

Identify each statement below with one of these key terms.

a. group
b. functional team

c. cross-functional team
d. self-managed team

_____ 21. At the Charlottesville Winery, the quality control department headed by a unit supervisor is in charge of testing all incoming ingredients to make sure only the best ingredients go into the company's wine.

_____ 22. At Richmond Technology Associates, a team with members from information technology, finance, customer service, and quality control oversaw an ambitious information system—an integration project that spanned operations in the United States and Canada.

_____ 23. In my department, a number of us sometimes get together to discuss ways of improving our work processes.

_____ 24. In my company, I work in a team where leadership roles are rotated and shared, with each of us taking initiative at appropriate times for the good of the group.

Learning Outcome 7   *Describe the benefits of using self-managed teams in organizations.*

The Benefits of Self-Managed Teams

A primary reason for growth in popularity of the self-managed team concept is the reported benefits by organizations (large and small) that have adopted it. Self-managed work teams are praised for bringing about results such as increased productivity, accelerated new product development and process improvements, greater product/service quality, improved worker participation, and better decisions overall.[119,120,121] These results have led to increases in job satisfaction, which in turn have been associated with other positive organizational and employee outcomes, such as lower absenteeism rates, less turnover, higher motivation levels and self-esteem, increased organizational citizenship behavior, and, ultimately, increased levels of profitability.[122,123]

Self-managed teams do create a context for a shared and emotionally grounded identity that allows for a shared set of guiding principles for decision making and action. Because any agreed-upon course of action is taken collectively, there is a strong commitment among all team members to make it successful. Pride in the team's accomplishment and a strong sense of belonging inspires SMT members to connect with their organization's vision and mission.

Self-managed teams reduce costs because of the reductions in managerial ranks throughout the organization. In a study examining the economic benefits of organizing field technicians into self-managed teams, it was found that SMTs absorb the monitoring and coordination tasks of supervisors, substantially reducing indirect labor costs but without adversely affecting quality and productivity.

It should be noted that self-managed teams do exhibit the same general advantages of teamwork discussed earlier in the chapter. It's a question of how much further these benefits go when conventional teams are replaced with SMTs. Exhibit 8.6 summarizes the benefits of self-managed teams. The next section discusses guidelines for improving SMT effectiveness and addresses organizational-level factors that can impact SMT effectiveness.

WORK Application 12

If you have been part of an SMT, describe the benefits that you derived from being part of the team. Be specific, matching your description to the list in Exhibit 8.6.

_____

_____

_____

_____

EXHIBIT 8.6 Benefits of Self-Managed Teams

- Greater improvements in quality, speed, process, and innovation.
- A sense of belonging and ownership in one's work.
- Greater employee motivation.
- Accelerated new product development.
- Greater employee participation.
- Reduced operational costs because of reductions in managerial ranks and greater efficiencies.
- Greater employee job satisfaction, commitment, and productivity, and lower turnover and absenteeism rates.

© Cengage Learning 2013

OPENING CASE APPLICATION

7. Do you think Gary Kelly is the type of leader who would embrace the self-managed team concept? Explain your answer.

In 2008 and 2010, Mr. Kelly asked the Mercer Group, a management-consulting firm, to conduct an employee survey to determine how employees felt about the company and areas of improvement. This shows that the CEO is willing to listen to his followers and take their suggestions seriously. Reflecting on the careers of some of his young managers, whom he hired as entry-level employees, Gary Kelly said, "it is not such a stretch to feel that you've helped raised these people. They helped raise me, for that matter." Coupled with Mr. Kelly's objective to make Southwest a happy place for its employees and make work fun, it is a good bet that he would readily embrace SMTs if employees wanted to give it a try. He seems to be a leader who will be adaptable and willing to learn from his followers.

Learning Outcome 8   *Describe top management's role in improving the success rate of self-managed teams.*

Improving the Success Rate of Self-Managed Teams

Despite the documented successes and benefits of SMTs, there is still much that needs to be done to improve their success rate. Many things can go wrong with self-managed teams, and adjusting to new behavioral expectations can be difficult. Many SMT initiatives are eventually abandoned.[124] For SMTs to succeed there has to be strong and sustained top management support. The introduction of SMTs does threaten the positions of managers who are asked to function as team members instead of team leaders. Some rank-and-file employees may not be ready to handle the responsibility, authority, and accountability that SMTs put on them. The SMT concept may go against the organization's culture and thus encounter resistance and even sabotage from other employees. Therefore, in planning the introduction of SMTs into the organization's structure, top management should abide by the following guidelines to ensure a higher rate of success:[125]

- Ensure that the whole organization has changed its culture, structure, and climate to support SMTs. This will address questions such as: Does the SMT have sufficient autonomy to perform its task and have access to information? Have conditions been created in which authority can shift between members to appropriately match the demands of their task? Are SMT participants adequately motivated and supported? Are there any psychological or functional walls preventing unity of purpose and action?

- Have a champion to support and defend the SMT from opponents who are threatened by the new concept and what it represents. *A self-managed team champion is an advocate of the self-managed team concept whose responsibility is to help the team obtain necessary resources, gain political support from top management and other stakeholders of the organization, and defend it from enemy attacks.* This advocacy role is especially critical when there is hostility and distrust by other managers who are afraid the self-managed teams will cause major shifts of power and authority in the organization. The SMT champion is therefore constantly engaged in getting others to "buy in" and gaining commitment at all levels, while communicating the benefits of the SMT.

- Allow adequate time for training so team members can bond with one another and form team skills. Effective team-building interventions will break down barriers and create opportunities for greater cooperation.

- Selecting members for SMTs should be a careful and judicious process. Team member skills and experiences should match task requirements. Team diversity should be emphasized.

- Provide specific goals and incentives.

- Ensure that the organization has the necessary resources to commit to this kind of change in time, money, and people.

- Avoid overreacting at the first sign of crisis. Team-building experts caution against over-reacting when an SMT starts experiencing problems. Top management should resist the urge to pull the plug on the new program or micro-management. Instead, a careful review and analysis of problem areas should be done before any action is taken.

The next sections examine the changing role of leadership in SMTs and the challenges of implementing SMTs.

CONCEPT APPLICATION 6
Improving the Success Rate of SMTs

Identify which guideline for improving the success rate of SMTs is implied by each statement below.

a. top management support and commitment
b. specific goals and incentives

(continued)

(Concept Application 6 continued)

c. SMT Champion

d. adequate and necessary resources

e. team composition

f. matching culture and structure

g. adequate team training time

_____ 25. The team members are not taking our new self-directed status seriously, because they believe SMTs are just the latest fad, that management will drop it for the next hot topic.

_____ 26. I get frustrated with this team because no one seems to know what we are doing or why we are doing it.

_____ 27. There are still a lot of people in this organization who don't know why we operate differently from other traditional teams and thus are not very supportive of our efforts. We need someone to defend and promote us.

_____ 28. The thing that bothers me is the fact that we are still missing some key people with specific skills and experiences to make the team complete.

_____ 29. Management expects us to get the job done but has not met our demands for better work space, new computers, and a travel budget.

The Changing Role of Leadership in Self-Managed Teams

If, as we defined it, self-managed teams are relatively autonomous teams whose members share or rotate leadership responsibilities and hold themselves mutually responsible for meeting team goals, then the obvious question is why a self-managed team would need a leader or manager? In its purest form, a self-managed team does not need a leader. Members have been highly trained to handle all of their own activities, including hiring, discipline, firing, motivation, performance appraisals, and training. Different persons lead as the needs of the team demand. We call this distributed or shared leadership. *In* **distributed leadership,** *multiple leaders take complementary leadership roles in rotation within the same SMT, according to their area of expertise or interest.*[126] In other words, different members of the SMT assume different leadership roles as circumstances and task requirements warrant. It is what some have described as peer leadership.[127]

Some organizations do assign a facilitator to self-managed teams. Where this is the case, the self-managed team reports to the facilitator. The purpose of the facilitator is to define the "broad parameters" for the self-managed team, clear the path in the organization for the team, and offer advice and counsel as needed. It is just as critical that the SMT facilitator possess the requisite skills and ability to effectively lead teams as was the case with conventional teams.[128] Therefore, we defined the **self-managed team facilitator** as *the external leader of a self-managed team, whose job is to create optimal working conditions so that team members take on responsibilities to work productively and solve complex problems on their own.*

A summary of the facilitator's team-building activities is presented in Exhibit 8.7. Employing these activities will enhance the chances of strong identification with the team, especially as pride in the team's accomplishments grows. These activities will also strengthen cohesiveness and the level of mutual cooperation among team members.

WORK Application 13
Describe which of the facilitator's team-building activities (see Exhibit 8.7) your SMT or other type of team facilitator employed in leading the team.

_____

_____

_____

_____

EXHIBIT **8.7**   **SMT Facilitator Team-Building Activities**

- Opening forums for resolving interpersonal conflicts.
- Creating opportunities for social interaction.
- Increasing mutual acceptance and respect among diverse team members.
- Maintaining an open communication policy.
- Highlighting mutual interest, not differences, of team members.
- Increasing team identification through the use of ceremonies, rituals, and symbols.
- Using team-oriented incentives to foster teamwork.

© Cengage Learning 2013

Learning Outcome 9   *Describe the challenges of implementing effective self-managed teams.*

The Challenges of Implementing Self-Managed Teams

To observe a highly effective self-managed team at work is truly a sight to behold. However, it is a difficult concept to implement. There are many reasons for this, not the least of which is the fact that management usually will not get out of the way. Some managers see the self-managed team as a threat to their future. Some have gone as far as to suggest that the use of self-managed work teams may signal the end of the middle manager.[129]

Even among members of the nonmanagerial ranks, the transition to SMTs has as much potential for frustrations and problems as it does for managers. This is usually due to unfamiliarity with the new structure and new routines, and adjusting to team responsibilities. Team members must learn new behaviors, like putting aside differences in order to make decisions that benefit the team. The need to adapt to a new working environment in which the definition of teamwork requires a personal, cultural, and behavioral adjustment, may be too much for some members and thus lead to personality and behavior conflicts.[130] The greatest challenge may lie in setting and enforcing new behavioral expectations made necessary by the absence of a traditional leader and the presence of new employee rights and responsibilities.

When SMT members and former managers are not working together, counterproductive workplace conflict and political activity increases; as does ill will and decrease in morale. Ultimately, when former managers now working as part of a self-managed team worry more about their egos and avoid communicating with other members, they set a poor example for the rest of the team. Changing old attitudes and mindsets is a major challenge to implementing SMTs.

Some of the disadvantages of working in teams in general discussed earlier in the chapter—such as social loafing and groupthink—are also likely to occur in self-managed teams.

The decision to use self-managed teams as a tool for re-engineering work in an organization is not always a guaranteed success. It requires a great deal of commitment, effort, and support from all members of the organization, especially senior management. In organizations where there has been careful planning, former managers become SMT facilitators and are retrained to function differently than they did in their previous role. Many of the difficulties associated with SMTs stem from the inability of some managers transitioning from a traditional command-and-control work environment to self-managed teams.[131] Team-building experts maintain that managers who have become accustomed to traditional, autocratic management and jaded at management fads that come and go may resist or undermine a self-managed team approach. In the long run, the benefits of SMTs to employee morale, productivity, quality, and economic savings are well worth the growing pains.

WORK Application **14**

Have you worked in a team in which former managers have been reassigned to function simply as members of the team? What was your experience with the behavior and attitude of these former managers in their new role as team members?

_____

_____

_____

_____

Chapter Summary

The chapter summary is organized to answer the ten learning outcomes for Chapter 8.

1. Discuss the advantages and disadvantages of working in teams.

Advantages: In a team situation it is possible to achieve synergy, whereby the team's total output exceeds the sum of individual member contributions. Team members often evaluate and add to one another's thinking, so there are fewer chances of errors and the quality of the decisions is improved. A team atmosphere contributes well toward effective problem solving, continuous improvement, and innovation. Also, being a team member makes it possible for someone to satisfy more needs than working alone; among these are the need for affiliation, security, self-esteem, and self-fulfillment.

Disadvantages: Some teams have the unhealthy practice of pressuring members to conform to lower group standards of performance and conduct. For example, a team member may be ostracized for being more productive than his or her coworkers. Shirking of individual responsibility, or social loafing, is another problem frequently noted in groups. Another well-known problem common in teams is the practice of groupthink, which happens when the team values getting along so much that dissenting views are quickly suppressed in favor of group consensus.

2. Briefly describe the ten characteristics of effective teams.

The characteristics of effective teams are: (1) highly publicized team charter and team norms, (2) widely shared goals and objectives, (3) strong team cohesion and high task interdependence, (4) a diversified team mix, (5) clearly defined roles and responsibilities, (6) positive interpersonal relationships, (7) clearly stated standard operating procedures, (8) trust and conflict management abilities, (9) effective interpersonal communication skills and (10) strong top management support. A team charter and team norms influence how a team's members perceive and interact with one another, approach decisions, and solve problems; they guide team members' behavior. Teams need effective leaders who will monitor the progress of the team to make sure that the team does not go off track, go too far or not far enough, lose sight of its goal, or become bogged down by conflict. Effective teams have high levels of cohesion and task interdependence. Highly cohesive teams are characterized by high group potency and strong self-efficacy.

Members of highly effective teams are more interactive and dependent on one another to get tasks done. Effective teams must have the appropriate mix of complementary skills, knowledge, and ability to successfully realize the team's objectives. Effective teams have structures that provide team members with broad participation in decision making. Effective teams have strong support from top management. Management support, both tangible and intangible, is critical for team success. It is top management's responsibility to create a work climate that supports and rewards teamwork. Finally, effective teams have clearly stated standard operating procedures, trust each other, manage conflicts constructively and communicate with each other on a regular basis.

3. What role can a team leader play in creating an effective team?

A team leader who is able to empower team members to think and act freely will increase the effectiveness of the team much faster than a team leader who practices a bureaucratic command and control leadership style. Team leadership is also about creating a team culture that supports teamwork. A team culture sets standards and values that govern team member behaviors, keeping everyone on the same plan. Finally, a team leader can play an active role in team effectiveness by doing some of the things suggested in Exhibit 8.1 such as: (1) matching members with the right assignments, (2) using group rewards and recognition, or (3) ensuring the availability of adequate time, money, and other resources for the team.

4. Describe how organizational climate can influence team creativity.

Creating the right organizational climate is the responsibility of top management. As such top management's role in influencing team creativity is significant. Creativity does not work in hierarchical command-and-control environments. Top management has the responsibility to create the appropriate setting and support systems that foster and nourish creativity. Top management activities that can influence creativity include providing teams with the following: (1) adequate and quality resources, (2) appropriate recognition and rewards, (3) flexibility and a minimum amount of structure, and (4) supportive culture.

5. Outline the three parts of conducting effective meetings.

Each meeting should cover the following:

1. *Identify objectives.* Begin the meeting on time. Begin by reviewing progress to date, the group's objectives, and the purpose/objective for the specific meeting. If minutes are recorded, they are usually approved at the beginning of the next meeting.

2. *Cover agenda items.* Be sure to cover agenda items in priority order. Try to keep to the approximate times, but be flexible. If the discussion is constructive and members need more time, give it to them; however,

if the discussion is more of a destructive argument, move ahead.

3. *Summarize and review assignments.* End the meeting on time. The leader should summarize what took place during the meeting. Were the meeting's objectives achieved? Review all of the assignments given during the meeting. Get a commitment to the task that each member should perform for the next or a specific future meeting. The secretary and/or leader should record all assignments.

6. Explain the differences between conventional and self-managed teams.

Self-managed teams differ from traditional teams in a number of ways. In self-managed teams, roles interchange frequently as members learn to be followers as well as leaders. Rather than functioning in their specialized units, SMT members develop multiskilled capabilities that make them very flexible in performing various tasks within the team. The nature of self-managed teams is one of group empowerment and accountability rather than individual empowerment and accountability. Team accountability is a significant responsibility, especially since SMT members determine how they will organize themselves to get the work done and are responsible not only for their own performance but for that of other team members as well.

7. Describe the benefits of using self-managed teams in organizations.

Self-managed teams (1) create a stronger sense of commitment to the work effort among team members; (2) improve quality, speed, and innovation; (3) have more satisfied employees and lower turnover and absenteeism; (4) facilitate faster new-product development; (5) allow cross-trained team members greater flexibility in dealing with personnel shortages due to illness or turnover; and (6) keep operational costs down because of reductions in managerial ranks and increased efficiencies.

8. Describe top management's role in improving the success rate of self-managed teams.

Senior management has the principal responsibility to create the right environment in which self-managed teams can grow and thrive. This involves undertaking activities to ensure that the whole organization has a changed culture, structure, and climate to support SMTs. This requires providing sufficient responses to questions such as whether the SMT has sufficient autonomy to perform its task and has access to information; whether conditions have been created in which authority can shift between members to appropriately match the demands of their task; and whether SMT participants are motivated, stimulated, and supported in a fashion that breaks down walls and creates unity of purpose and action.

Management must have a well thought-out vision of the way in which SMTs will fit into the scheme of the entire organization; allow time after training for the team members to bond with one another and form team skills; provide adequate training, so team member skills and experiences match task requirements; provide objective goals, incentives, and appropriate infrastructure; ensure that the organization has the necessary resources to commit to this kind of change (not only in time but also in money and people); and create a sense of empowerment, so SMTs take ownership of what they are doing and how they are going to do it.

9. Describe the challenges of implementing effective self-managed teams.

Many of the challenges of implementing SMTs stem from the difficulties of transitioning from a traditional command-and-control work environment to self-managed teams. Team-building experts contend that managers who have become accustomed to traditional, autocratic management and jaded at management fads that come and go may resist or undermine a team approach. Even among members of the nonmanagerial ranks, the transition to SMTs has as much potential for frustrations and problems as it does for managers. This is usually due to unfamiliarity with the new structure and new routines, and adjusting to team responsibilities. Team members must learn new behaviors, like putting aside differences in order to make decisions that benefit the team. The need to adapt to a new working environment in which the definition of teamwork requires a personal, cultural, and behavioral adjustment may be too much for some members and thus lead to personality and behavior conflicts. Thus, the greatest challenge may lie in setting and enforcing new behavioral expectations, made necessary by the absence of a traditional leader and the presence of new employee rights and responsibilities.

10. Define the following key terms (in order of appearance in the chapter).

Select one or more methods: (1) fill in the missing key terms from memory; (2) match the key terms from the following list with their definitions below; (3) copy the key terms in order from the list at the beginning of the chapter.

_____ is a collection of individuals who interact primarily to share information and to make decisions that enable each member to perform within his or her area of responsibility.

_____ is a unit of interdependent individuals with complementary skills who are committed to a common purpose and set of performance goals and to common expectations, for which they hold themselves accountable.

_____ is an understanding and commitment to group goals on the part of all team members.

_____ is the conscious or unconscious tendency by some team members to shirk responsibilities, by withholding effort toward group goals when they are not individually accountable for their work.

_____ is when members of a cohesive group tend to agree on a decision not on the basis of its merits but because they are less willing to risk rejection for questioning a majority viewpoint or presenting a dissenting opinion.

_____ has three components: (1) task performance—the degree to which the team's output (product or service) meets the needs and expectations of those who use it; (2) group process—the degree to which members interact or relate in ways that allow the team to work increasingly well together over time; and (3) individual satisfaction—the degree to which the group experience, on balance, is more satisfying than frustrating to team members.

_____ is the collective acquisition, combination, creation, and sharing of knowledge.

_____ are acceptable standards of behavior that are shared by team members.

_____ is the extent to which team members band together and remain committed to achieving team goals.

_____ is the creation of a valuable, useful, and novel product, service, idea, procedure, or process carried out via discovery rather than by a predetermined step-by-step procedure, by individuals working together in a complex social system.

_____ is a group of employees belonging to the same functional department, such as marketing, R&D, production, human resources, or information systems, who have a common objective.

_____ is made up of members from different functional departments of an organization who are brought together to perform unique tasks to create new and nonroutine products or services.

_____ is a team whose members are geographically distributed, requiring them to work together through electronic means with minimal face-to-face interaction.

_____ are relatively autonomous teams whose members share or rotate leadership responsibilities and hold themselves mutually responsible for a set of performance goals assigned by higher management.

_____ is an advocate of the self-managed team concept whose responsibility is to help the team obtain necessary resources, gain political support from top management and other stakeholders of the organization, and defend from enemy attacks.

_____ is the process by which multiple leaders take complementary leadership roles in rotation within the same SMT, according to their area of expertise or interest.

_____ is the external leader of a self-managed team, whose job is to create optimal working conditions so team members take on responsibilities to work productively and solve complex problems on their own.

Key Terms

cross-functional team, 291

distributed leadership, 306

functional team, 291

group, 278

groupthink, 281

self-managed team champion, 305

self-managed team facilitator, 306

self-managed teams (SMTs), 293

social loafing, 281

team, 279

team cohesion, 284

team creativity, 288

team effectiveness, 283

team learning, 283

team norms, 284

teamwork, 280

virtual team, 292

Review Questions

1. What is groupthink, and under what conditions is it most likely to occur?

2. Describe the factors that generally contribute high levels of team cohesion.

3. Creativity is usually thought of as a characteristic of individuals, but are some teams more creative than others?

4. What is team-centered leadership, and how does it differ from the leader-centered approach?

5. Describe how a leader can avoid conducting nonproductive meetings.

6. What is the depth of decision-making latitude commonly found in self-managed teams?

7. Briefly discuss some of the potential benefits and drawbacks of using self-managed teams.

Critical Thinking Questions

The following critical-thinking questions can be used for class discussion and/or as written assignments to develop critical thinking skills. Be sure to give complete explanations for all questions.

1. Teams are often credited with making better decisions than individuals, yet they are also criticized for groupthink. What are some strategies for creating effective teams that are not victims of the groupthink phenomenon?

2. Identify and describe any team you have been a member of, or know about otherwise, that has a strong norm of teamwork that all members buy into. What role did the team leader play in making this possible?

3. What are some of the key indicators of team dysfunction?

4. What is the key to creating cross-functional teams in which team members put the good of the team ahead of functional self-interest?

5. How can virtual teams work well together from far apart?

6. What would you describe as some of the do's and don'ts of team leadership?

7. Describe an organization whose culture, structure, and leadership philosophy clearly support creativity and innovation.

CASE

Frederick W. Smith—FedEx

Since 1971, Federal Express, now known simply as FedEx, remains the market leader in an industry it helped create. The name FedEx is synonymous with overnight delivery. The person in charge of providing the strategic direction for all FedEx Corporation companies is its founder, Frederick W. Smith, the Chairman, President, and Chief Executive Officer. To position the company for the 21st century, Smith has organized FedEx into the following Strategic Business Units: FedEx Express, FedEx Ground, FedEx Freight, FedEx Office, FedEx Custom Critical, FedEx Trade Networks, FedEx Supply Chain, and FedEx Services. These companies serve more than 220 countries and territories with operations that include 697 aircraft and more than 80,000 vehicles. With more than 290,000 team members worldwide, FedEx handles more than 8.5 million shipments each business day.

FedEx has expanded far beyond what Smith started with back in 1971. FedEx has continued to strengthen its industry leadership over the past 40 years and has been widely acknowledged for its commitment to total quality service. Federal Express was the first service company to win the Malcolm Baldrige National Quality Award in 1990. In addition, FedEx has consistently been ranked on *Fortune* magazine's industry lists, including "World's Most Admired Companies," "America's Most Admired Companies," "100 Best Companies to Work For," and "Blue Ribbon Companies." In 2011 *Fortune* ranked FedEx No. 8 among the "World's Most Admired Companies."

With growth come difficulties of coordination, maintaining efficiency, meeting customer expectations, and managing employees. Smith realized that a rigid hierarchy of command-and-control leadership would only magnify these difficulties. To give his employees the flexibility and freedom they need to move quickly and help FedEx remain the dominant overnight delivery service in the world, Smith decided to restructure FedEx by emphasizing the team approach to getting work done. He directed his executive team to create and empower more teams by giving them the authority and the responsibility to make the changes needed to improve productivity and customer satisfaction throughout the FedEx system. This directive is consistent with the operational strategy of the corporation put forth by Mr. Smith and his executive team. It is evident from the corporation's Web site that teamwork is a core component of its strategic orientation as revealed in this statement:

The unique FedEx operating strategy works seamlessly—and simultaneously—on three levels:

- **Compete collectively** by standing as one brand worldwide and speaking with one voice.

- **Operate independently** by focusing on our independent networks to meet distinct customer needs.
- **Manage collaboratively** by working together to sustain loyal relationships with our workforce, customers, and investors.[132]

An example of the successful implementation of Mr. Smith's directive can be found in Springfield, Virginia. With strong support from their managers, employees formed the Quality Action Team to overhaul their package-sorting techniques. The improvements they introduced put couriers on the road 12 minutes earlier than before, and halved the number of packages they delivered late. The success of teams at departmental or local levels encouraged Smith and his leadership team to also assign employee teams to companywide projects. Facing growing competition from United Parcel Service, the U.S. Postal Service, and Airborne Express, FedEx organized its clerical employees into "super-teams" of up to 10 people. These teams operated as self-managed teams with little direct supervision from managers. One team cut service glitches, such as incorrect bills and lost packages by 13 percent. Another team spotted—and worked until they eventually solved—a billing problem that had been costing the company $2.1 million a year.

FedEx teams have worked so well because Fred Smith sets standards and reinforces them. He spearheaded the concept of the "golden package," the idea that every package FedEx handles is critical and must be delivered on time. Whenever there's a crisis, whether due to competitive pressure or to Mother Nature threatening to ground the company's planes, the team with the golden package takes charge to figure out how to make the delivery on time. Smith reinforces group performance by presenting a monthly Circle of Excellence award to the best FedEx station. He encourages innovative thinking by creating a "job-secure environment." He takes the position that "if you hang people who try to do something that doesn't quite work, you'll get people who don't do anything."

Managers are by no means obsolete at FedEx. Smith has redefined their roles. There has been a shift in mindset from the traditional leader-centered to the team-centered leadership approach. Managers are expected to formulate clear, attainable goals for their teams, solicit employee ideas, and act on the best employee suggestions. FedEx managers perceive their role as facilitators—and sometimes they are players. During emergencies at the Memphis hub, senior managers have been known to hurry down from the executive suite to help load packages onto the conveyor belts that feed the company's planes. They practice team leadership by doing, not by telling.

According to one company executive, "FedEx has built what is the most seamless global air and ground network in its industry, connecting more than 90 percent of the world's economic activity." It is evident that FedEx's open, flexible, and team-based organizational structure and culture has been instrumental in keeping the company's lead position in overnight package service. CEO Smith's team leadership deserves much of the credit.

GO TO THE INTERNET: To learn more about Fred Smith and FedEx, their Web site **(http://www.fedex.com)**.

Support your answers to the following questions with specific information from the case and text or with other information you get from the Web or other sources.

1. How do the standards set by Fred Smith for FedEx teams improve organizational performance?

2. What motivates the members of FedEx to remain highly engaged in their teams?

3. Describe the role FedEx managers play in facilitating team effectiveness.

4. What type of teams does FedEx use? Provide evidence from the case to support your answer.

5. Leaders play a critical role in building effective teams. Cite evidence from the case that FedEx managers performed some of these roles in developing effective teams.

CUMULATIVE CASE QUESTIONS

6. The Big Five model of personality categorizes traits into dimensions of surgency, agreeableness, adjustment, conscientiousness, and openness to experience (Chapter 2). Which of these dimensions do you think Fred Smith possesses?

7. The normative leadership model identifies five leadership styles appropriate for different situations that users can select to maximize decisions (Chapter 5). Which of the five leadership styles is practiced by FedEx team leaders?

8. The case reveals that at the Memphis hub senior managers have been known to hurry down from the executive suite to help load packages during emergencies in order to get the plane off on time. FedEx leaders want to be seen as coaches, not managers. Specific guidelines can help a leader become an effective coach (Chapter 6). Which of the guideline(s) does the example above represent?

9. Research on followership describes five types of followership (see Exhibit 7.3, Chapter 7). Which of these types will work best in FedEx's team environment as described in the case, and why?

CASE EXERCISE AND ROLE-PLAY

Preparation: You are senior vice president for operations at FedEx. FedEx's monthly Circle of Excellence Award is presented to the best FedEx station. This time the best station was one that truly represented the spirit of teamwork in problem solving. The station manager spotted a loading problem that was costing the company millions of dollars a year and decided to leave it up to the station as a group to find ways of solving the problem. After a series of group meetings and key decisions, a solution was found that successfully took care of the loading problem and was adopted by the rest of the company. It has come to Fred Smith's attention that a key reason for the station's success is the leadership role played by the team leader during this process. Smith has asked that you use the award ceremony as an opportunity to highlight the virtues of the group-centered approach of leadership, particularly with respect to decision making in teams. Develop the key parts of the speech you will give on this occasion.

Your instructor may elect to break the class into groups to share ideas and put together the speech or simply ask each student to prepare an independent speech. If you do a group speech, select one leader to present the speech to the entire class.

Role-Play: One person (representing oneself or a group) may give the speech to the entire class, or break into groups of five or six and deliver speeches one at a time.

VIDEO ▶❙❙ CASE

The NEADS Team: People and Dogs

The National Education for Assistance Dog Services (NEADS) functions with teams of people. But another type of teamwork is also central to the mission of NEADS: the team of human and dog. NEADS acquires, raises, trains, and matches service dogs to meet the needs of people with limited physical mobility or deafness. It takes about two years to train a service dog—and that requires a lot of teamwork. Volunteer families become part of the team when, at four months of age, the puppies are placed in foster care. These families agree to feed, love, and raise the puppies so they become accustomed to the distractions and energy of the real world. Professional dog trainers from NEADS visit regularly to work with the families and dogs to ensure that the dogs receive the proper training in preparation for their later work. The puppies live in their foster homes until they are about a year and a half old; then they return to the NEADS farm to continue their education. Here, they receive advanced training from professional dog trainers. When a dog's training is complete, its new owner arrives on campus for a two-week stay, during which the person and the dog become a team. The person and dog have been matched through an extensive interview process that involves a team of people interviewers and dog trainers.

1. Describe the characteristics of a typical NEADS team, using the information discussed in the chapter.

2. What factors determine the cohesiveness of NEADS teams?

Behavior Model Skills Training

This behavior model skills training on leadership decision making has four parts. You should first read how to use the model. Then, you may view the behavior model video that illustrates all four decision-making styles for the same decision. Parts III and IV are together in Developing Your Leadership Skills Exercise 1, which gives you the opportunity to develop your ability to select the leadership decision-making style most appropriate for a given situation. Lastly, you further develop this skill by using the model in your personal and professional life.

Leadership Decision-Making Model

(Part I)

Deciding Which Leadership Decision-Making Style to Use

Read the instructions for using the leadership decision-making model, and see Model 8.1. You may want to refer to the model as you read.

Managers today realize the trend toward participation in decision making, and managers are open to using participation. It is sometimes difficult for managers to decide when to use participation and when not to, and what level of participation to use. You are about to learn how to use a model that will develop your skill at selecting the appropriate leadership style to meet the needs of the situation. First, let's examine ways in which groups can be used to generate solutions.

Selecting the Appropriate Leadership Decision Style

We have the same four variables as in the Situational Communication Model 6.6 in Chapter 6—time, information, acceptance, and capability level.

Step 1 Diagnose the situation. The first step you follow as a leader involves diagnosing the situational variables—including time, information, acceptance, and follower capability.

Time. You must determine whether there is enough time to include followers in decision making. Time is viewed as yes (you have time to use participation) or no (there is no time to use participation). If there is no time, you should use the autocratic style (S1A in Model 6.6 – chapter 6), regardless of preference. When there is no time to include employees in problem solving and decision making, you ignore the other three variables; they are irrelevant if there is no time. If you say yes there is time, then the consultative, participative, or empowerment styles may be appropriate. You use the other three variables to select the style.

Time is a relative term. In one situation, a few minutes may be considered a short time period, but in another a month may be a short period of time. Time is not wasted when the potential advantages of using participation are realized.

Information. You must decide if you have enough information to make a quality decision alone. The more information you have, the less need for participation; the less information you have, the greater the need for participation. If you have all the necessary information, there is no need for follower participation, and the autocratic style (S1A) is appropriate. When you have some information, but need more, which can be obtained by asking questions, the consultative style (S2C) may be appropriate. If you have little information, the appropriate style may be participative (S3P—group discussion) or empowerment (S4E—group makes the decision).

Acceptance. You must decide whether employee acceptance of the decision is critical to implementation of the decision. The more the followers will like a decision, the less need there is for participation; the more the followers will dislike a decision, the greater the need for participation. If you make the decision alone, will the follower or group willingly implement it? If the follower or group will be accepting, the appropriate style is probably autocratic (S1A). If the follower or group will be reluctant, the appropriate style may be consultative (S2C) or participative (S3P). If they will probably reject the decision, the participative (S3P) or empowerment style (S4E) may be appropriate. When teams make decisions, they are more understanding, accepting, and committed to implementing the decision.

Capability. You must decide whether the follower or group has the ability and motivation to be involved in problem solving and decision making. Does the follower or group have the experience and information needed to be involved? Will followers put the organization's or department's goals ahead of personal goals? Do the followers want to be involved in problem solving and decision making? Followers are more willing to participate when the decisions personally affect them. If the follower or group capability level is low (C1), an autocratic style (S1A) may be appropriate. When capability is moderate (C2), a consultative style (S2C) may be appropriate. If capability level is high (C3), a participative style (S3P) might be adopted. If capability is outstanding (C4), choose the empowerment style (S4E). Remember that an employee's or group's capability level can change from situation to situation.

Step 2 Select the appropriate leadership style. After considering the four variables, you select the appropriate style. In some situations, all variables will indicate that the same style is appropriate, whereas in other cases, the appropriate style is not so clear. For example, you could be in a situation in which you have time to use any style, may have all the information necessary (autocratic), followers may be reluctant (consultative or participative), and their capability may be moderate (consultative). In situations where different styles are indicated for different variables, you must determine which variables should be given more weight. In the above example, assume that acceptance was critical for successful implementation of the decision. Acceptance takes precedence over information. Because the followers involved have moderate capability, the consultative style would be appropriate. Again, Model 8.1 summarizes use of the four situational communication styles in decision making.

MODEL 8.1   Leadership Decision Making

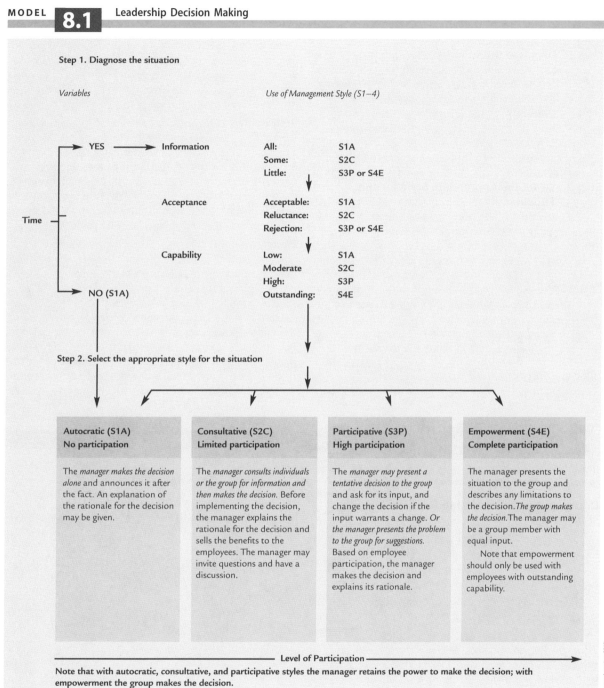

Step 1. Diagnose the situation

Variables   Use of Management Style (S1–4)

Time

YES ———▶ Information

All:	S1A
Some:	S2C
Little:	S3P or S4E

Acceptance

Acceptable:	S1A
Reluctance:	S2C
Rejection:	S3P or S4E

Capability

Low:	S1A
Moderate	S2C
High:	S3P
Outstanding:	S4E

NO (S1A)

Step 2. Select the appropriate style for the situation

Autocratic (S1A)
No participation

The *manager makes the decision alone* and announces it after the fact. An explanation of the rationale for the decision may be given.

Consultative (S2C)
Limited participation

The *manager consults individuals or the group for information and then makes the decision.* Before implementing the decision, the manager explains the rationale for the decision and sells the benefits to the employees. The manager may invite questions and have a discussion.

Participative (S3P)
High participation

The *manager may present a tentative decision to the group* and ask for its input, and change the decision if the input warrants a change. *Or the manager presents the problem to the group for suggestions.* Based on employee participation, the manager makes the decision and explains its rationale.

Empowerment (S4E)
Complete participation

The manager presents the situation to the group and describes any limitations to the decision. *The group makes the decision.* The manager may be a group member with equal input.

Note that empowerment should only be used with employees with outstanding capability.

————————————— **Level of Participation** ————————————▶

Note that with autocratic, consultative, and participative styles the manager retains the power to make the decision; with empowerment the group makes the decision.

Using the Leadership Decision-Making Model

We will apply the model to the following situation; additional similar situations are presented later with the skill-development exercise.

Manager Ben can give one of his followers a merit pay raise. He has a week to make the decision. Ben knows how well each employee performed over the past year. The followers really have no option but to accept getting or not getting the pay raise, but they can complain to upper management about the selection. The followers' capability levels vary, but as a group they have a high capability level under normal circumstances.

—— time —— information —— acceptance —— capability

Leadership style _____

Step 1 **Diagnose the situation.** Ben has plenty of time to use any level of participation (place a Y for yes on the "time" line below the situation). He has all the information needed to make the decision (place S1A on the "information" line). Followers have no choice but to accept the decision (place S1A on the "acceptance" line). And the group's capability level is normally high (place S3P on the "capability" line).

Step 2 **Select the Appropriate Style for the Situation.** There are conflicting styles to choose from (autocratic and participative): yes time; S1A information; S1A acceptance; S3P capability.

The variable that should be given precedence is information. The followers are normally capable, but in a situation like this they may not put the department's goals ahead of their own. In other words, even if followers know who deserves the raise, they may fight for it anyway. Such a conflict could cause future problems. Some ways to make the decision could include the following:

Autocratic (S1A). The manager would select the person to be given the raise without discussing it with any followers.

Ben would simply announce the decision after submitting it to the payroll department.

Consultative (S2C). The manager would get information from the followers concerning who should get the raise. Ben would then decide who would get the raise. He would announce the decision and explain the rationale for it. He may invite questions and discussion.

Participative (S3P). The manager could tentatively select the employee who gets the raise, but be open to change if a group member convinces him that someone else should. Or Ben could explain the situation to the group and lead a discussion concerning who should get the raise. After considering their input, Ben would make the decision and explain the rationale for it. Notice that the consultative style does not allow for discussion as the participative style does.

Empowerment (S4E). The manager would explain the situation and allow the group to decide who gets the raise. Ben may be a group member. Notice that this is the only style that allows the group to make the decision.

The autocratic style is appropriate for this situation. The consultative style is also a good approach. However, the participative and empowerment styles use too much participation for the situation. Your skill at selecting the appropriate decision-making leadership style should improve through using the model for the 10 situations in the skill-development exercise. However, the next step is to view the behavior video model.

Behavior Model Video 8.1 and Video Exercise

(Part II)

Deciding Which Leadership Decision-Making Style to Use

Objectives
To better understand the four leadership decision-making styles, and to select the most appropriate style for a given situation.

Video (*13 minutes*) Overview
The video begins by telling you how to use the model. Then it shows the human resources director, Richard, meeting with a supervisor, Denise, to discuss training changes. Each of the four styles is shown to illustrate how all four styles can be used in the same situation. Thus, you gain a better understanding of the four styles. During the video you will be asked to identify each of the four styles being used by Richard. The answers will be given by your instructor during or at the end of the video. In viewing the video, you should also realize that some styles are more appropriate than others for this situation. As a class, you may discuss which style would be the most effective, and at the end of the video, the recommended style is stated.

Preparation
You should have read the "Leadership Decision-Making Model" section of this leadership behavior-modeling skills training.

Procedure 1 (*10–20 minutes*) The instructor shows (or you view on your own) the video, "Decision Making." As you view each of the four scenes, identify the four leadership decision-making styles being used by Richard. Write the letters and number of the style on the line after each scene.

Scene 1. _____ Autocratic (S1A)

Scene 2. _____ Consultative (S2C)

Scene 3. _____ Participative (S3P)

Scene 4. _____ Empowerment (S4E)

Option A: View all four scenes and identify the style used by Richard. Select the one style that you would use in this situation. Are other styles also appropriate? Which style would you not use (is not appropriate) for this situation? Next to each style listed above, write the letter "a" for appropriate or "n" for not appropriate. After everyone is finished the instructor leads a class discussion and/or gives the correct answers.

Option B: After each scene the class discusses the style used by Richard. The instructor states the correct answer after each of the four scenes. Then discuss which style is the most effective for the situation.

Option C: Simply view the entire video without any discussion.

Conclusion

The instructor may lead a class discussion and/or make concluding remarks.

Developing Your Leadership Skills **1**

(Parts III & IV)

Deciding Which Leadership Decision-Making Style to Use

Preparation for This Exercise

Below are 10 situations calling for a decision. Select the appropriate decision-making style for each. Be sure to use Model 8.1 when determining the style to use. First determine the answers to the variables (S1A, S2C, S3P, S4E) and write them on the lines below the situation. Then place the selected style on the "Leadership style" line.

S1A autocratic   S2C consultative

S3P participative   S4E empowerment

1. You have developed a new work procedure that will increase productivity. Your boss likes the idea and wants you to try it in a few weeks. You view your followers as fairly capable, and believe that they will be receptive to the change.

  ___ time ___ information ___ acceptance ___ capability

Leadership style _____

2. There is new competition in your industry. Your organization's revenues have been dropping. You have been told to lay off 3 of your 15 followers in two weeks. You have been supervisor for over three years. Normally, your followers are very capable.

  ___ time ___ information ___ acceptance ___ capability

Leadership style _____

3. Your department has been facing a problem for several months. Many solutions have been tried and have failed. You've finally thought of a solution, but you're not sure of the possible consequences of the change required, or of acceptance by your highly capable followers.

  ___ time ___ information ___ acceptance ___ capability

Leadership style _____

4. Flextime has become popular in your organization. Some departments let each employee start and end work when he or she chooses. However, because of the cooperation required of your followers, they must all work the same eight hours. You're not sure of the level of interest in changing the hours. Your followers are a very capable group and like to make decisions.

  ___ time ___ information ___ acceptance ___ capability

Leadership style _____

5. The technology in your industry is changing too fast for the members of your organization to keep up. Top management hired a consultant who has made recommendations. You have two weeks to decide what to do about the recommendations. Your followers are usually capable; they enjoy participating in the decision-making process.

  ___ time ___ information ___ acceptance ___ capability

Leadership style _____

6. Top management has handed down a change. How you implement it is your decision. The change takes effect in one month. It will affect everyone in your department. Their acceptance is critical to the success of the change. Your followers are usually not interested in making routine decisions.

  ___ time ___ information ___ acceptance ___ capability

Leadership style _____

7. Your boss called to tell you that someone requested an order for your department's product; the delivery date is very short. She asked you to call her back in 15 minutes with a decision about taking the order. Looking over the work schedule, you realize that it will be very difficult to deliver the order on time. Your followers will have to push hard to make it. They are cooperative, capable, and enjoy being involved in decision making.

___ time ___ information ___ acceptance ___ capability

Leadership style _____

8. Top management has decided to make a change that will affect all of your followers. You know that they will be upset because it will cause them hardship. One or two may even quit. The change goes into effect in 30 days. Your followers are very capable.

___ time ___ information ___ acceptance ___ capability

Leadership style _____

9. You believe that productivity in your department could be increased. You have thought of some ways to increase it, but you're not sure of them. Your followers are very experienced; almost all of them have been in the department longer than you have.

___ time ___ information ___ acceptance ___ capability

Leadership style _____

10. A customer offered you a contract for your product with a quick delivery date. The offer is open for two days. To meet the contract deadline, followers would have to work nights and weekends for six weeks. You cannot require them to work overtime. Filling this profitable contract could help get you the raise you want and feel you deserve. However, if you take the contract and don't deliver on time, it will hurt your chances of getting a big raise. Your followers are very capable.

___ time ___ information ___ acceptance ___ capability

Leadership style _____

Doing This Exercise in Class

Objective

To develop your skill at knowing which level of participation to use in a given decision-making situation. You will learn to use the leadership decision-making model.

The primary AACSB learning standard skills developed through this exercise are leadership, analytic skills, and teamwork.

Experience

You will try to select the appropriate decision-making style for each of 10 situations in preparation for this exercise.

Preparation

You should have completed the preparation for this exercise, unless told not to do so by your instructor. There is an option to do the preparation in class as part of the exercise.

Procedure 1 *(8–12 minutes)* The instructor may review the leadership decision-making model (Model 8.1) and will explain how to use it to select the appropriate leadership style for the first situation.

Procedure 2 *(4–8 minutes)* Students, working alone, complete situation 2 using the model, followed by the instructor going over the recommend answers. If the instructor will be testing you on leadership decision making, you may be told the details.

Procedure 3 *(10–20 minutes)* Break into teams of two or three. Apply the model to situations 3 through 5 as a team. You may decide to change your original answers. The instructor goes over the recommended answers and scoring for situations 3 through 5. Your instructor may tell you not to continue on to situation 6 until he or she goes over the answers to situations 3 through 5.

Procedure 4 *(10–20 minutes)* In the same teams, select decision-making styles for situations 6 through 10. The instructor will go over the recommended answers and scoring.

Conclusion

The instructor may lead a class discussion and/or make concluding remarks.

Apply It *(2–4 minutes)* What did I learn from this experience? How will I use this knowledge in the future? Identify when you will practice this skill.

_____

_____

_____

Sharing

In the group, or to the entire class, volunteers may give their answers to the "Apply It" questions.

Developing Your Leadership Skills **2**

Individual Versus Group Decision Making

Preparation for This Exercise

To complete this exercise you must answer the questions in Concept Applications 1 through 4 in the chapter.

Doing This Exercise in Class

Objective

To compare individual and group decision making, to better understand when to use a group to make decisions

The primary AACSB learning standard skills developed through this exercise are analytic skills and teamwork.

Preparation

As preparation, you should have answered the questions in Concept Applications 1 through 4.

Experience

You will work in a group, each member of which will answer the same 20 questions, and then analyze the results to determine if the group or one (or more) of its members had the higher score.

Procedure 1 *(1–2 minutes)* Place your answers to the 20 questions in the "Individual Answer" column in the table on page 320.

Procedure 2 *(15–20 minutes)* Break into teams of five, with smaller or larger groups as necessary. As a group, come to an agreement on the answers to the 20 questions. Place the group answers in the "Group Answer" column. Try to use consensus rather than voting or majority in arriving at the answers.

Procedure 3 *(4–6 minutes)* **Scoring.** The instructor will give the recommended answers. Determine how many you got right as an individual and as a group. Total your individual and the group's score.

Compute the *average* individual score by adding all the individual scores and dividing by the number of group members. Write it here: _____.

Now calculate the difference between the average individual score and the group score. If the group's score is higher

than the average individual score, you have a gain (+) of points; if the group score is lower, you have a loss (−) of points. Write it here, _____ and circle one (+ or −).

Determine the highest individual score. Write it here: _____.

Determine the number of individuals who scored higher than the group's score: _____.

Procedure 4 *(5–10 minutes)* **Integration.** As a group, discuss the advantages or disadvantages of being in a group while making the decisions in this exercise. Go back to the text and review the advantages and disadvantages of team-centered decision making listed on pages 295–296 and discuss. Then try to agree on which of the advantages and disadvantages your group had.

Overall, were the advantages of using a group greater than the disadvantages? If your group were to continue to work together, how could it improve its decision-making ability? Write your answer below.

_____

_____

_____

Conclusion

The instructor may lead a class discussion and/or make concluding remarks.

Apply It *(2–4 minutes)* What did I learn from this experience? How will I use this knowledge in the future? Specifically, what will I do the next time I'm in a group to help it make better decisions? When will I have the opportunity?

_____

_____

_____

Sharing

In the group, or to the entire class, volunteers may give their answers to the "Apply It" questions.

Question Number	Individual Answer	Group Answer	Recommended Answer	Individual Score	Group Score
CA 1: 1					
2					
3					
4					
5					
CA 2: 6					
7					
8					
9					
10					
CA 3: 11					
12					
13					
14					
15					
CA 4: 16					
17					
18					
19					
20					
Total scores					

PART THREE

ORGANIZATIONAL LEADERSHIP

9

Charismatic and Transformational Leadership

Learning Outcomes

After studying this chapter, you should be able to:

1. Briefly explain Max Weber's conceptualization of charisma. p. 324

2. Explain what is meant by the statement "locus of charismatic leadership." p. 325

3. Discuss the effects of charismatic leadership on followers. p. 326

4. Discuss how one can acquire charismatic qualities. p. 328

5. Explain the difference between socialized and personalized charismatic leaders. p. 329

6. Explain the difference between transformational and transactional leadership. p. 332

7. Explain the four stages of the transformation process. p. 334

8. List the qualities of effective charismatic and transformational leaders. p. 336

9. Describe the four behavior dimensions associated with transformational and charismatic leader behaviors. p. 340

10. Distinguish between charismatic and transformational leadership. p. 342

11. Explain the basis of stewardship and servant leadership. p. 345

12. Define the following **key terms** (in order of appearance in the chapter):

socialized charismatic leader (SCL)

personalized charismatic leader (PCL)

transactional leadership

vision

personal meaning

stewardship

servant leadership

OPENING CASE APPLICATION

The last episode of *The Oprah Winfrey Show* aired on Wednesday, May 25, 2011. The price for a 30-second commercial spot on the finale was $1 million, the rate usually charged for a prime-time spot. *The Oprah Winfrey Show* has been a top-rated program for 25 years, a record unmatched in TV history.

With over 30,000 guests and a million studio audience members, Oprah and her show have garnered 48 Emmys, among other awards and accolades. According to *Forbes*, her personal net worth is roughly $2.7 billion.[1]

Of all the TV celebrities we know, Oprah had the largest audience of trusted followers who listened and believed so strongly in everything she said. The question for many researchers was: why? Adam Hanft, CEO of marketing firm Hanft Projects responded this way, "Oprah's got a magical combination of extraordinary personal charisma, a telepresence, a back story that's full of high drama and suffering and triumph, and an ability to open herself up or appear to be very much willing to expose that. And the empathetic bond that's been created as a result is appealing and enduring."[2] Oprah's charisma is seen in the way she has influenced so many people and opinions. It seems everything she touched or mentioned became a household name. Her endorsements made the fortunes of housewives, authors, singers or even presidential candidates. She built schools and rescued abused children. As one writer puts it, Oprah could move from high literature to lowly undergarments in a heartbeat.[3]

Oprah, who is now 57, will take a more active role in her business empire, which includes her fledgling cable network, OWN (Oprah Winfrey Network), her popular magazine, *O*, and her satellite show *Oprah & Friends* on XM Satellite Radio. OWN is a 50-50 venture between Ms. Winfrey and Discovery Communications.

Oprah's legacy has established her as one of the most important figures in popular culture. Through her television, publishing, and film endeavors, Oprah will continue to entertain, enlighten, and empower millions of viewers around the world. She closed her last episode with these words: "I won't say goodbye. I'll just say 'until we meet again.' To God be the glory."

OPENING CASE QUESTIONS:

1. Why was Oprah (and possibly still is) such a popular and admired figure on TV?

2. What is the locus of Oprah's charisma?

3. What effects has Oprah's charisma had on her followers?

4. Does Oprah embody the example of a socialized charismatic leader or a personalized charismatic leader?

5. What qualities of charismatic leadership does Oprah possess?

6. Is Oprah a transformational leader, a charismatic leader, or both?

7. Oprah seems to have a clear sense of her personal meaning or purpose in life. What factors do you think have contributed to her understanding?

Can you answer any of these questions? You'll find answers to these questions and learn more about Oprah Winfrey's businesses and leadership style throughout the chapter.

To learn more about Oprah Winfrey, visit her Web site at **http://www.oprah.com**.

The last 20 years have witnessed a renewed interest in and scholarship focus on charismatic and transformational leadership. This growth in interest has coincided with significant geopolitical, social, and economic changes. Much higher levels of environmental turbulence, uncertainty, and global competition characterize today's work environment.

The challenge many institutions face is how to cope with these changes so they will survive and prosper. Organizations are faced with the need to adapt or perish. Adaptation requires that organizations learn to do things differently, such as the need to transform internal cultures and structures, empower organizational members, develop new technologies/products, eliminate boundaries, and inspire followers. Charismatic and transformational leadership are appropriately suited to these challenges.

Charismatic and transformational theories return our focus to organizational leadership. These theories shine the light on exemplary leaders whose influence impacts entire social, cultural, economic, and political systems. Charismatic and transformational leaders are able to influence followers to rally towards a shared goal/s. They generate emotion, energy, and excitement that cause followers to make significant personal sacrifices in the interest of the organization.

In this chapter, we will start by discussing charismatic leadership; second, we will discuss transformational leadership; third, we will take an integrated perspective where we examine issues common to both charismatic and transformational leadership; and finally, we will briefly explore the related topics of stewardship and servant leadership.

OPENING CASE APPLICATION

1. Why was Oprah (and possibly still is) is such a popular and admired figure on TV?

Oprah possesses the charisma and transformational qualities alluded to above. She has already left an indelible mark on the face of television. She has used her celebrity status to push for social change in our society. She has championed the cause for child abuse, poverty, domestic violence, illiteracy, and much more. Her audience represents a cross-section of the American ethnic landscape. As supervising producer and host of *The Oprah Winfrey Show*, Oprah has entertained, enlightened, and empowered millions of viewers not just in the United States, but around the world.

Charismatic Leadership

Charismatic leadership has generally been defined in terms of the effects the leader has on followers, or in terms of the relationship between leaders and followers. This section discusses the following topics: Max Weber's conceptualization of charisma, the locus of charismatic leadership, the effects of charismatic leaders on followers, how anyone can develop charismatic qualities, and the notion of charisma as a double-edged sword.

Learning Outcome 1   *Briefly explain Max Weber's conceptualization of charisma.*

Weber's Conceptualization of Charisma

The Greek word *charisma* means "divinely inspired gift." Like the term *leadership* itself, charisma has been defined from various organizational perspectives by researchers studying political leadership, social movements, and religious cults. Of the early theories of charisma, the sociologist Max Weber made what is probably the single most important contribution. Weber used the term "charisma" to explain a form of influence based not on traditional or legal–rational authority systems but rather on follower perceptions that a leader is endowed with the gift of divine inspiration or supernatural qualities.[4]

WORK Application 1
Think of a leader from your work experience or education whom you believe has charisma. Explain why.

_____

_____

_____

_____

Charisma has been called "a fire that ignites followers' energy and commitment, producing results above and beyond the ordinary."[5] Weber saw in a charismatic leader someone who single-handedly visualizes a transcendent mission or course of action that is not only appealing to potential followers, but compels them to act on it because they believe the leader is extraordinarily gifted.[6] Other attributes of charisma identified in the political and sociological literature include acts of heroism, an ability to inspire and build confidence, espousing of revolutionary ideals, oratorical ability, and a "powerful aura."[7]

Charisma is relational in nature. It is not something found solely in the leader as a psychological phenomenon, nor is it totally situation determined. Instead, charisma manifests itself in the interplay between the leader (his or her traits and behaviors) and the follower (his or her values, needs, perceptions, and beliefs).

Combining these attributes with relational dynamics between leaders and followers offers a richer perspective of this phenomenon. From this perspective, we define **charisma** as *a social construct between the leader and follower, in which the leader offers a transformative vision or ideal which exceeds the status quo and then convinces followers to accept this course of action not because of its rational likelihood of success, but because of their implicit belief in the extraordinary qualities of the leader*[8]

Learning Outcome 2   *Explain what is meant by the statement "locus of charismatic leadership."*

Locus of Charismatic Leadership

Over the years, researchers from different disciplines have examined and debated Weber's early conceptualization of charismatic leadership. Perhaps the most intense debate has been on the locus of charismatic leadership. The locus of charismatic leadership focuses on one question: what is the basis of charisma? This question centers on the debate over whether charisma is primarily the result of:

- The situation or social climate facing the leader
- The leader's extraordinary qualities
- A combination of the situation and the leader's qualities

There are those who believe that charismatic leadership could not take place unless the society was in a state of crisis. For those sharing this viewpoint, the charismatic leader is simply an opportunist who capitalizes on a crisis situation. Proponents of this view argue that before an individual with extraordinary qualities could be perceived as a charismatic leader, the social situation must be such that followers would recognize the need for the leader's qualities. The sociological literature, led by Weber, supports this viewpoint, emphasizing that charismatic leadership is born out of stressful situations. Under stressful situations, charismatic leaders are able to express sentiments that are different from the established order, and deeply felt by followers. Advocates of this position would then argue that neither Martin Luther King, Jr., Nelson Mandela, Adolph Hitler, nor Gandhi would have emerged as charismatic leaders without the prevailing socioeconomic and political crises in their respective countries.

On the other hand, there are those who argue that charisma need not be born out of distress but rather that charisma is primarily the result of leader attributes as seen by their followers. These attributes include a strong sense of vision, exceptional communication skills, strong conviction, trustworthiness, high self-confidence and intelligence, and high energy and action orientation. Advocates of this position would argue that none of the leaders mentioned above would have earned the label of charisma if they did not possess these qualities, regardless of the situation.[9]

Finally, there are those who believe that charismatic leadership does not depend on the leader's qualities or the presence of a crisis alone, but rather that it is the combination of the two. There is growing acceptance of this viewpoint. Most theorists now view charisma as the result of follower attributions, influenced not only by actual leader characteristics and behavior but also by the context of the situation. The next section discusses the effects of charismatic leadership on individuals and organizations.

OPENING CASE *APPLICATION*

2. What is the locus of Oprah's charisma?

The locus of Oprah's charisma can be attributed to her extraordinary qualities rather than to any external factor(s) in her environment. "Knowledge is power! With knowledge you can soar and reach as high as your dreams can take you," said Oprah. This belief has guided Oprah Winfrey on her brilliant journey from a troubled youth to international fame. Oprah Gail Winfrey was born in Kosciusko, Mississippi. Oprah lived with her grandmother until age 6, when she moved to Milwaukee to live with her mother, Vernita Lee. At the age of 9 she was sexually abused by a teenage cousin. Over the next five years, she was molested several times by a family friend and once by her uncle. She became a rebellious child and was reportedly headed toward juvenile detention. Fortunately, at the age of 14, she went to live with her father, Vernon Winfrey, a strict disciplinarian. This, she said, was the turning point in her life. Oprah Winfrey is a success story that the everyday person can relate to. She is an effective communicator and a passionate individual. She has the ability to inspire trust and loyalty. Her personal story is inspirational and pulls people in to form strong emotional bonds with her.

Learning Outcome 3

Discuss the effects of charismatic leadership on followers.

The Effects of Charismatic Leaders on Followers

An area of interest for many scholars of charisma concerns the effects that charismatic leadership has on follower motivations, job performance, and satisfaction, as well as on an organization's overall performance.[10]

Followers of charismatic leaders often develop a *strong sense of trust and bonding* with the leader that is hard to find in other leader–follower relationships.[11] The relationship between the charismatic leader and the followers is comparable to that of disciples to a master. Such a strong emotional bond is possible because the charismatic leader is believed to have the power to effect radical change by virtue of his or her transcendent vision—one that is different from the status quo. Followers stay with the charismatic leader, not out of fear or monetary inducement, but out of love, passionate devotion, trust, and commitment. There is the effect of *unconditional acceptance* of the charismatic leader by his followers that is not often seen with other types of leaders. Charismatic leaders are seen as generally more positive in their personality than noncharismatic leaders. This type of positiveness and the leader's capacity to spread it has an effect on followers. Followers develop a *strong sense of self-confidence and self-efficacy in realizing the leader's vision.* When this happens, a positive atmosphere permeates the organization and fuels excitement and energy for the leader's cause. Some scholars have found that this sentiment ultimately *increases followers' organizational citizenship behavior.*[12]

Followers of charismatic leaders tend to assume *greater risk* than they would with other types of leaders. Followers are willing to suffer whatever fate awaits the charismatic leader as he or she fights to change the status quo. They have absolute trust in the leader and his or her cause.[13] *There is an unquestioning loyalty and obedience to the leader.* This was the case with Gandhi and Martin Luther King Jr.'s followers, as they fought to bring about equality and freedom for all.

Another effect of charismatic leadership on followers is to motivate them *to set or aim for higher goals* and have greater confidence in their ability to achieve such goals.[14] By observing the leader display self-confidence, followers develop self-confidence as well. The charismatic leader is seen as an object of identification by followers who try to emulate his or her behavior. When the character of the leader is grounded on such core

WORK Application **2**

Refer back to Work Application 1 on the leader you thought has charisma. Briefly discuss examples of the effect his or her charisma had on your work ethic, job performance or job satisfaction.

values as integrity, hard work, responsibility, respect, and accountability, it has an effect on followers who already *desire to align their beliefs, self-concept, cognitions, and values with those of their leader*. We are all aware of business leaders—such as Steve Jobs (Apple), Richard Branson (the Virgin Group), and Mark Zuckerburg (Facebook)—who command an extraordinary level of respect and affection from their followers. The effect of the leader's character on followers is seen by some as more critical than charisma itself.

At the organizational level, there is an ongoing debate in academic circles about charismatic CEOs and organizational performance.[15] The question is whether charismatic CEOs achieve better organizational performance than their less charismatic counterparts. The results are mixed; some studies revealed that charismatic leadership showed a positive relationship to profit.[16] There are also those who say a charismatic leader may indeed make the organization more attractive to outside stakeholders such as investors, customers, suppliers, and activists groups. Exhibit 9.1 summarizes these effects.

EXHIBIT 9.1   The Effects of Charismatic Leaders on Followers

a. Inspires trust in the "rightness" of the leader's vision and a strong bond
b. Unconditional acceptance of the leader
c. Increased self-confidence and self-efficacy
d. Acceptance of higher or challenging goals
e. Increase in followers' organizational citizenship behavior
f. Tendency of followers to assume greater risks
g. Strong loyalty and obedience to the leader
h. Motivation to set or aim for higher goals
i. Follower desire to align their beliefs, self-concept, cognitions, and values with those of the leader.

Source: Based on R. J. House, and M. L. Baetx (1979). "Leadership: Some Empirical Generalizations and New Research Directions." In B. M. Staw (Ed.), *Research in Organizational behavior*, vol. 1 (Greenwich, CT: JAI Press, 1979), 399–401.

OPENING CASE *APPLICATION*

3. **What effects has Oprah's charisma had on her followers?**

The effects of charismatic leadership summarized in Exhibit 9.1 are very much applicable to Oprah and her followers. Oprah's followers and supporters seem to have an unquestioning loyalty to her and all that she stands for. There is a strong affection and unconditional acceptance of her, and a willingness to trust in the "rightness" of whatever cause she champions. For example, in a 1997 episode of *The Oprah Winfrey Show*, Oprah encouraged viewers to use their lives to make a difference in the lives of others, which led to the creation of the public charity Oprah's Angel Network in 1998. To date, Oprah's Angel Network has raised more than $30 million, with 100 percent of audience donations going to nonprofit organizations across the globe. Oprah's Angel Network has helped establish scholarships and schools, support women's shelters, and build youth centers and homes—changing the future for people all over the world. As John Grace, executive director of Interbrand Group, a New York–based brand consultant, puts it, "Oprah stands for a certain set of very specific American values that very few of her celebrity competitors can claim, like honesty, loyalty, and frankness. It's a value set that is rare in business institutions and celebrities."

CONCEPT APPLICATION 1
The Effects of Charismatic Leaders on Followers

Referring to the characteristics listed in Exhibit 9.1 on page 327, identify each statement by its characteristic using the letters a–i.

_____ 1. In our church, the relationship between some members and the pastor is comparable to that of disciples to a master. These followers obey every instruction he utters.

_____ 2. The members of the church referred to in No. 1 above believe that the pastor has the power to effect radical change by virtue of his transcendent vision, which is different from the status quo.

_____ 3. Our leader, who is very charismatic, has somehow convinced every one of us that we can do anything if only we believe in ourselves.

_____ 4. Your friend tells you that she is very uncomfortable with some of the comments her CEO makes about gays and minorities but does not want to say anything because of her strong commitment to his overall mission.

_____ 5. The commercial Nike ran a few years ago with the tagline "I want to be like Mike." To which effect of charismatic leadership on followers does this apply?

Learning Outcome 4   *Discuss how one can acquire charismatic qualities.*

How One Acquires Charismatic Qualities

There are those who believe that charisma is inborn and cannot be trained into someone. However, there are also those who believe that charismatic qualities can be acquired—that everyone has the potential to develop charismatic qualities. It is possible through training to improve one's communication skills, build self-confidence, and learn techniques to inspire others. There have been great charismatic leaders who did not reveal their charismatic qualities until much later in life. Hitler certainly was not born with charismatic qualities. He was living life on the fringes of society and failed in most of his early endeavors. However, gradually he developed his oratorical and interpersonal skills when he had the opportunity to influence others of like-minded thinking. Richard Branson (CEO and Founder of the Virgin Group Corp) and Jack Welch (former CEO of GE) are two very effective leaders who have been described as charismatic and transformational; yet they both overcame stuttering, a speech impediment that causes many others to avoid public speaking. In fact, the best picture in the 2011 Oscar awards ceremony went to *The King's Speech*, a movie about the King of England who had a terrible speech impediment; only through the help of a speech coach did he overcome this weakness. He became an effective speaker and gave some inspiring speeches during World War II.

Nelson Mandela, John F. Kennedy, and Martin Luther King, Jr., on the other hand, seemed to have had charismatic qualities early on as young adults. Suggested strategies for acquiring or enhancing one's charismatic qualities include:

- Through training and practice, you can improve your communication skills. A coach or speech therapist can help you overcome a speech impediment such as stuttering that may be hindering you from communicating effectively.

- Through education, you can develop your visionary skills by practicing the act of creating a vision in a college course like this one. The role-play exercise at the end of this chapter is directed at this issue.

WORK Application **3**
Identify a leader you have worked with or currently work with whom you think has charismatic potential. Describe one trait or characteristic of this individual that, if developed, can transform him or her into an effective charismatic leader.

_____

_____

_____

_____

- You can practice being candid. Although not insensitive, the charismatic person is typically forthright in giving his or her assessment of a situation, whether the assessment is positive or negative. Charismatic leaders are direct in their approach, so that there is no ambiguity about their position on issues.

- You can develop an enthusiastic, optimistic, and energetic personality. A major behavior pattern of charismatic leaders is their combination of enthusiasm, optimism, and a high energy level. As mentioned earlier, charisma is a relational concept and ultimately comes from the attributions of followers.

Learning Outcome 5 | *Explain the difference between socialized and personalized charismatic leaders.*

Charisma: A Double-Edged Sword

Most people agree that charisma can be a double-edged sword capable of producing both positive and negative outcomes. It is possible in reading about the personal magnetism, vision, self-confidence, masterful rhetorical skills, and empowering style of charismatic leaders to conclude that they are all good moral leaders whom others should emulate. We live in a society where hero worship is a common occurrence. It is foolish and even dangerous to follow a leader just because he/she is charismatic. Leaders such as Gandhi, Martin Luther King, Jr., John F. Kennedy, and Winston Churchill exhibited tremendous charisma.[17] So did leaders such as Osama bin Laden, Charles Manson, David Koresh, Adolph Hitler, and the Reverend Jim Jones of the People's Temple. This latter group of charismatic leaders represents the dark side of charisma.[18] These leaders and many others like them are prone to extreme narcissism that leads them to promote highly self-serving and grandiose goals.[19, 20] Therefore, charisma can cut both ways; it is not always used in the service of a greater good.

One method for differentiating between positive and negative charisma is in terms of the values and personality of the leader. Values research proposes that two opposing but complementary motives drive an individual's behavior: self-glorification and self-transcendence. The self-glorification motive is about the self-maintenance and self-enhancement of the leader. It seeks to protect, maintain, and enhance the leader's self-esteem and is consistent with negative or destructive charisma.[21,22] On the other hand, the self-transcendence motive is about the collective interest or good of the broader society. It seeks to build mutually supportive relationships with followers and is consistent with altruistic and empowering orientations of positive or constructive charisma.

Based on this concept of positive and negative charisma, two types of charismatic leaders are identified: the socialized or positive charismatic leader and the personalized or negative charismatic leader.[23] The **socialized charismatic leader (SCL)** *is one who possesses an egalitarian, self-transcendent, and empowering personality and uses charisma for the benefit of others.*[24] The **personalized charismatic leader (PCL)** *is one who possesses a dominant, self-centered, self-aggrandizing and narcissistic personality and uses charisma for self-glorification.* The PCL has a tendency to be exploitative. SCLs pursue organization-driven goals and promote feelings of empowerment, personal growth, and equal participation for followers; PCLs pursue leader-driven goals and promote feelings of obedience, dependency, and submission.[25] With socialized charismatic leaders, rewards are used to reinforce behavior that is consistent with the vision and mission of the organization; personalized charismatic leaders use rewards and punishment to manipulate and control followers, and information is restricted or used to preserve the image of the leader or to exaggerate external threats to the organization. Socialized charismatic leaders tend to have followers who are part of a cohesive team. They convey a values-based message that aligns with the mission and objectives of the organization.[26]

WORK Application **4**

Describe a leader in your work experience who manifested positive or negative charismatic qualities. How did this affect your relationship with the leader?

_____

_____

_____

_____

Personalized or negative charismatic leaders emphasize devotion to themselves more than to ideals. Decisions of these leaders are often self-serving. Group accomplishments are used for self-glorification. Ideological appeals are only a ploy to gain power, after which the ideology is ignored or arbitrarily changed to serve the leader's self-interest. In contrast, socialized or positive charismatic leaders seek to instill devotion to ideology more than devotion to self.

OPENING CASE *APPLICATION*

4. **Does Oprah embody the example of a socialized charismatic leader or a personalized charismatic leader?**

Oprah's philanthropic activities and the way she conducts herself would suggest that she is more of a socialized than a personalized charismatic leader. As explained above, the socialized charismatic leader is driven by a self-transcendence motive. The self-transcendence motive focuses on collective interest, provides meaning through supportive relationships with others, and is consistent with altruistic and empowering orientations of positive or constructive charisma. The Oprah Winfrey Foundation was established to support the inspiration, empowerment, education, and well-being of women, children, and families around the world. Through this private charity, Oprah has directly served the needs of low-opportunity people and has awarded hundreds of grants to organizations that carry out this vision. She has contributed millions of dollars toward providing a better education for underserved students who have merit but no means. She created the "Oprah Winfrey Scholars Program," which gives scholarships to students determined to use their education to give back to their communities in the United States and abroad.

9.1 *Obesity and Charismatic Ads*

The federal government has reported that obesity might overtake tobacco as the leading cause of death in the United States.[27] Some social activists are blaming part of the obesity problem on marketing junk food to kids,[28] and food makers and ad agencies are defending advertising to children.[29] Some companies use charismatic star performers and athletes to promote their junk food products to get people to eat more. At the same time, American health officials are trying to persuade people to lose weight. The government has taken out public service ads to convince people to get in shape and eat right. Part of the ads' success depends on whether people take personal responsibility for their own health and weight.

1. What is the reason for the increase in obesity in the United States? Are junk food ads using charismatic stars to promote their products contributing to the obesity problem?

2. Is it ethical for junk food sellers to use charismatic stars to promote their products?

3. Is it ethical and socially responsible for the government to try to get people to lose weight, through ads and other methods?

CONCEPT APPLICATION 2
Socialized Versus Personalized Charismatic Leaders

Identify each statement as being more characteristic of one or the other type of charismatic leadership:

a. socialized charismatic leader

b. personalized charismatic leader ship

(continued)

(Concept Application 2 continued)

_____ 6. A leader whose primary motive is self-glorification.

_____ 7. A leader whose primary motive is to achieve collective interest through close supportive relationships with all followers.

_____ 8. A leader who is more interested in protecting, maintaining, and enhancing his or her self-image.

_____ 9. A leader who wants obedience, dependency, and submission from his followers.

_____ 10. When information is restricted and only used to preserve the image of the leader or to exaggerate external threats to the organization, it is an example of _____.

Transformational Leadership

J. M. Burns first articulated the idea of transformational leadership in 1978 before Bernard Bass expanded on it almost a decade later. Burns proposed two leadership approaches for getting work done: transactional or transformational.[30] The transformation label comes from the assessments of a leader's past performance rather than follower attributions (as is the case with charisma). Transformational leaders are known for moving and changing things "in a big way," by communicating to followers a special vision of the future, and like charismatic leaders, tapping into followers' higher ideals and motives. The transformational leader seeks to transform a weak or declining organization by influencing followers to buy into a new vision and new possibilities.

Effective transformational leaders know that to move forward, they must first earn the trust, commitment, and respect of followers. When this happens, the transformational leader is more likely to achieve a collective "buy-in" to his vision. Followers willingly expend exceptional effort in achieving organizational goals. For a definition, we maintain that the **transformational leadership** *seeks to change the status quo by articulating to followers the problems in the current system and a compelling vision of what a new organization could be;* transactional leadership *seeks to maintain stability within an organization through regular economic and social exchanges that achieve specific goals for both leaders and their followers.*

We will examine the effects of transformational leadership, differentiate between transactional and transformational leadership, and highlight key steps in the transformation process.

The Effects of Transformational Leadership

As organizations continue to face global challenges, there is ever greater need for leaders who can successfully craft and implement bold strategies that will transform or align the organization's strengths and weaknesses with emerging opportunities and threats. Increased volatility and uncertainty in the external environment is seen as one of the contributing factors for the emergence of transformational leadership. Transformational leadership describes a process of positive influence that changes and transforms individuals, organizations, and communities.

Transformational leader effects apply to entire organizations as well as to individual followers of the leader. Some studies have found that transformational leadership positively correlates with *higher organizational performance.*[31] In a study examining the interaction between organizational change, transformational leadership, and organizational performance, the authors found that transformational leadership is more strongly associated with perceptions of organizational performance when the organization under-takes high changes (i.e., many organizational adjustments) as opposed to low changes (i.e., few organizational adjustments).[32]

Transformational leader effects have also been associated with *positive changes in organizational culture and learning.*[33] The results of one study found that managers assuming a charismatic style of leadership tend to promote team innovation by creating a sense of team identity and commitment, and encouraging team members to cooperate through the sharing of ideas and participation in decisions.[34] As mentioned in Chapter 8, teams with a strong team identity combined with cooperative behaviors are more inno-vative. By encouraging teamwork, cooperation, and innovation, the transformational leader in effect, creates a learning culture.[35,36]

At the individual level, an effective transformational leader has the effect of influencing followers *to shift from a focus on self-interest to a focus on collective interests.* Effective transformational leaders use their charisma and power to inspire and motivate followers to *trust and follow the leader's example.* They generate *excitement and energy* by presenting a compelling vision of the future. Followers associated with transformational leaders report *higher levels of job satisfaction and greater commitment* to change implementation.[37]

Learning Outcome 6   *Explain the difference between transformational and transactional leadership.*

Transformational versus Transactional Leadership

Begin this section by completing Self-Assessment 1 to determine if you are more of a transactional or a transformational leader.

SELF-ASSESSMENT 1   **Are You More of a Transformational Leader?**

Complete the following questions based on how you will act (or have acted) in a typical work or school situation. Use the following scale:

1 — 2 — 3 — 4 — 5
Disagree   *Agree*

_____ 1. I enjoy change and see myself as a change agent.

_____ 2. I am better at inspiring employees toward a new future than motivating them to per-form their current jobs.

_____ 3. I have/had a vision of how an organization can change for the better.

_____ 4. I see myself as someone who is comfort-able encouraging people to express ideas and opinions that differ from my own.

_____ 5. I enjoy taking risks, but am not reckless.

_____ 6. I enjoy spending time developing new solutions to old problems rather than implementing existing solutions.

_____ 7. I deliberate carefully before acting; I'm not impulsive.

_____ 8. I like to support change initiatives, even when the idea may not work.

_____ 9. I learn from my experience; I don't repeat the same mistakes.

_____ 10. I believe the effort to change something for the better should be rewarded, even if the final outcome is disappointing.

Add up the numbers on lines 1–10 and place your total score here and on the continuum below.

10 — 20 — 30 — 40 — 50
Transactional leader   *Transformational leader*

The higher the score, generally, the more you exhibit transformational leader qualities. However, transforma-tional leaders also perform transactional behaviors. It is also generally easier to be transformational at higher levels of management than at lower levels.

Using Weber's seminal work on charismatic leaders as his foundation, Burns conceptualized that leadership occurs in one of two ways—transformational or transactional.[38] The transactional leadership process involves an exchange of valued benefits, based on the values and motivations of both leaders and followers. It therefore revolves around the leader–follower exchange (LMX) model, in which the leader rewards the follower for specific behaviors and performance that meets with the leader's expectations and punishes or criticizes behavior or performance that does not meet expectations.[39] Such exchanges represent defined contingent reward and punishment behaviors that mostly cater to the self-interest of the followers; transformational leadership inspires followers to go beyond self-interest and act for the broader interest of the organization.

Transformational leadership motivates followers by appealing to higher ideals and moral values. A study aimed at examining the effects of both transformational and transactional leadership behavior on followers' reported level of moral identity found that transformational leadership behavior has a larger positive effect on follower moral identity than does transactional leadership behavior.[40]

Some scholars refer to transactional leaders as "managers" and transformational leaders as "leaders." Supporters of this view point argue that leadership and management are not interchangeable. In their view, leadership is about having a vision, establishing long-term objectives and selecting strategies for achieving the objectives; while management is about operations at the execution/implementation level. It is more focused on short-term annual goals. It could be said that managers operationalize the leader's vision and long-term goals.[41] Transformational leaders are described as visionaries while transactional leaders are described as task- and reward-oriented.

The transformational leader wants to change the status quo by articulating to followers the problems in the current system and a compelling vision of what a new organization could be. The transactional leader enters into specific contractual arrangements with followers. In exchange for meeting specific objectives or performing certain duties, the leader provides benefits that satisfy followers' needs and desires.[42] As such the quality of the leader–follower relationship is critical.[43] Perceptions of fairness, justice, and trust in the leader play a critical role in defining the relationship. An example of transactional leadership occurs when managers give monthly bonuses to salespeople for meeting and exceeding their monthly sales quotas, or to production people for exceeding quality standards.

Transactional leadership tends to be transitory in that once a transaction is completed the relationship between the parties may end or be redefined. Transformational leadership is more enduring because the emphasis is on the long-term vision of the leader. Transactional leaders value stability, while transformational leaders value change, especially change that improves on the status quo.

Because of the attention paid to both charismatic and transformational leaders, the tendency for some has been to diminish the importance that transactional leaders have on organizational success. Recent studies, however, are revealing that transactional leadership, in the form of contingent reward and punishment behaviors, does have substantial effects on employee attitudes, perceptions, and job performance.[44] Transactional leadership behavior has been found to enhance follower outcomes such as organizational citizenship behavior, commitment, and trust in the leader.[45]

Bernard Bass argued that contrary to Burns's assertion that transformational and transactional leadership are at opposite ends of a single continuum of leadership, the two approaches are actually interdependent and complementary. A meta-analytic test of the relative validity of transformational and transactional leadership styles confirmed Bass's assertion. The study revealed that both are valid approaches for achieving organizational objectives, with transformational leadership showing the highest overall results and transactional or contingent reward

WORK Application 5

Identify a leader you have worked for or is working with now. In your opinion, is this leader more of a transformational or transactional leader? Explain why and include examples leadership a close second.[46,47] A related study examining the relationship between leadership and knowledge management found that both transformational and transactional leadership are positively related to an organization's knowledge management practices.[48]

CONCEPT APPLICATION 3
Transformational or Transactional Leadership

Identify each statement as being more characteristic of one or the other style:

a. transformational leadership   b. transactional leadership

_____ 11. I like to think that as a leader, I inspire my followers to focus on higher ideals rather than self-interest.

_____ 12. My vision is one that changes the status quo of this organization to something bigger and better.

_____ 13. I just want to maintain the steady progress we have been making.

_____ 14. My job is to fulfil specific contractual arrangements with my employees, one individual at a time.

_____ 15. We need to keep looking forward to new opportunities.

Learning Outcome 7   *Explain the four stages of the transformation process.*

The Transformation Process

Transformational leaders are usually brought into an organization that is experiencing a crisis or approaching total collapse, to institute turnaround strategies that can rescue the organization. This often involves fundamental changes in follower behaviors and work ethic. A successful transformation process involves broad participation among organizational stakeholders with the ultimate goal of embracing a shared vision, negotiating priorities, minimizing risk, and creating action plans and commitments for change.[49] It is not an ad hoc, serendipitous process. Here, we present a four-stage model that starts with the transformational leader's ability to (1) challenge the status quo and make a convincing case for change, (2) inspire a shared vision for the future, (3) provide effective leadership during the transition, and (4) institutionalized the change. Exhibit 9.2 presents the four stages of the transformation process with suggested activities in each stage.

EXHIBIT 9.2   **The Transformation Process**

Stages	Suggested Activities
1. Make a compelling case for change	Increase sensitivity to environmental changes and threats.
	Challenge the status quo.
	Identify emerging opportunities and threats.
2. Inspire a shared vision	Encourage everyone to think of a new and brighter future.
	Involve others in seeing and moving toward the vision.
	Express new vision in ideological, not just economic, terms.

EXHIBIT 9.2   The Transformation Process (continued)

Stages	Suggested Activities
3. Lead the transition	Instill a sense of urgency for the change.
	Empower, support, foster collaboration, and strengthen followers.
	Help followers understand need for change.
	Increase followers' self-confidence and optimism.
	Establish priorities.
	Minimize risk.
	Avoid the temptation of a "quick fix."
	Recognize and deal openly with conflict and resistance.
4. Implant the change	Enable and strengthen followers with a "greatness attitude"; for example, recognize and celebrate accomplishments.
	Help followers find self-fulfilment with new vision.
	Help followers look beyond self-interests to collective interests.
	Change appraisal procedures and reward systems.
	Implement team-building interventions and personnel changes.
	Appoint a special task force to monitor progress.
	Encourage top leaders and managers to model the way.

Source: Based on Carolyn Hines and William Hines Jr., "Seminar on the Essence of Transformational Leadership (Leadership Training Institute)," *Nation's Cities Weekly* 25(9) (March 4, 2002): 8.

YOU Make the ETHICAL Call

9.2   *Breach of Privacy*

Recent news that smart phone devices like the iPhone and iPad had been recording and retaining locational information generated a lot of anger from customers, privacy advocates, and government officials. There is great concern that keeping a detailed history of user's geographical locations without consent violates their privacy. Apple, the maker of these devices, argued that the purpose of maintaining a comprehensive location database is to ensure quicker and more precise location services to its iPhone and iPad customers.[50]

The dilemma for Apple is that while for some customers, privacy supersedes all other considerations, for others, location data provides the services they want and expect. For these users, finding the location of an appointment, a restaurant in a new part of town, or networking with a friend, the geo-location feature is a must-have. For others who worry about privacy, this feature could be a problem when, for example, an abusive spouse is involved or when an overzealous government agency can collect information on an individual without legal authorization like a search warrant. Both sides want the government and/or Apple to take steps to address their worries.[51]

1. Is it ethical for Apple to record and store location data for its customers without their consent?

2. What about the rights of those who want this location feature? What if taking out the location feature causes these customers to switch phone brands? Will this be fair to Apple?

3. In your opinion, what is the ethical thing for Apple to do?

Charismatic and Transformational Leadership—An Integrated Perspective

In the literature, both charismatic and transformational forms of leadership are frequently discussed from two separate but interrelated perspectives: in terms of the effects that these leaders have on followers, and in terms of the relationships that exist between them and their followers. Despite some obvious differences between charismatic and transformational leadership theories, there is much that is common between the two.[52] More often than not, the qualities that describe effective charismatic leaders are not different from those that describe effective transformational leaders. Also, the influencing behaviors of charismatic leaders are not that different from those of transformational leaders. For these reasons and more, this section takes an integrated perspective of the two theories. We examine the qualities of effectiveness common to leadership types, the leader behaviors they share in common, and what sets them apart.

Learning Outcome 8   *List the qualities of effective charismatic and transformational leaders.*

Qualities of Effective Charismatic and Transformational Leadership

Effective charismatic and transformational leaders share certain qualities. Exhibit 9.3 summarizes these qualities. Some of the qualities may have greater applicability to one leadership type and not the other; however, both share the majority of these qualities.

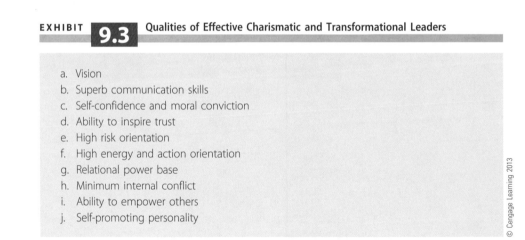

EXHIBIT 9.3   Qualities of Effective Charismatic and Transformational Leaders

a. Vision
b. Superb communication skills
c. Self-confidence and moral conviction
d. Ability to inspire trust
e. High risk orientation
f. High energy and action orientation
g. Relational power base
h. Minimum internal conflict
i. Ability to empower others
j. Self-promoting personality

© Cengage Learning 2013

Vision

Research has consistently emphasized the role of vision in charismatic and transformational leadership. Both leadership types articulate a transcendent vision that becomes the rallying cry of a movement or a cause. They have the ability to articulate an idealized vision of a future that is significantly better than the present. They quickly recognize fundamental discrepancies between the status quo and the way things can (or should) be. **Vision** *is the ability to imagine different and better conditions and the ways to achieve them.* A vision should uplift and attract followers. For this to happen, the process of crafting a vision must be a collaborative effort.[53] Both charismatic and transformational leaders lead the vision-formulation process by synthesizing seemingly disparate ideas, values, and problems from many sources (internal and external). They have a compelling vision of the future and are very passionate about it.

Superb Communication Skills

In addition to having a vision, charismatic and transformational leaders are known for their ability to communicate effectively.[54] In fact, this is one quality that sets charismatic leaders apart. Not only are they effective communicators, they are excellent orators when it comes to delivery of their message.[55] The charismatic leader's eloquent, imaginative, and passionate presentations awaken followers' desire for change and inspire them to embrace the leader's vision. Charismatic leaders use their superior rhetorical skills to stir dissatisfaction with the status quo while they build support for their vision of a new future. They employ rhetorical techniques such as metaphors, analogy, and stories to drive home their points so that their message will have a profound impact on followers. Fitting examples here include Martin Luther King, Jr.'s "I Have a Dream" speech, Hitler's "Thousand-year Reich," or Gandhi's vision of an India in which Hindus and Muslims live in harmony independent from British rule.[56]

Transformational leaders are able to make their case for change but not with the same passions and style known for charismatic leaders. Both leadership types are good at knowing what (facts) followers need to know, when (timing) they need to know, who (appropriate audience) needs to know, and where (media choice) the information needs to be for access. The distinction between the two leadership types often lies in how (oratorical ability) the information is delivered. Transformational leaders who are not very charismatic may use other means (written communication or a spokesperson) to communicate their ideas.

Self-Confidence and Moral Conviction

Charismatic and transformational leaders display an unshakable self-confidence and optimism as part of their persona. Charismatic leaders are, however, known to espouse messages of change that have religious and/or political overtones, thus emphasizing their strong faith and moral conviction in the message.[57] These qualities are critical in everyday interactions with followers, and all the more so for a leader who must convince others to join his or her cause.

Followers feel connected to leaders who are themselves optimistic and confident in the ultimate success of their mission. The leader's moral conviction in the rightness of his or her cause inspires followers' faith in the leader. Martin Luther King, Jr.'s "I Have a Dream" speech is an example of how a leader's self-confidence, faith, optimism, and strong moral conviction can inspire hope and faith in a better future, and move an entire nation.

Ability to Inspire Trust

Trust is critical in any relationship but even more so for transformational and charismatic leaders because of the magnitude of change they often present to their followers.[58] Constituents have to believe very strongly in the integrity of charismatic and transformational leaders to risk their careers, and even lives in some cases, for them. Charismatic and transformational leaders build support and trust by being honest with followers. Also, these leaders "talk the talk and walk the walk"; in other words, they model what they desire of their followers. This builds credibility with their followers and garners the support and cooperation of everyone. Effective charismatic and transformational leaders want to be role models to a new value system that is congruent with their articulations.

Gandhi represents an outstanding example of such systematic and intentional role modeling. He preached self-sacrifice, brotherly love, and nonviolent resistance to British rule. Repeatedly he engaged in self-sacrificing behaviors, such as giving up his lucrative law practice to live the life of a peasant, engaging in civil disobedience, fasting, and refusing to accept the ordinary conveniences offered to him by others.

High-Risk Orientation

Charismatic and transformational leaders are willing to take greater risk than the average leader. From a business standpoint, transformational leaders understand the risk/return relationship. They know that to earn high returns on any investment, one must take higher but calculated risks. Charismatic leaders on their part are willing to incur great personal risk to realize their objectives. The fearlessness of the charismatic leader romanticizes death as a real possibility. People admire the courage of those who take high risk. Putting themselves on the line is one way charismatic leaders affirm self-advocacy for their vision and thus gain the admiration and respect of their followers. It has been reported that Martin Luther King, Jr. received death threats against himself and his family almost every day during the civil rights movement. Yet, he persisted with his mission until his assassination.

In addition to assuming great risk, transformational and charismatic leaders use unconventional means to achieve success. Martin Luther King and his nonviolent campaign against angry violent opponents was a novel idea in the United States when he started. Contemporary examples of transformational leaders who have used unconventional methods to inspire followers include Herb Kelleher, former CEO of Southwest Airlines. Kelleher encouraged employees to break the rules, maintain their individuality, and have fun—a style he called "management by fooling around." It is a follower-centric style that has made Southwest Airlines employees the most productive in the industry. This is very similar to the laissez-faire approach employed by Richard Branson of Virgin Airlines.

High Energy and Action Orientation

All effective leaders share a tendency toward having high levels of energy and being always on the move. Charismatic and transformational leaders believe time is not on their side. They see urgency in the changes they want that demand higher levels of energy and action. Few people can match the daily routines of these leaders. Charismatic leaders in particular tend to be emotionally expressive, especially through nonverbal cues, such as warm gestures, movement, tone of voice, eye contact, and facial expressions. It is partly through nonverbal behavior that a charismatic leader is perceived to have a magnetic personality.

Relational Power Base

Effective leaders in general have close working relationships with followers. However, as mentioned earlier, a key part of charismatic leadership is the close emotional bond the leader has with followers.[59] Unlike other types of leadership, it is intensely relational and based almost entirely upon referent and expert power (Chapter 5), even when the leader occupies a formal organizational position. Followers are often in awe of the charismatic leader. There is a powerful identification with and emulation of such a leader and an unquestioning acceptance of and affection for him or her. The transformational leader's power source is typically positional and legitimate. They have reward and punishment power. However, effective transformational leaders do not rely solely on their positional power to influence followers; they try to develop close relations with their followers similar to the charismatic leader.

WORK Application 6

As part of your General Education Requirements, you have taken courses in the natural sciences, history, and literature. Identify a leader from any of these disciplines whom you believe was either a transformational or charismatic leader. How many of the qualities of charismatic and transformational leaders found in Exhibit 9.3, can you assign to your chosen leader?

_____

_____

_____

_____

Minimum Internal Conflict

Typically, charismatic and transformational leaders believe they are right in their vision and strategies for moving forward, which explains why they persist and stay the course, even through setbacks. Because of this conviction, they experience less internal guilt and discomfort even when faced with resistance and threats to themselves and their families.

Ability to Empower Others

Transformational and charismatic leaders understand that they cannot achieve their goals alone. They need help and support from their followers. They understand the need to empower followers to carry out necessary tasks. They do this by assigning followers to tasks that lead to successively greater positive experiences and self-confidence, thus persuading followers of their capabilities and creating an environment of positive emotions and heightened excitement.

Self-Promoting Personality

Even if no one will take up their cause, transformational and charismatic leaders are frequently out promoting themselves and their vision. Richard Branson and Donald Trump have relied on self-promotion to help build their business empires. These leaders are "not afraid to toot their own horn."

OPENING CASE APPLICATION

5. What qualities of charismatic leadership does Oprah possess?

"I am guided by the vision of what I believe this show can be. Originally our goal was to uplift, enlighten, encourage, and entertain through the medium of television. Now, our mission statement for _The Oprah Winfrey Show_ is to use television to transform people's lives, to make viewers see themselves differently and to bring happiness and a sense of fulfilment into every home." As seen in this quote, not only did Oprah have a vision for her show, she was and still is a superb communicator of this vision to her followers. She has self-confidence and a strong sense of moral conviction in everything she does. She has inspired and empowered millions of people through her show. She is of high energy and does not shy away from self-promotion. As revealed in the opening case, Oprah is described by those close to her as inspirational, brilliant, and personable. She is considered a sister by many of her key employees. She is one of the richest women in America; yet, she finds it hard to let all of her success go to her head. Oprah exemplifies all the qualities of charismatic and transformational leaders summarized in Exhibit 9.3 on page 336.

CONCEPT APPLICATION 4
Qualities of Effective Charismatic and Transformational Leaders

Referring to the characteristics listed in Exhibit 9.3 on on page 336, identify each statement by its characteristic using the letters a–j.

_____ 16. I see a future that is much better than the status quo. Let us grab the opportunity before it's too late.

_____ 17. As the leader of his fraternity, Justin has a way of using eloquent, imaginative, and passionate presentations to inspire his fraternity brothers.

_____ 18. Brooke has convinced each member of her cycling team that they have what it takes to win the Tour de France without resorting to using banned substances—i.e., dumping.

(continued)

(Concept Application 4 continued)

_____ 19. Jordan's honesty has had a significant impact on her followers; they seem to have more faith when it comes to following her directives.

_____ 20. Unlike her peer managers, Cullen has given his followers greater latitude and freedom in decisions affecting their jobs.

> **Learning Outcome 9** | *Describe the four behavior dimensions associated with transformational and charismatic leader behaviors.*

Transformational and Charismatic Leader Behaviors

To achieve their mission and objectives, transformational and charismatic leaders engage in a variety of behaviors.[60] Transformational leadership theory suggests that the leaders who are charismatic and transformational share some basic behaviors in common. This section focuses on some of these behaviors.

Bass and Avilio proposed that transformational leadership is composed of four behavior dimensions; they referred to them as the "four I's"—idealized influence, inspirational motivation, individual consideration, and intellectual stimulation.[61] The "four I's" can also play a role in explaining charismatic leader behaviors. The four behavior dimensions are discussed below.

- *Idealized influence (charisma)* is a fundamental factor in the transformation process. Transformational leaders with charisma possess the ability to develop great symbolic power that is then used to influence followers.[62] Followers idealize such a leader and often develop a strong emotional attachment. The charismatic and transformational leader engages in behavior that infuses followers with a strong sense of idealism.

- The second behavior dimension is *inspirational motivation*. Transformational and charismatic leaders tend to be inspirational individuals. Inspiration describes how the leader passionately communicates a future idealistic goal or situation that is a much better alternative to the status quo.[63] Both leadership types employ visionary explanations to depict what the work group can accomplish. Excited followers are then motivated and inspired to achieve challenging organizational goals. One study's findings suggested that an individual's commitment to a team and trust in team members was strengthened when the team leader possessed charismatic qualities and even more so in teams that were dispersed. This suggests that inspirational leaders are important in all contexts.[64]

- The third behavior dimension, *individual consideration*, is about the mentoring role often assumed by charismatic and transformational leaders. They serve as mentors to their followers. Effective charismatic and transformational leaders use an individualized developmental model that responds to follower needs and concerns.[65] Studies have found that in dyadic relationships characterized by strong individualized leader–follower exchanges, followers felt a greater sense of self-worth. Transformational leaders were found to support the development of these exchange relationships in greater measure.[66]

- Finally, *intellectual stimulation* describes the charismatic and transformational leader's creative and out-of-the-box way of thinking.[67] They encourage followers to approach old and familiar problems in new ways. By stimulating novel thinking, the leader inspires followers to question their own beliefs and learn to solve problems creatively. In a fast-changing environment such as we have today, innovation has come to be

WORK Application **7**

Think of a leader in our society today who is generally perceived to be a charismatic or transformational leader. In your opinion, which of the behavioral dimensions of charismatic and transformational leadership described in the text can be attributed to him or her?

seen as a strategic imperative for organizational survival. Because of the strategic significance of innovation, leader behaviors must focus on intellectual stimulation of followers. Leaders have to take a leading role in building and enhancing innovative capabilities of the organizations. This includes an emphasis on creativity, risk-taking, and experimentation. The organizational culture should embrace change and constantly challenge the status quo.[68]

A leader who exemplifies these four behavior dimensions is Nelson Mandela. Nelson Mandela led the change that is depolarizing a nation racially polarized for decades. Mandela's transformational leadership humanized apartheid South Africa and led to the emergence of a nation deserving of global recognition. His charismatic effect softened the hardest stances of the haves and have-nots and aligned them in pursuit of a constructive common cause.

Martin Luther King, Jr. was both a charismatic and a transformational leader like Nelson Mandela. A study focused on examining his legacy concluded that he personified the four behavior dimensions listed above. The study emphasized Martin Luther King's efforts at building follower confidence, challenging taken-for-granted assumptions, developing follower needs, and upholding high moral values.[69]

EXHIBIT 9.4 Transformational and Charismatic Leader Behaviors

Behavioral Dimension	Description
Idealized Influence	Behavior that conveys an ideal future that is much better than the present. The leader's behavior is aimed at inspiring followers to share in his or her vision.
Inspirational Motivation	Passionate communications of better days ahead that motivates followers to buy into the leader's vision
Individual Consideration	Behavior that employs an individualized developmental model that responds to follower needs and concerns
Intellectual Stimulation	Behavior that challenges followers to think "outside of the box" and re-examine old ways and methods

Source: Based on B. M Bass and B. J. Avilio, *Improving Organizational Effectiveness Through Transformational Leadership* (Thousand Oaks, CA: Sage, 1994); and P. M. Podsakoff, S. B. Mackenzie, R. H. Moorman, and R. Fetter, "Transformational Leader Behaviors and Their Effects on Followers' Trust in Leader, Satisfaction, and Organizational Citizenship Behavior," *Leadership Quarterly 1*(2) (1990): 107-142.

OPENING CASE APPLICATION

6. **Is Oprah a transformational leader, a charismatic leader, or both?**

A cursory review of the creation and evolution of *The Oprah Winfrey Show* and Harpo Productions is enough to conclude that Oprah is definitely a transformational leader. In 1986, Oprah formed her own production company, Harpo Productions, to bring quality entertainment projects into production. Two years later, television history was made when Harpo Productions announced that it had assumed ownership and all production responsibilities for *The Oprah Winfrey Show* from Capital Cities/ABC, making Oprah Winfrey the first woman in history to own and produce her own

(continues)

(Opening Case Application 7 continued)

talk show. Today, Harpo is well on its way to becoming a formidable force in film and television production. That growth has meant financial success. Oprah's Harpo Entertainment Group, the corporate umbrella over her film and TV production operations, is privately held and executives do not publicly talk about its finances. However, published reports say Oprah is well on her way to becoming the first African-American billionaire, with an estimated net worth of $675 million, according to *Forbes* magazine.

Oprah's venture into magazine publishing is another example that she has the ability to start and transform any venture she embarks upon. In April 2000, Oprah and Hearst Magazines introduced *O, Tthe Oprah Magazine*, a monthly magazine that has become one of today's leading women's lifestyle publications. It is credited as being the most successful magazine launch in recent history and currently has an audience of over 2 million readers each month. *O, Tthe Oprah Magazine*, is another medium through which Oprah connects with her audience and provides possibilities for transforming their lives. In April 2002, Oprah launched the first international edition of *O, Tthe Oprah Magazine*, in South Africa. Oprah is a transformational leader with charismatic qualities. She embodies both leadership styles.

Learning Outcome 10	*Distinguish between charismatic and transformational leadership.*

Differentiating between Charismatic and Transformational Leadership

Some authors make no distinction between the charismatic and the transformational leader, preferring to combine them into one theory. They refer to the two theories as charismatic because charisma is a central theme in both, either explicitly or implicitly. Others see charisma as just one of a collection of attributes that may explain transformational leadership behavior. The other attributes include honesty, optimism, communication skills, confidence, and consideration. From this perspective, it would appear that charisma and transformational theories are one and the same. However, this is not a complete picture of how the two theories mirror or differ from each other. How they work in practice does reveal another perspective: not all transformational leaders possess charismatic qualities.

The first notable area of difference is that both charismatic and transformational leadership theories are about change (regardless of the kind of change), but not all transformational leaders are charismatic. There are many examples of very successful transformational leaders who achieved great transforming results, but not through the charismatic effects of their personalities. These leaders are lacking in charisma but very effective as transformational leaders. Many will agree that leaders like Bill Gates, Warren Buffet, Abraham Lincoln, or Jack Welch are transformational, but few will label them as charismatic.[70] A more recent example is Mark Zuckerburg, the founder and CEO of Facebook. Not only is he leading the transformation of Facebook in the social network media industry, but he is also transforming our society in the ways we relate and communicate with each other. Yet he is described as shy, a recluse, a loner, and not very comfortable with the public.[71] No one will label him today as a charismatic leader; maybe he will develop charismatic qualities later in life. On the other hand, there are leaders such as Martin Luther King, Jr., John F. Kennedy, Adolf Hitler, Mahatma Gandhi, Nelson Mandela, Ronald Reagan, Bill Clinton, Richard Branson, and many others whose successful transforming results are to some extent attributed to their charismatic qualities. These leaders for the most part live by the tenets of consultation, persuasion, and cohabitation, and they shun coercion and domination.

A second area of difference is how one achieves the label of charisma or transformer. Attribution theory states that followers make attributions of heroic or extraordinary leadership abilities when they observe certain behaviors in their leader. These attributions form the basis upon which a leader is seen as possessing or not possessing charisma.[72] Such attributions of charisma then become the reason for follower unconditional loyalty, devotion, self-sacrifice, obedience, and commitment to the leader and his or her cause.[73] Transformational leaders, on the other hand, do not achieve their label from follower attributions. They are labeled as transformational leaders because they actually transformed the organizations they led. It is a reputation based on an individual's record of track record of past accomplishments.

A third area of difference is on the mind-set of charismatic and transformational leaders. Charismatic leaders tend to have a more activist mind-set. They see political and social causes as opportunities to influence change and provide a better life for their followers. Pursuing these causes provide charismatic leaders with meaning or sense of purpose for their existence. Charismatic leaders have a greater sensitivity to political, cultural, and economic conditions that are ripe for change. They magnify a climate of dissatisfaction by encouraging activism that heightens followers' willingness to change the status quo. When followers are going through periods of turmoil and collective stress, they may respond to a leader who is able to give meaning to their experiences in terms of a new social or political order. For example, Oprah's commitment to children led her to initiate the National Child Protection Act in 1991, when she testified before the U.S. Senate Judiciary Committee to establish a national database of convicted child abusers. On December 20, 1993, President Clinton signed the national "Oprah Bill" into law. Transformational leaders are more strategic in their approach. They find and exploit opportunities that maximize their gains and avoid threats. In fact, they try to steer away from political controversy. They are mostly driven by economic factors.

A fourth area of difference is on the career path that each leadership type is likely to follow. Transformational leaders do follow a career path of promotions and growth that ultimately puts them in a position of leadership where they can showcase their transformational qualities. In contrast, charismatic leaders are more likely to emerge in the throes of a crisis, when an organization or society is in turmoil because of conflicting values or belief systems. It is also the case that a leader could emerge from obscurity to prominence with or without a crisis simply because of his or her charismatic qualities. Such a leader could go on to pursue a career in public speaking without any track record of specific achievements.

A fifth area of difference between charismatic and transformational leaders is how each perceives their personal meaning or purpose in life. Charismatic leaders tend to express their personal meaning or purpose in life at a much earlier age and use it as a driving force behind their vision. We define **personal meaning** as *the degree to which people's lives make emotional sense and to which the demands confronted by them are perceived as being worthy of their energy and commitment.* Personal meaning is a major determinant of motivation, especially for individuals facing challenges. It is more often cited as the motivational force behind charismatic leader behaviors than transformational leader behaviors. You don't hear a transformational leader say their purpose in life has always been to become the CEO of Chrysler and turn it around.

Finally, the sixth area of difference between the charismatic and transformational leader is the degree of risk each faces from opponents of their vision. Often, the emotional levels of resistance and conflict towards charismatic leaders are more extreme than those toward transformational leaders. It seems there is more polarization between supporters and opponents for a charismatic leader's vision. This may explain why more charismatic leaders have met with violent deaths (such as Martin Luther King, Jr., John F. Kennedy, and Mahatma Gandhi) than transformational leaders. Mostly, transformational leaders lose their job or resign in the face of unrelenting resistance or conflict.

WORK Application 8

Identify a leader you have worked with or are working with now. In your opinion, is this leader more of a transformational or charismatic leader? Explain why and include examples.

————————

————————

————————

————————

OPENING CASE *APPLICATION*

7. Oprah seems to have a clear sense of her personal meaning or purpose in life. What factors do you think have contributed to her understanding?

Much has been published about Oprah in books and on the Internet. It is apparent from reading through these materials that her sense of personal meaning is intact. Oprah believes her purpose or personal meaning is to help others achieve their full potential in life. The Oprah Winfrey Foundation was established to support the inspiration, empowerment, education, and well-being of women, children, and families around the world. Through this private charity, Oprah has directly served the needs of low-opportunity people and has awarded hundreds of grants to organizations that carry out this vision. She has contributed millions of dollars toward providing a better education for underserved students who have merit but no means. She created the "Oprah Winfrey Scholars Program," which gives scholarships to students determined to use their education to give back to their communities in the United States and abroad. The Oprah Winfrey Foundation continues to expand Oprah's global humanitarian efforts in developing countries. In December 2002, Oprah brought a day of joy to tens of thousands of children with "ChristmasKindness South Africa," an initiative that included visits to orphanages and rural schools in South Africa where children received gifts of food, clothing, athletic shoes, school supplies, books, and toys. Sixty-three rural schools received libraries and teacher education, which continued throughout 2003. In addition, Oprah announced a partnership with South Africa's Ministry of Education to build a model leadership school for girls. The Oprah Winfrey Leadership Academy for Girls–South Africa recently graduated its first class of young high school women. More than 90 percent of whom are headed for university studies. Oprah spoke openly of her strong faith and spirituality on her TV show every day; the same way she now does on her radio show—Oprah XM Radio.

SELF-ASSESSMENT 2   Are You More Charismatic, Transformational, or Both?

There are no right or wrong answers, so be honest and you will really increase your self-awareness. We suggest doing this exercise in pencil or making a copy before you write on it. We will explain why later.

Using the scale below, rate each of the 20 statements according to how accurately it describes you. Place a number from 1 to 7 on the line before each statement.

Like me		Somewhat like me			Not like me	
7	6	5	4	3	2	1

_____ 1. I do enjoy getting up in front of audiences and giving passionate presentations on topics I care about.

_____ 2. I tend to associate my faith and religious values to issues I care very much about.

_____ 3. I enjoy change and see myself as a change agent.

_____ 4. I have always seen myself as someone who has the ability to inspire trust with my fellow students.

_____ 5. On occasions when I have made a difficult moral decision (or if I had to make a moral decision), I was (or will be) guided by the desire to not seem like a hypocrite if my actions became public.

_____ 6. I see myself as someone who, if given a leadership opportunity, will influence my followers and colleagues based on who I am not what I am (my position).

_____ 7. When I walk into a room of people (other students), I generally feel like my presence evokes a "powerful aura" or immediate attention.

_____ 8. I make friends easily and feel like I am extraordinarily gifted in more ways than others.

_____ 9. I am pretty good at making people feel empowered and self-confident.

_____ 10. If I believe in something, I will not give up trying to achieve it even if my life is threatened because of it.

_____ 11. I want to be remembered for something special I did beyond just being a loving member of my family.

_____ 12. I am better at inspiring employees toward a new future than motivating them to perform their current jobs.

(continued)

(Self-Assessment 2 continued)

_____ 13. I have/had a vision of how an organization can change for the better.

_____ 14. I see myself as someone who is comfortable encouraging people to express ideas and opinions that differ from my own.

_____ 15. I enjoy taking risks but am not reckless.

_____ 16. I enjoy spending time developing new solutions to old problems rather than implementing existing solutions.

_____ 17. I deliberate carefully before acting; I'm not impulsive.

_____ 18. Being in a position to turn a struggling organization around will be more attractive to me than leading a stable (no big changes required) type organization.

To determine whether you are more charismatic, transformational, or both: (1) In the blanks, place the number from 1 to 7 that represents your score for each statement. (2) Add up each column. Your total should be a number from 5 to 35. (3) On the number scale, circle the number that is closest to your total score. Each column in the chart represents an attribute of charismatic or transformational leadership.

1 Charismatic		2 Transformational		3 Both	
	35		35		35
	30		30		30
____ 1.	25	____ 12.	25	____ 3.	25
____ 2.	20	____ 14.	20	____ 4.	20
____ 7.	15	____ 15.	15	____ 5.	15
____ 8.	10	____ 16.	10	____ 6.	10
____ 10.	5	____ 17.	5	____ 9.	5
____ 11.		____ 18.		____ 13.	
____ Total	Scale	____ Total	Scale	____ Total	Scale

The higher the total number, the stronger you are in that particular leadership type. As discussed in the text, you can always improve your weak areas if you want to be a better charismatic or transformational leader or both.

Learning Outcome 11

Explain the basis of stewardship and servant leadership.

Stewardship and Servant Leadership

Stewardship and servant leadership represent a shift in the leadership paradigm from a focus on leading to a focus on serving. Stewardship and servant leadership are related to charismatic and transformational leadership, in that they emphasize empowering followers to accomplish organizational goals.[74] Traditional leadership theories elevate the leader and his or her role in effecting organizational success. The leader is the authority from whom followers take their orders. Advocates of stewardship and servant leadership view the leader as a steward and servant of the people. They believe that leadership has less to do with directing other people and more to do with serving people by placing others' needs ahead of yours.[75] Proponents of servant leadership and stewardship believe strongly in the positive relationship between spirituality and leadership in the conduct of business.[76,77]

Not everyone agrees with this model of leadership. To some the word *servant* implies a lower status for the person serving. Its use connotes negative feelings about leadership, especially for those who have traditionally thought of leaders as powerful visionaries leading the pack—the "great man" theory of leadership. However, the servant as someone who is assisting others, promoting the interests of others, or fighting for others implies a much greater noble purpose and a sense of duty to serve. In this section, we provide a definition of stewardship and servant leadership and a brief discussion of the attributes of effective steward and servant leaders.

Defining Stewardship and Servant Leadership

Stewardship and *servant leadership* describe leaders who lead from positions of moral influence, not power, and who are very follower-centric. Both leadership styles call for empathy, kindness, honesty, humility, and respect for others, especially the less powerful or influential. These attributes are important in identifying leaders who can be effective in the role of servant leader or stewardship. Some have used the term *values-based* **leadership** to describe steward and servant leadership. The values-based leadership perspective is seen by some as the moral foundation underlying the decisions and actions of servant and steward leaders.[78] For a definition of these leadership types, we offer that **stewardship** *is an employee-focused form of leadership that empowers followers to make decisions and have control over their jobs*; while **servant leadership** *is leadership that transcends self-interest to serve the needs of others, by helping them grow professionally and personally*.

Though some may view these two concepts of leadership as synonymous and use them interchangeably, they are not exactly identical. While both shine the spotlight on followers, servant leadership goes a step further. Servant leadership calls for the highest level of selflessness—a level that some doubt exists in the real world.

The Effective Steward Leader

Leaders who embody the stewardship philosophy are sincerely concerned about their followers and want to assist them to grow, develop, and achieve both personal and organizational goals. A fundamental purpose of stewardship is commitment to people's growth and building community. An effective steward leader creates the environment for team empowerment where decision making is highly decentralized. Therefore, stewardship is more about facilitating than actively leading. Another critical element in steward leadership is trust. Ethical stewardship is when followers perceive the leader's behavior as trustworthy.[79] Exhibit 9.5 presents guidelines to effective stewardship

EXHIBIT 9.5 Guidelines to Effective Stewardship

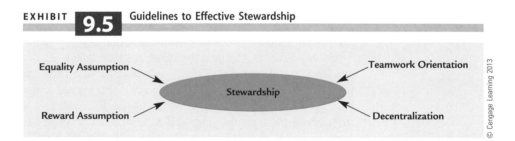

© Cengage Learning 2013

Strong Team Orientation

Steward leadership works best in environments where leaders and followers come together as a team to formulate goals, strategies, and policies for achieving them. Here, the steward leader's role is less dominant and more supportive of the process. Where a strong team spirit is present, the steward leader is just one of the team members. His job is more of a coach than leader of the team.

Decentralized Decision Making and Power

The steward leader is most effective when authority and decision making is decentralized and brought to the level where work gets done and employees are encouraged to take an active role in self-leadership. In this environment, the steward leader is highly effective, given the empowered status of followers and the positive exchange relationship between the steward leader and followers.

Equality Assumption

Stewardship works best when there is perceived equality between the steward leader and followers. It is a partnership of equals rather than a hierarchical leader–follower command and control relationship. The role of the steward leader is to find opportunities to serve rather than dictate orders. Honesty, respect, and mutual trust prevail when there is equality; these are values that enhance the success of stewardship. The absence of an assumption of equality makes stewardship almost inoperable.

Reward Assumption

Stewardship puts greater responsibility in the hands of employees. Increased responsibilities should be matched with an appropriate reward structure. Employees with more responsibility and authority who are compensated accordingly flourish under stewardship because they are motivated and committed to the organization's mission. Without this reward assumption, it is hard to sustain stewardship.

Stewardship leaders are not known for their great deeds but for empowering others to achieve great deeds. These leaders don't just lead, they coach (Chapter 6) followers to do the leading. This encourages followers to be more involved and committed to their jobs.

The Effective Servant Leader

At the core of servant leadership is self-sacrifice for others without regard to what one might receive in return.[80] The leader makes a conscious decision to hold followers in high regard. The leader is driven to serve, not to be served. According to retired AT&T executive Robert K. Greenleaf, servant leadership begins with the natural feeling that one wants to serve. Robert Greenleaf first introduced the concept of the leader as a servant more than three decades ago. Today, there is a Greenleaf Center for Servant Leadership with a global reach that includes 11 branch offices located around the world.[81]

Servant leaders approach leadership from a strong moral standpoint. The servant leader operates from the viewpoint that we all have a moral duty to one another and that as leaders, we have to both serve and lead. Leadership is seen as an opportunity to serve at the ground level, not to lead from the top. It is a leadership approach that is centered on a strong service orientation and moral–spiritual grounding. Servant leaders exhibit personality traits high on agreeableness, active listening, empathy, and integrity.[82,83]

Mother Teresa founded the Missionaries of Charity, a Catholic order of nuns dedicated to helping the less fortunate. Begun in Calcutta, India, the Missionaries of Charity grew to help the poor, the dying, orphans, lepers, and AIDS sufferers in over a hundred countries. Mother Teresa's selfless effort to help those in need has caused many to regard her as a model servant leader. Exhibit 9.6 presents the attributes of effective servant leadership.

EXHIBIT 9.6 Attributes of Effective Servant Leadership

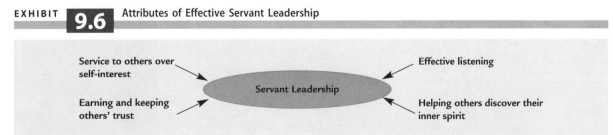

Source: *Based on* R. K. Greenleaf, *Servant Leadership: A Journey into the Nature of Legitimate Power and Greatness* (Mahwah, NJ: Paulist Press, 1977), 7.

Helping Others Discover Their Inner Spirit

The servant leader's role is to help followers discover the strength of their inner spirit and their potential to make a difference. This requires servant leaders to be empathetic to the circumstances of others. Servant leaders are not afraid to show their vulnerabilities. Mother Teresa was able to inspire hundreds of followers to join her order and serve others.

Earning and Keeping Others' Trust

Servant leaders earn followers' trust by being honest and true to their word. They work hard to preserve their integrity. They don't have any hidden agendas, and they are not afraid to give up power, recognition, or control to followers if it helps move the organization forward. It is how servant leaders build strong working relationships with followers. Servant leadership is about influence that is based on trust, not power.

WORK Application 9

In your college or work experience, identify one leader you have come across whom you can say fits the bill of either a steward or servant leader. Explain why?

_____

_____

_____

_____

Service over Self-Interest

The hallmark of servant leadership is the desire to help others, rather than the desire to attain power and control over others. Doing what's right for others takes precedence over protecting one's position. Servant leaders make decisions to further the interests of the group rather than their own interests.

Effective Listening

Servant leaders do not impose their will on the group; rather, they listen carefully to the problems others are facing and then engage the group to find solutions. They show love, acceptance, and encouragement for their followers and are very empathetic.

The discussion in this chapter has emphasized leadership approaches (charismatic, transformational, stewardship, and servant leadership) that operate under the premise that change is inevitable and not every leader is capable of managing it successfully. We have identified and discussed different leadership theories that deal with change effectively. Self-Assessment 3 provides the opportunity to link these leadership approaches to one personality type.

SELF-ASSESSMENT 3 **Personality and Charismatic and Transformational Leadership**

Charismatic leaders have charisma based on personality and other personal traits that cut across all of the Big Five personality types. Review the ten qualities of charismatic leaders in Exhibit 9.3 on page 336. Which traits do you have?

_____

_____

If you have a high surgency Big Five personality style and a high need for power, you need to focus on using socialized, rather than personalized, charismatic leadership.

Transformational leaders tend to be charismatic as well. In Self-Assessment 1 on page 332 you determined if you were more transformational or transactional. How does your personality affect your transformational and transactional leadership styles?

_____

_____

Chapter Summary

The chapter summary is organized to answer the 12 learning outcomes for Chapter 9.

1. Briefly explain Max Weber's conceptualization of charisma.

Weber used the term *charisma* to explain a form of influence based on follower perceptions that the leader is endowed with the gift of divine inspiration, not a traditional or legal mandate of authority. This gift of divine inspiration is the force behind a charismatic leader's ability to focus society's attention on both the crisis it faces and the leader's vision for a new and better future. According to Weber, charismatic individuals emerge as leaders during times of great social crisis and inspire people to do more than they would under normal circumstances.

2. Explain what is meant by the statement "the locus of charismatic leadership."

The question scholars have entertained since Weber's conception of charisma is whether charisma is a function of the prevailing social climate, the leader's extraordinary qualities, or an interaction between the two. Supporters of the view that charismatic leadership could not take place unless the society were in a tumultuous, unstable situation argue that without a crisis and followers' need for change, a leader's charismatic qualities would be hard to notice or appreciate. Therefore, the locus of charismatic leadership is the status of the society. Opponents argue that charismatic leadership is primarily the result of leader attributes, not the situation. They argue that without strong leader characteristics (such as vision, exceptional communication skills, trustworthiness, self-confidence, and focus on empowering others), leaders like Martin Luther King, Jr. or Gandhi would never have emerged as leaders of their respective followers, regardless of the situation. Finally, there is an emerging view that charismatic leadership is a convergence of follower perceptions and reactions influenced by leader characteristics and the prevailing social situation.

3. Discuss the effects of charismatic leadership on followers.

Charismatic leaders tend to have a strong emotional bond with their followers. The effects of such a bond are that followers are inspired enthusiastically to give unconditional loyalty, devotion, obedience, and commitment to the leader and to the cause the leader represents. A sense of fulfillment and satisfaction is derived from the pursuit of worthwhile activities and goals and having positive beliefs and values about life as presented by the charismatic leader. Implicitly, the charismatic leader is seen as an object of identification by which a follower emulates his or her behavior; thus, followers model their behavior, values, and cognitions after the leader. For example, followers are more likely to set or

accept higher goals and have greater confidence in their ability to contribute to the achievement of such goals. By observing the leader display self-confidence, followers develop self-confidence as well.

4. Discuss how one can acquire charismatic qualities.

There are suggested strategies for acquiring or enhancing charismatic qualities. Through training and education, people can enhance their communication skills and learn techniques of crafting visionary statements, as well as how to empower followers. Through practice and self-discipline, an individual can build his or her self-confidence and develop a personality profile that is warm, positive, enthusiastic, and optimistic.

5. Explain the difference between socialized and personalized charismatic leaders.

The charismatic leader seeks to achieve the unconditional commitment and devotion of followers to his or her ideological goals. However, negative charismatic leaders emphasize devotion to themselves more than to ideals, and positive charismatic leaders seek the opposite. It is against this backdrop that negative charismatics are said to have a personalized power orientation and positive charismatics have a socialized power orientation. In the former, ideological appeals are only a ploy to gain power and manipulate and control followers. In the latter, ideological appeals are organization-driven and seek to empower followers to achieve the vision and mission of the organization. Personalized charismatic leaders seek self-glorification, and socialized charismatic leaders seek organizational transformation through empowerment of followers.

6. Explain the difference between transformational and transactional leadership.

Transactional leadership tends to be transitory, in that once a transaction is completed, the relationship between the parties may end or be redefined. Transformational leadership is more enduring, especially when the change process is well designed and implemented. Transactional leaders promote stability, while transformational leaders create significant change in both followers and organizations. Transformational leadership inspires followers to go beyond their own self-interest for the good of the group. Transactional leadership seeks to satisfy followers' individual needs as a reward for completing a given transaction.

7. Explain the four stages of the transformation process.

A transformational leader who is brought into an organization facing a serious crisis or approaching total collapse has to institute a turnaround strategy. Turnaround strategies are often radical transformations that put the organization on a different path for future growth and prosperity. The magnitude of the task and the high risk of failure require that it be approached in a systematic fashion. Thus, the transformation process is a four-phase approach that *starts with the recognition of the need for change.* This provides the opportunity for the leader to formulate and introduce a new vision for the organization that promises a better and brighter future than the present. Once there is *acceptance of the leader's vision,* the third phase involves *implementing the new vision and effectively managing the transition.* Here, instilling in managers a sense of urgency for change, raising followers' self-confidence and optimism, and recognizing and dealing with resistance will greatly increase the chances of a successful transformation. The last phase is *institutionalizing the change* so that it is not a short-lived transformation. Effective strategies for institutionalizing change are outlined in the text.

8. **List the qualities of effective charismatic and transformational leaders.**

The qualities that effective charismatic and transformational leader share are vision, superb communication skills, self-confidence and moral conviction, ability to inspire trust, high risk orientation, high energy and action orientation, relational power base, minimum internal conflict, ability to empower others, self-promoting personality, selflessness and having an activist mind-set.

9. **Describe the four behavior dimensions associated with transformational and charismatic leader behaviors.**

The four behavior dimensions, also known as the four "I's" are idealized influence, inspirational motivation, individual consideration, and intellectual stimulation. *Idealized Influence—*behavior that conveys an ideal future that is much better than the present. The leader's behavior is aimed at inspiring followers to share in his or her vision.

*Inspirational Motivation—*passionate communications of better days ahead that motivates followers to buy into the leader's vision.

*Individual Consideration—*behavior that employs an individualized developmental model that responds to follower needs and concerns.

*Intellectual Stimulation—*behavior that challenges followers to think "outside of the box" and re-examine old ways and methods. It implores followers to be creative and innovate.

10. **Distinguish between charismatic and transformational leadership.**

The two leadership types are similar in that charisma and vision are central concepts in both of them. Also, both leadership types share the ability to influence followers to believe in their vision. They are different in many ways:

- Charismatic leaders are by nature transformational (regardless of the kind of transformation they seek), but not all transformational leaders are charismatic.
- How one achieves the label of charisma or transformation is different for the two. Charisma is attributed

to an individual by followers who believe he or she possesses charismatic qualities. Transformational is an earned title based on past accomplishments.

- Charismatic leaders tend to have a more activist mind-set than transformational leaders. They use political and social causes as opportunities to influence change and provide a better life for their followers. Transformational leaders are more strategic in their approach.
- Charismatic leaders tend to have a sense of their purpose or personal meaning much earlier in life than transformational leaders. Transformational leaders follow a career path that brings them to the point of leadership where they then display their transformational abilities.
- The level of resistance and conflict towards charismatic leaders are more extreme than those toward transformational leaders. This may explain why more charismatic leaders have met with violent deaths than have transformational leaders.

11. **Explain the basis of stewardship and servant leadership.**

The basis of stewardship and servant leadership is serving rather than directing other people. It is leadership based on placing others ahead of oneself. Both shine the spotlight on the employees who actually perform the day-to-day task of meeting organizational goals and objectives. The key to successful stewardship is the presence of four supporting values: equal treatment for all, reward for work, teamwork attitude, and decentralized decision making and authority. The key to successful servant leadership is based on four guiding principles as well: service to others over self-interest, trust, effective listening, and empowering others to discover their inner strength.

12. **Define the following key terms (in order of appearance in the chapter).**

Select one or more methods: (1) fill in the missing key terms from memory; (2) match the key terms from the following list with their definitions below; (3) copy the key terms in order from the list at the beginning of the chapter.

_____ is the degree to which people's lives make emotional sense and to which the demands confronted by them are perceived as being worthy of energy and commitment.

_____ is a distinct social relationship between the leader and follower, in which the leader presents a revolutionary idea, a transcendent image, or ideal which goes beyond the immediate or the reasonable; the follower accepts this course of action not because of its rational likelihood of success, but because of an effective belief in the extraordinary qualities of the leader.

_____ is the ability to imagine different and better conditions and the ways to achieve them.

_____ is one who possesses an egalitarian, self-transcendent, and empowering personality.

_____ is one who possesses a dominant, Machiavellian, and narcissistic personality.

_____ serves to change the status quo by articulating to followers the problems in the current system and a compelling vision of what the new organization could be.

_____ seeks to maintain stability within an organization through regular economic and social exchanges that achieve specific goals for both the leaders and their followers.

_____ is an employee-focused form of leadership that empowers followers to make decisions and have control over their jobs.

_____ is leadership that transcends self-interest to serve the needs of others, by helping them grow professionally and personally.

Key Terms

personal meaning, 343

personalized charismatic leader (PCL), 329

servant leadership, 346

socialized charismatic leader (SCL), 329

stewardship, 346

transactional leadership, 331

vision, 336

Review Questions

1. Describe the various sources from which one can draw his or her personal meaning.

2. Citing specific examples, explain how charismatic leaders of the past used vision and superb communication skills to make their case.

3. Describe the leading characteristics of charismatic leaders.

4. Martin Luther King, Jr., Gandhi, John F. Kennedy, Adolph Hitler, Nelson Mandela, David Koresh (of the Branch Davidians), Herb Kelleher (of Southwest Airlines), and Richard Branson (of the Virgin Group) are/were charismatic leaders. Can you associate with each name a characteristic (see Exhibit 9.3 on page 336) of charisma you think best describes the individual? Note: If you are not familiar with these individuals, do library or Internet research on them before attempting an answer.

5. Why is the theory of charisma described as a double-edged sword?

6. Describe the limitations of charismatic leadership theory.

7. Describe four key behaviors characteristic of transformational and charismatic leaders.

8. Describe some key attributes/qualities of transformational leaders.

9. What is servant leadership?

Critical Thinking Questions

The following critical-thinking questions can be used for class discussion and/or as written assignments to develop communication skills. Be sure to give complete explanations for all questions.

1. A strong emotional attachment and loyalty to a charismatic leader can have both beneficial and detrimental effects on followers. Explain both types of effects on followers.

2. Charismatic leaders are said to possess special traits that influence their behaviors. Three such traits described in the chapter are envisioning, empathy, and empowerment. Explain how each of these traits influences how followers perceive the charismatic leader.

3. In Chapter 5, different types of power—legitimate, reward, coercive, referent, expert, connection, and information power—and influencing tactics were discussed. What type of power is the charismatic leader most likely to be associated with and why?

4. Explain the importance of effective communication skills for charismatic and transformational leaders.

5. Servant leadership emphasizes being able to serve and lead. In your opinion, is this contradictory or doable?

6. Do you believe everyone has the same capability to become a servant leader, or are some people by their nature more inclined to be servant leaders?

Ursula Burns: Xerox's Chairwoman and CEO

In July 2009, Ursula Burns became the Chairwoman and CEO of Xerox, taking over from her former boss Ann Mulcahy. Xerox Corporation, a $22 billion global enterprise for business process and document management, is ranked No. 121 on the 2011 list of Fortune 500 companies.

Her elevation marked two milestones: the first time an African-American woman was named CEO of a major American corporation, and the first time a woman succeeded another woman in the top job at a company of this size.[84] Ms. Burns's story is the quintessential tale of the American Dream. She has defied the odds. She was raised in a housing project on Manhattan's Lower East Side by a hard-working single mother who cleaned, ironed, did child care—anything to see that Ursula and her siblings got a good education. She attended an all-girls Catholic High School in New York. She then went on to obtain a BS in Mechanical Engineering from Polytechnic Institute of NYU in 1980 and a master's in Mechanical Engineering from Columbia University a year later.

She joined Xerox as a summer intern in 1980. Ms. Burns, who is now 52, has never been shy about speaking her mind. On more than one occasion, her outspokenness caught the attention of higher-ups in the Xerox corporate office. It's how she ended up working with two of Xerox's former CEOs early on in her career. Referring to Ms. Burns, Mr. Hicks (former CEO) said, "She was enormously curious," she wanted to know why we were doing some things at the time, and she was always prepared in a way that I thought was very refreshing." Her hard work, determination, and dedication paid off. After a number of mid-level assignments, she eventually entered the executive ranks of Xerox. She was named a senior vice president in 2000 and became president of two different business groups over the next two years. Ann Mulcahy, the CEO at the time, told Ursula that she needed her help on the turnaround team. The pair worked closely together for almost a decade in a relationship that both women describe as a true partnership. Ms. Burns was named president of Xerox in 2007, a signal to investors and employees that she was the heir apparent.

African-Americans with Burns's background were not common at Xerox, but she never saw her race or low socio-economic status as a liability. "My perspective comes in part from being a New York black lady, in part from being an engineer," she said. "I know that I'm smart and have opinions that are worth being heard." When asked who her big influences were before joining Xerox, Ms. Burns had this to say: "150 percent my mother. My mother was pragmatic, focused and exceedingly practical and she was the ultimate self-determining person." Burns describes her mother as a value-driven single mother who believed in the mantra, "where you are, is not who you are" and who viewed a good education as a way "up and out."[85]

It is obvious that Ms. Burns is not comfortable being in the spotlight or getting all the recognition and praise that the media and others have heaped on her since being named to the top job at Xerox. "The accolades that I get for doing absolutely nothing are amazing—I've been named to every list, literally, since I became the CEO," Ms. Burns says. "In the first 30 days, I was named to a list of the most impressive XYZ. The accolades are good for five minutes, but then it takes kind of a shine off the real story. The real story is not Ursula Burns. I just happen to be the person standing up at this point representing Xerox."

She is taking over at a time when investors are eager to see Xerox build both revenue and earnings. She wants its 130,000 employees to get over the past, take more initiative, and become more fearless. She is encouraging them to take risks but not be reckless. She defines Xerox's culture as one of teamwork and the entrepreneurial spirit. Another contributing factor to Team Xerox's success is a shared vision. As Ms. Burns explains it, "The importance of having the people in the company completely aligned around a common set of goals, and using that alignment to drive a sense of urgency, focus and commitment, is crucial." Imploring all her followers to step up and take more initiative in solving problems, she said, "I cannot be viewed as the solution to all problems in this company."[86,87]

About accomplishments that have taken place since she became CEO, such as major product announcements, launches of new businesses, acquisitions, and major operational efficiencies, she said they are all the "collective accomplishments of Team Xerox." This in fact is an example of her modesty and desire to share credit for an action that many analysts and investors criticized her for taking. According to the *Wall Street Journal*, the cornerstone of

Ms. Burns's strategy, which she dubbed Xerox 2010, was the acquisition of Dallas-based service company Affiliated Computer Services (ACS) for $6.4 billion. At the time critics said it was the wrong move because it was too costly in the midst of a recession and too large—ACS had 74,000 employees compared to Xerox's 54,000 at the time. A year later, Ms. Burns is being lauded for the move. The service sector of Xerox is now bringing in nearly half of the company's total revenue.[88]

In a recent speech to investors and analysts at the New York Stock Exchange, Ms Burns talked about "the new Xerox." "A lot has changed. We have been working on transforming the company. We're confident we have the right strategy, the competitive advantage and a disciplined focus on executing," she said. She is intent on transforming Xerox into a service-based business. This is a defensive strategy aimed at protecting the Xerox from the growing threat posed by digital technology to its traditional hardware line.[89] There is no doubt that her influence inside and outside Xerox is growing. She was recently named by President Barack Obama to help lead the White House national program on STEM (science, technology, engineering, and math) in November 2009 and was appointed vice chair of the President's Export Council in March 2010.

GO TO THE INTERNET: To learn more about Ursula Burns and Xerox, visit its Web site **(http://www.xerox.com)**

Support your answers to the following questions with specific information from the case and text or with other information you get from the Web or other sources.

1. In your opinion is Ursula Burns more of a charismatic leader, transformational leader, or both?

2. Exhibit 9.5 identifies transformational and charismatic leader behaviors. In your opinion, which of the behavioral components does Ms. Burns exemplify?

3. A key attribute of servant leadership is that it transcends self-interest to serve the needs of others. Does Ursula Burns fit this bill?

4. Exhibit 9.4 identifies the qualities of charismatic and transformational leaders. Based on your knowledge of Ms. Burns, which of the 12 qualities can you directly attribute to her?

5. Every leader has a sense of his or her personal meaning, described in the text as the degree to which people's lives make emotional sense and to which the demands confronted by them are perceived as being worthy of

energy and commitment Based on the facts of the case, what is/are the sources from which Burns derives her personal meaning? (Note: personal meaning is discussed in the chapter as one of the factors used to differentiate between charismatic and transformational leadership).

CUMULATIVE CASE QUESTIONS

6. According to the leadership continuum model of Tannenbaum and Schmidt, where would you put Ursula Burns based on the facts of the case (see Chapter 5)?

7. Communication is a major competency for leaders (Chapter 6). Would you agree that this is a quality that Burns likely possesses, to have been as effective as she has been so far?

8. Leader–member exchange theory describes the type of relationship that often develops between leaders and followers (Chapter 7). How would you describe the dyadic relationship between Anne Mulcahy and Ursula Burns?

9. One of the characteristics of effective teams is the presence of a capable and competent team leader (Chapter 8). Chapter 8 describes different activities of the team leader in creating an effective team (see Exhibit 8.1 on page 283), including turning obstacles into opportunities. Would you describe Ursula Burns as an effective team leader?

CASE EXERCISE AND ROLE-PLAY

Preparation: Assume you are part of the leadership of an organization or organizational unit that is in need of redirection in a changing market environment. Your task is to formulate a new vision and mission statement that would transform your organization.

Role-Play: The instructor forms students into small groups to develop an inspiring vision of no more than 15 words and a mission statement of no more than 100 words. Here are some guidelines:

1. Identify key environmental trends or changes that have influenced your group's vision.

2. Make up a list of core values that your organization holds, or you would want it to have, and incorporate these in your mission statement.

3. Share your vision and mission statement with other members of the class and vote on who has the most inspiring and compelling vision and mission.

VIDEO ▶❚❚ CASE

Timbuk2: Former CEO Sets a Course

Making decisions is a big part of any manager's job. Making decisions that determine the direction a company will take is the job of a CEO. Mark Dwight, former CEO of Timbuk2, a manufacturer of bicycle messenger bags, was comfortable with this role, even though it meant sometimes making unpopular decisions—or even making mistakes. Most of the decisions Dwight made at Timbuk2 were nonprogrammed decisions—such as the design of a new product or the type of fabric to use. These decisions can affect sales, the brand image, and even overall performance of the company. "Mark is the guy with the vision," said marketing manager Macy Allatt. "He will drive decision making, but he's very open to taking input from other people. When decisions need to be made, everyone sits down and we hash it out, and when we come out of the room, we feel like we're going to make some progress." Just about every decision Mark Dwight faced at Timbuk2 had some degree of uncertainty. He knew that he wanted Timbuk2 to achieve $25 million in sales in five years; he knew that he wanted the firm to reach new markets; he knew that the firm needed to find new distribution channels. But there was no guarantee that a single decision would be the right one.

1. Would you describe Timbuk2 former CEO Mark Dwight as a charismatic leader? Why or why not?

2. Does Mark Dwight possess any characteristics of a transformational leader? If so, what are they?

Developing Your Leadership Skills **1**

Is the President of the United States a Charismatic Leader?

Preparing for This Exercise

Rate the current president of the United States on each of the ten characteristics of charismatic leaders. For each characteristic, rate the president as high (H), medium (M), or low (L). Be sure to provide a specific example (what the president did or said) for why you rate the president as H, M, or L for each characteristic.

1. Vision

2. Superb communication skills

3. Self-confidence and moral conviction

4. Ability to inspire trust

5. High risk orientation

6. High energy and action orientation

7. Relational power base

8. Minimum internal conflict

9. Ability to empower others

10. Self-promoting personality

Based on the text, what specific things do you recommend the president do or say to improve his charismatic leadership?

_____

_____

_____

Preparing for This Exercise in Class

Objective

To develop your ability to assess and advise a leader on charismatic leadership

The primary AACSB learning standard skills developed through this exercise are analytic skills and reflective thinking.

Procedure *(10–30 minutes)*

Option A: As a class, go over the preparation and rate the president as high, medium, or low on each charismatic leadership characteristic, and give an overall rating.

Option B: Break into groups of four to six, go over the preparation, and rate the president as high, medium, or low on each charismatic leadership characteristic, giving an overall rating. Be sure to provide a specific example (what the president did or said) for why your group rated the president as H, M, or L for each characteristic.

Option C: Same as B, but also select a spokesperson to present the group's answers to the entire class.

Conclusion

The instructor may lead a class discussion and/or make concluding remarks.

Apply It *(2–4 minutes)*

What did I learn from this experience? How will I use this knowledge in the future?

_____

_____

_____

Sharing

In the group, or to the entire class, volunteers may give their answers to the "Apply It" questions.

10

Leadership of Culture, Ethics, and Diversity

Learning Outcomes

After studying this chapter, you should be able to:

1. Explain the power of culture in the strategy execution process. p. 359

2. Describe the characteristics of low- and high-performing cultures. p. 360

3. Distinguish between symbolic and substantive leadership actions for shaping organizational culture. p. 364

4. Briefly describe the four types of culture commonly found in organizations. p. 366

5. Describe Hofstede's theory of National Culture Identities. p. 368

6. Briefly explain examples of organizational practices that can help foster an ethical work environment. p. 372

7. Discuss the validity of the assertion that authentic leadership has its roots in moral and ethical theory of leadership. p. 374

8. Explain the benefits of embracing diversity. p. 376

9. Describe the key factors that can enhance and support a pro-diversity culture. p. 378

10. Define the following **key terms** (in order of appearance in the chapter):

culture	low-uncertainty-avoidance culture	ombudsperson
cooperative culture		whistle-blowing
adaptive culture	high-power-distance culture	self-awareness
competitive culture	low-power-distance culture	diversity
bureaucratic culture	long-term orientation	demographic diversity
individualism	short-term orientation	ethnocentrism
collectivism	masculinity	glass ceiling
high-uncertainty-avoidance culture	femininity	
	ethics	

OPENING CASE *APPLICATION*

Andrea Jung has been CEO of Avon Company since November 1999. The oldest child of Chinese immigrants, Jung grew up speaking both English and Mandarin Chinese. Ten years ago, Avon, the world's largest direct seller of women's cosmetics, was experiencing some difficulties. Increasing sales in a market saturated with beauty products and savvy consumers was proving to be a daunting task even for a giant of Avon's stature. Jung gave the company what can only be described as "an extreme makeover," pouring millions into research and development, launching new lines of skin cream and expanding into overseas markets.

By all accounts, it appeared Jung's strategies were paying off, and then the 2008 recession struck. It has been described as the worst recession since the 1930s Great Depression. Avon's profit picture looked bleak as sales and sales rep counts dropped. To boost profit, Ms. Jung has controlled costs by implementing a hiring freeze. The company also lowered advertising expenses by 15 percent, particularly in China. Just as the market was beginning to question Ms. Jung's abilities to turn things around, the *Wall Street Journal* reported in May 2011 that Avon's first-quarter profit more than tripled as demand rose across different product categories from fragrance to personal-care products. She's also shifting more of the spending on initiatives that will help to boost morale and increase Avon's more than 6 million sales representatives, who are traditionally known as Avon Ladies and are the face of the brand and key to its future growth.[1]

Avon embraces diversity in the workforce and continues to be a leader in taking affirmative action to ensure that doors are opened to talented individuals, and that all associates and employees have opportunities for development and advancement. Avon also strives to create a work environment that values and encourages the uniqueness of each individual, and is committed to creating a culture that supports associates as they balance their many, and sometimes competing, work and personal responsibilities. Andrea Jung has definitely transformed Avon and, in the process, some believe she has given herself a career makeover, with her name cropping up on short lists of candidates to turn around bigger companies.

Opening Case Questions:

1. Is Avon's culture a contributing factor to its success? Explain.

2. The text points out that an organization's culture serves two important functions: (1) it creates internal unity, and (2) it helps the organization adapt to the external environment. Has this been the case at Avon?

3. The chapter discusses the characteristics of a high-performance (strong) culture. What is the evidence that Avon has a strong culture?

4. Is Avon's culture competitive, adaptive, bureaucratic, or cooperative? Support your answer.

5. What role has Andrea Jung played in fostering a climate of strict ethical standards at Avon?

6. What is Avon's stance on diversity, and has Avon lived up to it so far?

Can you answer any of these questions? You'll find answers to these questions and learn more about Avon and its leadership throughout the chapter.

To learn more about Avon and Andrea Jung, visit Avon's Web site at **http://www.avoncompany.com.**

I n this chapter we examine issues of organizational culture, ethics, and diversity—and the leader's role in shaping them. Regardless of the type of business or the size, organizations that consistently achieve outstanding results share a common characteristic—they all have what we call a high-performing culture. Organizations with high-performing cultures have an unmistakable profile that sets them apart from average performers—a profile that includes distinctive characteristics of a strong corporate culture, a reputation for ethical leadership, and a talented and diversified workforce. The three main topics featured in this chapter are organizational culture, ethics, and diversity.

What Is Organizational Culture?

The conceptual formation of culture traces its roots to anthropology, sociology, and the work of Edgar Schein.[2] Organizational culture is seen as a variable that affects organizational effectiveness. An organization's culture is manifested in the values, beliefs, and expectations that leaders preach and practice; in its employees' attitudes and behavior; in ethical guidelines; in operating policies; and in the stories people repeat about events in the organization.[3] Culture gives meaning to each individual's membership in the workplace and, in so doing, defines the organization's essential nature.[4] Organizational culture gives identity to an organization.[5]

An organization's culture is fairly enduring. It is the operating system that gives meaning to the underlying core values of the organization. Some have described organizational culture as a "shared mental model" or the "social glue" that holds an organization together.[6] From this background, we define culture as *the aggregate of beliefs, norms, attitudes, values, assumptions, and ways of doing things that is shared by members of an organization and taught to new members.* Cultural values are often anchored in the morals, customs, and practices of an organization.

Culture creation is a slowly evolving process. It can come from within the organization or be imposed from outside. An organization's core values and beliefs can come about from the experiences gained or lessons learned during trying times of the organization's life. The lessons learned during these hard times ultimately serve as the basis for role expectations that guide future behavior, and become embedded in the memory bank of organizational members.[7] Shared by leaders and followers, these expectations persist as new employees are encouraged to embrace them. One study called this the *feedforward learning flow model of culture creation.*[8] We should note that values and norms can also be learned during times of success and achievement. These shared memory of core values become the building blocks of the organization's culture. Eventually, these concepts become so deeply rooted in the culture that organizational members are no longer consciously aware of them. This organic process is consistent with the long-held view that culture emerges from the history and experiences of individuals and groups in that particular organization's context.

From the outside, culture can also be imposed on an organization by a new leader's desire to change an existing culture so it aligns with his or her personal values, strategies, and vision.[9] Changing an existing culture takes time but a determined leader can use power, status, rewards, and other mechanisms to change or modify culture.[10] It can be a difficult undertaking if the new leader's values are incongruent with those of the organization's members. Unwelcomed changes to an entrenched culture can provoke emotional reactions, often of an intense nature. However, when followers' values are congruent with those of the leader, they tend to react to change more positively. One study suggested that when followers' emotions to a proposed culture change are acknowledged and treated with respect, people become more engaged with the change.[11] The classical model for effecting change is the three-phase approach of unfreezing, cognitive restructuring, and refreezing. This model has been presented by some as the best approach for implementing cultural change.[12] We will discuss this model as part of the change management process in Chapter 11.

A culture is sustained as each successive generation of leaders and followers embraces and passes it to the next through mechanisms such as stories, artifacts, rituals, slogans, symbols, and special ceremonies. These mechanisms reproduce as well as reinforce the accepted culture.[13] They make up the cultural DNA that gives organizations and individuals their identities.[14] An example of this would be Sam Walton's conception of Walmart's culture from its early years. The essence of Walmart's culture is a commitment to customer satisfaction, zealous pursuit of low costs, and strong work ethic. To show his commitment to upholding these cultural values, Sam Walton instituted his ritualistic Saturday morning executive meetings at headquarters to exchange ideas and review problems. Also, he required company executives to visit stores, talk to customers, and solicit suggestions from employees. This tradition has carried on long after Mr. Walton's death. Creating and sustaining a high-performing culture at Walmart has been critical to its success.

In this section, we will examine the power of culture, differentiate between high- and low-performing cultures, explore the role of leaders in influencing culture, and highlight examples of different types of organizational culture.

OPENING CASE *APPLICATION*

1. **Is Avon's culture a contributing factor to its success? Explain.**

Yes, Avon's culture is a significant contributing factor to the company's success. The culture of the organization is encapsulated in what it calls "The Five Values of Avon," which are trust, respect, integrity, belief, and humility. According to the company's management, these five values have served as a continuing source of strength throughout Avon's proud history and will remain at the heart of who they are as a company. Avon enjoys a proud legacy and commitment to women.

Learning Outcome 1   *Culture serves two important functions in organizations. Briefly describe what they are.*

The Power of Culture

An organization's culture determines the way that it responds to changes in its external and internal environments. The response to changes in the external environment such as emerging opportunities and threats are reflected in the organization's vision, mission, objectives, and core strategies. The response to internal matters such as how power and status are determined, how resources are allocated, membership criteria, or how leaders and followers relate and interact with each other, is reflected in the organization's policies, procedures, and principles. Organizational performance is enhanced when strategy, structure, and capabilities are aligned to culture.[15] Experts and scholars on organizational culture have long maintained that culture serves two important functions in organizations: (1) it creates internal unity, and (2) it helps the organization adapt to the external environment.[16]

Internal Unity

Organizational culture defines a normative order that serves as a source of consistent behavior inside an organization. To the extent that culture provides organizational members with a way of making sense of their daily lives and establishes guidelines and rules for how to behave, it is a social control mechanism. A supportive culture provides a system of informal rules and peer pressures, which can be very powerful in influencing behavior, thus affecting organizational performance.[17] A strong culture provides a value system that regulates behavior and promotes strong employee identification with the organization's vision, mission, goals, and strategy. Culturally approved behavior thrives and is rewarded, while culturally disapproved behavior is discouraged and even punished. Culture offers a shared understanding about the identity of an organization. The right culture can make employees feel that they are valued participants and, as such, become self-motivated to take on the challenge of realizing the organization's mission and work together as a team. It can transform an organization's workforce into a source of creativity and innovative solutions.

External Adaptation

Culture determines how the organization responds to changes in its external environment. Depending on the volatility in the business environment, some changes are significant enough to force members to question aspects of their organization's identity and purpose. Culture plays a role in informing and supporting sense-making or meaning when external changes are severe enough to force members to re-evaluate aspects of their organizational identity and purpose. Having the right culture can ensure that an organization responds quickly to rapidly changing customer needs or the actions of a competitor. For example, if the competitive environment requires a strategy of superior customer service, the organizational culture should encourage and support such values as listening to customers, empowering employees to make decisions, and rewarding employees for outstanding customer service deeds.[18] The power of culture is in its potential to bring employees together to create a team rather than a collection of isolated individuals or factions when faced with threats from the external environment.[19]

OPENING CASE *APPLICATION*

2. The text points out that an organization's culture serves two important functions: (1) it creates internal unity, and (2) it helps the organization adapt to the external environment. Has this been the case at Avon?

Avon's employee-centered culture is what helps to guide and sustain its employees' productive behavior. Its emphasis on social responsibility, participation, and empowerment appeals strongly to Avon's employees. Avon strives to create a work environment that values and encourages the uniqueness of each individual, and it is committed to creating a culture that supports associates as they balance their many, and sometimes competing, work and personal responsibilities. The culture of Avon is certainly a factor in explaining the strong bond or internal unity that exists among company employees and also between sales representatives and their customers.

In terms of the culture facilitating external adaptation, Andrea Jung can be credited with directing the successful transformation of Avon. She is revitalizing Avon's reputation as the world's foremost direct seller of beauty products while leading the company into exciting new lines of business, launching a series of bold and image-enhancing initiatives, and expanding career opportunities for women around the world. She expanded the number of products offered to longtime customers by introducing a line of lingerie and casual wear, proving that she was not afraid to take risks. This generated new revenue from an established consumer base. "We were the first to come out with an alpha hydroxide acid product," she says, as she explains the need to constantly be on the lookout for new products. These are all changes that were responses to emerging opportunities and threats in the external environment.

Despite the empirical evidence of a positive relationship between organizational culture and performance, not too many organizations have credible claims to owning a high-performing culture. The next section focuses the discussion on the characteristics of low- and high-performing cultures.

Learning Outcome 2 — *Describe the characteristics of low- and high-performing cultures.*

Low- and High-Performing Cultures

A growing body of literature documents the economic benefits of investing in a performance-oriented culture.[20] A unique corporate culture is hard to duplicate or imitate and thus helps to sustain a firm's competitive advantage. Organizational cultures vary widely in the extent to which they are woven into the fabric of the organization's practices and behavioral norms. The strength of any culture depends on the degree to which these norms and practices are widely shared and strongly held throughout the organization. A weak culture symbolizes a lack of agreement or shared mind-set on key values and norms; a strong culture symbolizes a strong agreement or shared mind-set on key values and norms, with leaders playing a key role. The strong culture is described as distinctive and very tight—so much so, that members whose values don't match the organization's are more likely to have a short tenure because they are either forced to quit or voluntarily quit. Strong cultures are generally associated with high performance and weak cultures are generally associated with low performance.

The reference to performance is in terms of the many studies that have investigated the impact of organizational culture on performance indicators such as revenue and profit growth, quality,[21] customer satisfaction, innovation,[22] turnover and absenteeism rates, workforce productivity, employee job satisfaction,[23,24] creativity, [25,26,27] commitment,[28,29] and learning outcomes. Weak(low)-performing cultures share certain characteristics that distinguish them from strong(high)-performing cultures.

Characteristics of Low-Performing Cultures

Weak cultures are more likely to be associated with low performance. As mentioned above, an organization's culture is weak when there is little agreement on the values, beliefs, and norms governing member behavior. This could be because the leader has not effectively implanted the right culture or because members have not bought into the existing culture. In a weak culture, members of the organization typically show no deeply felt sense of identity with the organization's vision, mission, long-term objectives, and strategy. In such organizations, culture has no meaning to the employees and managers. In a weak culture, negative behaviors like gossiping, manipulation, favoritism, lack of communication, and internal conflict prevail. Without knowledge of what the organization stands for, weak cultures work against or hinder strategy implementation and thus are low performers. See the characteristics shared by low-performing cultures in Exhibit 10.1 and a brief discussion of each.

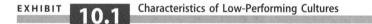

EXHIBIT 10.1   Characteristics of Low-Performing Cultures

- Insular thinking
- Resistance to change
- Politicized internal environment
- Unhealthy promotion practices

© Cengage Learning 2013

Insular Thinking

In a low-performing culture, there is a tendency to become insular. Managerial arrogance and inward thinking often prevent the organization from making the necessary cultural adaptation as external conditions change, thus leading to a decline in company performance.

Resistance to Change

Low-performing cultures tend to resist change when confronted by fast-changing domestic and global business conditions. The lack of leadership in encouraging and supporting employee initiatives or new ideas destroys creativity. Low-performing cultures want to maintain the status quo; as a result, avoiding risk and not making mistakes become more important to a person's career advancement than entrepreneurial successes and innovative accomplishments.

Politicized Internal Environment

Low performing cultures are characterized by a political environment that allows influential managers to operate their units autonomously—like personal kingdoms. In a politically charged culture, many issues or problems get resolved along the lines of power. Vocal support or opposition by powerful executives, as well as personal lobbying by key individuals or groups with vested interests in a particular outcome, may stifle important change. Such a culture has low performance because what's best for the organization is secondary to the self-interests of individual players.

Unhealthy Promotion Practices

Low-performance cultures tend to promote employees into higher leadership positions without serious consideration to abilities, experiences, and training. No effort is made to match the skills and capabilities of the appointee to the tasks requirements of the new position; instead, promotions are based on personal considerations (friendship, family ties, favoritism, and so forth).[30]

Characteristics of High-Performing Cultures

An organization's culture is considered strong and cohesive when it conducts its business according to a clear and explicit set of principles and values that are widely shared. In this culture, management commits considerable time to communicating these principles and values and explaining how they relate to the mission and strategies of the organization.

Ultimately, high-performing cultures have what some have described as a culture of discipline—where everyone is responsible to the values of the company, to its expectations, and to the purpose it serves. See the characteristics shared by high-performing cultures in Exhibit 10.2 and a brief discussion of each.

EXHIBIT 10.2   Characteristics of High-Performing Cultures

- Effective use of culture reinforcement tools
- Intensely people oriented
- Results oriented
- Emphasis on excellence

© Cengage Learning 2013

Effective Use of Culture-Reinforcement Tools

Culture-reinforcement tools include ceremonies, rewards, rituals, symbols, stories, language, and policies. High-performing cultures use ceremonies and other social events to reinforce dramatic examples of what the company values. Ceremonies recognize and celebrate high-performing employees. Also, in high-performing cultures, leaders tell stories to new employees to illustrate the company's primary values, which then create a shared understanding among workers. They also use symbols, rituals, and specialized language (such as slogans) to convey meaning and values. These mechanisms are the means by which high-performing cultures ensure that accepted norms and values are maintained and transmitted.

Intensely People Oriented

Organizations with high-performing cultures see their employees as their number one asset. They treat employees with dignity and respect, grant them greater autonomy, involve them in decision making, celebrate individual and team achievements, and use the full range of rewards and punishment to enforce high performance standards.

A reciprocal relationship develops when organizations are able to attract, retain, and reward outstanding performers. Such employees are more likely to behave in ways that help the organization succeed. This cycle of success is like a "virtuous spiral" that reinforces the reciprocal pattern again and again. Trust, responsibility, accountability, and integrity are defining features of relationships between leaders and their followers in high-performing cultures. These culture attributes are firm-specific assets that provide unique value, and because they are hard for competitors to imitate, offer the best means for building and sustaining a competitive advantage.

Results Oriented

High-performing cultures are very results oriented. Controls are developed to collect, analyze, and interpret employee performance data. High-performing cultures have a strong desire to establish linkages between reward systems and performance.[31] All employees and their managers are trained in the goal-setting process. Employees take ownership of their goals and as such demonstrate a higher commitment and motivation to achieve them. These goals form the basis of leader–follower performance evaluations and feedback. In high-performing cultures, leaders seek out reasons and opportunities to give out pins, buttons, badges, certificates, and medals to those who stand out in their performance.

WORK Application **1**
Would you describe the organization where you work or have worked as a low- or high-performance culture? Explain your answer.

_____

_____

_____

_____

Emphasis on Excellence

High-performing cultures create an atmosphere in which there is constructive pressure to be the best. Management pursues policies that benchmark best practices in the industry. When an organization performs consistently at or near peak levels, over time the pursuit of excellence becomes a way of life and a key part of the culture.

OPENING CASE APPLICATION

3. The chapter discusses the characteristics of a high-performing (strong) culture. What is the evidence that Avon has a strong culture?

Andrea Jung has led the way in not only communicating but also modelling the principles and values that Avon espouses. The Avon story, according to Jung, is all about bringing together women from all walks of life who through work, want to change their lives. Everyone at Avon seems to share the same dream and aspiration. There is an emotional bond with the mission of the company, and every employee works hard to realize the long-term goals set by Jung and her senior leadership team. She implores her senior leadership to communicate with the rank-and-file openly and frequently.

CONCEPT APPLICATION 1
Characteristics of Low- and High-Performing Cultures

a. Effective use of culture reinforcement tools
b. Intensely people oriented
c. Results oriented
d. Emphasis on excellence

e. Insular thinking
f. Resistance to change
g. Politicized internal environment
h. Unhealthy promotion practices

(continued)

(Concept Application 1 continued)

Identify each statement with a characteristic associated with a high- or low-performing culture. Write the appropriate letter in the blank before each item.

_____ 1. I like the way management just tells us what it wants done. It lets us do the job our way, as long as we meet the goals.

_____ 2. I wonder: how many of the top executives here got to where they are today on merit?

_____ 3. We have always done things here in a certain way and it's worked so far. I see no need to change that which is not broken.

_____ 4. Here, you have a big role in setting your own goals, but once they are set, you are held to them.

_____ 5. I know that Jean Claude started the company, but he died 10 years ago. His story and founding principles are still being told to all new and current employees today.

_____ 6. We get together regularly to celebrate one thing or another and it really motivates people.

_____ 7. One thing I like about this place is that I have greater autonomy in how I do my job.

_____ 8. I think every department in the company has a copy of the mission statement on the wall somewhere.

_____ 9. I find it a bit frustrating because top management seems to change its mind about our priorities whenever it suits them. That is why I am not going along this time.

_____ 10. Every division here is striving to be No. 1 or 2 in its industry; it is very challenging, yet motivating.

Learning Outcome 3

Discuss the leader's role in influencing culture.

The Leader's Role in Influencing Culture

Influencing the culture of an organization so that it aligns with strategy, structure, and HR policies and practices is a vital leadership responsibility.[32] Also, it is important for organizations to consider the "fit" between the current or desired organizational culture and CEO characteristics when it comes to new appointments. Studies on the subject have found that matching CEO personality traits and values to an organization's cultural values enhances successful outcomes.[33]

Leaders can initiate many different types of policies, programs, and practices to change, modify, or sustain an organization's culture. Some of these actions are substantive, while others are simply symbolic; yet taken together, they can shape the culture of an organization according to the expectations of the leader.[34] Substantive actions are explicit and highly visible and are indicative of management's commitment to a new way of doing things. These are actions that everyone will understand are intended to establish a new culture more in tune with the organization's mission and strategy. Symbolic actions are valuable for the signals they send about the kinds of behavior and expectations leaders wish to encourage and promote. In his book, Schein uses the terms *primary* and *secondary mechanisms* to distinguish between symbolic and substantive actions.[35]

Substantive Actions

Substantive actions that a leader can employ to influence culture include aligning culture to HR policies and practices, strategy, and structure; matching rewards/incentives to the culture outcomes; and designing physical work environments that match espoused cultural norms.[36,37]

The strongest sign that management is truly committed to creating a new culture is replacing old-culture members who are unwilling to change with a new breed of employees. This can be accomplished through new HR criteria for recruiting, selecting, promoting, and firing employees. These new criteria should match the values and expectations of the new culture. This matching process is what some have described as an HR-organizational culture fit and an HR-business strategy fit.[38] Existing policies and practices that impede the execution of new strategies must be changed. Through these actions, leaders let other members know what is important.

In rapidly changing business environments, the capacity to introduce new strategies is a necessity if a company is to perform well over long periods of time. Strategic agility and fast organizational response to new opportunities require a culture that quickly adapts to environmental change rather than a culture that resists change. Another name for this type of culture is the *organizational learning culture*.[39] It is the leader's responsibility to select a strategy that is compatible with the prevailing culture or to change the culture to fit the chosen strategy. The lack of a "fit" will hinder or constrain strategy execution. The culture of an organization naturally evolves over time, and without strong leadership it can change in the wrong direction. For example, incompatible subcultures may develop in various departments of the organization, leading to a culture of isolation rather than teamwork and cooperation.

Tying rewards and incentive programs directly to new measures of strategic performance is a culture-shaping action because it gives the leader leverage to reward only those performances that are supportive of the strategy and culture.[40] It is often the case that in many organizations, when strategies change, changes in the reward structure tend to lag behind. Imagine an organization in which the CEO has articulated an integration-based strategy that will require leaders at all levels to think and act across departmental or divisional boundaries and act on behalf of the entire enterprise. However, the organizational reward system only offers incentives for achieving unit success. Such reward/incentive misalignments weaken an organization's culture.[41]

Finally, leaders can design the physical work environment to reflect the values they want to promote within the organization. For example, having common eating facilities for all employees, no special parking areas, and similar offices is consistent with a value of equality. An open office layout with fewer walls separating employees is consistent with a value for open communication. In designing its headquarters, Google wanted to provide open work spaces and an environment that promoted coworker contact and interaction. By providing a clear sense of place and purpose for its employees, Google succeeded in communicating an employee-friendly culture through its facility design, with the architecture and comfort of the setting reinforced by the cultural and aesthetic elements in the building.

Symbolic Actions

Symbolic actions that a leader can employ to influence culture include modeling expected behavior, recognizing and celebrating accomplishments, and being visible. Senior executives are role models, and the stories they tell, decisions they make, and actions they take reveal an implicit cultural expectation for followers. Employees learn what is valued most in an organization by watching what attitudes and behaviors leaders pay attention to and reward, and whether the leaders' own behaviors match the espoused values. Employees want to see that their leaders "walk the walk." For example, when top executives lead a cost-reduction effort by curtailing executive perks, or when they emphasize the importance of responding to customers' needs by requiring members of the top management team to spend a portion of each week talking with customers and understanding their needs, these actions set a good example. The message employees get when a leader institutes a policy but fails to act in accordance with it is that the policy is really not important or necessary.[42]

WORK Application 2

Identify and briefly explain which of the leadership actions for shaping culture have been used by a leader where you work or have worked.

_____

_____

_____

_____

Leaders can schedule ceremonies to celebrate and honor people whose actions and performance exemplify what is called for in the new culture. Ceremonies reinforce specific values and create emotional bonds by allowing employees to share in important moments. A culture that celebrates accomplishments helps to retain valued employees. Ceremonies often include the presentation of awards.

Another symbolic action a leader can use to influence culture is simply being visible. A leader who appears at ceremonial functions to praise followers who exemplify the values and practices of the new culture is making a symbolic, yet instructive gesture. Effective leaders will also make special appearances at nonceremonial events (such as employee training workshops) to stress key priorities, values, cultural norms, and ethical principles. To followers, the mere appearance of the executive—and the things he or she chooses to emphasize—clearly communicates management's commitment to the new culture. Exhibit 10.3 summarizes the substantive and symbolic actions that leaders can use to influence or shape organizational culture.

EXHIBIT 10.3   **Leadership Actions for Shaping Culture**

Substantive Actions
a. Instituting new policies and practices
b. Aligning strategy and structure to culture
c. Matching rewards/incentives to the culture
d. Matching work environment design to culture

Symbolic Actions
a. Modeling expected behavior
b. Recognizing and celebrating accomplishments
c. Being visible

© Cengage Learning 2013

Learning Outcome 4   _Briefly describe the four types of culture commonly found in organizations._

Types of Culture

Rather than looking at culture as either good or bad, it should be viewed as a construct that varies according to an organization's business environment, the leader's personality, past history, and attitudes of current employees. There is no one best organizational culture. The ideal culture is that which supports the organization's mission and strategy. Organizational culture types such as the learning, innovative, team, clan, market, or adhocracy cultures have been studied for their impact on employee outcomes such as creativity,[43] productivity, job satisfaction,[44] or turnover.[45,46] Other names used to describe an organization's culture include the _cooperative, adaptive, competitive_, and _bureaucratic_ cultures.[47] We will focus our discussion on this later group. These culture types are not mutually exclusive; an organization's culture may reveal characteristics that will fit one or more of these groupings. However, high-performing organizations with strong cohesive cultures tend to emphasize or lean more toward one particular culture type—a shared mind-set.

Cooperative Culture

The **cooperative culture** _represents a leadership belief in strong, mutually reinforcing exchanges and linkages between employees and departments._ In this type of culture, operating policies, procedures, and practices are all designed with one goal in mind—to encourage cooperation, teamwork, power sharing, and camaraderie among employees. Management thinking is predicated on the belief that organizational success is influenced more by effective cooperative relationships inside the organization than by external relationships (resource-based view theory of the firm). It is an internally focused culture. Proponents of the cooperative culture argue that in today's dynamic work environment—characterized by constant changes and fluid projects—creating a work environment in which workers collaborate with each other and work in highly effective teams creates synergy and increases productivity.[48] It is a culture where employees are empowered to act and think like owners rather than hired hands.

Adaptive Culture

The **adaptive culture** *represents a leadership belief in active monitoring of the external environment for emerging opportunities and threats and adapting to them.* This culture is made up of policies, procedures, and practices that support employees' ability to respond quickly to changing environmental conditions. In adaptive cultures, members are encouraged to take risks, experiment, innovate, and learn from these experiences.[49] Management thinking is based on the belief that organizational success is influenced more by events outside the organization than by internal factors (the industrial organization view theory of the firm). Therefore, employees are empowered to make decisions and act quickly to take advantage of emerging opportunities and avoid threats. There is greater individual autonomy and tolerance for failure. There is a spirit of doing what is necessary to ensure both short-term and long-term organizational success, provided core values and business principles are upheld in the process. The adaptive culture is generally known for its flexibility and innovativeness.[50] The core principles of the adaptive culture are similar to those of organizational learning culture (OLC)[51] discussed in Chapter 12.

Competitive Culture

The **competitive culture** *represents a leadership mind-set that encourages and values a highly competitive work environment.* Organizational policies, procedures, work practices, and rules are all designed to foster both internal competition (employee versus employee, department versus department, or division versus division) and external competition (company versus competitors). An organization with a competitive culture operates in a mature market environment in which competition is intense. Competitive cultures focus on specific targets such as growth in market share, revenue, or profitability. This is a numbers-driven culture that values competitiveness, personal initiative, aggressiveness, achievement, and the willingness to work long and hard for you or your team. The drive to win either against one another internally or against an external competitor is what holds the organization together.

PepsiCo and Coca-Cola are two companies that exemplify the competitive culture. Each company socializes its members to view the other's employees as enemies and to do whatever is necessary to defeat them in the marketplace. High performance standards and tough reviews are used to weed out the weak and reward the strong. At PepsiCo, for example, former CEO Wayne Calloway was known to set backbreaking standards and then systematically raise them each year. Executives who met his standards were generously rewarded—stock options, bonuses, rapid promotions—and those who did not felt the pressure to produce or risk negative consequences such as demotions, transfers, or job termination.

Bureaucratic Culture

The **bureaucratic culture** *represents a leadership mind-set that values order, stability, status, and efficiency.* Bureaucratic cultures emphasizes strict adherence to set rules,

WORK Application **3**

Describe which of the four types of organizational cultures exist where you work or have worked. Does it lean towards one type or is it a compilation of the four types?

_____

_____

_____

_____

policies, and procedures, which ensure an orderly way of doing business. Organizations with bureaucratic cultures are highly structured and efficiency driven. The bureaucratic culture may work for an organization pursuing a low-cost leadership strategy but not for one pursuing a differentiation strategy. The bureaucratic culture is becoming increasingly difficult to sustain even for low-cost driven companies. Faced with the increasing threat of globalization, many leaders are forced to make the shift away from bureaucratic cultures because of the need for greater flexibility and adaptation.

OPENING CASE *APPLICATION*

4. **Is Avon's culture competitive, adaptive, bureaucratic, or cooperative? Support your answer.**

Avon's culture fits with three of the four culture types. Avon wants its saleswomen to share ideas with each other and to work together as a team. To facilitate this, Avon provides opportunities for employees to network among themselves. This qualifies Avon as having a cooperative culture. However, Avon is also cognizant of the need to adapt to market and technological changes. According to CEO Andrea Jung, these days, "you have to be part of a technology-driven and technology-resourced beauty company to win over the long run." Avon can also be described as having a competitive culture in the sense that the company is aware of its competitors and is constantly positioning and repositioning its marketing strategies vis-à-vis its competitors. The 2005 restructuring described in the opening case application was implemented with competition in mind. Andrea Jung did not want to lose ground to her competitors, and that's why she took bold moves to cut costs, launch new products, and increase advertising. The one thing that cannot be said about Avon's culture is that it is bureaucratic. Jung wants broad participation in decision making and encourages managers to meet with followers face-to-face to solicit feedback.

CONCEPT APPLICATION 2
Type of Organizational Culture

Identify each statement as characteristic of one of the types of organizational cultures. Write the appropriate letter in the blank before each item.

a. competitive   c. bureaucratic   e. team
b. adaptive   d. cooperative   f. clan

_____ 11. Being a young Internet company, we want our employees to work collaboratively with each other and share ideas/information.

_____ 12. Things don't change much around here. We just focus on performing our tasks according to standard operating procedures and keep costs low.

_____ 13. At Toyota, we focus on being flexible and responsive to changing customer needs and expectations.

_____ 14. In our industry, every action draws a counteraction from competitors; thus we keep a close eye on our prices to make sure we are not underpriced.

The following section describes a framework for understanding the bases of broad national cultural differences.

Learning Outcome 5   *Describe Hofstede's theory on National Culture Identities.*

National Culture Identities—Hofstede's Value Dimensions

Whether culture is analyzed from an organizational or national context, it is still a product of values, beliefs, and norms that people use to guide and control behavior. Relationships between leaders and members of an organization are based on shared values and norms. On a national level, a country's values and norms determine what kinds of attitudes and behaviors are acceptable or appropriate. There are significant interaction effects between organizational practices and national culture.[52] An organization's cultural archetype may have its roots or some of its roots in the national culture. The people of a particular country are socialized into the national culture as they grow up and thus, are influenced by it.[53] A well-known study on this subject is that of Geert Hofstede. Hofstede developed five key dimensions that distinguish a nation's culture from other nations.[54] Exhibit 10.4 summarizes these value dimensions, which are briefly discussed along with leadership implications. Each of these five dimensions is broken down into two opposing variables that are at opposite ends of a continuum.

EXHIBIT 10.4 A Framework of Value Dimensions for Understanding Cultural Differences

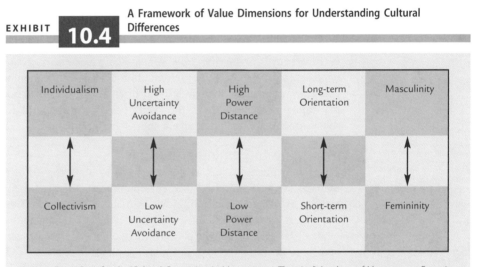

Source: From G. Hofstede, "Cultural Constraints in Management Theories," *Academy of Management Executive* 7 (1993), pp. 81–94. The Academy of Management review by Academy of Management. Copyright 1993. Reproduced with permission of Academy of Management (NY) in the format Textbook via Copyright Clearance Center.

Individualistic to Collectivistic Cultures

This dimension involves a person's source of identity in society. Some societies value individualism more than collectivism, and vice versa. **Individualism** *is a psychological state in which people see themselves first as individuals and believe their own interest and values are primary.* Other names for the individualistic culture are the autonomy culture or the self-expression culture. **Collectivism** *is the state of mind wherein the values and goals of the group—whether extended family, ethnic group, or company—are primary.*[55] The United States, Great Britain, and Canada have been described as individualistic cultures, while Greece, Japan, and Mexico are said to have collectivistic cultures.

High- to Low-Uncertainty-Avoidance Cultures

A society with a **high-uncertainty-avoidance culture** has *a majority of people who do not tolerate risk, avoid the unknown, and are comfortable when the future is relatively predictable and certain.* In a high-uncertainty-avoidance country like Japan, managers prefer well-structured and predictable situations. The other end of the continuum is a society where the majority of the people have low uncertainty avoidance. A low-uncertainty-avoidance culture *has a majority of* people *who are comfortable with and accepting of the unknown, and tolerate risk and unpredictability.* The United States, Australia, and Canada are associated with low-uncertainty-avoidance cultures while Argentina, Italy, Japan, and Israel are associated with high-uncertainty-avoidance cultures.

High- to Low-Power-Distance Cultures

This dimension deals with a society's view on power and status. The way in which people of different status, power, or authority should relate to each other as equals or un-equals is referred to as power distance. In a high-power-distance culture, *leaders and followers rarely interact as equals;* while in a low-power-distance culture, *leaders and their followers interact on several levels as equals.* It is also called the egalitarian culture. High-power-distance cultures include Mexico, Japan, Spain, and France. Low-power-distance cultures include Germany, the United States, and Ireland.

Long-Term to Short-Term Orientation Cultures

This dimension refers to a society's long- or short-term orientation toward life and work. People from a culture with a long-term orientation *have a future-oriented view of life and thus are thrifty (saving for the future) and persistent in achieving goals.* A short-term orientation *derives from values that express a concern for maintaining personal happiness and living in the present.* Immediate gratification is a priority. Most Asian countries, known for their long-term orientation, are also known for their high rate of per capita savings, whereas most European countries and the United States tend to spend more, save less, and have a short-term orientation.

WORK Application 4

Based on the five value dimensions discussed, briefly explain the level of cultural understanding that exists where you work or have worked.

Masculine to Feminine Cultures

This value dimension was used by Hofstede to make the distinction between the quest for material assets (which he called masculinity) and the quest for social connections with people (which he called femininity). In this context, masculinity *describes a culture that emphasizes assertiveness and a competitive drive for money and material objects.* At the other end of the continuum is femininity which *describes a culture that emphasizes developing and nurturing personal relationships and a high quality of life.*[56] Countries with masculine cultures include Japan and Italy; feminine cultures include Sweden and Denmark.

Implications for Leadership

The growing diversity of the workforce and the increasing globalization of the marketplace create the need for leaders with multicultural backgrounds and experiences. This trend explains why the AACSB list among required knowledge and skill areas the dynamics of the global economy and multicultural and diversity understanding.[57] In the academic community, there is greater recognition that future leaders need diversity competencies—in order to leverage a diverse workforce to create tangible benefits for their organizations.[58,59] Leaders have to recognize, for example, that although organizations in the United States may reward and encourage individual achievements, a different norm may apply in Japan, where the group makes important decisions. In the United States, competition between work-group members for career advancement is desirable. In collectivistic cultures however, members may resist competing with peers for rewards or promotions in order to avoid disrupting the harmony of the group or appearing self-centered.

Cross-cultural and international joint venture (IJV) studies often identify cultural differences as the cause of many interpersonal difficulties, including conflict and poor performance in postmerger and acquisition deals.[60] More and more organizations are relying on leaders with international experience to lead a multicultural workforce and compete in the global marketplace.[61]

10.1 *Buy American*

Organizational culture is also based on national culture. People tend to believe their country or company is the best. You most likely have heard the slogan "Buy American." Unions tend to ask Americans to buy products made in the United States to help save their jobs. On the other hand, some Americans ask why they should buy American products, especially if they cost more or they are inferior in quality or style to foreign-made products. Many (or most) Americans don't know the country of ownership of many products they buy, and some domestic products are made with more than half of the components coming from other countries—so is the product really made in America?

1. Is it ethical and socially responsible to ask people to buy American, or from their home country?

2. Is it ethical and socially responsible to buy foreign products?

Ethics Leadership

The importance of ethical leadership can be seen in the crises of the recent past. These crises revealed huge, and in some cases criminal, failures of both ethics and leadership in the banking and finance industry, the real estate subprime market, and government. The AACSB lists ethical understanding as an important competency.[62] This may explain why quite a few colleges and universities are adding ethics courses in their curriculum.[63] **Ethics** *are the standards of right and wrong that influence behavior.* Ethics provides guidelines for judging conduct and decision making. The discussion of ethics in Chapter 3 was from the individual's perspective. The emphasis was on how an individual's personality traits and attitudes, level of moral development, and the situational context affect ethical behavior.

In this section, we examine ethics from an organizational perspective: the role of leadership in creating an ethical work environment.[64] It is a concept that applies not only to larger corporations but also small and medium-sized enterprises. We also discuss the relatively new concept of authentic leadership—what it is, characteristics of authentic leaders, and how they influence follower behavior and attitudes. Before we begin, complete Self-Assessment 1 to determine your personal values in eight areas.

SELF-ASSESSMENT 1   **Personal Values**

Below are 16 items. Rate how important each one is to you on a scale of 0 (not important) to 100 (very important). Write the number 0–100 on the line to the left of each item.

0 — 10 — 20 — 30 — 40 — 50 — 60 — 70 — 80—90 — 100
Not important   Somewhat important   Very important

_____ 1. An enjoyable, satisfying job

_____ 2. A high-paying job

_____ 3. A good marriage

_____ 4. Meeting new people, social events

_____ 5. Involvement in community activities

_____ 6. My relationship with God/my religion

_____ 7. Exercising, playing sports

_____ 8. Intellectual development

_____ 9. A career with challenging opportunities

_____ 10. Nice cars, clothes, home, and so on

_____ 11. Spending time with family

(continued)

(Self-Assessment 1 continued)

———— 12. Having several close friends

———— 13. Volunteer work for not-for-profit organizations like the Cancer Society

———— 14. Meditation, quiet time to think, pray, and so on

———— 15. A healthy, balanced diet

———— 16. Educational reading, self-improvement programs, TV, and so on

Next, transfer your rating numbers for each of the 16 items to the appropriate columns. Then add the two numbers in each column.

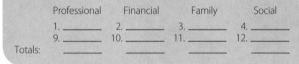

	Professional	Financial	Family	Social
	1. ————	2. ————	3. ————	4. ————
	9. ————	10. ————	11. ————	12. ————
Totals:	————	————	————	————

	Community	Spiritual	Physical	Intellectual
	5. ————	6. ————	7. ————	8. ————
	13. ————	14. ————	15. ————	16. ————
Totals:	————	————	————	————

The higher the total in any area, the higher the value you place on that particular area. The closer the numbers are in all eight areas, the better rounded you are.

Think about the time and effort you put forth in your top three values. Is it sufficient to allow you to achieve the level of success you want in each of those areas? If not, what can you do to change? Is there any area in which you feel you should have a higher value total? If yes, which, and what can you do to change?

Learning Outcome 6

Briefly explain examples of organizational practices that can help foster an ethical work environment.

Organizational Practices That Foster an Ethical Work Environment

For an organization to display consistently high ethical and socially responsible behavior, effective leaders must create and maintain a culture of ethics that permeates the entire organization.[65] An ethical work environment emphasizes openness and integrity.[66] One study suggested that an ethical work environment is mission- and values-driven, stakeholder balanced, and effectively managed.[67] Some of the tools available for creating and maintaining this type of ethical work environment are discussed below.

Code of Ethics

Many organizations have a written code of ethics or code of conduct that displays the values and principles governing employee behavior. Written statements have the advantage of explicitly stating the company's position on ethical and moral issues, and they serve as benchmarks for judging both company decisions and actions and individual conduct. A growing number of organizations have added a code of ethics to their list of formal statements and public pronouncements.[68] They are seen as tools for highlighting an organization's socially responsible culture.

Leaders must constantly communicate to members the value of not only observing ethical codes but also reporting ethical violations. "Gray areas" must be identified and openly discussed with members, and offer guidelines when disagreements arise.[69] It is generally believed that the more an organization's employees are informed of ethical expectations, the more likely they are to do the right thing. A code of ethics is of no consequence if an ethical corporate culture and top management support are lacking.[70]

Ethics Committees

Having a code of ethics is no guarantee that everyone will behave ethically. Enforcing the ethical code is critical. In order to ensure consistency and keep the ethical culture an ongoing part of organizational life, effective leaders are also requiring the creation of ethics committees charged with resolving ethical violations and updating ethical standards. In other organizations the responsibility is given to an ombudsperson. *An ethics* ombudsperson *is a single person entrusted with the responsibility of acting as the organization's conscience.* He or she hears and investigates complaints and points out potential ethics failures to top management. In many large corporations, ethics departments with full-time staff are now part of the organizational structure and charged with helping employees deal with day-to-day ethical problems or questions.

Training and Education Programs

Training and education provide the opportunity for everyone in the organization to be informed and educated on the company's code of ethics and social responsibility obligations. Training teaches employees how to incorporate ethics into daily behavior. In short, training helps to align member behaviors with the organization's values. As mentioned earlier, the AACSB has included ethical understanding and reasoning abilities as one of its knowledge and skill areas and encouraged business schools to add it to the curriculum. Many scholars and practitioners now believe that business schools need to play a greater role in instilling ethical values in their students, who are, after all, future business leaders. Organizations must train their employees to focus not only on the economic imperative of profit generation but also the fiduciary imperative of ethically anchored and socially responsible behavior.

Disclosure Mechanisms

WORK Application 5

In your school, look around or investigate if any of the tools discussed here for enforcing an ethical and socially responsible work environment is present. Describe briefly what it is, where it is located, and what behavior it regulates.

As part of enforcing ethical conduct, proactive organizations have also instituted disclosure mechanisms to encourage employees to report any knowledge of ethical violations. Whistle-blowing *is employee disclosure of illegal or unethical practices on the part of the organization.* In 2002, the scandals surrounding companies such as Enron and WorldCom left many people wondering why no one blew the whistle on these practices sooner. Later that year, *Time* magazine named three women, including Sherron Watkins of Enron Corporation, as People of the Year. Sherron Watkins is the one who first attempted to blow the whistle on the Enron scandal but no one would listen. Whistle-blowing can be risky for those who choose to do it—they have been known to suffer consequences including being ostracized by coworkers, demoted or transferred to less-desirable jobs, and even losing their jobs. Policies that protect employees from going through these setbacks will signal management's genuine commitment to enforce ethical behavior. Some organizations have done this by setting up hotlines to give employees a confidential way to report unethical or illegal actions.

OPENING CASE *APPLICATION*

5. What role has Andrea Jung played in fostering a climate of strict ethical standards at Avon?

Andrea Jung has always maintained that only by adhering to the highest ethical conduct can Avon look forward to continued success in the future. Avon's impeccable reputation, she said, is built upon a proud heritage of doing well by doing right. "For more than a century," she said, "we have been setting the very highest example of integrity and ethics in all of our relationships—with our shareholders, associates, and representatives; our suppliers and competitors; governments; and the public. Our values and principles are the bedrock not only of Avon's past—but of its future."

On Avon's company Web site, the following declaration is posted: "At Avon, we strive always to maintain the highest standards of integrity and ethical conduct, consistent with our Company values and in compliance with both the letter and spirit of all applicable laws and regulations. Each Avon Associate is individually responsible for strict compliance with the policies applicable to their work. Information published on this site reflects our commitment to upholding the highest of standards in the area of ethics, corporate governance and compliance." One can safely assume that Andrea Jung's leadership has played a significant role in shaping Avon's culture and ethical climate.

In a *Wall Street Journal* article on May 5, 2011, it was reported that Avon was widening its internal investigation into possible bribery of foreign officials. The investigation so far had uncovered more potential wrongdoing, with evidence of improper payments to government officials found in several countries beyond the probe's original focus of China. A person familiar with the case said that internal investigators at the door-to-door beauty seller have turned up millions of dollars of questionable payments to officials in Brazil, Mexico, Argentina, India, and Japan in amounts that are "not insignificant."[71]

This is a violation that falls under the Foreign Corrupt Practices Act, which basically says that it is illegal and a criminal act for U.S. company officials to bribe foreign government officials to curry business favors. Over the years, many have questioned this law given that other countries don't punish or forbid the same practice. If anything, it is encouraged. The view of opponents of the law is that it puts American businesses at a disadvantage since bribery is a way of doing business in many cultures; especially developing countries.

1. Do you think this law is fair to American businesses?

2. An Avon official has already been suspended. Is Avon doing the right thing?

3. Is it ethical that other countries are allowing or even encouraging this practice?

Learning Outcome 7

Discuss the validity of the assertion that authentic leadership has its roots in moral and ethical theory of leadership.

Authentic Leadership

In the wake of corporate scandals involving companies like Enron, WorldCom, Siemens, Samsung, and Tyco—not to mention the severe economic crises we are all currently living through—the need to have confidence in institutions and leaders is ever more critical. Reliability, integrity, and authenticity will be especially required of our business leaders.[72] Many people now say we need authentic leaders, people of the highest integrity, committed to building enduring organizations—leaders who have a deep sense of purpose and are true to their values. We need leaders who have the courage to tell their followers the hard truths even if it's not what they want to hear.[73] The interest in authentic leadership has led some to pose the question whether authentic leadership is the next big thing in leadership, or just wishful thinking.[74] To fully appreciate this new leadership model, we focus on three questions: what is authentic leadership, what are the characteristics of the authentic leader, and what is its impact on follower behavior, attitudes, and performance?

What Is Authentic Leadership?

Authenticity is about genuineness. It is a psychological construct that focuses on knowing, accepting, and acting in accordance with one's core values, beliefs, emotions, and preferences. The authentic leader holds him- or herself to a higher standard of integrity, character, and accountability. It is rooted in the notion of a "true self."[75] Authentic leadership has an introspective quality that allows leaders to reflect on whether their actions are consistent with who they are, ensuring that their values and ethics take precedence over external pressures, and not vice versa.[76] Authentic leaders try to convey a message of hopefulness, optimism, and resiliency to their followers. The authentic leader is driven by a value system that calls for being visible to others, focusing on what is ethical or the right thing to do, staying the course even at personal risk, making empowerment of others a priority, and maintaining open communication with all followers.[77] Authentic leadership theory is grounded in moral and ethical foundations of leadership. It is closely associated with other positive leadership models such as charismatic, transformational, servant, and values-based leadership.[78]

In their study on authentic leadership theory, Gardner and his associates describe four underlying components of authentic leadership: self-awareness, balanced information processing, authentic behavior, and relational transparency.[79] **Self-awareness** is defined as *a process where one continually comes to understand his or her unique talents, strengths, sense of purpose, core values, beliefs and desires.*[80] Balanced information processing is the second component of authentic leadership. Leaders form an objective view of their "true self" by balancing both positive and negative attributes and qualities. They try to be realistic and genuine in their self-assessment. The third component, authentic behavior, is a desire by the leader to match his or her espoused values to actions. This builds the leader's integrity and credibility with followers. The fourth and final component, relational transparency, is about openness and self-disclosure. This enhances followers' trust in the leader, and trust happens to be the cornerstone of authentic leadership.

Characteristics of Authentic Leaders

Authentic leaders are effective communicators and good decision makers. They don't shy away from making tough decisions, because they are motivated not by the desire to be liked, but by their values and purpose. They know who they are and are not afraid of being themselves. Authentic leaders are also known to exhibit a strong commitment to achieving their organization's goals and the premiums they place on the contribution their followers make to achieve such goals. Because it is a leadership model that centers on trust and keeping one's word, authentic leaders don't want to fail; they don't want to risk letting down the people who have invested so much trust in them.[81]

Authentic leadership is also about courage and character. Character provides the moral compass for decision making, especially for the tough decisions. When faced with difficult decisions, authentic leaders know what they stand for, and they have the courage to act on their principles even if the decision is unpopular. Courageous leaders are able to speak out to right wrongs, admit to personal weaknesses, and own up to mistakes.

How Authentic Leaders Influence Follower Behaviors and Attitudes

How a leader's authenticity influences follower behavior and attitudes is really the essence of authentic leadership. Followers take their cue from the leader, which is why the role of the leader in creating an ethical work environment is so critical. Trust is seen as the primary intervening variable linking authentic leadership to follower attitudes and behaviors.[82,83] Authentic leadership emphasizes a transparent and high-quality exchange relationship between leaders and followers. This allows for the formation of positive leader–member exchange relationships. This increases follower organizational citizenship behavior, job satisfaction, and retention. Because authentic leaders are consistent in their behavior, followers know what to expect from their leader and what is expected of them. Leader authenticity leads to higher levels of identification with the leader. The findings of one study revealed that leader authenticity is associated with higher ratings of transformational leadership behaviors.[84] The significance of authentic leadership in enhancing team and individual performance has been widely debated, with some studies finding strong support and others only partial support.

Diversity Leadership

Diversity *is the inclusion of all groups at all levels in an organization.* During the past three decades, the U.S. workplace has become more multiculturally diverse. A number of factors have contributed to this trend; among these are the Civil Rights Acts, which outlawed most types of employment discrimination; increased immigration, which has resulted in a more racially and ethnically mixed population; and changing demographics and the passage of the Americans with Disabilities Act (ADA) which has further broadened the scope of diversity in the workplace.

In this section, we explore changing demographics and its impact on workforce diversity, the benefits of embracing diversity, creating a culture the supports diversity, and the effects of globalization on diversity leadership.[85]

Changing Demographics and Workforce Diversity

Demographic diversity *is any characteristic that serves as a basis for social categorization and self-identification.* Demographic diversity describes differences resulting from age, gender, race, ethnicity, religion, and sexual orientation. National demographic changes, as well as greater minority representation in the workforce, have accounted for the most significant increase in workforce diversity.[86] The latest census revealed an increasing number of Hispanics, African-Americans, and Asians in the U.S. workforce. The population of these minority groups is growing at a faster rate than the overall population. This is accelerating what has been called the cultural diversity of the U.S. population.[87] The 2010 U.S. Census revealed that the number of Hispanics now stands at 16.3 percent (a 43 percent increase from 2000–2010). It is now the largest minority group and growing the fastest. The percentage of African-Americans is 12.6 percent, a 12.3 percent increase from 2000–2010. Longer term, Caucasians are projected to become a minority by 2050. Four states (California, Hawaii, New Mexico, and Texas) currently have the distinction of having a combined minority population greater than white populations, which only grew by 5.7 percent in the last census.

In the new work environment, workers must often share work duties and space with the handicapped. The passage of the Americans with Disabilities Act (ADA) has further broadened the scope of diversity in the workplace. Today, the chances of working with a disabled coworker are much higher than a decade ago.[88]

Another demographic trend is the age mix. The aging trend has now created what some have called generational or age diversity in the workplace.[89] For the first time, four distinct generations comprise today's workforce—the Traditionalists (1900–1945), the Baby Boomers (1946–1964), the Generation Xers (1965–1980), and the Millennials (1981–2000). Different generations have different attitudes and values, making the job of managing a team of mixed generations challenging to say the least.[90]

A greater likelihood exists that individuals will find themselves leading or under the leadership of someone demographically different from them.[91] As the U.S. workforce diversity continues to grow rapidly, effective leaders must create a workplace culture that allows workers from diverse backgrounds to succeed.[92] There is a growing interest in adding diversity management competency as part of leadership development programs.[93] Diversity competency training will enable leaders to understand how various leadership styles interact with followers' cultural value orientations to influence follower affective, cognitive, and behavioral outcomes.[94] Also, more corporate boards are recommending that top management teams be diversified.[95]

WORK Application 6

Describe diversity where you work or have worked. For example, approximately what percentages are male versus female, Caucasian versus non-Caucasian, older versus younger, and so on?

_____

_____

_____

_____

Learning Outcome 8   *Explain the benefits of embracing diversity.*

Benefits of Embracing Diversity

Decades of research have confirmed what many in the business world already know—that diversity makes for good business.[96,97] From a purely humanistic perspective, some believe that there is an ethical and moral imperative to pursue a policy of inclusion rather than exclusion. Advocates of this position believe that it is a matter of fairness, and that an inclusionary policy signals a company's commitment to uphold the dignity of every person regardless of their circumstance.

From a legal perspective, embracing diversity is in compliance with laws that have precedent and historical foundations. From a practical perspective, shifting demographics and increasing globalization have significantly changed the composition of the workforce, forcing corporations to respond or suffer economic loss. Organizations are forced to change their views and their approach to diversity in order to reflect this new reality.

Regardless of the moral, legal, or practical imperative of diversity, it must also have a positive link to the "bottom line." Many studies have examined the relationship between workforce diversity and organizational performance. There is a general acknowledgment that effective management of diversity initiatives/programs does produce positive outcomes.[98] Diversity initiatives that succeed in the short and long term are those that have a tangible impact on shareholder, customer, and employee values.[99,100] Some of the economic benefits that make the case for embracing diversity include the following:[101,102]

1. Embracing diversity can offer a company a marketing advantage.[103] More organizations are highlighting diversity in their advertising, because they are competing for talent in a tight labor market, and they recognize that demographic shifts are going to dramatically change their marketplace over the next 20 years. A diversified workforce may offer insight into understanding and meeting the needs of diverse customers. A diversified workforce is suitable to serve a diversified market place because employees who share similar cultural traits with the customers may be able to develop better, longer-lasting customer relationships.[104] Diversity, therefore, can enable a company to gain access in markets that others may not find easy to access.

2. Companies that embrace diversity will be able to recruit from a larger pool, train and retain superior performers, and maximize the benefits of a diverse workforce. When an organization has a reputation for valuing diversity, it tends to attract the best job candidates among women and other culturally diverse groups. For example, many HR recruiters have discovered that focusing on diversity in recruitment advertising helps attract more applicants from diverse backgrounds. Minority job seekers may feel more comfortable applying for employment with companies that have a proven diversity record.

3. Embracing diversity can be cost effective. Organizations that wholeheartedly embrace diversity and make everyone feel valued for their contributions can increase the job satisfaction of diverse groups, thus decreasing turnover and absenteeism and their associated costs. Diversity management practices can lead to positive effects on employees' organizational commitment.[105]

4. Embracing diversity may provide a broader and deeper base of creative problem solving and decision making. Creative solutions to problems are more likely to be reached in diverse work groups than homogeneous groups. In diverse groups, people bring different perspectives, knowledge, information, expertise, and skills to problems—resulting in better solutions and greater innovation. In innovative companies, leaders are challenged to create organizational environments that nurture and support creative thinking and the sharing of diverse viewpoints.

There is no consensus on the direct effects of diversity on the business bottom line (profitability). There are those who feel that diversity leads to better outcomes (such as those listed above) because of the richness of diverse perspectives and these benefits indirectly affect the bottom line; however, there are also those who feel that diversity impedes performance because diverse teams may be less cohesive and that there is no direct link between diversity and profitability. The latter group belongs to the minority. The majority of opinions support the hypothesis that effective diversity leadership is good for business. The next section takes a look at the downside of diversity.

The Downside of Diversity

Despite its benefits, diversity, if not effectively managed, can also bring about negative outcomes. Research suggests that, left unmanaged, workforce diversity is more likely to damage morale, increase turnover, and cause communication difficulties and ultimately conflict. This may occur because, in general, people feel more comfortable dealing with others who are like themselves. It has often been suggested that heterogeneity in teams can reduce intra-group cohesiveness, resulting in conflicts and misunderstandings which, in turn, can negatively impact employee satisfaction, citizenship behaviors, and turnover. Rather than a unified team, competition with and even distrust toward one another may characterize a diverse work environment; and ultimately lead to a decline in performance.[106]

A leader in a diverse work unit may spend more of his or her time and energy dealing with interpersonal conflicts than trying to achieve organizational objectives. Therefore, effective management of diversity requires creating an environment where all workers can succeed professionally and personally. Managing diversity has emerged as a much sought-after managerial skill and has spawned an industry of diversity training programs.

Experts caution that simply responding to legislative mandates does not seem to automatically result in meaningful, substantive changes in behaviors and attitudes. Rather, change aimed at valuing diversity must have top management support and commitment, have broad participation through empowerment, involve multiple initiatives, and require constant reinforcement.

The next section focuses on the leader's responsibility to create a culture that supports diversity.

Learning Outcome 9   *Describe the key factors that can enhance and support a pro-diversity culture.*

Creating a Pro-Diversity Culture

There is growing recognition that effective management of diversity at the organizational level (and led from the top) is a key component for achieving and sustaining a competitive advantage in an increasingly global economic environment. However, there are still reported accounts of racial and minority groups experiencing feelings of discomfort, alienation, and frustration as they try to assimilate into the workplace. For organizations to embrace and value diversity, the concept itself must be embedded in the culture of the organization.[107]

An organization that has a strong culture of diversity has a commitment to attract, retain, and promote employees of minority backgrounds and offers a system that rewards diversity initiatives throughout the organization. The best companies look beyond diversity compliance (with its focus on simply managing the numbers) to diversity institutionalization (with its focus on results). Saying you have a diversity program and being a diversified organization are two different things. It is the gap that exists between formal ethical policies and actual practices.[108] Some call it *decoupling*—a practice that allows organizations to publicize compliance programs that are nothing but window dressing, symbolic gestures designed to give the appearance of satisfying regulatory and social responsibility expectations without changing their practices substantively.[109,110] That is why diversity experts and scholars emphasize the importance of corporate leadership and organization-wide participation.[111]

Over the years, the literature has identified a number of factors that can enhance and promote a strong culture of diversity.[112] Exhibit 10.5 identifies seven such factors, which are briefly discussed below.

EXHIBIT 10.5 Factors That Support a Pro-Diversity Culture

Source: From J. A. Gilbert and J. M. Ivancevich, "Valuing Diversity: A Tale of Two Organizations," *Academy of Management Executive 14*(1) (2000): 93–105. The Academy of Management review by Academy of Management. Copyright 2000. Reproduced with permission of Academy of Management (NY) in the format Textbook via Copyright Clearance Center.

Top Management Support and Commitment

Publishing a statement that says an organization supports diversity does not guarantee success; unless it is woven into the fabric of organizational life in such a way that all employees, regardless of race, creed, age, or gender, feel welcomed to be a part of the organization. This is where top management support and commitment makes a difference. The commitment of the CEO and his or her top management team to diversity will filter down to individual operating units, thus making diversity an institutionalized concept. Leaders who talk diversity must "walk the walk." CEO commitment is considered to be the cornerstone of any successful diversity initiative.[113]

To achieve full diversity, leaders are challenged to institute policies that give women, as well as African-Americans, Hispanics, and other minorities, equal opportunities to move up the corporate ladder into leadership positions.[114] Though slowly changing, it is still the case that top leadership positions in most of corporate America are occupied by white males, despite the growing population of women and other minorities in the work place.

An indication that diversity has become a way of life for an organization is what happens to diversity programs during an economic downturn. In the past, corporate leaders viewed diversity programs as discretionary—something to be indulged in when times were good but quickly eliminated when the going got tough. More and more, companies are sticking with their diversity programs even during an economic downturn, which indicates the seriousness with which they now take diversity.

Organizational Philosophy

For diversity to succeed there has to be an explicit organizational philosophy that unambiguously disavows any kind of discrimination. Organizations that have achieved high levels of diversity have a philosophy that goes beyond simply responding to legislative mandates. It is a company-wide pro-diversity mind-set. Diversity is viewed as a strategic imperative to the organization's success. In such organizations, every effort is made to remove diversity blockers or obstacles. Diversity blockers are company policies and practices that result in intended or unintended consequences such as stereotypes and prejudices, ethnocentric belief, the "glass ceiling" effect, and, ultimately, an unfriendly work environment.

A stereotype is an assumption, without evidence, that people who are not part of the mainstream culture (Hispanics, African-Americans, and other minorities) are inherently inferior, less competent at their jobs, and less suitable for leadership positions. Unchecked, stereotypes can lead to prejudice and discrimination. **Ethnocentrism** *is the belief that one's own group or subculture is naturally superior to other groups and cultures.* It is easy to see how this kind of mind-set can be an obstacle to diversity and, at its worst, lead to discrimination. The "glass ceiling" effect is the concentration of women and minorities at the lower rungs of the corporate ladder, where their skills and talents are not fully utilized. *The* **glass ceiling** *is defined as an invisible barrier that separates women and minorities from top leadership positions.* A corporate philosophy that does not tolerate this phenomenon signals top leadership's commitment to creating a truly diversified work environment. The truth is that women and minorities are still vastly underrepresented in the board rooms and upper management positions. Despite college and graduate school enrollments among women that exceed those of men and despite a workforce participation rate since the mid-1960s that has resulted in three-fourths of all working-age women now in the labor force, the upper echelon of most U.S. corporations is still a decidedly male bastion.[115]

WORK Application **7**
Identify and briefly explain which of the obstacles to diversity exist and/or have been removed where you work or have worked.

Pro-Diversity HR Policies and Practices

Policies express an organization's intentions and provide a blueprint for action. One could argue that policies document the organization's "diversity talk" while practices represent the organization's "diversity walk." Unfortunately, it is not always the case that the two go hand-in-hand. We've all heard of the phrase "talk is cheap." To ensure that organizations "talk the talk" and "walk the walk," top leaders must put in place pro-diversity policies and practices. The HR department is the gateway through which all prospective employees pass in order to become members of an organization. As such, HR policies on hiring, training, promotion, compensation, and retirement or layoffs must be examined to make sure that minorities are not unfairly treated by actions taken in these areas.[116]

The work environment for many minorities can be a lonely, unfriendly, and stressful place, particularly at the executive level where Caucasian men outnumber women and minorities. Sexual harassment, intimidation, bullying, and social rejection are all examples of behavior that make the work place unfriendly. Minorities and women may be excluded from social activities in or out of the office, which often leads to feelings of alienation and despair. This in turn often leads to job dissatisfaction and high turnover among minority groups. HR practices such as periodic audits of recruitment, retention, compensation, performance appraisal, employee development, and promotion would ensure that diversity gains are not reversed.[117]

Organizational Communications on Diversity

Organizational efforts to communicate the message of diversity are an important factor for diversity success. Organizational communication in the form of newsletters, posters, calendars, and coffee mugs celebrating diversity achievements, and regular surveys of employee attitudes and opinions, are ways to heighten awareness of diversity. Repeated exposure to diversity themes would help to promote the message that diversity is a normal and accepted part of everyday life in the organization. Also, such in-house communications and newsletters would encourage employee involvement and help transmit the diversity message.

WORK Application 8

Identify and briefly explain which of the six factors related to creating a pro-diversity culture exist or do not exist where you work or have worked.

Including Diversity as a Criterion for Measuring Success

Creating a culture that supports diversity also means adding diversity objectives to criteria for measuring managerial performance. Rewards and incentives must be tied to diversity goal metrics and progress. Organizational objectives such as recruiting and promoting more minorities into managerial positions, developing and implementing regular diversity refresher workshops, or addressing diversity concerns in a timely manner can be tied to managerial compensation by requiring that a certain percentage of the manager's pay be dependent on meeting these diversity objectives. Not rewarding accomplishment of diversity goals could send a message that diversity is not a top management priority.[118]

Training and Education

Finally, sustaining a culture of diversity takes continuous training and education.[119] New employees learn the organization's culture while existing employees need refresher courses to keep them from backsliding into old habits.[120] Training sessions are aimed at increasing people's awareness of and empathy for people from different cultures and backgrounds.[121] Diversity training can include but is not limited to activities such as:[122]

WORK Application 9

Does the organization you work or have worked for offer diversity-awareness training and education? If you are not sure, contact the human resources department to find out. If it does, briefly describe the program.

- Role-playing, in which participants act out appropriate and inappropriate ways to deal with diverse employees

- Self-assessment activities, in which participants discover how their own hidden or overt biases influences their thinking about specific individuals and groups

- Sensitivity projects in which participants learn about others who differ from them in race, gender, culture, and so on

Diversity training programs can last hours or days. They can be conducted by outside experts, or by internal staff members. Small organizations are more likely to rely on outside assistance while larger organizations often have their own in-house diversity training staff. The primary objectives of diversity training programs may include one or more of the following:[123]

- Helping employees of different cultures communicate effectively with one another

- Learning the skills to effectively resolve diversity-related conflicts and tensions

- Changing perceptions so differences are viewed as strengths, not weaknesses

- Increasing members' appreciation and understanding of other cultures

Diversity training is most likely to be successful when it is not a one-time event, but an ongoing activity, and when there are follow-up activities to see whether the training objectives were accomplished.

As recommended by the AACSB, colleges and universities should incorporate multicultural and diversity understanding in their curriculum. Through education, students develop their knowledge of different cultures and ethnicities.[124] They learn that diversity is a strength, not a weakness. Through education, diversity blockers like stereotypes, prejudice, ethnocentrism, and other negative attitudes that can lead to discrimination are removed.

10.3   *Gender Discrimination*

On June 20, 2011, the Supreme Court ruled that a class action lawsuit filed against Wal-mart could not go forward. The majority opinion said each case was different from the other, casting doubt the claim that it was an intentional company-wide policy to discrimi-nate against women.[125] Therefore, the case did not meet the standard for a class action lawsuit. The plaintiffs can still pursue the case but on an individual basis. Walmart had been accused of denying women workers equal pay and opportunities for promotion. The suit claimed that even if Walmart policies were not clearly discriminatory, its organiza-tional culture perpetuated gender stereotypes that lead to differences in pay and promo-tion between men and women. It is estimated that up to 1.6 million women had join the class action suit. Walmart strongly disagreed with the lower court's decision to proceed with a class action lawsuit, and appealed to the Supreme Court. Since the lawsuit was filed, Walmart's CEO Lee Scott has initiated workplace-diversity moves to achieve full diver-sity. Walmart hired a director of diversity and set diversity targets, and executive bonuses are cut if the company doesn't meet the objectives. Walmart now posts management openings on its company-wide computer network.

1. Do you believe that organizational culture can lead to discrimination? Why or why not?

2. Do you agree with the Supreme Court ruling?

3. What's your opinion of Walmart's actions on diversity after the lawsuit was filed? Do you believe Walmart would have initiated the changes without the law suit?

CONCEPT APPLICATION 3
Factors That Support a Pro-Diversity Culture

Match each statement to one of the factors below. These are factors that show the extent to which an organization's policies and practices support a pro-diversity culture. Write the appropriate letter in the blank before each item.

a. Top Management Support and Commitment
b. Organizational Philosophy
c. Pro-Diversity HR Policies and Practices
d. Organizational Communications on Diversity
e. Diversity as a Criterion for Measuring Success
f. Training and Education

_____ 15. Making sure that hiring, training, promotion, compensation, and retirement or layoffs decisions don't unfairly treat minorities is an example of which factor?

_____ 16. Removing diversity blockers such as stereotypes and prejudices, ethnocentrism, the "glass ceiling" and an unfriendly work environment are part of which factor?

_____ 17. This particular factor is considered to be the alpha and omega of organizational efforts to create a culture that supports diversity.

_____ 18. Creating diversity awareness through newsletters, posters, and calendars, and conducting regular surveys of employee attitudes and opinions on diversity issues is part of which factor?

_____ 19. Requiring that a certain percentage of a manager's pay be dependent on meeting diversity objectives is associated with which factor?

_____ 20. A company-wide pro-diversity mind-set that views diversity as a strategic imperative to the organization's success refers to which factor?

The Effects of Globalization on Diversity Leadership

Corporations are becoming more global and hence more ethnically diverse.[126] Globalization has led firms to originate, produce, and market their products and services worldwide. A global labor market is emerging, dominated by Brazil, Russia, India, and China ("BRIC" countries). United States–based companies such as Pepsi-Cola, Coca-Cola, Procter & Gamble, and many others have established a significant presence in China and India, partly motivated by cheap labor and a sizable consumer market. They face competition from European companies such as Daimler-Benz, Nestlé of Switzerland, Canada's Northern Telecom, and many others with a significant presence in the United States. These corporations have to deal with a diverse cross-cultural workforce, customers, competitors, suppliers, and financial institutions. Collaboration among these companies is becoming the most effective way to deal with global competition and overcome the growing threat of nationalism—the tendency to want to purchase products from one's own country rather than a foreign country.[127]

In this global environment, understanding cultural differences and learning to deal effectively with partners from different cultures will be critical.[128,129,130] This may partially explain why the number of foreign-born managers being appointed to lead U.S. companies is increasing. Multinational companies are interested in recruiting leaders who have multicultural experiences.[131]

OPENING CASE APPLICATION

6. **What is Avon's stance on diversity, and has it lived up to it so far?**

Avon embraces diversity in the workforce, and continues to be a leader in taking affirmative action to ensure that doors are open to talented individuals, and that all associates and employees have opportunities for development and advancement. Avon has more women in management positions than any other Fortune 500 company, and half of its board of directors is women. In the United States and elsewhere, Avon has internal networks of associates including a Parents' Network, a Hispanic Network, a Black Professional Association, an Asian network, and a Gay and Lesbian network. The networks act as liaisons between associates and management, to bring voice to critical issues that impact the workplace and the marketplace.

Now that you have learned about culture and diversity as described in this chapter, you may find it interesting to see how your own personality traits match up. Complete Self-Assessment 2.

SELF-ASSESSMENT 2   Personality, Culture, Values, and Diversity

Culture and Values

If you scored high on the Big Five personality dimension of conscientiousness (high need for achievement), you tend to be a conformist and will most likely feel comfortable in an organization with a strong culture. If you have a high agreeableness (high need for affiliation) personality, you tend to get along well with people, can fit into a strong culture, and would do well in a cooperative culture that values collectivism, low power distance, and femininity. If you have surgency (high need for power), you like to dominate and may not like to fit into a strong culture that does not reflect the values you have. You would tend to do well in a competitive culture that values individualism, high-power distance (if you have it), and masculinity.

(continued)

(Self-Assessment 2 continued)

On the Big Five, if you are open to new experience you will do well in an adaptive culture that values low-uncertainty-avoidance, whereas if you are closed to new experience, you will tend to do well in a bureaucratic culture that values high-uncertainty-avoidance. Would you like to work in an organization with a weak or strong culture? What type of culture and values interest you?

_____

_____

Diversity

If you have a Big Five agreeableness personality type (high need for affiliation), are open to experience, and are well adjusted, you will tend to embrace diversity and

get along well with people who are different from you. However, if you have a surgency personality type (high need for power), are closed to experience, and are not well adjusted, you will tend to want to have things done your way (melting pot versus salad bowl) and may have problems with a diverse group of people who don't want to give you the power. If you have a conscientiousness personality type (high need for achievement), are well adjusted, and have openness to experience, you will tend to work with those who share your achievement values regardless of other differences. Do you enjoy working with a diversity of people?

_____

_____

Chapter Summary

The chapter summary is organized to answer the ten learning outcomes for Chapter 10.

1. Culture serves two important functions in organizations. Briefly describe what they are.

An organization's culture determines the way that it responds to changes in its external and internal environments. The two important functions served by culture are directly tied to this concept. They are: (1) that culture creates internal unity, and (2) that culture helps the organization adapt to the external environment. Culture provides a value system in which to operate, and when all employees buy into such a value system, there is internal unity. Culture determines how the organization responds to changes in its external environment. Appropriate cultural values can ensure that the organization responds quickly or proactively to emerging trends, rather than reacting.

2. Describe the characteristics of low- and high-performing cultures.

When there is little or no consensus on the values and norms governing member behavior, the culture of an organization is considered to be weak. On the other hand, a strong culture is one in which values are shared widely across the organization, from top management to rank-and-file employees. The characteristics of low-performance cultures include insular thinking, resistance to change, a highly politicized internal environment, and poorly conceived promotion or advancement practices for employees. The characteristics of high-performance cultures include a reputation for valuing their employees, being very results-oriented, emphasizing everyday outstanding performance

and excellence, and using diverse culture reinforcement mechanisms such as ceremonies, rituals, symbols, slogans, stories, and language (ceremonies honor and recognize achievement; slogans, symbols, language, and stories communicate the organization's primary values and provide a shared understanding among members).

3. Discuss the leader's role in influencing culture.

Leaders can initiate many different types of policies, programs, and practices to change, modify, or sustain an organization's culture. Some of these actions are substantive, while others are simply symbolic; yet taken together, they can shape the culture of an organization according to the expectations of the leader. Substantive actions are explicit and highly visible and are indicative of management's commitment to a new way of doing things. These are actions that everyone will understand are intended to establish a new culture more in tune with the organization's mission and strategy. Symbolic actions are valuable for the signals they send about the kinds of behavior and expectations leaders wish to encourage and promote.

4. Briefly describe the four types of culture commonly found in organizations.

The cooperative culture emphasizes teamwork amongst its employees. Collaboration is seen as critical to achieving organizational goals. The belief is that empowering, respecting, rewarding, and trusting employees is the key to capitalizing on external opportunities. The adaptive and cooperative cultures are often referred to as cultures of innovation, for their flexibility and creativity in responding to environmental changes. Competitive cultures are common in mature markets in which the emphasis is on the achievement of specific targets (such as market share, revenue growth, and profitability). The bureaucratic culture emphasizes strict adherence to set rules, procedures, and authority lines. Organizations with bureaucratic cultures are highly structured and efficiency-driven. Change is slow in bureaucratic cultures.

5. Describe Hofstede's theory of National Culture Identities.

The conceptual framework for understanding global cultural differences proposes that national cultures differ by the values they espouse. Researchers have associated different value dimensions with the cultures of different nationalities and/or regions of the world. Leading this effort is the work of Geert Hofstede, whose research identified five value dimensions for understanding global cultural differences. Each value dimension represents a continuum, with selected countries and regions located at various points along the continuum. The five value dimensions making up the framework are:

a. Individualism–collectivism
b. High–low uncertainty avoidance
c. High–low power distance
d. Long-term–short-term orientation
e. Masculinity–femininity

6. Briefly explain examples of organizational practices that can help foster an ethical work environment.

Organizational practices that can promote an ethical work environment include the following: a jointly developed code of ethics that everyone is well informed of its contents, creating ethics committees to oversee and process ethical violations, making ethical training part of employee development programs, and ensuring that there are available and safe disclosure mechanisms such as a whistle-blowing program for reporting ethical violations.

7. Discuss the validity of the assertion that authentic leadership has its roots in moral and ethical theory of leadership.

Authenticity is a psychological construct that focuses on knowing, accepting, and acting in accordance with one's core values, beliefs, emotions, and preferences. The authentic leader holds him or herself to a higher moral standard. It is rooted in the notion of a "true self." Authentic leadership theory has an introspective quality that allows leaders to reflect on whether their actions are consistent with who they are, ensuring that their values and ethics take precedence over external pressures, and not vice versa. The authentic leader is driven by a value system that calls for being moral and focusing on what is ethical or the right thing to do. Therefore, it is a valid assertion that authentic leadership has its roots in moral and ethical theory of leadership.

8. Explain the benefits for embracing diversity.

Changing demographics and increasing globalization have significantly changed the composition of the workforce. With more women and minorities entering the workforce and the growing interdependence between global companies, the need to embrace and value diversity is more critical than ever. The value of diversity is evident in studies that have found, among other things, that a diversified workforce offers an advantage in understanding and meeting the needs of diverse customers; some of the best job candidates are found among women and other culturally diverse groups; embracing and valuing diversity can lower an organization's cost attributed to high turnover and/or absenteeism among minority groups; and diverse work groups are more creative and innovative than homogeneous work groups.

9. Describe the key factors that can enhance and support a pro-diversity culture.

An organization that has a strong culture of diversity has a commitment to attract, retain, and promote employees of minority backgrounds and a system that rewards diversity initiatives throughout the organization. The best companies look beyond diversity compliance (with its focus on simply managing the numbers) to diversity institutionalization (with its focus on results). Saying you have a diversity program and being a diversified organization are two different things. Some of the factors that promote a culture of diversity include: top management support and commitment, a pro-diversity corporate philosophy, including diversity as a criterion for assessing and rewarding managerial performance, consistent and constant organizational communications taunting the company's diversity stance, pro-diversity HR practices and policies, and regular training and education workshops on diversity.

10. Define the following key terms (in order of appearance in the chapter).

Select one or more methods: (1) fill in the missing key terms from memory; (2) match the key terms from the following list with their definitions below; and (3) copy the key terms in order from the list at the beginning of the chapter.

_____ is the aggregate of beliefs, norms, attitudes, values, assumptions, and ways of doing things that is shared by members of an organization and taught to new members.

_____ represents a leadership belief in strong, mutually reinforcing exchanges and linkages between employees and departments.

_____ represents a leadership belief in active monitoring of the external environment for emerging opportunities and threats.

_____ represents a leadership mind-set that encourages and values a highly competitive work environment.

_____ represents a leadership mind-set that values order, stability, status, and efficiency.

_____ are generalized beliefs or behaviors that are considered by an individual or a group to be important.

_____ is a single person entrusted with the responsibility of acting as the organization's conscience.

_____ is employee disclosure of illegal or unethical practices on the part of the organization.

_____ is a psychological state in which people see themselves first as individuals and believe their own interest and values are primary.

_____ is the state of mind wherein the values and goals of the group—whether extended family, ethnic group, or company—are primary.

_____ has a majority of people who do not tolerate risk, avoid the unknown, and are comfortable when the future is relatively predictable and certain.

_____ has a majority of people are comfortable with and accepting of the unknown, and tolerate risk and unpredictability.

_____ leaders and followers rarely interact as equals.

_____ leaders and their members interact on several levels as equals.

_____ describes a culture that emphasizes assertiveness and a competitive drive for money and material objects.

_____ *have a future-oriented view of life and thus are thrifty (saving for the future) and persistent in achieving goals*

_____ *derives from values that express a concern for maintaining personal happiness and living in the present.*

_____ describes a culture that emphasizes developing and nurturing personal relationships and a high quality of life.

_____ is any characteristic that serves as a basis for social categorization and self-identification.

_____ is the inclusion of all groups at all levels in an organization.

_____ is the tendency to form an adverse opinion without just cause about people who are different from the mainstream in terms of their gender, race, ethnicity, or any other definable characteristic.

_____ is the belief that one's own group or subculture is naturally superior to other groups and cultures.

_____ is an invisible barrier that separates women and minorities from top leadership positions.

_____ a process where one continually comes to understand his or her unique talents, strengths, sense of purpose, core values, beliefs, and desires.

Key Terms

adaptive culture, 367

bureaucratic culture, 367

collectivism, 369

competitive culture, 367

cooperative culture, 366

culture, 358

demographic diversity, 376

diversity, 376

ethics, 371

ethnocentrism, 380

femininity, 370

glass ceiling, 380

high-power-distance culture, 370

high-uncertainty-avoidance culture, 369

individualism, 369

long-term orientation, 370

low-power-distance culture, 370

low-uncertainty-avoidance culture, 370

masculinity, 370

ombudsperson, 373

self-awareness, 375

short-term orientation, 370

whistle-blowing, 373

Review Questions

1. What are the similarities and differences between the cooperative culture and the adaptive culture?

2. How does a code of ethics help enforce ethical behavior in an organization?

3. What potential problems could develop in a case in which a leader is from a high-power-distance

culture, but his followers are from a low-power-distance culture?

4. Describe the four underlying components of authentic leadership presented by Gardner and his associates.

5. What are the major obstacles often encountered in trying to achieve diversity?

Critical Thinking Questions

The following critical-thinking questions can be used for class discussion and/or as written assignments to develop communication skills. Be sure to give complete explanations for all questions.

1. Based on your knowledge of the Enron case (Google it), what part did culture play in its actions and ultimate demise?

2. Describe some of the practices, policies, and norms that you would expect to find in an organization that prides itself on building a culture of respect and trust.

3. Describe the different generations that make up what some people are now referring to as "generational diversity" and identify their unique characteristics. What are the implications of generational diversity on effective leadership?

4. Despite the benefits of diversity, some have described it as a "double-edged sword." Explain why.

5. What is the difference between diversity compliance and diversity institutionalization?

6. In your opinion, what would be some strategies for developing a diversity sensitive orientation (DSO)?

CASE

Governor Deval Patrick—Commonwealth of Massachusetts

Deval Patrick was re-elected to a second term as Governor of the Commonwealth of Massachusetts in November 2010. In his inaugural address, he renewed his commitment to expanding opportunity and prosperity in Massachusetts. Much has changed in Massachusetts since Governor Patrick assumed the leadership of the state five years ago. Governor Patrick funded public education at the highest levels in the history of the Commonwealth and his school reform initiatives earned Massachusetts the top spot in the national Race to the Top competition. And through targeted initiatives that play to the Commonwealth's unique strengths, like his landmark 10-year, $1 billion program to promote the state's life sciences industry, the Governor has positioned the state as a global leader in biotech, biopharmaceuticals, and IT, and as a national leader in clean energy, including making Massachusetts home to the country's first offshore wind farm. Governor Patrick committed the state to renewing its aging and neglected infrastructure and oversaw the expansion of affordable health care insurance to over 98 percent of Massachusetts residents. The Patrick administration also accomplished major reforms that had eluded decades of other elected leadership, reforming the state's pension systems, ethics laws, and transportation bureaucracy. It seems he has instituted a results-oriented culture in his administration. It is what we have described in this chapter as a high(strong)-performing culture.

Deval Patrick describes the story of his life—from growing up on welfare in Chicago to thriving in business and politics—as "improbable." From where he started and where he is now, it seems truly improbable. Long before he became Governor of the Commonwealth of Massachusetts, Deval Patrick was a 4-year-old boy watching his father walk away from him and his mother. Deval talks of chasing his father down the street pleading with him not to leave. More than 50 years later, Gov. Patrick says that the day his father left their basement apartment on Chicago's South Side is burned into his memory. That's why the title of his new memoir, *A Reason to Believe: Lessons from an Improbable Life* is quite fitting. Speaking with *Morning Edition* co-host Renee Montagne, Patrick says his success stems from having supportive family and teachers—and from learning to look at life's lessons as "gifts."[132] He says he has been guided throughout his life by the advice of his grandmother: hope for the best and work for it.

As he puts it, "My life is often described as "improbable." Because I grew up in a broken home and in poverty, my academic career at Harvard College and Harvard Law School is sometimes called "improbable." My legal career, which included winning an argument before the U.S. Supreme Court and suing an Arkansas governor named Bill Clinton, who later appointed me assistant attorney general for civil rights, is called "improbable." My corporate career, which included service as a senior executive at two of the most highly recognized companies in America, Texaco and Coca-Cola, is called "improbable." My political career is described variously as "improbable" or "impossible": In my first race for elective office, lacking name recognition, connections, and money, I became the first African-American governor in the history of Massachusetts."[133] Governor Patrick has indicated that the purpose of his book is to share some of the lessons that have imbued him with core values, shaped his identity, and made him want to be a better man.

Here is a brief outline of Gov Patrick's meteoric rise to power. The first in his family to attend college, Deval Patrick went on to graduate from of Harvard College and the Harvard Law School. Following law school, he served as a law clerk to a federal appellate judge before joining the NAACP Legal Defense and Education Fund as a staff attorney. He then went on to lead a successful career in the private sector as an attorney and business executive, rising to senior executive positions at Texaco and Coca-Cola. In 1994, President Clinton appointed Patrick Assistant Attorney General for Civil Rights, the nation's top civil rights post. At the Justice Department, Patrick worked on a wide range of issues, including prosecution of hate crimes, and the enforcement of employment discrimination, fair lending, and disabilities rights laws. In 1997, Patrick was appointed the first chairperson of Texaco's Equality and Fairness Task Force where he led a company-wide effort to create a more equitable workplace environment. In 2006, he was elected to his first term as Governor of Massachusetts. It was his first race for elected office. In 2010, he was comfortably reelected.

Gov. Patrick has shown in his appointments that he is a strong supporter of diversity, especially at the highest levels of government. In May 2011, Gov. Patrick's nominee, Barbara Lenk was confirmed to serve on the State Supreme Court. She is the Court's first openly gay member. Patrick's other judicial appointments include the court's first black chief justice, Roderick Ireland, and the first Asian-American member, Fernande Duffly. Recently, Governor Patrick signed an executive order protecting state workers from discrimination on the basis of gender identity. "This Executive Order ensures that all employees in the executive branch will continue to be able to perform their duties free of discrimination," Patrick spokesman Alex Goldstein said in a statement.

S-Comm is a Federal program that was designed with the best of intentions, but critics say its implementation mostly targeted illegal immigrants. Critics belief that due to pressure from the federal government, Gov. Patrick agreed to participate in the program. However, when confronted with the reality of the program, he showed the courage of his convictions by standing up to the federal government

and saying no. He was praised for his courage to say no in the face of both a powerful federal government and widespread prejudice against immigrants. Governor Patrick showed the compassion, conviction, and common sense approach that got him elected in the first place. When Patrick was elected for a second term, he said to the immigrant community in Massachusetts, "I want you to know that you are welcome here in this Commonwealth. This is your Commonwealth. This is your home." His decision with the S-Comm program showed that he doesn't just talk the talk. He walked the walk, said another person.

When faced with difficult decisions, authentic leaders like Gov. Deval Patrick know what they stand for, and have the courage to act on their principles regardless of external pressures. He has been a visionary and very effective leader so far.

GO TO THE INTERNET: To learn more about Governor Deval Patrick, visit the official Web site of the Commonwealth of Massachusetts at **www.Mass.gov**

Support your answers to the following questions with specific information from the case and text or with information you get from the Web or another source.

1. In your opinion, would you characterize Governor Patrick's administration as a low- or high-performing culture? Support your answer with evidence from the case.

2. In what ways has Governor Patrick shown that he and his administration embrace and support diversity?

3. What is the evidence in the case to support the assertion that Governor Patrick exemplifies the principles of authentic leadership?

4. What are some the factors in Governor Patrick's life that have influenced his values?

CUMULATIVE CASE QUESTIONS

5. Based on your overall impression of Governor Deval Patrick, describe the quality of the exchange relationship (Chapter 7) he would most likely have with his followers. Explain your answer.

6. In Chapter 8 we discussed how organizational climate can influence team creativity and the role of top leaders in creating such a climate. Has Gov. Patrick created a climate for creativity and innovation in his state? Support your answer.

7. Transformational versus transactional leadership describes two leadership styles commonly associated with senior leaders of corporations (Chapter 9). Which of these leadership types is more representative of Governor Patrick? Support your answer.

CASE EXERCISE AND ROLE-PLAY

Preparation: Put yourself in Governor Patrick's position. You are about to have a news conference announcing your choice for the state Supreme Court nomination. You anticipate a lot of questions about the fact that she is a lesbian, and some have accused you of pandering to gay and lesbians for political reasons, not because of any deeply held values or principles. Prepare your response to such a question(s).

In-Class Groups: Break into groups of four to six members to share ideas and develop the response.

Role-Play: One student (representing themselves or their group) may give the response to the entire class, with the class acting like members of the media. Use information from the case and the discussion on diversity for input.

VIDEO ▶️ CASE

Diversity at PepsiCo

Imagine trying to manage and accommodate the needs of more than 185,000 people at once. Imagine a variety of voices, languages, cultures, ethnic backgrounds, families, lifestyles, ages, and geographies all vying for attention, all bearing the name PepsiCo. From the top down, PepsiCo embraces diversity and inclusion in its worldwide workforce. Top executives believe that nurturing diversity in the organization is not only a matter of responsible ethics but also good business. The Frito-Lay North American Diversity/Inclusion Model is a good example of how PepsiCo builds a measurable framework for diversity. The model addresses five key areas, ranging from "evolving the culture" to "leveraging our people systems." By following a structure, the human resources department and other managers can develop and implement specific programs to meet the needs of their employees.

1. Why is it important for upper-level managers at PepsiCo to receive diversity and inclusion training?

2. Do you think that PepsiCo's encouragement of employee networks actually works against diversity and the formation of multicultural teams? Why or why not?

Developing Your Leadership Skills 1

Identifying and Improving Organizational Culture

Preparing for This Exercise

1. Select one organization you work for or have worked for. Identify its culture by answering Work Applications 1 (is it a high- or low-performance culture?), 2 (which of the ten leadership actions are used?), 3 (which of the four types of organizational cultures does it have?), and 5 (what are the five dimensions of the culture?). Your answers can be between the two poles for Work Applications 2 and 5 (on each of the five dimensions); however, try to identify which end of the spectrum the culture is closest to.

2. What are the mission and values of the organization? Does the culture support the mission and values of the organization? Explain why or why not. If the organization does not have a clearly written mission and values, that would be a good starting point.

3. Based on the organization's mission and values, how can the culture be improved? Be specific.

Doing This Exercise in Class

Objective

To improve your ability to identify and improve an organizational culture in order to support its mission and values

The primary AACSB learning standard skill developed through this exercise is global and multicultural trends, diversity, and ethics.

Preparation

You should have completed the preparation for this exercise.

Procedure *(10–45 minutes)*

A. The instructor calls on students to give their answers to the preparation, with or without a class discussion.

B. Break into groups of four to six and share your answers to the preparation.

C. Same as B, but select one group member to present their answer to the entire class.

Conclusion

The instructor may lead a class discussion and/or make concluding remarks.

Apply It *(2–4 minutes)* What did I learn from this exercise? When will I implement my plan?

_____

_____

_____

Sharing

In the group, or to the entire class, volunteers may give their answers to the "Apply It" questions.

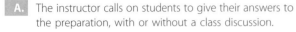

Developing Your Leadership Skills 2

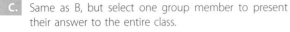

Diversity Training

Preparing for This Exercise

In preparation for the in-class exercise, write out the answers to the following questions.

Race and Ethnicity

_____ 1. I am of _____ race and ethnicity(ies).

_____ 2. My name is _____. It is significant because it means _____ and/or I was named after _____.

_____ 3. One positive thing about being this race/ethnicity is _____.

_____ 4. One difficult or challenging thing is _____.

Religion

_____ 1. I am of _____ religion/nonreligious/atheist.

_____ 2. One positive thing about it is _____.

_____ 3. One difficult or challenging thing about it is _____.

Gender

_____ 1. I am of _____ gender.

_____ 2. One positive thing about being this gender is _____.

_____ 3. One difficult or challenging thing is _____.

_____ 4. Men and women are primarily different in _____ because _____.

Age

_____ 1. I am _____ years old.

_____ 2. One positive thing about this age is _____.

_____ 3. One difficult or embarrassing thing about being this age is _____.

Ability

_____ 1. I am of _____ (high, medium, low) ability in college and on the job. I do/don't have a disability.

_____ 2. One positive thing about being of this ability is _____.

_____ 3. One difficult or challenging thing about being of this ability is _____.

Other

_____ 1. The major other way(s) in which I'm different than other people is _____.

_____ 2. One positive thing about being different in this way is _____.

_____ 3. One difficult or challenging thing about being different in this way is _____.

Prejudice, Stereotypes, Discrimination

Identify how you have been prejudged, stereotyped, and discriminated against.

_____

_____

_____

Doing This Exercise in Class

Objective

To increase your understanding of the value of diversity and being different. The more you value diversity, the more effort you will place on developing good human relations with a diversity of people.

The primary AACSB learning standard skill developed through this exercise is global and multicultural trends, diversity, and ethics.

Preparation

You should have answered the preparation questions for this exercise.

Procedure 1 *(2–3 minutes)* Break into groups of four to six with as much diversity as possible. The instructor will check the diversity levels and reassign people to groups to improve diversity, if necessary. Select a spokesperson to give the group's best one or two answers to the "Prejudice, Stereotype, Discrimination" question; it is not necessary to report on any other areas.

Procedure 2 *(10–30 minutes)* The instructor sets a time limit and selects the topics in the preparation to be discussed. Start with different areas first, but be sure to allow time (about 5 minutes) to complete the "Prejudice, Stereotypes, and Discrimination" question. If you finish the question to be reported before the time is up, go over other areas of difference that were not assigned by the instructor.

Procedure 3 *(5–20 minutes)* The spokesperson from each group gives the one or two best examples of prejudice, stereotypes, and discrimination.

Conclusion

The instructor may lead a class discussion and/or make concluding remarks.

Apply It *(2–4 minutes)* What did I learn from this experience? How will I use this knowledge in the future? More specifically, what will I do differently to personally embrace diversity? How will I encourage others to embrace diversity?

_____

_____

_____

Sharing

In the group, or to the entire class, volunteers may give their answers to the "Apply It" questions.

Developing Your Leadership Skills **3**

Developing an Effective Multicultural Team

Preparing for This Exercise

Assume you are part of a team and your task is to develop a brand new product called the Mind Reader 2010. It will make it possible for you to tell what someone is thinking by simply focusing the device in their direction. There is currently no product or substitute like it on the market—but time is of the essence and this product has to be on the market within a very short time; otherwise, other competing groups will beat you to it. You are a multicultural team with members from the following countries: United States, Japan, Argentina, Mexico, and Sweden. As discussed in the text section (pp. 369–370), "National Culture Identities—Hofstede's Value Dimensions," researchers have found key dimensions that explain broad cultural differences among selected nationalities. The following table summarizes the value dimensions of five countries from which team members are to be selected.

Doing This Exercise in Class

Objective

To learn how to deal with the different values, norms, and attitudes that characterize different cultures. Leaders have to recognize that cultural differences can lead to conflicts in multicultural team settings, and finding common ground where value differences exist is key to effective teamwork.

The primary AACSB learning standard skills developed through this exercise are teamwork and global and multicultural trends, diversity, and ethics.

Preparation

Read and understand the meaning of each value dimension in Exhibit 10.4 on page 369. Review the table in this exercise for the particular value dimensions of each country.

Procedure 1 *(3–5 minutes)* Break up into groups of four to six with as much diversity as possible. The instructor will check to ensure that each group is well diversified and reassign students to groups needing more diversity, if possible. Select a leader who will present the findings of the group's deliberations.

Procedure 2 *(10–20 minutes)* The instructor sets a time limit on the deliberations. If quality, teamwork, and speed are critical to successfully completing this project, what adaptations in behavior would your group have to make, given the different countries your group members are from? Be mindful of the values associated with each country and team member. For example, somebody from an individualistic culture or a high-uncertainty avoidance culture may have difficulty working as part of a team or working with people who are comfortable with and accepting of the unknown, and who tolerate risk and unpredictability. What ideas does the group have to help this individual adapt to the needs of the team to finish the project on time? Other potential areas of conflict exist. Identify them based on the composition of your team, and deliberate on possible solutions, keeping the objective in mind.

| Country | Masculinity | Femininity | Time Orientation | | Individualism | Collectivism | Uncertainty Avoidance | | Power Distance | |
			Long Term	Short Term			High	Low	High	Low
United States			X		X					
Japan	X			X		X	X			
Argentina								X		
Mexico						X			X	
Sweden		X						X		X

Procedure 3 *(15–20 minutes)* The leader from each group presents the potential conflicts introduced by the differences in the value dimensions of team members, and the team's solutions for dealing with such conflicts in order to achieve the desired objectives.

Conclusion

The instructor may lead a class discussion and/or make concluding remarks.

Apply It *(2–4 minutes)*

What did I learn from this experience? How will I use this knowledge in the future?

_____

_____

_____

Sharing

In the group, or to the entire class, volunteers may give their answers to the "Apply It" questions.

Strategic Leadership and Change Management

Learning Outcomes

After studying this chapter, you should be able to:

1. Discuss the role of strategic leadership in the strategic management process. p. 396

2. Describe the relevance of analyzing the internal and external environment to the strategic management process. p. 400

3. Explain the various components in the strategy formulation phase of the strategic management process. p. 402

4. Explain the relationship between corporate goals and strategies. p. 404

5. Explain the importance of strategy evaluation in the strategic management model. p. 409

6. Describe the change management process using three-stage model of change. p. 415

7. Identify the major reasons for resisting change. p. 416

8. Discuss some of the recommendations for minimizing resistance to change. p. 419

9. Define the following **key terms** (in order of appearance in the chapter):

strategic leadership	value
executive intuition	core competence
strategic management	organizational identity
strategic vision	organizational change
mission statement	survival anxiety
strategy	learning anxiety

OPENING CASE *APPLICATION*

While attending Stanford University, Larry Page met Sergey Brin, a native of Moscow, and together they launched Google in 1998. On April 4, 2011, Google announced that Page will take over from Eric Schmidt who has been CEO since 2001. Larry Page will take over the day-to-day operations of Google as CEO. Schmidt, who assumed the title of executive chairman, said he will focus on building relationships with customers, business partners, and the government. Many in the industry have long considered Larry the firm's thought leader and strategist. Brin will continue to focus his energy on new product/service development. Tech analysts don't expect a big shift in the firm's strategic framework. During Eric Schmidt's tenure, Google became one of the world's most dominant companies, employing more than 24,000 employees worldwide. Google is available in 160 local country domains and 117 languages and in 20 countries worldwide. Google's mission is to organize the world's information and make it universally accessible and useful. By providing the best user experience, Google and its leadership team believe that they can build a company that will create more value, not just for its users, but ultimately also for its shareholders.

Google's strength rests in its culture, which emphasizes teamwork, flexibility, transparency, and innovation. There is little in the way of corporate hierarchy. Google's hiring policy is aggressively nondiscriminatory and favors ability over experience. The result is a staff that reflects the global audience the search engine serves.

Google continues to pursue an aggressive growth strategy via acquisition of related tech firms. Page is now in charge of leading Google's expansion into the mobile phone market with its Android software, which has pitted the search firm against Apple and its iPhone platform.

The corporation's successful business model is based on the sale of ads that appear alongside its search engine results. During the fourth quarter of 2010, Google earned $2.54 billion in profits, a 29 percent increase compared to the same period a year ago. Yet the firm will have to navigate challenges as it builds on its dominance. One of those challenges is Facebook, the world's largest social-networking site, who in 2010 surpassed Google to become the most popular site on the Web. Google has not had much success launching its own social networking service.

Google's leaders aren't afraid to experiment—they are willing to question conventional wisdom and trust their own judgment. As Schmidt himself said, "For the last 10 years, we have all been equally involved in making decisions. This triumvirate approach has real benefits in terms of shared wisdom, and we will continue to discuss the big decisions among the three of us. But we have also agreed to clarify our individual roles so there's clear responsibility and accountability at the top of the company."[1] Many wait to see what the next 10 years under Larry Page will be like.

OPENING CASE QUESTIONS:

1. How effective has the executive leadership team of Schmidt, Page, and Brin been in providing the kind of strategic leadership that Google seen so far?

2. Describe Google's business environment. How well is Google adapting to it?

3. Critique Google's mission statement.

4. How well do Google's long-term objectives balance with the interests of its stakeholders?

5. What type of growth strategy is Google pursuing, and why do you think the leadership team has chosen such a course rather than the alternatives?

6. What are some of the factors contributing to Google's effective strategy implementation?

7. Do you agree with the analysts who say the change from Schmidt to Page will have minimal effect on Google's performance or strategic direction? Explain your answer.

8. Why have Schmidt, Page, and Brin encountered less resistance in bringing about changes at Google than most companies experience?

Can you answer any of these questions? You'll find answers to these questions and learn more about Google and its leadership throughout the chapter.

To learn more about Google and its leadership team, visit the company's Web site at **http://www.google.com**.

S trategic management is about organizational performance in the long-term. Successful organizations are not only capable of satisfying the needs of their present market(s), but also able to adapt to changing market requirements with new strategies.[2] Organizations are operating in increasingly complex environments, in which adaptation to environmental changes is an imperative. The attempt by an organization to align its vision, mission, goals, capabilities and strategies with external environmental trends is really the essence of strategic management. Many scholars and practitioners agree that the success of an organization's strategy is influenced by the degree of fit between its internal strengths and externalities in the macroenvironment. This process is strongly influenced by the interpretations strategic leaders make of environmental trends.[3]

There are a number of themes that have steadily permeated the teaching and practice of strategic management. The four most cited are globalization, environmental sustainability, hypercompetition, and technological transformations. The integration of these themes into the strategic management curriculum has gone from being a marginal issue to a center-stage topic of discussion. It has become standard practice to add these themes to the content of strategic management textbooks.

To succeed in the era of hypercompetition, globalization, environmental changes, and technological revolution, it is imperative that organizations act smart and fast. Strategists must respond quickly to marketplace demands for immediate action. This is where the need for effective strategic planning comes into play. The focus of this chapter is on strategic leadership and the strategic management process, and change leadership. However, before delving into these topics, we will briefly explore the subject of globalization and environmental sustainability.

Globalization and Environmental Sustainability

One area in which change is unmistakable is the increasingly global competitive marketplace. Virtually every company, large or small, faces competition for critical resources and market opportunities, not just from competitors in the home market but also more and more from distant and often little-understood regions of the world. In his book, *The World Is Flat*, Thomas Friedman eloquently makes the case that labor, jobs, information, knowledge, and capital readily move across borders with far less restrictions and at greater speed than was possible only a few years ago.[4] How successful a company is at exploiting emerging opportunities and dealing with associated threats depends crucially on leadership's ability to cultivate a global mind-set among managers and their followers.[5] International experience is now considered key for anyone aspiring to top leadership in their organization.

Beginning in the later part of the 20th century, there has been increasing attention paid to the idea of environmental sustainability. There seems to be emerging a collective understanding that the natural environment (which includes physical resources, wildlife, and climate) cannot sustain itself if human behavior towards the air, water, land, natural resources, flora, and fauna does not change.[6] Leaders today have a responsibility to ensure that they reduce side effects such as pollution, deforestation, and greenhouse gas emissions. Sustainability is about conservation of natural resources and minimization of waste in operations through actions such as recycling. The common phrase used nowadays to refer to this trend is "going green." Companies are increasingly seeking to develop and market environmentally friendly products.[7] Stakeholders increasingly expect corporations to take account of their impact on society and the environment in the ways they operate.[8] These stakeholder groups (customers, employees, government, or activists) maintain that an organization's continuous survival will depend not only upon the greater economic and social system of which it is a part, but also upon the natural ecosystem in which the firm is embedded.[9] This has led to calls for strategic leaders to formulate strategies that will help sustain the environment. It is also being socially responsible. Social responsibility is about the ethical and discretionary responsibilities an organization owes its stakeholders.[10]

There is research evidence that being pro-environment is also financially good for business. The importance of environmental sustainability can be seen in the growing number of higher education programs focused on sustainability.[11, 12] In fact, there is now an Association for the Advancement of Sustainability in Higher Education. While it is still the goal of strategic leaders to develop and grow their organizations, there is now talk of sustainable development—development that caters to the needs of today's generation without short-changing the ability of future generations to meet their own needs.[13]

In a recent article titled "How Siemens Got Its Geist Back," the new CEO Peter Loscher said "We very early focused on megatrends such as green business to assure the company's future." The article goes on to say that Loscher has increased the chunk of Siemens that sells sustainability-focused customers everything from light bulbs to high-speed trains to factory control systems. Because of these changes, one analyst declared that Siemens is very well positioned to achieve above-average growth.[14]

The next section focuses on the role of strategists in providing the right type of leadership in the global marketplace and protecting the natural environment in the process. We will also examine why some strategists fail at these responsibilities.

Learning Outcome 1   *Discuss the role of strategic leadership in the strategic management process.*

Strategic Leadership

Achieving organizational success is not a chance occurrence. It is determined largely by the decisions strategic leaders make.[15] Strategic leadership refers to the top management function that is usually conducted by the CEO of an organization in coordination with an executive team. The executive team may include the Chief Operating Officer (COO) or President and several vice presidents of divisions or functional areas. Each of the vice presidents then puts together a team of operational leaders (also called functional managers) to implement the organization's strategies. Each operational leader in this second tier is responsible for assembling his or her team of third-tier managers to carry out the day-to-day tasks of implementing strategy. These are the project managers, foremen, and supervisors. Even though it is generally recommended that strategic management should involve everyone in the organization, strategic leaders (the CEO and the executive team) are held responsible for the strategic management and performance of the organization by its board of directors. The CEO in turn holds his VPs and their operational teams responsible for strategy implementation and meeting assigned goals.

Strategic leadership involves leading the strategic management process to help organizations cope with change that seems to be increasing exponentially in today's globalized environment.[16] Strategic leadership is critical to an organization's ability to adapt, evolve, and prevail amid turbulent disruptions.[17] It applies to for-profit as well as not-for-profit organizations.[18,19] The strategic management process is discussed next.

Although many authors have provided varying definitions of the concept of strategic leadership, they all seem to revolve around the same themes: vision, change, people, and performance. We define **strategic leadership** as *a person's ability to anticipate, envision, maintain flexibility, think strategically, and work with others to initiate changes that will create a viable future for the organization.*[20,21] It is a process of providing the direction and inspiration necessary to create and implement a firm's vision, mission, and strategies to achieve organizational objectives.[22]

Strategic leaders are responsible for the organization's near-term performance, as well as for creating conditions that will ensure the organization's long-term competitiveness.[23,24]

Over the years, there has been a general acknowledgment amongst scholars and practitioners that an effective strategic leadership model is one that features a number of key components, which include establishing the organization's strategic direction; creating and sustaining distinctive competencies; developing human capital; building and maintaining an effective corporate culture; enforcing ethical practices; and instituting strategic controls.[25, 26] Therefore, the effective strategic leader must be capable of:[27,28,29,30]

- Anticipating and forecasting events in the external environment that have the potential to impact business performance—they observe from the outside in

- Finding and sustaining competitive advantage by building core competencies and selecting the right markets in which to compete

- Evaluating strategy implementation and results systematically, and making strategic adjustments

- Building a highly effective, efficient, and motivated team of employees

- Selecting, developing, and mentoring a talented team of top leaders[31]

- Deciding on appropriate goals and priorities

- Communicating effectively[32]

A strategic leader can choose to concentrate decision-making power at the executive level or spread it throughout the organization. Each approach has implications on follower motivation and commitment. For example, shifting much of the decision-making responsibility (especially operational decisions) away from the strategic leaders and onto operational or functional leaders frees top leaders to think strategically and gives them more time to address key issues.[33] However, as mentioned above, shifting strategic responsibilities to other leaders, especially less-qualified ones is too risky a move and does not absorb the strategic leader of any failures.

Strategic Leadership Failures

Focusing on the positive is not a new trend. While CEO successes are often heralded in the press, less attention is paid to failed expectations. The failed CEO is often let go quietly or with some public statement that strains to avoid mention that the reason has to do with failure to meet expectations. In some rare cases, boards have been known to be blunt about the reason a CEO is being let go. Some will argue that there is much to be learned from CEO failures and we need to share their lessons so others won't make the same mistakes.[34,35] "Failure" in the existing scholarly literature is largely confined to quantifiable measures of poor performance of a leader's direct actions.[36]

There are many reasons why strategic leaders fail, the most common of which is poor decision making during the strategic management process. Senior executives fail when (1) their strategic vision for the organization does not align with positive environmental trends; (2) they deviate from the mission to pursue actions that favor their personal interests and not enough of their constituents' and organization's interests; (3) they set long-term goals that are either too low or too high; (4) they engage in or condone unethical conduct; (5) they select the wrong strategies; (6) they fail to effectively lead the strategy implementation process; and (7) they pay little or no attention to performance standards. A perfect example of this will be GM and Chrysler and their near bankruptcy but for a government bailout in 2008.[37,38]

From a competency point of view, failures have also been attributed to the fact that leaders who are lacking in experience or training for the job may rely too much on intuition to the exclusion of rational analysis. **Executive intuition** *is the instinctive ability to respond to problems without the benefit of concrete facts and information.* Sometimes such intuition may fuel imagination, creativity, and innovation, and contribute to corporate success; other times it may result in spectacular blunders. While some see this as too risky, others argue that intuitive decisions, especially from strategic leaders with much experience, are needed in highly volatile, globally competitive business environments—in which time is of the essence. It is more likely the case that effective strategic decision making requires a balancing of intuition and rationality.

As mentioned above, ethical and moral lapses in judgment have led to the failure of CEOs from companies like Tyco, Enron, WorldCom, and Qwest.[39] The ultimate goal of the strategic leader should be to build sustainable integrity programs into the strategic management framework that encourage positive self-regulation of ethical behavior as a matter of routine within the organization. This will not happen unless the leader also demonstrates integrity. Integrity impacts the credibility and reputation of the strategic leader.[40]

SELF-ASSESSMENT 1   Strategic Leadership

Identify each of the 16 statements according to how accurately it describes you. Place a number from 1–5 on the line before each statement.

5 — 4 — 3 — 2 — 1
More like me   Less like me   Not me at all

_____ 1. I have a tendency to plan ahead instead of waiting until the last minute before acting on issues/problems.

_____ 2. I am a very flexible person when it comes to dealing with people or issues.

_____ 3. As a student, I often find myself playing the role of a leader rather than a follower.

_____ 4. When the stakes are high, I am comfortable being the one to make the final decision.

_____ 5. I am very good at setting personal goals and prioritizing events in my life.

_____ 6. I tend to consider the long-term consequences of my decisions and actions today rather than just the immediate consequences.

_____ 7. When I contact businesspeople who can help me, I praise their accomplishments.

_____ 8. I am the type that likes to sit back and try to envision my future to see where or what I will be in 10 years.

_____ 9. When it comes to working with others, I am more of a team player than a loner.

_____ 10. I am the type that would want the ball with the play clock counting down to zero and the chance to make the winning basket.

_____ 11. I am the type that would be very comfortable mentoring, training, and motivating others to meet team goals.

_____ 12. When it comes to interacting with people, I can communicate effectively with all kinds of people.

_____ 13. When it comes to solving problems or completing group projects, I will describe myself as more analytical than most of my peers.

_____ 14. I like to keep things the way they are (especially if they are working just fine) rather than trying to change them.

_____ 15. I have a strong desire to one day become the CEO of an organization.

_____ 16. I am a very ethical person when it comes to dealing with others or acting according to accepted norms.

Add up your score and place it here _____ and on the continuum below.

80 — 70 — 60 — 50 — 40 — 30 — 16
Strong Strategic Leadership   Weak Strategic Leadership
Potential   Potential

This self-assessment exercise is similar to the first one in Chapter 1 except this focuses on your potential to lead from the top. Generally, the higher your score on the continuum above, the greater your potential for strategic leadership. However, the key to realizing your aspirations is education, hard work, and persistence, not simply potential. You can develop your strategic leadership ability through this course by applying the principles and theories to your personal and professional life.

1. How effective has the executive leadership team of Schmidt, Page, and Brin been in providing the kind of strategic leadership that Google has utilized so far?

Together, this trio has put together a profitable business model built around keyword advertising. Since going public in 2004, Google has exceeded analysts' estimates for its financial performance in all but one quarter, and profits exceeded $2 billion in the last quarter of 2010 and continued into 2011. Google's stock is currently trading at over $530 per share. There is no doubt that its long-term objective of maximizing shareholder value is being met and exceeded. The Google team of strategic leaders is performing exceptionally well in all the areas of leadership responsibility identified above, especially in the implementation of its strategies.

Strategic Management Framework

In today's rapidly changing global environment, leaders are bombarded with so much information, often conflicting, that making effective decisions becomes a challenge. The complexity of the environment and the uncertainty of the future make the task of the strategic leader more difficult.[41] The fundamental question in strategic management is why some firms meet and even exceed market expectations while others barely survive, or worse, go out of business. The answer lies in the role that strategic leadership plays in creating an effective strategic road map for the organization.[42] The process of developing a strategic road map is called strategic management. **Strategic management** *is the set of decisions and actions used to formulate and implement specific strategies that are aligned with the organization's capabilities and its environment, so as to achieve organizational goals.*[43]

This section focuses on the strategic management process shown in Exhibit 11.1. It is often summarized as a four-step process: environmental scanning, strategy formulation,

EXHIBIT **11.1** Strategic Management Framework

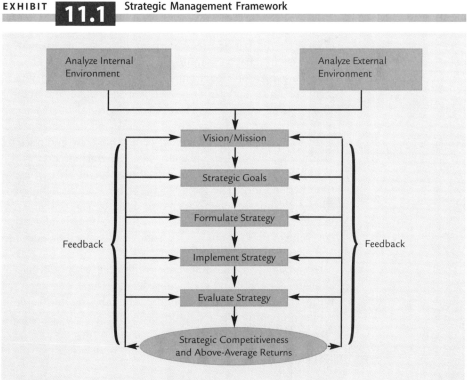

strategy implementation, and strategy evaluation and control. Great companies know how to put together an effective strategic road map for success, and the strategic management model or framework is the tool that makes it possible. It greatly facilitates preparation and planning for an uncertain future.

11.1 *Strategic Leadership and Management*

An important part of strategic leadership and management is creating the business model of how the business competes. The University of Miami Online High School (UMOHS) is in partnership with The University of Miami. UMOHS is for young athletes and performers (grades 8–12) who are too busy to attend traditional classes; it gives them more time to train and to travel to compete/perform. It wants to become the establishment school in the sports and performing world. UMOHS also accepts international students who want an American diploma. Some argue that online high school deprives a child of a traditional education and prevents a kid from being a kid and enjoying childhood.

1. How do you feel about high school students enrolling in an online school and missing the experience of attending traditional classes?

2. Is it ethical and socially responsible to offer an online high school for athletes and performers?

Learning Outcome 2 · *Describe the relevance of analyzing the internal and external environment to the strategic management process.*

Environmental Scanning

Environmental scanning is the first step in the strategic management process because it enables strategic leaders to identify relevant environmental factors and industry drivers that weigh on the organization's vision, mission, objectives, strategy, and business model. As the business environment becomes increasingly complex, the demand for greater environmental scanning has grown significantly.[44]

An organization's environment is both external and internal. The external environment presents opportunities and threats while the internal environment presents strengths and weaknesses. The external environment is generally thought of as consisting of three main levels: the natural, general, and task environments. The natural environment includes physical resources, wildlife, and climate. These elements make up the ecological system of our planet. The general environment includes the economic, technological, political, and sociocultural forces that influence an organization's long term performance. The forces in the natural and general environments indirectly affect all organizations, though to varying degrees. The task environment (also known as the industry environment) includes forces that directly affect an organization such as the government, local communities, suppliers, competitors, customers, creditors, employees, and activist groups.[45]

Increasingly, organizations are confronted with external environmental complexities, ambiguous signals, and conflicting demands that if ignored may end up threatening the future economic prospects of an organization, and if acted upon in a timely manner may result in opportunities for future economic growth. To survive and thrive, strategic leaders must be skilled at managing such environmental complexities and uncertainties. To thrive in such turbulent environments requires agility.[46] As one study points out, the agility capability comes in three forms: operational agility (which is the capacity to seize opportunities to improve operations and processes within a focused business model); portfolio agility (which is the ability to reallocate resources out of less-promising units and into attractive ones); and strategic agility (which is the ability to identify major opportunities in the external environment and respond promptly).[47]

Advances in telecommunications, the need to balance work–family life as more women enter the workforce, the rising cost of gasoline, increased traffic delays, and time scarcity are all trends that have led to a flexible and distributed working arrangement called telecommuting. With telecommuting, workers are able to work from home or even foreign country locations. Companies that are slow to respond to these changes or have yet to respond are losing out on recruiting and utilizing talented employees who prefer this type of work structure. The discussion in Chapter 8 on the growing use of virtual self-managed teams is an example of this trend.

From the task environment, it is essential to learn and understand the concerns of customers, the availability and bargaining power of suppliers and customers, the actions of competitors, market trends, and other stakeholder groups. From a competitive standpoint, knowing what your competitors are doing and how to respond is clearly important to a firm's survival. The systematic gathering, analysis, and assimilation of information is input into the strategic planning process.[48]

WORK Application **1**

Think of your college or university. Prepare a SWOT analysis that identifies one opportunity and one threat facing your institution in the next five years. Also identify a strength and a weakness that you think your institution has.

An organization's internal environment focuses on assessing its strengths and weaknesses in key functional areas such as marketing, finance/accounting, HR, R&D, and production/operations. Examples of an organization's strengths will include its brand name, product lines, reputation, talented employees, loyal customers, strong cash position, leverage position, patents, distribution networks, etc. The combined analysis of the external environment (to identify opportunities and threats) and internal environment (to identify strengths and weaknesses) is commonly referred to as SWOT (Strengths, Weaknesses, Opportunities, and Threats) analysis. The effectiveness of an organization's strategies is influenced by the degree of fit or alignment between the organization's internal capabilities/resources and its environmental opportunities.[49,50]

Accurate interpretation of the three types of environments requires considerable analytical and cognitive skills, such as the conceptual skills to think critically, identify and make sense of several complex trends, and streamline available information into a concise plan of action.[51] Accurate and timely interpretation of environmental trends plays a large part in the future actions and the continuing effectiveness of an organization. The importance of speed in recognizing and responding to environmental trends has been dramatically accentuated by the highly competitive landscape facing most organizations. As a result, some strategic leaders believe that it is much better to be a first-mover or pioneer and make mistakes occasionally than to be a follower.[52]

OPENING CASE APPLICATION

2. Describe Google's business environment. How well is Google adapting to it?

Google operates in the high-tech Internet environment, a sector that is undergoing significant transformations. The competition between Google, Facebook, Yahoo!, and Microsoft for supremacy is intense. The technologies for serving user needs in the industry are constantly changing. Major demographic changes are taking place among the user market. The world's economy is now one boundaryless global market with as much universality as diversity in customer needs. Google has adapted well to this turbulent business environment. With math, science, and computer technology backgrounds, Brin and Page created an economical, distributed system, based on thousands of servers built around

(continues)

(Opening Case Application 2 continued)

commodity PC hardware to support the gathering, storage, and analysis of Web content on a huge scale. Their focus on technological innovation and operating costs has created a search engine that is currently number one in its industry. Not only are there changes in the technological and competitive environment; the sociocultural environment is also changing as the world's population undergoes major demographic changes (see Chapter 10 on the growing demographic diversity of the U.S. population).

Learning Outcome 3   *Explain the various components in the strategy formulation phase of the strategic management process.*

Strategy Formulation

Strategy formulation focuses on selecting strategies that reveal a strategic fit between external opportunities (O) and internal strengths (S) while avoiding external threats (T) and improving internal weaknesses (W). This is generally referred to as the SWOT technique of strategy formulation. There is a general perception that a firm can measure its performance against competitors by evaluating its strengths, weaknesses, opportunities, and threats.[53] Strategy formulation is about selecting appropriate strategies for achieving an organization's objectives. Therefore, strategies are the means to the ends (objectives). However, there is more to this phase than just selecting appropriate strategies. Other relevant aspects of strategy formulation include the following: crafting a vision and mission statement, developing strategic objectives, and establishing appropriate policies.[54] Each of these components is discussed next.

Vision and Mission Statements

Strategic leadership starts with the creation of meaning and purpose for the organization with a compelling vision and mission. It is generally believed that a leader's inspiring vision motivates followers to focus on reaching a desirable future state that is better than the present state.[55] A mission statement on the other hand specifies an organization's present purpose—its market niche (customers), products/services offerings, operating principles, and business model. Getting the behaviors of diverse workers to coalesce around a common purpose is a major challenge for top management. As such, vision and mission statements have emerged as strategic tools for accomplishing this task. The values espoused in the mission and vision can act as a powerful force in bringing people together to perform effectively. Formulating an effective vision and mission requires careful consideration of fundamental questions relating to organizational beliefs and values. These questions include: Who are we (core ideology)? Why do we exist (core purpose)? What do we believe in (core values)? What inspires us (envisioned future)? Where are we going (vision statement)? And, finally, what will the future look like when we get there (vivid description)? These questions embody the essence of a strategic vision and mission statement.

A **strategic vision** is defined *as an ambitious view of the future that everyone in the organization can believe in and that is not readily attainable, yet offers a future that is better in important ways than what now exists.*[56] It is important for the CEO to convey a vision of the organization's future and to do it in such a way that followers accept it as their vision as well.[57] The leader must have a clear idea of where he or she wants to take the organization and the strength to persist even in the face of setbacks and even failures.

John F. Kennedy demonstrated vision when he promised that an American would land on the moon during the 1960s, because at the time of his announcement, NASA was in its infancy and the state-of-the-art technology for space exploration was Sputnik.

WORK Application 2

Write an inspiring vision statement for an organization you work or worked for. If the company has one, you may use it or revise it. Explain why you think it has an inspirational appeal.

It is only fitting that this chapter is being completed during the same week (July 8, 2011) that NASA just launched space shuttle Atlantis on its last voyage to space, 50 years after President Kennedy's vision was announced. To be motivating, a vision must be expressed in ideological terms, not just in economic terms, to help people develop a personal connection with the organization.[58] A clear and inspiring vision serves a number of important functions, including:[59,60]

- Facilitating decision making, in that it helps people determine what is good or bad, important or trivial

- Inspiring followers by appealing to their fundamental human need to feel important and useful, and to be a part of something great

- Linking the present to the past by rationalizing the need for changing old ways of doing work

- Giving meaning to work by explaining not just what people do but why they do it

- Establishing a standard of excellence

Effective leaders understand that creating a vision involves content, process, and implementation. To be widely accepted, vision creation should be a shared experience. The role of the leader in bringing together all the key partners to the visioning process is critical.[61] To make a difference, a vision must be based on the input and values of followers and other key stakeholders. A well-crafted vision is one that is the result of teamwork, simple enough to be understood, appealing enough to energize and garner commitment, and credible enough to be accepted as realistic and attainable.[62] Some examples of companies with simple yet inspiring vision statements include the following:

- Komatsu: "Encircle Caterpillar"

- Coca-Cola: "People, Planet, Portfolio, Partners, and Profit—the five Ps"

- Citibank: "To be the most powerful, the most serviceable, the most far reaching world financial institution that has ever been"

- Nike: "To crush the enemy"

- American Express: "To be the world's most respected service brand"

A **mission statement** *is an enduring statement of purpose that distinguishes one organization from other similar enterprises.* It is the organization's core purpose and reason for existence. It answers the question, "What business are we in?" A well-crafted mission statement can provide many benefits to an organization, including providing direction and focus, forming the basis for objectives and strategies, inspiring positive emotions about the organization, ensuring unanimity of purpose, and helping resolve divergent views among managers. The two components that are often featured in a mission statement are the core values and the core purpose. The *core values* outline the guiding principles and ethical standards by which the company will conduct business, no matter the circumstance.

The *core purpose* doesn't just describe goods and services; it describes the broad needs (immediate and anticipated) of the people served by the organization. For 3M, the mission is "To solve unsolved problems innovatively"; for Merck, it is "To preserve and improve human life"; for the Army, it is "To be all that you can be"; and for Ford, it is to make "Quality job one." In these and many other examples, there is no mention of the specific products or services these organizations manufacture or serve.

Examples abound of organizations that have been adversely affected by poorly crafted mission statements. The railroad industry almost brought about its own demise by

WORK Application **3**
Write an inspiring mission statement for an organization you work or worked for. If the company has one, you may use it or revise it. Explain the core values and core purpose of your mission statement.

defining its mission as being in the railroad business rather than the transportation business. The March of Dimes' original mission was "to cure polio," until a cure was discovered and the organization found itself without a purpose. Today, its mission is to advance human health. Motorola and Zenith were once successful competitors in the manufacture and sale of televisions. Yet, while Zenith has lost ground, Motorola has continued to grow and expand. The difference is that Motorola, unlike Zenith, defined its mission as "applying technology to benefit the public," not as "making television sets."

A good mission statement should focus on the needs that the organization's products/ services are meeting. The mission should be broad but not so broad that it does not distinguish the organization from its competitors. It should be specific but not so specific that it creates rigidity and resistance to new ideas. Finding an appropriate balance between specificity and generality is difficult, but worth the effort. It is generally believed that mission-driven organizations stand a better chance of succeeding and thus creating long-term shareholder value than those that are not mission-driven.

A vision statement represents a future aspiration, whereas the mission statement represents the enduring character, values, and purpose of the organization in the present. The job of strategic leadership is to ensure that the vision and mission of the organization are effectively communicated and embraced by all employees.[63]

OPENING CASE APPLICATION

3. Critique Google's mission statement.

Google's mission is to organize the world's information and make it universally accessible and useful. It succinctly identifies Google's purpose. It focuses on the need (information) that Google's product/service (search engine technology) provides. It is neither too broad nor too narrow. Of the two components often featured in mission statements—core values and core purpose—Google's mission statement only identifies its core purpose; however, Google has a separate document called "Google's Code of Conduct" that identifies its core values. Overall, Google's mission statement is well-designed.

Learning Outcome 4

Explain the relationship between organizational goals and strategies.

Organizational Goals

Goals are the desired long-term outcomes that an organization seeks to achieve for its various stakeholders—employees, customers, stockholders, and others.[64] They represent a clear and unambiguous articulation of what the organization seeks to achieve.[65] Companies develop both financial and strategic goals. Financial goals may include measures such as return on investment, sales, profits, earnings per share, or return on equity. Strategic goals may include acquiring new customers, opening new market, or creating new products.

Commitment to organizational goals is achieved when there is broad participation in goal setting, and rewards are linked to goal achievement.[66] Goal-setting theory suggests that people with specific goals perform better than those with vague goals (such as "do your best") or easily attained goals. An effective goal is one that is **s**pecific, **m**easurable, **a**chievable, **r**esults-based, and **t**ime-specific—a "SMART" goal. Refer to Chapter 3 for details on how to write effective objectives (see Model 3.1 in Chapter 3).

Goals are essential because they help focus everyone in the same direction; they offer feedback on how well an organization's strategy is working; they create synergy; they are the means by which organizations reveal their priorities; and they are the basis for planning, organizing, leading, and controlling activities.[67]

OPENING CASE APPLICATION

4. How well do Google's long-term objectives balance the interests of its stakeholders?

Google's executive leadership team under CEO Larry Page believes that in the long term, Google's obligation is to maximize shareholder and customer value by providing the best user experience. Google is a company that has remained relentlessly focused on the end user by continuously improving on the quality of its search results. To accomplish this, Google has brought together a highly talented and motivated workforce. The media has regularly featured stories on Google touting its generous incentives and compensation package for its employees. The focus on quality has brought in more users and consequently more advertising revenues and profits. Google's philanthropic causes include disease prediction and prevention, improvement of public services by informing and empowering people, and the increase of economic growth and job creation through stimulating small- and medium-sized enterprises. Google is a company that understands the needs and interests of its various stakeholders (employees, customers, community groups, shareholders, the government, etc.) and is doing a great job trying to serve each group.

Selecting Appropriate Strategies

A **strategy** *is an integrated, overarching plan of how an organization will achieve its objectives.* Armed with a vision and mission statement, organizational objectives, and factors in the internal and external environment, strategic leaders then try to formulate strategies that align with each of these components. It must reflect the vision and mission of the organization. It must be able to achieve the desired objectives of the organization. And finally, it must have a strategic fit with external opportunities and internal strengths, while avoiding external threats and improving internal weaknesses. This is what some scholars have called the planned mode of strategy selection. Others maintain that strategy selection is more of an emergent process. According to this emergent mode, organizations unintentionally and randomly create patterns in their strategic decisions from which ultimately emerge strategic patterns.[68]

Examples of strategy types include diversification, joint ventures, mergers and acquisitions, new product development, new market development, restructuring, re-engineering, and bankruptcy. Selecting among these strategy alternatives is a critical managerial activity, requiring careful consideration of various factors. As one study cautions, it is important to understand the underlying antecedents to managerial behavior that may influence strategy selection. A leader's cognitive, psychological, and affective processes will affect how he or she makes decisions.[69] Some leaders are prone to be very aggressive and others are more cautious.

For companies operating in high-velocity or turbulent environments, staying competitive requires a strategy of launching multiple product innovations in quick succession. Some strategists do this through internal development processes (develop your own products) while others pursue growth through external means (acquisitions and mergers). The opening case highlights Google's acquisition of several small technology-based firms as part of its aggressive growth strategy. Companies operating in high-velocity environments may seek what researchers call a "first mover" advantage. The "first mover" firm proactively enters a new market or launches a new product with the expectation of enjoying a temporal competitive advantage over follower firms pursuing an imitation or "second mover" strategy.[70] It is the old saying that "the early bird gets the worm."

To maintain a competitive edge over rivals, effective strategic leaders develop strategies that:

- Enhance value to the customers
- Create synergistic opportunities
- Build on the company's core competence[71]

Delivering value to the customer should be central to any strategy. **Value** *is the ratio of benefits received to the cost incurred by the customer.* At the end of the day, every strategy is designed to satisfy the needs or expectations of a customer. Firms that meet or exceed the customer's expectations succeed while the rest fail.[72] Synergy occurs when a chosen strategy (such as in related diversification) calls for organizational units or systems to interact and produce a joint result that is greater than the sum of the parts acting independently—the "2 + 2 = 5" outcome. Synergistic benefits include lower cost, greater market power, or superior employee skills and capabilities. Finally, the third component to maintaining a competitive edge over rivals is having a distinctive or unique core competence. Strategies that are based on a company's unique core competencies are harder to copy and thus have a better chance of improving the company's performance.[73] A **core competence** *is a capability that allows an organization to perform extremely well in comparison to competitors.*

A strategic leader's job is to identify the organization's unique strengths—what differentiates the organization from its competitors. Core competencies are a source of sustainable competitive advantage when they are rare, hard to imitate, not easily substitutable, and create value for the firm. Arguably, the most distinctive and hard-to-imitate resource available to firms is knowledge, especially people-based knowledge. Unlike physical resources, which are depleted when used, core competencies increase (in terms of their efficient application) as they are used. Such employee-based competencies are what some have referred to as *human capital.*[74,75]

The shared actions and interactions of employees across functional boundaries help to create an organizational identity that differentiates the organization from rivals. **Organizational identity** is the *members' consensual understanding of "who we are as an organization" that emerges from that which is central, distinctive, and enduring to the organization as a whole.*[76] Organizations like Southwest Airlines, Nike, Walmart, Google, Facebook, and many others are well known for fostering an identity that separates them from their competitors.

WORK Application 4
Identify a core competence of an organization you work or worked for. Explain how it differentiates the organization from its competitors.

OPENING CASE *APPLICATION*

5. What type of growth strategy is Google pursuing, and why do you think the leadership team has chosen such a course rather than the alternatives?

Google is pursuing a growth strategy of mergers and acquisitions with other related businesses. This strategy is preferred because it allows Google to quickly adopt new technologies and processes rather than trying to develop them internally. Given the rapid changes the industry is undergoing, timing is critical. Acquisitions and partnerships make more sense.

CONCEPT APPLICATION 1
Strategic Management Process

Match each statement to one of the strategic management concepts (a through f) below.

a. threat/opportunity
b. vision
c. mission

d. goal
e. strategy
f. value

g. core competency
h. strength/weakness

(continued)

(Concept Application 1 continued)

_____ 1. Motorola: The Apple iPhone is taking away our sales.

_____ 2. Microsoft: A personal computer on every desk in every home.

_____ 3. UVA's College at Wise: We educate students in spirit, mind, and body for leadership in service to humanity.

_____ 4. YMCA: We are the only child care provider to offer gym and swim classes as part of our programs.

_____ 5. Jiffy Lube: Electric cars don't have engines that need oil changes.

_____ 6. GM: To increase revenue by 10% from 2010 to 2011.

_____ 7. Discover: Our small-business credit card is the only one that will give you 5 percent back on your office supplies and gas purchases.

_____ 8. InBev: To merge with Anheuser-Busch to become the world largest beer brewer.

_____ 9. Avon Cosmetics: To give unlimited opportunity to women.

_____ 10. Google: We are number 1 because we offer the best search engine for free to our users.

Strategy Implementation

The third step in the strategic management process is strategy implementation. It is the action phase of the process. Strategy implementation takes place through the basic organizational architecture (structure, policies, procedures, systems, incentives, and governance) that makes things happen. Strategy implementation has been described as the most important and most difficult step of the strategic management process.[77] Strong leadership is considered one of the most important requirements for successful strategy implementation. The style of leadership and an abundance of managerial skills and experience make a difference. As was revealed in Chapter 2, some successful leaders employ a directive and task-oriented leadership style while others are equally successful by being more consultative, participative, and people-oriented. Managerial skills such as persuasiveness, administrative experience, communication, knowledge about team dynamics, social skills, creativity, and conceptual skills have been found to strongly affect strategy implementation efforts and ultimately firm performance.[78]

Strategy implementation requires galvanizing the organization's employees and managers at all levels to turn formulated strategies into action. Collaboration at all levels is critical for effective strategy implementation.[79] An excellent strategy that is poorly executed will yield the same poor results as a bad strategy. Therefore, careful consideration must be paid not just to strategy formulation but to its implementation as well.[80]

There are other obstacles to effective strategy implementation. Strategies may fail for lack of appropriate or adequate resources. The leader must prioritize and make resources available during strategy implementation. Rewards and other forms of compensation must be aligned with the goals that employees are seeking to accomplish. Also, time is of the essence in strategy implementation. Being careful and rational during strategy formulation is important but not sufficient if managers are slow to initiate actions. Managers must avoid becoming trapped in the vicious cycle of rigidity and inaction that prevents them from acting in a timely fashion. We call it "paralysis by analysis."

Strategy implementation is considered to be the most difficult stage because it involves bringing together people who may have varying levels of motivation, commitment, and dedication. These differences can result in interpersonal conflicts that, if left unresolved, can significantly affect implementation efforts and performance.[81] Successful strategy implementation rests on the shoulders of managers who must be able to motivate employees to cooperatively perform at high levels—a task that is not always easy to undertake when the right employees are not in place or the leader lacks people skills.[82,83]

Another factor that makes strategy implementation a difficult process is related to the many components that need to be integrated in order to turn a chosen strategy into action. Leadership decisions in key areas such as structure, culture, pay or reward systems, budget allocation, and organizational policies and procedures will determine the success or failure of strategy implementation.[84] Decisions in these areas must match the requirements of the chosen strategy, mission, and objectives of the company.

A company pursuing a strategy of differentiation through innovation in a bureaucratic, hierarchical organizational structure will be an example of a mismatch between strategy and structure. However, a company pursuing a strategy of internal efficiency and stability, aimed at offering customers lower prices than competitors, is more likely to succeed with this type of centralized hierarchical structure because of its strict controls on cost containment. A lack of fit between strategy elements (for example, a strategy–culture, strategy–structure, or strategy–environment misalignment) increases the chances of failure.[85] Assessing the extent to which stated goals or expectations have been achieved or not achieved after implementation is strategy evaluation.

OPENING CASE *APPLICATION*

6. **What are some of the factors contributing to Google's effective strategy implementation?**

The following factors have supported and continue to support Google's effective strategy implementation:

- Its highly talented leadership team and workforce
- The strength of its culture that emphasizes teamwork, flexibility, transparency, and innovation
- Its structure—there is little in the way of corporate hierarchy
- Its aggressive hiring policy—it is nondiscriminatory and favors ability over experience

CONCEPT APPLICATION 2
Strategic Leadership

Identify in each statement if the view expressed is reflective of a strategic leader or operational manager.

a. strategic leader   b. operational manager

_____ 11. It is my responsibility to ensure that we have the right strategy to achieve our long-term objectives and mission.

_____ 12. My goal is to motivate and lead my team to meet our production quota every week and not worry about other departments.

_____ 13. I am concerned that our technology is not keeping up with the latest technological trends and our culture is not aligned with the rest of our strategic framework.

_____ 14. I am not worried about the future because our current portfolio of products is meeting our customers' present needs just fine.

_____ 15. I get paid to deliver results today, not to worry about the future.

_____ 16. It makes good sense for good leaders to frequently ask themselves the question, "What will the future of this industry look like?"

(continued)

(Concept Application 2 continued)

_____ 17. I spend my time focusing on solving the day-to-day problems.

_____ 18. We are not concerned about developing skills or capabilities that cannot help us to perform our present tasks.

_____ 19. A company cannot reach its full potential without an inspiring vision.

_____ 20. In our business, the environment changes very quickly. Therefore, we have to constantly monitor it for emerging opportunities and threats.

Learning Outcome 5   *Explain the importance of strategy evaluation in the strategic management process.*

Strategy Evaluation and Control

Strategy evaluation and control is the last and final phase of the strategic management process. This phase compares actual results (outcomes) with expected results (stated objectives), which then provides feedback for necessary adjustments throughout the model. It is the primary means of determining the overall effectiveness or success of the strategic management process. Effective strategy evaluation involves three key activities or steps: (1) reviewing internal and external factors that are the bases for the current strategies, (2) measuring actual performance against stated objectives, and (3) taking corrective action.[86]

When step 2 reveals discrepancies, it is the responsibility of senior leaders to support change efforts. It is the task of the strategic leader to encourage meaningful communication and interaction among managers and employees across hierarchical levels, so that feedback from strategy evaluation can be shared throughout the organization and necessary changes implemented. A popular tool used to measure the effectiveness of the strategic management process is the balance scorecard. The balance scorecard translates elements of the strategic management process into a comprehensive set of objectives and performance measures that can be quantified and appraised.[87] Let us conclude this section by reviewing an example of strategic management in action at Coca-Cola.

Strategic Management in Action

We should disclose that the parties mentioned in the example below are no longer with the Coca-Cola Company. However, the example is still a relevant and instructive illustration of the strategic management process in action. We should also note that in April 2009, Mr. Neville Isdell retired from Coca-Cola after 43 Years of Service. The Board of Directors elected Muhtar Kent as chairman of the Board and CEO of the company. Ms. Cynthia McCague retired from Coca-Cola in December 2009 after 28 years of service. She was replaced by Ms. Eberly, a 19-year veteran of the company. Her title is Chief People Officer, with responsibility for leading the Company's global People Function (formerly Human Resources).

Back in 2004, Coca-Cola's board of directors called Neville Isdell out of retirement to lead the 122-year-old beverage company back to growth and profitability after two failed reorganization attempts. Isdell's first move was to bring in a new Human Resources Vice President, Cynthia McCague. Isdell reorganized the HR function so that instead of reporting to the general counsel's office, it reported directly to him. This move signaled the beginning of an important partnership between HR and strategic leadership at Coca-Cola.

With this change in place, the HR V.P. and other senior managers embarked on a seven-month-long internal analysis of the company. A survey of the top 400 managers of Coca-Cola revealed some hard truths about the feelings of employees. For example, there was a feeling that the company and its people lacked a clear direction and a common purpose, had low employee morale, and demonstrated a lack of teamwork. Another group of 150 senior managers from around the globe met several times to review the survey results and interviews. Working in groups called "workstreams," they came up with solutions. Each workstream was led by two senior executives and included operational and functional managers. One workstream helped formulate new vision, mission, and values statements for Coca-Cola. The implementation of "workstream" recommendations was again a team effort. HR partnered with public affairs and communication specialists to roll out the plan. Communication was highly stressed with many interactions taking place via face-to-face meetings, intranet, webTV, and BlogBlast.

The results, after implementation of the changes, were very positive. Isdell attributed the success to the process of looking inward, working collaboratively to create solutions, and engaging employees in implementation. This example illustrates how strategic leadership and strategic management interacted to bring about successful change. It was an internal environmental analysis that revealed critical weaknesses that were hampering the company's ability to exploit attractive opportunities in the external environment. Coca-Cola needed to make a strategic change, and the board brought Isdell out of retirement to make it happen after two failed attempts. Leading change is a key aspect of strategic leadership and is the subject of the next section.

Leading Change

Strategy is often described as the management of change. Recall that change is part of our definition of leadership (Chapter 1); *leadership is the process of influencing leaders and followers to achieve organizational objectives through change.* As the discussion on charismatic, transformational, and strategic leadership has revealed, the focus of each of these leadership disciplines is change, not status quo. The central objective of this section is to understand how leaders can effectively manage the change processes in order to improve organizational success. Organizational change is defined as *an alteration in an organization's alignment with its external environment.*[88]

In today's turbulent environment, where change is a fact of life, organizations must constantly cope with unfamiliar events or situations in order to survive and stay competitive. Implementing change in an environment characterized by increased complexities and uncertainties makes it much more difficult and challenging.[89] Corporations and government institutions spend millions of dollars on change efforts. Examples of change efforts include attempts to re-engineer or restructure business practices, to develop new technologies/products, or to create a new organizational culture or a change in leadership.

Change can be transformational or incremental, and sometimes an incremental change can emerge or amplify into a much larger and radical change than was first anticipated. In some cases, radical change may require a redefinition of an organization's vision and mission, and consequently a shift in the organization's objectives and strategies.[90] In essence, organizational change is any transition that requires a change in human behavior. Change is about people doing things differently. In this section, we will discuss the need for change, the role of leadership in implementing change, the change process, why people resist change, and strategies for minimizing resistance to change.

YOU Make the ETHICAL Call

11.2   *Change through Upgrading*

SAP is a world-leading software company, headquartered in Germany. Fluor Corporation is one of the world's largest publicly owned engineering, procurement, construction, and maintenance services organizations.

Fluor and other businesses have accused SAP and other software companies of forcing them to upgrade their software. Fluor claims that SAP upgrades are often minor and not needed, yet Fluor is required to purchase the upgrades. In fact, Fluor dropped part of the products it had licensed from SAP and tried to take over its own software, hiring its own Chief Information Officer (CIO) at a cost of about $13 million. However, SAP told Fluor that it would have to install a new version or pay even higher annual fees to get updates, fixes for bugs, and access to SAP's technicians.

1. Do you believe that companies come out with upgrades just to make more money (sometimes called planned obsolescence), or do you believe companies are being honestly innovative and customers are just resistant to change?

2. As a sales rep, would you push selling an upgrade to a customer who doesn't really need one so that you can make a commission?

3. What would you do if your boss pressured you to sell unneeded upgrades?

4. Is it ethical and socially responsible to "require" updates to continue using a product or service?

The Need for Change

Rapid environmental changes are causing fundamental transformations that are having a dramatic impact on organizations and presenting new opportunities and threats for leadership. Organizational change is an alteration of not only structures, systems, and processes, but also a cognitive leadership reorientation. There is little doubt that implementing strategic change is one of the most important responsibilities of any strategic leader. Leaders must be ready and able to make necessary changes when conditions warrant such actions. Successful implementation of strategic change can re-energize a business while failure can lead to disastrous results.[91]

A key first step in managing change is to identify and analyze the need for change before embarking on any implementation plan. A comprehensive analysis of an organization's internal and external environment is the best place to start looking for answers as to why change is necessary.[92] Just about every type of organization is facing an external environment characterized by rapid technological changes, a global economy, changing market requirements, and intense domestic and international competition. These changes have created opportunities such as larger, underserved markets in developing economies and falling trade barriers. Threats in the form of more domestic and foreign competition, increased rates of technological obsolescence, increased speed in new innovations, shortened product life cycles, and global competition are also part of the external environment.

Internally, the need for change is more likely when a long-time CEO retires and a new CEO is brought in, especially if the new CEO is an outsider charged with a mandate for change by the board of directors. A steady trend of mediocre performance in an organization would also signal the need for a change in leadership, employee ranks, or strategies. The end-of-chapter case on Nike and the board's decision to replace William Perez with Mark Parker illustrates this point. Even a one-time strategic blunder that results in a significant decline in key performance metrics (profitability, stock price, and so on) may trigger calls for a change in leadership. Such was the case with Citigroup and American Express, where high-performing CEOs were fired due to huge losses resulting from bad investments in the subprime housing market.

Many will agree that real change does not start to happen until the organization is experiencing some external threat or imminent danger of significant loss due to an internal weakness. When an organization is in crisis, the need for change increases because there is a sense of urgency.[93,94] People need to know that change is needed—now—and why. This is what Edgar Schein—Sloan Fellows Professor of Management Emeritus and senior lecturer at MIT's Sloan School of Management—refers to as "survival anxiety." **Survival anxiety** *is the feeling that unless an organization makes a change, it is going to be out of business or fail to achieve some important goals.* According to Schein, survival anxiety is a necessary but not by itself a sufficient stimulus to change. He argues that the reason survival anxiety alone is not a sufficient stimulus for change is because the prospect of learning something new produces anxiety, what he calls "learning anxiety," and this can create resistance to change even with a high survival anxiety.[95] **Learning anxiety** *is the prospect of learning something new in itself.* Change often requires people to learn new skills, new technologies, or new processes. It is for this reason that a "buy in" by followers is crucial for change to succeed. This topic will be further discussed in a later section on why people resist change. Awareness of the need for change, and a leader's ability to inspire followers to transcend their own immediate interests for the sake of the organization's needs, underscores the importance of effective leadership in implementing change. The next section discusses the leader's role in managing change.

OPENING CASE APPLICATION

7. Do you agree with the analysts who say the change from Schmidt to Page will have minimal effect on Google's performance or strategic direction? Explain your answer.

For now, yes! There would have been a greater chance of significant change in strategic direction if Google had hired an outsider or if Eric Schmidt was retiring or going to another company. As it is right now the same trio that has always made joint decisions for the company are still in place. Only the titles have changed. As environmental conditions change and as Larry Page gets more comfortable in the CEO chair, he may decide to go a different route than Schmidt would have chosen. Larry, Eric and Sergey will like to maintain the confidence that the market has in Google's continued growth and profitability by not making any unnecessary changes.

The Leader's Role in Managing Change

Given the current economic climate, the question of how leaders can steer their organizations through needed strategic changes is a valid one. The very nature of change implies some type of movement (forward or backwards from the status quo). Growth strategies imply a change forward while retrenchment strategies imply a change backwards. Therefore, for many organizations, even those pursuing a stability strategy, change is inevitable. Unfortunately, a lot of change initiatives do not succeed or meet expectations.

Various contributing factors have been suggested for this poor outcome including the fact that operating managers in charge are not equipped or experienced in managing change, cultural inertia, resistance to change, and the lack of leadership from the top.[96,97,98] A critical issue for many leaders is managing people during the change process and dealing with conflict and resistance.[99,100] Cultural inertia is a rigid, outdated culture that goes against anything new or different from the old ways. When a proposed change goes against the organization's culture, it is more likely to encounter resistance.[101] Resistance to change is discussed in greater detail later in the chapter.

Studies on institutional change have stressed the role of change agents (leaders) in effectively managing the process, focusing on how they need to infuse new values, expectations, and beliefs into the organization's social structure by garnering collective action in support of change initiatives.[102] There are many options leaders can employ to effect successful change. Examples include:[103,104,105,106]

- Articulating a compelling reason for change
- Having a road map for implementation including training programs for required skills/competencies
- Forming a coalition of supporters and experts during the early stages of the change process
- Staying the course in spite of perceived difficulties
- Recognizing and rewarding the contributions of followers to the process
- Carefully managing resources and priorities
- Keeping the process transparent
- Having a plan for dealing with resistance

Senior leaders must make every effort to eliminate policies, procedures, and behaviors that undermine the change efforts. Followers who are charged with implementing change must see in the behavior of their leaders an honest effort to share in the challenges of the change. A leader must embody the change that he or she wants to see in followers. Gandhi put it best when he said, "We must become the change we want to see." Finally, effective change agents must be good listeners. Listening helps a leader to have a better understanding of the root causes of resistance.

Ultimately, the objective of any leader is to implement change that results in positive organizational performance; however, the question has always been how to do it effectively and successfully, given the stress, discomfort, and dislocation that change often brings. For example, a change in leadership may affect members' initial trust in the new leader, communications, motivation to perform, job satisfaction, and even turnover. An organized and systematic change management process enhances the chances of successful change implementation and the likelihood that more people will support and commit to the change rather than resist it. The next section focuses on the change management process.

The Change Management Process

Change is a process that leads to a desired end-result. The change process is the means for a leader to transform the organization, a way to realize a new vision for the organization. It requires moving through several stages and executing different tasks, including performing an organizational audit, planning, formulating the change strategy, communicating, persuading others, making and consolidating the change.[107] It takes effective transformational leadership (at the individual, group, and organizational levels) to accomplish all these activities.[108]

One of the earliest and most widely used change process theories is Lewin's classic three-stage theory of change. The three stages are (1) "unfreezing" an existing state, (2) moving to a new, desirable state, and then (3) "refreezing" that new state.[109] (See Exhibit 11.2). Edgar Schein provided further detail for a more comprehensive model of change calling his approach "cognitive redefinition." More recent attempts have developed Schein's model and extended his ideas further. Kotter's Eight Steps to Effective Change is one such example.[110, 111] As its name implies, this model presents eight steps for implementing change. They are as follows:

1. Establish a sense of urgency.
2. Form a support platform (prochange coalition).
3. Develop a compelling vision.
4. Diffuse the vision throughout the organization.
5. Train and empower followers to act on the vision.
6. Allow for short-term accomplishments and reward performance.
7. Consolidate gains by changing the culture, systems, policies, and structures to align with the new vision.
8. Institutionalize the change in the organizational culture.

We will combine the three-stage and the eight-step models into one comprehensive model of change implementation (see Exhibit 11.2).

EXHIBIT 11.2 **Change Implementation Process**

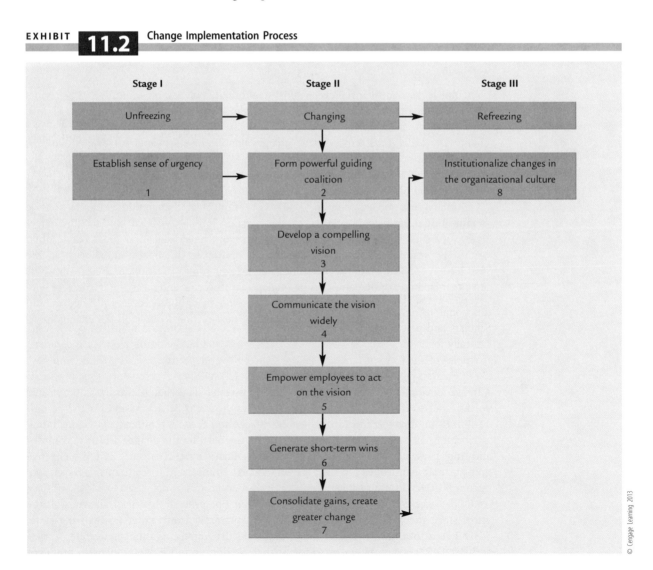

Describe the change management process using the three-stage model of change.

Unfreezing Phase

Instigated by the actions of a charismatic, strategic, or transformational leader, people in an organization may become aware of the need for change. In other words, a leader may inspire people with a vision of a better future that is sufficiently attractive to convince them that the old ways of doing business are no longer adequate. This recognition may occur as a result of an immediate crisis, or it may result from the efforts of a transformational leader who is able to describe threats and opportunities not yet evident to most people in the organization. The key is to identify the problems or threats facing the organization that make for an urgent need to change. It is important to invest the time at this early stage to uncover not just the threat, but its root cause(s) because the rest of the steps will focus on the specific threat. People have to be convinced of the need for change, and a focus on the wrong threat and/or root causes can complicate later stages of the change process. When followers are not convinced of the need for change or don't understand it, there is a greater likelihood of resistance. Other mechanisms for creating a motivation to change include the disconfirming of present behaviors or attitudes, creation of guilt, discomfort or anxiety with the status quo, and creation of psychological safety by reducing barriers to change. The second phase of the force-field model of change management is the actual change itself.

Changing Phase

This phase is also known as cognitive restructuring because it is where the actual change takes place. The key at this stage is developing new attitudes, beliefs, values, and behaviors based on new information. Here, people look for a leader with an inspiring vision. Lack of a carefully designed plan of action at this stage can lead to failure. The difference between the three-stage and the eight-stage model is what happens during the changing phase. The eight-stage model prescribes six additional steps that are in essence part of the changing phase in the three-stage model. This is an extension of the classic three-step model referred to above. As shown in Exhibit 11.2, these are steps 2 through 7. These intermediate steps are tactics that a leader can use to strengthen change implementation.

The first change implementation tactic is for the leader to form a powerful guiding coalition that supports the change initiative. One way to do this is by forming a cross-functional team with the necessary expertise and power to guide the change process. Scholars and practitioners generally agree that a support platform of influential people who can rally followers to "buy into" the change effort should be the number one consideration. Examples of such persons include people who are well respected, seen as credible, and well liked. Another recommendation is that such a pro-change coalition should consist of people who are effective communicators and who understand the roadblocks, inertia, fears, and political issues that could impede adoption of change initiatives.

With a pro-change coalition in place, the second change implementation tactic is for the leader to develop and articulate a compelling vision that will guide the change effort and selected strategies. To be committed to the change process, people need to believe in the leader's vision of a promising future that is significantly better than the present to justify the costs and hardships that the transformation will bring. The context for change needs to be established by the CEO and his top leadership team. Also, a shared vision must be the result of debate and consensus hammered out by a representative group.

The third change implementation tactic is active communication of the new vision and plan of action. The leader's excellent communication skills and ability to mobilize widespread participation is critical for success. It is generally believed that the most effective leaders have strong interpersonal skills that blend the instrumental and charismatic qualities of change leadership.

The fifth tactic describes the importance of empowering employees throughout the organization to act on the change. The leader must empower people by providing resources, information, and discretion to make decisions. Successful implementation depends on winning employee support and enthusiasm for proposed changes, rather than merely overcoming resistance. Empowerment must also include removing obstacles to change, which may include adapting the infrastructure (systems, structure, policies, procedures, and culture) to match the requirements of the change effort.[112]

The sixth and seventh tactics require the leader to organize the change activities in ways that highlight and celebrate short-term accomplishments. Major change takes time to complete, and without some visible signs of progress, the transformation effort may lose momentum. Charismatic and transformational leaders understand that actions speak louder than words in creating and sustaining internal momentum for change, even if such actions are merely symbolic. Confidence, enthusiasm, and pride gained via short-term wins will create the drive and motivation to tackle bigger challenges and bring about a faster completion of the change. This leads us to the last phase of the force-field model of change—the refreezing phase.

Refreezing Phase

For any change to become routine and accepted into the everyday practices of an organization, the change process must follow through to the final stage of refreezing the new change. A variety of strategies may be adopted to achieve this, including new rules, attitudes, traditions, regulations, and reward schemes to reinforce the new changes and maximize the desired behaviors of all organizational members. This will prevent a reversion to the old ways after implementation. Complete transformation can only occur when the desired change in behavior becomes habitual. This is step 8 of the eight-stage model. The refreezing phase is critical because, as the saying goes, "old habits die hard." Resistance that may have been resolved during the changing phase can resurface in the form of resentment towards those who supported and committed to the change.

Though stages in the change process generally overlap, each phase is critical for success. An attempt to start implementing change without first unfreezing old attitudes is likely to meet with strong resistance. Not refreezing new attitudes and behaviors may result in the change being reversed soon after implementation. Understanding these phases is important for change-oriented leaders, who must exercise good judgment throughout the process.

It should be noted that following these steps does not guarantee success; it only enhances the chances of success. It increases the likelihood that the majority of organizational members will commit to, rather than resist, the change. Even with the best change implementation efforts, a few people will always resist the change. However, it is generally the case that these holdouts tend to come around when confronted by fellow group members whose majority membership is committed to the change.

WORK Application **5**
Think of a time when a major change initiative at an organization you were or are affiliated with succeeded or failed. Identify possible reasons for the success or failure, and tie them to the three phases of the change model—unfreezing, changing, and refreezing.

Learning Outcome 7   _Identify the major reasons for resisting change._

Why People Resist Change

Although indispensable for long-term economic growth, organizational changes are frequently met with resistance. Change can disrupt the status quo and lead to stress, discomfort, and for some even dislocation. These negative outcomes often motivate people to resist change.[113] Resistance is a natural response by employees who want to protect their self-interest in the organization. For some, change is often perceived as a win–lose proposition; leaders see it as a positive way to strengthen the organization while followers view it as a threat to their status and livelihood. Change has to be perceived as a win–win proposition for both leaders and followers.

People realize that trying to learn something new could be risky for a number of reasons. First, it may make them look less capable: second, it may expose them to rejection by valued groups; and third, it may even cause them to lose their job or position. This can lead to learning anxiety. As mentioned above, survival anxiety is a necessary but insufficient stimulus for change because the prospect of learning something new itself produces anxiety, which then makes people react defensively by denying the reality or validity of the information that triggered the survival anxiety. This then allows for rationalization that the change is not needed. Effective change agents/leaders can create a psychological safety net for followers by finding ways to reduce learning anxiety. An example will be providing ample opportunities for training and education. Focused education and training can equip employees with the new skills and capabilities that match the change.

Effective leaders do not downplay resistance or perceive it as a discipline problem to be dealt with through punishment or coercion. Turning resistance into positive momentum can focus the energy where it will do the most good. One way to do this is for leaders to become good listeners and be open to feedback from followers.[114] Exhibit 11.3 summarizes some of the reasons why people resist change.

EXHIBIT 11.3   Reasons for Resisting Change

  a. Threat to one's self-interest
  b. Uncertainty
  c. Lack of confidence that change will succeed
  d. Lack of conviction that change is necessary
  e. Distrust of leadership
  f. Threat to personal values
  g. Fear of being manipulated

© Cengage Learning 2013

Threat to One's Self-Interest

An employee's self-interest in protecting his or her power, position, prestige, pay, and other company benefits is a major reason for opposing change. When an organization embarks on a major change, such as pursuing a new strategy, it often results in a shift in the relative power structure and the status of individuals and units within the organization. For example, changes in job design or technology may require knowledge and skills not currently possessed by employees. For these employees, the fear of losing their jobs or status is a major impetus for resisting change, regardless of the benefits to the organization. This is what was referred to as learning anxiety.

Uncertainty

Uncertainty represents a fear of the unknown. Lack of information about a change initiative creates a sense of uncertainty.[115] When employees don't have full knowledge of how a proposed change will affect them, they may worry that replacing skills they have mastered over the years with new ones may prove too difficult to achieve.

Lack of Confidence That Change Will Succeed

A proposed change may require such a radical transformation from the old ways of doing business that some will question its likelihood of succeeding. In this case, even though there may be a general acknowledgment of problems and the need for change, the lack of confidence that the change will succeed creates resistance. Also, if there have been instances of past failures, this may create cynicism and doubt of future change proposals.

Lack of Conviction That Change Is Necessary

People may resist change if the leader has failed to articulate a real need and urgency for change.[116] This is especially true in cases where employees believe that the current strategy is working just fine and there is no need to change. It's that old adage of "if it's not broken, don't fix it."

Distrust of Leadership

Trust between parties is the basic requirement for sustaining any relationship. The absence of trust will cause people to resist change, even if there are no obvious threats. Change is resisted if people suspect that there are hidden consequences or motives that management is not revealing. Trust is a valuable currency for leaders to have, because it is the basis upon which the benefits of a proposed change can be sold to employees who may suffer personal losses from such action. One study's survey found that most employees were skeptical of corporate change initiatives, but were willing to put their trust in change efforts which are supported by influential peers.[117]

Threat to Personal Values

WORK Application **6**

Give an example of when you were resistant to change. Be sure to identify your resistance by one of the seven reasons in Exhibit 11.3.

When a proposed change threatens a person's values, it ignites powerful feelings that fuel resistance to change. Any proposed change must take into account its impact on the values of those who are affected by the change, especially values that are closely aligned with an entrenched organizational culture. If threatened, values that are aligned with an entrenched organizational culture will ignite resistance that is organization-wide rather than isolated.

Fear of Being Manipulated

When people perceive change as an attempt by management to manipulate them, they will resist. However, when people understand and accept the need for change and believe that they have a voice in determining how to implement the change, resistance is lessened.

In the end, leaders who regard resistance as a distraction rather than a real and legitimate concern will find it hard to move beyond the first stage of the change model (see Exhibit 11.2). Effective leaders will not only follow the steps in the model but also employ the best implementation techniques or strategies to minimize employee resistance.

OPENING CASE *APPLICATION*

8. Why have Page, Schmidt, and Brin encountered less resistance in bringing about changes at Google than most companies experience?

Google's leadership style and its culture have largely contributed to the lack of resistance. At Google, there is a sense of "we are in this together." There is little in the way of corporate hierarchy, and everyone wears several hats. Everyone realizes that they are an important part of Google's success. Though growing rapidly, Google still maintains a small-company feel. At its headquarters, almost everyone eats in the Google café (known as "Charlie's Place"), sitting at

(continues)

(Opening Case Application 8 continued)

whatever table has an opening and enjoying conversations with Googlers from different departments. Google's culture of transparency and open communication minimizes the chances that the reasons given in Exhibit 11.3 for resisting change will develop among employees.

CONCEPT APPLICATION 3
Resistance to Change

Using the letters a through g that accompany the reasons listed in Exhibit 11.3, identify which reason for resisting change explains each employee statement.

_____ 21. I'm not too sure about this new program. Is it really going to make a difference or just another fad?

_____ 22. Why should our company go through with the merger? What do we know about that foreign company anyway?

_____ 23. If we get these new machines, we will need fewer operators and there goes my job.

_____ 24. Why do we have to put in a new system when the current one is only a year old and is working fine?

_____ 25. How can management ask us to take a pay cut when they are the ones who are making all the money? We shouldn't let them take advantage of us.

Learning Outcome 8   *Discuss some of the recommendations for minimizing resistance to change.*

Minimizing Resistance to Change

A few basic guidelines, if followed, can significantly reduce the level of resistance encountered during the change implementation process. From a humanistic point of view, resistance to change has a cognitive, emotional, and behavioral dimension. From a cognitive standpoint, there is a rational calculation that change cannot occur unless the forces driving the need for change are stronger than the forces resisting it. There is a concerted effort to increase the forces of resistance against the forces of support. From an emotional standpoint, the fear of loss (status, position, job, pay, and so forth) and fear of the unknown causes a lot of frustration and anger. Capitalizing on such anger can really heighten resistance. Resistance to change as a behavior focuses on the actions of members opposed to the change. Examples of such actions include sabotage and intentional work slowdowns. Strategies for minimizing resistance to change ultimately focus ways of addressing the cognitive, emotional, and behavioral states of organizational members.

Recommendations for Minimizing Resistance

Effective leaders ensure that they keep employees informed, supportive, and motivated about any change initiatives. Effective communication before, during, and after change has been implemented will prevent misunderstandings, false rumors, and conflict. It is important that those affected by change not learn about it from secondhand sources. Employees should be informed of *what* is changing, *why* it is changing, *who* is affected, *how* the change will affect individuals, and *when* the change will start and end.[118] Another way to put this is for change agents to pay attention to the "5-Ps"—*purpose, priorities, people, process, and proof.* A stated purpose describes what is changing with specific targets identified and prioritized, people potentially affected by the change, a process that employs appropriate levels of participation and consultation, and proof that the change will accomplish its stated goals. Also, because major change involves adjustments, disruptions, and dislocation, training, education and mentoring are needed to help employees acquire skills and capabilities for their role in the implementation process or for their new responsibilities. This underscores the importance that HR can play in the change process.[119]

There are also process, policy, and structural changes that leaders can make to minimize resistance to change. Some call this business process reengineering (BPR).[120] Leaders can minimize the incidence of resistance through BPR by adjusting existing structures, procedures, and processes to align with the requirements of proposed change initiatives. For example, some strategic leaders are finding out that adopting flatter, more agile structures and empowering teams/individuals to make decisions are better ways of minimizing resistance to change. Although it is time-consuming, getting employees involved in designing change activities pays off in that it gives people a sense of control. Exhibit 11.4 summarizes these and many other suggested recommendations that leaders can employ to minimize resistance to change.

EXHIBIT **11.4**   **Recommendations for Minimizing Resistance**

To reduce or eliminate resistance to change, effective leaders:
- Show relentless support and unquestionable commitment to the change process.
- Communicate the need and the urgency for change to everyone.
- Maintain ongoing communication about the progress of change.
- Avoid micromanaging and empower people to implement the change.
- Ensure that change efforts are adequately staffed and funded.
- Anticipate and prepare people for the necessary adjustments that change will trigger, such as career counseling and/or retraining.

© Cengage Learning 2013

Now that you have learned about strategic leadership and change leadership, complete Self-Assessment 1 to determine how your personality affects your strategic planning and ability to change.

SELF-ASSESSMENT 2   **Personality, Leadership, and Change**

Strategic leadership is less based on personality than is charismatic or transformational leadership. Management level also has a lot to do with strategic planning and leadership, as it is primarily a function of top-level managers. Are you a strategic thinker with a focus on long-term planning? Do you have any business or personal plans for three to five years from now, or do you take things as they come without planning for the future?

_____

_____

_____

Change leadership is based on the Big Five personality type openness to experience. Charismatic, transformational, and strategic leadership all require being receptive to change and influencing others to change. Are you open to trying new things and to change, or do you tend to like the status quo and resist change? Do you attempt to influence others to try new things?

_____

_____

_____

Chapter Summary

The chapter summary is organized to answer the nine learning outcomes for Chapter 11.

1. Discuss the role of strategic leadership in the strategic management process.

Strategic leaders establish organizational direction through vision and strategy. They are responsible for analyzing the organization's environment, considering how it may be different in the future, and setting a direction everyone can believe in and work toward. Strategic leaders must then craft the organization's mission, which includes its core values and purpose for existence. Strategy formulation is the leader's responsibility: He or she must guide the selection among alternative plans and choose the best option for translating goals and objectives into action. The final step is strategy implementation and evaluation. Successful completion of the strategic management process and the attainment of superior organizational performance is not a chance occurrence. It is determined by the decisions and actions that strategic leaders take during the process.

2. Describe the relevance of analyzing the internal and external environment to the strategic management process.

The underlying tenet of strategic management is that organizations need to formulate strategies to take advantage of external opportunities and to avoid or reduce the negative impact of external threats. This takes place by monitoring customer behavior, supplier and vendor activities, actions of competitors, market trends, economic conditions, government policies, and technological advances. Analyzing the internal environment focuses on assessing the organization's position in the market, financial position, capabilities, core competencies, culture, and structure. This process reveals the organization's strengths and weaknesses. The combined analysis of the external environment (i.e., to identify opportunities and threats) and internal environment (i.e., to identify strengths and weaknesses) is commonly referred to as SWOT or situation analysis.

3. Explain the various components in the strategy formulation phase of the strategic management process.

Many organizations develop both a vision and a mission statement. Whereas the vision statement answers the question, "What do we want to become?" the mission statement answers the question, "What is our business?" Both the vision and mission statements ensure unanimity of purpose within the organization and make important statements about "who the firm is" and "what it wants to become" to outside stakeholders. In other words, reaching agreement on formal mission and vision statements can greatly facilitate the process of reaching agreement on the other components of the strategy formulation phase—setting long-term objectives, selecting appropriate strategies, and establishing policies

and standard operating procedures. Organizational success depends on tying all of these components together.

4. Explain the relationship between corporate goals and strategies.

Goals are the desired outcomes that an organization seeks to achieve for its various stakeholders. Strategies are the means by which goals will be realized. It is for this reason that the mission and goals of an organization are established before the strategy formulation phase in the strategic management model.

5. Explain the importance of strategy evaluation in the strategic management model.

Note in the strategic management model that feedback is critically important. Changes can occur that impact all strategic management activities. The strategy evaluation stage allows these changes to be identified and adjustments to be made. The feedback that results from the strategy evaluation process promotes the creation of a climate for two-way communication throughout the organization. Strategy evaluation involves three fundamental activities: (1) reviewing internal and external factors that are the bases for the current strategies; (2) measuring performance against stated objectives; and (3) taking corrective action. Corrective action utilizes the feedback that results from the strategy evaluation process.

6. Describe the change management process using the three-stage model of change.

The force-field model proposes that the change process can be divided into three phases: unfreezing, changing, and refreezing. During the unfreezing phase, the leader establishes the need for change by establishing the problems associated with the current situation and presenting a vision of a better future. Awareness of the need for change and acceptance of a new vision sets the stage for the changing phase. It is during the second phase that the proposed vision is implemented. It is action oriented. The leader must actively and effectively communicate the vision with a tone of urgency. He or she must empower followers to act on the vision by giving them resources, information, and discretion to make decisions. Empowerment must also include removing obstacles to change, which may include adapting the infrastructure to the new strategy or strategies of the organization. Other motivational strategies for achieving success at this stage are described in the text. The third phase, refreezing, involves cementing the new vision in the organizational culture so that the change is not reversed soon after it is implemented. The change must be institutionalized so that old habits, values, traditions, and attitudes are permanently replaced.

7.   Identify the major reasons for resisting change.

Change is not a risk-free proposition. Change often brings with it pain and stress. Some people get demoted, reassigned, relocated, or even fired from their jobs. With all of these negative possibilities, the first reaction of most people is to resist any attempts at making a change. Some of the major reasons why people resist change are the threat to one's self-interest, lack of conviction that change is necessary, fear of being manipulated, threat to personal values, lack of confidence that change will succeed, distrust of leadership, and uncertainty. These reasons are further elaborated on in the text.

8.   Discuss some of the recommendations for minimizing resistance to change.

To overcome resistance to change, effective managers must think in terms of people actions and task actions. People actions involve undertaking the following: anticipate change and prepare people for the necessary adjustments that change will trigger, avoid micromanaging and empower people to implement the change, ensure that change efforts are adequately staffed and funded, communicate a strong message about the urgency for change, celebrate and maintain ongoing communication about the progress of change, and show a strong commitment to the change process. Task-based actions include assembling a coalition of supporters inside and outside the organization, recruiting and filling key positions with competent and committed supporters, aligning the organizational structure and other infrastructure with the new strategy, using qualified task forces to shape and support implementation activities, and recognizing and rewarding others' contributions to the change process.

9.   Define the following key terms (in order of appearance in the chapter).

Select one or more methods: (1) fill in the missing key terms from memory; (2) match the key terms from the following list with their definitions below; and (3) copy the key terms in order from the list at the beginning of the chapter.

_____ is a person's ability to anticipate, envision, maintain flexibility, think strategically, and work with others to initiate changes that will create a viable future for the organization.

_____ *is the instinctive ability to respond to problems without the benefit of concrete facts and information.*

_____ is the set of decisions and actions used to formulate and implement specific strategies that aligned with the organization's capabilities and its environment, so as to achieve organizational goals.

_____ is an ambitious view of the future that everyone in the organization can believe in and that is not readily attainable, yet offers a future that is better in important ways than what now exists.

_____ is an enduring statement of purpose that distinguishes one organization from other similar enterprises.

_____ is an integrated, overarching plan of how an organization will achieve its objectives.

_____ is the ratio of benefits received to the cost incurred by the customer.

_____ is a capability that allows an organization to perform extremely well in comparison to competitors.

_____ is an alteration in an organization's alignment with its external environment.

_____ is members' consensual understanding of "who we are as an organization" that emerges from that which is central, distinctive, and enduring to the organization as a whole.

_____ is the feeling that unless an organization makes a change, it is going to be out of business or fail to achieve some important goals.

_____ is the prospect of learning something new in itself.

Key Terms

core competence, 406

executive intuition, 397

learning anxiety, 412

mission statement, 403

organizational change, 410

organizational identity, 406

strategic leadership, 396

strategic management, 399

strategic vision, 402

strategy, 405

survival anxiety, 412

value, 406

Review Questions

1.   Discuss how an organization's objectives may affect its search for opportunities.

2.   What are the key elements of the strategic management process?

3. What is the difference between a strategic vision and a mission statement?

4. The essence of the strategic management process is adapting to change. Discuss.

5. Describe the role of leadership in successful change implementation.

6. What are the phases of the eight-stage model of planned change?

7. Why is change often perceived as a win–lose proposition between leaders and followers?

8. What is the difference between people- and task-centered strategies for minimizing resistance to change?

Critical Thinking Questions

The following critical-thinking questions can be used for class discussion and/or as written assignments to develop communication skills. Be sure to give complete explanations for all questions.

1. What, in your opinion, are the risks and benefits of the leadership arrangement at Google, where the two founders (Larry Page and Sergey Brin) elected to bring in Eric Schmidt to be the CEO while they function as presidents under him?

2. Comment on this statement: "Google is so successful it does not need to change anything in its strategic framework."

3. As leaders make strategic decisions, they must balance the interests of various stakeholders—employees, customers, shareholders, suppliers, unions/activists, and the community. Describe the best approach for doing this.

4. Many decisions made by strategic leaders benefit some people at the expense of others, thus raising ethical issues. Give specific examples for each of the following categories of unethical behavior:

- Breaking laws or evading regulations
- Legal but unethical behavior
- Acts of omission rather than commission

5. For CEOs and many other senior executives, strategic leadership is an important role they must perform well. Briefly describe some of the specific actions or responsibilities of the CEO that strategic leadership entails.

6. Resistance to change is more likely to succeed if the forces resisting the change are stronger than the forces driving the need for change. Describe some of the specific tactics that resisters would employ to thwart change efforts.

CASE

Nike—CEO Mark Parker and His Executive Team Impress Shareholders and Analysts

In late 2004, when Nike was looking to fill the CEO position after Phil Knight offered to step down, Mark Parker, a seasoned 27-year veteran of the company, was passed on in favor of William Perez, an outsider. Many at the time quietly wondered if Mr. Knight's action was an indication that he was not confident in the leadership abilities of Mark Parker. Then in 2006, just 13 months into the job, Phil Knight and the rest of the Nike board decided to replace Perez with Mark Parker. Why Mr. Parker was passed on in the first place was baffling to some because of his past track record at Nike. Parker, 54, joined Nike in 1979 and has served in various management capacities in product design, development, marketing, manufacturing, research, design and brand management. He is widely recognized as the product visionary for the Nike Air franchise and many other industry-leading

product design and performance innovations. Mr. Parker was appointed divisional Vice President in charge of development in 1987, corporate Vice President in 1989, General Manager in 1993, Vice President of Global Footwear in 1998, and President of the NIKE Brand in 2001.[121] Even Phil Knight described him as an experienced, talented executive who has played an instrumental role in building and making the Nike brand as strong as it is today. So why was he not selected in the first place was the question many people had in mind.

Given the way Mr. Parker came to the job, there has been interest in how well he will perform as CEO. It is worth looking back to see how Mr. Parker has defied the odds and surprised those who doubted his readiness for the job in the first place.

Since assuming the role of CEO of Nike, Parker's team has overhauled the way Nike runs, shifting the brand away from the previous sub-brand and product-based structure to a customer-driven structure. He has structured Nike into six "customer-focused" categories, such as running, basketball, and women's fitness. Parker has personally shaped Nike's innovation processes. For example, even before becoming CEO, he established a group for pursuing long-range innovation, called Explore. He described Explore as a multidisciplinary group pursuing "deep space" innovation possibilities with academics, inventors, and other companies. Explore, he pointed out, was chiefly responsible for the cooperation with Steve Jobs and Apple that led to the launch of the Nike Plus program in 2006. The Nike + iPod is a wireless system that allows Nike + footwear to talk with your iPod nano to connect you to the ultimate personal running and workout experience. According to most analysts, Parker's biggest strength is his ability to key into consumer trends.

Mark Parker took the helm of Nike at the time when the stakes in the U.S. market were particularly high, especially as Adidas was becoming more powerful with the acquisition of Reebok. Parker said at the time that he believed he was the right person to lead Nike through the challenges of the future. He said it was his job to help carry the torch into the future. He has always maintained that all Nike employees work for one boss—the consumer.

We discussed the concept of globalization and environmental sustainability. Nike has what it calls "Nike Sustainable Business + Innovation" program. Nike believes it can use the power of its brand, the energy and passion of its people, and the scale of its business to create meaningful change. Nike believes the opportunity is greater than ever for sustainable principles and practices to deliver business returns and create a positive social and environmental impact in the world.[122]

Parker isn't an attention-seeking sort of CEO, so until now it has been hard to get a sense of him. But the imprint he is making as CEO is turning out to be as meaningful as his design work. Putting his stamp on Nike as forcefully as the much splashier cofounder Phil Knight did, Parker has reorganized the company into units based on particular sports, "a conscious decision to sharpen each piece of the business so we're not some big fat dumb company," he says; reshuffled its regions to put new emphasis on China and Japan; streamlined the reporting process and removed regional middle management; handled a rare round of layoffs; and weathered yet another scandal involving a high-profile endorser. He describes this set-up as more of a framework than a process.[123]

On June 27, 2011, Nike reported financial results for its fiscal 2011 fourth quarter and full year ended May 31, 2011. Revenues and earnings per share (EPS) for both the quarter and full year hit record highs. Significantly better than analysts expected. Commenting on the results, Mark Parker said, "We delivered exceptional results in extraordinary times." Forbes has described Parker as an effective leader of NIKE.

For the future, Parker has set some big goals for Nike: increase sales by more than 40 percent, to $27 billion by 2015; meet a set of equally ambitious sustainability benchmarks; grow earnings 7 percent a year; and keep 33,000 employees thinking as nimbly as possible.[124]

Today, Nike's passion for real innovation continues to thrive. Nike is still the world's largest sportswear company with over $20 billion in annual sales, employing more than 30,000 employees, and operating in more than 160 countries. Nike's mission is to bring inspiration and innovation to every athlete in the world. It is evident by the goals Mr. Parker has put out that he intends to push forward with this mission and continue Nike's leadership in the industry.

GO TO THE INTERNET: (http://www.nike.com) Support your answers to the following questions with specific information from the case and text or with other information you get from the Web or other sources.

1. What external and internal pressures did Mark Parker face when he assumed the leadership of Nike, and how did he respond to these challenges?

2. Strategic management is about formulating strategies that align an organization's internal capabilities with external opportunities while avoiding or minimizing threats. How effective has Mark Parker been as a strategist so far?

3. What is the evidence that Mark Parker and Nike understand the impact of environmental sustainability on their business practices?

4. As revealed in the text, an effective strategist develops strategies that (1) enhance value to its customers, (2) create synergistic opportunities, and (3) build on the company's core competencies. What evidence shows that Mark Parker is pursuing this course or shares this viewpoint?

CUMULATIVE CASE QUESTIONS

5. According to the Big Five Model of Personality, what traits would Mark Parker consider critical for his managers to possess (Chapter 2)?

6. The interactions among power, politics, networking, and negotiation are a common occurrence in organizational life (Chapter 4). CEOs have to deal with various stakeholders (shareholders, employees, board of directors, customers, suppliers, unions, government and state regulators, and so on). Describe how a CEO like Mark Parker would employ power, politics, networking, and negotiation as effective tools of leadership.

7. Communication, coaching, and conflict management are said to be skills that have a direct and significant impact on a leader's career success (Chapter 6). Given the weak market and financial position that Nike was in prior to Mark Parker's appointment, how critical are these skills in his efforts to reposition the company and address its weaknesses?

CASE EXERCISE AND ROLE-PLAY

Preparation: Assume you are part of the leadership of an organization or organizational unit that is in need of training the management team of its foreign subsidiary to embrace and practice diversity at the highest levels. Under Mark Parker, Nike is leading the way in diversity. Nike's vision is for every team to be high performing, diverse, and inclusive. To achieve this vision, Nike strategy is to:

- Cultivate diversity and inclusion to develop world-class, high-performing teams
- Ignite change and inspire critical conversations around diversity, inclusion, and innovation
- Create venues and environments for open dialogue, diverse opinions, and a multitude of perspectives

A multinational corporation like Nike wants to ensure that all its subsidiaries around the world have high diversity standards (visit Nike's Web site at **www.nike.com** for more information). Your task is to help your foreign subsidiary develop diversity standards for its respective units that are in congruence with the overall diversity standards of the parent corporation.

Role-Play: The instructor forms students into small groups (representing top leadership of the foreign subsidiary or partner) to develop a diversity statement of no more than 100 words. Here are some guidelines:

1. Make a case for diversity by identifying key benefits of a diversified workforce.
2. Create a list of core values that your organization now holds or you would want it to have, and incorporate them into your diversity statement.
3. Share your diversity statement with other members of the class, and vote on who has the best diversity statement.

VIDEO ▶❚❚ CASE

Original Penguin Spreads Its Wings

Chris Kolbe is a master of change. Now president of Original Penguin, Kolbe essentially runs the division for its parent company, Perry Ellis International. Original Penguin was a 1950s icon—the penguin logo appeared on Munsingwear Penguin knit sport shirts for men. Eventually, its popularity faded, and Perry Ellis International later acquired the brand. Chris Kolbe was working in merchandising at retailer Urban Outfitters when he conceived the idea of rejuvenating the penguin—but with a new twist and for a new market. Starting with a few new shirts, which sold out almost immediately, the "new" Original Penguin began to grow, and

Perry Ellis tapped Kolbe to complete the transformation as head of a new venture team. Kolbe recognizes that the fashion industry is a hotbed of change—and any clothing company that wants to survive must embrace innovation. He also understands that change takes time and patience.

1. Why has it been important for Perry Ellis International to give freedom to a new venture team in order to relaunch Original Penguin?

2. In what respects does Original Penguin represent a cultural change for Perry Ellis?

Developing Your Leadership Skills **1**

Strategic Planning

Preparing for This Exercise

Think of a business that you would like to start someday. Develop a simple strategic plan for your proposed business by following steps 1 through 4 below. If you cannot think of a business you would like to start, select an existing business. Do not select a company if you are familiar with their strategic plan. What is the name and location of the business?

_____

1. What would be some of your strengths and weaknesses, opportunities and threats, compared to your competitors? It may be helpful to think about your answer to step 4 below before doing your SWOT analysis.

_____

_____

2. Develop a vision statement for your business.

_____

_____

3. Develop a mission statement for your business.

_____

_____

4. As part of the strategy formulation, identify your core competencies. Be sure they answer the questions, "What will your business do better or different than your competitors? Why should someone do business with you rather than your competitors?" This stage is related to the SWOT analysis in step 1 above.

_____

_____

Doing This Exercise in Class

Objective

To develop a simple strategic plan for a business you would like to start someday

The primary AACSB learning standard skill developed through this exercise is strategic management.

Procedure *(10–30 minutes)*

Option A: Break into groups of 3 to 6 and share your strategic plans. Offer each other suggestions for improvements.

Option B: Same as A, but select the best strategy from the group to be presented to the entire class. Each group's selected strategy is presented to the class.

Conclusion

The instructor may make concluding remarks.

Apply It *(2–4 minutes)* What did I learn from this exercise? How will I use this knowledge in the future?

_____

_____

_____

Sharing

In the group, or to the entire class, volunteers may give their answers to the "Apply It" questions.

Developing Your Leadership Skills **2**

Planning a Change Using the Force-Field Model

Preparing This Exercise

Select a change at work or in your personal life that you would like to make, and develop a plan as follows.

1. Unfreezing. Briefly describe the change and why it is needed.

_____

_____

2. Changing. State the beginning-of-change date and end-of-change date. Develop a plan for making the change.

_____

_____

_____

_____

_____

3. Refreezing. Identify plans for maintaining the new change.

_____

_____

_____

Doing This Exercise in Class

Objective

To develop a personal plan for change

The primary AACSB learning standard skill developed through this exercise is analytic skills.

Procedure *(10–30 minutes)*
Option A: Break into groups of 3 to 6 and share your change plans. Offer each other suggestions for improvements.

Option B: Same as A, but select the best plan from the group to be presented to the entire class. Each group's selected plan is presented to the class.

Conclusion
The instructor may make concluding remarks.

Apply It *(2–4 minutes)* What did I learn from this experience? How will I use this knowledge in the future? Relist your beginning and ending target dates for the change.

_____

_____

_____

Sharing
In the group, or to the entire class, volunteers may give their answers to the "Apply It" questions.

Developing Your Leadership Skills **3**

Managing Change at Your College

Doing This Exercise in Class

Objective

To develop a large-scale plan for change

The primary AACSB learning standard skills developed through this exercise are analytic skills and strategic management.

Procedures *(10–30 minutes)*
As an individual, group, or class, select a change you would like to see implemented at your college. Answer the following questions and conduct the force-field analysis.

1. State the change you want.

_____

2. State which of the four types of change it is.

_____

3. Identify possible resistance to the change.

_____

_____

4. Select strategies for overcoming the resistance.

_____

_____

_____

5. Conduct a force-field analysis for the change. Below, write the present situation in the center and the forces that hinder the change and the forces that can help get the change implemented.

Hindering Forces $\longrightarrow$ Present Situation $\longleftarrow$ Driving Forces

Conclusion
The instructor may make concluding remarks.

Apply It *(2–4 minutes)* What did I learn from this experience? How will I use this knowledge in the future?

_____

_____

_____

Sharing
In the group, or to the entire class, volunteers may give their answers to the "Apply It" questions.

12

Crisis Leadership and the Learning Organization

Learning Outcomes

After studying this chapter, you should be able to:

1. Explain why crisis leadership competence is an important consideration when hiring new leaders. p. 430

2. Identify the benefits of precrisis planning. p. 434

3. Identify three key components of the precrisis planning phase. p. 435

4. Describe the five-step process for crisis risk assessment. p. 436

5. Describe the role of the CEO and communication in managing a crisis. p. 438

6. List five or more attributes that can be used to describe the learning organization. p. 446

7. Distinguish between the traditional organization and the learning organization. p. 448

8. Describe the role of leadership in creating a learning organization. p. 451

9. Define the following **key terms** (in order of appearance in the chapter):

crisis	learning organization
press release	organizational knowledge
press kit	discontinuous change

OPENING CASE APPLICATION

Vikram Pandit is the CEO of Citigroup, a multinational financial institution with approximately 200 million customer accounts and activities in more than 160 countries and jurisdictions. Born in India, the Pandit family immigrated to the United States when Vikram was only 16. He enrolled in Columbia University, earning BS and MS degrees in engineering and later earned his PhD in finance from the same institution in 1986.

Pandit was named the new CEO of Citigroup on December 11, 2007. He replaced Chuck Prince, who resigned in November 2007. At the time of Chuck Prince's resignation, Citigroup's financial performance was abysmal to say the least. The company was deeply involved in the subprime mortgage crisis that began in 2007. As was true of most banking/financial institutions at the time, many experts believed that righting the ship at Citigroup would be a large challenge for anyone. And while Citigroup was not the only bank to take a loss from exposure related to subprime mortgages, there was a feeling within the company that it had not lived up to its potential.

As if the current problems facing the company were not enough, Mr. Pandit added to the company's woes with some early decisions he made. Testifying before Congress on February 11, 2009, Pandit struck an apologetic tone for letting the bank consider completing the purchase of a private jet plane after receiving some $45 billion in bailout money. In another strategic move at damage control, Pandit told Congress that he had declared to his board of directors, "my salary should be $1 per year with no bonus until we return to profitability."

With his appointment, Pandit embarked on a plan to refocus, recapitalize, and restructure Citigroup during the most challenging economic environment since the Great Depression. With the goals of long-term profitability and growth on his mind, Pandit's strategy for building a new Citigroup centered on the company's strengths and distinctive competitive advantages: its global franchise, strong emerging market footprint, innovative spirit, and talented and diverse employee base. In a conference call with journalists, Citigroup's chief financial officer, John C. Gerspach, indicated that after clawing its way back from the brink of collapse during the financial crisis; Citigroup has been engaged in an ambitious plan to transform from a sprawling financial supermarket to a leaner, more focused company. He said Citigroup has been hiring dozens of investment bankers, dialing up advertising, and drawing up plans to add several hundred branches worldwide, including more than 200 in major cities across the United States. "The company was on its deathbed, and the

investing they were doing was to make sure they survived," said Gerard Cassidy, a banking analyst at RBC Capital Markets."

Hoping to avoid a future crisis, Pandit has made Responsible Finance a priority. According to Pandit, Citigroup is committed to providing choice, control, and transparency for clients, managing risk responsibly and contributing to economic growth. From innovative foreclosure prevention programs that have kept more than a million Americans in their homes to a new, disciplined approach to risk management, Responsible Finance is being ingrained throughout Citigroup's practices and culture. Pandit has been successfully downsizing assets, improving risk management, and severing the bank's ties with the federal government by paying down bailout money.

Citigroup reported second quarter 2011 net income of $3.3 billion, compared to $2.7 billion in second quarter 2010. Earnings per share of $1.09 versus $0.90 in second quarter 2010. After posting five consecutive quarterly profits, Citigroup announced a $23.2 million retention award to Mr. Vikram Pandit in 2011, making him one of the highest paid CEOs.[1]

OPENING CASE QUESTIONS:

1. Describe the nature of the crisis that Citigroup was in prior to Mr. Pandit's appointment.

2. In your opinion, would precrisis planning have helped Citigroup avert the crisis it faced?

3. How effective was CEO Pandit in managing the crisis he inherited and the ones he created?

4. In your opinion, has Mr. Pandit been an effective communicator in the way he has handled the crisis?

5. What are some of the changes Mr. Pandit has instituted to avoid a repeat of a similar crisis in the future?

6. Describe the threats facing Citigroup in its external environment. Do these threats support or go against adopting a learning organizational culture?

7. In your opinion, does Citigroup represent the traditional organization or the learning organization?

8. What additional steps will you recommend that Vikram Pandit take in order to make Citigroup more of a learning organization?

Can you answer any of these questions? You'll find answers to these questions and learn more about Citigroup and its leadership throughout the chapter.

To learn more about Citigroup and Vikram Pandit, visit Citigroup's Web site at **http://www.citi.com**.

A key aspect of a strategic leader's responsibility is dealing with crisis. From natural disasters to the debt-ceiling crisis that threatened to shut down the U.S. government in the summer of 2011, crises know no boundaries. A crisis can strike any organization without warning. Far from a passing fad, crisis planning and management is now an integrated part of effective organizational leadership.[2] The British Standards Institute has formed a Crisis Management Steering Group, sponsored by the UK Cabinet Office through its education arm, the Emergency Planning College.[3] A crisis by its very nature is an event that could not be predicted or anticipated prior to its occurrence. Therefore, avoidance is rarely possible.

Crises are indeed damaging to an organization if not properly managed. In a crisis, revenue, profits, and stock prices can plummet while operating costs escalate, causing both short- and long-term financial losses. A crisis that is mismanaged can also damage an organization's reputation and diminish consumer confidence in the organization and in some cases lead to its demise altogether.[4] In a crisis, organizations that adopt a defensive stance are more vulnerable to attacks from competitors. An effective strategist must also have the relevant skills to manage a crisis successfully. Increasingly, organizations are investing a lot of resources in preparing for crises such as threats, disasters, sabotage, and scandals.[5]

The first half of this chapter discusses crisis leadership in depth. The second half of the chapter focuses on the important topic of organizational learning and knowledge management. The learning organization is one that emphasizes creativity, innovation, and knowledge creation as a way of maintaining its competitiveness.

Learning Outcome 1 *Explain why crisis leadership competence is an important consideration when hiring new leaders.*

Crisis Leadership

A **crisis** *is a low-probability, high-impact event that threatens the viability of the organization and is characterized by ambiguity of cause, effect, and means of resolution, as well as by a belief that decisions must be made swiftly.*[6] Today, more than ever, there is a great need for leaders from all walks of life to show that they possess the skills and competence to lead during times of crisis.[7] Mismanaging a crisis has ended the careers of many CEOs. The CEO of BP lost his job over his handling of the BP oil spill off the Gulf coast in 2010. It is not always the case that an effective leader is also effective at crisis management. Crisis leaders often face challenges that are clearly different from normal operations. Crisis leadership requires the application of skills, knowledge, and abilities that go beyond those required for day-to-day work.[8] That is why the incorporation of crisis planning in every organization's strategic plan is critical. We are all aware of the headlines involving corporate scandals, accounting fraud, ethical lapses in judgment, and allegations of workplace discrimination. According to Warren Bennis, crises are always crucibles of leadership in that sooner or later some transformative event or experience comes along that is central to finding one's voice, learning how to engage others through shared meaning, and acquiring the other skills of leadership.[9]

In today's volatile global marketplace, many experts believe that organizations (whether for-profit or not-for-profit) should recognize the inevitable—that crises can and will emerge. Unfortunately, crisis response plans are not as widespread as one would expect. Many experts and scholars agree that while a precrisis response plan will not prevent a crisis, it can minimize financial loss and long-term damage to a firm's reputation.

Some proactive corporations are now putting in place strategic crisis readiness plans. These organizations are taking appropriate steps to design systems and procedures to respond effectively to a crisis when it happens. Strategic crisis leadership requires three things:

1. Using environmental monitoring techniques to identify events that could trigger crises in the future.
2. Integrating crisis management into the strategic management framework so it remains a regular part of the overall strategy-evaluation process.[10]
3. Establishing a culture that embraces crisis awareness and preparation as a way of life.

Crises come in many forms—natural disasters (the 2010 earthquake in Haiti and the 2011 earthquake in Japan and subsequent nuclear accident), terrorist attacks (the July 24, 2011, mass shootings in Oslo, Norway, where more than 70 people were killed), product failures (the Toyota recall crisis of 2010), human error disasters (the BP *Deepwater Horizon* well exploding in April 2010 that sent oil gushing for three months into the Gulf), unexpected death of a CEO (McDonald's CEO and Chairman, Jim Catalupo), and system failures (*the Challenger* accident and Chernobyl nuclear plant explosion). Also, many crises don't always make the front pages of newspapers or aren't featured in the TV news, such as sexual harassment, executive misconduct, sabotage, and succession crisis.[11,12]

In July 2011, two branches of the U.S. government—the legislative and executive—began to operate in a state of crisis. The crisis concerned the ongoing debate over whether the debt ceiling of the United States should be raised and, if so, by what amount. The law specifies that if the Treasury does not collect enough in revenue to pay for expenditures by the Federal Government, it is authorized by Congress to issue debt (in other words, borrow money) to pay for the federal budget deficit. The debt ceiling is a limit on the amount the Treasury can borrow to pay for the unpaid obligations already incurred. In the past, this has been a routine process where Congress passes the legislation authorizing that the debt ceiling be raised and the President signs it with very little fanfare. It has turned into a crisis of historical proportions over Republican demands that spending and tax reforms be tied to raising the debt ceiling. They argue that trillions of U.S. debt is burdening the economy and threatening our long-term future. The debate between the Democrats and Republicans has focused on two key questions: (1) What future spending policies and/or tax code policies should be associated with the action to increase the debt ceiling? and (2) What structural changes for future budgeting processes if any (for example, spending caps, revenue increases, and/or a balanced budget amendment to the U.S. Constitution) should be associated with raising the debt ceiling?

Many crisis management experts and scholars have been closely watching how the President and Congressional leaders are handling this crisis. With negotiations going nowhere and the deadline approaching, Standard and Poors (one of three credit rating agencies) indicated that it would downgrade the U.S. credit rating if a meaningful deal was not reached before the deadline. In the end, a deal to cut the deficit by 2.8 trillion dollars was reached and the debt ceiling raised with only hours to go before the deadline expired. If the debt ceiling had not been raised by August 2, 2011, the United States would have defaulted, with many economists predicting catastrophic consequences. Despite this action, Standard and Poors did downgrade the U.S. credit rating, citing paralysis in the political process between democrats and republicans to work together in resolving the crisis. S and P also indicated that the $2.8 trillion was insignificant given the amount of the deficit and projected growth trend. Following this action the stock market has lost a lot of value as investors sell stocks in anticipation of a slowdown, or worst, a recession in the economy. As in past studies of political crisis, the postcrisis analysis will focus on leaders' behaviors (who negotiated in good faith, who was the best at communicating the message, who stroke the right balance or who was more ethical), the presence of the president during the crisis and the role of prudence in his decision-making given the stakes.[13] The repercussions of this crisis will be long-lasting.

Regardless of the nature of the crises, what they all have in common is the stress and pressure they place on key organizational resources and systems. Any weaknesses that may have been present in the system prior to a crisis are exposed and further compound the negative consequences of the crisis. A crisis has the potential for damaging a firm's reputation, credibility, integrity, and financial position.[14,15] It is therefore imperative that organizations prepare their leaders on managing a crisis. This takes leadership training and development.

Crises Leadership Training

Given the potential for major disruptions that a crisis can cause in an organization, there is agreement that leadership training in crises management is critical.[16,17] In times of crisis, how an organization comes out is highly dependent on the quality of leaders it had going into the crisis.[18] Strong and effective leadership is imperative to organizational survival. However, many organizations make the mistake of assuming that leaders who are good at managing day-to-day issues are just as good when it comes handling a crisis. Nothing could be further from the truth. During a crisis, a leadership style that might have been appropriate under normal situations may not work in a crisis. Also, during a crisis, a leader becomes the symbol of order and authority, with considerable power to influence employee behaviors. An effective crisis leader should be aware of the types of power he or she possesses and the best way to apply each type in resolving a crisis. The crisis leader must be prepared to adapt quickly to change and deal with higher levels of uncertainty and complexity.[19] How the leader behaves or reacts during a crisis can have a negative or positive effect on followers. For example, a CEO admitting personal mistakes or offering positive feedback can calm follower anxieties during difficult times.[20] These are valued lessons that leaders can acquire through good training and development programs.

Leadership training for organizational crises should involve exposure to various learning approaches such as modeling, simulations, or learning from others (mentorship) who have experienced crises or narrowly avoided failure. Acceptance and Commitment Therapy (ACT) is an evidence-based modern cognitive-behavior therapy approach that has been used in crisis training. Through this approach, leaders develop a repertoire of crisis resiliency skills.[21] The objective of any leadership development program should be to equip leaders with well-practiced patterns of effective problem-solving skills that can be replicated during a crisis.[22] Training and development programs should emphasize traits of effective crises leaders such as decisiveness, self-confidence, communication, and problem solving. These traits are what some experts describe as crisis management competencies.[23]

The Crisis Management Plan (Exhibit 12.2) and the Recommendations for Effective Crisis Communication (Exhibit 12.3), discussed later in the chapter are effective tools for crises leadership training.

The Impact of Environmental Factors

There are emerging threats in the current business environment that if not properly monitored and managed could create serious financial crisis for some organizations. Rising oil prices, high unemployment, political grid-lock in Congress, the weak housing market, threat of Greek default and credit crunch, and talk of another recession are all factors that can stymie even the best-prepared CEOs. More than ever, people are looking for leaders who can provide stability, reassurance, confidence, and a sense of control during and after a crisis.[24]

Technological advances involving the Internet and communication networks allow millions to analyze and critique virtually every aspect of an organization's response to a crisis—such as a violent act on the job, a major accident, or a product recall. Technologies such as e-mail, Web pages, twitter, cable news, and social-networking sites are weapons for affected organizations and the outside world to use during a crisis.[25] A crisis is instantly visible and viral with the potential to inflict terminal damage on the affected organization. These technologies have diminished an organization's ability to control crisis communications by opening alternate channels that others can use to disseminate their views and build support.[26]

A company today may have only minutes, not hours, to contain a crisis. In many cases, there is a minute-by-minute real-time analysis of the financial implications of the crisis by investors, customers, and analysts, as Internet and cable television are linked with investment portfolios. Stakeholders may have more information at their fingertips about an ongoing crisis than the company itself. To stay ahead, effective leaders are incorporating crisis management into their strategic management models and updating their skills in crisis leadership.

Anticipating the kinds of crises that an organization can encounter is not an easy task for any leader. Literally thousands of incidents can turn into crises and handicap an organization's attempts to achieve its strategic goals. The challenge is detecting the signals that warn of a crisis. Many organizations are presented with early warning signals of an impending crisis but fail to recognize and heed them.[27] Therefore, the same degree of care invested in putting together a strategic plan for growth must be devoted to precrisis planning.

A crisis can present the opportunity for an organization to learn and adapt when the next crisis hits. Some leaders start paying attention to precrisis planning only after they encounter a crisis. Up until a crisis hits, it is an often neglected part of leadership in some organizations.[28] This approach is dangerous because there may not always be a second chance to learn from your mistakes. The next section discusses crisis management planning using the three-stage crisis planning model.

OPENING CASE *APPLICATION*

1. Describe the nature of the crisis that Citigroup was in prior to Mr. Pandit's appointment.

Citigroup's crisis came about as a result of poor leadership decisions during the real estate boom from 2000 to 2006. Like many other financial institutions, Citigroup overinvested in the housing market, failing to see the signs that what looked like a never-ending upward trend in real estate was a bubble about to burst. When the bubble did burst in 2007, Citigroup lost a lot of money from bad real estate loans—in what became known as the subprime mortgage crisis. So many home owners had mortgages that they could not afford and the banks had to foreclose on many of those loans. Adding to this crisis, the economy turned sour as unemployment went up and consumer spending went down. Citigroup was in a crisis of survival and the federal government had to step in and bail it out so it would not go bankrupt. There was a lack of leadership in anticipating the impending meltdown of the housing market—therefore making it a man-made or human error crisis. Also, conditions in the external environment contributed to worsen the crisis.

Crisis Management Plan

Crises by nature are not part of the regular work environment; therefore, effectively managing crisis situations requires leaders to be well prepared for the unknown. Though suffering some loss is almost unavoidable, proper preparation and management can reduce the duration of a crisis, enhance or retain a corporation's image and reputation, and secure future profitability. Effective crisis management depends on planning and people.[29]

According to experts in the field, an effective crisis management plan is one that is (1) comprehensive, with clear leadership, team, and individual assignments in the form of roles and responsibilities; (2) upgraded frequently and supported by training and periodic drill sessions; and (3) coordinated and controlled across levels and units of the organization. Collectively, all three requirements seem to be pointing to the important role that effective crisis leadership plays in crisis management. From an organizational perspective, readiness to respond to a crisis is a function of:

- Knowing and accepting one's assigned role in the crisis management plan
- Sufficient training specific to the assigned role to enable one to perform his or her responsibilities competently[30]
- Complementary and integrated roles and responsibilities at all levels of the organization, so the crisis management response is controlled and coordinated.[31]

A crisis management plan should address what happens before, during, and after a crisis. A precrisis plan is the first step of any crisis management program. It allows an organization to establish procedures and practices for risk analysis, early signal detection, and preventative measures. During a crisis, successful execution of a prepared plan improves damage control and recovery; after the crisis, organizational learning and change are vital for future survival.[32]

In the next section, we propose a three-stage crisis management model—precrisis planning, managing during a crisis, and managing after a crisis—for effective crisis leadership.

EXHIBIT 12.1 **Three-Stage Crisis Management Model**

Precrisis Planning
· Designate Crisis Leader
· Form Crisis Response Team
· Develop Risk Assessment Model
Managing During a Crisis
· The Role of Senior Leaders
· Effective Crisis Communication
· Actions of Crisis leader and Team
· Crisis Resolution
Managing After a Crisis
· Evaluation of Crisis Response
· Lessons Learned
· Preventing a Future Crisis

© Cengage Learning 2013

WORK Application **1**
Find out if your college or university has a precrisis plan. If you find one, read and critique it for its effectiveness and present your findings to your classmates. If there is none, present an argument for having one.

Learning Outcome 2 *Identify the benefits of precrisis planning.*

Precrisis Planning

Although no one can develop a precrisis plan that would accurately anticipate and address every possibility in the future, such a plan is still the best way to mitigate the negative consequences of any crisis. Leading an organization through a crisis requires rational decision making. A precrisis plan enables leaders and their followers to make good decisions under severe pressure in the most difficult and unpleasant circumstances.[33] Many people seldom contemplate the possibility that a fire, coworker violence, robbery, or natural disaster could occur where they work. The tendency is to develop a mental detachment from the issue—it happens to other people, not to me or our organization. Some leaders rationalize that the present systems are adequate to deal with such crises should they arise, while others find solace in the "positive thinking" (nothing bad will happen) approach. Denial of the occurrence of these low-probability, high-impact events makes thinking the unthinkable a major leadership challenge.[34] Leaders who are able to overcome these psychological roadblocks and perceive risks realistically can approach precrisis management in a logical and systematic way.

Learning Outcome 3   *Identify the three key components of the precrisis planning phase.*

Every organization (large, small, for-profit, or non-profit) should have a precrisis plan. Precrisis planning entails putting together a comprehensive crisis response plan that includes the following three components: (1) *appointing a crisis leader*, (2) *creating a crisis response team*, and (3) *assessing risk*. We will briefly describe each one of these separately.

Crisis Leader   Given the dynamic environment of business, proactive organizations have found it prudent to designate one or more senior executives with the task of scanning and monitoring the internal and external environments for potential threats or warning signs of a crisis. In the event of a crisis, the leader must be visible, in control, and overseeing all aspects of the plan's execution. The crisis leader may report directly to the CEO or to the head of communications or public relations. The primary duties of the crisis leader may include activities such as the following:

- Requiring individuals or departments to keep logs of complaints or incidents
- Monitoring customer and employee complaints and behavior
- Identifying emerging patterns or trends in the regulatory environment, competitive landscape, and social environment
- Coordinating the activities of the crisis management team to ensure that the members work well together

The ability of crisis leaders to grasp the impact of events in the early stages of development has helped some organizations avert a crisis and has even helped others turn would-be crises into opportunities. The attributes or qualities of an effective crisis leader include expertise coupled with real experience dealing with crises, insight, influence, decisiveness, and pragmatism.[35] As mentioned before, these are qualities that can be acquired through leadership training and development.

To be effective, a crisis leader must have the power, resources, position, and stature to influence events when a crisis erupts. For example, an organization must empower the crisis leader to make a critical decision such as shutting down a production line if a defect is suspected, or halting operations on an assembly line if multiple injuries or malfunctions have occurred.

Crisis Response Team   Having a standing crisis response team increases an organization's ability to respond to a crisis in a timely and effective manner. A crisis response team should involve a good mix of representatives from all sectors of the organization. It should draw on critical internal resources (e.g., human resources) and external resources (e.g., trauma counselors). In most medium- or large-sized organizations, the crisis response team is led by a senior-level executive and composed of representatives from a cross section of all the functional disciplines. Diversity in the makeup of the crisis management team is critical and necessary.

In the precrisis planning phase, a leader wants a team that is hardworking, creative, organized, and motivated. During an actual crisis, the team whose members are calm, capable, self-confident, assertive, decisive, and dependable is more likely to succeed than a team whose members have the opposite traits.

Unfortunately, it is often the case that during a crisis, people who must work together have no history of doing so because they have never practiced or rehearsed the plan; thus, they have no understanding of each other's roles and responsibilities. It is also sometimes the case during a crisis that resources brought to bear may have never been deployed to see how well they function together. This is due to the fact that often crisis personnel receive little or no training. Senior Leaders must develop comprehensive training programs for crisis-response team personnel and engage them in frequent drills that simulate actual crisis situations.[36]

This coordinated team approach contrasts with actual organizational practices that often divide and spread the duties of crisis management throughout the organization without a central command. Experience shows that this divided approach often results in turf wars and conflict—sometimes motivated by varying ideologies, resource limitations, or office politics—over just who will be singularly responsible for leading a crisis. In these situations, it is not uncommon to have the leaders of various company departments argue that they and their staff are best equipped to lead a crisis, often to the disapproval of other leaders.

An effective crisis team functions as one unit with one voice under a single unit command. Such a team is made up of members who can challenge one another's ideas without resorting to personal attacks, engage in debates without coercion or blame, and unite behind decisions once they are made. Members don't circumvent or undermine each other; instead they work cooperatively, sharing information, and encouraging teamwork. This unity and spirit prevent the team from becoming dysfunctional. In the words of one expert, "If a team is dysfunctional before a crisis, that team is more likely to have a dysfunctional response during an incident." A crisis will reveal the quality of leadership in an organization.[37]

Because the warning signals of an impending crisis may be too weak to identify or accurately interpret, they are often missed or ignored. For this reason, an increasing number of organizations are employing techniques to monitor and assess the risks of potential crises before they happen.

WORK Application **2**
Identify someone who has been or is part of a crisis prevention and management team, preferably someone on your campus's crisis prevention and management team. Ask him or her to describe the makeup and function of the team.

_____

_____

_____

_____

Learning Outcome 4

Describe the five-step process for crisis risk assessment.

Crisis Risk Assessment Risk assessment is a common tool used in crisis planning. Borrowing from the field of risk management, crisis teams set out to identify potential incidents that could hit the organization and then determine the probability of their occurrence and the degree of preparedness necessary. A crisis will negatively impact an organization's people, its financial condition, or its image. The crisis leader and crisis team members begin the risk assessment process by engaging in "what-if" scenario analysis that focuses on creating realistic incidents under each crisis category. Scenario analysis and planning is a tool that helps leaders prevent or respond to crises through decision-making skills based on possible outcomes of crises. Members may entertain questions such as, "What could happen? Where are we vulnerable? What is the worst-case scenario? What are the short- and long-term outlooks?"[38] This series of "what-if" scenarios set the stage for a five-step risk assessment plan. See Exhibit 12.2 for the model depicting these steps.

The five-step process for risk assessment consists of (1) risk identification, (2) risk assessment and ranking, (3) risk reduction, (4) crisis prevention, and (5) crisis management.[39]

EXHIBIT **12.2**   Risk Assessment Model

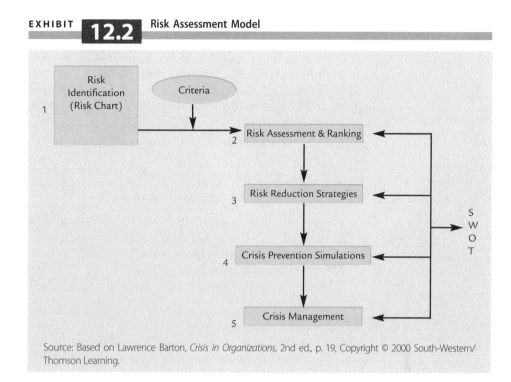

Source: Based on Lawrence Barton, *Crisis in Organizations*, 2nd ed., p. 19, Copyright © 2000 South-Western/ Thomson Learning.

Step 1. **Risk identification.** Crisis team members will begin by first identifying the worst-case incidents that could have severe consequences on people, the organization's financial position, or its image. This process is described as risk identification and results in the creation of a risk chart.

Step 2. **Risk assessment and ranking.** Next, these incidents are analyzed and ranked using criteria such as loss of life, injuries, emotional trauma, or minimal inconvenience for each incident's human impact. On the financial and image side, ranking criteria such as extraordinary impact (i.e., it will bankrupt the organization), serious but insured (i.e., we are covered), or small impact (i.e., nothing to worry about) may be employed. This information is then used as the basis for launching the third step, which is risk reduction.

Step 3. **Risk reduction.** During the risk reduction step, the crisis leader shares the risk chart created during risk assessment and ranking with team members or larger audiences, and they begin debating and formulating strategies for countering each crisis or threat. SWOT analysis comes into play as a tool in determining what resources and capabilities are available or needed to better manage each crisis. For instance, say the organization is a chemical plant. An item on the risk chart may indicate the risk of a "poisonous gas leak" as a likely event. A SWOT analysis of this particular risk may progress as follows: the crisis team identifies strengths the organization has if such an incident should occur (such as poison gas scientists and materials), weaknesses (such as the present lack of a poisonous gas leak response plan), opportunities (such as community support for the plant because of its economic impact on the area), and threats (such as environmentalists who are likely to protest and demand that the plant be closed). Based on this analysis, the crisis team may recommend as a risk-reduction plan that the organization begin safety awareness programs and conduct joint meetings with local emergency response teams.

Step 4. Crisis prevention. During crisis prevention, precrisis drills such as simulations are conducted to test employees under pressure. Again, SWOT analysis information is used to fine-tune this step. This step helps to sensitize the organization to the need for crisis planning. After the tests and simulations and the resulting discussions, evaluations, and feedback from managers at all levels of the organization, the crisis team can then rest easy with the assurance that the organization is better prepared to handle a crisis.

Step 5. Crisis management. A team is assembled and is ready to respond in the event of a real crisis.

WORK Application 3
Using your college or university as a reference, identify five risk areas that could result in crisis if nothing is done now. Recommend a risk reduction plan or strategy that can help your school avert or deal with a crisis for one of these risk areas.

Ultimately, the best gauge to determine an organization's readiness to respond to a crisis is how it rates according to the following five factors:

1. Quality of strategic crisis plan
2. Awareness and access to crisis management information
3. Readiness for a quick response
4. Effective communication plan in place
5. Effective crisis leadership

The benefits of a precrisis response plan are obvious: faster response time, better judgments, ready and available resources, fewer costly mistakes, less panic, and quicker resolution of the crisis. As mentioned earlier, unless the crisis response plan is rehearsed and practiced regularly, it becomes just another document collecting dust on the bookshelf.

OPENING CASE *APPLICATION*

2. In your opinion, would precrisis planning have helped Citigroup avert the crisis it faced?

The short answer is yes. Precrisis planning entails putting together a comprehensive crisis response plan that includes the following three components: (1) *appointing a crisis leader*, (2) *creating a crisis response team*, and (3) *assessing risk*. Let's focus on item number 3, risk assessment. We said the five-step process for risk assessment consists of (1) risk identification, (2) risk assessment and ranking, (3) risk reduction, (4) crisis prevention, and (5) crisis management. A precrisis plan would have identified the housing bubble as a potential crisis and seek to reduce Citi's exposure to the risk. Also, failure to anticipate the downturn in the economy is something that could have been picked up in precrisis planning.

It is a fact of life that in spite of all the crisis-prevention planning that organizations undergo, sooner or later a crisis will emerge and an organization will have to deal with it. The next section focuses on crisis management during an actual crisis.

Learning Outcome 5

Describe the role of the CEO and communication in managing a crisis.

Managing during a Crisis

When a crisis erupts, a rapid response is vital. Some leaders go into denial about the urgency and severity of a crisis. Without acknowledging that there is a crisis, it is hard to proceed to the next step of developing a response plan. An immediate and effective response to a crisis is critical to an organization's survival. An organization should make itself accessible as quickly and as openly as possible. It is generally believed that within an hour of becoming aware that a crisis situation may exist, company officials must be prepared to issue an initial statement to the media and other key stakeholder groups—providing facts as they are known and an indication of when additional details will be made available. The purpose of an immediate response on the part of the affected organization is to fill an information vacuum with facts and perspectives. Such quick action can help to preserve the credibility and reputation of the organization and its leaders during the crisis.[40] Experience has shown that the longer companies wait, the more likely the vacuum will be filled with inaccurate statements and outright misinformation that becomes accepted as truth.

The Role of Senior Leaders   Effective leadership from the top is critical during a crisis.[41] When there is a crisis, employees will look to the CEO or the most senior leader on how to cope with the situation. Unfortunately, some senior leaders have been known to retreat behind closed doors when a crisis hits. They delegate to lower managers the task of facing the media and other relevant stakeholder groups. Three key principles of crisis leadership are: (1) stay engaged and lead from the front, (2) focus on the big picture and communicate the vision, and (3) work with your crisis management team.[42]

An example of how not to lead during a crisis is the leader who digs deeper into his or her foxhole after a crisis hits. The familiar tale of Nero playing the fiddle while Rome burned illustrates the importance of a leader's presence. A leader's physical presence is a matter of moral importance even when it lacks immediate practical value. Being there conveys moral solidarity, commitment, and concern, apart from the leader's actual empathy or sensitivity.[43,44]

Effective leaders rely on the values and principles found in their mission statements to guide their decision. There is an unwavering faith that they and their followers will prevail. They have the persistence and courage to keep going forward.[45]

Effective leaders view crisis management as a team effort. In a time of crisis, a team with a balance of complementary skills and talents can move quickly and effectively. This is where having gone through precrisis planning and risk assessment pays big dividends. Not only should a leader seek wise counsel from the team, he or she should also instill a greater feeling of camaraderie among all employees by allowing them to share their emotions and feelings with each other in group settings.[46] Effective leaders understand that their job during a crisis includes caring for their followers or taking responsibility for them—what one study calls the ethics of care.[47]

WORK Application **4**

Think of a leader whom you have observed in a crisis situation, either in person or on TV. Critique the leader's handling of the crisis using the text discussion as your guide.

_____

_____

_____

_____

YOU
Make the
ETHICAL
Call

12.1   *Toyota Recall Crisis*

The Toyota recall crisis of 2010 prompted much criticism in media circles, national business forums, and automotive trade publications. The original complaint from some customers was that the brakes were failing and causing accidents. One such case was a driver on the freeway who had called 911 to report an ongoing crisis he was experiencing as his Toyota was not responding to repeated attempts to stop. Toyota did its own tests and kept saying that they had found nothing wrong with the brakes. At some point, as the media attention mounted, Toyota said they had concluded that the floor mats were causing the problem. Many lawsuits were filed against Toyota. Later, it was reported that the driver on the freeway had staged the supposed problem he was reporting about. There are those who think Toyota waited too long to take the complaints seriously and others who think it was unfair the way the American media targeted Toyota without waiting for the facts. It so happens that all this was happening at the same time that the American auto industry was going

(continued)

through its worst crisis. Some have speculated that the Toyota crisis did help the American auto manufacturers as many people switched from Toyota to American models.

A recent survey on this subject revealed the following: From a total of 109 participants that included 72 business college students and 37 adults from the local community, a majority (57 percent) of the sample felt that Toyota leadership's handling of the recall was somewhat disappointing or very poor. Moreover, few respondents (18 percent) had any confidence in the veracity of public statements from Toyota. With regard to ethics, 50 percent of the sample felt that Toyota's decision- making is unethical to some degree. In addition, a majority (56 percent) expressed little faith in Toyota's transparency during this crisis. Noteworthy is that only 13 percent felt that Toyota would probably not regain its prominence in the auto sector.[48]

1. In your opinion, was the media coverage of the crisis fair and ethical?

2. What would you criticize of the survey results and the methodology for collecting the data?

3. If 50 percent of the sample felt that Toyota's decision making is unethical to some degree, why then is it that only 13 percent felt that Toyota would probably not regain its prominence in the auto sector?

How a company deals with a crisis from a communications standpoint can make or break it. The next section focuses on the importance of effective communication during a crisis.

OPENING CASE APPLICATION

3. How effective was CEO Pandit in managing the crisis he inherited and the ones he created?

Upon his appointment, Pandit embarked on a plan to refocus, recapitalize, and restructure Citigroup during the most challenging economic environment since the Great Depression. With the goals of long-term profitability and growth on his mind, Pandit's strategy for building a new Citigroup centered on the company's strengths and distinctive competitive advantages: its global franchise, strong emerging market footprint, innovative spirit, and talented and diverse employee base. Citigroup has been hiring dozens of investment bankers and adding several hundred branches worldwide, including more than 200 in major cities across the United States.

Pandit was out in front communicating what Citi was doing to weather the crisis and what his role was in making it happen. He testified before Congress and apologized for what some criticized as poor judgment on his part to approve the purchase of an expensive luxury corporate jet at a time when taxpayers were bailing out the company from its bad investments.

The bank's financial results so far seem to bear out the success of Pandit's aggressive growth strategies. Citi has posted five consecutive quarterly profits including the recent second quarter 2011 reported revenue and profits growth. There is a sense of optimism about Citi's future under Pandit that was not present when he took over. There is a perception by some analysts that through his actions, Citi has weathered the crisis.

Crisis Communication

Leaders must be able to communicate quickly and effectively during crises.[49] Over the past few years, it has become increasingly clear that opening communication lines with primary stakeholders—employees, customers, board members, the news media, and regulatory bodies—is critical for survival when a crisis hits.[50] Effective precrisis planning should have designated who will speak for the organization in the event of a crisis. Public relations staff may field questions from the media while legal staff may respond to legal inquiries. This avoids both the mistake of putting out mixed messages from multiple sources and potential power-struggles over jurisdiction. These problems create confusion and hurt crisis response effectiveness.

Four questions that often emerge after a crisis are: (1) What happened? (2) How did it happen? (3) What's being done to address the crisis? and (4) What has been done to ensure it never happens again? Providing honest, accurate, and timely answers to these questions is the essence of effective crisis communication. The crisis response team must guard against releasing information too late or not countering rumors and myths in real time.[51]

Another potential problem during crisis communication is the seniority level of the person representing the organization. As mentioned before, it is important for the CEO or the most senior leader in the organization to show up rather than retreat to the background. The level of seniority demonstrates to the public the seriousness with which the incident is viewed. The organization does not want to send the message that it does not care or take the crisis seriously. Leaders who retreat into their foxholes during a crisis are more likely to engage in a blame game—trying to assign responsibility and accountability to someone else.[52]

A well-designed crisis communication system should inform employees at all levels whom to call, what procedures to follow, and what they should and should not say to a variety of individuals and agencies. Internally, everyone should know what role(s) they would play in the event of a crisis, and how communication will be handled within and between departments. There should be no power-struggles over jurisdiction. Getting the message right is critical, and so is choosing the right communications medium.[53]

Investing time and other resources in developing an effective crisis communication system with employees has significant short- and long-term benefits. In the short term, well-informed employees will assist the organization in presenting accurate facts to the outside world on the current crisis. Invariably, someone from outside is going to ask an employee what happened, how it happened, or what the organization is doing to remedy the situation. Also, employees, even those at the lower levels of the organization, may have excellent insight on the incident and valuable suggestions on solution alternatives. Their immediate input may provide the pathway to a quick recovery. In the long term, the organization will have won over the confidence, loyalty, and commitment of the employees, who appreciate being included and listened to during the crisis. Employees' sense of belonging and self-worth is enhanced, and a culture of teamwork and cohesion is created. The postcrisis feeling of "we did it together" can carry over into other areas as the organization moves forward.

The literature is rich with several "dos" and "don'ts" when it comes to effective crisis response. Some of these "dos" and "don'ts" are presented later in the chapter under the section titled, the principles of effective crisis communication.

OPENING CASE *APPLICATION*

4. In your opinion, has Mr. Pandit been an effective communicator in the way he has handled the crisis?

Effective communication is the key. The CEO should be out there communicating the what, how, and when. People need to know the facts and what leadership is doing to address the crisis. Testifying before Congress on February 11, 2009, Pandit struck an apologetic tone for letting the bank consider completing the purchase of a private jet plane after receiving some $45 billion in bailout money. Also, Pandit told Congress that he had informed his board of directors that he will only earn a $1 per year with no bonus until Citi return to profitability. Not only was Pandit out communicating what the company was doing to address the problems that had led to the crisis, he was taking responsibility for the company's past actions and self-imposing an unheard-of compensation reduction. He did not rely on press releases or spokespersons; he was out there speaking for the corporation himself. These actions endeared him to many and helped gain the goodwill towards Citi that other financial institutions lacked.

Managing after a Crisis

It is quite possible for an organization to experience growth and prosperity after a crisis. Effective leaders know how to turn a negative event such as a crisis into a growth and learning experience. It is about looking beyond the present crisis and into the future. Most forward-looking organizations do a post mortem. That is, in the aftermath of a crisis, top management authorizes a review (preferably conducted by an objective third party) of the organization's effectiveness in managing the crisis. When done well, such a review should include effectiveness in communicating with key stakeholder groups and effectiveness in addressing the root cause(s) of the crisis. Other questions should focus on how effective the crisis team performed, how the organization handled victims and family members, and what worked the best in mitigating the crisis. These questions and the answers they generate offer lessons that if learned that can help prevent future crises.

At the end of the day, the most basic lesson of crisis leadership is to prepare for crises, respond quickly, act with integrity, and disclose fully. Another lesson is to be mindful of the "three As"—acknowledge, action, and avoid. *Acknowledge* or admit the crisis, specify what *action* you are taking to contain or repair the damage, and tell the public what you are going to do to *avoid* a repeat in the future.[54]

Organizations must resist the tendency to rush through the postcrisis review and focus on image protection.[55] In July 2011, a Chinese high-speed rail crashed and killed about 70 passengers. From the reporting on NPR, it seems the Chinese government was more interested in covering up the accident and the facts than providing the truth about the cause of the accident to relatives of the victims and the media. Within hours of the accident, it was reported that the mangled parts of the train were buried and contradicting explanations given for the cause of the accident—all of this before the government-appointed commission to investigate the accident even started deliberating. As a sign that China is very concerned about protecting its image, the government has announced that it is going to reduce the speed of its trains.

OPENING CASE *APPLICATION*

5. What are some of the changes Mr. Pandit has instituted to avoid a repeat of a similar crisis in the future?

Hoping to avoid a future crisis, Pandit has made Responsible Finance a priority. According to Pandit, Citigroup is committed to providing choice, control, and transparency for clients and managing risk responsibly. From innovative foreclosure prevention programs that have kept more than a million Americans in their homes to a new, disciplined approach to risk management, Responsible Finance is being ingrained throughout Citigroup's practices and culture. The key phrases here are "a new, disciplined approach to risk management" and "Responsible Finance."

Principles of Effective Crisis Communication

It is generally believed that the first 24 hours of a crisis are crucial because of the media's need to know what happened so they can tell their audiences. There is an information vacuum that, if left unfilled, will be filled by others. The longer companies wait, the more likely falsehoods will become accepted as truths.[56] The key is to be open, straightforward, and transparent. Tell the truth and tell it quickly. Telling the truth up front is the simplest and most effective way of defusing public hostility, no matter how bad the incident.[57] Rather than being preoccupied with protecting itself from liability, a company must demonstrate a strong sense of integrity, responsibility, and commitment. Getting out in front of the crisis with honest accounts of the facts and accepting responsibility will build confidence and credibility with all stakeholders.[58]

An organization can use a number of media and approaches to inform the public or tell its side of the story to weather the storm brought on by a crisis. These include press releases, press kits, news conferences, and one-on-one interviews with the various media. *A press release is a printed statement that describes how an organization is responding to a crisis and who is in charge. A press kit is a package of information about a company, including names and pictures of its executives, a fact sheet, and key milestones in the company's history.* In the event of a crisis, the last item included in the press kit is a specific press release related to the current incident. This package is ready for distribution to the media when a crisis breaks.

Telling what your organization is doing to address a crisis is especially important to family or close relatives of victims. These family members must be handled with utmost sensitivity. Leaders must avoid paternalistic attitudes that treat victims or the public as unintelligent or uninformed. The absence of genuine concern and empathy can lead to a perception of arrogance. It is also important to add to the discussion of what is being done, a plan showing how a similar crisis will be avoided in the future.[59] In addition to providing an overview of the progress being made to address the crisis, the spokesperson should involve technical specialists to provide more expert and detailed background information. This is especially critical during a press conference. Also, enlisting the support of objective third parties to speak on the organization's behalf can lessen the damage. Exhibit 12.3 presents 10 simple communication rules to remember during a crisis.[60,61]

EXHIBIT 12.3 Principles of Effective Crisis Communication

a. Be present.
b. Don't "spin." Tell it like it is.
c. Communicate the plan of action for resolving the crisis.
d. Be sensitive with affected parties.
e. Avoid conflicting messages.
f. Show a plan for how you will avoid a repeat in the future.
g. Don't make excuses for yourself or the leader.
h. Go the extra mile. Go beyond the requirements of the situation.
i. When things are going good, take credit for it without being self-absorbed.
j. The media is your friend and link to the public. Be honest and straightforward with them.

© Cengage Learning 2013

YOU Make the ETHICAL Call

12.2 *The Debt Ceiling Crisis*

Refer to the discussion we presented at the beginning of this chapter on the debt ceiling crisis and the ensuing debate between Republicans and Democrats on how to resolve it. You can Google the topic for more information.

Some Democrats say the Republicans were holding the debt ceiling hostage in order to advance their agenda of small government through spending cuts. The Republicans on their part say our national debt is too high and is threatening our future. The Democrats want a balanced solution that includes spending cuts and taxes. The Republicans say the primary source of the problem has been too much spending and thus only want spending cuts.

1. In your opinion, does this debate have ethical implications and what are the ethical issues?

2. What is your opinion on the contrasting positions of the two sides on how to resolve the crisis?

(continued)

3. Some say this is a man-made crisis because raising the debt ceiling has never been tied to any condition(s) and this is the first time since its inception be used as a bargaining chip. In your opinion, is this good politics or poor judgment on the part of Republicans?

4. Based on what you remember of the media coverage of the crisis, which party or leaders did a good job of communicating their position to the American people?

5. In your opinion, will this issue be a major factor in the next election for politicians of both parties? Explain.

CONCEPT APPLICATION 1
Principles of Effective Crisis Communications

Using the letters a through j that accompany the guidelines in Exhibit 12.3, identify which guideline is explained by each statement below.

_____ 1. After the Concorde crashed, the French authorities along with British Airways immediately grounded all Concorde flights until the designers came up with a fuel tank protection solution.

_____ 2. Family or close ones of victims, or those affected, are brought to a central location and provided with services such as counselling, support, and other facilities that might be needed to help them cope.

_____ 3. Information is held back or filtered to say only what the leaders or those in charge want you to know about a crisis.

_____ 4. The CEO of a company is on vacation when a crisis breaks out, but refuses to cancel his vacation and return home to deal with the crisis.

_____ 5. Expect and treat victims and/or family members' emotional outbursts with empathy.

_____ 6. The Public Relations person addresses the media and says something that is later contradicted by the CEO in his own press conference.

_____ 7. The accident happened because we relied on faulty instruments from our subcontractor who designed the part. Without their error, this would never have happened.

_____ 8. I don't like the press because they tend to overemphasize the negative as if we have never done anything good in this community. From now on, I will only tell them what they need to know.

_____ 9. After our post-crisis analysis (managing after a crisis), I realized that we did everything just right to address the crisis despite the criticisms that we received early on from various groups. It is a good thing we did not listen to them; after all what do they know about crisis management?

_____ 10. The Principal of a high school where a fatal shooting has just taken place appears before parents to explain what he and the security team are doing in response to the crisis. Many of the parents criticize him afterwards for not having much to say about the incident.

A Spotlight on the African Crisis

African today is a continent in crisis. Except for a handful of states such as South Africa, Ghana, and Liberia, there are many failed states in the continent that cannot provide for their citizens without foreign aid. There is abject poverty, high mortality, and high unemployment and social unrest throughout the continent. This massive crisis has its roots in corruption, leadership ineptitude, absence of democratic institutions, and the lack of structured foundations for economic development. Here we are in the 21st century, when many economies are benefiting from the forces of innovation, infrastructure expansion, information and communication technology, and major medical advances, while the African continent remains enmeshed in crises of all kinds—natural and man-made. The images of babies dying of hunger in what is called "the horn of Africa" (Somalia, Ethiopia, Kenya) are now appearing on TV screens in the West and other developed countries. At the same time, you have pictures of so-called rebel soldiers roaming city streets threatening to kill any outside groups attempting to come in and help with food distribution. The question many have is: Where are the governments of these states? How is it that on a continent so rich with natural resources and with so much human capital can so many lack the most basic needs—food, shelter, healthcare, etc?[62]

Corruption permeates every facet of life in Africa. It is so endemic that it will take decades to address and put the continent on the path to recovery. It is not uncommon to find situations where teachers need bribes to teach kids in their classes and even doctors and nurses ask for bribes to treat patients. So much for the Hippocratic Oath ("first do no harm"). There are no government services that one can access (getting a passport, a driver's license, a business permit, employment, admission into schools, etc.) without first offering a bribe. Security services (like police officers) only attend to a crime victim after they have been paid. The criminal gangs are often aligned with the security forces. The fight to address this crisis of corruption is going to take a holistic instead of a selective approach. It has become a continent where the only ethical principle in decision making is self-preservation.

Africa is a continent in need of reform across the board. Government policies have to be redirected at infrastructure building, free enterprise, youth empowerment through education and training, and a whole new way of governance that is people-centered rather than power-centered. A new generation of African leaders who want to start tackling this crisis will need to employ all the leadership theories and skills we have covered in this text. These nations are in need of transformational leaders who can offer visions of a better future and how it can be reached, model optimism and confidence, promote confidence, empower followers, and lead by example. They need leaders with social modeling skills to help focus the nation on its priorities; leaders who can put together a strategic plan that addresses the needs of the country in the immediate and long-term; leaders who can change the culture of the country so that attitudes and values will no longer tolerate or condone corruption and other vices; and, most critical, they need leaders who understand the urgency of the situation and are willing to sacrifice personal interests for the greater good.

We should note that there is corruption in every culture and economy; however, it is much worse in many developing economies. The picture we have painted for the majority of African nations is very much the same for many countries in South America, parts of Asia, and much of Eastern Europe (especially those breakaway nations from the former Soviet Union block).

If there is one certainty in organizational life today, it is that change will happen. More and more organizations are discovering that they operate in highly turbulent environments where the level of change is rapid and discontinuous. Therefore, future success will depend on an organization's ability to learn and adapt. In the second half of this chapter, we explore the emerging concept of the learning organization and knowledge management.

The Learning Organization and Knowledge Management

It is an established fact that the United States and most of the developed world are transitioning from a production-based to a knowledge-based economy.[63] As a result, organizations are increasingly dependent on innovative knowledge to create value for their customers.[64] In a knowledge-based economy, employee learning is becoming increasingly relevant for organizational competitiveness.[65,66] The question for many leaders is how to organize people, systems, and processes within the organization to generate and exploit new forms of knowledge.[67] In his book, *The Fifth Discipline*, Peter Senge makes a compelling case that an organization's survival is linked to its ability to learn and adapt. He describes a true learning organization as one that can develop not only new capabilities but also a fundamental mind-set transformation.[68] To stay competitive, organizations must continuously innovate.

The responsibility of any organization desirous of change and innovation in a rapidly changing environment must be for its leaders to make it a priority to build and maintain a learning culture that engages employees in learning activities and that enables them to master new knowledge, skills and abilities.[69,70] Organizational learning is seen as a fundamental component of the knowledge-creation process.[71,72]

In this section, we examine what a learning organization represents, how a learning organization differs from a traditional organization, and the role of leadership in creating a learning organization culture.

Learning Outcome 6   List five or more attributes that can be used to describe the learning organization.

What Is a Learning Organization?

The learning organization is described as an idealized vision of an organization where work patterns, structures, and routines are open to continuous adaptation and improvement, where everyone engages in continuous learning, where the culture is supportive of continuous learning, and where strategic decision making is informed by and responsive to relevant data analysis and feedback.[73] From this description, it is clear that the learning organization concept is linked to the type of environment in which an organization operates. In a stable environment, change is slow and incremental, and employee skills and abilities remain relevant for long periods of time; thus the need to learn, innovate, and adapt is not as urgent or acute.

In rapidly changing environments, characterized by increasing globalization, hyper-competition, changing demographics, and technological shifts, employee skills and abilities can quickly become obsolete and irrelevant. In this type of environment, there is increasing pressure on employees to upgrade their job skills and knowledge to match the requirements of a new labor market that no longer guarantees long-term employment and job security. Therefore, employees who engage in continuous learning activities are more likely to be a source of competitive advantage for their organizations. Organizations must learn to create and assimilate new knowledge at an increasing pace, encourage innovation, and learn to compete in new ways. The culture of the organization is instrumental in keeping the process of learning continuous and accepted as a way of life in the organization, thus leading it to become a learning organization.[74,75]

We define a **learning organization** as one that *is skilled at creating, acquiring, and transferring knowledge, and at modifying behavior to reflect new knowledge and insights.*[76] It is through learning that knowledge is created. In the past, organizations generally viewed learning as formal training workshops that took place during specified periods of the year. However, many now recognize that learning should be an on-going practice that is embedded within the daily work environment of each employee. Each assignment, job responsibility, temporary or permanent project, and other daily tasks are opportunities for expansive learning.[77] Leaders, especially those in top positions, must create the type of environment that supports and nurtures collective learning (also known as organizational learning),[78] for it is through this process that members acquire new knowledge and develop innovative capabilities that result in new products/services.[79,80]

Organizational learning involves external and internal sources. Externally, an organization can learn from its customers, suppliers, competitors, industry and academic publications, business partners, and consultants. Internally, organizations can learn from their employees. Every employee, especially those who work directly with customers, is a great source of new ideas.

What Is Knowledge Management?

Creating, storing, and leveraging knowledge are integral to knowledge management processes. Leveraging knowledge is manifested in learning, and thus knowledge management and organizational learning are intricately related.[81,82] **Organizational knowledge** *is the tacit and explicit know-how that individuals possess about products, services, systems, and processes.* Explicit or formal knowledge is expressed in a system of rules and is easily communicated and shared. It is often codified in manuals, databases, and information systems. Tacit or informal knowledge is highly personal, difficult to communicate, strongly rooted in action, and highly contextual in nature. Unlike explicit knowledge, such as the design of a product or the description of a business process, tacit knowledge is the instinct and intuition that an experienced practitioner possesses.[83] Organizational knowledge has been referred to as intellectual capital that is used to produce financial or other benefits for an organization.[84,85]

Knowledge has been identified as one of the most important resources that contribute to the competitive advantage of an organization.[86] Superior performance is achieved when newly acquired knowledge is interpreted and integrated with existing knowledge and applied to problem solving.

OPENING CASE APPLICATION

6. Describe the threats facing Citigroup in its external environment. Do these threats support or go against adopting a learning organizational culture?

Citigroup, like many other multinational corporations, is facing major threats from the technological, economic, political/legal, sociocultural, competitive, and demographic environments. Technological innovations in the way financial services are delivered are moving at a fast pace and causing Citi to play catch-up or react to competitor moves in this area. The economy has been going through some uncertain times, and some think it is sliding into a recession due to high unemployment, a weak housing market, and the debt crisis. Politically, there is increased regulation of the financial industry in a variety of areas including interest rate charges, mortgage contract conditions, and a newly created consumer financial protection agency. From a competitive standpoint, there is intense competition from other financial institutions like Morgan Stanley, Goldman Sachs, American Express, Bank of America, Wells Fargo, and many others. Demographically, the consumer market is global and undergoing some significant transformations. The Baby Boomers are getting older and changing their tastes and desires to align with their needs. The younger generations (GenX, GenY, and the Millenials) are savvy consumers who are not easily swayed by promotions and rely on their own judgments for brand choice. They are the cell phone, Internet, iPod, Facebook, and twitter generation that has information available at their fingertips. This type of environment requires an organization like Citi to make learning and knowledge management a priority.

Before we get into the details of the learning organization and knowledge management, complete Self-Assessment 1.

SELF-ASSESSMENT 1   Learning Organizations

Select an organization you work or have worked for and rate it for each question on a scale of 1–5. If you are not sure, rate it as 3.

5 — 4 — 3 — 2 — 1
Describes organization   Does NOT describe organization

_____ 1. The organization has a flat structure, few layers of management, and makes decisions quickly.

_____ 2. Decision making is decentralized; lower-level managers make important decisions.

_____ 3. There are no job descriptions, or they are very general and focused on getting the job done.

_____ 4. There is a focus on continuous improvement and change.

_____ 5. Everyone has easy access to communicate with anyone.

_____ 6. Managers encourage creative thinking.

_____ 7. Managers listen to and implement employee ideas for improvement.

_____ 8. The climate encourages experimentation of new ideas.

_____ 9. There are incentives for learning new things.

_____ 10. There are incentives for contributing new ideas and innovations.

_____ 11. Employees are encouraged to identify and solve problems.

_____ 12. There are no departmental boundaries; people don't focus on developing departmental power.

_____ 13. When new methods are developed, they are shared for everyone throughout the organization to use.

_____ 14. The focus is on teamwork, not individual accomplishments.

_____ 15. When employees implement new ideas that fail, they are encouraged to keep trying rather than being punished.

Add up your score. Place the score here and on the continuum below.

75—70—65—60—55—50—45—40—35—30—25—20—15
Learning organization   NOT a learning organization

The higher the score, the more characteristic the firm is of a learning organization. Most organizations group around the middle.

Learning Outcome 7 *Distinguish between the traditional and the learning organization.*

Differentiate between the Traditional and Learning Organization

By all accounts, most organizations today operate in environments characterized by continuous change, and for some—like the high-tech companies—the level of change is even discontinuous. **Discontinuous change** *occurs when anticipated or expected changes bear no resemblance to the present or the past.* The emergence of better and cheaper technologies, rivals' introduction of new or better products and services, competition from low-cost foreign competitors, and demographic shifts represent major threats to the profitability and even survival of many organizations. In stable environments, organizations focus on being efficient and on achieving stated objectives through highly structured command systems with strong vertical hierarchies and specialized jobs. However, given the realities of the current dynamic environment, this traditional organizational form is being replaced by the learning organizational form. The two are separated by a different mind-set and culture. See Exhibit 12.4 for a comparison of the two organization types.

EXHIBIT **12.4** Key Differences between the Traditional and the Learning Organization

Traditional (efficiency driven)	Learning (learning driven)
• Stable environment	• Changing environment
• Vertical structure	• Flat horizontal structure
• Strategy is formulated from the top and passed down	• Strategy is a collaborative effort within the organization and with other companies
• Centralized decision making	• Decentralized decision making
• Rigidly defined and specialized tasks	• Loose, flexible, and adaptive roles
• Rigid culture that is not responsive to change	• Adaptive culture that encourages continuous improvement and change
• Formal systems of communication tied to the vertical hierarchy with lots of filters	• Personal and group networks of free, open exchanges with no filters

© Cengage Learning 2013

Characteristics of the Traditional Organization

The traditional organization has the following characteristics:

- The traditional organization is based on the bureaucratic model that emphasizes a command-and-control structure, centralized decision making, highly formalized systems and specialized tasks. These vertical structures are effective under stable environmental conditions where the pace of change is slow or incremental at best.

- The culture of the traditional organization is oriented toward the individual, and rewards are individualized. This fosters competition among individuals.

- The mind-set of leaders is that there is a "right way" to do things, and only when that way is followed will the organization be successful. An elaborate formal system of reporting allows leaders to closely monitor work operations. This formal system is a powerful tool for controlling information and often acts as a filter in determining what information leaders decide to pass down to lower-level employees.

- Because the traditional organization is efficiency driven, deviating from standard operating procedures is frowned upon and mistakes are viewed as a symptom of poor performance. Therefore, employees don't take chances, and mistakes and problems are hidden.

Characteristics of the Learning Organization

The learning organization has the following characteristics:

- The learning organization culture is open, proactive, and creativity driven.[87,88]

- In learning organizations, the vertical structure is abandoned for a flat, horizontal structure. The horizontal structure is constituted around work flows or processes rather than functional specialties. The learning organization recognizes that work processes and procedures are the means to satisfying customer needs rather than ends in themselves. Flexible structures facilitate innovation.[89]

- Interdisciplinary teams and network systems are highly valued tools in learning organizations. Network systems facilitate open communication and exchange throughout the organization and with other external entities. The exchange between teams facilitated by highly efficient network systems enhances an organization's learning capacity and subsequent competitiveness.[90,91] Networks that connect teams provide access to knowledge, resources, markets, and technologies.[92]

- To encourage innovation and creativity in meeting current challenges, learning organizations are designing tasks that are much looser, free flowing, and adaptive.[93] There are fewer restrictions on how things should be done.[94] Responsibility and authority are decentralized to lower-level workers, empowering them to think, debate, create, learn, and solve problems at their level.[95,96]

- Organizational learning is a multilevel process, bringing together individual, group, and organizational levels of analysis.[97] It involves multiple learning processes (intuition, integrating, interpreting, and institutionalization) that allow learning to feed forward to the organizational level and feed back to the group or individual. The most successful learning organizations compound their advantage by encouraging employees at all levels to collect and share information across boundaries rather than hoarding it. This is facilitated through communication and information hubs that make knowledge sharing a way of life.[98]

- The learning organization embraces the idea that people will learn if encouraged to be creative, face challenges, experiment, fail, and reflect on their experiences. Involving everyone in the planning of learning activities and creating a sense of collective ownership of the process can be an important motivational factor.[99] On the question of whether we learn more from failures or from successes, one study concluded that organizations learn more effectively from failures than successes because knowledge from failure tends to depreciate more slowly than knowledge from successes.[100]

Examples of learning organizations today include Google, Facebook, Apple, Toyota, W. L. Gore & Associates, Xerox, 3M, Johnson & Johnson, Procter & Gamble, and many others. These companies are finding that success is more about nurturing the imagination, creativity, and passion of employees to solve customer problems than focusing on costs and profits.

WORK Application 5

Explain whether where you work or have worked is more of a traditional organization or a learning organization.

OPENING CASE *APPLICATION*

7. **In your opinion, does Citigroup represent the traditional organization or the learning organization?**

Organizations that operate in highly turbulent environments need to adopt a learning organization culture. As we have documented in question number 7, Citigroup is operating in a fast-changing domestic and global business environment. It is for this reason that Mr. Pandit's first set of decisions had to do with making the organization leaner and more responsive to customer needs and market trends. As was revealed in the opening case, upon his appointment, Mr. Pandit embarked on a plan to refocus, recapitalize, and restructure Citigroup. With the goals of long-term profitability and growth on his mind, Pandit's strategy for building a new Citigroup centered on the company's strengths and distinctive competitive advantages: its global franchise, strong emerging market footprint, innovative spirit, and talented and diverse employee base. The innovative spirit and a talented and diverse workforce are characteristics of learning organizations. Citi clearly represents an organization that is moving away from the traditional to the learning organization culture or mind-set.

CONCEPT APPLICATION 2
Differentiating between the Traditional and Learning Organization

Identify each statement by its type of organization. Write the appropriate letter in the blank before each item.

a. traditional
b. learning

(continued)

(Concept Application 2 continued)

_____ 11. With a union, we have clearly defined jobs and are not allowed to do other work.

_____ 12. Top-level managers make all the important decisions around here.

_____ 13. In our organization, employees are encouraged to experiment and take risk without fear of punishment when they fail.

_____ 14. There aren't many levels of management in our company.

_____ 15. Our organization's structure can be described as flat or horizontal with much decision-making responsibility delegated downward.

The Learning Organizational Culture and Firm Performance

Increasingly, researchers are finding that the higher the level of learning and knowledge acquisition, the greater the level of firm financial and nonfinancial performance.[101,102] It is believed that a learning organization is more likely to develop and maintain its competitiveness than one without a learning ability.[103] Different studies have focused on the relationship between the constructs represented by the learning organization, knowledge management, and performance. Here are a few examples:

- Studies investigating the relationship between knowledge creation and value creation found that a firm's ability to create and share knowledge is positively related to new product development success.

- Productivity and profits increase in organizations that embrace a learning culture.[104]

- Supportive learning cultures have been found to have a positive and direct influence on a team's creativity and its collaborative knowledge creation practices.[105]

- Organizational learning and knowledge creation have a direct positive influence on the level of creativity and innovation.

- The learning organizational culture has a positive direct impact on employee, customer, and supplier satisfaction levels.[106,107]

- The learning organization culture is significantly associated with organizational citizenship behavior, knowledge-sharing intention, interpersonal trust, and organizational commitment.[108,109]

Learning Outcome 8

Describe the role of leadership in creating a learning organization.

The Role of Leaders in Creating a Learning Organization Culture

Researchers generally agree that leadership is an important factor in influencing the development of a learning organization. They suggest that creating a shared vision of the future, empowering and training followers to handle environmental challenges, modeling learning behavior, and fostering a learning culture are critical skills for leaders of a learning organization.[110] Part of fostering a learning culture is creating the appropriate climate so that people can share and build upon each other's ideas and suggestions. Leaders are seen as an important motivational force behind employee engagement in learning activities that result in new knowledge.[111] The learning organization is driven to innovate.

As we discussed in Chapter 7, the nature of the relationship between leaders and their followers (LMX) does influence employee outcomes such as job performance, job satisfaction, organizational citizenship behavior, commitment, retention, and employee creativity.[112] A recent study on the subject found that employee learning is in fact enhanced by the relationship that employees have with their leader and is a shared responsibility between the leader, the employee, and the organization as a whole.[113] From this point of view, some experts have argued that failed efforts to create a learning organization should be at least in part blamed on poor leadership.

Leaders in learning organizations face a dual challenge to maintain efficient operations and create a flexible and adaptive organization at the same time. For example, leaders have to balance the need for employee learning versus the pressures of the job; investing in strategic learning initiatives versus the need to keep organizational operating costs low; and encouraging creativity and flexibility versus organization-wide standards that emphasize efficiency and accountability.[114] These are leadership conundrums that must be tackled for the learning culture to succeed. In Exhibit 12.5, we suggest ways in which leaders can create conditions conducive to learning and knowledge creation.[115,116]

EXHIBIT 12.5 Recommendations for Fostering a Learning Organizational Culture

- Encourage creative thinking.
- Create a climate in which experimentation is encouraged.
- Provide incentives for learning and innovation.
- Build confidence in followers' capacity to learn and adapt.
- Encourage systems thinking.
- Create a culture conducive to individual and team learning.
- Institute mechanisms for channeling and nurturing creative ideas for innovation.
- Create a shared vision for learning.
- Broaden employees' frame of reference.
- Create an environment in which people can learn from their mistakes.

© Cengage Learning 2013

Encourage Creative Thinking

The learning organization encourages creativity because it is regarded as the building block for innovation. Innovation enhances organizational adaptability and growth. Creativity takes place at the individual, group, and organizational levels. Creativity is generally initiated by employees themselves; however, the relationship between individuals and their leaders (or between team members and their leader) does play a key role in fostering or dampening creativity. As discussed in Chapter 7, individuals or members of a team who have a high-quality relationship with each other and with the leader (LMX and TMX) tend to exhibit higher levels of self-efficacy, and self-efficacy has been shown to have a positive impact on creativity.[117] At the organizational level, creativity is affected by leadership style, culture, climate, structure, and systems that the organization has in place. Also, the resources and reward system that the organization has will play a role.

At the individual level, leaders can enhance learning by encouraging members to "think outside the box"—in other words, consider possibilities that do not already exist. Rather than responding to known challenges, employees are encouraged to create the future. People with maverick ideas or out-of-the-ordinary proposals have to be welcomed and given room to operate in a learning organization. People who advocate radical or different ideas must not be looked on as disruptive or troublesome.

Another approach to enhance creative thinking is to encourage employees to research and learn from some of the best in the industry. This process, known as *benchmarking,* allows a company to imitate the best practices of others. However, mere imitation does not yield a competitive advantage; it is a follower strategy. An organization must improve upon the best practices of competitors and launch innovations ahead of competitors.

Create a Climate in Which Experimentation Is Encouraged

Learning is more likely to take place in an organization in which experimentation on a small scale is encouraged and permitted. The purpose of an experiment is to learn by trial in a controlled environment. The costs of failure are not as significant as in a real attempt. People who are afraid of failing and risking their reputations or careers may be more likely to try something new or be creative on a small scale. The leader must create a culture that nurtures and celebrates experimentation and innovation. Everybody is encouraged to contribute ideas, show initiative, and pursue continuous improvement. One way to do this is to inspire people to see change and innovation as a necessity and way of life in the organization. Another way is to reward those who fail, because it symbolizes the importance of taking risks.

Provide Incentives for Learning and Innovation

The use of incentives and rewards is a powerful tool that leaders can apply to encourage learning and innovation. Increasingly, innovation is seen as a key driver of competitiveness.[118] However, organizations are often criticized for proclaiming themselves as champions of learning and innovation but not being able to provide workers with the kind of tangible support needed to motivate them. Rewards for successful ideas and innovations must be large and visible for others to notice. Rewards and incentives reinforce positive learning and innovation in the organization. CEOs must take steps to encourage and support learning and innovation in the workplace.

Build Confidence in Followers' Capacity to Learn and Adapt

The environment of the learning organization is one of rapid change, wherein survival depends on a timely response to threats and opportunities. Providing opportunities for employees to solve problems will increase their confidence and pride in the process. With each celebrated success comes greater confidence in dealing with new challenges. Over time, familiarity with the change process will create an appreciation for flexibility and learning.

Encourage Systems Thinking

To enhance learning, the leader should help members regard the organization as a system in which everybody's work affects the work of everybody else. Therefore, everyone in the organization must consider how their actions affect other parts/functions of the organization. The emphasis on the whole system reduces boundaries both within the organization and with other companies, which allows for collaboration and continuous learning. Members begin to see how relationships with other companies can lower costs, increase sales, or bring in new competencies. Rigid loyalties to one's department or functional area gradually disappear.

12.3 *Departmentalization*

Colleges and universities are known to have rigid departments, such as economics, management, marketing, accounting, and finance. At some schools, these departments are more concerned about themselves (related to budgets and number of faculty and courses) than serving students and cooperating with other departments. For example, some economics faculty have stated that they are concerned with theory and don't need to teach anything practical. There is also overlap in some courses offered by different departments, such as strategy being taught in management and marketing courses. In the business world, there is a trend to break down the barriers between departments and to be much more cooperative. However, academia doesn't seem to be following this trend.

1. Should the faculty's top priority be students, their department, or cooperating with other departments?

2. Should faculty move away from a focus on theory to more practical applications to business?

3. Should colleges follow the business trend of breaking away from departments and cooperate more? Or are they different from businesses, thus needing clear departments differentiated by discipline?

Create a Culture Conducive to Individual and Team Learning

Personal development and a lifetime of learning must be strong cultural values in learning organizations. Leaders must create a culture in which each person is valued, and the organization promotes and supports people to develop to their full potential. This type of learning culture encourages self-initiated activity, serendipity, and intracompany communications. In this type of learning culture, top leadership offers total support; employees take ownership of their work; and managers function more like facilitators than taskmasters. Another aspect of creating a culture conducive to team learning is the concept of team diversity (discussed in Chapter 10). Leaders must ensure that diversity is present in their teams. Studies have found that diverse teams enhance learning because members from different diverse backgrounds combine to generate novel insights or knowledge.

Institute Mechanisms for Channeling and Nurturing Creative Ideas for Innovation

The birth of a new idea or knowledge begins with the individual. Making personal knowledge available to others is the central activity of the knowledge-creating organization. Knowledge that is shared can help an employee with a difficult problem or provide the opportunity for employees from different parts of the organization to interact with each other, getting advice and providing support about common problems. Ideas generated within or outside an organization may become the source of new products or innovations. Venture teams, task forces, information systems networks, seminars, and workshops can be used to diffuse knowledge and to channel creative ideas to appropriate locations for evaluation and application. Once this process is institutionalized, knowledge creation and exchange become part of the culture.

Create a Shared Vision for Learning

Creating a shared vision enhances learning as organization members develop a common purpose and commitment to make learning an ongoing part of the organization. If employees all believe that the organization is headed toward greatness, they will be motivated to be part of it by learning and contributing their best ideas and solutions. As discussed in Chapters 9 and 10, this is a role suitable to the transformational and strategic leader; this explains the interest of some scholars in exploring the role of transformational leadership in the development of the learning organization.[119]

Broaden Employees' Frame of Reference

A person's frame of reference determines how he or she sees the world. The ways we gather, analyze, and interpret information—and how we make decisions based on such information—are affected by our personal frames of reference. A frame of reference determines what implicit assumptions people hold, and those assumptions, consciously or unconsciously, affect how they interpret events. To enhance employees' ability to learn, it is helpful for leaders to broaden the frames employees use to see the organization and its external environment. Learning is constrained when leaders and their followers fail to see the world from a different and more enlightened perspective and therefore are unable to help their organization adapt to changes taking place in such environments. Broadening employees' frames of reference or perspective provides for a greater variety of approaches to solving problems and thus facilitates learning and continuous improvement.

Create an Environment in Which People Can Learn from Their Mistakes

WORK Application 6

The workplace should be a place of learning but some critics argue that not all of them have a culture that encourages learning. Of the ten recommendations for fostering a learning organizational culture in Exhibit 12.5, how many would you say are true of your current or past workplace?

_____

_____

_____

_____

Some of the most important inventions or scientific breakthroughs resulted from investigating failed outcomes. Unfortunately, in many organizations, when experiments or full-scale ventures fail, the tendency is to immediately abandon the activity to save face or avoid negative consequences. This is often the wrong approach, because more learning takes place from things that go wrong than from things that go right. After all, when things turn out as expected, it just confirms existing theories or assumptions. New insights are more likely when there is an investigation into why expected outcomes were not realized. Therefore, to encourage learning, leaders must communicate the view that failure is tolerated. Then, they must provide opportunities for people to engage in post-activity reviews regardless of outcome. Creating a culture that rewards those who succeed, as well as occasionally rewarding those who fail, sends a message that the organization encourages risk-taking.

Learning is a never-ending exercise. Leaders must communicate the message that learning and continuous improvements are imperative in today's highly dynamic business environment. Leaders must take the lead in challenging the status quo and creating organizational conditions that are conducive to learning and continuous innovation.

OPENING CASE *APPLICATION*

8. What additional steps will you recommend that Vikram Pandit take in order to make Citigroup more of a learning organization?

CEO Pandit can employ many of the guidelines for enhancing organizational learning listed in Exhibit 12.5 and described in this section. Action on all or any number of these guidelines will increase Citi's efforts to become a greater learning organization.

Now that you have learned about crisis leadership and the learning organization, you may find it interesting to see how your own personality traits match up. Complete Self-Assessment 2.

SELF-ASSESSMENT 2   Personality and Crisis and the Learning Organization

Crisis

When facing a crisis, surgency personalities tend to take the leadership position to solve the crisis, and agreeableness personalities are glad to follow. Those with adjustment problems tend to get emotional under the pressure of a crisis and often get defensive and deny there is a problem, whereas conscientious personalities with an openness to experience tend to want to resolve the crisis. How do you handle crisis situations? How can you improve?

Learning Organization

The key personality trait that differs between the traditional organization and the learning organization is openness to new experience. If you are closed to new experience, you will tend to like a traditional organization in which change is slow and top management makes the decisions. If you are open to new experience, you will tend to enjoy a learning organization in which you are encouraged and valued for implementing change and making many of your own decisions. Would you be more comfortable in a traditional or learning organization? Why?

Chapter Summary

The chapter summary is organized to answer the nine learning outcomes for Chapter 12.

1. Explain why crisis leadership competence is an important consideration when hiring new leaders.

Crises are inevitable. It is not a question of "if" a crisis will happen, but "when." A crisis can inflict severe damage to an organization if not properly managed. In a crisis, stock prices plummet and operating costs escalate, causing both short- and long-term financial losses. A crisis that is mismanaged can also damage an organization's reputation and diminish consumer confidence in the organization's mission, or in some cases can lead to its demise altogether. As the economy limps on and speculation of it sliding into a recession builds, the real prospect exists that many corporations are going to face a crisis of survival. Rising oil prices, the housing downturn, the subprime crisis, the credit crunch, and talk of possible inflation and recession are all ingredients that could stymie even the best-prepared CEOs.

2. Identify the benefits of precrisis planning.

Precrisis planning buys you time. You are ready when a crisis strikes. Many organizations are presented with early warning signals of an impending crisis but fail to recognize and heed them. The problem is detecting the signals that warn of a crisis. It is for this reason that experts recommend precrisis planning for any size of business. Precrisis planning allows you to create systems and procedures for detecting signals that warn of an impending crisis before it happens. Effective precrisis planning leads to effective crisis management during and after a crisis.

3. Identify three key components of the precrisis planning phase.

Three components to precrisis planning that every organization (large, small, for-profit, or nonprofit) should address are: (1) appointing a crisis leader, (2) creating a crisis response team, and (3) assessing risk.

4. Describe the five-step process of crisis risk assessment.

The five-step process for risk assessment consists of: (1) risk identification, (2) risk assessment and ranking, (3) risk reduction strategies, (4) crisis prevention simulations, and (5) crisis management. In step 1, crisis team members begin by first identifying the worst-case incidents that could have severe consequences on people, the organization's financial position, or its image. This process is described as risk identification and results in the creation of a risk chart. Next, these incidents are analyzed and ranked. During the risk reduction step, the crisis leader shares the risk chart created during risk assessment and ranking with team members or larger audiences, and they begin debating and formulating strategies for countering each crisis or threat. The fourth step in the risk assessment process is crisis prevention. Here, tests and simulations are conducted to test employees under pressure. The fifth step of risk assessment is crisis management. A team is assembled and readied to respond in the event of a real crisis.

5. Describe the role of the CEO and communication in managing a crisis.

The CEO must be out leading the charge before, during, and after a crisis. The CEO's involvement demonstrates to the public the seriousness with which the incident is viewed. Before a crisis, the CEO should be actively involved in precrisis planning. During a crisis, he or she cannot develop a bunker mentality. As mentioned in the chapter, the three key tenets of crisis leadership are (1) stay engaged and lead from the front, (2) focus on the big picture and communicate the vision, and (3) work with your crisis management team. During a crisis, the CEO must have answers to the following questions: What happened? How did it happen? What are you doing to address the crisis? And after the crisis, what you going to do to ensure that it never happen again? For all of these things to happen, the organization must have in place a well-designed communication system and the leader must be an effective communicator.

6. List five or more attributes that can be used to describe the learning organization.

- Learning from mistakes and past experience
- Learning from others
- Systematic problem solving
- Experimentation
- Sharing knowledge
- Strong leadership support

7. Distinguish between the traditional organization and the learning organization.

The traditional, efficiency-driven organization has a bureaucratic structure (a tall pyramid), starting with the CEO at the top and everyone else functionally organized in layers below. Decision making is centralized at the top of the hierarchy, which controls and coordinates all functional units throughout the organization. To ensure reliable and predictable results, tasks are rigidly defined and broken down into specialized jobs. Strict formal rules and procedures for performing each task are enforced. Though repetitive, boring, and unchallenging, it is an efficient way of keeping the production line running smoothly. An elaborate formal system of reporting allows leaders to closely monitor work operations and maintain efficient, steady performance. This formal system is a powerful tool for controlling information and often acts as a filter in determining what information leaders decide to pass down to lower-level employees.

By contrast, in learning organizations the vertical structure is abandoned for a flat, horizontal structure. The horizontal structure is constituted around work flows or processes rather than functional specialties. To encourage innovation and creativity in meeting current challenges, learning organizations are designing tasks that are much looser, free flowing, and adaptive. Few strict rules and procedures prescribe how things should be done. The term *organic* has been used to describe this type of organization. Responsibility and authority are decentralized to lower-level workers, empowering them to think, experiment, create, learn, and solve problems at their level.

8. Describe the role of leadership in creating a learning organization culture.

The learning organization represents a paradigm shift in the approach organizations take to managing their internal and external relationships. In today's rapidly changing business environment, organizations must transform into active learning organisms or risk becoming extinct. To succeed, organizations must be proactive and anticipatory, which requires continuous improvement. Thus, the traditional organization model that emphasized efficiency and stability is being replaced by a model that is learning driven and adaptable.

Leaders play a critical role in effecting this transformation. Without effective leadership from the top and throughout the organizational structure, it is hard to imagine how the learning organization can succeed. A shared vision and mission are the basis for the emergence of strategy in a learning organization, and this is the responsibility of leadership. Leaders can play a key role in enhancing organizational learning by encouraging creative thinking, creating a climate in which experimentation and risk taking are encouraged, providing incentives for learning and innovation, building confidence in followers' capacity to learn and adapt, encouraging systems thinking, and creating a culture conducive to individual and team learning.

9. Define the following key terms (in order of appearance in the chapter).

Select one or more methods: (1) fill in the missing key terms from memory; (2) match the key terms from the following list with their definitions below; and (3) copy the key terms in order from the list at the beginning of the chapter.

_____ is a low-probability, high-impact event that threatens the viability of the organization and is characterized by ambiguity of cause, effect, and means of resolution, as well as by a belief that decisions must be made swiftly.

_____ is a printed statement that describes how an organization is responding to a crisis and who is in charge.

_____ is a package of information about a company, including names and pictures of its executives, a fact sheet, and key milestones in the company's history.

_____ is one that is skilled at creating, acquiring, and transferring knowledge, and at modifying behavior to reflect new knowledge and insights.

_____ is the tacit and explicit knowledge that individuals possess about products, services, systems, and processes.

_____ occurs when anticipated or expected changes bear no resemblance to the present or the past.

Key Terms

crisis, 430

discontinuous change, 448

learning organization, 446

organizational knowledge, 447

press kit, 443

press release, 443

Review Questions

1. Strategic crisis leadership is about a leader taking action in three key areas. What are these areas?

2. How has the Internet affected the way crises are perceived in our society today?

3. What are the main components of a precrisis plan?

4. The precrisis response plan requires the appointment of a crisis leader. Describe the responsibilities of this person.

5. The best indicator of an organization's readiness to respond to a crisis is how it rates on five factors. What are these five factors?

6. What is the appropriate role of an organization's top leadership during a crisis?

7. What does it mean to say that organizational learning is a multilevel sharing process?

8. What factors account for the fact that the learning organization is described as more creative and innovative than the traditional organization form?

Critical Thinking Questions

The following critical-thinking questions can be used for class discussion and/or as written assignments to develop communication skills. Be sure to give complete explanations for all questions.

1. Describe why a senior leader's physical presence is critical during a crisis.

2. What are the purpose and benefits of creating a comprehensive crisis response plan before a crisis happens?

3. What advice would you give to a leader who wants to improve his or her organization's communications function so that it is more effective during a crisis?

4. How important to an organization is internal (employee) communication during a crisis?

5. What message does it send when the organizational culture encourages employees to view mistakes/problems as opportunities for improvement rather than reasons to blame or punish those involved?

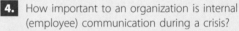

CASE

Merck CEO Ken Frazier: First African-American Leading a Major Pharmaceutical Company

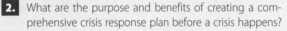

The opening case featured Citigroup, a company that was clearly in crisis mode when its new CEO took over. This end-of-chapter case features Merck, a pharmaceutical company that was doing just fine when it brought in a new CEO. We selected Merck because it operates in an environment where learning and knowledge management are critical for success. Also, unlike the Citigroup case, where a leadership change was triggered by a crisis and poor performance, Merck's change in leadership was the result of an orderly succession plan. Merck's outgoing CEO Richard T. Clark was stepping down after reaching Merck's mandatory retirement age of 65.

Merck is a global healthcare leader that employs 100,000 people worldwide, 42,000 in the United States NJ is part of USMerck operates in more than 140 countries to deliver innovative health solutions. In 2009, Merck spent $41.1 billion to acquire rival drug maker Schering-Plough. This mega merger made the combined company the second-largest healthcare company in the world. Merck's leadership saw a lot of synergistic benefits in the merger. They rationalized that both companies are strong, science-based companies. Both have a common mission—and passion—to improve health and well-being around the world. And both share a long-standing commitment to putting customers first and to being there for people in times of need. Drug research is a high-risk and time-consuming process. Only 1 out of every 5000–10,000 compounds screened becomes an approved drug. It takes an average of 10 to 15 years at an average cost of more than US$1 billion to develop a successful medicine.[120] Therefore, knowledge management and the organizational learning are what a company like Merck is all about.

On November 30, 2010, Merck announced that its Board of Directors had elected Kenneth C. Frazier to be its next chief executive officer (CEO) and president, as well as a member of the board, effective January 1, 2011. Mr. Frazier succeeded Richard T. Clark, who had served as Merck's CEO since 2005, who would continue as chairman of the board.

Mr. Frazier received his bachelor's degree from The Pennsylvania State University and holds a JD from Harvard Law School. Prior to being appointed president, Mr. Frazier served as executive vice president and president, Global Human Health, from 2007 to 2010. Frazier is the first African-American to lead a major U.S. pharmaceutical company. Mr. Frazier grew up in North Philadelphia, where his father raised three children on a janitor's salary after the death of Mr. Frazier's mother when he was 12.

Mr. Frazier made his name in Merck as the lawyer who masterminded the company's strategy of defending the pain drug Vioxx. Patients were claiming that the drug was responsible for heart attacks, leading to the deaths of many who had been on the drug. From Wall Street's perspective, Vioxx was nothing short of a crisis. Frazier was the strategist calling the shots, initially deciding to defend the company against thousands of lawsuits by fighting every case separately instead of as a joint action. He eventually structured a $4.85 billion settlement to resolve the remaining lawsuits. Wall Street had expected that Merck would have to pay even more. "He managed the Vioxx litigation extraordinarily well, and there were a lot of doubting Thomases, especially on Wall Street," said Barbara Ryan, an analyst who follows drug companies for Deutsche Bank. Mr. Frazier has maintained that the pillar of Merck's strategy will remain innovation, with a focus on emerging markets led by China and Brazil. "The most important thing is to continue on the strategy" that Mr. Clark established, Mr. Frazier said.[121] Richard Clark, Ken's predecessor, said Frazier demonstrated his leadership skills during the merger of Merck and Schering Plough. "Ken spent time in the field understanding the customer needs of our markets in a way that I hadn't seen done

before," Clark said. "It showed you his dedication and enthusiasm."

Speaking on behalf of Merck's Board of Directors, William B. Harrison said, "During the board's succession planning process, it became clear to us that Ken Frazier has the strategic vision, operational experience, and passion to lead Merck. Ken is a proven executive who has played a key role in shaping Merck's business strategy. With his understanding of the global health care environment, the board is confident in Ken's ability to take the helm at Merck and guide the continued implementation of our long-term strategy."

Supporters of Ken Frazier believe he has the strategic breadth and depth to advance Merck's innovative strategy and make it a competitive player in the highly competitive pharmaceutical industry.[122] Others, however, are more skeptical. While Frazier's legal experience is extensive, his experience running the operations of a company is limited and may cause doubt for some investors, observed Bowe, an industry expert. "Does leading a big pharma company in a very challenging and changing environment require more operational experience?" Bowe said. "That's the question."[123] This question is raised because Mr. Frazier is not a scientist and his experience at Merck and other places were in the legal department. Only the future will tell!

GO TO THE INTERNET: To learn more about Ken Frazier and Merck, visit **www.merck.com**.

Support your answers to the following questions with specific information from the case and text or with other information you get from the Web or other sources.

1. In what way(s) has Ken Frazier demonstrated his effectiveness as a crisis leader?

2. Given our discussion on the distinction between a traditional and learning organization, what type of organization is Merck? Support your answer.

3. Mr. Frazier has maintained that the pillar of Merck's strategy will remain innovation. Suggest some ideas he can institute to enhance innovation.

4. Describe the strategy that Ken Frazier has articulated for moving Merck forward.

5. What are some of the supporting factors that the Merck Board of Directors used in making the decision to appoint Ken Frazier Merck's next CEO?

6. Drug research is a high-risk and time-consuming process. What evidence is there to support this assertion?

7. What specific personality and leadership traits does Ken Frazier possess that align with leading a learning- and knowledge-driven organization like Merck?

CUMULATIVE CASE QUESTIONS

8. What is CEO Frazier's source of power? Also, what type of power and influencing tactics has he been using, and is it the appropriate power type? If not, which power type should he be using (Chapter 5)?

9. Chapter 6 discusses communication, coaching, and mentoring as ways to develop the leadership skills of underlings by senior leaders. What is the evidence from the case that Mr. Frazier is a beneficiary of effective mentoring and coaching?

10. Strategic leadership is about having a vision that aligns with future environmental trends and working with and through others to realize it (Chapter 11). What evidences is there that Ken Frazier is an effective strategic leader?

CASE EXERCISE AND ROLE-PLAY

Preparation: Put yourself in the position of Ken Frazier. There has been a major incident involving one of Merck's drugs. Patients using the drug have been experiencing some serious side effects. The law suits are beginning to mount. You and the crisis management team are getting ready for a news conference with the media on the crisis. Prepare a list of questions you anticipate the media will be asking and what your response should be. What other preparations do you have to make prior to the news conference?

In-Class Groups: Break into groups of four to six members, and discuss the preparation questions.

Role-Play: Taking turns, one group will represent the crisis management team led by Mr. Frazier. Let another group play the role of the media. They should select no more than three questions from their prepared list to ask. The rest of the class should listen and judge the performance of the Merck crisis management team in addressing the media. Each group should take turns role-playing the media, the Merck crisis management team, or the judges. Each team playing the role of the media should ask a different set of questions, so the same questions are not repeated during each round.

Observer Role: As the rest of the class members watch the role-play, they should judge (1) the opening remarks of the crisis management team—their demeanor, body language, tone, style, and substance; (2) the quality of questions that the media team asked; and (3) the quality of responses given by Mr. Frazier and his team—how honest and truthful they are with their answers. Did Mr. Frazier take a leading role or did he stay in the background and let others do the talking? Use the guidelines for effective crisis communication as the tool to judge Merck's crisis management team performance during the news conference. Look for things that the person playing Mr. Frazier did well or did not do well during the news conference.

Discussion: After the role-plays, the class votes for the crisis management team that did the best job addressing the news media with its opening remarks and responding to questions. The instructor should weigh in with his or her opinion on which team did the best job in the questioning and which team did the best job in responding to the questions. Which team member playing Mr. Frazier did the best job and why? Where did the others fall short?

VIDEO ▶❚❚ CASE

Managing in Turbulent Times at Second City Theater

Managers today are expected to deal with uncertainty, unexpected events, diversity, and change. They must demonstrate flexibility, foster trust, and engage the hearts and minds of employees. The managers at Second City Theater have a leg up in developing these skills and dealing with these situations because Second City has been doing it for years—on stage. In 1975, owner and executive producer Andrew Alexander started the Second City television series (SCTV) in response to the new trend of television sketch comedy.

Later, the company opened the Second City Training Center, an educational center offering classes in improvisation, acting, writing, and other skills. Most recently, Second City opened a corporate communications division, which provides training in the areas of internal communications, external marketing and branding, and learning development. With its focus on human skills, Second City demonstrates all of the qualities of a learning organization. The managers at Second City foster a climate where experimentation and learning are encouraged.

1. Many students of the Second City Training Center are businesspeople looking to gain skills for the corporate context. What skills from the world of improvisational comedy would be valuable to a business manager?

2. What do you think would be the challenges of a manager in a learning organization? Why?

Developing Your Leadership Skills 1

Handling a Crisis

Preparation for This Exercise

Research the business news and find an organization that has just had a crisis. Below, identify the firm and the crisis. Also, read Procedure 2 below and think of your "Three As" response to the crisis.

_____

_____

_____

Doing This Exercise in Class

Objective

To develop your ability to handle a crisis

The primary AACSB learning standard skill developed through this exercise is strategic management.

Preparation

You should have selected a business in crisis.

Procedure 1 *(3–5 minutes)* Break into crisis teams of four to six and select one business crisis that the group will work on resolving.

Procedure 2 *(10–15 minutes)* Develop a crisis communication plan, identifying your "Three As".

Acknowledge: _____

_____

_____

Action: _____

_____

_____

Avoid: _____

_____

_____

Procedure 3 *(10–20 minutes)* Each crisis team selects a spokesperson who tells the class the organization chosen and its crisis followed by the team's "Three As" plan.

Conclusion

The instructor may lead a class discussion and/or make concluding remarks.

Apply It *(2–4 minutes)* What did I learn from this experience? How will I use this knowledge in the future?

_____

_____

_____

Sharing

In the group, or to the entire class, volunteers may give their answers to the "Apply It" questions.

Developing Your Leadership Skills 2

The Learning Organization

Preparation for This Exercise

Return to Self-Assessment 1, Learning Organizations, on page 00. Below, identify the firm you assessed and its score.

_____

Select any 3 of the 15 characteristics of learning organization questions that can be improved. Below, list the numbers and develop a plan on how the organization can improve on each of the three characteristics.

_____

_____

_____

_____

Doing This Exercise in Class

Objective

To develop your skill to improve a firm's ability to learn

The primary AACSB learning standard skill developed through this exercise is strategic management.

Preparation

You should have developed plans to improve learning on three characteristics of learning organizations.

Procedure 1 _(10–15 minutes)_ Break into teams of four to six and share your preparation plans. Help each other improve the plans.

Procedure 2 _(10–20 minutes)_ Each team selects a spokesperson who tells the class the organization chosen and the plans to improve learning.

Conclusion

The instructor may lead a class discussion and/or make concluding remarks.

Apply It _(2–4 minutes)_ What did I learn from this experience? How will I use this knowledge in the future?

_____

_____

_____

Sharing

In the group, or to the entire class, volunteers may give their answers to the "Apply It" questions.

Leadership and Spirituality in the Workplace

Judith Neal, PhD[*]

T he purpose of this appendix is twofold: (1) It provides an overview of the concept of faith and spirituality in the workplace; and (2) it provides spiritual principles that have been useful to many leaders in their personal and professional development.

Spirituality in the Workplace

Tom Aageson, former Director of Aid to Artisans—a nonprofit organization that helps artists in third-world countries—takes an annual retreat in which he contemplates questions about the purpose of his life, and evaluates how well he is living in alignment with his values. Angel Martinez, former CEO of Rockport Shoes, invited all his top executives to a retreat that included exploring the integration of each person's spiritual journey with his or her work journey. At Integrated Project Systems (IPS) in San Francisco, former CEO Bill Kern created a document called "The Corporate Stand" that is very explicit about "The Integrity of the Human Spirit." These are key principles that employees live by at IPS. Rodale Press, publisher of such well-known magazines as *Prevention, Men's Health, Runner's World*, and *Organic Gardening*, has a "kiva room" at corporate headquarters where employees may go to meditate, pray, or just spend quiet time when things get too stressful. ANZ Bank in Australia and New Zealand sends all its employees through personal transformation programs, conducts an audit based on levels of corporate consciousness, and allows each bank branch to design its own meditation/quiet room. Tyson Foods has over 120 workplace chaplains on the payroll and is committed to being a "faith-friendly workplace."

Stories like these are becoming more and more common in all kinds of workplaces. Academic and professional conferences are offering an increasing number of sessions that have words such as *Faith, Spirituality, Consciousness*, or *Soul* in the title. There is a new openness in management education to recognition of our spiritual nature. This recognition can be on a personal level, such as when a person explores his or her own spiritual journey and struggles with what this means regarding work. It is also on a conceptual level, as both academics and practitioners explore the role that spirituality might have in bringing meaning, purpose, and increased performance to organizational

[*]Appendix written by Judith A. Neal, Ph.D., Executive Director, International Center for Spirit at Work, http://www.spiritatwork.org. © 2011 by Judith Neal; used by permission of the author.

life. A major change is going on in the personal and professional lives of leaders, as many of them more deeply integrate their spirituality and their work. And most would agree that this integration is leading to positive changes in their relationships and their effectiveness.

Defining Spirituality in the Workplace

Spirituality is difficult to define. The Latin origin of the word "spirit" is *spirare*, meaning, "to breathe." At its most basic, then, spirit is what inhabits us when we are alive and breathing; it is the life force. Spirituality has been defined as "that which is traditionally believed to be the vital principle or animating force within living beings—that which constitutes one's unseen intangible being, or the real sense or significance of something."[1] A fairly comprehensive definition, part of which is provided here, is as follows:

> *One's spirituality is the essence of who he or she is. It defines the inner self, separate from the body, but including the physical and intellectual self.... Spirituality also is the quality of being spiritual, of recognizing the intangible, life-affirming force in self and all human beings. It is a state of intimate relationship with the inner self of higher values and morality. It is a recognition of the truth of the inner nature of people.... Spirituality does not apply to particular religions, although the values of some religions may be a part of a person's spiritual focus. Said another way, spirituality is the song we all sing. Each religion has its own singer.*[2]

Perhaps the difficulty people have had in defining spirituality is that they are trying to objectify and categorize an experience and way of being that is at its core very subjective and beyond categorizing. For this reason, some have resorted to poetry as a way of trying to capture the essence of the experience of spirituality. Lee Bolman did this very effectively in his keynote presentation on spirituality in the workplace to the Eastern Academy of Management in May 1995. He quoted the Persian poet Rumi:[3]

> *All day I think about it, then at night I say it*
> *Where did I come from and what am I supposed to be doing?*
> *I have no idea*
> *My soul is elsewhere, I'm sure of that*
> *And I intend to end up there.*

James Autry, a successful *Fortune 500* executive, wrote a poem called "Threads." Here is an excerpt from that poem:[4]

> *Listen.*
> *In every office*
> *You hear the threads*
> *of love and joy and fear and guilt,*
> *the cries for celebration and reassurance,*
> *and somehow you know that connecting those threads*
> *is what you are supposed to do*
> *and business takes care of itself.*

Spirituality in the workplace is about people seeing their work as a spiritual path, as an opportunity to grow personally and to contribute to society in a meaningful way. It is about learning to be more caring and compassionate with fellow employees, with bosses, with subordinates and customers. It is about integrity, being true to oneself, and telling the truth to others. Spirituality in the workplace can refer to an individual's attempts to live his or her values more fully in the workplace. Or it can refer to the ways in which organizations structure themselves to support the spiritual growth of employees.

In the final analysis, the understanding of spirit and of spirituality in the workplace is a very individual and personal matter. There are as many expressions of these concepts as there are people who talk or write about them.

Approaches to Implementing Spirituality in the Workplace

In practice, organizations are implementing spirituality in the workplace utilizing one or more of the following four approaches:[5]

1: Individual Development

At this level, programs focus on helping the individual employee understand more about his or her values, spiritual principles, and sense of purpose. The organization is committed to helping individuals live in alignment with their faith and spiritual path, may offer meditation rooms or courses on spiritual practices and/or teachings, and may bring in speakers who talk about spiritual development. There is an understanding that if people can discover and respond to their own "calling" or sense of purpose, they will be more creative, committed, and service-oriented.

2: Leadership and Team Development

Organizations are offering courses to leaders with titles like "Authentic Leadership," "Leading with Soul," and "Spiritual Leadership." Leaders are encouraged to apply spiritual values such as humility, trust, courage, integrity, and faith to their work with teams. They may offer courses such as "Team Spirit" and "Noble Purpose" developed by Barry Heerman.[6] Some organizations are offering lunchtime Spirit at Work discussion groups. Others are offering team-building courses that incorporate spiritual values or practices.

3: Total System Development

A growing number of CEOs and organizational leaders have become personally committed to creating organizations that nurture the human spirit of the company's employees, customers, and other stakeholders. Several systemic approaches have been developed to help organizations evolve to a higher level of congruence with spiritual values. These include "Corporate Tools" by Richard Barrett,[7] "Spiral Dynamics" by Don Beck and Chris Cowan,[8] "Appreciative Inquiry" by David Cooperrider and colleagues,[9] "Positive Organizational Scholarship" and "The Abundance Framework" by Kim Cameron,[10] and "Open Space Technology" by Harrison Owen.[11] The key aim in each of these organizational development processes is to help an organization move beyond just a focus on profits and the bottom line to a commitment to human development and a positive contribution to society.

4: Redefining the Role of Business

A new paradigm is emerging among business leaders that redefines the purpose of business as the solution to solving problems in society and around the globe, rather than being a contributor to them. The focus is on using the creative energy and talent of their employees, along with their vast capital resources and international reach, to truly make a positive difference in the world. Willis Harman, cofounder of the Institute of Noetic Sciences and of the World Business Academy, was probably the first person to speak about the important role of business in increasing consciousness in the world.[12] More recently, Case Western Reserve's Wetherhead School of Management has created a Center of Excellence called the *Center of Business as an Agent of World Benefit*

(BAWB), which has sponsored an ongoing inquiry research project into the ways business is making a positive difference in the world.

Each organization is unique in terms of its values, vision, and readiness for spirituality in the workplace, so there is no one formula that leaders can use to implement spiritual values and practices in their organizations. The best thing to do is to learn as much as possible from organizations that have been successful in this integration. A great place to start is to study the organizations that have received the International Spirit at Work Award for their explicit spiritual practices and commitment to nurturing the human spirit of their employees; for more information, go to **http://tfsw.uark.edu.**

Before we discuss guidelines for leading from a spiritual perspective, complete the self-assessment below to better know thyself.

SELF-ASSESSMENT 1 Spiritual Intelligence at Work

Instructions: Please read each statement below and decide to what degree you either agree or disagree with the statement.

1 = Strongly Disagree
2 = Somewhat Disagree
3 = Neither Agree or Disagree
4 = Somewhat Agree
5 = Strongly Agree

_____ 1. I am very aware of my values and beliefs at work.

_____ 2. It is important to accept that others in my workplace may not have the same values and beliefs that I do.

_____ 3. I have had one or more transcendent experiences that have affected the way I feel about my work.

_____ 4. People I work with describe me as calm and nonjudgmental.

_____ 5. When someone has done something that makes me angry, I find it very difficult to forgive them.

_____ 6. I try to have daily contact with my Higher Power, the Divine, God, or Universal Consciousness.

_____ 7. In difficult situations, I find that a calm part of me can remain detached and observe my thoughts, feelings, and behaviors.

_____ 8. I have a great deal of compassion for the leaders of my organization.

_____ 9. When I need special help or guidance in my work, I turn to prayer, meditation, or other spiritual guidance.

_____ 10. I do not feel the need to grow or develop myself at work.

_____ 11. It is important to keep business life and personal life separate in my relationships at work.

_____ 12. I feel divinely guided to the work I am doing.

_____ 13. I have a regular spiritual or religious practice that I find helpful to me in my work.

_____ 14. I often feel a real sense of love and caring for the people I interact with at work.

_____ 15. I do not believe that there is anything greater than myself and know that the only way to make it in my life and career is to rely on my own abilities.

_____ 16. If I found myself in a work situation where I was asked to compromise my values, I would have to stick to my values, even if it hurt me or my career.

_____ 17. My primary motivation at work is to be of service to others.

_____ 18. I am deeply concerned about the effects of some business practices on the planet.

_____ 19. The reality of business is that sometimes you just have to compromise your values for the sake of the company or for your career.

_____ 20. Dealing with people at work is a great cause of frustration for me.

_____ 21. It is important to me that my organization operates in a way that is respectful of all life.

_____ 22. I have a real sense of calling about the work I do.

(continued)

(Self-Assessment 1 continued)

———— 23. I really try to get to know the people I work with on a deeper level than just work-related issues.

———— 24. I believe that my work is part of a larger divinely guided plan.

———— 25. My mission in life is very clear to me.

———— 26. People in my workplace often come to me to talk about personal or spiritual issues.

———— 27. I feel a sense of the sacred in my workplace.

———— 28. I often feel stressed at work.

———— 29. I work hard at having authentic and caring relationships with people at work.

———— 30. Because of my belief in something greater than myself, I try to live in alignment with key virtues such as trustworthiness, humility, justice, and unity.

Spiritual Intelligence at Work—

Scoring Key Instructions:

1. Transpose the numbers from the questionnaire to the columns below. For starred items (*), reverse the scoring by subtracting your answer from 6. For instance, if you responded to question 5 with a "4", 6−4 = 2, so put a "2" in item 5 below.
2. Add up the totals for each column.

Column A	Column B	Column C
1. ————	2. ————	3. ————
4. ————	*5. ————	6. ————
7. ————	8. ————	9. ————
*10. ————	*11. ————	12. ————
13. ————	14. ————	*15. ————
16. ————	17. ————	18. ————
*19. ————	*20. ————	21. ————
22. ————	23. ————	24. ————
25. ————	26. ————	27. ————
*28. ————	29. ————	30. ————
Totals:		
Column A: ————	Column B: ————	Column C: ————

Spiritual Intelligence at Work—

Interpretation of Scores

Spiritual Intelligence is the ability to feel a connection to self, a connection to others, and a connection to something greater than oneself. Column A provides you the score for "Connection to Self," Column B for "Connection to Others," and Column C for "Connection to the Transcendent." Make note of your highest score and your lowest score and write your thoughts about that here:

————————————————————————

————————————————————————

————————————————————————

Connection to Self

Spiritual Intelligence must begin with some sense of self-awareness. As the Delphi Oracle declared, "Know Thyself." Of the five dimensions of work (physical, intellectual, emotional, volitional, and spiritual), "Connection to Self" is most related to the "Intellectual" dimension because of its emphasis on self-development. People who have a strong connection to self are in touch with their values and beliefs, have a strong degree of emotional intelligence, and have done enough spiritual practice or self-development work so that they can calmly observe themselves and gain mastery over their thoughts, feelings and behaviors. Other people experience people who are high in connection to self as calm, able to act competently in chaotic situations, and as having serene competence.

40–50 You have a strong connection to self and may want to help others develop this capacity through your coaching or mentoring.

30–39 You are fairly self-aware with room for development. You may want to think about taking on a spiritual practice such as meditation or prayer, or receiving coaching or mentoring from someone who has a highly developed sense of connection to self.

20–29 You may often feel out of touch, confused by others' responses to you, and unsure of your sense of purpose or mission in life. It may be useful to take personal or spiritual growth workshops or to take time for a personal retreat where you can have time to reflect on yourself, your goals, and the kind of person you want to be.

0–19 You may feel fairly disconnected from yourself, and may be focusing most of your time and energy on external activities or on pleasing other people to your own detriment. You should give serious thought to the value of increasing your self-awareness of your beliefs, values, behavior, and goals in life. Therapy, spiritual direction, and support groups can all be very helpful in increasing your connection to self.

(continued)

(Self-Assessment 1 continued)

Connection to Others

It is not enough to just be self-aware and concerned with your own growth. People with high Spiritual Intelligence use this self-knowledge as a basis for understanding others better and for developing meaningful relationships. Of the five dimensions of work (physical, intellectual, emotional, volitional, and spiritual), "Connection to Others" is most related to the "Emotional" dimension because of its emphasis on the interpersonal aspects of the work environment. People who have a strong connection to others are very respectful of differences in values, beliefs, and cultural background and often curious to learn more. They are caring, compassionate, and able to forgive. They see the Divine in others and treat each person as unique and as a sacred being.

40–50 You have a strong connection to others and are probably good at team building and at creating a sense of community. People tend to trust you and you take that very seriously.

30–39 You are fairly good at relationship building with room for development. People are generally pretty comfortable with you and find you open and supportive. However, occasionally there may be things you say or do that are out of character. When this happens, take the time to reflect on your behavior and the underlying values, beliefs or attitudes that you may want to change.

20–29 You may often feel uncomfortable in your relationships at work. You may either find yourself feeling angry or resentful a lot, or intimidated or unappreciated. It can be easy to blame others for this, but it may be worth taking a look at your own behavior. Consider taking courses or workshops in interpersonal skills such as communication, assertiveness training, or conflict resolution. It is also helpful to ask someone you trust for feedback on your behavior.

0–19 You may feel fairly isolated from others, and find yourself preferring to work alone to avoid the uncomfortableness of difficult relationships. It is helpful to spend time reflecting on how you can take responsibility for improving the situation. Interpersonal skills workshops, such as those mentioned above, may be helpful. You might also consider hiring a professional coach to help you improve your relationships.

Connection to the Transcendent

Perhaps the major element that distinguishes Spiritual Intelligence from other forms of human intelligence is its emphasis on the connection to something greater than ourselves—what people may refer to as God, the Universe, the Divine, the Transcendent, or similar terms. Of the five dimensions of work (physical, intellectual, emotional, volitional, and spiritual), "Connection to the Transcendent" is most related to the "Spiritual" dimension because of its emphasis on the sacredness of human beings and all life. People who are high in "Connection to the Transcendent" have a belief in something greater than themselves, and find themselves guided and led by the Transcendent. They tend to have a clear sense of their greater purpose in life and are concerned with moral issues such as justice and respect.

40–50 You have a strong connection to the Transcendent and find yourself guided by a greater wisdom. You see your work as part of a much larger plan that contributes to the human race and the good of the planet. Because of your vision and your spiritual connection, others turn to you for leadership and inspiration.

30–39 You value your connection to the Transcendent, but it may not be a part of your daily awareness. You have a desire to deepen this relationship but may either think you don't have the time to do this, or it may be that you don't know how. It may be helpful to explore the spiritual traditions of your childhood, or to read some of the inspiring books on the relationship to the Transcendent, such as "How to Know God," by Deepak Chopra.

20–29 You may feel somewhat disconnected from the spiritual dimension of your life, although you turn to your Higher Self or Higher Power on occasion when there are difficult situations at work. You are probably not that interested in larger issues of justice, respect, or morality at work, but may find yourself getting upset if you feel that a personal injustice has been done to you, or someone has shown you a lack of respect. It may be helpful to focus on some basic principles such as The Golden Rule (see Chapter 2) or the concept of Unity.

0–19 A connection to the Transcendent is not a big part of your life, and you may feel a lack of inspiration or sense of purpose about your work. It's possible that you may be dealing with basic survival issues and cannot focus on the bigger picture at this time. If you wish to enhance this part of your Spiritual Intelligence, you must develop the "Volitional" dimension of work—i.e., the will to change for the better. To improve your connection to the Transcendent, you will need to make a commitment to a spiritual practice such as prayer, meditation, journaling, or spending time in nature. As part of your practice, ask the Transcendent for guidance on how to improve your connection. Make note of your reactions to your scores and list one or two areas you would like to develop further.

_____

_____

_____

Guidelines for Leading from a Spiritual Perspective

Following are five spiritual principles that have been useful to many leaders in their personal and professional development.

Know Thyself

All spiritual growth processes incorporate the principle of self-awareness. That is why we included the self-assessment on spiritual intelligence at work, and here are some other ways to know thyself. Leading provides a great opportunity to become more self-aware. Examine why you respond to situations the way you do. Take a moment in the morning to reflect on the kind of leader you would like to be today. At the end of the day, take quiet time to assess how well you did, and to what extent you were able to live in alignment with your most deeply held core values. It is also helpful to take personal and leadership assessment tools, such as the one in this appendix and the Myers-Briggs Type Indicator. You might also consider taking the *Spiritual Intelligence Assessment* developed by Cindy Wigglesworth at Deep Change.

Act with Authenticity and Congruency

Followers learn a lot more from who we are and how we behave than from what we say. Authenticity means being oneself, being fully congruent, and not playing a role. Many managers really get into the role of "leader," and they see managing as a place to assert their superiority and control. They would never want employees to see the more human, softer parts of them. Yet we are finding that managers who are more authentic, humble, and congruent tend to be more effective.[13]

It is a real challenge to be authentic and congruent in the workplace. Most people feel that if they are truly themselves and if they say what they are really thinking, it will be the end of their careers. But I believe that if we don't do this, we sell a little bit of our souls every time we are inauthentic, and that saps our creative energy and our emotional intelligence. It also reduces our sense of commitment to the work we do, and we cannot perform at our highest level. Experiment with greater authenticity and with showing more of your humanness. You will be surprised at how positively people will respond.

It is also important to create a climate in which employees are encouraged to behave authentically and congruently. This means that they should be comfortable expressing feelings as well as thoughts and ideas. Contrary to popular opinion, humility accompanied by a strong will does create an enduring organization, and is a much more powerful tool for success than a strong ego.

Respect and Honor the Beliefs of Others

It can be very risky and maybe even inappropriate to talk about your own spirituality in the workplace. Yet if spirituality is a guiding force in your life and your leading, and if you follow the guideline of authenticity and congruency, you cannot hide that part of yourself. It is a fine line to walk.

What seems to work best is to build a climate of trust and openness first, and to model an acceptance of opinions and ideas that are different from yours. Then, if an appropriate opportunity comes up in which you can mention something about your spiritual beliefs, you should emphasize that they are yours alone. Explain that people have different beliefs and that you respect those differences. It is extremely important that employees do not feel that you are imposing your belief system (spiritual, religious, or otherwise) on them. At the same time, it is worthwhile to do anything that you can do to nurture spiritual and ethical development in your employees in a way that allows them to explore their own deepest values and beliefs.

Be as Trusting as You Can Be

This guideline operates on many levels. On the personal level, this guideline of "being as trusting as you can be" applies to trusting oneself, one's inner voice, or one's source of spiritual guidance. This means trusting that there is a Higher Power in your life and that if you ask you will receive guidance on important issues. It also operates on the interpersonal, team, and organizational level. If you truly learn to see yourself as trustworthy, and believe that it is our essential nature as humans to be trustworthy, then you will naturally feel trusting of colleagues and subordinates. And you will also feel more trusting that the processes and events that are happening have a higher purpose to them if you look for it and amplify it.

WORK Application

A-1. Give an example of spirituality in the place where you work or have worked.

A-2. Have you or anyone you know struggled with spiritual journey and what this means for work? Explain.

Maintain a Spiritual Practice

In a research study on people who integrate their spirituality and their work, the most frequently mentioned spiritual practice is spending time in nature. Examples of other practices are meditation, prayer, reading inspirational literature, hatha yoga, shamanistic practices, writing in a journal, and walking a labyrinth. People reported that it is very important for them to consistently commit to whatever individual spiritual practice they have chosen. The regular involvement in a chosen practice appears to be the best way to deepen one's spirituality.[14]

When leaders faithfully commit to a particular spiritual practice they are calmer, more creative, more in tune with employees and customers, and more compassionate.[15]

Resources on the Web

- *Center of Business as an Agent of World Benefit (BAWB)* at Case Western Reserve's Wetherhead School of Management. http://worldbenefit.case.edu.

- *Spiritual Intelligence Assessment* developed by Cindy Wigglesworth at Deep Change, www.deepchange.com. Note: The instrument is free if it is used as a part of a research project.

- *Tyson Center for Faith and Spirituality in the Workplace*, Sam M. Walton College of Business, University of Arkansas. http://tfsw.uark.edu. This Web site has research papers, dissertations, podcasts, videos, and many other resources for those interested in the integration of faith and spirituality in the workplace.

Appendix Summary

There is a growing trend to talk more openly about spirituality and to want to integrate spiritual principles into all aspects of life—relationships, community, and work. This appendix has presented some resources for leaders who are interested in more fully integrating their spirituality and their leadership. A newly emerging field expands beyond just the focus on spirituality in the workplace. It goes by such names as Faith at Work, Spiritual Capitalism, Compassionate Capitalism, and Conscious Capitalism. Leading-edge thinkers are now exploring ideas about spiritual and humanistic values applied to economic and political systems.

Living more congruently with deeply held spiritual principles is never easy, but it is extremely rewarding and meaningful. I hope that some of the resources provided here will help to make the journey a little easier.

Review Questions

1. Spirituality is about learning to be more caring and compassionate in the workplace. Should we be more caring and compassionate with others at work? Why or why not?

2. Spirituality is about integrity, being true to oneself, and telling the truth to others in the workplace. Should we be honest with others at work? Why or why not?

3. Is knowing oneself important to leading from a spiritual perspective? Why or why not?

4. Should leaders let followers see the more human, softer parts of them (truly be themselves)? What effect would this have on productivity?

Critical Thinking Questions

The following critical-thinking questions can be used for class discussion and/or as written assignments to develop communication skills. Be sure to give complete explanations for all questions.

1. There is no single accepted definition of spirituality in the workplace. What is your definition?

2. Are managers who have a spiritual practice more effective leaders than those who do not?

3. Do you have a spiritual practice? If yes, what is it?

4. If our capitalistic system were based on spiritual principles, what would it look like? How would business and government be different?

Glossary

A

achievement motivation theory attempts to explain and predict behavior and performance based on a person's need for achievement, power, and affiliation

acquired needs theory proposes that people are motivated by their need for achievement, power, and affiliation

adaptive culture represents a leadership belief in active monitoring of the external environment for emerging opportunities and threats

adjustment personality dimension traits related to emotional stability

agreeableness personality dimension traits related to getting along with people

alienated follower someone who is low on involvement yet is high on critical thinking

arbitrator a neutral third party who makes a binding decision to resolve a conflict

attitudes positive or negative feelings about people, things, and issues

attribution theory used to explain the process managers go through in determining the reasons for effective or ineffective performance and deciding what to do about it

B

BCF model describes a conflict in terms of behavior, consequences, and feelings

behavior individual behavior that is discretionary, not directly or explicitly recognized by the formal reward system, and that in the aggregate promotes the effective functioning of the organization

behavioral leadership theories attempt to explain distinctive styles used by effective leaders, or to define the nature of their work

big five model of personality categorizes traits into dimensions of surgency, agreeableness, adjustment, conscientiousness, and openness to experience

bureaucratic culture represents a leadership that values order, stability, status, and efficiency

C

coaching the process of giving motivational feedback to maintain and improve performance

coaching feedback based on a good, supportive relationship; it is specific and descriptive; and it is not judgmental criticism

coercive power involves punishment and withholding of rewards to influence compliance

collectivism the state of mind wherein the values and goals of the group—whether extended family, ethnic group, or company—are primary

communication the process of conveying information and meaning

competitive culture represents a leadership that encourages and values a highly competitive work environment

conflict exists whenever people are in disagreement and opposition

conformist follower someone who is high on involvement but low on critical thinking

connection power based on the user's relationships with influential people

conscientiousness personality dimension traits related to achievement

content motivation theories focus on explaining and predicting behavior based on people's needs

contingency leadership model style is task- or relationship-oriented, and if the situation (leader–member relationship, task structure, and position power) matches the leader's style to maximize performance

contingency leadership theories attempt to explain the appropriate leadership style based on the leader, followers, and situation

cooperative culture represents a leadership belief in strong, mutually reinforcing exchanges and linkages between employees and departments

core competence a capability that allows an organization to perform extremely well in comparison to competitors

crisis a low-probability, high-impact event that threatens the viability of the organization and is characterized by ambiguity of cause, effect, and means of resolution, as well as by a belief that decisions must be made swiftly

cross-functional team is made up of members from different functional departments of an organization who are brought together to perform unique tasks to create new and nonroutine products or services

culture the aggregate of beliefs, norms, attitudes, values, assumptions, and ways of doing things that is shared by members of an organization and taught to new members

D

decisional leadership roles entrepreneur, disturbance-handler, resource-allocator and negotiator

decision-making skills are based on the ability to conceptualize situations and select alternatives to solve problems and take advantage of opportunities.

delegation model (1) explain the need for delegating and the reasons for selecting the employee; (2) set objectives that define responsibility, level of authority, and deadline; (3) develop a plan; and (4) establish control checkpoints and hold employees accountable

delegation the process of assigning responsibility and authority for accomplishing objectives

demographic diversity any characteristic that serves as a basis for social categorization and self-identification

descriptive leadership models identify contingency variables and leadership styles without specifying which style to use in a given situation

discontinuous change occurs when anticipated or expected changes bear no resemblance to the present or the past

distributed leadership multiple leaders take complementary leadership roles in rotation within the same self-managed team, according to their area of expertise or interest

diversity the inclusion of all groups at all levels in an organization

dyad the individualized relationship between a leader and each follower in a work unit

dyadic theory an approach to leadership that attempts to explain why leaders vary their behavior with different followers

E

equity theory proposes that people are motivated when their perceived inputs equal outputs

ethics the standards of right and wrong that influence behavior

ethnocentrism the belief that one's own group or subculture is naturally superior to other groups and cultures

evidence-based management (EBM) means that decisions and organizational practices are based on the best available scientific evidence

executive intuition instinctive ability to respond to problems without the benefit of concrete facts and information.

expectancy theory proposes that people are motivated when they believe they can accomplish the task, they will get the reward, and the rewards for doing the task are worth the effort

expert power based on the user's skill and knowledge

F

feedback the process of verifying messages and determining if objectives are being met

femininity describes a culture that emphasizes developing and nurturing personal relationships and a high quality of life

follower a person who is being influenced by a leader

followership the behavior of followers that results from the leader–follower influence relationship

functional team a group of employees belonging to the same functional department, such as marketing, R&D, production, human resources, or information systems, who have a common objective

G

giving praise model (1) Tell the employee exactly what was done correctly. (2) Tell the employee why the behavior is important. (3) Stop for a moment of silence. (4) Encourage repeat performance

glass ceiling an invisible barrier that separates women and minorities from top leadership positions

goal-setting theory proposes that specific, difficult goals motivate people

group is a collection of individuals who interact primarily to share information and to make decisions that enable each member to perform within his or her area of responsibility

groupthink when members of a cohesive group tend to agree on a decision not on the basis of its merit but because they are less willing to risk rejection for questioning a majority viewpoint or presenting a dissenting opinion

H

hierarchy of needs theory proposes that people are motivated through five levels of needs—physiological, safety, belongingness, esteem, and self-actualization

high-power-distance culture leaders and followers rarely interact as equals

high-uncertainty-avoidance culture not tolerating risk, avoiding the unknown, and being comfortable when the future is relatively predictable and certain

I

impressions management a follower's effort to project a favorable image in order to gain an immediate benefit or improve long-term relationship with the leader

individualism a psychological state in which people see themselves first as individuals and believe their own interest and values are primary

influencing the process of a leader communicating ideas, gaining acceptance of them, and motivating followers to support and implement the ideas through change

information power based on the user's data desired by others

informational leadership roles monitor, disseminator, and spokesperson

ingratiation the effort to appear supportive, appreciative, and respectful

in-group includes followers with strong social ties to their leader in a supportive relationship characterized by high mutual trust, respect, loyalty, and influence

initiating conflict resolution model (1) plan a BCF statement that maintains ownership of the problem; (2) present your BCF statement and agree on the conflict; (3) ask for, and/or give, alternative conflict resolutions; and (4) make an agreement for change

integrative leadership theories attempt to combine the trait, behavioral, and contingency theories to explain successful, influencing leader–follower relationships

interpersonal leadership roles figurehead, leader, and liaison

interpersonal skills involve the ability to understand, communicate, and work well with individuals and groups through developing effective relationships

J

job instructional training (1) trainee receives preparation; (2) trainer presents the task; (3) trainee performs the task; and (4) trainer follows up

L

leader motive profile (LMP) includes a high need for power, which is socialized; that is, greater than the need for affiliation and with a moderate need for achievement

leader motive profile theory attempts to explain and predict leadership success based on a person's need for achievement, power, and affiliation

leader–member exchange (LMX) the quality of the exchange relationship between an employee and his or her superior

leadership the influencing process of leaders and followers to achieve organizational objectives through change

leadership continuum model determines which one of seven styles to select, based on the use of boss-centered versus subordinate-centered leadership, to meet the situation (boss, subordinates, situation/time) in order to maximize performance

leadership grid   identifies five leadership styles: 1,1 impoverished; 9,1 authority compliance; 1,9 country club; 5,5 middle of the road; and 9,9 team leader

leadership model   an example for emulation or use in a given situation

leadership paradigm   a shared mindset that represents a fundamental way of thinking about, perceiving, studying, researching, and understanding leadership

leadership style   the combination of traits, skills, and behaviors leaders use as they interact with followers

leadership theory   an explanation of some aspect of leadership; theories have practical value because they are used to better understand, predict, and control successful leadership

leadership theory classifications   trait, behavioral, contingency, and integrative

leadership trait theories   attempt to explain distinctive characteristics accounting for leadership effectiveness

learning anxiety   the prospect of learning something new in itself

learning organization   one that is skilled at creating, acquiring, and transferring knowledge, and at modifying behavior to reflect new knowledge and insights

legitimate power   based on the user's position power, given by the organization

levels of analysis of leadership theory   individual, group, and organizational

locus of control   is on a continuum between an external and internal belief over who has control of a person's destiny

long-term orientation   future-oriented view of life and thus are thrifty (saving for the future) and persistent in achieving goals

low-power-distance culture   leaders and their members interact on several levels as equals

low-uncertainty-avoidance culture   being comfortable with and accepting of the unknown, and tolerating risk and unpredictability

M

management to the leadership theory paradigm   a shift from the older autocratic management style to the newer participative leadership style of management

managerial role categories   interpersonal, informational, and decisional

masculinity   describes a culture that emphasizes assertiveness and a competitive drive for money and material objects

mediator   a neutral third party who helps resolve a conflict

mentoring   a form of coaching in which a more-experienced manager helps a less-experienced protégé

message-receiving process   listening, analyzing, and checking understanding

mission statement   enduring statement of purpose that distinguishes one organization from other similar enterprises

moral justification   the process of reinterpreting immoral behavior in terms of a higher purpose

motivation   anything that affects behavior in pursuing a certain outcome

motivation process   people go from need to motive to behavior to consequence to satisfaction or dissatisfaction

N

negotiating   a process in which two or more parties are in conflict and attempt to come to an agreement

networking   a process in which two or more parties are in conflict and attempt to come to an agreement

normative leadership model   a time-driven and developmental-driven decision tree that enables the user to select one of five leadership styles (decide, consult individually, consult group, facilitate, and delegate) appropriate for the situation (seven questions/variables) to maximize decisions

O

ohio state university leadership model   identifies four leadership styles: low structure and high consideration, high structure and high consideration, low structure and low consideration, and high structure and low consideration

ombudsperson   a single person entrusted with the responsibility of acting as the organization's conscience

one-minute self-sell   an opening statement used in networking that quickly summarizes your history and career plan and asks a question

openness-to-experience personality dimension traits related to being willing to change and try new things

oral message-sending process (1) develop rapport; (2) state your communication objective; (3) transmit your message; (4) check the receiver's understanding; and (5) get a commitment and follow up

organizational change an alteration in an organization's alignment with its external environment

organizational citizenship an alteration in an organization's alignment with its external environment

organizational identity members' consensual understanding of "who we are as an organization" that emerges from that which is central, distinctive, and enduring to the organization as a whole

organizational knowledge the tacit and explicit knowledge that individuals possess about products, services, systems, and processes

out-group includes followers with few or no social ties to their leader, in a strictly task-centered relationship characterized by low exchange and top-down influence

P

paraphrasing the process of having the receiver restate the message in his or her own words

passive follower someone who is neither high on critical thinking nor involvement

path–goal leadership model selects the leadership style (directive, supportive, participative, or achievement-oriented) appropriate to the situation (subordinate and environment) to maximize both performance and job satisfaction

performance formula explains performance as a function of ability, motivation, and resources

personal meaning the degree to which people's lives make emotional sense and to which the demands confronted by them are perceived as being worthy of energy and commitment

personality a combination of traits that classifies an individual's behavior

personality profiles identify individual stronger and weaker traits

personalized charismatic leader (PCL) one who possesses a dominant, Machiavellian, and narcissistic personality

pragmatic follower exhibits a little of all four styles—depending on which style fits the prevailing situation

prescriptive leadership models tell the user exactly which style to use in a given situation

process motivation theories focus on understanding how people choose behavior to fulfill their needs

pygmalion effect proposes that leaders' attitudes toward and expectations of followers, and their treatment of them, explain and predict followers' behavior and performance

R

reciprocity involves creating obligations and developing alliances, and using them to accomplish objectives

referent power based on the user's personal relationship with others

reinforcement theory proposes that through the consequences for behavior, people will be motivated to behave in predetermined ways

reward power based on the user's ability to influence others with something of value to them

S

self-awareness relates to being conscious of your emotions and how they affect your personal and professional life

self-concept the positive or negative attitudes people have about themselves

self-efficacy a person's beliefs in his or her capabilities to produce at a certain level of performance

self-managed team champion an advocate of the self-managed team concept whose responsibility is to help the team obtain necessary resources, gain political support from top management and other stakeholders of the organization, and defend it from enemy attacks

self-managed team facilitator the external leader of a self-managed team, whose job is to create optimal working conditions so team members take on responsibilities to work productively and solve complex problems on their own

self-managed teams (SMTs) relatively autonomous teams whose members share or rotate leadership responsibilities and hold themselves mutually responsible for a set of performance goals assigned by higher management

self-promotion   the effort to appear competent and dependable

servant leadership   leadership that transcends self-interest to serve the needs of others, by helping them grow professionally and personally

short-term orientation   values that express a concern for maintaining personal happiness and living in the present

social capital   the set of resources that inheres in the structure of relations between members of the group, which helps them get ahead

social loafing   the conscious or unconscious tendency by some team members to shirk responsibilities by withholding effort toward group goals when they are not individually accountable for their work

socialized charismatic leader (SCL)   one who possesses an egalitarian, self-transcendent, and empowering personality

stakeholder approach to ethics   creates a win-win situation for relevant parties affected by the decision

stewardship   an employee-focused form of leadership that empowers followers to make decisions and have control over their jobs

strategic leadership   a person's ability to anticipate, envision, maintain flexibility, think strategically, and work with others to initiate changes that will create a viable future for the organization

strategic management   the set of decisions and actions used to formulate and implement specific strategies that will achieve a competitively superior fit between the organization and its environment, so as to achieve organizational goals

strategic vision   an ambitious view of the future that everyone in the organization can believe in and that is not readily attainable, yet offers a future that is better in important ways than what now exists

strategy   an integrated, overarching plan of how an organization will achieve its objectives

substitutes for leadership   include characteristics of the subordinate, task, and organization that replace the need for a leader or neutralize the leader's behavior

surgency personality dimension   leadership and extraversion traits

survival anxiety   the feeling that unless an organization makes a change, it is going to be out of business or fail to achieve some important goals

T

360-degree feedback   a formal evaluation process based on receiving performance evaluations from many people

team   a unit of interdependent individuals with complementary skills who are committed to a common purpose and set of performance goals and to common expectations, for which they hold themselves accountable

team cohesion   the extent to which team members band together and remain committed to achieving team goals

team creativity   the creation of a valuable, useful, and novel product, service, idea, procedure, or process carried out via discovery rather than a predetermined step-by-step procedure, by individuals working together in a complex social system

team effectiveness   has three components: (1) task performance—the degree to which the team's output (product or service) meets the needs and expectations of those who use it; (2) group process—the degree to which members interact or relate in ways that allow the team to work increasingly well together over time; and (3) individual satisfaction—the degree to which the group experience, on balance, is more satisfying than frustrating to team members

team learning   the collective acquisition, combination, creation, and sharing of knowledge

team norms   acceptable standards of behavior that are shared by team members

team-member exchange (TMX)   a team member's social exchanges with peers in terms of the mutual exchange of ideas, support, camaraderie, and feedback

teamwork   an understanding and commitment to group goals on the part of all team members

technical skills   involve the ability to use methods and techniques to perform a task

theory X and theory Y attempt to explain and predict leadership behavior and performance based on the leader's attitude about followers

traits distinguishing personal characteristics

transactional leadership seeks to maintain stability within an organization through regular economic and social exchanges that achieve specific goals for both the leaders and their followers

two-factor theory proposes that people are motivated by motivators rather than maintenance factors

V

value the ratio of benefits received to the cost incurred by the customer

virtual team one whose members are geographically distributed, requiring them to work together through electronic means with minimal face-to face interaction

vision the ability to imagine different and better conditions and the ways to achieve them

W

whistle-blowing employee disclosure of illegal or unethical practices on the part of the organization

writing objectives model (1) To + (2) action verb + (3) singular, specific, and measurable result to be achieved + (4) target date

Endnotes

Chapter 1

1. Groupon Web site (www.groupon.com), retrieved April 1, 2011.
2. M. Hickins, "Groupon Review Hits $760 Million, CEP Memo Shows," *Wall Street Journal* (February 26-27, 2011): B3.
3. Wikipedia (www.wikipedia.com) and M. F. Coburn, "On Groupon, and Its Founder, Andrew Mason," *Chicago Mag.com*, retrieved April 1, 2011.
4. M. F. Coburn, "On Groupon, and Its Founder, Andrew Mason," *Chicago Mag.com*, retrieved April 1, 2011.
5. B. Weiss, "Group's $6 Billion Gambler," *Wall Street Journal* (December 18-19, 2010): A15.
6. R. W. Stackman and K. Devine, "Leadership and Emotional-Rational Coherence: A Start? *Academy of Management Perspectives* 25(1) (2011): 42–44.
7. R. S. Rubin and E. C. Dierdorff, "On the Road to Abilene: Time to Manage Agreement About MBA Curricular Relevance," *Academy of Management Learning & Education* 10(1) (2011): 148–161.
8. D. S. DeRue, S. B. Sitkin, and J. M. Podolny, "Call for Papers—Teaching Leadership." *Academy of Management Journal* 53(4) (2010): 922–923.
9. E. Morrison, "From the Editors." *Academy of Management Journal* 53(5) (2010): 932–936.
10. K. Y. Ng, L. V. Dyne, and S. Ang, "From Experience to Experiential Learning: Cultural Intelligence as a Learning Capability for Global Leader Development," *Academy of Management Learning & Education* 8(1) (2009): 511–526.
11. C. Rose, "Charlie Rose Talks to Mike Duke," *BusinessWeek* (December 6-2, 2010): 30.
12. D. S. DeRue, S. B. Sitkin, and J. M. Podolny, "Call for Papers—Teaching Leadership." *Academy of Management Learning & Education* 9(1) (2010): 158–159.
13. Staff, "Preserve Your Health Like Your Wealth," *Wall Street Journal* (April 15, 2009): D5–D6.
14. The Atlantic, "The CEO Conundrum," *BusinessWeek* (June 15, 2009): 12.
15. The Atlantic, "The CEO Conundrum," *BusinessWeek* (June 15, 2009): 12.
16. D. Brady, "Speed Dial Warren Bennis," *BusinessWeek* (September 27-October 2, 2010): 22.
17. The Atlantic, "The CEO Conundrum," *BusinessWeek* (June 15, 2009): 12.
18. J. S. Lublin, "Some CEOs Face Big Repair Jobs in 2011," *Wall Street Journal* (January 4, 2011): B6. Online Poll, "Who has the Toughest Turnaround Challenge? *Fortune* (March 21, 2011): 10.
19. D. S. DeRue, S. B. Sitkin, and J. M. Podolny, "Call for Papers—Teaching Leadership." *Academy of Management Journal* 53(4) (2010): 922–923.
20. J. D. Hoover, R. C. Giambatista, R. L. Sorenson, W. H. Bommer, "Assessing the Effectiveness of Whole Person Learning Pedagogy in Skill Acquisition," *Academy of Management Learning & Education* 9(2) (2010): 192–203.
21. Groupon Web site (www.groupon.com), retrieved April 1, 2011
22. B. Weiss, "Group's $6 Billion Gambler," *Wall Street Journal* (December 18-19, 2010): A15.
23. C. Steiner, "The Next Web Phenom," *Forbes* (August 30, 2010): 58–62.
24. E. Holmes, "Small Businesses Get Savvy," *Wall Street Journal* (March 24, 2011): B1, B4.
25. G. Williams, "Comic Belief: Is Leadership Really a Crock?" *Entrepreneur* (April 2003): 28.
26. D. S. DeRue and S. J. Ashford, "Who Will Lead and Who Will Follow? Social Process of Leadership Identity Construction in Organizations," *Academy of Management Review* 35(4) (2010): 627–647.
27. J. R. Knapp, "Book Review," *Academy of Management Review* 33(3) (2008): 776–777.
28. D. S. DeRue and S. J. Ashford, "Who Will Lead and Who Will Follow? Social Process of Leadership Identity Construction in Organizations," *Academy of Management Review* 35(4) (2010): 627–647.
29. D. S. DeRue and S. J. Ashford, "Who Will Lead and Who Will Follow? Social Process of Leadership Identity Construction in Organizations," *Academy of Management Review* 35(4) (2010): 627–647.
30. J. R. Knapp, "Book Review," *Academy of Management Review* 33(3) (2008): 776–777.
31. J. Immelt, GE Annual Shareowners Meeting, April 26, 2006, http://www.ge.com/pdf/investors/events/068/ge_annualshareownersmeeting_042606_en.pdf.
32. B. M. Galvin, P. Balkudi, and D. A. Waldman, "Spreading the Word: The Role of Surrogates in Charismatic Leadership Processes." *Academy of Management Review* 35(3) (2010): 477–494.
33. D. Skube, "The Interpersonal Edge." *Costco Connection* (January 2011): 67.
34. K. W. Mossholder, H. A. Richardson, and R. P. Settoon, "Human Resource Systems and Helping in Organizations: A Relational Perspective." *Academy of Management Review* 36(1) (2011): 33–52.
35. J. R. Knapp, "Book Review," *Academy of Management Review* 33(3) (2010): 776–777.
36. M. Clark, "Book Review," *Academy of Management Perspectives* 23(3) (2009): 103–105.
37. K. Y. Ng, L. V. Dyne, and S. Ang, "From Experience to Experiential Learning: Cultural Intelligence as a Learning Capability for Global Leader Development," *Academy of Management Learning & Education* 8(1) (2009): 511–526.

38. B. Stone and D. MacMillan, "Are Four Words Worth $25 Billion?" *BusinessWeek* (March 21-March 27, 2011): 70–75.

39. R. Hooiberg and N. Lane, "Using Multisource Feedback Coaching Effectively in Executive Education," *Academy of Management Learning & Education* 7(1) (2008): 108–123.

40. K. Y. Ng, L. V. Dyne, and S. Ang, "From Experience to Experiential Learning: Cultural Intelligence as a Learning Capability for Global Leader Development," *Academy of Management Learning & Education* 8(1) (2009): 511–526.

41. D. S. DeRue, S. B. Sitkin, and J. M. Podolny, "Call for Papers—Teaching Leadership." *Academy of Management Journal* 53(4) (2010): 922–923.

42. P. Navarro, "The MBA Core Curricula of Top-Ranked U.S. Business Schools: A Study in Failure?" *Academy of Management Learning & Education* 8(1) (2009): 511–526.

43. L. Dragoni, P. E. Tesluk, J. E. A. Russell, and I. S. Oh, "Understanding Managerial Development: Integrating Developmental Assignments, Learning Orientation, and Access to Developmental Opportunities, in Predicting Managerial Competencies." *Academy of Management Journal* 52(4) (2009): 731–743.

44. R. E. Ployhart, J. A. Weekley, and J. Ramsey, "The Consequences of Human Resource Stocks and Flows: A Longitudinal Examination of Unit Service Orientation and Unit Effectiveness." *Academy of Management Journal* 52(5) (2009): 996–1015.

45. P. Navarro, "The MBA Core Curricula of Top-Ranked U.S. Business Schools: A Study in Failure?" *Academy of Management Learning & Education* 8(1) (2009): 511–526.

46. B. Weiss, "Group's $6 Billion Gambler," *Wall Street Journal* (December 18-19, 2010):.A15.

47. B. Stone and D. MacMillan, "Are Four Words Worth $25 Billion?" *BusinessWeek* (March 21-March 27, 2011): 70–75.

48. R. S. Rubin and E. C. Dierdorff, "On the Road to Abilene: Time to Manage Agreement About MBA Curricular Relevance," *Academy of Management Perspectives* 25(1) (2011): 148–161.

49. V. Lombardi, "Quote." *SBANC Newsletter* (May 19, 2009): 1.

50. R. S. Rubin and E. C. Dierdorff, "How Relevant is the MBA? Assessing the Alignment of Required Curricula and Required Managerial Competencies." *Academy of Management Learning & Education* 8(2) (2009): 208–224.

51. D. S. DeRue, S. B. Sitkin, and J. M. Podolny, "Call for Papers—Teaching Leadership." *Academy of Management Learning & Education* 9(1) (2010): 158–159.

52. J. D. Hoover, R. C. Giambatista, R. L. Sorenson, W. H. Bommer, "Assessing the Effectiveness of Whole Person Learning Pedagogy in Skill Acquisition." *Academy of Management Learning & Education* 9(2) (2010):. 192–203.

53. D. S. DeRue, S. B. Sitkin, and J. M. Podolny, "Call for Papers—Teaching Leadership." *Academy of Management Journal* 53(4) (2010): 922–923.

54. Stanford University, "Margin Note." *Fortune* (March 21, 2011): 64.

55. G. Sheffer, "GE Responds." *Fortune* (March 21, 2011): 17.

56. D. A. Waldman, P. A. Balthazard, and S. J. Peterson, "Leadership and Neuroscience: Can We Revolutionize the Way That Inspirational Leaders Are Identified and Developed? *Academy of Management Perspectives* 25(1) (2011): 60–74.

57. R. E. Ployhart, J.A. Weekley, and J. Ramsey, "The Consequences of Human Resource Stocks and Flows: A Longitudinal Examination of Unit Service Orientation and Unit Effectiveness." *Academy of Management Journal* 52(5) (2009): 996–1015.

58. L. Dragoni, P. E. Tesluk, J. E. A. Russell, and I. S. Oh, "Understanding Managerial Development: Integrating Developmental Assignments, Learning Orientation, and Access to Developmental Opportunities, in Predicting Managerial Competencies." *Academy of Management Journal* 52(4) (2009): 731–743.

59. R.W. Stackman and K. Devine, "Leadership and Emotional-Rational Coherence: A Start? *Academy of Management Perspectives* 25(1) (2011): 42–44.

60. J. D. Hoover, R. C. Giambatista, R. L. Sorenson, W. H. Bommer, "Assessing the Effectiveness of Whole Person Learning Pedagogy in Skill Acquisition." *Academy of Management Learning & Education* 9(2) (2010): 192–203.

61. J. C. Santora, "Quality Management and Manufacturing Performance: Does Success Depend on Firm Culture?" *Academy of Management Perspective* 23(2) (2009): 103–105.

62. R. B. Kaiser and R. B. Kaplan, "The Deeper Work of Executive Development: Outgrowing Sensitivities," *Academy of Management Learning & Education* 5(4) (2006):.463–483.

63. P. Navarro, "The MBA Core Curricula of Top-Ranked U.S. Business Schools: A Study in Failure?" *Academy of Management Learning & Education* 8(1) (2009): 511–526.

64. C. Verzat, J. Byrne, and A. Fayolle, "Tangling With Spaghetti: Pedagogical Lessons from Games," *Academy of Management Learning & Education* 8(3) (2009): 356–369.

65. R. B. Kaiser and R. B. Kaplan, "The Deeper Work of Executive Development: Outgrowing Sensitivities," *Academy of Management Learning & Education* 5(4) (2006): 463–483.

66. P. Navarro, "The MBA Core Curricula of Top-Ranked U.S. Business Schools: A Study in Failure?" *Academy of Management Learning & Education* 8(1) (2009): 511–526.

67. K. M. Bloomfield and R. A. Price, "So You Want to be a Billionaire," *Forbes* (August 30, 2010): 64–67.

68. R. W. Stackman and K. Devine, "Leadership and Emotional-Rational Coherence: A Start? *Academy of Management Perspectives* 25(1) (2011): 42–44.

69. G. A. Ballinger and K. W. Rockmann, "Chutes Versus Ladders: Anchoring Events and a Punctuated-Equilibrium Perspective on Social Exchange Relationships." *Academy of Management Review* 35(3) (2010): 373–391.

70. A. C. Cosper, "How to be Great," *Entrepreneur* (March 2010): 12.

71. M Hilton, "Skills for Work in the 21st Century: What Does the Research Tell Us?" *Academy of Management Perspective* 22(4) (2008): 63–78.

72. L. Dragoni, P. E. Tesluk, J. E. A. Russell, and I. Oh, "Understanding Managerial Development: Integrating Developmental Assignments, Learning Orientation, and Access to Developmental Opportunities in Predicting Managerial Competencies," *Academy of Management Journal* 52(4) (2009): 731–742.

73. C. Verzat, J. Byrne, and A. Fayolle, "Tangling With Spaghetti: Pedagogical Lessons from Games," *Academy of Management Learning & Education* 8(3) (2009): 356–369.

74. M. Clark, "Book Review." *Academy of Management Perspectives* 23(3) (2009): 103–105.

75. J. W. Rudolph, J. B. Morrison, J. S. Carroll, "The Dynamics of Action-Oriented Problem Solving: Linking Interpretation and Choice." *Academy of Management Review* 34(4) (2009): 733–756.

76. G. A. Van Kleef, A. C. Homan, B. Beersma, D. Van Knippenberg, and F. Damen, "Searing Sentiment or Cold Calculation? The Effects of Leader Emotional Displays on Team Performance Depend on Follower Epistemic Motivation," *Academy of Management Journal* 52(3) (2009): 562–580.

77. M. J. Mills, "High-Involvement Work Practices: Are They Really Worth It?" *Academy of Management Perspectives* 23(3) (2009): 93–95.

78. R. S. Rubin and E. C. Dierdorff, "How Relevant Is the MBA? Assessing the Alignment of Required Curricula and Required Managerial Competencies," *Academy of Management Learning & Education* 8(5) (2009): 208–224.

79. T. V. Mumford, M. A. Campion, and F. P. Morgeson, "The Leadership Skills Strataplex: Leadership Skill Requirements Across Organizational Levels." *Leadership Quarterly* 18(1) (2007): 154–166.

80. B. Weiss, "Group's $6 Billion Gambler," *Wall Street Journal* (December 18-19, 2010): A15.

81. Wikipedia (www.wikipedia.com) and M.F. Coburn, "On Groupon, and Its Founder, Andrew Mason," *Chicago Mag.com*, retrieved April 1, 2011.

82. D. C. Wyld, "What Matters More in Growth Companies: Leader or Idea? *Academy of Management Perspectives* 23(2) (2009): 95–96.

83. R. W. Stackman and K. Devine, "Leadership and Emotional-Rational Coherence: A Start? *Academy of Management Perspectives* 25(1) (2011): 42–44.

84. R. S. Rubin and E. C. Dierdorff, "How Relevant is the MBA? Assessing the Alignment of Required Curricula and Required Managerial Competencies." *Academy of Management Learning & Education* 8(2) (2009): 208–224.

85. L. Dragoni, P. E. Tesluk, J. E.A. Russell, and I. S. Oh, "Understanding Managerial Development: Integrating Developmental Assignments, Learning Orientation, and Access to Developmental Opportunities, in Predicting Managerial Competencies." *Academy of Management Journal* 52(4) (2009): 731–743.

86. H. Mintzberg, *The Nature of Managerial Work* (New York: Harper & Row, 1973).

87. The Atlantic, "The CEO Conundrum." *BusinessWeek* (June 15, 2009): 12

88. K. M. Bloomfield and R. A. Price, "So You Want to be a Billionaire." *Forbes* (August 30, 2010): 64–67.

89. J. Helyar and C. Hymowitz, "The Recession is Gone, and The CEO Could be Next." *BusinessWeek* (February 7-13, 2011): 24–26.

90. P. Navarro, "The MBA Core Curricula of Top-Ranked U.S. Business Schools: A Study in Failure?" *Academy of Management Learning & Education* 7(1) (2008): 108–123.

91. D. Brady, "Speed Dial Warren Bennis." *BusinessWeek* (September 27-October 2, 2010): 22.

92. E. Morrison, "From the Editors." *Academy of Management Journal* 53(5) (2010): 932–936.

93. A. Murray, "The End of Management," *Wall Street Journal* (August 21-22, 2010): W3.

94. E. Holmes, "Small Businesses Get Savvy," *Wall Street Journal* (March 24, 2011): B1, B4.

95. G. A. Ballinger and K.W. Rockmann, "Chutes Versus Ladders: Anchoring Events and a Punctuated-Equilibrium Perspective on Social Exchange Relationships." *Academy of Management Review* 35(3) (2010): 373–391

96. J. S. Lublin, "Coaching Urged for Women." *Wall Street Journal* (April 4, 2011): B8.

97. M. J. Canyan, "Executive Compensation and Incentives," *Academy of Management Perspectives* 20(1) (2006): 25–44.

98. M. Krantz and B. Hansen, "CEO Pay Soars While Worker's Pay Stalls," *USA Today* (April 1, 2011): B1–B2.

99. I. Filatotchev and D. Allcock, "Corporate Governance and Executive Remuneration: A Contingency Framework," *Academy of Management Perspectives* 24(1) (2010): 20–33.

100. D. S. DeRue and S. J. Ashford, "Who Will Lead and Who Will Follow? Social Process of Leadership Identity Construction in Organizations," *Academy of Management Review* 35(4) (2010): 627–647.

101. A. Murray, "The End of Management," *Wall Street Journal* (August 21-22, 2010): W3.

102. A. Murray, "The End of Management," *Wall Street Journal* (August 21-22, 2010): W3.

103. L. A. Burke and B. Rau, "The Research-Teaching Gap in Management," *Academy of Management Learning & Education* 9(1) (2010): 132–143.

104. R. Chia and R. Holt, "The Nature of Knowledge in Business Schools," *Academy of Management Learning & Education* 7(4) (2008): 471–486.

105. D. S. DeRue, S. B. Sitkin, and J. M. Podolny, "Call for Papers—Teaching Leadership." *Academy of Management Learning & Education* 9(1) (2010): 158–159.

106. G. B. Graen, "Educating New Management Specialists From an Evidence-Based Perspective: A Proposal," *Academy of Management Learning & Education* 8(2) (2009): 255–258.

107. R. W. Stackman and K. Devine, "Leadership and Emotional-Rational Coherence: A Start? *Academy of Management Perspectives* 25(1) (2011): 42–44.

108. T. Reay, W. Berta, and M. K. Kohn, "What's the Evidence of Evidence-Based Management?" *Academy of Management Perspectives* 23(4) (2009): 5–18.

109. AACSB, *AACSB Standards 2011 Update Report.* p. 72.

110. E. Salas, J. L. Wildman, and R. F. Piccolo, "Using Simulation-Based Training to Enhance Management Education," *Academy of Management Learning & Education* 8(4) (2009): 559–573.

111. C. Verzat, J. Byrne, and A. Fayolle, "Tangling With Spaghetti: Pedagogical Lessons from Games," *Academy of Management Learning & Education* 8(3) (2009): 356–369.

112. K. Y. Ng, L. V. Dyne, and S. Ang, "From Experience to Experiential Learning: Cultural Intelligence as a Learning Capability for Global Leader Development," *Academy of Management Learning & Education* 8(1) (2009): 511–526.

113. AACSB, *AACSB Standards 2011 Update Report.*

114. M. Sorcher and A. P. Goldstein, "A Behavior Modeling Approach in Training," *Personnel Administration* 35 (1972): 35–41.

115. D. S. DeRue, S. B. Sitkin, and J. M. Podolny, "Call for Papers—Teaching Leadership." *Academy of Management Learning & Education* 9(1) (2010): 158–159.

116. P. Newcomb, "Business Person of the Year," *Fortune* (December 6, 2010): 137.

117. J. Hempel and B. Kowitt, "Smartest People in Tech," *Fortune* (June 26, 2010): 82–83.

118. P. Newcomb, "Business Person of the Year," *Fortune* (December 6, 2010): 137.

119. "The Richest People in America," *Forbes* (October 11, 2010): 302.

120. "The World's Most Admired Companies," *Fortune* (March 21, 2011): 110.

121. "The 50 Most Innovative Companies," *BusinessWeek* (April 25, 2010): 38.

122. B. Stone and P. Burrows, "The Essence of Apple," *Business-Week* (January 24-30, 2011): 6–8.

123. Y. I. Kane and S. E. Ante, "Apple Profit Muscles Past IBM," *Wall Street Journal* (October 19, 2010): B1.

124. "America's Most Admired Companies," *Fortune* (March 17, 2008): 116–133.

125. J. Hempel and B. Kowitt, "Smartest People in Tech," *Fortune* (June 26, 2010): 82–83.

126. "When Good Bosses Go Bad," *Fortune* (September 27, 2010): 22.

127. Y. I. Kane and R. Adams, "Apple Opens a Door, Keeps Keys," *Wall Street Journal* (February 16, 2011): B1.

128. Y. I. Kane and E. Smith, "Apple Opens Locker for Songs," *Wall Street Journal* (June 7, 2011): B1, B9.

129. B. Stone and P. Burrows, "The Essence of Apple," *Business-Week* (January 24-30, 2011): 6–8.

130. P. Newcomb, "Business Person of the Year," *Fortune* (December 6, 2010): 137.

131. B. Stone and P. Burrows, "The Essence of Apple," *Business-Week* (January 24-30, 2011): 6–8.

132. B. Stone and P. Burrows, "The Essence of Apple," *Business-Week* (January 24-30, 2011): 6–8.

133. P. Elkind, "The Trouble with Steve Jobs," *Fortune* (March 17, 2008): 68–74.

134. J. Hempel and B. Kowitt, "Smartest People in Tech," *Fortune* (June 26, 2010): 82–83.

135. S. Weinberg and A. Efrati, "Tech Rivals Wage War of Words," *Wall Street Journal* (October 20, 2010): B6.

136. A. Vance, "Jobs: All Your Chips now Belong to Us," *BusinessWeek* (March 14-29, 2011): 37–38.

137. B. Stone and P. Burrows, "The Essence of Apple," *Business-Week* (January 24-30, 2011): 6–8.

138. G. A. Fowler, and N. Wingfield, "Apple's Showman Takes the Stage," *Wall Street Journal* (March 3, 2011): B1.

139. Y. I. Kane, "Apple's Jobs Calls Shots From Home," *Wall Street Journal* (February 11, 2011): B1.

140. Y. I. Kane and E. Smith, "Apple Opens Locker for Songs," *Wall Street Journal* (June 7, 2011): B1, B9.

141. Y. I. Kane, "Steve Job's Latest Project iSpace," *Wall Street Journal* (June 9, 2011): B7.

Chapter 2

1. Information taken from the DuPont Website May 11, 2011.

2. Staff, "The Fortune 500," *Fortune* (May 3, 2010): 48–49.

3. Staff, "Global 500," *Fortune* (July 26, 2010): 153, F7.

4. G. Colvin, "The World's Most Admired Companies,' *Fortune* (March 21, 2011): 109–111.

5. J. R. Knapp, "Book Review," *Academy of Management Review* 33(3) (2008): 776–777.

6. S. S. Wang, "Why So Many People Can't Make Decisions," *Wall Street Journal* (September 28, 2010): D1–D2.

7. E. Morrison, "From the Editors." *Academy of Management Journal* 53(5) (2010): 932–936.

8. E. Bernstein, "Do You Get an A in Personality?" *Wall Street Journal* (April 5, 2011): D1–D2.

9. E. Bernstein, "Do You Get an A in Personality?" *Wall Street Journal* (April 5, 2011): D1-D2

10. R. Hooiberg and N. Lane, "Using Multisource Feedback Coaching Effectively in Executive Education," *Academy of Management Learning & Education* 7(1) (2008): 108–123.

11. J. Z. Bergman, J. W. Westerman, J. P. Daly, "Narcissism in Management Education," *Academy of Management Learning & Education* 9(1) (2010): 119–131.

12. E. Bernstein, "Do You Get an A in Personality?" *Wall Street Journal* (April 5, 2011): D1–D2.

13. E. Bernstein, "Do You Get an A in Personality?" *Wall Street Journal* (April 5, 2011): D1–D2.

14. T. A. Judge, R. Ilies, J. E. Bono, and M. W. Gerhardt, "Personality and Leadership: A Qualitative and Quantitative Review," *Journal of Applied Psychology* 87(4) (2002): 765–768.

15. S. S. Wang, "Why So Many People Can't Make Decisions," *Wall Street Journal* (September 28, 2010): D1–D2.

16. M. Rosenwald, "The Origin of C-Suites," *BusinessWeek* (January 24–30, 2011): 116–117.

17. J. B. Kahnweiler, "Why Introverts Can Make the Best Leaders," *Forbes* (December 28, 2009): 8.

18. E. Kearney, D. Gebert, and S. C. Voelpel, "When and How Diversity Benefits Teams: The Importance of Team Members' Need for Cognition," *Academy of Management Journal* 52(3) (2009): 581–598.

19. M. Rosenwald, "The Origin of C-Suites," *BusinessWeek* (January 24–30, 2011): 116–117.

20. E. Bernstein, "Do You Get an A in Personality?" *Wall Street Journal* (April 5, 2011): D1–D2.

21. G. Colvin, "Why Talent is Over Rated," *Fortune* (October 27, 2008): 138–146.

22. E. Kearney, D. Gebert, and S. C. Voelpel, "When and How Diversity Benefits Teams: The Importance of Team Members' Need for Cognition," *Academy of Management Journal* 52(3) (2009): 581–598.

23. D. A. Waldman, P. A. Balthazard, and S.J. Peterson, "Leadership and Neuroscience: Can We Revolutionize the Way That Inspirational Leaders Are Identified and Developed? *Academy of Management Perspectives* 25(1) (2011): 60–74.

24. M. W. Morgan and M. M. Lombardo, *Off the Track: Why and How Successful Executives Get Derailed* (Greensboro, NC: Center for Creative Leadership, January 1988), Technical Report nos 21 & 34.

25. E. Bernstein, "Do You Get an A in Personality?" *Wall Street Journal* (April 5, 2011): D1–D2.

26. K. M. Hmieleski and R. A. Baron, "Entrepreneurs' Optimism and New Venture Performance: A Social Cognitive Perspective," *Academy of Management Journal* 52(3) (2009): 473–488.

27. M. Jokisaari and J. E. Nurmi, "Change in Newcomers' Supervisor Support and Socialization Outcomes After Organizational Entry," *Academy of Management Journal* 52(3) (2009): 527–544.

28. D. B. McNatt, "Negative Reputation and Biased Student Evaluations of Teaching: Longitudinal Results From a Naturally Occurring Experiment," *Academy of Management Learning & Education* 9(2) (2010): 225–242.

29. F. Walter, M. S. Cole, and R. H. Humphrey, "Emotional Intelligence: Sine Qua Non of Leadership or Folderol?" *Academy of Management Perspectives* 25(1) (2011): 45–59.

30. R. E. Boytzis and D. Goleman, *The Emotional Competence Inventory* (Boston: Hay Group, 2001).

31. G. A. Van Kleef, A. C. Homan, B. Beersma, D. Van Knippenberg, B. Van Knippenberg, and F. Damen," "Searing Sentiment or Cold Calculation? The Effects of Leader Emotional Displays on Team Performance Depend on Follower Epistemic Motivation," *Academy of Management Journal* 52(3) (2009): 562–580.

32. J. Z. Bergman, J. W. Westerman, J. P. Daly, "Narcissism in Management Education," *Academy of Management Learning & Education* 9(1) (2010): 119–131.

33. R. S. Dalal, H. Lam, H. M. Weiss, E. R. Welch, and C. L. Hulin, "A Within-Person Approach to Work Behavior and Performance: Concurrent and Lagged Citizenship-Counterproductivity Associations, and Dynamic Relationships with Affect and Overall Job Performance," *Academy of Management Journal* 52(5) (2011): 1051–1066.

34. R. E. Johnson and L. Q. Chang, "Commitment and Motivation at Work: The Relevance of Employee Identity and Regulatory Focus," *Academy of Management Review* 35(2) (2009): 226–245.

35. R. S. Rubin and E. C. Dierdorff, "On the Road to Abilene: Time to Manage Agreement About MBA Curricular Relevance," *Academy of Management Learning & Education* 10(1) (2011): 148–161.

36. G. Colvin, "Why Talent is Over Rated," *Fortune* (October 27, 28): 138–146.

37. D. B. Montgomery and C. A. Ramus, "Calibrating MBA Job Preferences for the 21st Century," *Academy of Management Learning & Education* 10(1) (2011): 9–26.

38. R. Karlgaard, "Scary Smart: The Next Trillion-Dollar Industry," *Forbes* (October 25, 2010): 26.

39. M. E. Egan and M. K. Ozanian, "The World's 100 Most Powerful Women," *Forbes* (October 25, 2010): 57–76.

40. J. Shambora and B. Kowitt, "50 Most Powerful Women," *Fortune* (October 18, 2010): 129–131.

41. P. Newcomb, "Businessperson of the Year," *Fortune* (December 6, 2010): 134–139.

42. Information taken from the DuPont Website May 11, 2011.

43. P. Newcomb, "Businessperson of the Year," *Fortune* (December 6, 2010): 134–139.

44. D. McClelland, *The Achieving Society* (New York: Van Nostrand Reinhold, 1961); and D. McClelland and D. H. Burnham, "Power Is the Great Motivator," *Harvard Business Review* (March/April 1978): 103.

45. D. C. McClelland and R. E. Boyatzis, "Leadership Motive Pattern and Long-Term Success in Management," *Journal of Applied Psychology* 6 (1982): 737–743.

46. D. C. McClelland, *Human Motivation* (Glenview, IL: Scott Foresman, 1985).

47. P. Newcomb, "Businessperson of the Year," *Fortune* (December 6, 2010): 134–139

48. S. S. Wang, "Why So Many People Can't Make Decisions," *Wall Street Journal* (September 28, 2010): D1–D2.

49. M. Jokisaari and J. E. Nurmi, "Change in Newcomers' Supervisor Support and Socialization Outcomes After Organizational Entry," *Academy of Management Journal* 52(3) (2009): 527–544.

50. R. E. Johnson and L. Q. Chang, "Commitment and Motivation at Work: The Relevance of Employee Identity and Regulatory Focus," *Academy of Management Review* 35(2) (2009): 226–245.

51. D. McGregor, *Leadership and Motivation* (Cambridge, MA: MIT Press, 1966).

52. Mind Tools Web site "Comparing Theory X and Theory Y," (www.mindtools.com), retrieved May 25, 2011.

53. Mind Tools Web site "Comparing Theory X and Theory Y," (www.mindtools.com), retrieved May 25, 2011.

54. J. S. Livingston, "Pygmalion in Management," in Harvard Business Review, *Harvard Business Review on Human Relations* (New York: Harper & Row, 1979).

55. R. E. Johnson and L. Q. Chang, "Commitment and Motivation at Work: The Relevance of Employee Identity and Regulatory Focus," *Academy of Management Review* 35(2) (2009): 226–245.

56. P. Newcomb, "Businessperson of the Year," *Fortune* (December 6, 2010): 134–139.

57. M. Jokisaari and J. E. Nurmi, "Change in Newcomers' Supervisor Support and Socialization Outcomes After Organizational Entry," *Academy of Management Journal* 52(3) (2009): 527–544.

58. R. Audi, "Objectivity Without Egoism: Toward Balance in Business Ethics," *Academy of Management Learning & Education* 8(2) (2009): 263–274.

59. AACSB, *AACSB Standards 2011 Update Report.* p. 72.

60. P. Navarro, "The MBA Core Curricula of Top-Ranked U.S. Business Schools: A Study in Failure?" *Academy of Management Learning & Education* 7(1) (2008): 108–123.

61. J. F. Veiga, "'Special Topic' Ethical Behavior in Management, Bringing Ethics into the Mainstream: An Introduction to the Special Topic," *Academy of Management Executive* 18(2) (2004): 37–38.

62. Y. Mishina, B. J. Dykes, E. S. Block, T. G. Pollock, "Why Good Firms Do Bad Things: The Effects of High Aspirations, High Expectations, and Prominence on the Incidence of Corporate Illegality," *Academy of Management Journal* 53(4) (2010): 701–722.

63. M. E. Graebner, "Caveat VEnditor: Trust Asymmetries in Acquisitions of Entrepreneurial Firms," *Academy of Management Journal* 52(3) (2009): 435–472.

64. D. W. Lehman and R. Ramanujam, "Selectivity in Organizational Rule Violations," *Academy of Management Review* 34 (4) (2009): 643–657.

65. B. E. Litzky, K. A. Eddleston, and D. L. Kidder, "The Good, the Bad, and the Misguided: How Managers Inadvertently Encourage Deviant Behaviors," *Academy of Management Perspectives* 20(1) (2006): 91–103.

66. D. B. Montgomery and C. A. Ramus, "Calibrating MBA Job Preferences for the 21st Century," *Academy of Management Learning & Education* 10(1) (2011): 9–26.

67. D. O. Neubaum, M. Pagell, J. A. Drexler, F. M. M. Ryan, and E. Larson, "Business Education and Its Relationship to Student Personal Moral Philosophies and Attitudes Toward Profits: An Empirical Response to Critics," *Academy of Management Learning & Education* 8(1) (2009): 9–24.

68. Information taken from the DuPont Website May 13, 2011.

69. V. Tonoyan, R. Strohmeyer, M. Habib, and M. Perlitz, "Corruption and Entrepreneurship: How Formal and Informal Institutions Shape Small Firm Behavior in Transition and Mature Market Economies," *Entrepreneurship Theory and Practice* 34(5) 2010: 803–831.

70. Y. Mishina, B. J. Dykes, E. S. Block, T. G. Pollock, "Why Good Firms Do Bad Things: The Effects of High Aspirations, High Expectations, and Prominence on the Incidence of Corporate Illegality," *Academy of Management Journal* 53(4) (2010): 701–722.

71. R. Audi, "Objectivity Without Egoism: Toward Balance in Business Ethics," *Academy of Management Learning & Education* 8(2) (2009): 263–274.

72. Bill & Melinda Gates Foundation Web site (www.gratesfoundation.org), retrieved May 27, 2011.

73. "The Richest People in America," *Forbes* (October 2010): 294.

74. B. Schlender, "Bill Gates: Life After Microsoft," *Fortune* (July 5, 2010): 94.

75. B. Schlender, "Bill Gates: Life After Microsoft," *Fortune* (July 5, 2010): 94.

76. "The World's 100 Most Powerful Women," *Forbes* (October 25, 2010): 74.

77. For more information on Zig Ziglar training go to his Web site (www.ziglar.com).

Chapter 3

1. Trader Joe's Web site (www.traderjoes.com), retrieved May 30, 2011.

2. B. Kowitt, "Inside Trader Joe's," *Fortune* (September 6, 2010): 86–96.

3. See note 2.

4. See note 2.

5. L. Dragoni, P. E. Tesluk, J. E. A. Russell, and I. S. Oh, "Understanding Managerial Development: Integrating Developmental Assignments, Learning Orientation, and Access to Developmental Opportunities, in Predicting Managerial Competencies." *Academy of Management Journal* 52(4) (2009): 731–743.

6. R. S. Rubin and E. C. Dierdorff, "On the Road to Abilene: Time to Manage Agreement About MBA Curricular Relevance," *Academy of Management Learning & Education* 10(1) (2011): 148–161.

7. A. Joshi and H. Roh, "The Role of Context in Work Team Diversity Research: A Meta-Analytic Review," *Academy of Management Journal* 52(3) (2010): 599–627.

8. See note 5.

9. R. Hooiberg and N. Lane, "Using Multisource Feedback Coaching Effectively in Executive Education," *Academy of Management Learning & Education* 7(1) (2008): 108–123.

10. E. Morrison, "From the Editors." *Academy of Management Journal* 53(5) (2010): 932–936.

11. D. S. DeRue, S. B. Sitkin, and J. M. Podolny, "Call for Papers—Teaching Leadership." *Academy of Management Journal* 53(4) (2010): 922–923.

12. S. Shellenbarger, "How to Keep a Resolution," *Wall Street Journal* (December 22, 2010): D1–D2.

13. K. Lewin, R. Lippitt, and R. K. White, "Patterns of Aggressive Behavior in Experimentally Created Social Climates," *Journal of Social Psychology* 10 (1939): 271–301.

14. R. E. Johnson, C. H. Chang, and L. Q. Yang, "Commitment and Motivation at Work: The Relevance of Employee Identity and Regulatory Focus," *Academy of Management Review* 35(2) (2009): 226–245.

15. R. Likert, *New Patterns of Management* (New York: McGraw-Hill, 1961).

16. R. M. Stogdill and A. E. Coons, eds., *Leader Behavior: Its Description and Measurement* (Columbus: Ohio State University Bureau of Business Research, 1957).

17. T. A. Judge and J. D. K. Mueller, "Happiness as a Social Value," *Academy of Management Perspectives* 25(1) (2011): 30–41.

18. P. G. Norhouse, *Leadership* 5e (Los Angeles, Sage, 2010).

19. See note 18.

20. R. Blake and J. Mouton, *The Managerial Grid* (Houston, TX: Gulf Publishing, 1964); R. Blake and J. Mouton, *The New Managerial Grid* (Houston, TX: Gulf Publishing, 1978); R. Blake and J. Mouton, *The Managerial Grid III: The Key to Leadership Excellence* (Houston, TX: Gulf Publishing, 1985); and R. Blake and A. A. McCanse, *Leadership Dilemmas—Grid Solutions* (Houston, TX: Gulf Publishing, 1991). "R. Blake and J. Mouton: The Managerial Grid," *Thinkers* (March 2002).

21. B. M. Fisher and J. E. Edwards, "Consideration and Initiating Structure and Their Relationship with Leader Effectiveness: A Meta-Analysis," *Proceeding of the Academy of Management* (August 1988): 201–205.

22. T. Talevich, "From Losers to Winners," *Costco Connection* (January 2011): 37–38.

23. E. G. Love, D. W. Love, and G. B. Northcraft, "Is the End in Sight? Student Regulation of In-Class and Extra-Credit Effort in Response to Performance Feedback," *Academy of Management Learning & Education* 9(1) (2008): 81–97.

24. See note 14.

25. B. L. Rich, J. A. Lepine, and E. R. Crawford, "Job Engagement: Antecedents and Effects on Job Performance," *Academy of Management Journal* 53(3) (2010): 617–635.

26. J. C. Dencker, "Outliners: The Story of Success," *Academy of Management Perspectives* 24(3) (2010): 97–99.

27. A. Thompson, "The Secrets Behind Goal Setting and Achievement," *Costco Connection* (January 2011): 29–30.

28. See note 6.

29. See note 10.

30. N. Bozionelos, "Happiness Around the World: Is There More to It than Money?" *Academy of Management Perspectives* 24(4) (2010): 96–97.

31. See note 17.

32. A. Murray, "The End of Management," *Wall Street Journal* (August 21-22, 2010): W3.

33. J. Bennett, "What's in It for Me?" *Entrepreneur* (December 2010): 104.

34. K. Blanchard, D. Hutson, and E. Wills, *The One Minute Entrepreneur* (New York: Currency, 2008).

35. See note 2.

36. See note 1.

37. See note 2.

38. A. Maslow, "A Theory of Human Motivation," *Psychological Review* 50 (1943): 370–396.

39. "Using the Malsow Hierarchy of Needs Theory," Mind Tools Web site (www.mindtools.com), retrieved June 7, 2011.

40. D. R. Hekman, G. A. Bigley, H. K. Steensma, and J. F. Hereford, "Combined Effects of Organizational and Professional Identification on the Reciprocity Dynamic for Professional Employees," *Academy of Management Journal* 52(3) (2009): 506–526.

41. See note 1.

42. F. Herzberg, "The Motivation-Hygiene Concept and Problems of Manpower," *Personnel Administrator* (1964): 3–7; and F. Herzberg, "One More Time: How Do You Motivate Employees?" *Harvard Business Review* (January–February 1968): 53–62.

43. A. M. Grant and J. W. Berry, "The Necessity of Others is the Mother of Invention: Intrinsic and Prosocial Motivations, Perspective Taking and Creativity," *Academy of Management Journal* 54(1) (2011): 73–96.

44. "Motivation-Hygiene Theory," Mind Tools Web site (www.mindtools.com), retrieved June 7, 2011.

45. See note 43.

46. See note 44.

47. D. B. Montgomery and C. A. Ramus, "Calibrating MBA Job Preferences for the 21st Century," *Academy of Management Learning & Education* 10(1) (2011): 9–26.

48. See note 25.

49. N. A. Ashkanasy, "International Happiness," *Academy of Management Perspectives* 25(1) (2011): 23–29.

50. D. C. Wyld, "Does More Money Buy More Happiness on the Job?" *Academy of Management Perspectives* 25(1) (2011): 101–102.

51. See note 25.

52. "Implementing a Job Enrichment Program," Mind Tools Web site (www.mindtools.com), retrieved June 7, 2011.

53. See note 41.

54. H. Murray, *Explorations in Personality* (New York: Oxford University Press, 1938). J. Atkinson, *An Introduction to Motivation* (New York: Van Nostrand Reinhold, 1964). D. McClelland, *The Achieving Society* (New York: Van Nostrand Reinhold, 1961); and D. McClelland and D. H. Burnham, "Power Is the Great Motivator," *Harvard Business Review* (March/April 1978): 103.

55. "McClelland," Mind Tools Web site (www.mindtools.com), retrieved June 7, 2011.

56. See note 1.

57. M. J. Gorgievski, M. E. Ascalon, and U. Stephan, "Small Business Owners' Success Criteria, a Values Approach to Personal Differences," *Journal of Small Business Management* 49(2) (2011): 207–232.

58. G. E. Kreiner, E. C. Hollensbe, M. L. Sheep, "Balancing Borders and Bridges: Negotiating the Work-Home Interface Via Boundary Work Tactics," *Academy of Management Journal* 52(4) (2009): 704–730.

59. J. S. Adams, "Toward an Understanding of Inequity," *Journal of Abnormal and Social Psychology* 67 (1963): 422–436.

60. "How to Apply Adam's Equity Theory," Mind Tools Web site (www.mindtools.com), retrieved June 6, 2011.

61. M. Crouch, "Get Hired, Not Fired," *Readers Digest* (April 2011): 130–139.

62. See note 1.

63. V. Vroom, *Work and Motivation* (New York: John Wiley & Sons, 1964).

64. L. F. Edelman, C. G. Brush, T. S. Manolova, and P. G. Greene, "Start-up Motivations and Growth intentions of Minority Nascent Entrepreneurs," *Journal of Small Business Management* 48(2) (2010): 174–196.

65. D. Ilgen, D. Nebeker, and R. Pritchard, "Expectancy Theory Measures: An Empirical Comparison in an Experimental Simulation," *Organizational Behavior and Human Performance* 28 (1981): 189–223; W. Van Eerde and H. Thierry, "Vroom's Expectancy Models and Work-Related Criteria: A Meta-Analysis," *Journal of Applied Psychology* 81 (October 1996): 548–556; and R. Fudge and J. Schlacter, "Motivating Employees to Act Ethically: An Expectancy Theory Approach," *Journal of Business Ethics* 18 (February 1999): 295–296.

66. M. Jokisaari and J.E. Nurmi, "Chance in Newcomers' Supervisor Support and Socialization Outcomes After Organizational Entry," *Academy of Management Journal* 52(3) (2009): 527–544.

67. See note 10.

68. E. A. Locke and G. P. Latham, "Has Goal Setting Gone Wild, or Have Its Attackers Abandoned Good Scholarship?" *Academy of Management Perspective* 23 (1) (2009): 17–23.

69. G. Hirst, D. Van Knippenberg, and J. Zhou, "A Cross-Level Perspective on Employee Creativity: Goal Orientation, Team Learning Behavior, and Individual Creativity," *Academy of Management Journal* 53(5) (2010): 932–936.

70. J. Jargon, "KFC Savors Potential in Africa," *Wall Street Journal* (October 18, 2010): B1.

71. "Chinese Auto Market," *Businessweek* (April 25-May 1, 2011): 29.

72. A. Cremer and T. Higgins, "Volkswagen Rediscovers America," *Businessweek* (May 23-29, 2011): 11–12.

73. C. Rauwald and V. Fuhrmans, "Volkswagen Unions Aim to Take Cup to 3% Voting Stake in Care Maker," *Wall Street Journal* (June 9, 2011): B3.

74. "China Wants Nuclear Reactors—Fast," *Businessweek* (December 6-12, 2010): 15.

75. L. D. Ordonez, M. E. Schweitzer, and M. H. Bazerman, "Goals Gone Wild: The Systematic Side Effects of Overprescribing Goal Setting." *Academy of Management Perspective* 23 (1) (2009): 6–16.

76. See note 75.

77. See note 23.

78. See note 75.

79. R.C. Litchfield, "Brainstorming Reconsidered: A Goal-Based View," *Academy of Management Review* 33(3) (2008): 649–668.

80. G. Colvin, "Why Talent is Over Rated," *Fortune* (October 27, 2008): 138–146.

81. See note 14.

82. See note 79.

83. See note 75.

84. R. S. Rubin and E. C. Dierdorff, "How Relevant is the MBA? Assessing the Alignment of Required Curricula and Required Managerial Competencies." *Academy of Management Learning & Education* 8(2) (2009): 208–224.

85. See note 27.

86. See note 75.

87. See note 68.

88. K. M. Bloomfield and R. A. Price, "So You Want to be a Billionaire." *Forbes* (August 30, 2010): 64–67.

89. See note 80.

90. See note 27.

91. B. F. Skinner, *Beyond Freedom and Dignity* (New York: Alfred A. Knopf, 1971).

92. K. W. Mossholder, H. A. Richardson, and R. P. Settoon, "Human Resource Systems and Helping in Organizations: A Relational Perspective." *Academy of Management Review* 36(1) (2011): 33–52.

93. A. D. Stajkovic and F. Luthans, "Differential Effects of Incentive Motivators on Work Performance," *Academy of Management Journal* 44(4) (2001): 580–590.

94. K. H. Queen, "Carrot or Stick?" *Costco Connection* (December 2010): 19–20.

95. See note 12.

96. N. Wingfield, "Why We Can't Stop Playing," *Wall Street Journal* (November 30, 2010): D1.

97. See note 94.

98. S. Kerr, "On the Folly of Rewarding A, While Hoping for B," *Academy of Management Executive* 9 (February 1995): 32–40.

99. See note 12.

100. See note 40.

101. See note 39.

102. See note 94.

103. Friedmans Appliances Web site (www.friedmansappliances. com), retrieved June 9, 2011.

Chapter 4

1. PepsiCo Web site (www.pepsico.com), retrieved June 21, 2011.

2. S. Cendrowski, "Finding the Fizz in Pepsi Stock," *Fortune* (March 21, 2011): 60.

3. "Fortune 500," *Fortune* (May 23, 2011): F1–F26.

4. "Global 500," *Fortune* (July 26, 2010): 153, F1–F5.

5. "The World's Most Admired Companies," *Fortune* (March 21, 2011): 109–111.

6. J. Shambora and B. Kowitt, "50 Most Powerful Women," *Fortune* (October 18, 2010): 129–138.

7. The World's 100 Most Powerful Women," *Forbes* (October 25, 2010): 57–68.

8. See note 6.

9. D. Stanford, "*BusinessWeek* (April 4-10, 2011): 25–26.

10. See note 1.

11. See note 7.

12. R. Greenwood and D. Miller, "Tackling Design Anew: Getting Back to the Heart of Organizational Theory," *Academy of Management Perspectives* 24(4) (2010): 78–84.

13. J. Helyar and C. Hymowitz, "The Recession is Gone, and the CEO Could be Next." *BusinessWeek* (February 7-13, 2011): 24–26.

14. G. A. Van Kleef, A. C. Homan, B. Beersma, D. Van Knippenberg, B. Van Knippenberg, and F. Damen," "Searing Sentiment or Cold Calculation? The Effects of Leader Emotional Displays on Team Performance Depend on Follower Epistemic Motivation," *Academy of Management Journal* 52(3) (2009): 562–580.

15. L. Dragoni, P. E. Tesluk, J. E. A. Russell, and I. S. Oh, "Understanding Managerial Development: Integrating Developmental Assignments, Learning Orientation, and Access to Developmental Opportunities, in Predicting Managerial Competencies." *Academy of Management Journal* 52(4) (2009): 731–743.

16. C. M. Christensen and P. R. Carlile, "Course Research: Using the Case Method to Build and Teach Management Theory," *Academy of Management Education & Learning* 8(2) (2009): 240–251.

17. I. Filatotchev and D. Allcock, "Corporate Governance and Executive Remuneration: A Contingency Framework," *Academy of Management Perspectives* 24(1) (2010): 20–33.

18. M. Farjoun, "Beyond Dualism: Stability and Change as a Duality," I. Filatotchev and D. Allcock, "Corporate Governance and Executive Remuneration: A Contingency Framework," *Academy of Management Review* 35(2) (2010): 202–225.

19. M. C. Sonfield and R. N. Lussier, "Gender in Family Business Ownership and Management: A Six Country Analysis," *International Journal of Gender and Entrepreneurship*" 1(2) (2009): 96–117.

20. K. Y. Ng, L. V. Dyne, and S. Ang, "From Experience to Experiential Learning: Cultural Intelligence as a Learning Capability for Global Leader Development," *Academy of Management Learning & Education* 8(1) (2009): 511–526.

21. S. Nadkarni and P. Herrmann, "CEO Personality, Strategic Flexibility, and Firm Performance: The Case of the Indian Business Process Outsourcing Industry," *Academy of Management Journal* 53(5) (2010): 1050–1073.

22. B. L. Kirkman, G. Chen, J. L. Farh, Z. X. Chen, and K. B. Lowe, "Individual Power Distance Orientation and Follower Reactions to Transformational Leaders: A Cross-Level, Cross-Cultural Examination," *Academy of Management Journal* (2009), 52(4) 744–764.

23. S. D. Sidle, "Building a Committed Global Workforce: Does What Employees Want Depend on Culture?" *Academy of Management Perspectives* (2009) 23(1): 79–80.

24. S. Hamm, "The Globe is IBM's Classroom," *Business Week* (March 23 & 30, 2009): 56–57.

25. R. J. House; et al., eds. *Culture, leadership, and organizations: the GLOBE study of 62 societies* (Sage, 2004).

26. See note 2.

27. F. E. Fiedler, *A Theory of Leadership Effectiveness* (New York: McGraw-Hill, 1967); F. E. Fiedler and M. M. Chemers, *Improving Leadership Effectiveness: The Leader Match Concept*, 2nd ed. (New York: Wiley, 1982).

28. See note 18.

29. See note 15.

30. A. Joshi and H. Roh, "The Role of Context in Work Team Diversity Research: A Meta-Analytic Review," *Academy of Management Journal* 52(3) (2010): 599–627.

31. R. S. Dalal, H. Lam, H. M. Weiss, E. R. Welch, and C. L. Hulin, "A Within-Person Approach to Work Behavior and Performance: Concurrent and Lagged Citizenship-Counterproductivity Associations, and Dynamic Relationships with Affect and Overall Job Performance," *Academy of Management Journal* 52(5) (2011): 1051–1066.

32. M. J. Strube and J. E. Garcia, "A Meta-Analytical Investigation of Fiedler's Contingency Model of Leadership Effectiveness," *Psychology Bulletin* 90 (1981): 307–321; and L. H. Peters, D. D. Hartke, and J. T. Pohlmann, "Fiedler's Contingency Theory of Leadership: An Application of the Meta-Analysis Procedure of Schmidt and Hunter," *Psychological Bulletin* 97 (1985): 274–285.

33. F. E. Fiedler, "A Rejoinder to Schriesheim and Kerr's Premature Obituary of the Contingency Model," in J. G. Hunt

and L. L. Larson, eds., *Leadership: The Cutting Edge* (Carbondale, IL: Southern Illinois University Press, 1977): 45–50; and F. E. Fiedler, "The Contingency Model: A Reply to Ashour," *Organizational Performance and Human Behavior* 9 (1973): 356–368.

34. R. Tannenbaum and W. H. Schmidt, "How to Choose a Leadership Pattern," *Harvard Business Review* (March–April 1958): 95–101; R. Tannenbaum and W. H. Schmidt, "How to Choose a Leadership Pattern," *Harvard Business Review* (May–June 1973): 166.

35. R. Tannenbaum and W. H. Schmidt, excerpts from "How to Choose a Leadership Pattern," *Harvard Business Review* (July–August 1986): 129.

36. R. J. House, "A Path-Goal Theory of Leader Effectiveness," *Administrative Science Quarterly* 16(2) (1971): 321–329; and M. G. Evans, "The Effects of Supervisory Behavior on the Path-Goal Relationship," *Organizational Behavior and Human Performance* 5 (1970): 277–298; and R. N. House and R. J. Aditya, "The Social Scientific Study of Leadership: Quo Vadis?" *Journal of Management* 23 (May–June 1997): 409–474.

37. See note 21.

38. See note 15.

39. J. C. Wofford and L. Z. Liska, "Path-Goal Theories of Leadership: A Meta-Analysis," *Journal of Management* 19 (1993): 858–876; and P. M. Podsakoff, S. B. MacKenzie, M. Ahearne, and W. H. Bommer, "Searching for a Needle in a Haystack: Trying to Identify the Illusive Moderators of Leadership Behavior," *Journal of Management* 21 (1995): 423–470.

40. V. H. Vroom and P. W. Yetton, *Leadership and Decision Making* (Pittsburgh: University of Pittsburgh Press, 1973); V. H. Vroom and A. G. Jago, *The New Leadership: Managing Participation in Organizations* (Englewood Cliffs, NJ: Prentice-Hall, 1988); and V. H. Vroom, "Leadership and the Decision-Making Process," *Organizational Dynamics* 28 (Spring 2000): 82–94.

41. V. H. Vroom, "Leadership and the Decision-Making Process," *Organizational Dynamics* 28 (Spring 2000): 82–94.

42. J. B. Miner, "The Uncertain Future of the Leadership Concept: An Overview," in J. G. Hunt and L. L. Larson, eds., *Leadership Frontiers* (Kent, OH: Kent State University, 1975); R. H. G. Field, "A Critique of the Vroom-Yetton Contingency Model of Leadership Behavior," *Academy of Management Review* 4 (1979): 249–257; R. H. G. Field, "A Test of the Vroom-Yetton Normative Model of Leadership," *Journal of Applied Psychology* (October 1982): 523–532; and R. H. G. Field, P. C. Read, and J. J. Louviere, "The Effect of Situation Attributes on Decision Method Choice in the Vroom-Jago Model of Participation in Decision Making," *Leadership Quarterly* 1 (1990): 165–176.

43. V. H. Vroom and A. G. Jago, *The New Leadership: Managing Participation in Organizations* (Englewood Cliffs, NJ: Prentice-Hall, 1988).

44. See note 13.

45. See note 21.

46. See note 16.

47. S. Kerr and J. Jermier, "Substitutes for Leadership: Their Meaning and Measurement," *Organizational Behavior and Human Performance* 22 (1978): 375–403.

48. P. M. Podsakoff, S. B. MacKenzie, and W. H. Bommer, "Meta-Analysis of the Relationships between Kerr and Jermier's Substitutes for Leadership and Employee Job Attitudes, Role Perceptions, and Performance," *Journal of Applied Psychology* 81 (August 1996): 380–400.

49. F. Balfour and T. Culpan, "Chairman Gou," *BusinessWeek* (September 13-19, 2010): 58–69.

50. J. Bussey, "Measuring the Human Cost of an iPad Made in China," *Wall Street Journal* (June 3, 2011): B11.

51. Foxconn Web site (www.foxconn.com), retrieved June 23, 2011.

52. See note 49.

53. T. Culpan, A. Lifei, and B. Einhorn, "How to Beat the High Cost of Happy Workers," *BusinessWeek* (May 19-15, 2011): 39–49.

54. See note 49.

55. See note 51.

56. See note 53.

57. See note 51.

58. See note 49.

59. "The Changing Face of Asian Business," *Fortune* (May 2, 2011): 79–84.

60. See note 49.

Chapter 5

1. Forbes Web site (www.forbes.com/profile/mark-cuban), retrieved June 24, 2011.

2. Wikipedia Web site (www.wikipedia.com), retrieved June 24, 2011.

3. B. M. Galvin, P. Balkudi, and D. A. Waldman, "Spreading the Word: The Role of Surrogates in Charismatic Leadership Processes," *Academy of Management Review* 35(3) (2010): 477–494.

4. N. Levina and W. J. Orlikowski, "Understanding Shifting Power Relations within and across Organizations: A Critical Genre Analysis," *Academy of Management Journal* 52(4) (2009): 672–703.

5. E. G. Foldy, P. Rivard, and T. R. Buckley, "Power, Safety, and Learning in Racially Diverse Groups," *Academy of Management Learning & Education* 8(1) (2009): 25–41.

6. N. Levina and W. J. Orlikowski, "Understanding Shifting power Relations within and across Organizations: A Critical Genre Analysis," *Academy of Management Journal* 52(4) (2009): 672–703.

7. E. Morrison, "From the Editors," *Academy of Management Journal* 53(5) (2010): 932–936.

8. J. Helyar and C. Hymowitz, "The Recession Is Gone, and the CEO Could Be Next," *BusinessWeek* (Feb. 7-13, 2011): 24–26.

9. A. Murray, "The End of Management," *Wall Street Journal* (Aug. 21-22, 2010): W3.

10. J. R. P. French and B. H. Raven, "The Bases of Social Power," in D. Cartwright, Ed., *Studies of Social Power* (Ann Arbor, MI: Institute for Social Research, 1959): 150–167.

11. F. Rojas, "Power through Institutional Work: Acquiring Academic Authority in the 1968 Third World Strike," *Academy of Management Journal* 53(6) (2010): 1263–1280.

12. R. Pinheiro, "SuperFreakonomics," *Academy of Management Perspectives* 25(2) (2011): 86–87.

13. See note 11.

14. See note 11.

15. See note 5

16. See note 3..

17. See note 3.
18. See note 5.
19. B. Vissa, "A Matching Theory of Entrepreneurs' Tie Formation Intentions and Initiation of Economic Exchange," *Academy of Management Journal* 54(1) (2011): 137–158.
20. See note 11.
21. See note 11.
22. See note 5.
23. See note 2.
24. Wikipedia Web site (www.wikipedia.com), retrieved June 24, 2011.
25. D. R. Soriano, "Political Skills in Organizations: Do Personality and Reputation Play a Role?" *Academy of Management Perspectives* 22(1) (2008): 66–68.
26. See note 25.
27. C. H. Chang, C. C. Rosen, and P. E. Levy, "The Relationship between Perceptions of Organizational Politics and Employee Attitudes, Strain, and Behavior: A Meta-Analytic Examination," *Academy of Management Journal* 52(4) (209): 779–801.
28. D. R. Hekman, G. A. Bigley, H. K. Steensma, and J. F. Hereford, "Combined Effects of Organizational and Professional Identification on the Reciprocity Dynamic for Professional Employees," *Academy of Management Journal* 52(3) (2009): 506–526.
29. See note 27.
30. S. Nadkarni and P. Herrmann, "CEO Personality, Strategic Flexibility, and Firm Performance: The Case of the Indian Business Process Outsourcing Industry," *Academy of Management Journal* 53(5) (2010): 1050–1073.
31. See note 28.
32. G. A. Ballinger and K. W. Rockmann, "Chutes Versus Ladders: Anchoring Events and a Punctuated-Equilibrium Perspective on Social Exchange Relationships," *Academy of Management Review* 35(3) (2010): 373–391.
33. See note 27.
34. P. J. Frederickson, "Political Skill at Work," *Academy of Management Perspectives* 20(2) (2006): 95–96.
35. K. Blanchard, D. Hutson, and E. Wills, *The One Minute Entrepreneur* (New York: Currency/Doubleday, 2008).
36. K. M. Bloomfield and R. A. Price, "So You Want to be a Billionaire," *Forbes* (Aug. 30, 2010): 64–67.
37. D. M. De Carolis, B. E. Litzky, and K. A. Eddleston, "Why Networks Enhance the Progress of New Venture Creation: The Influence of Social Capital and Cognition," *Entrepreneurship Theory and Practice* 33(2) (2009): 527–545.
38. See note 38.
39. J. Shambora, "Fortune's Best Networker," *Fortune* (Feb. 7, 2011): 27.
40. C. Lechner, K. Frankenberger, and S. W. Floyd, "Task Contingencies in the Curvilinear Relationships between Intergroup Networks and Initiative Performance," *Academy of Management Journal* 53(4) (2010): 865–889.
41. I. Hughes, "Constant Connectivity," *Entrepreneur* (Oct. 2010): 78.
42. See note 30.
43. This section is adapted from A. Gumbus and R. N. Lussier, "Career Development: Enhancing Your Networking Skill," *Clinical Leadership & Management Review* 17(1) (Jan.–Feb. 2003).
44. C. Brogan, "The Network Is Everything," *Entrepreneur* (Oct. 2010): 56.

45. K. M. Bloomfield and R. A. Price, "So You Want to Be a Billionaire," *Forbes* (Aug. 30, 2010): 64–67.
46. S. S. Wong and W. F. Boh, "Leveraging the Ties of Others to Build a Reputation for Trustworthiness among Peers," *Academy of Management Journal* 53(1) (2010): 129–148.
47. See note 41.
48. See note 19.
49. See note 44.
50. See note 44.
51. See note 44.
52. See note 44.
53. See note 44.
54. "Social Networking: Trouble at the Virtual Water Cooler," *BusinessWeek* (May 2-6, 2011): 31–32.
55. G. A. Fowler, "Are You Talking to Me?" *Wall Street Journal* (Apr. 25, 2011): R5.
56. R. Cheng, "So You Want to Use Your iPhone for Work? Uh-oh." *Wall Street Journal* (Apr. 25, 2011): R1, R4.
57. See note 54.
58. See note 56.
59. See note 55.
60. See note 55.
61. See note 2.
62. See note 5.
63. P. Navarro, "The MBA Core Curricula of Top-Ranked U.S. Business Schools: A Study in Failure?" *Academy of Management Learning & Education* 8(1) (2009): 511–526.
64. R. S. Rubin and E. C. Dierdorff, "On the Road to Abilene: Time to Manage Agreement About MBA Curricular Relevance," *Academy of Management Perspectives* 25(1) (2011): 148–161.
65. H. R. Bowles and F. Flynn, "Gender and Persistence in Negotiation: A Dyadic Perspective," *Academy of Management Journal* 53(4) (2010): 769–787.
66. See note 4.
67. G. E. Kreiner, E. C. Hollensbe, and M. L. Sheep, "Balancing Borders and Bridges: Negotiating the Work-Home Interface Via Boundary Work Tactics," *Academy of Management Journal* 52(4) (2009): 704–730.
68. D. Skube, "The Interpersonal Edge," *Costco Connection* (Jan. 2011): 67.
69. See note 41.
70. C. Fiedler, "Defusing Conflict," *Costco Connection* (Dec. 2010): 57–58.
71. See note 68.
72. See note 70.
73. W. Amos, "No Equals Yes," *Costco Connection* (Dec. 2010): 11.
74. P. H. Kim, K. T. Dirks, and C. D. Cooper, "The Repair of Trust: A Dynamic Bilateral Perspective and Multilevel Conceptualization," *Academy of Management Review* 34(3) (2009): 401–422.
75. See note 46.
76. See note 70.
77. See note 73.
78. See note 46.
79. See note 70.
80. See note 70.
81. Y. Mishina, B. J. Dykes, E. S. Block, and T. G. Pollock, "Why Good Firms Do Bad Things: The Effects of High Aspirations, High Expectations, and Prominence on the Incidence of

Corporate Illegality," *Academy of Management Journal* 53(4) (2010): 701–722.

82. M. E. Graebner, "Caveat Venditor: Trust Asymmetries in Acquisitions of Entrepreneurial Firms," *Academy of Management Journal* 52(3) (2009): 435–472.

83. R. Pinheiro, "SuperFreakonomics," *Academy of Management Perspectives* 25(2) (2011): 86–87.

84. G. A. Fowler and A. Efati, "Facebook Hired Firm to Target Google," *Wall Street Journal* (May 13, 2011): B1, B-2.

85. This is an actual case, but the names have been changed to protect identities.

Chapter 6

1. Information taken from personal interviews with the Clarks and The Ranch Web site: http://www.theranchgolfclub.com, retrieved July 1, 2011

2. P. Navarro, "The MBA Core Curricula of Top-Ranked U.S. Business Schools: A Study in Failure?" *Academy of Management Learning & Education* 8(1) (2009): 511–526.

3. C. Verzat, J. Byrne, and A. Fayolle, "Tangling with Spaghetti: Pedagogical Lessons from Games," *Academy of Management Learning & Education* 8(3) (2009): 356–369.

4. R. S. Rubin and E. C. Dierdorff, "How Relevant Is the MBA? Assessing the Alignment of Required Curricula and Required Managerial Competencies," *Academy of Management Learning & Education* 8(2) (2009): 208–224.

5. M. Clark, "Book Review," *Academy of Management Perspectives* 23(3) (2009): 103–105.

6. W. P. Smith and F. Tabak, "Monitoring Employee E-mail: Is There any Room for Privacy?" *Academy of Management Perspectives* 23(4) (2009): 33–48.

7. A. Biterktine, "Toward a Theory of Social Justice Judgments of Organizations: The Case of Legitimacy, Reputation, and Status," *Academy of Management Review* 36(1) (2011): 151–179.

8. D. B. Montgomery and C. A. Ramus, "Calibrating MBA Job Preferences for the 21st Century," *Academy of Management Learning & Education* 10(1) (2011): 9–26.

9. J. D. Hoover, R. C. Giambatista, R. L. Sorenson, and W. H. Bommer, "Assessing the Effectiveness of Whole Person Learning Pedagogy in Skill Acquisition," *Academy of Management Learning & Education* 9(2) (2010): 192–203.

10. K. Y. Ng, L. V. Dyne, and S. Ang, "From Experience to Experiential Learning: Cultural Intelligence as a Learning Capability for Global Leader Development," *Academy of Management Learning & Education* 8(1) (2009): 511–526.

11. B. M. Galvin, P. Balkudi, and D. A. Waldman, "Spreading the Word: The Role of Surrogates in Charismatic Leadership Processes." *Academy of Management Review* 35(3) (2010): 477–494.

12. E. De Haan, C. Bertie, A. Day, and C. Sills, "Clients' Critical Moments of Coaching: Toward a "Client Model" of Executive Coaching," *Academy of Management Learning & Education* 9(4) (2010): 607–621.

13. K. Rosman, "Y U Luv Texts, H* Calls," *Wall Street Journal* (Oct. 14, 2010): D1–D2.

14. "Dear E-Mail: Die Already. Love, Facebook," *BusinessWeek* (Nov. 22-28, 2010): 50–51.

15. C. Brogan, "Brevity Rules," *Entrepreneur* (Mar. 2011): 62.

16. See note 11.

17. A. Hwang and A. M. Francesco, "The Influence of Individualism-Collectivism and Power Distance on Use of Feedback Channels and Consequences for Learning," *Academy of Management Learning & Education* 9(2) (2010): 243–257.

18. See note 11.

19. D. Skube, "The Interpersonal Edge," *Costco Connection* (Jan. 2011): 67.

20. See note 15

21. See note 15.

22. P. Johnson, "Listening and Telling the Truth," *Forbes* (Apr. 26, 2010): 17.

23. J. Chatzky, "Every Employee Counts," *Fortune* (May 3, 2010): 34.

24. See note 6.

25. Public Radio, News Broadcast, WFCR 88.5, aired May 28, 2010.

26. C. Brogan, "The New Attention Deficit," *Entrepreneur* (Dec. 2010): 70.

27. J. Robinson, "E-mail Is Making You Stupid?" *Entrepreneur* (Mar. 2010): 61–63.

28. See note 26.

29. See note 19.

30. R. C. Litchfield, "Brainstorming Reconsidered: A Goal-Based View," *Academy of Management Review* 33(3) (2008): 649–668.

31. G. Colvin, "Why Talent Is Over Rated," *Fortune* (Oct. 27, 2008): 138–146.

32. See note 9.

33. See note 32.

34. See note 19.

35. R. Hooiberg and N. Lane, "Using Multisource Feedback Coaching Effectively in Executive Education," *Academy of Management Learning & Education* 7(1) (2008): 108–123.

36. See note 11.

37. See note 36.

38. M. Clark, "What Got You Here Won't Get You There," *Academy of Management Perspectives* 23(3) (2009): 103–105.

39. See note 4.

40. See note 36.

41. See note 12.

42. See note 10.

43. See note 36.

44. See note 19.

45. See note 36.

46. J. Falvey, "To Raise Productivity, Try Saying Thank You," *Wall Street Journal* (Dec. 6, 1982): B1.

47. D. W. Lehman and R. Ramanujam, "Selectivity in Organizational Rule Violations," *Academy of Management Review* 34(4) (2009): 643–657.

48. See note 32.

49. J. S. Lublin, "Coaching Urged for Women." *Wall Street Journal* (Apr. 4, 2011): B8.

50. See note 32.

51. L. Rapp, "Will You Be My Mentor?" *Entrepreneur* (Jan. 2011): 22.

52. E. G. Foldy, P. Rivard, and T. R. Buckley, "Power, Safety, and Learning in Racially Diverse Groups," *Academy of Management Learning & Education* 8(1) (2009): 25–41.

53. D. R. Hekman, G. A. Bigley, H. K. Steensma, and J. F. Hereford, "Combined Effects of Organizational and

Professional Identification on the Reciprocity Dynamic for Professional Employees," *Academy of Management Journal* 52(3) (2009): 506–526.

54. P. H. Kim, K. T. Dirks, and C. D. Cooper, "The Repair of Trust: A Dynamic Bilateral Perspective and Multilevel Conceptualization," *Academy of Management Review* 34(3) (2009): 401–422.

55. See note 54.

56. H. R. Bowles and F. Flynn, "Gender and Persistence in Negotiation: A Dyadic Perspective," *Academy of Management Journal* 53(4) (2010): 769–787.

57. Margin Note, *Entrepreneur* (Feb. 2007): 26.

58. See note 4.

59. A. Joshi and H. Roh, "The Role of Context in Work Team Diversity Research: A Meta-Analytic Review," *Academy of Management Journal* 52(3) (2010): 599–627.

60. See note 60.

61. K. A. Jehn, S. Rispens, and S. M. B. Thatcher, "The Effects of Conflict Asymmetry on Work Group and Individual Outcomes," *Academy of Management Journal* 53(3) (2010): 595–616.

62. C. Fiedler, "Defusing Conflict," *Costco Connection* (Dec. 2010): 57–58.

63. See note 62.

64. See note 63.

65. See note 57.

66. S. Nadkarni and P. Herrmann, "CEO Personality, Strategic Flexibility, and Firm Performance: The Case of the Indian Business Process Outsourcing Industry," *Academy of Management Journal* 53(5) (2010): 1050–1073.

67. See note 63.

68. See note 67.

69. See note 63.

70. See note 63.

71. One of the authors uses this technique at work.

72. See note 67.

73. See note 63.

74. See note 63.

75. See note 53.

76. M. V. Copeland, "Reed Hastings: Leader of the Pack," *Fortune* (Dec. 6, 2010): 212–130.

77. M. Jarzemsky, "Netflix to Enter Latin America," *Wall Street Journal* (July 6, 2011): B5.

78. See note 77.

79. C. Rose, "Charlie Rose Talks to Reed Hastings," *Business-Week* (May 9-15, 2011): 26.

80. See note 77.

81. See note 77.

82. See note 77.

83. See note 80

84. See note 77.

85. See note 77.

86. N. Wingfield and S. Schechner, "Netflix Rattles Rivals as It Expands on Web," *Wall Street Journal* (Dec. 6, 2010): B1, B5.

87. Netflix Web site (www.netflix.com), retrieved July 11, 2011.

88. K. Swisher, "What's Playing—and Where," *Wall Street Journal* (June 6, 2011): R4.

89. See note 78.

90. See note 89.

91. See note 89.

92. See note 80.

93. See note 88.

94. Information taken from a mail advertisement in July 2011.

95. N. Wingfield, "Netflix Plays Down DVDs," *Wall Street Journal* (July 13, 2011): B2.

96. See note 87.

97. See note 77.

Chapter 7

1. R. Stengel, "Person of the Year," *Time* (Dec. 15, 2010); J. A. Vargas, "The Face of Facebook," *The New Yorker* (September, 20, 2010); "M. Zuckerburg," *New York Times* (Jan. 3, 2011).

2. B. Schyns and D. Day, "Critique and Review of Leader-Member Exchange Theory: Issues of Agreement, Consensus, and Excellence." *European Journal of Work & Organizational Psychology*, 19(1) (2010): 1–29.

3. C. R. Gerstner and D. V. Day, "Meta-Analytic Review of Leader-Member Exchange Theory: Correlates and Construct Issues," *Journal of Applied Psychology*, 82(6) 1997: 827–844.

4. G. B. Graen and M. Uhl-Bien, "Relationship-Based Approach to Leadership: Development of Leader-Member Exchange (LMX) Theory of Leadership Over 25 Years: Applying a Multi-Level Multi-Domain Perspective," *Leadership Quarterly* 6(2) 1995: 219–247.

5. G. Graen, "Letter to the Editor," *Academy of Management Perspectives* 21(1) (2007):

6. F. J. Yammarino and F. Dansereau, "Individualized Leadership: A New Multiple-Level Approach," *Journal of Leadership & Organizational Studies* 9 (Summer 2002): 90–100.

7. A. Joshi, H. Liao, and S. Jackson, "Cross-Level Effects of Workplace Diversity on Sales Performance and Pay," *Academy of Management Journal* 49(3) (2006): 459–481.

8. See note 4.

9. See note 2.

10. L. Raymond, M. Yina, and N. Hang-yue, "Linking Leader-Member Exchange and Employee Work Outcomes: The Mediating Role of Organizational Social and Economic Exchange," *Management & Organization Review* 5(3) (2009): 401–422.

11. A Perumalu, I. Kandan, and I Ali, "A Correlation Study of Leader-Member Exchange and Organizational Citizenship Behavior in a Public Sector Organization," *Journal of Global Business & Economics* 1(1) (2010): 62–78.

12. D. S. Kang and J. Stewart, "Leader-Member Exchange (LMX) Theory of Leadership and HRD: Development of Units of Theory and Laws of Interaction," *Leadership & Organizational Journal* 28(6) (2007): 531–551.

13. J Manzoni and J. Barsoux, *The Set-Up-to-Fail Syndrome. How Good Managers Cause Great People To Fail* (Boston: Harvard Business School Press, 2002)

14. B. Erdogan, R. Liden, and L. Kraimer, "Justice and Leader–Member Exchange: The Moderating Role of Organizational Culture," *Academy of Management Journal* (149) (2006): 395–406.

15. See note 10.

16. R. Cropanzano and M. S. Mitchell, "Social Exchange Theory: An Interdisciplinary Review," *Journal of Management* 31(6) (2005): 874–900.

17. R. Sparrowe, B. Soetjipto, and M. Kraimer, "Do Leaders' Influence Tactics Relate to Members' Helping Behavior? It Depends on the Quality of the Relationship," *Academy of Management Journal* 49(6) (2006): 1194–1208.

18. J. R., Mesmer-Magnus and L. A. DeChurch, "Information Sharing and Team Performance: A Meta-Analysis," *Journal of Applied Psycholog*, 94(2009): 535–546.

19. H. H. M. Tse, M. T. Dasborough and N. M Ashkanasy, "A Multi-Level Analysis of Team Climate andIinterpersonal Exchange Relationships at Work," *Leadership Quarterl*, 19 (2008): 195–211.

20. A. Seers, "Interpersonal Workplace Theory at a Crossroads." In G. B. Graen (Ed.), *New frontiers of leadership, LMX leadership: The series*, 2(2004): 1–31, (Greenwich, CT: Information Age).

21. J. B Wu, A. S Tsui, and A. J. Kinicki, "Consequences of Differentiated Leadership in Groups," *Academy of Management Journal* 53(1) (Feb. 2010): 90–106.

22. G. B. Graen, C. Hui, and E. A. Taylor, "Experienced-Based Learning about LMX Leadership and Fairness in Project Teams: A Dyadic Directional Approach," *Academy of Management Learning & Education* 5(4) (2006): 448–460.

23. See note 22.

24. S. Anand, P. R. Vidyarthi, R.C. Liden, and D. M. Rousseau, "Good Citizens in Poor-Quality Relationships: Idioyncratic Deals as a Substitute for Relationship Quality," *Academy of Management Journal* 53(5) (2010): 970–988.

25. H. Liao, D. Liu, and R. Loi "Looking at Both Sides of the Social Exchange Coin: A Social Cognitive Perspective on the Joint Effects of Relationship Qaulity and Differnetiation on Creativity," *Academy of Management Journal* 53(5) (2010): 1090–1109.

26. K. S. Wilson, H-P. Sin, and D. E. Conlon, "What About the Leader in Leader-Member Exchange? The Impact of Resource Exchanges and Substitutability on the Leader," *Academy of Management Review* 35(3) (2010): 358–372.

27. R. L Loi, Y. M. Mao, and H. Ngo, "Linking Leader-Member Exchange and Employee Work Outcomes: The Mediating Role of Organizational Social and Economic Exchange,." *Management & Organization Review* 5(3) (2009): 401–422.

28. J. B. Wu, A.S. Tsui, and A. J. Kinicki, "Consequences of Differentiated Leadership in Groups," *Academy of Management Journal* 53(1) (2010): 90–106.

29. See note 3.

30. R. Ilies, J. D., Nahrgang, and F. P. Morgeson, "Leader Member Exchange and Citizenship Behaviors: A Meta-Analysis," *Journal of Applied Psychology* 92(2007): 269–277.

31. See note 11.

32. See note 27.

33. K. M., Sherony and S. G. Green, "Co-Worker Exchange Relationships between Co-Workers, Leader-Member Exchange, and Work Attitudes," *Journal of Applied Psycholog*, 87(3) (2002): 542–548.

34. S. M. S. Malar, "Right Attitude: Grab it!" *IUP Journal of Soft Skills* 3 (Sep 2009): 19–25.

35. See note 17.

36. D. Rolf, N. Quaquebeke, R. Kerschreiter, and A. Buxton, "Two Lighthouses to Navigate: Effects of Ideal and Counter-Ideal Values on Follower Identification and Satisfaction with

Their Leaders," *Journal of Business Ethics* 93(2) (2010): 293–305.

37. R. G., Lord and D. J. Brown, *Leadership Processes and Follower Self-Identity* (Mahwah, NJ: Lawrence Erlbaum Associates, Inc., 2004).

38. R. G. Lord, D. J. Brown, and S. J. Freiberg, "Understanding the dynamics of leadership: The role of follower self-concepts in the leader/follower relationship," *Organizational Behavior and Human Decision Processes* 78 (1999): 167–203.

39. D. Van Knippenberg, B. van Knippenberg, D. De Cremer, and M. A. Hogg, "Leadership, self, and identity: A review and research agenda." *Leadership Quarterly* 15 (2004): 825–856.

40. See note 11.

41. See note 2.

42. W. Lam, X. Huang, and E. Snape, "Feedback Seeking Behavior and Leader–Member Exchange: Do Supervisor Attributed Motives Matter?" *Academy of Management Journal* 50 (2007): 348–363.

43. See note 26.

44. See note 22.

45. See note 26.

46. E L. Mouriño-Ruiz, "Leader-Member Exchange (LMX) The Impact of Leader-Employee Relationships in the 21st Century Workplace (Implications for Research on Latinos in the Workforce)," *The Business Journal of Hispanic Research* 4(1) (2010): 35–42.

47. See note 26.

48. See note 27.

49. See note 25.

50. M. Brewer, "The Importance of Being We: Human Nature And Intergroup Relations," *The American Psychologist* 62 (2007): 728–38.

51. H. Oh, M.-H. Chung, and G. Labianca, "Group Social Capital and Group Effectiveness: The Role of Informal Socializing Ties," *Academy of Management Review* 4(7) (2004): 860–875.

52. See note 25.

53. See note 22.

54. See note 14.

55. See note 24.

56. See note 11.

57. L. Lapierre, and L. Hackett, "Trait Conscientiousness, Leader–Member Exchange, Job Satisfaction and Organizational Citizenship Behavior: A Test of an Integrative Model," *Journal of Occupational and Organizational Psychology* 80 (2007): 539–554.

58. See note 25.

59. See note 25.

60. See note 2.

61. See note 3.

62. See note 47.

63. R. D. de Jong, "The Art of Followership: How Great Followers Create Great Leaders and Organizations," Ed. Ronald Riggio, Ira Chaleff, and Jean Lipman-Blumen, *Personnel Psychology*, 62(3) (2009): 636–639.

64. M. Vugt, R. Hogan, and R. Kaiser, "Leadership, Followership, and Evolution: Some Lessons from the Past," *The American Psychologist* 63 (2008): 182–196.

65. R. E. Kelley,. "Power of Followership: How to Create Leaders People Want to Follow and Followers Who Want to Lead Themselves," (1991). Double Day Publishing

66. R. G. Lord and D. J. Brown, "Leadership Processes and Follower Self-Identity," *Personnel Psychology* 57 (Summer 2004): 517–521.

67. R. E. Kelley, *The Power of Followership* (New York: Doubleday, 1992).

68. I. Chaleff, *The Courageous Follower: Standing up to and for Our Leaders*, (2nd ed) (San Fransisco: Berrett-Koehler, 2003).

69. B. Kellerman, "What Every Leader Needs to Know about Followers," *Harvard Business Review* 85 (December 2007): 84–91.

70. R. E. Kelley, "In Praise of Followers," *Harvard Business Review* (Nov/Dec 1988): 142–148.

71. See note 72.

72. See note 65.

73. J. M. Howell and B. Shamir, "The Role of Followers in the Charismatic Leadership Process: Relationships and Their Consequences," *Academy of Management Review* 30(1) (2005): 96–112.

74. A. Bandura, "Self-efficacy, in V. S. Ramachaudran (Ed.), *Encyclopedia of human behavior* (Vol. 4, pp. 71–81). (New York: Academic Press; repr. in H. Friedman [Ed.], *Encyclopedia of Mental Health* (San Diego: Academic Press, 1998).

75. See note 65.

76. G. Dixon, "Can We Lead and Follow?" *Engineering Management Journal* 21(1) (March 2009): 34–41.

77. A. J. DeLellis, "Clarifying the Concept of Respect: Implications for Leadership," *Journal of Leadership Studies* 7 (Spring 2000): 2–37.

78. See note 66.

79. D. Cavell, "Leadership or Followership: One or Both? All Successful Leaders Need Good Followers," *Healthcare Financial Management* 61 (November 2007): 142–143.

80. P. M. Buhler, "Managing in the New Millennium: The Top Ten Managerial Mistakes," *Supervision* 65 (August 2004): 15–18.

81. C. Kauffman, "Employee Involvement: A New Blueprint for Success," *Journal of Accountancy* 209 (May 2010): 46–49.

82. C. Kauffman, "Employee Involvement: A New Blueprint for Success," *Journal of Accountancy* 209(5) (May 2010): 46–49.

83. K. N. Corazzini, R. A. Anderson, C. G. Rapp, C. Mueller, E. S. McConnell, and D. Lekan, "Delegation in Long-Term Care: Scope of Practice or Job Description?" *Online Journal of Issues in Nursing* 15(2) (2010): 4–40.

84. P. Danby, "Setting the Right Direction," *Business Strategy Review* 20(4) (Winter 2009): 58–63.

85. See note 85.

86. C. Hymowitz, "A Vacationing Boss Should Take a Break; Let Staffers Step Up," *The Wall Street Journal* (August 20, 2007): B1.

87. www.huffingtonpost.com/.../tom-coburn-john-ensign_n_861287.html, retrieved May 25, 2011.

88. T. A. Sykes, "Get Time on Your Side: Accomplish More Using Less Energy," *Black Enterprise* 34 (June 2004): 312–313.

89. F. Dalton, "Improving Delegation: When 'Just Do It' Just Won't Do It," *Contract Management* 44 (Nov. 2004): 4–7.

90. E. Yariv, "The Appraisal of Teachers' Performance and Impact on the Mutuality of Principal-Teacher Emtions," *School Leadership & Management* 29(5) (Nov. 2009): 445–461.

91. S. Onyett, A. Rees, C. Borrill, D. Shapiro, and S. Boldison, "The Evaluation of a Local Whole Systems Intervention for Improved Team Working and Leadership in Mental Health Services," *Innovation Journal* 14(1) (2009): 1–18.

92. E. Sones, "360 Assessment, an Easier Pill to Swallow: Implantation of Peer Assessment for Captain's Career Course Students and Staff," *U.S. Army Medical Department Journal* (2009): 59–63.

93. R. Vecchio and R. Anderson, "Agreement in Self-Other Ratings of Leader Effectiveness: The Role of Demographics and Personality," *International Journal of Selection & Assessment* 17(2) (June 2009): 165–179.

94. T. Walser, "An Action Research Study of Student Self-Assessment in Higher Education," *Innovative Higher Education* 34 (5) (Dec. 2009): 299–306.

95. C. L. Howe, P. A. Auflick, and G. Freiburger, "Upward Evaluation at the Arizona Heaslth Sciences Library," *Journal of the Medical Library Association* 99(1) (Jan. 2011): 91–94.

96. Information taken from the W. L. Gore & Associates Web site: http://www.gore.com, rerieved July 8, 2008. Update to May 2011

97. G. Hamel, "W. L. Gore: Lessons from a Management Revolutionary,". *The Wall Street Journal*, March 18, 2010; G. Hamel, W. L. Gore: Lessons from a Management Revolutionary, Part 2. *The Wall Street Journal*, April 2, 2010.

Chapter 8

1. www.southwest.com; Steve Heaser, "Gary Kelly on 2010 4Q Earnings" www.blogsouthest.com; Candace Carlisle, "Gary Kelly Selected as DBJ's CEO of the Year," *Dallas Business Journal* (Jan. 7, 2011).

2. F. J. Landy and J. M. Conte, *Work in the 21st Century: An Introduction to Industrial and organizational Psychology* (3rd ed.). (Wiley-Blackwell, 2010).

3. A. Seers, A. "Interpersonal Workplace Theory at a Crossroads." In G. B. Graen (Ed.), *New frontiers of leadership, LMX leadership:* The series, 2: 1–31 (Greenwich, CT: Information Age (2004); T. L. Baker and T. G. Hunt, "An Exploratory Investigation Into the Effects of Team Composition on Moral Orientation," *Journal of Managerial Issues* 15 (Spring 2003): 106–120; E. E. Lawler, III, S. A. Mohrman, and G. E. Ledford, Jr., *Creating High Performance Organizations: Practices and Results of Employee Involvement and Total Quality Management in Fortune 1000 Companies* (San Francisco, CA: Jossey-Bass Publishers, 1995); and J. Gordon, "Work Teams: How Far Have They Come?" *Training* 29 (1992): 59–65.

4. D. C. Jones and K. Takao, "The Impact of Teams on Output, Quality, and Downtime: An Empirical Analysis Using Individual Panel Data," *Industrial & Labor Relations Review* 64(2) (Jan. 2011): 215–240.

5. R. Th. A. J., Leenders, J. M. L. van Engelen, and J. Kratzer, "Systematic Design Methods and the Creative Performance of New Product Teams: Do they contradict or complement each other?" *Journal of Product Innovation Management* 24 (2007): 166–179; E. E. Lawler, S.A. Mohrman, and G. E. Ledford, *Creating High Performance Organizations: Practices and Results of Employee Involvement and Total Quality*

Management in Fortune 1000 companies (San Francisco: Jossey-Bas, 1995).

6. L. Schlenkrich and C. Upfold, "A Guideline for Virtual Team Managers: the Key to Effective Social Interaction and Communication," *Electronic Journal of Information Systems Evaluation* 12(1) (2009): 109–118.

7. M. E. Burbach, G.S. Matkin, K. M. Gambrell, K. M., and H. E. Harding, "The Impact of Preparing Faculty in the Effective Use of Student Teams," *College Student Journal* 44(3) (2010): 752–761.

8. G. B. Graen, C. Hui, and E. A. Taylor, "Experience-Based Learning about LMX Leadership and Fairness in Project Teams: A Dyadic Directional Approach," *Academy of Management Learning & Education* 5(4) (2006): 448–460.

9. H. E. Harding, et al. "The Impact of Preparing Faculty in the Effective Use of Student teams," *College Student Journal* 44(3) (2010): 752–761.

10. M. Butler, "Our HR columnist," *People Management* 13 (Nov. 2007): 43.

11. A. Ellis, "System Breakdown: The Role of Mental Models and Transactive Memory in the Relationship between Acute Stress and Team Performance," *Academy of Management Review* 49(3) (2006): 576–589.

12. J. Allen, "Building a Group into a Team," *Internet Journal of Healthcare Administration* 6(1) (2009): 3.

13. S. Sidle, "Do Teams Who Agree to Disagree Make Better Decisions?" *Academy of Management Perspectives* 21(2) (May 2007): 74–75.

14. R. J. Trent, "Becoming an Effective Teaming Organization," *Business Horizons* 47 (March–April 2004): 33–41.

15. L. Hsieh and S. Chen, "A Study of Cross-Functional Collaboration in New Produce Development: A Social Capital Perspective," *International Journal of Productivity and Quality Management* 2 (Nov. 2006): 23.

16. L. Cheng-Chen, and P. Tai-Kuang, "From Organizational Citizenship Behaviour to Team Performance: The Mediation of Group Cohesion and Collective Efficacy," *Management & Organization Review* 6(1) (2010): 55–75.

17. J. N. Choi, "Collective Dynamics of Citizenship Behaviour: What Group Characteristics Promote Group-Level Helping?" *Journal of Management Studies* 46(8) (2009): 1396–1420.

18. R. Batt, "Who Benefits from Teams? Comparing Workers, Supervisors, and Managers," *Industrial Relations* 43 (Jan. 2004): 183–212.

19. B. Dineen, R. Noe, J. Shaw, M. Duffy, and C. Wiethoff, "Level and Dispersion of Satisfaction in Teams: Using Foci and Social Context to Explain the Satisfaction–Absenteeism Relationship," *Academy of Management Journal* 50 (2007): 623–643.

20. See note 20.

21. R. Kidwell and S. Valentine, "Positive Group Context, Work Attitudes, and Organizational Misbehavior: The Case of Withholding Job Effort," *Journal of Business Ethics* 86(1) (2009): 15–28.

22. K. Price, D. Harrison, and J. Gavin, "Withholding Inputs in Team Contexts: Member Composition, Interaction Processes, Evaluation Structure, and Social Loafing," *Journal of Applied Psychology* 91 (Nov. 2006): 1375–1384.

23. E. Stark, J. Shaw, and M. Duffy, "Preference for Group Work, Winning Orientation, and Social Loafing Behavior Groups," *Group & Organization Management* 32 (Dec. 2007): 699–723.

24. K. McFarland, "Where Group-Think Is Good; Groups Often Provide the Best Answers to Business Problems—Provided You Know How to Structure the Team," *Business Week Online* (April 2007).

25. B. K. Brockman, M. E. Rawlston, M. A. Jones, and D. Halstead, "An Exploratory Model of Interpersonal Cohesiveness in New Product Development Teams," *Journal of Product Innovation Management* 27(2) (2010): 201–219.

26. M. Baer, R. J. Leenders, G. R. Oldham, and A. K. Vadera, "Win or Lose the Battle for Creativity: The Power and Perils of Intergroup Competition," *Academy of Management Journal* 53(4) (2010): 827–845.

27. P. Lencioni, "The Five Dysfunctions of a Team: A Leadership Fable," Reviewed by J. R. Hackman and E. Pierce, *Academy of Management Perspectives* 20 (2006): 122–125.

28. J. Bunderson and P. Boumgarden, "Structure and Learning in Self-Managed Teams: Why 'Bureaucratic' Teams Can Be Better Learners," *Organization Science* 21(3) (2010): 609–624.

29. D. Derue, J. Hollenbeck, D. Ilgen, and D. Feltz, "Efficacy Dispersion in Teams: Moving Beyond Agreement and Aggregations," *Personnel Psychology* 63(1) (2010): 1–40.

30. M. Pryor, L. Singleton, S. Taneja, and L. Toombs, "Teaming as a Strategic and Tactical Tool: An Analysis with Recommendations," *International Journal of Management* 26(2): 320–333.

31. L. Lynam, M. McCord, and L. Michaelsen, "Designing Effective Team Assignments: Kolb's Learning Cycle modified by the 4 S Method," *Business Education Innovation Journal* 2(1) (2010): 67–75.

32. M. Martinsuo, "Teaching the Fuzzy Front End of Innovation: Experimenting with Team Learning and Cross-Organizational Integration," *Creativity & Innovation Management* 18(3) (2009): 147–159.

33. R. Rico, M. Sanchez-Manzanares, F. Gil, and C. Gibson, "Team Implicit Coordination Processes: A Team Knowledge-Based Approach," *Academy of Management Review* 33 (2008): 163–184.

34. M. Zellmer-Bruhn and C. Gibson, "Multinational Organization Context: Implications for Team Learning and Performance," *Academy of Management Journal* 49(3) (2006): 501–518.

35. J. T. Byrd and M. R. Luthy, "Improving Group Dynamics: Creating a Team Charter," *Academy of Educational Leadership Journal* 14(1) (2010): 13–26.

36. M. D. Johnson, J. R. Hollenbeck, S. E. Humphrey, D. R. Ilgen, D. Jundt, and C. Meyer, "Cutthroat Cooperation: Asymmetrical Adaptation to Changes in Team Reward Structures," *Academy of Management Journal* 49(1) (2006): 103–119.

37. D. Jones, P. Kalmi, and A. Kauhanen, "How Does Employee Involvement Stack Up? The Effects of Human Resource Management Policies on Performance in a Retail Firm," *Industrial Relations* 49(1) (2010): 1–21.

38. See note 31.

39. M. Barrick, B. Bradley, A. Brown, and A. Colbert, "The Moderating Role of Top Management Team Interdependence: Implications For Real Teams and Working Groups," *Academy of Management Journal* 50 (2007): 544–557.

40. See note 25.

41. See note 29.

42. H. Liao, D. Liu, and R. Loi, "Looking at Both Sides of the Social Exchange Coin: A Social Cognitive Perspective on the Joint Effects of Relationship Quality and Differentiation on Creativity," *Academy of Management Journal* 53(5) (2010): 1090–1109.

43. D. Sluss and B. Ashforth, "Relational Identity and Identification: Defining Ourselves Through Work Relationships," *Academy of Management Review* 32(1) (2007): 9–32.

44. T. Kline and J. O'Grady, "Team Member Personality, Team Processes and Outcomes: Relationships Within a Graduate Student Project Team Sample,", *North American Journal of Psychology* 11(2) (2009): 369–382.

45. J. A. LePine, R. F. Piccolo, C. L. Jackson, J. E. Mathieu, and J. R. Saul, "A Meta-analysis of Teamwork Processes: Tests of a Multidimensional Model and Relationships with Team Effectiveness Criteria," *Personnel Psychology* 61 (2008): 273–307.

46. K. Voutsas, "Effects of Heterogeneity in Work Teams: Creativity or Conflict?" *Insights to a Changing World Journal* 5 (2011): 115–120.

47. D. Harrison and S. Humphrey, "Designing for Diversity or Diversity for Design? Tasks, Interdependence, and Within-Unit Differences at Work," *Journal of Organizational Behavior* 31(12/3) (2010): 328–337.

48. R. B. Bouncken and V.A. Winkler, "National and cultural diversity in transnational innovation teams," *Technology Analysis & Strategic Management* 22(2) (2010): 133–151.

49. G. P. Huber and K. Lewis, "Cross-Understanding: Implications for Group Cognition and Performance," *Academy of Management Review* 35(1) (2010): 6–26.

50. N. Davies, "Build an Effective Team," *Nursing Standard* 23(129) (2009): 72.

51. H. M. Williams, S. K. Parker, S. K., and N. Turner, "Proactively Performing Teams: The Role of Work Design, Transformational Leadership, and Team Composition," *Journal of Occupational & Organizational Psychology* 83(2) (2010): 301–324.

52. M. Prewett, A. Walvoord, F. Stilson, M. Rossi, and M. Brannick, "The Team Personality-Team Performance Relationship Revisited: The Impact of Criterion Choice, Pattern of Workflow, and Method of Aggregation," *Human Performance* 22(4) (2009): 273–296.

53. W. Davies, "Groupwork as a Form of Assessment: Common Problems and Recommended Solutions," *Higher Education* 58(4) (2009): 563–584.

54. See note 32.

55. See note 59.

56. R. Hollister and C. Mejia, "Navigating Team Whirlpools," *Journal of the Quality Assurance Institute* 23(2) (2009): 16–19.

57. G. Clark, "The Seeds of Excellence," *Profit* 28(5) (2009): 19.

58. See note 62.

59. B. A. De Jong and T. Elfring, "How Does Trust Affect the Performance of Ongoing Teams? The Mediating Role of Reflexivity, Monitoring, and Effort," *Academy of Management Journa*, 53(3) (2010): 535–549.

60. M. Mach, S. Dolan, and S. Tzafrir, "The Differential Effect of Team Members' Trust on Team Performance: The Mediation Role of Team Cohesion," *Journal of Occupational & Organizational Psychology* 83(3) (2010): 771–794.

61. M. Lang, "Conflict Management: A Gap in Business Education Curricula," *Journal of Education for Business* 84(4) (2009): 240–245.

62. C. Shu-Cheng Steve, H. Chiung-Yi, and C. Artemis, "Safety Climate and Relational Conflict in the Eyes of Team Memgers: Examining the Role of Need for Closure," *Social Behavior & Personality: An International Journal* 38(1) (2010): 103–114.

63. D. Sethi and M. Seth, "Interpersonal Communication: Lifeblood of an Organization," *IUP Journal of Soft Skills* 3 (Sep. 2009): 32–40.

64. See note 69.

65. C. Kauffman, "Employee Involvement: A New Blueprint for Success," *Journal of Accountancy* 209 (May 2010): 46–49.

66. See note 56.

67. See note 71.

68. See note 57.

69. H. J. Thamhain, "Leadership Lessons from Managing Technology-Intensive Teams," *International Journal of Innovation & Technology Management* 6(2) (2009): 117–133.

70. V. S. Anantatmula, "Project Manager Leadership Role in Improving Project Performance," *Engineering Management Journal* 22(1) (2010): 13–22.

71. S. Sarin and G. O'Connor, "First among Equals: The Effect of Team Leader Characteristics on the Internal Dynamics of Cross-Functional Product Development Teams," *Journal of Product Innovation Management* 26(2) (2009): 188–205.

72. P. Wellington and N. Foster, "21st century teamwork," *Engineering & Technology (17509637)* 4(118) (2009): 72–75.

73. J. B. Wu, A. S. Tsui, and A. J. Kinicki, "Consequences of Differentiated Leadership in Groups," *Academy of Management Journal* 53(1) (2010): 90–106.

74. K. T. Jones, "I'm in Charge Now? Understanding Your Role as a Leader Will Benefit Both You and Your Employees," *Journal of Property Management* 69 (July–August 2004): 72.

75. A. Srivastava, K. M. Bartol, and E. Locke, "Empowering Leadership in Management Teams: Effects on Knowledge Sharing, Efficacy, and Performance," *Academy of Management Journal* 49(6) (2006): 1239–1254.

76. G. Chen, R. Kanfer, B. Kirkman, D. Allen, and B. Rosen, "A Multilevel Study of Leadership, Empowerment, and Performance in Terms," *Journal of Applied Psychology* 92 (2007): 331–346.

77. B. V. Knippenberg and D. V. Knippenberg, "Leader Self-Sacrifice and Leadership Effectiveness: The Moderating Role of Leader Self-Confidence," *Journal of Applied Psychology* 90 (Jan. 2005): 25–38; and D. D. Cremer and D. V. Knippenberg, "Leader Self-Sacrifice and Leadership Effectiveness: The Moderating Role of Leader Self-Confidence," *Organizational Behavior & Human Decision Processes* 95 (Nov. 2004): 140–156.

78. P. J. Schroeder, "Changing Team Culture: The Perspectives of Ten Successful Head Coaches," *Journal of Sport Behavior* 33(1) (2010): 63–88.

79. X. Liu and R. Batt, "How Supervisors Influence Performance: A Multilevel Study of Coaching and Group Management in Technology-Mediated Services," *Personnel Psychology* 63(2) (2010): 265–298.

80. J. Birkinshaw, C. Bouquet, and T. Ambos, "Leaders Relate," *Business Strategy Review* 17 (2006): 19–23.

81. D. Derue, J. Hollenbeck, D. Ilgen, D. Feltz, "Efficacy Disperson in Teams: Moving Beyond Agreement and Aggregation," *Personnel Psychology* 63(1) (2010): 1–40.

82. H. Oh, G. Labianca, and M. Chung, "A Multilevel Model of Group Social Capital," *Academy of Management Review* 31 (2006): 569–582.

83. L. Chin-Yun, A. Pirola-Merlo, Y. Chin-Ann, and H. Chih, "Disseminating the Functions of Team Coaching Regarding Research and Development Team Effectiveness: Evidence from High-Tech Industries in Taiwan," *Social Behavior & Personality: An International Journal*, 37(1) (2009): 41–57.

84. E. Duygulu and N. Ciraklar, "Effects of Leadership Roles on Team Effectiveness," *Ege Academic Review* 9 (2009): 389–400.

85. C. J. Hobson, D. Strupeck, and J. Szostek, "A Behavioral Roles Approach to Assessing and Improving the Team Leadership Capabilities of Managers," *International Journal of Management* 27(1) (2010): 3–15.

86. See note 26.

87. See note 48.

88. See note 77.

89. A. Carr, H. Kaynak, and S. Muthusamy, "The Cross-Functional Coordination Between Operations, Marketing, Purchasing, and Engineering and the Impact on Performance," *International Journal of Manufacturing Technology and Management* 13 (Dec. 2007): 55.

90. See note 95.

91. B. Ebrahimi, R. McGowan, and T. Chung, "Key Success Factors in New Product Development," *International Journal of Management and Decision Making* 7(12–3) (Mar. 6, 2006): 313.

92. T. L. Legare, "How Hewlett-Packard Used Cross-Functional Teams to Deliver Healthcare Industry Solutions," *Journal of Organizational Excellence* 20(4) (Autumn 2001): 29–38.

93. C. O. Longenecker, and M. Neubert, "Barriers and Gateways to Management Cooperation and Teamwork," *Business Horizons* 43(5) (Sep./Oct. 2000): 37–44.

94. A. Joshi, N. Pandey, and G. Han, "Bracketing Team Boundary Spanning: An Examination of Task-Based, Team-Level, and Contextual Antecedents," *Journal of Organizational Behavior* 30(6) (2009): 731–759.

95. H. Peelle, "Appreciative Inquiry and Creative Problem Solving in Cross-Functional Teams," *Journal of Applied Behavioral Science* 42 (Dec. 2007): 447–467.

96. D. D. Greenand G. E. Roberts, "Personnel Implications of Public Sector Virtual Organizations," *Public Personnel Management* 39(1) (2010): 47–57.

97. C. Brad Crisp, et al., "Can You Hear Me Now? Communication in Virtual Product Development Teams," *Journal of Product Innovation Management* 26(2) (2009): 139–155.

98. P. Dvorak, "How Teams Can Work Well Together From Far Apart," *The Wall Street Journal* (Sep. 17, 2007).

99. N. A. Ebrahim, S. Ahmed, and Z. Taha, "Virtual Teams: a Literature Review," *Australian Journal of Basic & Applied Sciences* 3(3) (2009): 2653–2669.

100. K. Siakas and E. Siakas, "The Need for Trust Relationships to Enable Successful Virtual Team Collaboration in Software Outsourcing," *International Journal of Technology, Policy, and Management* 8 (Dec. 2007): 593.

101. T. Clemmensen, M. Khryashcheva, and O. Podshibikhina, "Combining Bases of Trust Development in Virtual Teams," *International Journal of Networking and Virtual Organisations* 5 (Dec. 2007): 17.

102. S. A. Furst, M. Reeves, B. Rosen, and R. S. Blackburn, "Managing the Life Cycle of Virtual Teams," *Academy of Management Executive* (May 2004): 6–20; L. L. Martins, L. L. Gilson, and M T. Maynard, "Virtual Teams: What Do We Know and Where Do We Go From Here," *Journal of Management* 30(6) (2004): 805–835.

103. C. B. Gibson and J. L. Gibbs, "Unpacking the Concept of Virtuality: The Effects of Geographic Dispersion, Electronic Dependence, Dynamic Structure, and National Diversity on Team Innovation," *Administrative Science Quarterly* (Sep. 2006): 451–495.

104. United States Office of Personnel Management (2009). *Status of Telework in the Federal Government*, http://www.telework. gov/Reports, retrieved.

105. See note 102.

106. R. S. Colfax, A. T. Santos, and J. Diego, "Virtual Leadership: A Green Possibility in Critical Times. But Can It Really Work?" *Journal of International Business Research* 8 (June 2009): 133–139.

107. See note 112.

108. A. Ismail, N. Zainuddin, and Z. Ibrahim, "Linking Participative and Consultative Leadership Styles to Organizational Commitment as an Antecedent of Job Satisfaction," *UNITAR e-Journal* 6(1) (2010): 11–26.

109. See note 114.

110. See note 114.

111. X. Huang, J. Iun, A. Liu, A, and Y. Gong, "Does Participative Leadership Enhance Work Performance by Inducing Empowerment or Trust? The Differential Effects on Managerial and Non-managerial Subordinates," *Journal of Organizational Behavior* 31(1) (2010): 122–143.

112. M. Seo and L. Barrett, "Being Emotional During Decision Making—Good or Bad? An Empirical Investigation," *Academy of Management Journal* 50 (2007): 923–940.

113. I. Bens, "Facilitating With Ease! Core Skills for Facilitators, Team Leaders and Members, Managers, Consultants, and Trainers," Reviewed by J. K. Williams, *Academy of Management Learning & Education* 6(2) (June 2007): 294.

114. See note 119.

115. M. R. Haas, "The Double-Edged Swords of Autonomy and External Knowledge: Analyzing Team Effectiveness in a Multinational Organization," *Academy of Management Journal* 53(5) (2010): 989–1008.

116. See note 57.

117. N. Watersand M. Beruvides, "An Empirical Study Analyzing Traditional Work Schemes Versus Work Teams," *Engineering Management Journal* 21(4) (2009): 36–43.

118. See note 123.

119. I. P. Vlachos, "The Effects of Human Resource Practices on Firm Growth," *International Journal of Business Science & Applied Management* 4(2) (2009): 17–34.

120. See note 57.

121. See note 121.

122. A. Fazzariand J. Mosca, "'Partners in Perfection': Human Resources Facilitating Creation and Ongoing Implementation of Self-Managed Manufacturing Teams in a Small Medium

Enterprise," *Human Resource Development Quarterly* 20(3) (2009): 353–376.

123. Z. Omar, A. Zainal, F. Omar, and R. Khairudin, "The Influence of Leadership Behaviour on Organisational Citizenship Behaviour in Self-Managed Work Teams in Malaysia," *South African Journal of Human Resource Management* 7(1) (2009): 196–206.

124. C. Langfred, "The Downside of Self-Management: A Longitudinal Study of the Effects of Conflict on Trust, Autonomy, and Task Interdependence in Self-Managing Teams," *Academy of Management Journal* 50 (2007): 885–900.

125. M. Moravec, O. J. Johannessen, and T. A. Hjelmas, "The Well-Managed SMT," *Management Review* 87 (June 1998): 56–58.

126. J. Carson, P. Tesluk, and J. Marrone, "Shared Leadership in Teams: An Investigation of Antecedent Conditions and Performance," *Academy of Management Journal* 50 (Oct. 2007): 1214–1231.

127. David Gelormo, et al., "Are In-Class Peer Leaders Effective in the Peer-Led Team-Learning Approach?" *Journal of College Science Teaching* 38(4) (2009): 62–67.

128. See note 91.

129. L. Gratton, "The End of the Middle Manager," *Harvard Business Review* 89(11/2) (2011): 36.

130. See note 130.

131. M. Bolino, S. Valcea, and J. Harvey, "Employee, Manage Thyself: The Potentially Negative Implications of Expecting Employees to Behave Proactively," *Journal of Occupational & Organizational Psychology* 83(2) (2010): 325–345.

132. www.fedex.com, retrieved May 30, 2011.

Chapter 9

1. A. Cheney, "Oprah Winfrey Signs Off," *Wall Street Journal*, May 25, 2011.

2. A. Oldenburg, *USA TODAY*, May 21, 2011.

3. A. Stanley, "Television Diva Gives Thanks and Signs Off," *The New York Times*, May 25, 2011.

4. N. S. Hopkins, "Charisma and Responsibility: Max Weber, Kurt Eisner, and the Bavarian Revolution of 1918," *Max Weber Studies* 7(2): 185–211, Academic Search Complete, EBSCO*host*, retrieved June 6, 2011.

5. A. B. Seligman, "Charisma and the Transformation of Grace in the Early Modern Era," *Social Research* 58(3) (1991): 591–620.

6. C. Adair-Toteff, "Max Weber's Charisma," *Journal of Classical Sociology* 5(2) (2005): 189–204, Academic Search Complete, EBSCO*host*, retrieved June 6, 2011.

7. M. G. Scott, "Max Weber: On Charisma and Institution Building (Book)," *British Journal of Sociology* 21(4) (1970): 458–460, Academic Search Complete, EBSCO*host*, retrieved June 6, 2011.

8. T. E. Dow, Jr., "The Theory of Charisma," *Sociological Quarterly* 10 (1969): 306–318.

9. M. Bligh and J. Robinson, "Was Gandhi "Charismatic? Exploring the Rhetorical Leadership of Mahatma Gandhi," *Leadership Quarterly* 21(5) (2010): 844–855.

10. J. Rowold and L. Laukamp, "Charismatic Leadership and Objective Performance Indicators," *Applied Psychology: An International Review* 58, (4) (2009): 602–621.

11. B. Michaelis, R. Stegmaier, and K. Sonntag, "Affective Commitment to Change and Innovation Implementation Behavior: The Role of Charismatic Leadership and Employees' Trust in Top Management," *Journal of Change Management* 9(4) (2009): 399–417.

12. M. Babcock-Roberson and O. Strickland, "The Relationship Between Charismatic Leadership, Work Engagement, and Organizational Citizenship Behaviors," *Journal of Psychology* 144(3) (2010): 313–326.

13. See note 11.

14. J. B. Wu, A. S. Tsui, and A. J. Kinicki, "Consequences of Differentiated Leadership in Groups," *Academy of Management Journal* 53(1) (2010): 90–106.

15. A. Tikhomirov and W. Spangler, "Neo-Charismatic Leadership and the Fate of Mergers and Acquisitions: An Institutional Model of CEO Leadership," *Journal of Leadership & Organizational Studies* 17(1) (2010): 44–60.

16. See note 10.

17. M. Bligh and J. Robinson "Was Gandhi 'Charismatic'? Exploring the Rhetorical Leadership of Mahatma Gandhi," *Leadership Quarterly* 21(5) (2010): 844–855.

18. G. Gregory, "Pseudocharismatic Leaders from Either Side of the Podium: An Introduction to Mitigation Methods for Followers of Toxic Leaders," *Conference Papers, Midwestern Political Science Association*, p. 1.

19. E. E. Osaghae, "The Limits of Charismatic Authority and the Challenges of Leadership in Nigeria," *Journal of Contemporary African Studies* 28(4) (2010): 407–422.

20. R. Rigby, "Charisma Is a Dangerous Quality," *Human Resources (09648380)* (2009)): 62.

21. J. Humphreys, D. Zhao, K. Ingram, J. Gladstone, and L. Basham, "Situational Narcissism and Charismatic Leadership: A Conceptual Framework," *Journal of Behavioral & Applied Management* 11(2) (2010): 118–136.

22. See note 19.

23. See note 21.

24. R. Nielsen, J. Marrone, and H. Slay, "A New Look at Humility: Exploring the Humility Concept and Its Role in Socialized Charismatic Leadership," *Journal of Leadership & Organizational Studies* 17(1) (2010): 33–43.

25. P. Varella, M. Javidan, and Dr. Waldman, "Leadership, Group Behavior, and Density of Instrumental Ties in Organizational Groups," *Academy of Management Annual Meeting Proceedings* (2010): 1–5.

26. M. Brown and L. Trevifio, "Leader-Follower Values Congruence: Are Socialized Charismatic Leaders Better Able to Achieve It?" *Journal of Applied Psychology* 94(2) (2009): 478–490.

27. www.cdc.gov, retrieved June 3, 2011.

28. http://www.thehealthcarecenter.com/child_obesity_from_fast_food.html, retrieved June 3, 2011.

29. www.fastfoodmarketing.org, retrieved June 3, 2011.

30. J. M. Burns, *Leadership*. (New York: Harper & Row, 1978).

31. L. Paarlberg and B. Lavigna, "Transformational Leadership and Public Service Motivation: Driving Individual and Organizational Performance," *Public Administration Review* 70(5): 710–718.

32. I. Boga, I and N. Ensari, "The Role of Transformational Leadership and Organizational Change on Perceived Organizational Success," *Psychologist-Manager Journal* 12(4): 235–251.

33. H. Zagoršek, V. Dimovski, and M. Škerlavaj, "Transactional and Transformational Leadership Impacts on Organizational Learning," *Journal for East European Management Studies* 14 (2) (2009): 144–165.

34. N. Paulsen, D. Maldonado, V. Callan, and O. Ayoko, "Charismatic Leadership, Change and Innovation in an R&D Organization," *Journal of Organizational Change Management* 22(5) (2009): 511–523.

35. "Organization Development and Change," Conference Paper Abstracts, *Academy of Management Annual Meeting Proceedings* (2010): 1–30, Business Source Complete, EBSCOhost, retrieved June 8, June 2011.

36. X. Zhang and K. M. Bartol, "Linking Empowering Leadership and Employee Creativity: The Influence of Psychological Empowerment, Intrinsic Motivation, and Creative Process Engagement," *Academy of Management Journal* 53(1) (2010): 107–128.

37. Z. Hinduan, E. Wilson-Evered, S. Moss, and E. Scannell, "Leadership, Work Outcomes and Openness to Change Following an Indonesian Bank Merger," *Asia Pacific Journal of Human Resources* 47(1) (2009): 59–78.

38. See note 30.

39. R. L. Loi, Y. M. Mao, and H. Ngo, "Linking Leader-Member Exchange and Employee Work Outcomes: The Mediating Role of Organizational Social and Economic Exchange," *Management & Organization Review* 5(3) (2009): 401–422.

40. Z. Weichun, R. Riggio, B. Avolio, and J. Sosik, "The Effect of Leadership on Follower Moral Identity: Does Transformational/Transactional Style Make a Difference?" *Journal of Leadership & Organizational Studies* 18(2) (2011): 150–163.

41. A. Zaleznik, "Managers and Leaders: Are They Different?" in W. W. Rosenbach and R. L. Taylor (Eds.), *Contemporary Issues in Leadership* (Oxford: Westview Press, 1993): 36–56.

42. A. Ismail, M. Mohamad, H. Mohamed, N. Rafiuddin, and K. Zhen, "Transformational and Transactional Leadership Styles as a Predictor of Individual Outcomes," *Theoretical & Applied Economics* 17(6) (2010): 89–104.

43. J. Whittington, R. Coker, V. Goodwin, W. Ickes, and B. Murray, "Transactional Leadership Revisited: Self-Other Agreement and Its Consequences," *Journal of Applied Social Psychology* 39(8) (2009): 1860–1886.

44. N. Podsakoff, P. Podsakoff, and V. Kuskova, "Dispelling Misconceptions and Providing Guidelines for Leader Reward and Punishment Behavior," *Business Horizons* 53(3) (2010): 291–303.

45. See note 43.

46. B. M. Bass, B. J. Avolio, D. I. Jung, and Y. Berson, "Predicting Unit Performance by Assessing Transformational and Transactional Leadership," *Journal of Applied Psychology* 88 (2) (April 2003): 207–219.

47. T. Judge and R. Piccolo, "Transformational and Transactional Leadership: A Meta- Analytic Test of Their Relative Validity," *Journal of Applied Psychology* 89(5) (Oct. 2004): 755–768.

48. N. Hai Nam and S. Mohamed, "Leadership Behaviors, Organizational Culture and Knowledge Management Practices," *Journal of Management Development* 30(2) (2011): 206–221.

49. E. Davis, J. Kee, and K. Newcomer, "Strategic Transformation Process: Toward Purpose, People, Process and Power," *Organization Management Journal* 7(1) (2010): 66–80.

50. A. Thierer, "Apple, The iPhone and a Locational Privacy Techno-Panic," *Forbes*, May 2011.

51. S. Thurm and Y. I. Kane, "Your Apps Are Watching You: A WSJ Investigation Finds That iPhone and Android Apps Are Breaching the Privacy of Smartphone Users," Wall Street Journal (Dec. 17, 2010).

52. B. Brocato, and S. Gold, "Leadership Ambiguity and Ambivalence: A Critical Solution," *Global Management Journal* 2(2): 5–15.

53. J. Zenger, J. Folkman, and S. Edinger, "Inspiring Leaders," *Leadership Excellence* 26(6) (June 2009): 20–20.

54. K. Levine, R. Muenchen, and A. Brooks, "Measuring Transformational and Charismatic Leadership: Why Isn't Charisma Measured?" *Communication Monographs* 77(4) (2010): 576–591.

55. See note 54.

56. See note 17.

57. J. Sosik, J. Juzbasich, and J. Chun, "Effects of Moral Reasoning and Management Level on Ratings of Charismatic Leadership, In-role and Extra-role Performance of Managers: A Multi-source Examination," *Leadership Quarterly* 22(2) (2011): 434–450.

58. See note 11.

59. B. Galvin, P. Balkundi, and D. Waldman, "Spreading the Word: the Role of Surrogates in Charismatic Leadership Process," *Academy of Management Review* 35(3) (2010): 477–494.

60. F. Walter and H. Bruch, "An Affective Events Model of Charismatic Leadership Behavior: A Review, Theoretical Integration, and Research Agenda," *Journal of Management* 35(6) (2009): 1428–1452.

61. B. M. Bass and B. J. Avilio, *Improving Organizational Effectiveness Through Transformational Leadership* (Thousand Oaks, CA: Sage, 1994).

62. See note 34.

63. R. De Vries, A. Bakker-Pieper, and W. Oostenveld, "Leadership = Communication? The Relations of Leaders' Communication Styles with Leadership Styles, Knowledge Sharing and Leadership Outcomes," *Journal of Business & Psychology* 25(3) (2010): 367–380.

64. A. Joshi, M. Lazarova, M, and H. Liao, "Getting Everyone on Board: The Role of Inspirational Leadership in Geographically Dispersed Teams," *Organization Science* 20(1) (2009): 240–252.

65. See note 14.

66. N. Wallis, F. Yammarino, and A. Feyerherm, "Individualized Leadership: A Qualitative Study of Senior Executive Leaders," *Leadership Quarterly* 22(1) (2011): 182–206.

67. See note 36.

68. A. Oke, N. Munsh, and F. Walumbwa, "The Influence of Leadership on Innovation Processes and Activities," *Organizational Dynamics* 38(1) (2009): 64–72.

69. D. McGuire and K. Hutchings, "Portrait of a Transformational Leader: The Legacy of Dr. Martin Luther King Jr.," *Leadership & Organization Development Journal* 28 (2007): 154–166.

70. M. Cusumano, "Technology Strategy and Management: The Legacy of Bill Gates," *Communications of the ACM* 52(1) (2009): 25–26.

71. R. Stengel, "Person of the Year," *Time* (Wednesday, Dec. 15, 2010); J. A. Vargas, "The Face of Facebook," *The New Yorker* (Sep., 20, 2010); "M. Zuckerburg," *New York Times* (Jan. 3, 2011).

72. D. Jung and J. Sosik, "Who Are the Spellbinders? Identifying Personal Attributes of Charismatic Leaders," *Journal of Leadership & Organizational Studies* 12 (2006): 12–26.

73. J. M. Howell and B. Shamir, "The Role of Followers in the Charismatic Leadership Process: Relationships and Their Consequences," *Academy of Management Review* 30(1) (Jan. 2005): 96–112.

74. See note 36.

75. M. McCuddy and M. Cavin, "The Demographic Context of Servant Leadership," *Journal of the Academy of Business & Economics* 9(2) (2009): 129–139.

76. D. R. Ebener, "Servant Leadership and a Culture of Stewardship," *Priest* 67(2): 17–21.

77. "Management Spirituality and Religion," Conference Paper Abstracts, 2010, *Academy of Management Annual Meeting Proceedings*, pp. 1–17, Business Source Complete, EBSCO-host, retrieved June 8, 2011.

78. M. Ahn, L. Ettner, and A. Loupin, "From Classical to Contemporary Leadership Challenges," *Journal of Leadership Studies* 5(1) (2011): 6–22.

79. C. Caldwell, L. Hayes, and D. Long, "Leadership, Trustworthiness, and Ethical Stewardship," *Journal of Business Ethics* 96(4) (2010): 497–512.

80. L. C. Spears, "Servant Leadership," *Leadership Excellence* 26 (5) (2009): 20.

81. R. K. Greenleaf, Servant *Leadership: A Journey into the Nature of Legitimate Power and Greatness* (Mahwah, NJ: Paulist Press, 1977), 7.

82. See note 75.

83. L. Spears, "Servant-Leaders," *Personal Excellence* 15(2) (2010): 14.

84. A. Bryant, "Xerox's New Chief Tries to Redefine Its Culture," *New York Times* (Feb. 20, 2010).

85. "Chairwoman and CEO of Xerox Corporation Ursula Burns Addresses the Executives' Club of Chicago at the J" (June 1, 2011), http://centennial.executivesclub.org.

86. "Entrepreneurial Spirit: Ursula Burns, Chief Executive Officer, Xerox Corporation," info@outputlinks.com, retrieved June 9, 2011.

87. See note 84.

88. D. Mattioli, "Xerox Chief Looks Beyond Photocopiers Towards Services," *Wall Street Journal*, (Monday June 13, 2011): B9.

89. See note 88.

Chapter 10

1. A. Cheng, "Avon's Profit More than Triples; Shares Gain," *Wall Street Journal* (May 3, 2011).

2. E. Schein, *Organizational Culture and Leadership* (San Francisco: Jossey-Bass, 1985),.

3. G. S. McNeal, "Organizational Culture, Professional Ethics, and Guantanamo," *Case Western Reserve Journal of International Law* (2010): 125–149.

4. M. Dull, "Leadership and Organizational Culture: Sustaining Dialogue between Practitioners and Scholars," *Public Administration Review*: 857–866.

5. S. Cheung, P. Wong, and A. Wu, "Towards an Organizational Culture Framework in Construction," *International Journal of Project Management* 29(1) (2011): pp. 33–44.

6. R. J. Taormina, "Organizational Socialization: The Missing Link between Employee Needs and Organizational Culture," *Journal of Managerial Psychology* 24(7) (2009): 650–676.

7. W. Wines and J. Hamilton, "On Changing Organizational Cultures by Injecting New Ideologies: The Power of Stories," *Journal of Business Ethics* 89(3) (2009): 433–447.

8. J. Yuhee and N. Takeuchi, "Performance Implications for the Relationships among Top Management Leadership, Organizational Culture, and Appraisal Practice: Testing Two Theory-Based Models of Organizational Learning Theory in Japan," *International Journal of Human Resource Management* 21(111) (2010): 1931–1950.

9. F. Duarte, "Working with Corporate Social Responsibility in Brazilian Companies: The Role of Managers' Values in the Maintenance of CSR Cultures," *Journal of Business Ethics* 96(3) (2010): 355–368.

10. See note 3.

11. R. Smollan and J. Sayers, "Organizational Culture, Change and Emotions: A Qualitative Study," *Journal of Change Management* 9(4) (2009): 435–457.

12. E. Schien, *Organizational Culture and Leadership*, 3rd ed. (San Francisco, CA: Jossey-Bass, 2004); H. M. Trice and J. M. Beyer, *The Cultures of Work Organizations* (Englewood Cliffs, NJ: Prentice-Hall, 1993); M. J. Hatch, "The Cultural Dynamics of Organizing and Change," in N. M. Ashkanasy, C. P. M. Wildreon, and M. F. Peterson (Eds.), *Handbook of Organizational Culture and Climate* (Thousand Oaks, CA: Sage, 2000): 245–260.

13. M. Dacin, K. Munir, and P. Tracey, "Formal Dining at Cambridge Colleges: Linking Ritual Perforance and Institutional Maintenance," *Academy of Management Journal* 53(6) (2010): 1393–1418.

14. See note 7.

15. W. Zheng, B. Yang, and G. McLean, "Linking Organizational Culture, Structure, Strategy, and Organizational Effectiveness: Mediating Role of Knowledge Management," *Journal of Business Research* 63(7) (2010): 763–771; D. Ravasi and M. Schultz, "Responding to Organizational Identify Threats: Exploring the Role of Organizational Culture," *Academy of Management Journal* 49 (2006): 433(126); M. Muafi, "The Effects of Alignment Competitive Stragecy, Culture, and Role Behavior on Organizational Performance in Service Firms," *International Journal of Organizational Innovation* 2(1) (2009): 106–134.

16. E. Schien, *Organizational Culture and Leadership*, 2nd ed. (San Francisco, CA: Jossey-Bass, 1992).

17. M. Braunscheidel, N. Suresh, and A. Boisnier, "Investigating the Impact of Organizational Culture on Supply Chain Integration," *Human Resource Management* 49(5) (2010): 883–911.

18. S. Chakravorti, "Managing Organizational Culture Change and Knowledge to Enhance Customer Experiences: Analysis and Framework," *Journal of Strategic Marketing* 19(2) (2011): 123–151.

19. M. Baughn and P. Finzel, "A Clash of Cultures in a Merger of Two Acquisition Project Offices," *Engineering Management Journal* 21(2) (2009): 11–17.

20. B. Gregory, S. Harris, A. Armenakis, and C. Shook, "Organizational Culture and Effectiveness: A Study of Values, Attitudes, and Organizational outcomes," *Journal of Business Research* 62(7) (2009): 673–679.

21. J. C. Santora, "Quality Management and Manufacturing Performance: Does Success Depend on Firm Culture?" *Academy of Management Perspectives* 23(2) (2009): 103–105.

22. J. Naranjo-Valencia, D. Jiménez-Jiménez, and R. Sanz-Valle, "Innovation or Imitation? The Role of Organizational Culture," *Management Decision* 49(1) (2011): 55–72.

23. B. Aydin and A. Ceylan, "What Is the Joint Effect of Employee Satisfaction and Customer Orientation on the Organizational Culture in Metal Working Manufacturing?" *International Journal of Human Resource Management* 22(5): 1203–1215.

24. E. Zavyalova and D. Kucherov, "Relationship between Organizational Culture and Job Satisfaction in Russian Business Enterprises," *Human Resource Development International* 13(2): 225–235.

25. B. Joo, "Organizational Commitment for Knowledge Workers: The Roles of Perceived Organizational Learning Culture, Leader–Member Exchange Quality, and Turnover Intention," *Human Resource Development Quarterly* 21(1) (2010): 69–85.

26. M. Simosi and A. Xenikou, "The Role of Organizational Culture in the Relationship between Leadership and Organizational Commitment: An Empirical Study in a Greek Organization," *International Journal of Human Resource Management* 21(110) (2010): 1598–1616.

27. A. Hon and A. Leung, "Employee Creativity and Motivation in the Chinese Context: The Moderating Role of Organizational Culture," *Cornell Hospitality Quarterly* 52(2) (2011): 125–134.

28. J. Baek-Kyoo and S. Ji Hyun, "Psychological Empowerment and Organizational Commitment: The Moderating Effect of Organizational Learning Culture," *Human Resource Development International* 13(4) (2010): 425–441.

29. R. Padma and V. Nair, "Organizational Culture and Its Impact on Organizational Commitment in Public and Private Organizations," *Global Management Review* 4(1) (2009): 32–39.

30. E. Castilla and S. Benard, "The Paradox of Meritocracy in Organizations," *Administrative Science Quarterly* 55(4) (2010): 543–576.

31. A. Chen, "Culture and Compensation—Unpicking the Intricate Relationship between Reward and Organizational Culture," *Thunderbird International Business Review* 52(3) (2010): 189–202.

32. See note 4.

33. T. Giberson, C. Resick, M. Dickson, J. Mitchelson, K. Randall, and M. Clark, "Leadership and Organizational Culture: Linking CEO Characteristics to Cultural Values," *Journal of Business & Psychology* 24(2) (2009): 123–137.

34. R., D. Davis, L. Thorndyke, "Transforming Culture Through Physician Leadership Development," *Physician Executive* 36(3) (2010): 38–44.

35. See note 16.

36. See note 8.

37. P. J. Schroeder, "Changing Team Culture: The Perspective of Ten Successful Head Coaches," *Journal of Sports Behavior* 33(1) (2010): 63–88.

38. I. Chow and S. Liu, "The Effect of Aligning Organizational Culture and Business Strategy with HR Systems on Firm Performance in Chinese Enterprises," *International Journal of Human Resource Management* 20(111) (2009): 2292–2310.

39. See note 28

40. See note 8.

41. K. M. Kuhn, "Compensation as a Signal of Organizational Culture: The Effects of Advertising Individual or Collective Incentives," *International Journal of Human Resource Management* 20(7) (2009): 1634–1648.

42. See note 37.

43. See note 27.

44. See note 24.

45. S. Liu, "Organizational Culture and New Service Development Performance: Insights from Knowledge Intensive Business Service," *International Journal of Innovation Management* 13(3) (2009): 371–392.

46. See note 17.

47. R. E. McClure, "The Influence of Organizational Culture and Conflict on Market Orientation," *Journal of Business & Industrial Marketing* 25(7) (2010): 514–524.

48. See note 37.

49. See note 28.

50. See note 22.

51. See note 25.

52. C. Webster and A. White, "Exploring the National and Organizational Culture Mix in Service Firms," *Journal of the Academy of Marketing Science* 38(6) (2010): 691–703.

53. S. D. Sidle, "Building a Committed Global Workforce: Does What Employees Want Depend on Culture?" *Academy of Management Perspectives* 23(1) (2009): 79–80.

54. G. Hofstede, "Cultural Constraints in Management Theories," *Academy of Management Executive* 7(1) (Feb. 1993): 81–94.

55. See note 53.

56. See note 53.

57. www.aacsb.edu (*AACSB Standards 2011 Update Report*, p. 72).

58. R. Stevens and E. Ogunji, "Managing Diverse Organizational Environments for Strategic Advantage: Exploring the Value of Developing Business Diversity Curriculum in Higher Education," *Journal of Management Policy & Practice* 11(4) (2010): 72–85.

59. S. Powell, "The Business Benefits of andPractical Challenges Involved in the Promotion of Workforce Diversity," *International Journal of Retail & Distribution Management* 32(8) (2004): 448–451.

60. L. Pinto, C. Cabral-Cardoso, and W. Werther, "Why Solidarity Matters (and Sociability Doesn't): The Effects of Perceived Organizational Culture on Expatriation Adjustment," *Thunderbird International Business Review* 53(3) (2011): 377–389.

61. G. Chen, B. L. Kirkman, K. Kim, C. C. Farh, and S. Tangirala, "When Does Cross-Cultural Motivation Enhance Expatriate Effectiveness? A Multilevel Investigation of the Moderating Roles of Subsidiary Support and Cultral Distance," *Academy of Management Journal* 53(5) (2010): 1110–1130.

62. See note 57.

63. P. Navarro, "The MBA Core Curricula of Top-Ranked U.S. Business Schools: A Study in Failure?" *Academy of Management Learning & Education* 7(1) (2008): 108–123.

64. D. Palmer, "Business Leadership: Three Levels of Ethical Analysis," *Journal of Business Ethics* 88(3) (2009): 525–536.

65. M. Brown and M. Mitchell, "Ethical and Unethical Leadership: Exploring New Avenues for Future Research," *Business Ethics Quarterly* 20(4) (2010): 583–616.

66. P. Verhezen, "Giving Voice in a Culture of Silence. From a Culture of Compliance to a Culture of Integrity," *Journal of Business Ethics* 96(2) (2010): 187–206.

67. A. Ardichvili, J. Mitchell, and D. Jondle, "Characteristics of Ethical Business Cultures," *Journal of Business Ethics* 85(4) (2009): pp. 445–451.

68. P. Erwin, "Corporate Codes of Conduct: The Effects of Code Content and Quality on Ethical Performance," *Journal of Business Ethics* 99(4) (2011): 535–548.

69. F. J. Flynn and S. S. Wiltermuth, "Who's with Me? False Consensus, Brokerage, and Ethical Decision Making in Organizations," *Academy of Management Journal* 53(5) (2010): 1074–1089.

70. C. Messikomer and C. Crika, "Constructing a Code of Ethics: An Experiential Case of a National Professional Organization," *Journal of Business Ethics* 95(1) (2010): 55–71.

71. E. Byron, "Avon Bribe Investigation Widens," *Wall Street Journal* (Thursday, May 5, 2011).

72. P. Blausten, "Can Authentic Leadership Survive the Downturn?" *Business Strategy Review* 20(1) (Spring 2009): 84–87.

73. L. Reynolds, "Authentic Leadership," *Training Journal* (Aug. 2009): 52–55.

74. See note 73.

75. D. Ladkin and S. Taylor, "Enacting the True Self: Towards a Theory of Embodied Authentic leadership," *Leadership Quarterly* 21(1) (Feb. 2010): 64–74.

76. M. Spitzmuller and R. Ilies, "Do They [all] See My True Self? Leader's Relational Authenticity and Followers' Assessments of Transformational Leadership," *European Journal of Work & Organizational Psychology* 19(3) (June 2010): 304–332.

77. C. Wong and G. Cummings, "The Influence of Authentic Leadership Behaviors on Trust and Work Outcomes of Health Care Staff," *Journal of Leadership Studies* 3(2) (2009): 6–23.

78. B. J. Avolio and W. L. Gardner, "Authentic Leadership Development: Getting to the Root of Positive Forms of Leadership," *Leadership Quartery* 16 (2005): 315–338.

79. W. L. Gardner, B. J. Avolio, F. Luthans, D. R. May, and F. Walumbwa, "Can You See the Real Me?" A Self-Based Model of Authentic Leaders and Follower Development," *Leadership Quarterly* 16 (2005): 343–372.

80. B. J. Avolio and W. L. Gardner, "Authentic Leadership Development: Getting to the Root of Positive Forms of Leadership," *Leadership Quarterly* 16 (2005): 315–338.

81. M. Sabatier, "Bring Back the Authentic Leaders," *Training Journal* (May 2010): 30–32.

82. B. J. Avolio, W. L. Gardner, F. O. Walumbwa, F. Luthans, and D. R. May, "Unlocking the Mask: A Look at the Process by which Authentic Leaders Impact Follower Attitudes and Behaviors," *Leadership Quarterly* (15) (2004): 801–823.

83. R. Clapp-Smith, G. R. Vogelgesang, and J. B. Avey, "Authentic Leadership and Positive Psychological Capital: The Mediating Role of Trust at the Group Level of Analysis," *Journal of Leadership & Organizational Studies* 15(3) (Feb. 2009): 227–240.

84. See note 77.

85. L. Shore, B. Chung-Herrera, M. Dean, K. Ehrhart, D. Jung, A. Randel, and G. Singh, "'Diversity in Organizations: Where Are We Now and Where Are We Going?" *Human Resource Management Review* 19(2) (2009): 117–133.

86. D. Pitts, A. Hicklin, D. Hawes, and E. Melton, "What Drives the Implementation of Diversity Management Programs? Evidence from Public Organizations," *Journal of Public Administration Research & Theory* 20(4) (2010): 867–886.

87. L. Leveson, T. Joiner, and S. Bakalis, "Managing Cultural Diversity and Perceived Organizational Support," *International Journal of Manpower* 30(4) (2009): 377–392.

88. R. Roessler, J. Hurley, and B. McMahon, "A Comparison of Allegations and Resolutions Involving Issues of Discharge Versus Constructive Discharge: Implications for Diversity Management," *Advances in Developing Human Resources* 12(4) (2010): 407–428.

89. S. van der Walt and T. du Plessis, "Age Diversity and the Aging Librarian in Academic Libraries in South Africa," *South African Journal of Library & Information Science* 76(1) (2010): 1–10.

90. K. L. Fessele, "Nursing Through the Ages: Benefits of a Generationally Diverse Staff Mix," *ONS Connect* 24(5) (2009): 8–12.

91. A. Eagly and J. Lau Chin, "Diversity and Leadership in a Changing World," *American Psychologist* 65(3) (2010: 216–224.

92. See note 86.

93. R. Stevens and E. Ogunji, "Preparing Business Students for the Multi-cultural Work Environment of the Future: A Teaching Agenda," *International Journal of Management* 28 (2) (2011): 528–544.

94. B. L. Kirkman, G. Chen, J. Farh, Z. Chen, and K. B. Lower, "Individual Power Distance Orientation and Follower Reactions to Transformational Leaders: A Cross-Level, Cross-Cultural Examination," *Academy of Management Journal* 52(4) (2009): 744–764.

95. C. Camelo, M. Fernández-Alles, and A. Hernández, "Strategic Consensus, Top Management Teams, and Innovation Performance," *International Journal of Manpower* 31(6) (2010): 678–695.

96. See note 85.

97. M. Roberge and R. van Dick, "Recognizing the Benefits of Diversity: When and How Does Diversity Increase Group Performance?" *Human Resource Management Review* 20(4) (2010): 295–308.

98. M. Jayne and R. Dipboye, "Leveraging Diversity to Improve business Performance: Research Findings and Recommendations for Organizations," *Human Resource Management* 43(4) (2004): 409–424.

99. G. B. Cunningham, "The Moderating Effect of Diversity Strategy on the Relationship Between Racial Diversity and Organizational Performance," *Journal of Applied Social Psychology* 39(6) (2009): 1445–1460.

100. See note 93.

101. M. L. Dixon and L. K. Hart, "The Impact of Path-Goal Leadership Styles on Work Group Effectiveness and Turnover Intention," *Journal of Managerial Issues* 22(1) (2010): 52–69.

102. See note 85.

103. See note 93.

104. M. Bendick Jr., M. Egan, and L. Lanier, "The Business Case for Diversity and the Perverse Practice of Matching Employees to Customers," *Personnel Review* 39(4) (2010): 468–486.

105. E. Magoshi and E. Chang, "Diversity Management and the Effects on Employees' Organizational Commitment: Evidence from Japan and Korea," *Journal of World Business* 44(1) (2009): 31–40.

106. See note 97,

107. A. Herdman and A. McMillan-Capehart, "Establishing a Diversity Program is Not Enough: Exploring the Determinants of Diversity Climate," *Journal of Business & Psychology* 25(1) (2010): 39–53, *Business Source Complete*, EBSCO. Web, retrieved May 3, 2011.

108. See note 107.

109. A. Tilcsik, "From Ritual to Reality: Demography, Ideology, and Decoupling in a Post-Communist Government Agency," *Academy of Management Journal* 53(6) (2010): 1474–1498.

110. T. L. MacLean and M. Behnham, "The Dangers of Decoupling: The Relationship between Compliance Programs, Legitimacy Perceptions, and Institutionalized Misconduct," *Academy of Management Journal* 53(6) (2010): 1499–1520.

111. J. Lau Chin, "Introduction to the Special Issue on Diversity and Leadership," *American Psychologist* 65(3) (2010): 150–156.

112. Y. Yang and A. Konrad, "Understanding Diversity Management Practices: Implications of Institutional Theory and Resource-Based Theory," *Group & Organization Management* 36(1) (2011): 6–38.

113. See note 58.

114. See note 87.

115. A. Jurkus, J. Park, and L. Woodard, "Women in Top Management and Agency Costs," *Journal of Business Research* 64(2) (2011): 180–186.

116. J. Shen, A. Chanda, B. D'Netto, and M. Monga, "Managing Diversity through Human Resource Management: An International Perspective and Conceptual Framework," *International Journal of Human Resource Management* 20(2) (2009): 235–251.

117. E. Nga and G. Sears, "The Effect of Adverse Impact in Selection Practices on Organizational Diversity: A Field Study," *International Journal of Human Resource Management* 21(9) (2010): 1454–1471.

118. See note 85.

119. See note 93.

120. M. Bell, M. Connerley, and F. Cocchiara, "The Case for Mandatory Diversity Education," *Academy of Management Learning & Education* 8(4): 597–609.

121. M. Yap, M. Holmes, C. Hannan, and W. Cukier, "The Relationship between Diversity Training, Organizational Commitment, and Career Satisfaction," *Journal of European Industrial Training* 34(6) (2010): 519–538.

122. M. Kormanik and H. Rajan, "Implications for Diversity in the HRD Curriculum Drawn From Current Organizational Practices on Addressing Workforce Diversity in Management Training," *Advances in Developing Human Resources* 12(3) (2010): 367–384.

123. See note 121.

124. C. Leicht-Scholten, A. Weheliye, and A. Wolffram, "Institutionalisation of Gender and Diversity Management in Engineering Education," *European Journal of Engineering Education* 34(5) (2009): 447–454.

125. J. Bravin and A. Zimmerman, "Wal-Mart Ruling to Have Wide Reach," *Wall Street Journal* (Tuesday, June 21, 2011).

126. See note 59.

127. P. Cappelli, H. Singh, J. Singh, J., and M. Useem, "The India Way: Lessons for the U.S.," *Academy of Management Perspectives* 24(2) (2010): 6–24.

128. See note 58.

129. L. Hao-Chieh and H. Sheng-Tsung, "Managerial Lessons from the East: An Interview with Acer's Stan Shih," *Academy of Management Perspectives* 24(4) (2010): 6–16.

130. C. Ming-Jer and D. Miller, "West Meets East: Toward an Ambicultural Approach to Management," *Academy of Management Perspectives* 24(4) (2010): 17–24.

131. See note 61.

132. *NPR Morning Edition*, June 18, 2011.

133. D. Patrick, *A Reason To Believe* (New York: Random House, 2011).

Chapter 11

1. J. L. Yang and I. Shapira, "Larry Page to Replace Eric Schmidt as Google CEO," *Washington Post* (Jan. 21, 2011); Austin Carr, "Google CEO Shakeup: Larry Page to Replace Eric Schmidt on April 4," *Fastcompany* (Jan. 20, 2011); Barry Schwartz, "Eric Schmidt Dodges Future Bullets by Stepping Down as CEO," Search Engine RoundTable (Jan. 20, 2011). http://www.seroundtable.com/page-schmidt-google-ceo-12833.html (retreived on August 14, 2011)

2. G. Gavetti, "The New Psychology of Strategic Leadership," *Harvard Business Review* 89(17/8) (2011): 118–125.

3. See note 2.

4. T. L. Friedman, *The World Is Flat* (New York: Farrar, Strauss & Giroux), 2005.

5. S. Khavul, M. Peterson, D. Mullens, and A. Rasheed, "Going Global with Innovations from Emerging Economies: Investment in Customer Support Capabilities Pays Off," *Journal of International Marketing* 18(4) (2010): 22–42.

6. J. Pfeffer, "Building Sustainable Organizations: The Human Factor," *Academy of Management Perspectives* 24(1) (2010): 34–45.

7. D. Rosa and P. Devashish, "Mainstreaming Green Product Innovation: Why and How Companies Integrate Environmental Sustainability," *Journal of Business Ethics* 95(3) (Sept. 2010): 471–486.

8. H. M. Haugh and A. Talwar, "How Do Corporations Embed Sustainability Across the Organization?" *Academy of Management Learning & Education* 9(3) (2010): 384–396.

9. T. L. Wheelen and J. D. Hunger, *Strategic Management & Business Policy: Achieving Sustainability*, 12th ed. (Upper Saddle River, NJ: Prentice Hall, 2010).

10. A. Delios, "How Can Organizations Be Competitive but Dare to Care?" *Academy of Management Perspectives* 24(3) (2010): 25–36.

11. P. Shrivastava, "Pedagogy of Passion for Sustainability," *Academy of Management Learning & Education* 9(3) (2010): 443–455.

12. S. Benn and A. Martin, "Learning and Change for Sustainability Reconsidered: A Role for Boundary Objects," *Academy of Management Learning & Education* 9(3) (2010): 397–412.

13. L. K. Audebrand, "Sustainability in Strategic Management Education: The Quest for New Root Metaphors," *Academy of Management Learning & Education* 9(3) (2010): 413–428.

14. R. Weiss and K. Benedikt, "How Siemens Got Its Geist Back," *Bloomberg Businessweek* (Jan. 31-Feb. 6, 2011).

15. J. Calandro Jr., "Henry Singleton: A Pioneer of Corporate Strategic Leadership and Value Creation," *Strategy & Leadership* 38(6) (2010): 29–37.

16. See note 2.

17. B. J. Davies "The Nature and Dimensions of Strategic Leadership," *International Studies in Educational Administration (Commonwealth Council for Educational Administration & Management (CCEAM))* 38(1) (2010): 5–21.

18. K. Phipps and M. Burbach, "Strategic Leadership in the Nonprofit Sector: Opportunities for Research," *Journal of Behavioral & Applied Management* 11(2) (2010): 137–154.

19. D. Fritz and N. Ibrahim, "The Impact of Leadership Longevity on Innovation in a Religious Organization," *Journal of Business Ethics* 96(2): 223–231.

20. A. Hagen, M. Hassan, and S. Amin, "Critical Strategic Leadership Components: An Empirical Investigation," *SAM Advanced Management Journal (07497075)* 63(3) (1998): 39.

21. B. Barron and M. Henderson, "Strategic Leadership: A Theoretical and Operational Definition," *Journal of Instructional Psychology* 22(2) (1995): 178.

22. J. C. Picken, et al. "Top Management Team Communication Networks, Environmental Uncertainty, and Organizational Performance: A Contingency View," *Journal of Managerial Issues* 22(4) (2010): 436–455.

23. N. Yazdani, "Organizational Democracy and Organization Structure Link: Role of Strategic Leadership & Environmental Uncertainty," *IBA Business Review* 5(2) (2010): 51–74.

24. K. Beatty and L. Quinn, "Strategic Command Taking the Long View for Organizational Success," *Leadership in Action* 30(1) (2010): 3–7.

25. B. Ettore, "A Strategy Session with C. K. Prahalad," *Management Review* 84(4) (1995): 50.

26. M. A. Hitt, R. D. Ireland, and R. E. Hoskisson, *Strategic Management: Competitiveness and Globalization Concepts* (St. Paul, MN: West Publishing Company, 1995).

27. T. Quong and A. Walker, "Seven Principles of Strategic Leadership," *International Studies in Educational Administration (Commonwealth Council for Educational Administration & Management (CCEAM))* 38(1) (2010): 22–34.

28. See note 17.

29. See note 15.

30. See note 2.

31. C. Boone and W. Hendriks, "Top Management Team Diversity and Firm Performance: Moderators of Functional-Background and Locus-of-Control Diversity," *Management Science* 55(2) (2009): 165–180.

32. See note 22.

33. See note 23.

34. J. Cangemi, H. Lazarus, T. McQuade, J. Fitzgerald, J. Conner, R. Miller, and W. Murphree, "Successful Leadership Practices during Turbulent Times," *Journal of Management Development* 30(1) (2011): 30–43.

35. T. Armstrong, "Learning from Failures in O.D. Consulting," *Organization Development Journal* 27(1) (2009): 71–77.

36. H. Liu, "When Leaders Fail: A Typology of Failures and Framing Strategies," *Management Communication Quarterly* 24(2) (2010): 232–259.

37. E. Wallace, "GM: Still Making the Same Mistakes," *BusinessWeek Online* (2009), p. 7.

38. D. Kiley, "Chrysler, Fiat: Back from the Brink?" *BusinessWeek Online* (2009), p. 12.

39. D. Cremer, A. Tenbrunsel, and M. Dijke, M., "Regulating Ethical Failures: Insights from Psychology," *Journal of Business Ethics* 95 (2010): 1–6.

40. J. Glanz, "Justice and Caring: Power, Politics and Ethics in Strategic Leadership," *International Studies in Educational Administration (Commonwealth Council for Educational Administration & Management (CCEAM))* 38(1) (2010): 66–86.

41. I. Gurkov, "Strategy Techniques for the Times of High Uncertainty," *Journal for East European Management Studies* 15(2) (2010): 177–186.

42. S. Saslow, "Taking the Lead in Executive Development," *Leadership in Action* 24(6): 21–23.

43. P. Daewoo, R. Chinta, M. Lee, J. Turner, and L. Kilbourne, "Macro-fit versus Micro-fit of the Organization with its Environment: Implications for Strategic Leadership," *International Journal of Management* 28(2) (2011): 488–492.

44. D. Liu, M. Shih, C. Liau, and C. Lai, "Mining the Change of Event Trends for Decision Support in Environmental Scanning," *Expert Systems with Applications* 36(2) (2009): 972–984.

45. J. Oreja-Rodríguez and V. Yanes-Estévez, "Environmental Scanning: Dynamism with Rack and Stack from Rasch Model," *Management Decision* 48(2) (2010): 260–276.

46. Y. Doz and M. Kosonen, "Embedding Strategic Agility: A Leadership Agenda for Accelerating Business Model Renewal," *Long Range Planning* 43(12/3) (2010): 370–382.

47. D. Sull, "How to Thrive in Turbulent Markets," *Harvard Business Review* 87(2) (2009): 78–88.

48. M. Jenkins, "Technological Discontinuities and Competitive Advantage: A Historical Perspective on Formula 1 Motor Racing 1950–2006," *Journal of Management Studies* 47(5) (2010): 884–910.

49. See note 44.

50. J. A. Parnell, "Strategic Capabilities, Competitive Strategy, and Performance among Retailers in Argentina, Peru and the United States," *Management Decision* 49(1) (2011): 130–155.

51. O. Olamade, T. Oyebisi, A. Egbetokun, and B. Adebowale, "Environmental Scanning Strategy of Manufacturing Companies in Southwestern Nigeria," *Technology Analysis & Strategic Management* 23(4) (2011): 367–381.

52. D. Cravens, N. Piercy, and A. Baldauf, "Management Framework Guiding Strategic Thinking in Rapidly Changing Markets," *Journal of Marketing Management* 25(11/2) (2009): 31–49.

53. E. Shea, "Health Check Up for Business," *Manufacturing Today* (2010): 13–15. http://www.business-ownermagazine.com/2011/02/a-health-checkup-for-your-business/

54. U. Asan and A. Soyer, "Identifying Strategic Management Concepts: An Analytic Network Process Approach," *Computers & Industrial Engineering* 56(2) (2009): 600–615.

55. D. Stam, D. van Knippenberg, and B. Wisse, "The Role of Regulatory Fit in Visionary Leadership," *Journal of Organizational Behavior* 31(4) (2010): 499–518.

56. S. Kantabutra and G. Avery, "The Power of Vision: Statements That Resonate," *Journal of Business Strategy* 31(1) (2010): 37–45.

57. F. Slack, J. Orife, and F. Anderson, "Effects of Commitment to Corporate Vision on Employee Satisfaction with their Organization: An Empirical Study in the United States," *International Journal of Management* 27(3) (2010): 421–436.

58. See note 58.

59. D. Stid and J. Bradach, "How Visionary Nonprofits Leaders Are Learning to Enhance Management Capabilities," *Strategy & Leadership* 37(1) (2009): 35–40.

60. See note 57.

61. See note 23.

62. See note 58.

63. "Mission vs. Vision," *Marketing News* 45(2) (2011): 10.

64. H. Sundin, M. Granlund, and D. Brown, "Balancing Multiple Competing Objectives with a Balanced Scorecard," *European Accounting Review* 19(2) (2010): 203–246.

65. D. Stacks and S. Bowen, "The Strategic Approach: Writing Measurable Objectives," *Public Relations Tactics* 18(5) (2011): 14.

66. See note 23.

67. J. González-Benito and I. Suárez-González, "A Study of the Role Played by Manufacturing Strategic Objectives and Capabilities in Understanding the Relationship between Porter's Generic Strategies and Business Performance," *British Journal of Management* 21(4) (2010): 1027–1043.

68. V. Titus, J. Covin, and D. Slevin, "Aligning Strategic Processes in Pursuit of Firm Growth," *Journal of Business Research* 64(5) (2011): 446–453.

69. R. Livengood and R. K. Reger, "That's Our Turf! Identity Domains and Competitive Dynamics," *Academy of Management Review* 35(1) (2010): 48–66

70. M. Semadeni and B. S. Anderson, "The Follower's Dilemma: Innovation and Imitation in the Professional Services Industry," *Academy of Management Journal* 53(5) (2010): 1175–1193.

71. See note 53.

72. R. Rumelt, "The Perils of Bad Strategy," *McKinsey Quarterly* 1 (2011): 30–39.

73. N. Ooncharoen and P. Ussahawanitchakit, "Internal Marketing, External Marketing, Organizational Competencies, and business Performance," *International Journal of Business Research* 10(1) (2010): 24–30.

74. M. Memon, R. Mangi, R, and R. Chandan Lal, "Human Capital a Source of Competitive Advantage: Ideas for Strategic Leadership," *Australian Journal of Basic & Applied Sciences* 3(4) (2009): 4182–4189.

75. E. J. McClean, "High Commitment HR Practices, Employee Effort, and Firm Performance," *Academy of Management Annual Meeting Proceedings* (2009): 1–6.

76. See note 70.

77. C. Prange and B. Schlegelmilch, "The Role of Ambidexterity in Marketing Strategy Implementation: Resolving the Exploration-Exploitation Dilemma," *Business Research* 2(2) (2009): 215–240.

78. T. Čater and D. Pučko, D. "Factors of Effective Strategy Implementation: Empirical Evidence from Slovenian Business Practice," *Journal for East European Management Studies* 15(3) (2010): 207–236.

79. A. Clarke and M. Fuller, "Collaborative Strategic Management: Strategy Formulation and Implementation by Multi-Organizational Cross-Sector Social Partnerships," *Journal of Business Ethics* 94 (2010): 85–101.

80. M. R. Shirey, "Strategic Leadership for Organizational Change. Addressing Strategy Execution Challenges to Lead Sustainable Change," *Journal of Nursing Administration* 41(1) (2011): 1–4.

81. B. Smith, "Turf Wars: What the Intraorganisational Conflict Literature May Contribute to Our Understanding of Marketing Strategy Implementation," *Journal of Strategic Marketing* 19(1) (2011): 25–42.

82. See note 81.

83. S. Cadwallader, C. Jarvis, M. Bitner, and A. Ostrom, "Frontline Employee Motivation to Participate in Service Innovation Implementation," *Journal of the Academy of Marketing Science* 38(2) (2010): 219–239.

84. R. Greenwood and D. Miller, "Tackling Design Anew: Getting Back to the Heart of Organizational Theory," *Academy of Management Perspectives* 24(4) (2010): 78–88.

85. A. Carmeli, R. Gelbard, and D. Gefen, "The Importance of Innovation Leadership in Cultivating Strategic Fit and Enhancing Firm Performance," *Leadership Quarterly* 21(3) (2010): 339–349.

86. See note 9.

87. W. B. Tayler, "The Balanced Scorecard as a Strategy-Evaluation Tool: The Effects of Implementation Involvement and a Causal-Chain Focus," *Accounting Review* 85(3) (2010): 1095–1117.

88. T. Karp and T. Helgø, "Reality Revisited: Leading People in Chaotic Change," *Journal of Management Development* 28(2) (2009): 81–93.

89. See note 89.

90. B. Leavy, "Leading Adaptive Change by Harnessing the Power of Positive Deviance," *Strategy & Leadership* 39(2) (2011): 18–27.

91. S. Sonenshein, "We're Changing—Or Are We?" Untangling the Role of Progressive, Regressive, and Stability Narratives during Strategic Change Implementation," *Academy of Management Journal* 53(3) (2010): 477–512.

92. See note 81.

93. See note 81.

94. See note 92.

95. J. C. Quick and J. H. Gavin, "The Next Frontier: Edgar Schein on Organizational Therapy," *Academy of Management Executive* 14(1) (2000).

96. M. Hartley, "Leading Grassroots Change in the Academy: Strategic and Ideological Adaptation in the Civic Engagement Movement," *Journal of Change Management* 9(3) (2009): 323–338.

97. I. Mostovicz, N. Kakabadse, and A. Kakabadse, "How Critical Is Leading through Strategic Change?," *Proceedings of the European Conference on Management, Leadership & Governance* (2009), pp. 117–124.

98. C. Matthew, "Leader Creativity as a Predictor of Leading Change in Organizations," *Journal of Applied Social Psychology* 39(1) (2009): 1–41.

99. J. Chamberlin, "Business Process Reengineering," *Management Services* 53(4) (2009): 38–43.

100. R. Singleton, L. Toombs, S. Taneja, C. Larkin, and M. Pryor, "Workplace Conflict: a Strategic Leadership Imperative,"

International Journal of Business & Public Administration 8(1) (2011): 149–163.

101. G. F. Latta, "A Process Model of Organizational Change in Cultural Context: The Impact of Organizational Culture on Leading Change," *Journal of Leadership & Organizational Studies* 16(1) (2009): 19–37.

102. J. Lok, "Institutional Logics as Identity Projects," *Academy of Management Journal* 53(6) (2010): 1305–1335.

103. K. Esty, "Lessons from Muhammad Yunus and the Grameen Bank," *OD Practitioner* 43(1) (2011): 24–28.

104. S. Tandon, "Who Killed Change? Solving the Mystery of Leading People through Change," *International Journal of Business Insights & Transformation* 3(1) (2009): 86–87.

105. L. Fagerström and S. Salmela, "Leading Change: A Challenge for Leaders in Nordic Health Care," *Journal of Nursing Management* 18(5) (2010): 613–617.

106. L. Anderson and D. Anderson, "Leading Change," *Leadership Excellence* 26(111) (2009): 3–4.

107. E. Schien, *Organizational Culture and Leadership*, 3rd ed. (San Francisco, CA: Jossey-Bass, 2004); H. M. Trice and J. M. Beyer, *The Cultures of Work Organizations*, (Englewood Cliffs, NJ: Prentice-Hall, 1993); M. J. Hatch, "The Cultural Dynamics of Organizing and Change," in N. M. Ashkanasy, C. P. M. Wildreon, and M. F. Peterson (Eds.), *Handbook of Organizational Culture and Climate* (Thousand Oaks, CA: Sage, 2000, pp. 245–260).

108. See note 81.

109. E. H. Schein, Kurt Lewin's Change Theory in the Field and in the Classroom: Notes Toward a Model of Managed Learning, www.a2zpsychology.com/articles/Kurt_Lewin's_Change_The-ory.htm (retrieved on August 14, 2011).

110. J. Kotter and H. Rathgeber, "*Our Iceberg Is melting: Changing and Succeeding Under Any Conditions*," Reviewed by James B. Avey, *Academy of Management Perspective* 23(3) (2009): 101–103.

111. A. Schulte, "Leading Bold Change," *Leadership Excellence* 27(4) (2010): 4.

112. "Human Resources Conference Paper Abstracts," *Academy of Management Annual Meeting Proceedings* (2010): pp. 1–65.

113. C. Peus, D. Frey, M. Gerkhardt, P. Fischer, and E. Traut-Mattausch, "Leading and Managing Organizational Change Initiatives," *Management Revue* 20(2) (2009): 158–175.

114. B. Gullickson, "Wisdom at the Edge," *Strategic Finance* 91(111) (2010): 21–22.

115. "Keep Leading through Change," *Managing People at Work* 333 (2009): 6.

116. "Leading Change and Managing Resistance," *Executive Leadership* 24(112) (2009): 1–2.

117. P. Brotherton, "Employees Skeptical of Change Efforts Look to Influential Peers," *T+D* 65(4) (2011): 27.

118. J. LaMarsh, "How Companies Reduce the Downside of Downsizing," *Global Business & Organizational Excellence* 29(1) (2009): 7–16.

119. C. Rees and H. Johari, "Senior Managers' Perceptions of the HRM Function during Times of Strategic Organizational Change," *Journal of Organizational Change Management* 23(5) (2010): 517–536.

120. See note 100.

121. www.nikebiz.com/company_overview/.../mark_parker.html

122. www.nikemedia.com

123. E. MCgirt, "How Nike's CEO Shook Up the Shoe Industry," *FastCompany* (Sept. 1, 2010). PP 1–6. www.fastcompany.com/magazine/148/artist-athlete-ceo.html - Cached-(retrieved August 14, 2011).

124. See note 124.

Chapter 12

1. www.citi.com; Eric Dash, "Citigroup Goes on the Offense: Hiring, Expansion," *San Francisco Chronicle*, (July 17, 2011): D-8; J. Weil, "What Vikram Pandit Knew, and When He knew it," *Bloomberg* (Feb. 23, 2011).

2. B. S. Gainey, "Crisis Management's New Role in Educational Settings," *Clearing House* 82(6) (2009): 267–274.

3. P. Power, "A Crisis Management Standard: Who Needs it?" *Journal of Business Continuity & Emergency Planning* 3(4) (2009): 302–311.

4. E. K. Stern, "Crisis Navigation: Lessons from History for the Crisis Manager in Chief," *Governance* 22(2) (2009): 189–202.

5. L. C. McLaren, "Crisis Leadership Now: A Real-world Guide to Preparing for Threats, Disaster, Sabotage and Scandal," *Journal of European Industrial Training* 33(7) (2009): 671–672.

6. A. Carmeli and J. Schaubroeck, "Organizational Crisis-Preparedness: The Importance of Learning from Failures," *Long Range Planning* 41(2) (Apr. 2008): 177–196.

7. M. Van Wart and N. Kapucu, "Crisis Management Competencies,". *Public Management Review* 13(4) (2011): 489–511.

8. S. L. Muffet-Willett and S. D. Kruse, "Crisis Leadership: Past Research and Future Directions," *Journal of Business Conti-nuity & Emergency Planning* 3(3) (2009): 248–258.

9. W. Bennis, "Crises Reveal the Quality of Leadership," *Leader to Leader* (154) (2009): 27–31.

10. C. Lalonde, "Managing Crises through Organizational Development: A Conceptual Framework," *Disasters* 35(2) (2011): 443–464.

11. See note 5.

12. K. S. Groves, "Six Steps for Confronting the Emerging Leadership Succession Crisis," *Graziadio Business Report* 13(1) (2010): 1–7.

13. J. Fousek and D. Wasserman, "Ethical Issues in U.S. Presidential Leadership," *Presidential Studies Quarterly* 40(1) (2010: 1–8.

14. See note 5. *Training*, 33(7), 671–672.

15. S. L. Smith and S. F. Kline, "Crisis Preparedness and Meeting Planners' Perceptions," *Journal of Convention & Event Tour-ism* 11(1) (2010): 62–78.

16. L. Chambers, J. Drysdale, and J. Hughes, "The Future of Leadership: A Practitioner View," *European Management Journal* 28(4) (2010): 260–268.

17. See note 15.

18. C. Piotrowski, "Earthquake in Haiti: The Failure of Crisis Management," *Organization Development Journal* 28(1) (2010): 107–112.

19. B. J. Reynolds and E. Earley, "Principles to Enable Leaders to Navigate the Harsh Realities of Crisis and Risk Communica-tion," *Journal of Business Continuity & Emergency Planning* 47(3) (2010): 262–273.

20. R. I. Sutton, "CEOs, Tough Times, and Emotions," *McKinsey Quarterly* (1) (2010): 58–59.

21. D. J. Moran, "ACT for Leadership: Using Acceptance and Commitment Training to Develop Crisis-Resilient Change Managers," *International Journal of Behavioral Consultation & Therapy* 6(4) (2010): 341–355.

22. B. E. Baran and M. Adelman, "Preparing for the Unthinkable: Leadership Development for Organizational Crises," *Industrial & Organizational Psychology* 3(1) (2010): 45–47.

23. See note 7.

24. See note 5.

25. I. Woodward and E. More, "Leadership Communication at the Edge," *Australian Journal of Communication* 37(1) (2010): 111–136.

26. A. Boin, "The New World of Crises and Crisis Management: Implications for Policymaking and Research," *Review of Policy Research* 26(4) (2009): 367–377.

27. C. Roux-Dufort, "The Devil Lies in Details! How Crises Build up Within Organizations," *Journal of Contingencies & Crisis Management* 17(1) (2009): 4–11.

28. J. A. Gruman, N. Chhinzer, and G. W. Smith, "An Exploratory Study of the Level of Disaster Preparedness in the Canadian Hospitality Industry," *International Journal of Hospitality & Tourism Administration* 12(1) (2011): 43–59.

29. See note 26.

30. See note 8.

31. See note 19.

32. See note 5.

33. D. Bauman, "Evaluating Ethical Approaches to Crisis Leadership: Insights from Unintentional Harm Research," *Journal of Business Ethics* 98(2) (2011): 281–295.

34. B. George, "Leading in Crisis," *Leader to Leader* (155) (2010): 24–29.

35. See note 8.

36. See note 8.

37. See note 9.

38. J. B. Moats, T. J. Chermack, and L. M. Dooley, "Using Scenarios to Develop Crisis Managers: Applications of Scenario Planning and Scenario-Based Training," *Advances in Developing Human Resources* 10(3) (June 2008): 397–424.

39. See note 5.

40. See note 33.

41. G. A. Magaliff and A. Miller, "In a Time of Change and Crisis: A Call for Extraordinary Leadership," *Journal of Jewish Communal Service* 85(1) (2010): 53–56.

42. See note 19.

43. J. B. Ciulla, "Being There: Why Leaders Should Not 'Fiddle' While Rome Burns," *Presidential Studies Quarterly* 40(1) (2010): 38–56.

44. M. Oliveira and P. Murphy, "The Leader as the Face of a Crisis: Philip Morris' CEO's Speeches during the 1990s," *Journal of Public Relations Research* 21(4) (2009): 361–380.

45. See note 34.

46. See note 34.

47. J. Ciulla, "Leadership and the Ethics of Care," *Journal of Business Ethics* 88(1) (2009): 3–4.

48. P. Chris and R. W. Guyette, Jr., "Toyota Recall Crisis: Public Attitudes on Leadership and Ethics," *Organization Development Journal* 28(2) (2010): 89–97.

49. See note 22.

50. D. R. Griffin-Padgett and D. Allison, "Making a Case for Restorative Rhetoric: Mayor Rudolph Giuliani & Mayor Ray Nagin's Response to Disaster," *Communication Monographs* 77(3) (2010): 376–392.

51. See note 19.

52. See note 26.

53. See note 25.

54. See note 26.

55. X. Liu, Z. Chang, and P. Zhao, "Is It Simply a Matter of Managerial Competence? Interpreting Chinese Executives' Perceptions of Crisis Management," *Public Relations Review* 35(3) (2009): 232–239.

56. See note 19.

57. S. Stern, "Truth, Not Secrets, for Better Leadership," *Strategic Communication Management* 15(3) (2011): 11.

58. See note 34.

59. See note 50.

60. See note 19.

61. See note 25.

62. E. J. Iheriohanma, "Capacity Building, Leadership Question and Drains of Corruption in Africa: A Theoretical Discourse," *Asian Social Science* 7(3) (2011): 131–138.

63. J. Marti, "ICBS Intellectual Capital Benchmarking System: A Practical Methodology for Successful Strategy Formulation in the Knowledge Economy," *Proceedings of the European Conference on Intellectual Capital* (2011): 461–474

64. S. Chakravorti, "Managing Organizational Culture Change and Knowledge to Enhance Customer Experiences: Analysis and Framework," *Journal of Strategic Marketing* 19(2) (2011): 123–151.

65. X. M. Bezuijen, P. T. van den Berg, K. van Dam, and H. Thierry, "Pygmalion and Employee Learning: The Role of Leader Behaviors," *Journal of Management* 35 (2009): 1248–1267.

66. S. Liao, W. Chang, and C. Wu, "An Integrated Model for Learning Organization with Strategic View: Benchmarking in the Knowledge-Intensive Industry," *Expert Systems with Applications* 37(5) (2010): 3792–3798.

67. N. Hai Nam and S. Mohamed, "Leadership Behaviors, Organizational Culture and Knowledge Management Practices," *Journal of Management Development* 30(2) (2011): 206–221.

68. P. M. Senge, *The Fifth Discipline: The Art and Practice of the Learning Organization* (Rev. ed.) (New York: Doubleday, 2006).

69. K. Singh, "An Analysis of Relationship between the Learning Organization and Organizational Culture in Indian Business Organization," *Organizations & Markets in Emerging Economies* 1(1) (2010): 142–165.

70. J. Šebestová and Ż. Rylková, "Competencies and Innovation within Learning Organization," *Economics & Management* 16 (2011): 954–960.

71. W. Zheng, B. Yang, and G. McLean, "Linking Organizational Culture, Structure, Strategy, and Organizational Effectiveness: Mediating Role of Knowledge Management," *Journal of Business Research* 63(7) (2010): 763–771.

72. U. Aktharsha and H. H. Anisa, "Knowledge Management System and Learning Organization: An Empirical Study in an Engineering Organization," *IUP Journal of Knowledge Management* 9(2) (2011): 26–43.

73. N. N. Antonoaie and C. C. Antonoaie, "The Learning Organization," *Bulletin of the Transilvania University of Brasov, Series V: Economic Sciences* (3) (2010): 105–108.

74. W. Zheng, B. Yang, and G. McLean, "Linking Organizational Culture, Structure, Strategy, and Organizational Effectiveness: Mediating Role of Knowledge Management," *Journal of Business Research* 63(7) (2010): 763–771.

75. K. Singh, "An Analysis of Relationship between the Learning Organization and Organizational Culture in Indian Business Organization," *Organizations & Markets in Emerging Economies* 1(1) (2010): 142–165.

76. P. M. Senge, *The Fifth Discipline: The Art and Practice of the Learning Organization* (Rev. ed.) (New York: Doubleday, 2006).

77. M. Gustavsson, "Facilitating Expansive Learning in a Public Sector Organization," *Studies in Continuing Education* 31(3) (2009): 245–259.

78. C. Argyris and D. A. Schon, *Organizational Learning: A Theory of Action Perspective* (Reading, MA: Addison-Wesley, 1978).

79. A. Hon and A. Leung, "Employee Creativity and Motivation in the Chinese Context: The Moderating Role of Organizational Culture,", *Cornell Hospitality Quarterly* 52(2) (2011): 125–134.

80. G. N. Chandler and D. W. Lyon, "Involvement in Knowledge-Acquisition Activities by Venture Team Members and Venture Performance," *Entrepreneurship: Theory & Practice* 33(3) (2009): 571–592.

81. U. Aktharsha and H. H. Anisa, "Knowledge Management System and Learning Organization: An Empirical Study in an Engineering Organization," *IUP Journal of Knowledge Management* 9(2) (2011): 26–43.

82. V. S. Anantatmula, "Designing Meaningful KM Processes to Improve Organizational Learning," *Trends in Information Management* 5(2) (2009): 219–245.

83. H. Hoang and F. Rothaermel, "Leveraging Internal and External Experience: Exploration, Exploitation, and R&D Project Performance," *Strategic Management Journal* 31(7) (2010): 734–758.

84. R. Bejinaru and S. Iordache, "Intellectual Capital Dynamics within the Learning Organization," *Proceedings of the European Conference on Intellectual Capital* (2011): 70–77.

85. J. G. Vargas-Hernández and M. Noruzi, "How Intellectual Capital and Learning Organization Can Foster Organizational Competitiveness?" *International Journal of Business & Management* 5(4) (2010): 183–193.

86. N. Akhtar and R. Khan, "Exploring the Paradox of Organizational Learning and Learning Organization," *Interdisciplinary Journal of Contemporary Research in Business* 2(9) (2011): 257–270.

87. K. Singh, "An Analysis of Relationship between the Learning Organization and Organizational Culture in Indian Business Organization," *Organizations & Markets in Emerging Economies* 1(1) (2010): 142–165.

88. N. Akhtar and R. Khan, "Exploring the Paradox of Organizational Learning and Learning Organization," *Interdisciplinary Journal of Contemporary Research in Business* 2(9) (2011): 257–270.

89. J. Šebestová and Ž. Rylková, "Competencies and Innovation within Learning Organization," *Economics & Management* 16 (2011): 954–960.

90. M. Lucchi, M. de Fátima Bianco, and P. Tadeu de Mello Lourenção, "Work in Multidisciplinary Teams: a Study about Mobilization of Knowledge and Learning in an Organization of Complex Products," *Brazilian Administration Review (BAR)* 8(3) (2011): 305–328.

91. Š. Miha, D. Vlado, and C. Kevin, "Patterns and Structures of Intra-organizational Learning Networks within a Knowledge-Intensive Organization," *Journal of Information Technology* 25(2) (2010): 189–204.

92. G. N. Chandler and D. W. Lyon, "Involvement in Knowledge-Acquisition Activities by Venture Team Members and Venture Performance," *Entrepreneurship: Theory & Practice* 33(3) (2009): 571–592.

93. T. Harding, "Fostering Creativity for Leadership and Leading Change," *Arts Education Policy Review* 111(2) (2010): 51–53.

94. A. Skennar, "Establishing and Building a Learning Culture in an Organisation," *Training & Development in Australia* (2009): 35–38.

95. S. G. Isaksen and G. Ekvall, "Managing for Innovation: The Two Faces of Tension in Creative Climates," *Creativity & Innovation Management* 19(2) (2010): 73–88.

96. B. Mishra and A. Bhaskar, "Empowerment: A Necessary Attribute of a Learning Organization?" *Organizations & Markets in Emerging Economies* 1(2) (2010): 48–70.

97. J. Davis and H. Davis, "The Learning Organization Implemented in Education Through Advisory Committees,: *Education* 130(1) (2009): 114–117.

98. B. Kieslinger, K. Pata, and C. Fabian, "A Participatory Design Approach for the Support of Collaborative Learning and Knowledge Building in Networked Organizations," *International Journal of Advanced Corporate Learning* 2(3) (2009): 34–38.

99. See note 104.

100. P. M. Madsen and V. Desai, "Failing to Learn The Effects of Failure and success on Organizational Learning in the Global Orbital Launch Vehicle Industry," *Academy of Management Journal* 53(3) (2010): 451–476.

101. H. Noubar, R. Rose, N. Kumar, and L. Salleh, "Learning Culture to Organizational Breakthroughs in Malaysian Companies," *Economics & Management* 16 (2011): 852–858.

102. T. Češnovar, "Influences of Implementing the Learning Organisation on Companies' Financial and Non-Financial Performances," *Managing Global Transitions: International Research Journal* 8(3) (2010): 285–306.

103. See note 72.

104. C. Newwbold and N. Pharoah, "What It Means to Be a Learning Organization," *Strategic HR Review* 8(3) (2009): 12–16.

105. Y. Seung Won, S. Ji Hoon, L. Doo Hun, and J. Baek-Kyoo, "Structural Determinants of Team Performance: The Mutual Influences of Learning Culture, Creativity, and Knowledge," *Human Resource Development International* 13(3) (2010): 249–264.

106. S. Chich-Jen, "Study on the Relations among the Customer Knowledge Management, Learning Organization, and Organizational Performance," *Service Industries Journal* 31(5) (2011): 791–807.

107. K. M. Dirani, "Measuring the Learning Organization Culture, Organizational Commitment and Job Satisfaction in the Lebanese Banking Sector," *Human Resource Development International* 12(2) (2009): 189–208.

108. J. Song, H. Kim, J. A. Kolb, "The Effect of Learning Organization Culture on the Relationship between Interpersonal

Trust and Organizational Commitment," *Human Resource Development Quarterly* 20(2) (2009): 147–167.

109. J. Sung Jun and B. Joo, "Knowledge Sharing: The Influences of Learning Organization Culture, Organizational Commitment, and Organizational Citizenship Behaviors," *Journal of Leadership & Organizational Studies* 18(3) (2011): 353–364.

110. S. Rijal, "Leading the Learning Organization," *Business Education & Accreditation* 1(1) (2009): 131–140.

111. X. Bezuijen, K. van Dam, P. T. van den Berg, and H. Thierry, "How Leaders Stimulate Employee Learning: A Leader-Member Exchange Approach," *Journal of Occupational & Organizational Psychology* 83(3) (2010): 673–693.

112. H. Liao, D. Liu, and R. Loi, "Looking at Both Sides of the Social Exchange Coin: A Social Cognitive Perspective on the Joint Effects of Relationship Quality and Differentiation on Creativity," *Academy of Management Journal* 53(5) (2010): 1090–1109.

113. See note 117.

114. S. Smith and A. Young, "Adapting to Change: Becoming a Learning Organization as a Relief and Development Agency," *IEEE Transactions on Professional Communication* 52(4) (2009): 329–345.

115. See note 73.

116. S. G. Isaksen and G. Ekvall, "Managing for Innovation: The Two Faces of Tension in Creative Climates," *Creativity & Innovation Management* 19(2) (2010): 73–88.

117. See note 118.

118. K. N. Dervitsiotis, "A Framework for the Assessment of an Organisation's Innovation Excellence,". *Total Quality Management & Business Excellence* 21(9) (2010): 903–918.

119. See note 116.

120. http://www.innovation.org/index.cfm/ToolsandResources/FactSheets/Innovation_by_the_Numbers

121. J. Rockoff, "Merck Names Frazier as CEO," *Wall Street Journal* (Dec. 1, 2010).

122. S. Todd, "Merck Names Ken Frazier as Its Next CEO," nj.com (Nov. 30, 2010). (http://www.nj.com/business/index.ssf/2010/11/merck_names_ken_frazier_as_its.html)

123. T. Randall, "Merck's New CEO Frazier Vows Innovation, Wider Markets," Bloomberg (Nov. 30, 2010).(http://www.businessweek.com/news/2010-11-30/merck-new-ceo-frazier-vows-innovation-wider-markets.html)

Index